Maryland

Maryland

Leonard M. Adkins

The Countryman Press ✳ Woodstock Vermont

FIRST EDITION

DEDICATION

For Ann and Denny Messick. Thank you for your friendship—and for Laurie.
—L. M. A.

We welcome your comments and suggestions. Please contact Explorer's Guide Editor, The Countryman Press, P.O. Box 748, Woodstock, VT 05091, or e-mail countrymanpress@wwnorton.com.

First Edition

ISBN: 0-88150-518-8
ISSN: 1542-1163

Maps by Moore Creative Design, © 2002 The Countryman Press
Cover and interior design by Bodenweber Design
Text composition by PerfecType, Nashville, TN
Front cover photograph by Camerique/Robertstock
Back cover photographs Leonard M. Adkins
Interior photographs by Leonard M. Adkins unless otherwise noted.

Published by The Countryman Press, P.O. Box 748, Woodstock, Vermont 05091

Distributed by W. W. Norton & Company, 500 Fifth Avenue, New York, NY 10110

Printed in the United States of America
10 9 8 7 6 5 4 3 2 1

There is no frigate like a book to take us lands away.

—Emily Dickinson

Also by Leonard M. Adkins

50 Hikes in Maryland: Walks, Hikes, and Backpacks from the Allegheny Plateau to the Atlantic Ocean

50 Hikes in Northern Virginia: Walks, Hikes, and Backpacks from the Allegheny Mountains to the Chesapeake Bay

50 Hikes in Southern Virginia: From the Cumberland Gap to the Atlantic Ocean

Adventure Guide to Virginia

The Appalachian Trail: A Visitor's Companion

Wildflowers of the Appalachian Trail

Walking the Blue Ridge: A Guide to the Trails of the Blue Ridge Parkway

The Caribbean: A Walking and Hiking Guide

Seashore State Park: A Walking Guide

© The Countryman Press

EXPLORE WITH US!

Welcome to the first edition of *Maryland: An Explorer's Guide,* the state's most comprehensive travel companion. All attractions, inns, and restaurants are chosen on the basis of merit, not paid advertising. The organization of the book is simple, but the following points will help to get you started on your way.

WHAT'S WHERE

In the beginning of the book is an alphabetical listing with thumbnail sketches of special highlights, important information, and advice on everything from where to obtain the best homemade ice cream to what to do if you get stung by a jellyfish.

LODGING

Lodging establishments mentioned in this book are selected on the basis of merit; no innkeeper or business owner was charged for inclusion. When making reservations, which almost all B&Bs require, ask about the policy on children, pets, smoking, and acceptance of credit cards. Many B&Bs do not accept children under 12, and some places have a minimum-stay policy, especially on weekends, holidays, and during special events.

Rates: The rates are for two people to stay in one room for one night and are weekend rates during what the establishment considers its high season. Weekday and off-season rates may be lower. However, please do not hold me or the respective innkeepers responsible for the rates listed as this book went to press. Changes are inevitable. State, local, and room taxes (which can be well above 10 percent) have not been included.

RESTAURANTS

Please note the distinction between *Dining Out* and *Eating Out.* By their nature, restaurants in the *Eating Out* section are less expensive and more casual.

KEY TO SYMBOLS

- ⑤ **Special value.** The special-value symbol appears next to lodgings and restaurants that offer a quality not often found at the price charged.
- ✍ **Child-friendly.** The crayon symbol appears next to places or activities that accept and/or appeal to young children, or have a children's menu.
- ♿ **Handicapped access.** The wheelchair symbol appears next to lodgings, restaurants, and attractions that are partially or completely handicapped-accessible.
- ❀ **Pets.** The pet symbol appears next to places, activities, and lodgings that accept pets. Almost all lodging accommodations require that you inform them of a pet when you make a reservation, and often request an additional fee.

Maryland Regions

REGIONS

1 The Eastern Shore
2 Central Maryland
3 Capital Region
4 Southern Maryland
5 Frederick and the Catoctin Mountains
6 The Mountains of Western Maryland

N

0   25   50

Miles

© The Countryman Press

CONTENTS

INTRODUCTION

I started the introduction to my book *50 Hikes in Maryland* (Backcountry Guides) with the tourism-bureau-inspired slogan, "So many things to do. So close together." I stand by that phrase to introduce you to this first edition of *Maryland: An Explorer's Guide*. From the waves of the Atlantic Ocean rolling onto the sands of the Eastern Shore, to the heights of the Allegheny Plateau shadowed by a setting sun in western Maryland, all areas of the state are within a few hours' drive of each other.

As you head to the beach in Ocean City, you could stop to take a fishing trip on the Chesapeake Bay, visit a maritime museum (or two, or three, or more) to learn how people make a living from those waters, watch migrating waterfowl fly overhead by the thousands, kayak a tidal stream, and still have time for an evening ride on a 1902 carousel and a fresh seafood dinner.

In Baltimore, you can take in the exhibits at the city's world-renowned art museums, watch dolphins at play in the aquarium, stand upon the parapets that gave birth to America's national anthem, ride a hot-air balloon 450 feet above Inner Harbor, dine on Spanish food in a jacket and tie, and finish the day munching a freshly made cannoli as you stroll the alleyways of Little Italy.

Within a 30-minute drive of this cosmopolitan atmosphere, you could be bicycling a 20-mile rail-trail through rural countryside, swimming in the Chesapeake Bay, or betting on a horse at Pimlico, home of the Triple Crown's Preakness Stake.

A half day's drive to western Maryland can introduce you to the 184.5-mile C&O Canal, Civil War battlefields at Monocacy and Antietam, one of the state's finest fine-arts museums, and the opportunity to go underground. You could learn of the upheaval of the land when Africa collided with North America ages ago, enjoy an historic steam-train ride through the forested mountains, go downhill skiing, and exhilarate in whitewater rafting.

To facilitate your explorations, this guide, the most comprehensive of its kind, has been divided into broad geographic regions. Individual chapters then cover areas that can easily be explored from their listed overnight accommodations.

Each chapter begins with an overview of the area, taking in its geographic features, historic aspects, and attraction highlights. There are listings on how to obtain further information, how to get to the area and get around once there, and places to obtain emergency help should the need arise.

Following those are the *To See* and *To Do* sections, which provide you with enough information to decide if a particular museum, historic home or site, family attraction, guided tour, golf course, hiking trail, lake, or other place or activity should fit into your travel plans.

I then give descriptions of places to stay, including B&Bs, inns, resorts, cottages, vacation rentals, and a few motels and hotels. Having stayed in them, or at least visited, I have based my descriptions on firsthand experiences and a propensity to snoop into hidden areas and out-of-the-way places. I try to be as honest as possible in my appraisals. What I saw and experienced is what I wrote about.

The same is true for the dining options provided. I gained quite a few pounds sampling the fare of the upscale restaurants *(Dining Out)* and that of the everyday places *(Eating Out),* in addition to bakeries, candy shops, ice cream parlors, and coffeehouses.

Listings of entertainment venues, outstanding businesses worthy of some of your shopping time, and special events that take place annually round out each chapter.

Within all of these hundreds of listings and descriptions you will find very few negative remarks (and those are usually small comments about something trifling). The reason is that I visited and dined in a few places that I simply did not include in the guide. If I was uncomfortable in a place or found it lacking in cleanliness, I felt that other lone travelers, couples, or families would, too. If a meal was not worth the calories consumed, or the atmosphere made for an unpleasant dining experience, the restaurant was not included. This does not mean that an inn had to be palatial or a restaurant serve five-star cuisine. It just means that you should get a good and fair experience for the money you spend.

I became acquainted with Maryland on an intimate basis when I first hiked the Appalachian Trail as I followed the state's 40 miles of the pathway along the crest of South Mountain. I came to appreciate more of what the state has to offer after I married Laurie, who was born and raised in Annapolis. Journeys to visit her relatives introduced to me to the places important to her childhood, while further explorations enabled both of us to discover boundless hiking, biking, canoeing, and other outdoor adventures.

History permeates the air over this land. The first settlement in the New World dedicated to true religious tolerance was established here in 1634. George Washington and many other movers and shakers of the American Revolution traveled throughout, fighting and preaching for the cause. Four of the state's citizens signed the Declaration of Independence, and when the new country needed a place for its capital, Maryland graciously donated the land on which Washington, D.C., is built.

As a border state, Maryland was the site of some of the most bitter fighting during the Civil War. The Battle of Antietam was the single bloodiest day in American war history, while the fight along the Monocacy River is credited with having saved Washington, D.C., from Confederate invasion.

I had fun doing the field research for this book. I had already experienced many wonderful adventures in Maryland, but the need for current, firsthand knowledge of the state set me off on new explorations.

From fly-fishing in a western Maryland creek to touring the hallowed halls of the capitol building in Annapolis, I had the perfect excuse to go to new places and engage in activities I had always wanted to explore but lacked the time. A walk along the C&O Canal, an afternoon nap upon the Ocean City beach, and a visit to the Calvert Marine Museum in Solomons returned me to places I had long yearned to see again. In addition, since the human body demands fuel and rest, I became privileged to sample the sumptuous offerings of some of the world's most innovative chefs, and engage in friendly and intriguing conversations with the guests and hosts of the state's excessively relaxing and historically rich B&Bs.

George Washington traveled often throughout Maryland and really did sleep here—in many places, in fact. You should, too. Happy exploring.

ACKNOWLEDGMENTS

I relied upon hundreds of people to help me along the way, to make arrangements, point me in the right direction, and introduce me to other people, places, and activities I would have overlooked. Without your unselfish aid, this book would never have been completed. May it reflect the confidence you had in me:

Barbara J. Beverungen and Heather Johnson, Carroll County Office of Tourism; Deb Clatterbuck, Garrett County Chamber of Commerce; Lisa Challenger & Debbie Keitt, Worcester County Tourism; Mary G. Calloway, Dorchester County Department of Tourism; Sheila Crites, Allegany County Convention and Visitors Bureau; Norma Dobrowolski and staff, Ocean City Convention and Visitors Bureau; Debbi Dodson, Barbara A. Reisert, and Gayle V. Keen, Talbot County Office of Tourism; Dianne Gleissner, St. Mary's County Division of Tourism; Kelly Groff, Conference and Visitors Bureau of Montgomery County; Julie Horner, Beth Somers, and staff, Somerset County Tourism; Deborah Ing, Howard County Tourism Council; Sandy Maruchi-Turner and Bob White, Cecil County Tourism; Diane Molner and Susan Hanna, Discover Harford County Tourism Council; Larry Noto, Baltimore Area Convention and Visitors Bureau; Terry B. Nyquist, Wicomico County Convention and Visitors Bureau; Craig Peddicord, Baltimore County Conference and Visitors Bureau; Beth Finneyfrock Rhoades, Tourism Council of Frederick County; Joanne Roland, Charles County Visitors Bureau; Herman E. Schieke, Jr., Calvert County, Maryland Department of Economic Development; Barbara Siegert, Queen Anne's County Department of Business and Tourism; Carl Smith, Jr., Prince George's County, Maryland Conference and Visitors Bureau; Bernadette Van Pelt, Kent County Office of Tourism; Anedra T. Wiseman and Clare Vanderbeek, Annapolis and Anne Arundel County Conference and Visitors Bureau; and Gigi Yelton, Hagerstown/Washington County Convention and Visitors Bureau. Every entry in this book represents hours that someone was willing to take out of a busy schedule to assist me. To those many hundreds more who can't be named here, thank you.

Connie Yingling, Maryland Office of Tourism Development—was I ever lucky that you stepped in to help. Dr. Stephen Lewis, Caroline Charonko, Terry Cumming, and Susie Surfas—life goes on, thanks to you. Nancy Adkins, Kathleen, John, Tim, and Jay Yelenic—thank you for understanding why my visits became so infrequent. Laurie—thank you for sharing Maryland with me, and me with Maryland. Life with you is all it should be.

WHAT'S WHERE IN MARYLAND

AREA CODES More than five areas codes exist in Maryland, with new ones to be added in the future. You must dial the area code on all phone calls, including those made locally. This means that every call is at least a 10-digit proposition.

ADMISSION FEES Admission fees of less than $5 per person are simply listed as "small admission fee." The actual cost is provided if higher. Please keep in mind that, as this book went to press, the rates quoted were accurate but are always subject to change.

AIR SERVICE The state is serviced primarily by three airports clustered around the Baltimore–Washington, D.C., area. **Baltimore/Washington International Airport** (1-800-I-FLY-BWI) is located between Baltimore and Annapolis. **Ronald Reagan Washington National Airport** (703-417-8000) is in Virginia across the Potomac River from the District of Columbia. **Dulles International Airport** (703-572-2700), in northern Virginia, may be a bit farther away but often has lower airfares. All three have airline companies with connections around the world.

Philadelphia International Airport (215-937-5400) may be a good choice for those traveling to Central Maryland or the northern part of the Eastern Shore, while **Pittsburgh International Airport** (412-472-3525) may be best for those wanting to explore western Maryland.

Smaller, regional airports have commuter connections and are noted in their respective chapters.

AMTRAK Despite its many troubles through the years, AMTRAK (1-800-USA-RAIL; www.amtrak.com) service for Maryland is quite extensive. It can get you close to the northern part of the Eastern Shore by dropping you off in Aberdeen, or take you deep into western Maryland at Cumberland. There is, of course, service to Baltimore, Washington, D.C., and several towns close to the two big cities.

ANTIQUES New Market has so many antiques shops that it has dubbed itself the "Antiques Capital of Maryland." Other areas with heavy concentrations of dealers include Havre de Grace; Kensington; Historic Savage Mill in Savage; and Fell's Point, Federal Hill, and Antique Row in Baltimore. Head to the Eastern Shore to find shops filled with nautical items of yesteryear.

The **Antiques Dealers Association of Maryland** (410-269-1440; www.antiquesinmd.com), 17 Conduit Street, Annapolis, 21401, publishes a pamphlet describing more than 50 of its members. A calendar of shows is included.

APPALACHIAN TRAIL The Appalachian Trail follows the crest of the Appalachian Mountains for more than 2,000 miles from Georgia to Maine. Forty miles of the pathway are in Maryland, entering at the C&O Canal across the Potomac River from Harpers Ferry, West Virginia. After following the canal eastward for a few miles, it climbs Weverton Cliffs for a spectacular view of the confluence of the Shenandoah and Potomac Rivers. Staying along the crest of South Mountain, the trail passes by several places of historic interest and one viewpoint after another. It leaves the state at the Mason-Dixon Line near Pen-Mar.

The **Appalachian Trail Conference** (304-535-6331; www.appalachiantrail.org), P.O. Box 807, Harpers Ferry, WV 25425, is the source for the *Appalachian Trail Guide to Maryland and Northern Virginia; The Appalachian Trail: A Visitor's Companion; Wildflowers of the Appalachian Trail;* and other publications and information.

AQUARIUMS You could spend hours, even days, experiencing everything the multilevel, multibuilding **National Aquarium** in Baltimore has to offer. Smaller, but still engaging, are the aquariums in the **Ocean City Life Saving Museum** and at the **Calvert Marine Museum** in Solomons.

ART GALLERIES Baltimore is the state's epicenter of art with the world-class **Baltimore Museum of Art** and **Walters Art Museum.** The eccentric exhibits in the **American Visionary Art Museum** enhance the reputation. The **Annapolis Marine Art Gallery** displays only works of living artists who portray life in and around the water. The architecture of the **Washington County Museum of Fine Arts** in Hagerstown is almost as impressive as its extensive collection of Old Masters and American works.

Smaller in size, but still impressive, are **Strathmore Hall** in North Bethesda, **Gudelsky Gallery** in Silver Spring, and **African Art Museum of Maryland** in Columbia. **Mattawoman Creek Art Center** near Marbury is in one of the most peaceful settings you will find, while the presentation of artwork in the commercial **Ocean Gallery World Center** in Ocean City fits in with the chaos and activity of its boardwalk location.

Many artist-owned galleries have become destinations unto themselves.

Places such as **L'Atelier** in Stevensville, **Troika Gallery** in Easton, and **Hidden Artisans' Studio** in St. Michaels contain the works of some of the state's best creators. Most colleges and universities also have a gallery or two, and do not overlook the *Crafts* section in each chapter.

The web site www.delmarweb. com/maryland/artgallery.html has an extensive list (but no descriptions) of galleries throughout the state.

ARTS COUNCILS Every county has an arts council that is funded, at least in part, by the **Maryland State Arts Council** (www.msac.org). As individual organizations, they vary greatly in how large they are and what they do. Most do sponsor classes in various media, theatrical and musical productions, and festivals. All of them have a gallery where the works of their members are displayed in changing exhibits. Several of the largest and most active are: **Academy Art Museum** in Easton; **Carroll County Arts Council Gallery** inside a refurbished 1928 art deco movie house; and **Washington County Arts Council** in Hagerstown.

The **Elkton Arts Center** in Elkton is a real standout. The **Garrett County Arts Council** has the only fine-arts gallery in its region.

BALLOONING Hot-air balloon rides are available from **Fantasy Flights** (301-417-0000; www.airtravel.com/fantasy) in Gaithersburg and **Friendship Hot Air Balloon Company** (410-442-5566) in West Friendship.

The **HiFlyer** (410-727-8120; www.portdiscovery.com) in Baltimore rises 450 feet above Inner Harbor and is tethered to a steel cable.

BEACHES **Ocean City** is, of course, the beach that comes to mind when you think of Maryland. And well it should. With its thousands of motel rooms, attractions by the score, and 10 miles of sand, it is the quintessential East Coast resort town. Just south of it is **Assateague Island** and 30 miles of beach with far fewer people (and amenities). If you are looking for even fewer people, know that hardly anyone ever takes advantage of the small public beach in **Public Landing.**

The beach on **Janes Island** in the Chesapeake Bay offers great seclusion, as it can only be reached by boat. Other beaches along the bay are easier to get to. **Betterton Beach** is the only one that has been completely free of sea nettles (jellyfish) for decades. **Sandy Point** near Annapolis is considered by many to be one of the bay's finest. **Chesapeake Beach** and neighboring **North Beach** were resort destinations in the early 1900s and are still nice, but now quieter, places. You have to take a hike to reach their beaches, but you can search for fossils once you are upon the sands of **Calvert Cliffs State**

Park and **Flag Ponds Nature Park** near Lusby, and **Purse State Park** close to Marbury.

Many state parks have beaches along their lakes, and other small public beaches are mentioned throughout this book.

BED & BREAKFASTS I don't list every one that is in operation, but I have stayed in close to 100 B&Bs in Maryland, and visited and inspected scores more. My selection ranges from modest homes to palatial mansions, and includes working farms, waterfront cottages, historic town houses in busy downtown areas, rustic lodges in isolated woodlands, and more.

Each B&B is different, and it is this diversity that makes each place a new experience. As opposed to staying in a hotel or motel, a visit at a B&B is a much more personal way to get to know the locals and the area in which they live. Although you can make reservations by other means, I like making mine over the phone, as it gives me a chance to chat with the host and establish a relationship before I arrive.

Rates were current when this book went to press, but as in all things monetary, they will probably be a bit higher by the time you visit. Be aware that a number of B&Bs do not accept credit cards.

BICYCLING The relatively flat terrain of the eastern portion of Maryland has always made it popular with bicyclists, and the activity's growth in recent years has made the state even more biker-friendly. The "Maryland Bicycle Map" provides information on more than 50 places to road and/or mountain bike, describing several major long-distance trails and even bike-friendly ferry and transportation systems. The pamphlet *Bicycling in Maryland* contains additional biking and contact information. Both are available from the **Department of Transportation** (1-800-252-8776). Local tourism offices usually have detailed information about their respective areas.

The 184.5-mile C&O Canal is probably the most popular biking route, but do not overlook the Northern Central Railroad Trail, Baltimore and Annapolis Trail, Capital Crescent Trail, Rock Creek Trail, Western Maryland Rail Trail, and ViewTrail 100 Bike Trail. Also, many of Maryland's Scenic Byways (see *Scenic Drives*) are great road-riding journeys. *25 Bicycle Tours in Maryland*, by Anne H. Oman, details additional road trips, while *Mountain Bike America: Washington–Baltimore*, by Martin Fernandez and Scott Adams, is for those looking for the thrill of the single track.

Tour de Shore (410-745-9011; 1-866-745-9011; www.biketds.com) in St. Michaels operates supported road trips on the Eastern Shore. **High Mountain Sports** (301-387-4199; www.highmountainsports.com) will take you on guided mountain bike explorations of the forests around **Deep Creek Lake** in western Maryland.

BIRDING **Waterfowl** migrating through Maryland during the spring and fall may be observed by the hundreds of thousands on the Eastern Shore in places such as **Blackwater National Wildlife Refuge, Eastern Neck National Wildlife Refuge,** and **Deal Island Wildlife Management Area.** *Birdwatcher's Guide to Delmarva* provides details on these and other Eastern Shore sites. **Sandy Point State Park** and **Point Lookout State Park** are a couple of hot spots on the Chesapeake Bay's western shore.

In addition to waterfowl, wide varieties of birds are often seen in **Merkle Wildlife Sanctuary, Greenwell State Park,** and **Patuxent Research Refuge. Clyburn Arboretum** is a favored Baltimore-area birding site, while a number of state-rare breeding species have been observed in **Finzel Swamp** and **Cranesville Swamp** in western Maryland. Rock outcrops along the route of the **Appalachian Trail** on South Mountain are the places to be for the **fall hawk migration.**

The Audubon Society leads bird walks at **Pickering Creek** and **Woodend.** The Wildfowl Trust of North America sponsors a number of walks each year in the **Horsehead Wetlands Center.**

As stands to reason, the Baltimore oriole is the state bird.

BOATBUILDING Chesapeake Wooden Boat Builders School (410-939-4800) in Havre de Grace has classes on antique canoe repair and restoration, model-ship building, and basic wooden-boat building.

BOAT AND SAILING EXCURSIONS To explore Maryland without taking a boating excursion of some kind or another is to miss an essential element of the state. Many of the outings are narrated (and are the ones I think you gain the most from), and you can go onto the water in everything from sailboats to working fishing boats to boats built solely to thrill with speed. The Eastern Shore towns of Ocean City, Cambridge, Hurlock, St.

Michaels, Stevensville, Grasonville, Rock Hall, Solomons, and Tilghman Island all offer excursions. Two boats I especially enjoyed were the **Nathan of Dorchester** in Dorchester and **Lady Patty** in Tilghman Island. Look to the harbors of Havre de Grace, Baltimore, and Annapolis for trips originating on the Chesapeake Bay's western shore.

A boating excursion of a different kind is the 1-hour round-trip ride on the mule-powered **Canal Clipper** on the C&O Canal at Great Falls.

BOAT RAMPS, PUBLIC The map "A Fisherman's Guide to Maryland Piers and Ramps" is available from the **Fisheries Service** (1-800-688-FINS) and highlights more than 240 public water-access areas throughout the state. *The Chesapeake Bay, Susque-hanna River and Tidal Tributaries Public Access Guide* provides even greater detail to those particular areas and may be obtained from the **Chesapeake Bay Program** (1-800-662-CRIS; www.chesapeakebay.net).

BOOKS It is always a good idea to read a few books to help you gain a greater awareness, enjoyment, and understanding of your surroundings. *Maryland: A Middle Temperament, 1634–1980*, by Brugger, Requardt, and Cottom, is an in-depth survey of the state's history. *Maryland: A New Guide to the Old Line State* by Brugger and Papenfuse covers the state's history by leading you on different driving tours; it would make a good companion to this book. It can be a little heavy on the technical aspects, but Edwin Danson's *Drawing the Line: How Mason and Dixon Surveyed the Most Famous Border in America* chronicles the task of delineating Maryland from Pennsylvania. *Maryland in the Civil War: A House Divided*, by Robert I. Cottom Jr. and Mary Ellen Haward, may be the best way to learn about the state's role during the war without having to read multiple volumes. *Home on the Canal* by Elizabeth Kytle is interesting for its historical information, but even more so when it provides firsthand accounts of those who lived and worked on the C&O Canal.

James Michener wrote what may be the best-selling Maryland novel of all time, *Chesapeake,* which describes life around the bay through the eyes of the early settlers and on up to those inhabiting the land in later years. William Martin's novel of intrigue and romance, *Annapolis,* uses the city as a background.

Tom Horton lived and worked among the local people so that he could write his imitate portrait, *An Island Out of Time: A Memoir of Smith Island in the Chesapeake. Chesapeake Almanac: Following the Bay Through the Seasons* is a collection of newspaper columns by John Page William Jr. that takes you through a year's worth of natural world events around the bay. *Chesapeake Bay: Nature of an Estuary,* by Christopher P. White, is another good book about the environment of the bay.

Baseball fans will enjoy Lois P. Nicholson's *From Maryland to Cooperstown: Seven Maryland Natives in Baseball's Hall of Fame.* In *Discovering Maryland Wineries*, Kevin M. Atticks describes not only the wineries and the wines but also the people behind them.

Maryland author Nora Roberts has sold more than 145 million copies of women's novels, a number of them set in Maryland, while mystery writer Martha Grimes turns out one book after another, some of which also feature locations in the state. The comments of the great Baltimore newspaper writer H. L. Mencken have been gathered into several volumes and should be looked over for their caustic wit and ironic observations.

If planning outdoor activities, I recommend you consult my guidebook *50 Hikes in Maryland* (Backcountry Guides), as well as *Hikes in Western Maryland* by the Potomac Appalachian Trail Club; *Birdwatcher's Guide to Delmarva;* and *Finding Wildflowers in the Washington, DC/Baltimore Area. Hiking, Biking, and Canoeing in Maryland,* by Bryan MacKay, focuses on outings appropriate for families with children.

BUS SERVICE Carolina Trailways (410-289-9307) services the Eastern Shore towns of Ocean City, Princess Anne, Cambridge, Easton, and Salisbury. **Greyhound** (1-800-229-9424) stops in Salisbury, Stevensville, and Elkton.

Trailways (703-691-3052) and Greyhound both have terminals in Baltimore. Greyhound also serves Aberdeen, Annapolis, Cumberland, Elkton, Frederick, Grantsville, Hagerstown, and Waldorf.

CAMPING Reservations for campsites and cabins in state parks may be made by calling 1-888-432-CAMP or on-line at www.reservations.dnr.state. md.us. A few are open year-round, but most of the parks' campgrounds are open from early spring to late fall. Backcountry camping is permitted in many state forests, but information (and payment of a fee) must be obtained from each state-forest office.

More than 30 campsites, with chemical toilets and drinking water (in-season), are strung along the **C&O Canal National Historical Park.** Only two, Antietam Creek and Fifteen Mile Creek, charge a fee; all others are free, and all are operated on a first-come, first-served basis. Contact 301-739-4200; www.nps.gov/ choh for more information. Reservations may be made for camping in **Assateague Island National Seashore** and **Greenbelt Park** by contacting 1-800-436-2267 or www.reservations.nps.gov. Call 301-663-9388 for camping reservations in **Catoctin Mountain Park.**

The largest percentage of commercial campgrounds listed in this book have hookups and other facilities for those traveling and camping with trailers or RVs.

CHESAPEAKE BAY If there is any one thing that defines Maryland, especially its eastern portion, it is water—and the Chesapeake Bay is the state's most immense body of water. As America's largest bay, it is the catch basin for a far-reaching drainage system that covers 64,000 square miles. Snowmelt that begins its downstream journey near Cooperstown, New York, meets and mingles in the bay with rainwater that fell on the higher elevations of the Allegheny Mountains on the western Maryland–West Virginia border. The bay is considered an *estuary,* a body of water in which tidal movements bring salt water upstream, where it comes in contact with the fresh water being carried toward the ocean by river currents.

There are many other estuaries throughout the world, such as Puget Sound in Washington, Cook Inlet in Alaska, and the fjords of Norway, but none of them is nearly as productive as the Chesapeake Bay. Well over 100 million pounds of seafood are harvested from the bay most years, including 50 percent of America's supply of **blue crabs** and a large percentage of its **oysters.** A number of conditions combine to make the bay this productive. Probably the two most important factors are the large amounts of fresh water coming into the bay and the vast acreages of marshlands surrounding it, which produce an abundance of detritus and other nutrients. These wetlands are home to numerous shorebirds and are also major resting areas on the **Great Atlantic Flyway** for migratory waterfowl.

The **Chesapeake Bay Gateways Network** is a system of parks, refuges, historic towns, and museums (most of which are described in this book), each of which tells a part of the bay's natural history and impact on Maryland's way of life. The brochure is available from the **Maryland Office of Tourism Development** (see *Information*); you can also consult www.baygateways.net.

CHESAPEAKE & OHIO (C&O) CANAL
The 184.5-mile C&O Canal, running from Georgetown to Cumberland, has excellent opportunities for hiking, biking, canoeing, camping, horseback riding, insights into history, and more for the entire family. I have included information on these activities in the appropriate chapters. Please consult the **C&O Canal National Historical Park** sidebar on page 301 to learn more about the colorful history of this national treasure and how you can best explore it.

CHILDREN, ESPECIALLY FOR The crayon symbol ✎ identifies activities and places of special interest to children and families.

CIVIL WAR As a border state, Maryland was a hotbed of activity during the Civil War. **Antietam National Battlefield** at Sharpsburg and **Monocacy National Battlefield** near Frederick preserve the sites of two of the war's most important battles. In Cambridge, the **Harriet Tubman Museum** sponsors guided tours that reveal the story of Ms. Tubman, who led more than 300 slaves to freedom along the Underground Railroad.

Baltimore Civil War Museum tells of the city's part during the war and in the Underground Railroad. The **National Museum of Civil War Medicine** in Frederick vividly portrays medicine's role. Other sites, battles, and museums of Civil War significance are detailed in their respective sections of each chapter.

The state is developing **Civil War Driving Trails,** and information may be obtained from the **Maryland Office of Tourism Development** (see *Information*).

COVERED BRIDGES Spanning a waterway within the Fair Hill Natural Resources Management Area is the **Big Elk Creek Covered Bridge.** About 3 miles north of North East on MD 272 is the **Gilpin Falls Covered Bridge,** the longest covered bridge still standing in the state. The circa-

1865 **Jericho Covered Bridge** is near Kingsville. **Utica Covered Bridge, Loy's Station Covered Bridge,** and **Roddy Road Covered Bridge** are all north of Frederick.

CRABS Blue crabs can be found from North America's Cape Cod to South America's Uruguay, and even in Egypt's Nile River. It is in the Chesapeake Bay, however, that they reach their greatest numbers, and Maryland crabs have the reputation of being the finest. The harvest fluctuates from year to year—and has been on a downward trend for a while—yet thousands of pounds are still caught and eaten each year. Crab houses serve up bushels of heavily spiced steamed crabs, and soft-shell crabs are considered a real delicacy, while the state's succulent **crabcakes** are known far and wide. I find it amusing that, as you travel around the state, you will find almost every restaurant that serves seafood has "the region's best crabcakes," "the Eastern Shore's best crabcakes," "the best crabcakes in Maryland," or even "the world's best crabcakes."

One of the most fun activities a visitor to the Chesapeake Bay can do is to go **crabbing** by becoming what the local folks call a "chicken necker." This is done by attaching a chicken neck (or any other bony piece of meat) to a string and casting it a few feet out into the water. Gradually pull the string in when you feel a tug on it. With luck, a crab will be hanging tenaciously on to the bait and you can slip a net under it before you lift it out of the water. Be careful of the claws when you turn the net over to gently shake the crab out! No license is required for recreational crabbing (if you take less than two dozen hard-shell crabs), but I suggest you follow what is the law for commercial crabbing and not keep a crab that is less than 5 inches from shell point to shell point.

The interesting lives of blue crabs are described in superbly entertaining and nontechnical detail in William Warner's Pulitzer Prize–winning *Beautiful Swimmers: Watermen, Crabs, and the Chesapeake Bay.* "Beautiful swimmers" is the English translation of the blue crab's genus/species name, *Callinectes sapidus.*

DECOY CARVING AND WILDLIFE ART Steve and Lem Ward are generally acknowledged as being the ones who elevated decoy carving into an art form. Their workshop in Crisfield has been preserved, while the **Ward Museum of Wildlife Art** in Salisbury exhibits their work and chronicles the history of decoy carving. Other significant decoy displays are in the **Upper Bay Museum** in North East and the **Havre de Grace Decoy Museum.** The **Ward World Championship Wildfowl Carving Competition,** held each spring in Ocean City, is the world's largest carving competition.

DELMARVA The word *Delmarva* refers to the entire Eastern Shore peninsula, which is composed of portions of Delaware, Maryland, and Virginia.

EMERGENCIES Hospitals with emergency rooms are noted near the beginning of each chapter. A few urgent-care facilities that can handle minor emergencies are also listed. Dialing **911** anywhere in the state will connect you to an emergency service. For highway accidents or assistance, the **state police** may be reached at 410-653-4200, on **CB Channel 9,** or **Cellular #77.**

EVENTS County fairs, arts and crafts demonstrations, fishing tournaments, skill competitions, historic reenactments, music concerts, crab festivals: Some kind of distinctive event or celebration takes places almost every day of the year. Leading annual events are noted in the *Special Events* section at the end of each chapter. *Maryland Celebrates,* available from the **Maryland Office of Tourism Development** (see *Information*), describes hundreds of events that will take place within the calendar year; a number of them are onetime occurrences.

FACTORY OUTLETS There are a number of modern, mall-type outlets, and they are noted in their respective chapter under *Selective Shopping*. There are also several true factory outlets where you purchase the product where it was produced. In Crisfield, the story behind **Carvel Hall**'s cutlery and seafood tools goes back to the late 1800s. You watch the craftsmen at work in **Salisbury Pewter** in Salisbury. Cumberland's **Biederlack of America** is a major manufacturer of rugs and throws.

FARMER'S MARKETS Farmer's markets may be found in every region of the state and are listed in the *Selective Shopping* section of each chapter. I love going to them, but be aware that the locations and operating days and times of farmer's markets have been known to change frequently.

FERRIES Relics of the past, only a few ferries remain in Maryland. Their historic aspect and the scenic beauty of the waterways they cross make using one as much of a fun excursion as a utilitarian necessity. The **Whitehaven Ferry** is connected to a fixed line and crosses the Wicomico River about 18 miles west of Salisbury. The **Upper Ferry** crosses the Wicomico River less than 10 miles west of Salisbury. The **Oxford–Bellevue Ferry** enables a circular driving tour of Easton, Oxford, and St. Michaels by making a crossing on the Tred Avon River. **White's Ferry,** the only remaining ferry across the Potomac River, permits you come into Maryland near Poolesville from US 15 just north of Leesburg, Virginia.

Much larger, the **Cape May, New Jersey–Lewes, Delaware Ferry** can save you hours and many miles of driving if you are arriving on the Eastern Shore from New Jersey.

FISHING The **Department of Natural Resources/Fisheries Service** (1-800-688-FINS) can supply the information you need about regulations and licenses, and has free publications geared toward tidal, freshwater, trout, fly-, and other types of fishing.

Within the *Fishing* section of the chapters are places to fish on your own, or companies and individuals who provide guided trips. The web site for the **Maryland Charter Boat Association** (www.marylandcharterboats.com) contains the largest list of charter-boat captains on the Chesapeake Bay, while local tourism offices (see *Guidance* in each chapter) maintain lists of reliable captains and fishing guides.

GOLF The courses listed under the *To Do* section in each chapter are public courses that do not require payment of a membership fee. The *Maryland Golf Guide,* available from the **Maryland Office of Tourism Development** (see *Information*), outlines public, semiprivate, and private courses.

HANDICAPPED ACCESS The wheelchair symbol ♿ appears next to lodgings, restaurants, and attractions that are partially or completely handicapped-accessible.

HIGHWAY TRAVEL The speed limit on interstates is 65 miles per hour unless otherwise noted. Driver and passengers are required to wear safety belts, and children under the age of 4 or those weighing less than 40 pounds must be in approved child-safety seats. Driving lights must be on whenever you are using windshield wipers. You may make a right turn at a red signal light after coming to a complete stop unless posted signs prohibit doing so.

Call the **State Highway Administration's Construction Hotline** (410-545-0300; 1-800-323-6742) 8–4:30, Monday through Friday, to obtain the latest information on construction projects that may impact your travel plans. The commission's web site (www.marylandroads.com) provides up-to-date road conditions during inclement weather and a wealth of road-travel information.

The official state highway map may be obtained from the **Maryland Office of Tourism Development** (see *Information*). Available at bookshops and many convenience stores, the *Maryland and Delaware Atlas and Gazetteer* (published by DeLorme) is an invaluable navigation tool.

HIKING I have included the state's best hiking excursions under the *Hiking* section of each chapter; look at the *Bicycling, Birding, Parks, Gardens,* and *Nature Preserves* sections for additional opportunities to walk outdoors.

Recommended resources include *Walks and Rambles on the Delmarva Peninsula* by Jay Abercrombie, *Country Walks Near Washington* by Alan Fisher, and *Country Walks Near Baltimore.* One of my own books, *50*

Hikes in Maryland (Backcountry Guides), covers the entire state with outings ranging from easy, 1-hour jaunts to multiday backpacking treks.

HORSEBACK RIDING Places to ride your own horse and businesses offering guided rides are listed under the *To Do* section of a chapter; additional places to ride can often be found by looking in the *Bicycling*, *Hiking*, and *Parks* sections of a chapter. **The Equiery** (1-800-244-9580) publishes a directory to rental stables and guided trail rides in the state.

HUNTING A comprehensive booklet, *Hunting and Trapping in Maryland*, may be obtained from the **Department of Natural Resources** (410-260-8540; www.dnr.state.md.us).

If you like the outdoors but are not a hunter, be aware that hunting is permitted in wildlife management areas, state forests, and some state parks. Although the law is under pressure to change, Sunday hunting was still prohibited as this book went to press.

ICE CREAM, HOMEMADE When I started adding them up, I was amazed at just how many places produce homemade ice cream; no wonder I put on a few pounds researching this book. **Dumser's Drive-In** at Ocean

City serves it within a few hours of making it. **Canal Creamery** is on the waterfront in Chesapeake City. **Gourmet by the Bay** in St. Michaels sells its frozen treats in pints only. There is often a line waiting get into Havre de Grace's **Bomboy's Homemade Ice Cream**. **Hoffman's** in Westminster has been using the same recipes since it opened in 1947. **Mother's Federal Hill Grille** and **Maggie Moo's** are located in Baltimore, while **Simple Pleasures Ice Café** may be found in Bowie. **Baugher's** in Westminster and **Queen City Creamery and Deli** in Cumberland serve their ice creams within a restaurant setting, while the peach ice cream at **Kent Fort Farm** in Stevensville is available only during the August Peach Festival.

The crème de la crème is **Lakeside Creamery** at Deep Creek Lake. The owner is such a master at his craft that people travel from foreign lands just to take his classes on producing homemade ice cream.

INFORMATION Regional information sources are described under the *Guidance* section near the beginning of each chapter. The **Maryland Office of Tourism Development** (410-767-3400; 1-800-634-7386; www.mdisfun.org), 217 East Redwood Street, Baltimore, 21202, publishes *Destination Maryland,* an annual guide to many attractions, outdoor opportunities, and lodging facilities throughout the state. The office can also be the source for numerous brochures on specialized topics such as golfing, biking, antiques, canoeing, fishing, and more.

INSECTS Warm weather brings no-see-ums, gnats, fleas, sand fleas, deerflies, mosquitoes, ticks, and more. Although the mountains have their fair share, the lowlands, marshes, and beaches of the eastern part of the state, especially southern Maryland and the Eastern Shore, can be nearly swarming with them at times. Bring lots of repellent on any outing from late spring through midfall. (And remember that one of the pleasures of travel during the colder months of the year is the absence of insects.)

KAYAKING AND CANOEING The kayaking and canoeing are soft and easy along the streams and creeks of the Eastern Shore and southern Maryland, while winds across the Chesapeake Bay can test the mettle of an experienced kayaker. The rushing waters of western Maryland can require such technical skill that they have been used for national and international competitions and by athletes training for the Olympics.

Included in the *Kayaking and Canoeing* section of the various chapters are guided trips by outfitters as well as places to paddle on your own. Also consult the *Boat Rentals* and *Parks* sections. The books **Maryland and Delaware Canoe Trails** by Edward Gertler and **Exploring the Chesapeake in Small Boats** by John Page Williams and William S. Portlock can provide additional information.

LIGHTHOUSES Lighthouses have helped provide safe passage for commercial and recreational boats navigating the Chesapeake Bay and other state waters for well over 100 years. Of the 44 once in Maryland, only 25 remain and most are no longer in service. **Hooper Straight Lighthouse** in St. Michaels and **Drum**

Point in Solomons have been moved to museums, and are two of the most visited. **Cove Point,** the oldest continuously used lighthouse in the state, is at the mouth of the Patuxent River north of Solomons.

Concord Point is along a waterside walkway in Havre de Grace, while **Turkey Point** is reached by a 1-mile hike in Elk Neck State Park. **Sevenfoot Knoll,** now in Baltimore's Inner Harbor, was moved from its original location at nearby Pier 5. **Piney Point** has an adjacent museum, while **Point Lookout** is open to the public only once a year; both are at the tip of southern Maryland where the Potomac River meets the bay.

MARITIME MUSEUMS The **Chesapeake Bay Maritime Museum** in St. Michaels is the state's largest and one of the finest on the East Coast. The **Calvert Marine Museum** in Solomons is another standout. At the head of the bay is the **Havre de Grace Maritime Museum,** while Cambridge on the Eastern Shore has the **Richardson Maritime Museum** and **Brannock Maritime Museum**.

Annapolis Maritime Museum tells the history of its Eastport neighborhood. **Baltimore Maritime Museum** has no real walls, as it consists of three ships docked about a block from each other.

MOTELS AND HOTELS For the most part, chain motels and hotels have not been listed because information about them is easily obtained from many sources and because their architecture and amenities tend to have a cookie-cutter sameness. Those that are included are in areas where lodging options are few, are in a desirable location, or are outstanding places to stay.

THE NATIONAL ROAD In 1775, British forces under General Edward Braddock, accompanied by a young George Washington, widened a Native American trail through Turners Gap to facilitate their march westward, where they were ambushed (and Braddock killed) by French and Indian troops in Pennsylvania. With funds provided by the state in 1806, the route was improved, extended from Baltimore to Cumberland, and named the **National Pike.** At the same time, the U.S. Congress also authorized federal funds for another road, this one to begin in Cumberland and head westward. Eventually the two roads came to be known as the National Road. As one of the major thoroughfares of the day, it was traveled by such luminaries as Abraham Lincoln, Daniel Webster, Henry Clay, and Presidents Jackson, William Henry Harrison, Polk, Taylor, and Van Buren.

US 40 in Maryland follows the route of what was once the National Road and was named an **"All American Road"** in 2002. As you explore Maryland, take a break from the interstate to travel the roadway and discover historic sites you would otherwise pass by.

NATURE TOURISM The **Department of Natural Resources** has embarked upon what I think is one of the most exciting and farsighted ventures to come along in years. By using state employees, contracts with private outfitters, and some volunteers, the Nature Tourism program offers recreational and educational opportunities for adults and children of all skill and fitness levels to experience the outdoors. Hiking, biking, rock climbing, caving, horseback riding, kayaking, canoeing, rafting, fishing, bird-watching, camping, and day camps are just a few of the many organized and guided activities the program has offered—usually at a fairly low cost. New ones are being added all the time. The great thing is that the department has hired Nature Tourism employees for each region of the state, so someone is out there on the local level arranging all of these activities. Contact 1-800-830-3974; www.dnr.md.us/outdoors for detailed information.

OLD LINE STATE One of Maryland's nicknames is the Old Line State. It does not refer to the Mason-Dixon Line as many people believe but goes back to the Revolutionary War. Maryland's Governor Smallwood had led a group of state volunteers to help George Washington in New York. The Marylanders held their line of defense against the British long enough to permit Washington's troops to escape and regroup to fight another day. He was so impressed that Washington ever after referred to Maryland as the "Old Line State."

PARKS, NATIONAL

Assateague Island National Seashore shares the barrier island with Maryland's **Assateague State Park** and Virginia's **Chincoteague National Wildlife Refuge.** Undeveloped, except for a couple of campgrounds and a few visitors centers, the island offers close to 30 miles of unbroken sandy beaches on which to beachcomb, swim, sunbathe, or surf fish. A hike of 25 miles can be accomplished by making use of designated campsites (and carrying plenty of water!). **Greenbelt Park,** close to Washington, D.C., has a campground and a trail system within a forest bordered by four-lane highways. **Catoctin Mountain Park,** north of Frederick, is home to the U.S. presidential retreat, **Camp David,** and miles of pathways leading to spectacular viewpoints.

Other components of the U.S. National Park Service are Antietam National Battlefield, C&O Canal National Historical Park, Fort Washington, Glen Echo Park, Oxon Hill Farm, Piscataway Park, and a number of historic buildings and structures, such as the Thomas Stone National Historic Site near Port Tobacco.

PARKS AND FORESTS, STATE

With more than 280,000 acres of land, there is a state park or forest within a 40-minute drive of any location in Maryland. Admission to the state forests and some of the state parks is free, but some have a nominal entrance or parking fee, usually in the $1–5 range. Many of the state parks have campgrounds and cabins for rent, and backcountry camping is permitted in some of the state forests (see *Camping* above). Consult the *Bicycling, Hiking, Kayaking and Canoeing,* and *Parks* sections in each chapter to find what is available in each region. The **Department of Natural Resources–State Forest and Park Service** (410-974-3771; 1-800-830-3974; www.dnr.state.md.us) can send you a packet brimming with all kinds of information.

PETS

The dog-paw symbol 🐾 appears next to places, activities, and lodgings that accept pets. Always inform a hotel, motel, B&B, or other lodging that you will be traveling with your pet; expect to pay an additional fee.

POPULATION

The state's population was 5,296,486 according to the 2000 federal census.

PICK-YOUR-OWN PRODUCE

There is just something about a strawberry, tomato, or peach that is picked ripe off the plant that grocery-store produce can't match. Farms and orchards that invite the public into their fields and orchards are listed in each chapter. Unless you don't mind just taking a drive in the country, it is a wise idea to call ahead to confirm what is ripe and at what time and day you may come out to pick.

The **Maryland Direct Farm**

Market Association (410-665-0154), 2526 Proctor Lane, Baltimore, 21234, publishes a directory of pick-your-own places and farms that have their own fruit and vegetable stands.

RAILROAD RIDES AND MUSEUMS Rail fans, and children, enjoy the excursions offered by the **Walkersville Southern Railroad** near Frederick and **Western Maryland Scenic Railroad** in Cumberland and Frostburg.

Baltimore's **B&O Railroad Museum** has 40 acres of locomotives, cars, and artifacts. Built around 1830, the **Ellicott City B&O Railroad Station Museum** is the oldest railroad terminal in America. **Brunswick Railroad Museum** features a model layout of the B&O line from Washington, D.C., to Brunswick. Hagerstown's **Roundhouse Museum** is from the days when five different lines converged on the city.

SAILING LESSONS Three excellent sailing schools make Annapolis, the "Sailing Capital of America," their home port. **Annapolis Sailing School** is one of the world's most well-respected institutions of sailing knowledge. **AYS Charters and Sailing School** offers sailing instructions

and charter-certification courses. **Womanship, Inc.**, has sailing instruction taught by and for women.

Rock Hall has two schools, the **Maryland School of Sailing and Seamanship** and the **Sailing Emporium.** North of Baltimore in Havre de Grace is **BaySail.** In western Maryland, you can learn to hoist a sail on a lake at the **Deep Creek Sailing School.**

SCENIC BYWAYS I had originally intended to point out quite a number of Maryland's scenic drives (and I do include a few), but when I discovered the excellent *Maryland Scenic Byways* book and accompanying "Scenic Byways Map," it seemed that the effort would be superfluous.

First of all, the 192-page book is free and may be obtained from most local tourism offices, state welcome centers, the **Maryland Office of Tourism Development** (see *Information*), or the **Maryland Scenic Byways, Office of Environmental Design** (1-877-MDBYWAY; www.sha. state.md.us/oed/bywaysprogram.htm).

Second, the book gives directions for more than 30 drives throughout the state with detailed background information on the human and natural history of the area driven through, sites along the route, recreational opportunities, and even side trips worth taking. The shortest byway is 5 miles in Baltimore; the longest is several hundred miles and stretches from the Atlantic Ocean to the Appalachian Mountains.

This a great explorer's resource—and remember, it is available free for the asking.

SEA NETTLES A jellyfish with long tentacles, and known as a sea nettle, increases in number as the temperatures of summer warm the Chesapeake Bay, its tributaries, and the Atlantic Ocean. Its sting can be a source of irritation for many hours. Alcohol, vinegar, baking soda, or meat tenderizer may help relieve the pain, but some people have severe allergic reactions that require them to be hospitalized.

SKIING, CROSS-COUNTRY New Germany and **Herrington Manor State Parks** have trails groomed and tracked just for cross-country skiing. The parks also provide ski rentals and warming huts. Information on the many miles of ungroomed trails around the **Deep Creek Lake** area may be obtained from the **Garrett County Chamber of Commerce** (301-387-4286; www.garrettchamber. com).

Piney Run Park near Sykesville, the **Catoctin Mountain Park, C&O Canal,** and **Appalachian Trail** all make for good cross-country ski outings when enough snow falls to cover the roots and rocks.

SKIING, DOWNHILL Wisp Ski and Golf Resort, at Deep Creek Lake, is the state's only downhill skiing spot. It has what is considered to be one of the best snowmaking systems in the world, so all that is really needed is cold weather for the trails to be open. Snowboarding, cross-country skiing, tubing, night skiing, and children's programs are also available.

SNOWMOBILING The Deep Creek Lake area welcomes snowmobilers. **Deep Creek Lake, Garrett State Forest, Potomac State Forest,** and **Savage River State Forest** have a combined total of 75 miles of marked

trails open for backcountry travel. The **Garrett County Chamber of Commerce** (301-387-4286; www.garrettchamber.com) can supply detailed information.

TAXES The state sales tax is 5 percent; lodging, meals, and amusement taxes can be well in excess of 10 percent.

WATERFALLS Swallow Falls State Park near Oakland has a 1.5-mile circuit hike that will lead you to four different waterfalls. **Muddy Creek Falls** is considered the highest in the state, **Lower Falls** and **Swallow Falls** are on the Youghiogheny River, and there is a sandy beach at **Toliver Falls.**

The round-trip journey to **Cunningham Falls** near Thurmont is an easy 1-mile hike. **Falling Branch,** in Rocks State Park near Jarrettsville, and **Great Falls** in the Potomac River, are on the fall line where the piedmont meets the Coastal Plain.

Incidentally, despite the name, there are no waterfalls in Gunpowder Falls State Park. *Falls* was a colonial term for "river."

WEATHER Maryland can have a wide range of temperatures and conditions.

Winters can be unpredictably cold or relatively mild, while summers can become hot and humid or may be rather temperate. Spring and autumn can be the most pleasant times of the year, as days warm up to a comfortable degree, nights cool down for easy sleeping, and crowds are fewer.

Snow is common in the mountains, moderate in the Capital and Central Regions, and quite infrequent in southern Maryland and the Eastern Shore. When heat and humidity have taken the joy and fun out of the eastern portion of the state, the mountains will beckon with temperatures that can be 10 or more degrees lower. Exploring Maryland can be a year-round activity.

WHITEWATER RAFTING Precision Rafting in Friendsville is the premier Maryland company that runs the Upper Youghiogheny River as it passes through a narrow, 5-mile gorge with nearly continuous Class IV and V rapids. **River and Trail Outfitters** in Knoxville and **Outdoor Excursions** in Boonsboro have runs along the (usually) calmer Potomac River.

The Eastern Shore

The Eastern Shore

THE EASTERN SHORE

Maryland's Eastern Shore is a land where time has stood still—or at least slowed down considerably.

In search of flounder, crabs, clams, oysters, and other delicacies of the deep, watermen still arise before dawn to venture onto the Chesapeake Bay or the Atlantic Ocean. Moving about in small craft often with a crew of just one or two people, they use many of the same techniques that their fathers and grandfathers used decades ago.

The area is unmarred by huge malls and strips of fast-food restaurants; the only industry in many of the unpretentious fishing villages are small seafood processing plants at water's edge. Thriving downtown districts still exist in a number of small towns. Blessed with a long growing season and fertile soil, the flat fields surrounding the towns produce a rich harvest of corn, beans, tomatoes, peppers, and other vegetables.

The completion of the Bay Bridge in 1952 opened the Eastern Shore to a rush of travelers and new residents. Although rising amounts of traffic and tourism have resulted in subtle changes in Eastern Shore lifestyles, outside influences have also helped bring about an increased awareness of the need to preserve the natural world.

Migrating shorebirds, waterfowl, raptors, and songbirds—including sandpipers, plovers, dowitchers, knots, whimbrels, ducks, geese, herons, egrets, swans, pelicans, falcons, and ospreys—make use of the islands, marshlands, and fields as major resting areas. Thousands of waterfowl, such as snow geese, black ducks, mallards, and pintails, winter here.

Maryland's Seaboard

MARYLAND'S SEABOARD—OCEAN CITY, ASSATEAGUE ISLAND, AND BERLIN

When Marylanders, especially those from the Baltimore-Annapolis area, say they are "goin' down'e ocean," they mean they will be spending time on the beach at Ocean City. My wife is a native Annapolitan, and her earliest vacation memories are of packing up the beach blankets and sand buckets and spending a few hours in the car anticipating the first whiff of salty air. It is such an entrenched tradition that generation after generation return here, going so far as to spend their vacation time in the exact same motel or B&B room as their parents or grandparents did.

The area began developing as a resort destination in 1869 when Isaac C. Coffin built the Rhode Island Inn. Within a few years, a group of developers received a land grant, and the Atlantic Hotel—still in operation—was opened in 1875.

The construction of a railroad bridge across the Sinepuxent Bay in 1880 connected the mainland to the resort, which was soon host to more than 5,000 visitors a year. Although Ocean City continued to grow in popularity, the city and surrounding area were struck by a major storm in 1933 that destroyed almost the entire infrastructure and nearly every building and road. The storm cut an inlet into the bay, separating the city from what is now called Assateague Island and creating ideal conditions for commercial and sportfishing. Boats could dock in the quiet waters of the bay but have quick access to the ocean for deep-sea fishing.

A four-lane bridge across the bay was constructed in 1941, and Ocean City has continued to grow in popularity since.

With its 10-mile-long beach, the city has many of the aspects of beach towns farther north, such as a 3-mile boardwalk, amusement parks and arcades next to and close to the beach, and an abundance of saltwater taffy and other goodies stores. Yet its waters are warmer and gentler, like those of the ocean resorts found in South Carolina and Georgia.

The southern end of the boardwalk, with arcades, an amusement park, and many fast-food spots, attracts the most people, while the central portion of the beach and the hotels located there tend to draw a young crowd. Those looking for a family atmosphere on the sand often book motels north of the boardwalk.

Almost everyone who visits Ocean City makes the short drive to Assateague

Island to catch a glimpse of the wild ponies made famous by Marguerite Henry's popular series of children's books, beginning with *Misty of Chincoteague* in 1947.

A barrier island, Assateague is the farthest east you can go to take a hike or camp in Maryland. Formed by sand that constant waves have raised from the gently sloping ocean floor, a string of such islands extends along the East Coast from Plum Island, Massachusetts, to Padre Island, Texas. Being prime beachfront property, many have been heavily developed and turned into typical high-rise resort areas.

The same thing almost happened to Assateague Island. Having purchased the largest majority of it in Maryland, the Ocean Beach Corporation began subdividing the island into small plots in the 1950s. Within a few years, there was a paved road running down the interior of the island, electric lines had been installed, close to 6,000 plots had been sold, and a number of houses already built.

A northeaster that struck the island in March 1962 drove the ocean completely across the island in several places. Almost every house was demolished, the power lines were downed and severed, and the road destroyed, with most of its pavement washed away. Realizing the enormous costs of trying to maintain a

ADDITIONAL SOURCES OF INFORMATION

A number of publications, such as *Sunny Day Guide to Ocean City, Ocean City Visitors Guide, Ocean City: Sea for Yourself,* and *Beachcomber,* are available free from the Convention and Visitors Bureau, the welcome center (see *Guidance*), merchants, and vending boxes on the streets. Not only do they provide up-to-date information on stores, restaurants, events, and points of interest, but some also contain a plethora of coupons that could end up saving you quite a few dollars.

WILD PONIES GRAZE ON ASSATEAGUE ISLAND.

modern way of life on the island, private investors began to shy away, and the
federal government was able to establish Assateague Island National Seashore
in 1965.

Today, the entire island is public land and administered as the national
seashore by the U.S. National Park Service, Assateague State Park under the
jurisdiction of the Maryland Department of Natural Resources, and, on the Virginia side of the island, Chincoteague National Wildlife Refuge within the aus-
pices of the U.S. Fish and Wildlife Service. What this means to you is that the
island's 37-mile beach has been left gloriously undeveloped, with just a few
minor amenities, such as couple of campgrounds, visitors centers, and a few
nature trails concentrated in two small areas.

COMMUNITIES **Berlin** has retained so much of its small-town look and atmosphere that Hollywood has chosen it as the setting for several movies. Two of the
most recent are the Julia Roberts and Richard Gere film *Runaway Bride,* and
Disney's 2002 release of *Tuck Everlasting.*

The town dates from a 1677, 300-acre land grant establishing the Burley Plantation. It was not named in honor of the German city; most historians believe the
name was derived from a local habit of quickly saying and slurring the name of
one of the town's inns, the "Burleigh Inn." Its fortunes were in many ways tied to
those of Ocean City, as it slowly prospered by becoming a stopping-over point or
an alternate destination for travelers headed to the beach.

Today, the Atlantic Hotel, built in
the late 1800s, sits in the center of
the town's well-preserved historic
district. Visitors now come to walk
the tree-lined streets, stopping to
admire structures dating from
America's Federal, Victorian, and
20th-century periods, and look
through the hidden treasures to be
found in numerous antiques stores.

The town of **Snow Hill** was chartered in 1686, and only eight years
later it was named a Royal Port,
reflecting its advantageous location.
The Chincoteague Bay and access
to the Atlantic Ocean were only 7
miles to the east, while the Chesapeake Bay at Pocomoke Sound was
less than 30 miles down the river.
Snow Hill retained its prominence
long into the 19th century, as the
railroad came through the center
of town. The town is the seat of
government for Worcester County,

PONY PENNING

One of the most exciting events of the
year in this area takes place on the last
continuous Wednesday and Thursday
of July when Virginia's famous herd of
ponies swims across the channel from
Assateague Island to Memorial Park on
Chincoteague Island in Virginia (call 757-
336-6161 for more information). Actually
owned by the Chincoteague Volunteer
Fire Department, some of the foals are
sold at auction, with proceeds aiding fire-
fighting efforts. Legend has long held that
the ponies are descendants of mustangs
that swam ashore after a Spanish ship
wrecked off the coast in the 16th century.
More likely, their ancestors were placed
on the island by mainland owners wanting to avoid taxation and the expense of
fencing.

and many of its old homes and other historic structures remain along its tree-shaded streets. The small business district is still located where it always was, close to the river—which is now a playground for recreational boaters.

Pocomoke City, also located along the Pocomoke River, shares much of the same history as Snow Hill. With deeper water, though, it was able to service much larger ships, which it still does today. The Victorian Costen House helps preserve the town's history, while the 1-mile boardwalked trail in Cypress Park is a great place to enjoy the area's natural habitats.

GUIDANCE The **Ocean City Convention and Visitors Bureau** (410-289-2800; 1-800-OC-OCEAN) operates a large information center adjacent to the Convention Center at 4001 Coastal Highway, Ocean City.

The **Ocean City Chamber of Commerce** (1-888-OCMD-FUN; www.ocean-city.org) has a **welcome center** just a few miles west of the beach on US 50 in West Ocean City.

Exhibits, an aquarium, and brochures about Assateague Island are available at the National Park Service's **Barrier Island Visitor Center** (410-641-1441; 410-641-3030), 7206 National Seashore Lane, Berlin.

The **Worcester County Tourism Office** (410-632-3110; 1-800-852-0335) is located on the corner of Pearl and Market Streets in Snow Hill.

GETTING THERE *By air:* The **Ocean City Airport** (410-213-2471) is available to private planes, while the **Salisbury/Ocean City Airport** (410-548-4827), which is located about 30 minutes west of the ocean, receives regularly scheduled flights via US Airways (1-800-428-4322).

By car: **US 50** is the route that will bring you into the city from points to the north, west, and south. If possible, plan your arrival for times other than Friday afternoon or evening and Saturday morning, and your departure other than Sunday. Doing so will permit you to avoid miles of bumper-to-bumper cars moving at a snail's pace. **US 113** is the main artery through Worcester County and provides access to major side routes.

By ferry: If coming from New Jersey and other places to the northeast, you can save yourself a number of hours and many miles by taking the **Cape May, New Jersey–Lewes, Deleware, Ferry** (1-800-64-FERRY for schedule and reservations) and driving through Rehoboth Beach to Ocean City.

By bus: **Carolina Trailways** (410-289-9307) has a station at 2nd Street and Philadelphia Avenue in Ocean City.

GETTING AROUND *By car:* Driving (and then parking) at any time during the summer season can be a real aggravation. To save driving into the resort area, you can park your car for free at the **Park and Ride** off US 50 in West Ocean City and take the shuttle bus to the 2nd Street Transit Center in Ocean City for only $1.

If you do drive into the resort area and happen to find a parking space, but don't want to drive anymore, you can ride a bus all the way from the Inlet to the

Delaware state line for only $1, all day, 24 hours a day. **Buses** run every 10 minutes during the summer; every 30 minutes at other times of the year. Routes include all of the major streets and roadways. Exact change required. Call 410-723-1607 for more information.

By train: The **Boardwalk Train** (410-723-1607), with open-air cars, runs the full length of the 2.9-mile boardwalk throughout the heaviest tourist months. $2.50, one way.

By taxi: **Sunshine Cab** (410-208-2828); **Whites Cab** (410-250-8294); **Ace Taxi** (410-641-4280).

By bus: The local bus service, **Worcester County** (410-632-3232), has a route that enables you to ride a loop from West Ocean City to Berlin. It is also possible to ride the length of Worcester County, making stops in Berlin, Newark, Snow Hill, Pocomoke City, Stockton, and points in between. Also see *By car,* above.

PARKING Meters in all municipal lots in Ocean City are in effect 24 hours a day; those on the street have varying times. No-parking zones are enforced, and businesses can be aggressive in their towing policies.

The Inlet parking lot has a gated time system. You get a ticket when you enter, and pay when you leave; no need to worry about feeding the meter. Often fills to capacity early in the day.

PUBLIC REST ROOMS In Ocean City, at the boardwalk at Worcester Street; boardwalk at Caroline Street; 3rd Street and St. Louis Avenue; boardwalk at 9th Street; boardwalk at 27th Street; and 4001 Coastal Highway.

MEDICAL EMERGENCY Ocean City: **10th Street Medical Center** (410-289-6241); **75th Street Medical Center** (410-524-0075); **126th Street Medical Center** (410-250-8000). Berlin: **Atlantic General Hospital** (410-641-1100), located at the intersection of US 50 and US 113; available for 24-hour emergency services.

✳ To See

MUSEUMS

Ocean City

✎ **Ocean City Life Saving Museum** (410-289-4991), boardwalk at the Inlet. Open 7 days a week May 1 through October 31; Saturday and Sunday, November through April. Once a lifesaving station, this museum chronicles the exploits of brave members of the U.S. Life Saving Service and Coast Guard who have saved more than 7,000 lives off the Maryland coast. In addition, there are items from Ocean City history, a whimsical look at bathing-suit styles through the years, several small aquariums, shipwreck items, and, what I found very interesting, over 200 samples of beach sand from around the world. Free kids' programs on the boardwalk during the summer.

Wheels of Yesterday (410-213-7329), 12708 Ocean Gateway (US 50). Owner Granville Trimper has been gathering his collection for years and shows about 30 antique cars at a time. One that is always on exhibit is Jack Benny's 1917 Overland. Others on display include the 1904 Oldsmobile used in the 2002 movie *Tuck Everlasting* and one of only 1,200 1962 Corvair pickups manufactured with a side bed entrance.

Newark

Queponco Railway Station (410-632-0950), 8378 Patey Wood Road. Donations accepted. Open first and third Saturday 1–4, May through October. A local group rescued this abandoned passenger station in 1991 and is gradually restoring and outfitting it to look as it did from 1910 to the 1960s.

Snow Hill

Julia A. Purnell Museum (410-632-0515), 201 West Market Street. Small admission charge. Tuesday through Saturday 10–4, April through October. Ms. Purnell created more than 1,000 needlework pictures during the last 15 years of her 100-year life. The works, most of them depicting the historic homes and buildings of Snow Hill, brought her such worldwide acclaim that she was inducted into the National Hobby Hall of Fame. Since its establishment in 1957, the museum has become a repository of not only her accomplishments but also of many items important to the history of the area. Exhibits include a general store, a tribute to local firefighters, and a display of Native American artifacts. The local museum of my childhood had a pair of dressed fleas that attracted many people from the surrounding area, and I was happy to see that the Purnell Museum also contains a pair, with one of them carrying a parasol! Docents tell me this is the museum's most popular display.

Mt. Zion One Room School Museum (410-632-1265), Ironshire and Church Streets. Small admission charge. Tuesday through Saturday 1–4, mid-June through Labor Day. Now moved from its original location, the Mt. Zion school served students from the northern part of the county from 1869 to 1931. Many of the original coat hooks and shelves remain, as well as some of the students' metal lunch pails. Docents provide a short guided tour.

THE QUEPONCO RAILWAY STATION

Pocomoke City

Sturgis One Room School Museum (410-957-1913), 209 Willow Street. Small admission charge. Wednesday and Saturday 1–4, May through October. The Sturgis one-room school served Worcester County's African American community from 1900 to 1937. Moved from its original site in the late 1990s, it continues to undergo restoration and outfitting.

HISTORIC HOMES **Calvin B. Taylor House** (410-641-1019), North Main and Baker Streets, Berlin. Donations accepted. Monday, Wednesday, Friday, and Saturday 1–4, Memorial Day weekend through October. Like so many historic buildings in America, the Taylor House, built around 1832, was slated to be torn down to make way for a parking lot. Rescued from destruction by the Berlin Heritage Foundation, it opened to the public as a museum in 1983. Guided tours take visitors throughout the period-decorated house and focus on its two most prominent occupants. The Harrison family operated the country's largest mail-order nursery business, shipping seedlings from their fruit trees to destinations the world over. In 1890, Calvin B. Taylor established the bank bearing his name, which is still in business. His bank desk and chair are on display along with other items from the town's history. Most impressive are the original flooring and 1830s quilts in the upstairs bedroom, and the portico's butterfly modillions atop the fluted columns.

Costen House (410-957-3110), 206 Market Street, Pocomoke City. Small admission charge. Wednesday and Saturday 1–4, May through October. Dr. Costen was known throughout the Eastern Shore for his courageous works and travels to treat victims of typhoid fever. Built around 1870, his home now helps present the life of a small town and of the doctor and his family. The Hall-Walton Garden on the property re-creates a landscape similar to that of the doctor's days.

HISTORIC SITES **Furnace Town** (410-632-2032), Furnace Town Road, Snow Hill. Small admission fee. Open 7 days a week 11–5, April 1 through October 31. Off-season the grounds and trails are open for walking during daylight hours. The smelting of iron during the 1800s was a labor-intensive process that required an entire village to support just one furnace. Through living-history demonstrations and reconstructed buildings, those days are brought back. Visit

---

1872 RULES FOR TEACHERS

- Each teacher will bring a bucket of water and a scuttle of coal for the day's session.
- Men teachers may take one evening each week for courting purposes, or two evenings a week if they go to church regularly.
- Women teachers who marry or engage in unseemly conduct will be dismissed.
- Any teacher who smokes, uses liquor in any form, frequents pool or public halls, or gets shaved in a barber shop will give good reason to suspect his worth, intention, integrity and honesty.
- The teacher who performs his labor faithfully and without fault for five years will be given an increase of 25 cents per week in his pay, providing the Board of Education approves.

—from the Worcester County one-room schoolhouses

FURNACE TOWN

the old furnace, observe the blacksmith at work, or stand on the pulpit of the church and preach a sermon. The broom maker explained to me what a niddy-noddy is; be sure to find out for yourself. The easy, 1-mile Paul Leiffer Nature Trail wanders through the Nassawango Cypress Swamp.

HISTORIC CHURCHES
Snow Hill

The **Gothic Revival Makemie United Presbyterian Church** (Market and Washington Streets) was built in 1890 and serves a congregation that can trace its origin to the end of the 1600s.

There are both Gothic and Victorian aspects to the **All Hallows Church** (Market and Church Streets), built around 1750. The purple and yellow panes in the roundheaded windows were added near the turn of the 20th century. Take a step inside to see the 1701 Bible printed in London and given to the congregation by Queen Anne.

✳ To Do
AIR RIDES
Ocean City

✈ **Island Parasail** (410-289-2896), 1st Street and the bay. Certainly not cheap, but a thrill nonetheless, Island Parasail has single and tandem flights for kids and adults. It is Ocean City's original parasail company and has completed over 100,000 flights with a perfect safety record while providing a different perspective on the ocean and the beach.

✈ **O. C. Parasail** (410-723-1464), 54th Street or Talbot Street Pier. O.C. Parasail also has a perfect safety record.

✈ **Bay Sports Unlimited** (410-289-2144), 22nd Street and the bay. Bay Sports offers single, tandem, and triple parasail rides. Waverunners are also rented.

Cloud Dancer (410-641-2484), Ocean City Airport. Two-passenger open-cockpit flights over the area in a vintage biplane.

Ocean City Sky Tours (410-289-TOUR; www.ocean-city.com/ocskytours), Ocean City Airport. Day, sunset, and night flights.

ARCADES, AMUSEMENT AND WATER PARKS, GO-CARTS
Ocean City

✈ **Jolly Roger Amusement Park** (410-289-4902), 30th Street and Coastal Highway. The city's largest amusement park with the Sky Coaster, Giant Ferris Wheel, and Titanic Slide.

✈ **Splash Mountain** (410-289-6962), 30th Street and Coastal Highway. Ten water slides, a lazy river, and a sea-creature walk. Adjacent to Jolly Roger (see above).

65th Street Slide and Ride (410-524-5270), 65th Street and the bay. In addition to three water slides, this place has several rides for young children.

Speed World (410-289-6088), 30th Street and Coastal Highway. Go-carts of every imaginable shape, such as Indy racers, LeMans, midget racers, family tracks, and even a speedboat course. Adjacent to Jolly Roger (see above).

Trimper's Rides (410-289-8617), between South Division and South 1st Streets, on the boardwalk. Fans of old carousels will love this amusement park with its 1902 Herschel-Spellman carousel. In continuous operation since its 1912 installation, its hand-carved horses, camels, roosters, tigers, zebras, and more have been maintained in excellent condition. Trimper's is the center of activity on the southern end of the boardwalk in the evening.

BICYCLING

Ocean City

Bicycle riding is permitted on Ocean City's **boardwalk,** but hours vary greatly according to the season, so check the posted signs.

Atlantic Bike Company (410-289-3305), 8th Street and the boardwalk. Bicycle and pedal-surrey rentals.

Mike's Bikes (410-289-5404), North Division and Baltimore Avenue, and North 1st Street and the boardwalk (410-289-4637). Open all year for bike rentals, sales, and service.

The **ViewTrail 100 Bike Trail** follows a circular path along country roads, through farms, woodlands, cypress swamps, and small towns for more than 100 miles in Worcester County. Numerous restaurants, historic sites, and accommodations along the way. (See *Guidance* for places to obtain the trail brochure.)

THE 1902 HERSCHEL-SPELLMAN CAROUSEL AT TRIMPER'S RIDES

BOAT EXCURSIONS

Ocean City
OC Rocket (410-289-3500; www.ocean-city.com/boatrides), Talbot Street Pier. A ride, at times up to 40 miles an hour, on this boat should be able to satisfy anyone's need for speed in the ocean. The 50-minute trip passes through the inlet and goes along the beach almost to the Delaware state line. Hold on to your seat when you bounce across the waves! Yee-Hah! Be sure to ask for the discounted price.

⚓ Located at the same pier as the *OC Rocket*, and owned by the same company, the **Assateague Adventure** is an easy pontoon-boat ride/nature tour. The boat glides into the Ocean City Fishing Center and along Sinepuxent Bay, and lands on Assateague Island. In addition to possibly seeing the wild ponies and hand-net dipping for crabs and clams, you'll hear naturalists narrate tidbits about island migration, saltwater marshes, sea lettuce, and more. Adults may wish for more depth of information, but it's a good

HAND-NET DIPPING FOR CRABS AND CLAMS OFF ASSATEAGUE ISLAND

introduction to the local environment.

Sea Rocket (410-289-5887), end of Dorchester Street, bayside. Claiming to be the world's largest speedboat, the *Sea Rocket* competes with the *OC Rocket* for customers. It is the one with the large rooster-tail wake.

⚓ The **Assateague Island Explorer,** operated by the owners of the *Sea Rocket,* provides trips much like those of the *Assateague Adventure* (see above).

⚓ **Sport Crabber** (410-289-7438; www.sportcrabber), Bahia Marina between 21st and 22nd Streets and the bay. Captain Bill and his crew entertain with genial banter as passengers drop lines baited with chicken necks in hopes of attracting a blue crab or two. Although you don't keep the catch, this is an entertaining (and educational) cruise, especially for younger family members.

BOAT RENTALS

Ocean City
Bahia Marina (410-289-7438), between 21st and 22nd Streets and the bay. Pontoon and skiff rentals.

Sailing Etc. (410-723-1144), 46th Street and the bay. Sailboats, Windsurfers, and kayaks for rent.

Bayside Boat Rentals (410-524-1948), 54th Street and the bay. Pontoon boats.

FAMILY ACTIVITIES

Ocean City
⚓ **Pirate Adventures on the Sea Gypsy** (410-213-1075), Ocean City Fishing Center, West Ocean City. Young kids really enjoy this cruise on a pirate ship in search of sunken treasure. The crew is in costume, the kids get their faces painted, cannons

"WHAT'S THAT?"

The boats with the tall booms and apparatuses that you see in the Ocean City Fishing Center dredge for clams in the waters around the resort area. Most of the catch is sent to Texas, where Campbell's Soup turns it into canned clam chowder.

CLAM-DREDGING BOATS IN OCEAN CITY FISHING CENTER

are fired, the boat is attacked, and everyone gets to take home a share of the loot.

🐚 ♿ **Frontier Town Western Theme Park** (410-289-7877; www.frontiertown.com), 3.5 miles south of US 50 on MD 611. Open 10–6; gate closes at 4:30. When my wife told me how much fun she had as a child coming here in the 1960s, my thought was that the children of today would look upon the theme park as a hokey bore. How wrong I was. Kids up to 12 years old were cheering on the good guy in the Gunfight at the OK Corral, joining in the (authentic) Native American dances, and hooting and hollering at the villain in the Trial of Lopez. The con-structed frontier town houses gift shops, a western saloon complete with a cancan show, and stagecoach, steam-train, and pony rides. Separate fees provide access to the Frontier Town Water Park and Frontier Town Campground.

FISHING

Ocean City

Headboats (first-come, first-served) and charter boats (reserved ahead of time) leave almost daily from nearly every marina in the Ocean City area. Most provide or rent the necessary equipment.

Ocean City Fishing Center (410-213-1121), West Ocean City. Just off US 50 on the mainland, the center claims to have the largest charter fleet in Ocean City.

Miss Ocean City (410-213-0926; 1-800-631-4848), US 50 and Shanty-town Road (at the Shantytown Lighthouse), West Ocean City. With a capacity of 80 anglers, *Miss Ocean City* goes on half-day trips as well as special night-fishing excursions (in-season).

Judith M (410-289-7438), Bahia Marina between 21st and 22nd Streets. Possibly the most recognized headboat around Ocean City, the *Judith M* goes on deep-sea fishing trips twice a day during the summer. In the evening she provides narrated 90-minute oceanfront cruises.

Bay Bee (410-213-1121; 1-800-322-3065), US 50 and Shantytown Road, West Ocean City. In search of sea bass, flounder, trout, snapper, blues, and croaker, the *Bay Bee* runs half-day trips.

Snow Hill
Captain Bruce Wooten (410-632-1431), 6661 Snow Hill Road. Captain Bruce, a licensed guide, specializes in bass fishing on the Pocomoke, Wicomico, Nanticoke, and Choptank Rivers. There are only one or two anglers on each 8-hour trip, so you will have the river and instruction, if needed, to yourself. Offered year-round.

GOLF
Berlin
The Bay Club (410-641-4081; 1-800-BAY-CLUB; www.thebayclub.com), 9122 Libertytown Road. 36 holes. The course at Bay Club East is one of the area's newest 18-hole courses. The Bay Club West course has been laud-ed by the *Washington Times*.

GOLF VACATIONS
Ocean City has become a golfer's destination, with more than a dozen courses nearby. Contact **Ocean City Golf Getaway** (410-213-7050; 1-800-462-4653; www.ocean-citygolf.com), 9935 Stephen Decatur Highway, Unit 141, Ocean City, 21842, to help you decide which ones to play—and to arrange special package deals with hotels and restaurants. **Ocean City Golf Groups** (1-888-465-3477; www.ocgolfgroups.com), 2200 Baltimore Avenue, Ocean City, 21842, provides the same type of service.

Eagle's Landing (410-213-7277; 1-800-2TEE-TIME), 12367 Eagle's Landing Road. Dr. Michael Hurdzan designed Ocean City's municipal 18-hole course with a par 72 and a length of 6,163 feet. The first certified Audubon sanctuary in Maryland; *Golf Digest* magazine rated it one of the state's top 10 courses.

Ocean City Golf and Yacht Club (410-641-1779; 1-800-442-3570), 11401 Country Club Drive. Two courses. One seaside and the other with marshes along Newport Bay.

River Run (410-641-7200; 1-800-733-RRUN; www.riverrungolf.com), 11605 Masters Lane. On this Gary Player Signature Course, the first nine holes bring to mind Scottish links, while the last nine are set among nat-ural marshes.

Rum Point Seaside Golf Links (410-629-1414; 1-888-809-4653; www.rumpointe.com), 7000 Rum Pointe Lane. This par-72 course, designed by Pete and P. B. Dye, over-looks Sinepuxent Bay and Assateague Island.

Bishopville
The Links at Lighthouse Sound (410-352-5767; 1-888-55HILLS; www.lighthousesound.com), 12723 St. Martin's Neck Road. One of the closest courses to Ocean City, it has views of the resort area's skyline. Par 72 with a 73.3 rating.

MINIATURE GOLF
Ocean City
❧ **Lost Galaxy Golf** (410-524-4FUN; www.planetmaze.com), 33rd Street and Coastal Highway. Miniature golf with an outer-space theme featuring spaceships, meteors, fire, and fog. Laser tag and the largest indoor/outdoor maze in Maryland are also at this location.

❧ **Old Pro Golf** (410-524-2645, main phone number; www.oldprogolf.com). Old Pro has eight miniature-golf courses throughout the city. People appeared to have the most fun at the Lost Civilization theme at 23rd Street and at the new indoor Under Sea course at 68th Street.

❧ **Lost Treasure Golf** (410-250-5678), 140th Street and Coastal Highway. Caves, waterfalls, and ancient ruins.

KAYAKING AND CANOEING OC
Kayak (410-213-2818; www.ockayak.com), Shantytown Village (US 50 and Shantytown Road), Ocean City. For an adrenaline rush, take OC Kayak's guided trip onto the surf of the ocean; great fun and no experience necessary. My trip onto one of the Eastern Shore's back creeks was an easy paddle on calm water, accompanied by

some great natural-history tidbits from the guide. They also rent kayaks if you wish to explore on your own.

Several inns and B&Bs have banded together to form the **"Inn-to-Inn Canoe Trail"** along the Pocomoke River. Tours are 3 or 5 days long, and everything is included: canoes, shuttles, three meals a day, and evening accommodations. All you have to do is paddle leisurely along the river enjoying the scenery and wildlife, knowing that soft beds await you. I can't imagine a better way to get to know the interior lands of the Eastern Shore. The **River House Inn** (410-632-2722; www.riverhouse.com), 210 East Market Street, Snow Hill, makes the arrangements. Tours begin at $600 for two people.

Pocomoke River Canoe Co. (410-632-3971), 312 North Washington Street, Ocean City, not only provides livery service for the inn-to-inn trips, but also provides shuttle service and rents canoes and kayaks for those wanting to explore the river on their own.

Rainy Day, Inc. (410-641-5029), Assateague Island. Rents canoes and bikes at the Assateague National Seashore from Memorial Day through Labor Day.

PERSONAL WATERCRAFT RENTALS (JET SKIS)
Ocean City
Action Watersports, Ltd. (410-524-4769; www.actionwatersportsltd.com), 106 52nd Street.

Island Jet Ski (410-289-2896), 1st Street and the bay.

Odyssea Watersports (410-723-4227), 50th Street and Coastal Highway.

Inlet Sea-Doos (410-289-1488), on the Inlet.

SAILING *Images* (443-366-7925), 12624 Balte Road, Ocean City. Everyone else seems to want you to fly across the water in a motor-powered boat, but Captain Art Hitch takes passengers on a 3-hour, nearly silent cruise aboard his 36-foot Irwin sloop.

SKATING Roller skating, skateboarding, and scooter riding are permitted on the boardwalk in Ocean City, but hours vary greatly according to the season, so check the posted signs.

Alfred Memorial Park (410-250-0125), 3rd Street, Ocean City. Within this city park is the Ocean Bowl Skate Park, open to skateboarders and in-line skaters. Facilities include a bowl, ramps, and a concrete street area.

TENNIS Public courts are located at 31st Street and the bay; 61st Street and the bay; 94th Street and the bay; and 136th Street and the bay in Ocean City.

WALKING TOURS Ocean City. A walking-tour brochure describing some of the older structures and sites along the southern end of the Ocean City boardwalk is available from the Convention and Visitors Bureau (see *Guidance*). It's nice to learn the stories behind the Violets Are Blue House, the Tarry-A-While, and St. Mary's of the Sea Catholic Church.

Berlin. The Historic District of Berlin contains structures from the 1790s to the early 20th century, and a walking-tour brochure available in the town offices (10 William Street) will direct you to the most historically and architecturally significant. Be sure to

seek out the **Burley House** and its narrow brick chimneys atop a steep gable roof.

Snow Hill. The Snow Hill Walking Tour brochure points out more than 50 historically or architecturally important structures within the town limits. Available from the Worcester County Tourism Office (see *Guidance*).

✳ Green Space

BEACHES All 10 miles of the **Ocean City** beach are free and open to the public 6 AM–10 PM. Beach Patrol members are on duty 10 AM–5:30 PM.

&. Access points to the beach for the physically challenged are identified by blue signs along Coastal Highway.

There are patrolled beaches in both the state park and national seashore on **Assateague Island** that are much less crowded than those in Ocean City. If you want a primitive beach experience, just walk a few hundred yards away from these designated areas and there is a good possibility of having the sand and surf all to yourself.

A small strip of beach in the settlement of **Public Landing** is open to the general public, yet very few people ever take advantage of it.

PARKS Northside Park, 125th Street and the bay, Ocean City. The park's 58 acres situated at the northern end of town on the bayside enable you to escape the noise and congestion of the rest of the resort area.

Pocomoke River State Park (410-632-2566), 461 Worcester Highway, Snow Hill. Canoeing, swimming, hiking, fishing, and two campgrounds.

WALKS Kerring Creek Nature Trail (410-632-2144), Keyset Point Road, West Ocean City. An easy-to-get-to escape from the resort area. The 1-mile loop trail passes by a pond and creek, through forested wetlands, and onto a small pine island with picnic tables.

Assateague Island. Within **Assateague State Park** and **Assateague Island National Seashore** (see *Lodging—Camping*) are miles of unspoiled beaches on which to walk. Three short interpretive trails—Life of the Dunes, Life of the Marsh, and Life of the Forest—are close to the National Seashore Campground. Those wanting a longer hike should consult *50 Hikes in Maryland* (Backcountry Guides), which describes a 2-day backpacking trip along the beach.

HIKING ⌂ About a 30-mile drive from Ocean City, the 1-mile circuit **Bald Cypress Nature Trail** in the Milburn Landing area of **Pocomoke River State Park** (see *Lodging—Camping*) is the place to take the kids after they have had enough of sun, surf, and sand and are badgering you about what to do next. The easy walk takes you by a few small swamps and underneath dozens of bald cypress trees, oddities within the world of trees. They are coniferous, meaning they develop cones like pines, firs, and hemlocks—all trees with evergreen needles. Yet while they may look like needles, the leaves of the bald cypress drop off as the weather turns colder, just as those on deciduous trees do. In addition, even though it is called a cypress, the bald cypress is actually a member of the redwood family. It is also a tree more common to the swamps of the South, just barely able to survive here at its very northern limits on the Eastern Shore.

PONIES SHARE THE BEACH WITH SUBATHERS ON ASSATEAGUE ISLAND.

✴ Lodging

MOTELS AND HOTELS

Ocean City, 21842

Atlantic Hotel (410-289-9111; 1-800-3-ATLANTIC; www.atlantichotel-ocmd.com), Wicomico Street and the boardwalk. There are no swimming pools, Jacuzzis, fitness rooms, or private balconies here. If you can accept this, you will enjoy staying in one of the oldest hotels in Ocean City with its sundeck overlooking the beach, six-over-six sash windows, and historic lobby. Do not come here looking for opulence, but do take advantage of the low rates. Owned by the same family since 1922. $95–135.

♿ **Coconut Malorie** (410-723-6100; 1-800-767-6060; www.coconutmalorie.com), 200 59th Street. The rooms with custom furniture, original Haitian art, and marble baths with Jacuzzi tubs all have nice views, but be sure to take the elevator to the English Library (rich dark wood) and Art Gallery (local artists) located in The Tower. Just by turning your head you can take in the Atlantic, Ocean City, and the bay. The hotel's lobby with its French door entrance and grand double stone staircase leading to the pool is equally impressive. $139–399.

♿ **Dunes Manor Hotel** (410-289-1100; 1-800-523-2888; www.dunes-manor.com), 2800 Baltimore Avenue. The only hotel in the city with all of its rooms facing the ocean. Invoking the grandeur of 19th-century seaside resorts, the Dunes Manor is furnished with antiques and decorated in a Victorian theme. The suites are exceptionally large. Without being pretentious, everything in the hotel is done with a touch of class. Only one block north of the boardwalk. Indoor/outdoor pool. $179–315. See *Dining Out* for the hotel's restaurant, the **Victorian Room.**

✏ ♿ **Dunes Motel** (410-289-4414), 2700 Baltimore Avenue. Owned by the same people as Dunes Manor, this is my sister's family's choice when they come to Ocean City. It is reasonably priced and caters to families (Disney Channel on TV and a kids'

PEOPLE-WATCHING ALONG THE OCEAN CITY BOARDWALK

wading pool). It is on the very north end of the boardwalk, which does not have the commercial activity and crowds found on the southern end. Ocean view, pool view, and efficiencies available. $99–279.

&✏ Holiday Inn Oceanfront (410-524-1600; 1-800-837-3588; www.ocmdhotels.com/holidayinn), 6600 Coastal Highway. Indoor/outdoor pools with baby pools. Oceanfront, ocean-view, and garden-view rooms and suites. Free children's summertime activities. $225–280. See *Dining Out* for **Reflections,** the hotel's restaurant.

& Princess Royale Oceanfront Hotel (410-524-7777; 1-800-4-ROYALE; www.princessroyale.com), 9100 Coastal Highway. One of the city's newer all-suite facilities. Oceanfront, ocean-view, and one- to three-room suites overlooking the Olympic-sized pool and atrium are available. Guests can have food delivered to them on the beach, and the kids can have fun playing rooftop miniature golf. $149–309.

& Ramada Limited Oceanfront (410-289-6444; 1-800-837-3589; www.ocmdmotels.com/ramada), 3200 Baltimore Avenue. All rooms are efficiencies with microwave oven, cookware, dishes, silverware, and toaster. The first-floor rooms open directly onto the hotel's picnic and play area but do not have a view of the ocean; other floors have the view. Complimentary continental breakfast and daily newspaper. $225–240.

INNS

Ocean City, 21842

& Lighthouse Club Hotel (410-524-5400; 1-888-371-5400; www.fagers.com), 56th Street On-The-Bay. The

OCEAN VIEWS IN OCEAN CITY
If you want to see the ocean, ask for a room on the third floor or above if your lodgings are north of 27th Street. The beach's sand dune blocks the views from the first, and often second, floors in this area.

custom-made Lawrence Peabody furniture and water views give this lighthouse-shaped inn the feel of a Caribbean resort. Certainly one of the most luxurious and romantic spots in Ocean City with a balcony, marble bath, whirlpool Jacuzzi, terry robes, and refrigerator in each suite. Even if you don't get a bay-view room, you can still enjoy a view of herons, geese, and ducks wandering around the inland marsh. To keep up with its growing clientele, the management opened **The Edge at the Lighthouse,** a hotel next door with the same amenities. All of this is part of the **Fager's Island Restaurant/** Lighthouse Club Hotel complex (see *Dining Out*). $245–295; includes continental breakfast.

Berlin, 21811

Atlantic Hotel (410-641-3589; 1-800-814-7672; www.atlantichotel.com), 2 North Main Street. The Atlantic Hotel was built in 1895 and has been faithfully maintained with its Victorian features. The impressive staircase adds a bit of grandeur to the small entranceway. Each of the 16 rooms is furnished with antiques and period pieces. I liked watching Berlin's life unfold from the windows of my second-floor front room, while another visit in one of the back rooms was a quiet one removed from the bustle of Main Street. Private bath, air-conditioning, television, and phone are in each room; deluxe rooms can accommodate up to five people. $95–180. Continental breakfast included. See *Dining Out* for the hotel's restaurant.

Snow Hill, 21863

🐾 ✍ ♿ **River House Inn** (410-632-2722; www.riverhouse.com), 210 East Market Street. Larry and Susanne Knudsen have been such successful innkeepers that they have added more buildings on their riverfront property just to keep up with guests' demands. The East and West Rooms in the 1860 Gothic Revival house are large and bright, and a screened-in porch overlooks the lawn, which slopes downs to the Pocomoke River. The 1834 cottage houses two suites, while the private accommodations in the 1890 Carriage Barn include a whirlpool tub. My favorite spot is the upstairs suite in the Riverview Hideaways. Not only can you enjoy the river from the 28-foot-long porch, but when you retire at night, the clouds painted on the bedroom ceiling provide a serene atmosphere to lull you to sleep. Furnishings in the older structures fit the period, while the decor of newer rooms is modern. The inn is a member of the **Inn-to-Inn Canoe Trail** (see *To Do— Kayaking and Canoeing*); canoes and kayaks are available for rent, and guests have free use of bicycles. Children and pets are welcome. All rooms have air-conditioning and private bath. $140–220.

Snow Hill Inn (410-632-2102), 104 East Market Street. All four rooms have quilts on the beds in this inn whose main portion dates from the late 1700s. Although the rooms are sort of small, they have the feel of an inn you might come across in Ireland or Scotland; and you can't beat the rates. $65–75. See *Dining Out* for the inn's restaurant.

BED & BREAKFASTS

Ocean City, 21842

🐚 **Atlantic House B&B** (410-289-2333; www.atlantichouse.com), 510 North Baltimore Avenue. Things may have changed by time you read this, as the owners were contemplating selling the Atlantic House. If still in business, it is one of the most convenient and lower-cost places to stay right on the boardwalk. The oceanside rooms let you watch the sunrise, while the bayside rooms catch the sunset's glow. $110–225.

Inn on the Ocean (410-289-8894; 1-877-466-6662; www.innontheocean.com), 1001 Atlantic Avenue. The city's only other B&B is also located on the boardwalk. All six rooms have private bath, TV, VCR, and air-conditioning. The Veranda Room opens directly onto the wraparound porch (where breakfast is often served), while my favorite, the Oceana Room, has a private balcony overlooking the ocean. Bicycles, beach equipment, and afternoon refreshments are complimentary. $190–290.

Berlin, 21811

✍ **Holland House B&B** (410-641-1956), 5 Bay Street. Jan and Jim Quick have been operating their B&B for well over a decade and have its operation down to a T. They both have outside jobs, but you would never know it. One or the other will serve you breakfast, and it seems that they are always around when a guest has a question. (They are a great repository of knowledge on where to eat or what to do in the area.) The Holland House was a doctor's residence at the turn of the 20th century, and the size of the rooms and the decor reflect the physician's middle-income status. Many guests enjoy coffee and the morning paper on the front porch. An outside shower enables you to wash off beach sand before dressing for dinner. Children are welcome, which adds to the family atmosphere. $90–125.

Snow Hill, 21863

Chanceford Hall (410-632-2900; www.chancefordhall.com), 209 West Federal Street. The gardens with the second oldest black walnut tree in Maryland, weeping cherry trees, magnolias, boxwoods, and hollies, along with the lap pool, make Chanceford Hall's backyard a visually pleasing yet relaxing place to read a selection from the B&B's extensive library. Host Alice Kesterson works in the publishing industry, so she is constantly adding new books to the collection. Her husband, Randy, is often the one to prepare the large gourmet breakfasts. Not only are they great conversationalists, but Alice and Randy also possess a great knowledge of area history and attractions. Rooms in the 18th-century manor house, built by the family of Robert Morris, financier of the American Revolution, are spacious and furnished with antiques. The luxurious feel of a pima cotton robe and 230-count sheets on the poster beds made me look forward to the end of the day. All 10 of the fireplaces are in working condition, so there is no doubt that you will be comfortable as you wander through the house appreciating the elaborate crown moldings, chair rails, paneled doors (with the original hardware), and wide-planked wood floors. Bicycles are free for guests' use. $130–150.

The Mansion House (410-632-389; www.mansionhousebnb.com), 4436 Bayside Road, Public Landing. There are two things I remember about the Mansion House: sunrise bathing the entire house, with its golden glow reflected off the waters of Chincoteague Bay, and an abundance of fireplaces. Not only does each guest room have a working fireplace, but there are also fireplaces on each end of the living room. The 1800s building has lots of common space, including a swing on the upstairs porch, in which to relax after a swim in the bay or a walk along the beach. $140–160.

VACATION RENTALS If you plan to spend a week or more in Ocean City, you will probably save quite a few dollars by renting a cottage, house, or condominium. Among the agencies handling these properties are **O'Conor, Piper and Flyn** (1-800-633-1000), **Ocean City Weekly Rentals** (1-800-851-8909), and **Moore, Warfield and Glick** (1-800-289-2821).

CAMPING

Ocean City, 21842

🦞 Ocean City Campground (410-524-7601; www.occamping.com), 105 70th Street. The only campground in Ocean City is open year-round (limited winter facilities) and has 200 sites, a laundry, and a small playground.

🐾 ✂ Frontier Town (410-641-0880; 1-800-228-5590; www.frontiertown. com), on MD 611 south of Ocean City. Only a 10-minute drive from Ocean City, this 500-site campground is part of the **Frontier Town Western Theme Park** complex (see *To Do—Family Activities*). There are tons of activities for the kids, a free shuttle to the beach, free access to the large water-slide park, a choice of primitive or deluxe sites, and even some trailers and cabins for rent. The cost of the primitive sites is a bargain given all of the extras guests are entitled to.

Whaleyville, 21872
🐾 ✐ **Fort Whaley Campground** (410-641-9785; www.fortwhaley.com), 11224 Dale Road. A companion campground to Frontier Town (see above), it has primitive and deluxe sites. Free admission to the miniature-golf course and Frontier Town's Water Park.

Berlin, 21811—Assateague Island
Assateague State Park (410-641-2120; 1-888-432-2267), 7307 Stephen Decatur Highway. April 1 through October 31. More than 300 sites are situated among the sand dunes; almost 40 have hookups. Bathhouse and concession building.

Assateague Island National Seashore (410-641-3030), 7206 National Seashore Lane. The National Park Service operates two campgrounds—one near the ocean, the other next to the bay—that offer more of a rustic experience than the other sites listed here. There are no hookups and only chemical toilets and cold showers. Some sites are open year-round. Primitive backcountry sites are available to those willing to walk anywhere from 4 to 11 miles. 50 *Hikes in Maryland* (Backcountry Guides) describes the hike in detail.

Snow Hill, 21863
Pocomoke River State Park (410-632-2566), 461 Worcester Highway. The **Shad Landing Campground** (off US 113) has a swimming pool,

marina, camp store, hookups, a dump station, and a playground.

🐾 Also within the park, the **Milburn Landing Campground** (off MD 364) is a bit more primitive, but it does permit pets.

✳ Where to Eat
DINING OUT
Ocean City
✐ ♿ **Fager's Island Restaurant** (410-524-5500; www.fagers.com), 60th Street on the bay. Open every day, all year, Fager's brings daylight hours to a close with the 1812 Overture. The music starts about 5 minutes before sunset and ends at the exact moment the sun drops out of view. Meals, either indoors or on the deck, can start with chicken skewers ($7) with jalapeño-peach BBQ sauce and tomato-mint salad, progress to bronzed salmon ($28) or prime rib with shaved horseradish ($27), and end with a lemon cream pie in a pecan cookie crust ($6). Fager's is part of the **Lighthouse Club Hotel** complex (see *Lodging—Inns*).

♿ **Fresco's** (410-524-8202), 8203 Coastal Highway. Native Italian Alex Frachetti opened his own place in 2001 after cooking for more than 20 years in other people's Ocean City restaurants. The variety at lunch is limited, but the quality of the evening entrées make this the resort town's obvious choice for Italian food. Forget the usual spaghetti and meatballs or lasagna; think more along the lines of penne with crabmeat ($17.95) or chicken Piccata ($17.95). The Zuppa de Pesce (shrimp, clams, mussels, and calamari served over linguine; $23.95) is one of the signature dishes, while the veal scaloppini sautéed with lobster medallions and finished with butter and cream ($26.95) is an exceedingly rich indulgence. Sunsets over the bay cast a reddish glow through the restaurant's picture windows. Fresco's was endorsed by a fellow B&B guest, a visitor from Florence, Italy, no less.

Galaxy Bar and Grill (410-723-6762), 6601 Coastal Highway. Ocean City native John Trader operated his wine shop, Liquid Assets, for more than a decade before opening the Galaxy, and its extensive wine list, ranging from $4 glasses to $550 bottles, reflects his knowledge of the vintner's craft. Yet everything is right on the mark here—not only the freshly inventive dishes, but everything from the mosaic floor in the dining area to the appealing decor in the rest rooms. John and his staff collaborate to create items such as melon gazpacho, herbed mushroom pancakes served with goat cheese and vanilla balsamic-glazed greens, and mustard seed and jack cheese encrusted catfish. The menu is ever-evolving. Leave room for the raspberry cheesecake set in a raspberry crème fraîche ($9). Lunch items $11–14; dinner entrées $20–33. Currently my favorite Ocean City restaurant; it takes on a nightclub atmosphere late at night.

& **The Hobbit Restaurant** (410-524-8100), 81st Street and the bay. The Hobbit has been under the same ownership and management since it opened in 1977, decades before the 2001 *Lord of the Rings* movie was even thought about. With a few figurines and paintings depicting characters from J. R. R. Tolkien's fantasy masterpiece decorating the walls, it is a favorite of Newt Gingrich and other Baltimore and Washington, D.C.,

politicos and celebrities. Casual fare in the café, such as the Hobbit burger or chicken sandwich, is $7.95 to $13.95, while the more formal menu in the dining room has items like roast duckling or prime rib up to $26.95.

& **Mario's** (410-289-9445), 22nd Street and Philadelphia Avenue. Dinner only. Restaurants come and go, but Mario's has been serving Ocean City since 1954. All meats are cut on the premises. Traditional Italian cooking making use of local seafoods. $13.95–29.95.

& **Reflections** (410-524-5252), 67th Street oceanfront. One of the most upscale and formal dining experiences in the city. The small fountain and low, golden lighting make it a place couples come to for a romantic setting. The ever-changing Continental menu has tableside flambé cooking, along with variations on seafood, pasta, and steak from $22.95 to $32.95. My early-bird special (5–6 PM) filet mignon ($13.95) was charbroiled to my liking and covered with bordelaise sauce. Inside the **Holiday Inn** (see *Lodging—Motels and Hotels*).

& **Victorian Room** (410-289-1100; www.dunesmanor.com), 28th Street and the oceanfront. Located in the **Dunes Manor Hotel** (*see Lodging—Motels and Hotels*). American cuisine with items from the sea and the land. $13.95–21.95.

& **Windows on the Bay** (410-723-3463), 61st Street and the bay. The upstairs location provides a panoramic view of sunsets. Windows is known for its Caesar salads, flambé dishes, and fresh catch of the day ($19.95). Other entrées $16.95–29.95. Early-bird menu $9.95–13.95.

Berlin

Atlantic Hotel (410-641-3589; 1-800-814-7672; www.atlantichotel.com), 2 North Main Street. Reservations are strongly suggested. The Atlantic (also see *Lodging—Inns*) is a winner of the Wine Spectator Award of Excellence. Its formal dining decor and the fresh ingredients in the seafood and beef dishes keep locals coming back whenever they have a special occasion to celebrate. The rockers on the front porch are a nice place to let things settle and digest. $18–30.

Across the hall in the hotel is the **Drummer's Café** with a more casual atmosphere and a lighter menu of soups, sandwiches, and some entrées. $6–15. Open for lunch and dinner.

Snow Hill

Snow Hill Inn (410-632-2102), 104 East Market Street. The menu changes on a regular basis at this historic inn (see *Lodging—Inns*). Guests

within the three small dining rooms recently had a choice of veal Bianco ($18.95), bourbon steak and shrimp ($23.95), or broiled salmon ($16.95). The crabcake sandwich served in the lounge, where other light fare is offered, is a great deal at $6.95.

✳ Eating Out

Ocean City

💰 ♿ **Angler Restaurant** (410-289-7924), Talbot Street and the bay. Breakfast, lunch, and dinner. The Angler gives a free coastline cruise with every evening meal. You are going to eat dinner anyway, so why not take them up on the offer? The daily catch (market price) can be prepared blackened, amandine, island style, or several other ways. There are 10 early-bird entrées under $12.

🦐 💰 ♿ **Atlantic Stand Diner** (410-289-7203), Wicomico Street and the boardwalk. With some dishes less than $2.50, Atlantic has some of the

TALBOT STREET PIER IN OCEAN CITY

lowest-cost breakfasts, lunches, and take-out food in the city. The most expensive item is a jumbo lump crab-cake for less than $8. In the same location since 1933.

* & **The Bayside Skillet** (410-524-7950; www.baysideskillet.com), 77th Street and the bay. The place for out-of-the-ordinary breakfasts. Choose a hot fudge sundae or peach melba crêpe, a seafood frittata (crab, shrimp, and scallops with marinara sauce), or pan-fried potatoes sautéed with bacon, onions, mushrooms, and cheddar cheese. The four-egg omelets are so large that the management recommends sharing (at no extra charge!). I ate about two-thirds of my Spanish omelet and did not eat again until late in the evening. Expect to spend $6–9 at this place, which is easily recognized by its bright pink exterior and lines of people waiting to get in from early morning on. Lunch and dinner are also served.

* **The Dough Roller.** There are five locations in Ocean City: South Division Street and the boardwalk (410-289-3501); 3rd Street and the boardwalk (410-289-2599); 41st Street and Coastal Highway (410-524-9254); 70th Street and Coastal Highway (410-524-7981); 125th and Coastal Highway (410-250-5664). My sister, by far one of the most severe of pizza critics, says Dough Rollers is the best "fast-food pizza" in the city. Eat in or pick up only; no deliveries.

* & **Phillips Crab House and Seafood Festival Buffet** (410-289-6821), 21st Street and Philadelphia Avenue. It seems that every ocean resort area in America now has the obligatory all-you-can-eat seafood buffet restaurants, and Ocean City is no exception. With decades of knowl-

edge in the commercial fishing industry, Phillips is the best of the lot, and is one of the few still offering steamed crabs on the buffet. Arrive around 4 PM to save a few dollars on the $25 charge. Kids' and regular menus available.

& **Seacrets Bar and Restaurant** (410-524-4900), 49th Street and the bay. Seacrets capitalizes on its reggae theme by providing 14 indoor and open-air bars. Most of the items on the menu, such as veggie, tuna salad, and spicy chicken sandwiches, or ribs and red snapper platters, have a bit of Jamaican heritage to them. Eat under palm trees or lounge on rafts in the water and have your food brought to you. There is live entertainment year-round, but when bands come to play at the height of the season, this place hops so much you might think you've walked into an MTV Spring Break party. Entrées $6–13.

* **The Shark** (410-723-1221; www.thesharkonthebay.com), 46th Street and the bay. The Shark puts a bit of a different twist on the typical Ocean City beach bar food. Try the crab bruschetta ($8.95) as your appetizer and the Creole rockfish ($18.95) as the entrée. Sandwiches (from $6.95) and other entrées (up to $22.95) are available.

Weitzel's Restaurant (410-524-6990), 51st Street and Beach Highway. Where the locals go for breakfast (cream chip beef, $6.75; western omelet, $6.50) and lunch (grilled ham and cheese, $3.50; marinated tuna steak, $5.50). The jalapeño poppers, mahi on a stick, or breaded crab claws ($4.95 each) are good choices to carry out to the beach.

* & **The Wharf Restaurant** (410-250-1001), 128th Street and Coastal

Highway. The emphasis here is on the seafood, much of which is obtained fresh daily from the Seafood and Spirits market next door. A raw bar, award-winning crabcakes, and separate adult and kid-friendly dining rooms. $13.95–27.95.

Berlin
An A Fare To Remember Café (410-629-0707; www.anafaretoremember.com), Pitts Street. Part gift shop and part coffee bar, the café serves gourmet-type sandwiches and select dishes from 11 AM to 5 PM (4 PM in the winter). The desserts are reason enough to come here. $5–15.

Snow Hill
Bailey's: A Café (410-632-3700), 104 West Green Street. With just six tables in a downtown location, Bailey's serves a full breakfast and a lunch menu of soups, salads, and sandwiches. The tuna salad ($5.75) is made with fresh yellowfin tuna, while the Dagwood sandwich ($5.50) provides enough protein to keep you going for the rest of the day. The Vegetarian Delight sandwich ($4.50) is especially tasty with grilled portobello mushrooms and large chunks of avocado.

CRABS
Ocean City
& **Bahama Mamas** (410-289-0291), 221 Wicomico Street. The outside deck overlooking Assateague Island is the appropriate place to be cracking open jumbo steamed blue crabs (market price)—obtained fresh from the restaurant's affiliated seafood outlet market just a few miles up the beach. Happy hour 4–7 PM.

& **Crab Alley** (410-213-7800), 9703 Golf Course Road, West Ocean City. Owned and operated by a local waterman and family. If you don't mind driving back onto the mainland, you will probably find some of the freshest steamed blue crabs here (market price). They serve other seafood (such as tuna steak, $18.95; seafood platter, $23.95) when available fresh. I like the children's menu—it simply says, "Half the food, half the price."

& **Captain's Galley** (410-213-2525), 12817 Harbor Road, West Ocean City. Fresh seafood purchased directly from the docks. It's great fun to sit on the outside deck overlooking the harbor and crack open steamed crabs by the dozen (market price).

Berlin
& **Assateague Crab House** (410-641-4330), MD 611. The post office address is Berlin, but you will find this restaurant on your way to Assateague Island, just south of the MD 611/MD 376 intersection. This is a typical crab house, so the decor is minimal, but the price on the crabcake sandwich served with french fries is certainly reasonable ($9). All-you-can-eat crabs and shrimp available at market prices.

SNACKS AND GOODIES
Ocean City
& **Dumser's Drive-In** (410-524-1588), 49th Street and Coastal Highway. Dumser's has been serving subs, burgers, and fries in Ocean City since 1939, but the real attraction is the ice cream made on the premises that is sold within a few hours of manufacture. The Hawaiian delight—cherries, pineapples, and bananas in vanilla ice cream—is one of the best-sellers. The three-dip super sundaes ($4.95) could easily fill up two hungry kids.

❧ **Candy Kitchens** (1-800-60-FUDGE), 5301 Coastal Highway. Ocean City's saltwater taffy connection for more than 50 years has multiple kitchens located throughout the resort area. Also offers homemade fudge, hand-dipped chocolates, and one of the newest features, "make-your-own ice cream sundae."

✳ Entertainment

MUSIC The Globe Theater (410-641-0784; www.globetheater.com), 12 Broad Street, Berlin. Mostly acoustic jazz, folk, classical, and rock music are presented on the weekends in a coffee house-type setting. Talent ranges from local to international. The bulk of the audiences come from the surrounding area, so this is the place to mingle with the natives.

NIGHTLIFE

Ocean City
Club 24/Embers Nightclub (410-289-3322), 24th Street and Coastal Highway. Laser light show and DJs nightly.

Caribbean Bar and Grill (410-289-0837), 2nd Street and the boardwalk. Live funk, reggae, or jazz bands nightly.

The Shark (410-723-1221), 46th Street and the bay. The Shark features live jazz, blues, and acoustic music presented on its private beach.

Shenanigan's Irish Pub (410-289-7181), 4th Street and the boardwalk. Irish entertainment each night on the oceanfront deck during the summer season.

The OC Jamboree (410-213-7581; www.ocjam.com), Route 611 and Marjan Lane, West Ocean City. Open all year, the jamboree tries to appeal to families with its Opryland/Branson-type variety musical entertainment.

THEATERS Beach House Restaurant (410-289-6846), 38th Street and the boardwalk, Ocean City. The restaurant produces a Murder Mystery Dinner every Thursday throughout the summer. Reservations required.

✳ Selective Shopping

ANTIQUES

Berlin
Town Center Antiques (410-629-1895), Main Street. A gallery-type shop with over 125 antiques dealers.

Stuart's Antiques (410-641-0435), Pitts Street. It would take a full afternoon to look over all of the furniture, glass figures and animals, estate jewelry, china, and silverware crammed into this shop.

ART GALLERIES

Ocean City
The Art League of Ocean City (410-524-9433; www.artleagueof-oceancity.org), 94th Street. Monthly exhibits of works primarily by members and other local artists.

Ocean Gallery World Center (410-289-5300; www.oceangallery.com), 2nd Street and the boardwalk. There is no mistaking this building, as its exterior is the most amazing hodge-podge of pieces of other buildings from around the world that fans of the gallery have donated to it. The inside is just as convoluted. There are thousands works of art, some by well-known painters, others of ambiguous origin and quality, stacked one against the other over four different floors. The experience is worth the visit.

While taking a lighthearted look at art, you just may find a hidden masterpiece.

Berlin
Worcester County Arts Council (410-641-0809; www.worcestercounty-artscouncil.org), Jefferson Street. Closed Saturday The council's small retail shop is an outlet for a variety of local artists and craftspersons. This is a chance to bring home something that has not been mass-produced.

BOOKSTORES See *Special Shops— Berlin.*

SPECIAL SHOPS
Ocean City
♬ **The Kite Loft.** With three locations in Ocean City: 5th Street and the boardwalk (410-289-6852); 45th Street Village (410-524-0800); and 131st Street and Coastal Highway (410-250-4970). Box, wind, diamond, airplane, bird-shaped, you-name-it; this shop has more—and different kinds—of kites than anywhere else in Maryland. Prices range from single to almost triple digits.

Shantytown Village (www.shanty-townvillage.com), US 50 and Shanty-town Road, West Ocean City. A constructed shopping village of small "shanties" located on the bay's waterfront, with more than 20 different businesses. I found the most unique to be **Crystal Underground** (410-213-1311) with crystals, jewelry, and clothing; **Mason Collection's** assortment of novelties (410-213-0041); and **Craft Patch's** handmade nautical souvenirs (410-213-2585).

Berlin
Dennisons Trackside Hobbies (410-641-2438), Main Street. A shop

for railroad and model enthusiasts. Not only is there a large selection of trains of all scales, new and used, but you will also find model and remote-control boats, cars, and airplanes.

Ta-Da (410-641-4430), William Street. Patty Falck markets a diverse collection of hand-painted furniture and glassware. Many locals come in to get her customized vases as wedding gifts.

Sassafras Station (410-641-0979), Main Street. Closed Sunday and Monday. A combination gift store, antiques shop, and local artists' gallery.

Findings (410-641-5049), 11538 Gum Point Road. Although it has a Berlin address, Findings is located on the north side of US 50 off MD 589. Good-quality primitive handcrafted cottage furniture and garden accessories.

Globe Theater (410-641-0784; www.globetheater.com), 12 Broad Street. Three different shops are crammed into the confines of Berlin's historic theater, each with a caliber of items not often found in tourist areas. On the upper floor is the **Balcony Gallery** of paintings, sculpture, jewelry, and pottery work. Many of the items are high quality, one-of-a-kind. The **Globe Café** serves light-fare food not often found in this part of Maryland. The gourmet sandwiches and soups are about as healthful as they are tasty. The Eastern Shore has a dearth of bookstores, so **Duck Soup Books and Gifts,** with no more than 10 square feet of books, can be a welcome spot.

Snow Hill
Pusey's Country Store (410-632-1992), 5313 Snow Hill Road. There's a little bit of everything here: wooden

buckets, handmade brooms, roasted peanuts, ammo boxes, jellies and preserves, an impressive selection of 50 microbrew beers, and, most importantly, the friendly members of the Pusey family.

OUTLETS Ocean City Factory Outlets (1-800-625-6696; www.ocfactory-outlets.com), Ocean Gateway (US 50) and Golf Course Road, West Ocean City. Includes outlets for Ann Taylor, Bugle Boy, Carter's for Kids, Tommy Hilfiger, Levi's, Dress Barn, and more than 30 other manufacturers.

FARMER'S MARKETS Berlin. Located at North Main Street. Held on Wednesday and Friday from 1 PM till sold out, May through October.

Pocomoke City. From April through November you can find fresh produce and other farmer's market items on Monday through Saturday 8–6 at Market Street next to Cypress Park.

PICK-YOUR-OWN FARMS Milton's Produce (410-632-2633), 6230

Worcester Highway, Newark. A wide variety of fruits and vegetables are available for picking, 7 AM–7 PM, during their seasons.

✳ Special Events

January: **Nautical and Wildlife Art Festival; North American Craft Show** (410-524-9177). Both held in the Convention Center, 40th Street, Ocean City.

March: **St. Patrick's Day Parade** (410-289-6156). From 61st Street to 44th Street, Ocean City.

April: **Easter Arts and Crafts and Kids Fair** (410-524-7020), Convention Center, Ocean City. Egg hunts, clowns, storytellers, and the Easter Bunny. **Ward World Championship Wildfowl Carving Competition** (410-742-4988), Convention Center, Ocean City. Not to be missed by those who have the slightest interest in decoy art. The largest and, without a doubt, the most prestigious competition of wildfowl art. More than 150 exhibitors and artists.

THE WILD PONIES OF ASSATEAGUE ISLAND

May: **Springfest** (410-289-2800), Inlet Parking Area, Ocean City. A 4-day festival under big-top tents.

June: **Strawberry Day** (410-632-2032), Furnace Town, Snow Hill. Lots of food created from strawberries; contests and tastings.

July: **Annual Ocean City Tuna Tournament** (410-213-1121), Ocean City Fishing Center. **Greek Festival** (410-524-0990), Convention Center, Ocean City. Greek food and goodies, dancing, and entertainment. **Penning of the Ponies** (757-336-6161), Chincoteague Island, nearby in Virginia (see sidebar on page 39). Watch the ponies swim across the channel from Assateague Island to Chincoteague Island. Draws extremely large crowds.

August: **White Marlin Open** (410-289-9229; www.whitemarlinopen.com), Ocean City. Offshore fishing competition for white and blue marlin, tuna, and shark. This is not a small-time event; prize money totals well over $1 million. **Worcester County Fair** (410-632-1972), Furnace Town, Snow Hill.

September: **Sunfest** (410-289-2800), Inlet Parking Area, Ocean City. Autumn's equivalent of the Springfest. Includes the Kite Festival, considered by many to be America's largest gathering of kite fliers. Competitions and aerial exhibits.

November through early January: **Winterfest of Lights** (410-289-2800), Ocean City. Holiday lights and animated displays throughout the city.

TANGIER SOUND AREA— CRISFIELD AND PRINCESS ANNE

I n *Beautiful Swimmers*, William W. Warner aptly describes Crisfield as "A town built upon oyster shells, millions of tons of it." And he is right, both figuratively and literally.

When large beds of oysters were discovered in Tangier Sound in the mid-1800s, John W. Crisfield recognized the importance of the find. He brought the railroad from Salisbury so that the oysters could be economically transported to the important markets of the Northeast. In order to bring the tracks right to the water's edge, the land was artificially extended upon a base of compacted oyster shells.

In its heyday, Crisfield's population numbered well over 10,000, and more sailing ships were registered here than in any other port in the country. Close to 150 seafood processing plants, many of them also built upon oyster shells, clustered around the water. Agricultural packing houses and a sewing industry also moved into the area to take advantage of the railroad.

When the oysters began to play out, the watermen turned their attention to blue crabs and other seafood. Even though the bay's bounty has declined in recent years, Crisfield remains essentially a working town—and this is the reason to visit. Observing the activity on the city dock could occupy you for a full day. Ferries come and go to Smith Island, tons of seafood are unloaded, and sportfishermen head out with hopes high. Do not expect fancy shops, gourmet food, or theme parks, but the opportunity to observe an industrious way of life.

Princess Anne was chartered in 1733 and became the Somerset County seat in 1742. Until the turn of the 20th century, large ships were able to sail up the Manokin River, bringing growth and prosperity. Many of the town's historic mansions and homes, most notably Teackle Mansion, have

THE CRISFIELD CITY DOCK

Tangier Sound

13

50

50

349 Salisbury

349

352

Coxs Corner Green Hill

Nanticoke River

University of
Maryland
Eastern Shore
& Teackle Mansion

13

349

Wicomico River

Monie Bay

Mount Vernon Jason

Oakville

388

Princess Anne

*Old St. Peter's
Church*

363

Chance

DEAL ISLAND
WILDLIFE
MANAGEMENT
AREA

627

Oriole

Deal

Tangier

Wenona

640

Manokin River

Westover Greenhill Cokesbury

361 Manokin

13

Fairmount

Kingston

Hudsons
Corner 667 Pocomoke City

413

Big Annemessex River

Sound

667 Rehobeth

667

Marion

JAMES ISLAND
STATE PARK Hopewell 357

*J. Millard Tawes Mansion
& Ward Brothers' Workshop* 667

Ewell Bedsworth

Crisfield 380

Birdtown

VIRGINIA

Smith Island

Pocomoke Sound

13

N

0 1 2 3 4 5   10
Miles

© The Countryman Press

been well preserved and make a walking tour of the city worthwhile, while the University of Maryland Eastern Shore attracts visitors with its cultural events.

COMMUNITIES The small fishing villages of **Deal** and **Wenona** on Deal Island are worth driving through just to catch a glimpse of a lifestyle that may be on its way out.

GUIDANCE Somerset County Tourism (410-651-2968; 1-800-521-9189) maintains offices at 11440 Ocean Highway, Princess Anne, 21853, and inside the **J. Millard Tawes Museum** (410-968-2501), Somers Cove Marina, Crisfield, 21817.

GETTING THERE *By car:* **US 13** is the route that will bring you into the area, with **MD 413** going south to Crisfield.

By bus: **Carolina Trailways** (410-289-9307) makes a stop at the Chevron station, 106 Somerset Avenue, Princess Anne, 21853.

MEDICAL EMERGENCY McCready Health Services maintains a full-service hospital in Crisfield (410-968-1200), and clinics in Princess Anne (410-651-5883) and Dames Quarter (410-651-0585).

✳ To See

COLLEGES Founded as the Delaware Conference Academy in 1886, the **University of Maryland Eastern Shore** (410-651-2200) in Princess Anne is the cultural hub of the area. Its library contains more than 150,000 books, and diverse programs are presented in the **Ella Fitzgerald Performing Arts Center.** The 700-acre campus can be a quiet place for an afternoon's walk.

MUSEUMS J. Millard Tawes Museum (410-968-2501), Somers Cove Marina, Crisfield. Small admission charge. Monday through Saturday 9–4:30, October through April; Monday through Saturday 9–6, May through September. J. Millard Tawes was a native of Crisfield and Maryland's 54th governor. In addition to paying homage to his life, the museum chronicles the history of the area, from Native Americans to how the catch of the watermen gradually moved from oysters to crabs. The decoys of the Ward Brothers, models of various boats that worked Tangier Sound, and a mural that provides a sweeping overview of Chesapeake Bay chronology make the museum worth the small price of admission.

HISTORIC HOMES Teackle Mansion (410-651-2238), 11736 Mansion Street, Princess Anne. Small admission charge. Wednesday, Saturday, and Sunday 1–3, April through mid-December. Sunday 1–3, mid-December through March. The home of Littleton Teackle, prominent educator, banker, and statesman, is so large it took from 1802 to 1819 to complete. Its center has a Flemish-bond brick facade and decorative plasterwork above the door and first-floor windows. The adherence to Federal-style architecture, with its strict sense of symmetry, is as amusing as it is amazing. The house is furnished in period pieces, many from the Teackle family, and tour guides point out the family Bible, prints by artists

TEACKLE MANSION, PRINCESS ANNE

Teackle met in England, banknotes, and a "Report of the State's Bank."

HISTORIC SITES Ward Brothers' Workshop, Crisfield. Crisfield natives Steve and Lem Ward are generally acknowledged as being the ones who elevated decoy carving into an art form. Their workshop, which was rapidly deteriorating, has recently been stabilized, but not glamorized. Wood chips from the brothers' work remain on the floor, their ripped vinyl chairs have not been replaced, and even the color of the walls remains the same. This is one of few the historic places in which you get a real feel for what went on inside it. This is a highly recommended stop, but you must contact the J. Millard Tawes Museum (see *Museums*) to gain access.

HISTORIC CHURCHES Within the **Asbury United Methodist Church** in Crisfield is a painting of Daniel in the lion's den done by Lem Ward. However, he did not like the way it turned out, so he signed it as having been done by "Balkuaves."

The old **St. Peter's Church** in Oriole was founded in 1782, and the congregation is still going strong.

The original congregation of the **Metropolitan United Methodist Church** (30522 East Broad Street, Princess Anne) consisted entirely of slaves. The present building was erected in the late 1800s.

GUIDED TOURS The Port of Crisfield Escorted Walking Tour is sponsored by the J. Millard Tawes Historical Museum (see *Museums*). It makes the usual stops at historic sites, churches, and homes, but the tours of the seafood processing plants are the big treat. At the **Metompkin Bay Oyster Company** you can watch the amazing ability of workers who shuck hundreds of oysters per hour, while the walk through **Southern Connection Seafood** will enlighten you on how soft-shell crabs are harvested.

✳ To Do

BIRDING Woodlands, bay shoreline, and brackish marshes are the reason that **Deal Island Wildlife Management Area** (410-543-8223; MD 363 west of Princess Anne) has such a diversity of bird life: bald eagles, short-eared owls, tundra swans, marsh wrens, black rails, the rare peregrine falcon, and Maryland's only nesting population of black-necked stilts.

BOAT EXCURSIONS

Crisfield
⚓ *LEARN-IT* (410-968-9870), sails from the Captain's Galley Restaurant

on the Crisfield City Dock. Be sure to make reservations ahead of time, as the *LEARN-IT*'s schedule has been somewhat erratic. Captain Larry Laird Jr. takes passengers into Tangier Sound to watch how crabs and oysters are harvested, and to learn about the natural history of the bay. An excellent introduction to the estuary, especially for kids.

FISHING

Crisfield

Tangier Sound has some of the best fishing on the bay with flounder, striped bass, drum, trout, croaker, and perch being the catch for sportfishermen. Among the many charter-boat captains operating out of Crisfield are **Keith Ward** (410-968-0074; www.crisfield.com/prim), **Gilbert Howard** (410-968-0291), **Vernon Ricker** (www.crisfield.com/naturesbest), and **Curtis Johns** (410-623-2310).

Captains Joe and John Asanovich (410-957-2562; www.crisfield.com/barbara) operate headboats that leave at 7 AM daily from the Somers Cove Marina.

Somerset County Tourism (see *Guidance*) can provide you with a list of additional charter captains operating in and around Tangier Sound.

GOLF ⚐ **Great Hope Golf Course** (410-651-5900; 1-800-537-8009; www.greathope.com), 8380 Crisfield Highway, Westover. Closed only on Christmas Day. Five sets of tees at each hole allow you to pick your challenge on the 7,049-yard golf course designed by Dr. Michael Hurzdan. A children's discount is available.

HIKING See *Green Space—Parks.*

> "You have to think like a crab if you want to catch a crab."
> —Charles Bradshaw of Southern Connection Seafood

KAYAKING AND CANOEING Tangier Sound Outfitters (TSO) (410-968-1803; www.crisfield.org/TSO.html), 27582 Farm Market Road, Marion. A certified partner in the state's Nature Tourism program, TSO offer lessons, rentals, sales, shuttle services, and guided trips on Tangier Sound, Nassawango Creek, Pocomoke River, and Smith Island. A rarity on the Eastern Shore, they can arrange for backcountry paddle/camping trips.

✳ Green Space

BEACHES See *Parks.*

GARDENS The **Boxwood Garden** at the corner of Somerset Avenue and Washington Street in Princess Anne dates from the mid-1800s.

PARKS Janes Island State Park (410-968-1565), 40 Alfred Lawson Drive, Crisfield. The park is divided into two areas, the 300-acre **Hodson**

FISHING FROM THE PIER IN CRISFIELD

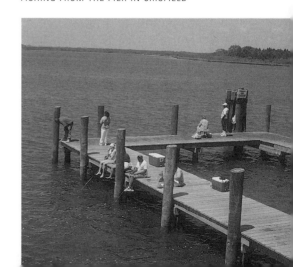

Memorial Area on the mainland and, separated from it by the Daugherty Creek Canal, Janes Island itself. Within the memorial area are a marina with boat-launch capabilities, a 104-site campground with modern amenities, picnic areas, and rental cabins. Although this area has two hiking trails, each a mile in length, it is the 3,000-acre island that is most worth spending your foot-travel time upon.

Except for a small boat dock and some ruins of a former fishing village on its southern end, Janes Island is completely undeveloped. Bordered by Tangier Sound, it is the quintessential Chesapeake Bay island, with a landscape barely above sea level. You will find windswept beaches, salt marshes, ponds, low-growing vegetation, and an assortment of creatures that exist only in this type of environment. To come here is to be brought back in time, to what many of the islands looked like when Captain John Smith made his famous exploration of the bay in the 1600s.

✳ Lodging

BED & BREAKFASTS

Crisfield, 21817

Bea's B&B (410-968-0423; www.beasbnb.com), 10 South Somerset Avenue. Built in 1909 by the founder of the Handy Soft Shell Crab Company, the house has many of the features common to fine houses of its day: pocket doors, stained-glass windows, and a grand foyer. The pink rose wallpaper in the Deborah Room gives it a feminine touch. The lace curtains in the Jennifer Room catch the morning sun. $75–85

🐾✒ **Washington Tull House** (410-

968-1891; www.bbonline.com/md/tull), 3296 Sackertown Road. Children over the age of 6 are welcomed in Sonia Coulbourn's home built around the turn of the 20th century. A Christian library, along with other books, is located in each room. Grab a book and curl up next to the fireplace in the parlor. $65.

Princess Anne, 21853

Hayman House (410-651-1107), 30491 Prince William Street. On a quiet side street just one block from the Teackle Mansion (see *To See—Historic Homes*), Hayman House is the perfect spot to stay for parents visiting their student-children at the nearby University of Maryland Eastern Shore. The Victorian parlor with its cranberry-tiled fireplace is a gathering place for quiet conversations, and the carved woodwork and oak floors add a warmth to the interior. Morning coffee is best appreciated on the porch. Hosts Carol and Charles Pinkerman enjoy relating the history of the area—and they prepare a great breakfast. Choice of private or shared bath. $80–100.

♿ **Waterloo County Inn** (410-651-0883; waterloocountryinn.com), 28822 Mt. Vernon Road. I could go on for pages about what makes the Waterloo such a splendid place to stay, but just a listing of a few of the many things will have to suffice: a historical home built in the mid-1700s; 317 acres of working farmland and woods to wander upon; free bicycles and canoes to explore the countryside; an outdoor pool; Jacuzzis; a choice of six rooms or suites, each decorated in appropriate furnishings but in a manner reflecting the Swiss origin of the inn's hosts. The Monie Room, where I stayed, has a king bed, a desk, a sitting area with wing chairs, and more. To top it all off, hosts Therese and Erwin Kraemer speak German, French, Italian, and English, so expect to meet visitors from a number of other countries. $105–245.

CAMPING **Janes Island State Park** (410-968-1565), 40 Alfred Lawson Drive, Crisfield, 21817. The state park's campground has sites on the shoreline overlooking the water and the island. Rental cabins also overlooking the water are often reserved a year in advance.

Lake Somerset Family Campground (410-957-9897), 8658 Lake Somerset Lane, Westover, 21871. Caters primarily to those with an RV. There are hookups, a general store, swimming pool, boat rentals, 5-acre fishing pond, and rental cabins and trailers.

Princess Anne Campground (410-651-1520), along US 13 south of Princess Anne, 21853. RV and trailer sites packed together with a few tent sites. Short nature trails, free firewood, and hot showers.

✳ Where to Eat

DINING OUT ☙ **Watermen's Inn** (410-968-2119), 901 West Main Street, Crisfield. Closed Monday. Chef Brian Julian and partner Kathy Berezpski both have degrees in culinary arts from Johnson and Wales University in Rhode Island, and they must have studied well. Brian only uses fresh local seafood and organically grown produce in his cooking. The grilled tiger shrimp with artichokes and tomatoes over black pepper fettuccine ($15.95) was one of

the best shrimp meals I've had on the Eastern Shore. The menu ranges from fried chicken ($9.95) to veal Piccata sautéed with capers ($14.95). Save room for Kathy's inventive desserts. Breakfast and lunch also served. Do not be misled by the modest exterior; dinner is a fine dining experience.

EATING OUT

Crisfield

☙ **Captain's Galley Restaurant** (410-968-3313), Main Street and city dock. With a great view of Tangier Sound, Captain's Galley serves everything from steamed crabs (market price) to stuffed mushrooms ($6.75) to a 24-ounce porterhouse ($21.95). Kids' menu with items under $5.

Tropical Chesapeake (410-968-3622), 712 Broadway. Serves breakfast, lunch, and dinner. Good sandwiches ($3.75–8.50) for a light lunch; try the baked egg sandwich for a different twist on breakfast. (Also see *Selective Shopping.*)

Circle Inn Restaurant (410-968-1969), 4012 Crisfield Highway. Serves breakfast, lunch, and dinner. This is where the locals come for low-cost home cooking. A full breakfast can be had for less than $3, while the most expensive dinner is the 12-ounce T-bone for $9.40.

Gordon's Confectionery (410-968-0566), 931 West Main Street. This is the place to come if you want to soak up the local color. It opens at 4 AM to serve the watermen, and is known for its coffee, old-fashioned fountain service, and a drink called a Zip (primarily chocolate or strawberry milk served over crushed ice). The ever-present group of guys in the back never tires of discussing fishing or politics.

✐ **Peppy's** (410-968-2727), 821 West Main Street. I let you decide what category to put this restaurant in. You can order pizza ($4–16.95), a 1-pound steamed shrimp basket ($14.95), country-fried steak with gravy ($5.95), crabcakes with two vegetables ($13.95), baked lasagna ($6.95), steamed crabs (market price), and more. Items on the kids' menu are less than $4.

Princess Anne
Peaky's (410-651-1950), 30361 Mt. Vernon Road. Serves breakfast, lunch, dinner. Known for their fried chicken ($6.95). Many of the lunch and dinner items, such as broiled flounder ($12.95) or pork chops ($9.95), are the same price at both lunch and dinner.

China Chef (410-651-5768), 12087 Somerset Avenue. Open for lunch and dinner. The China Chef has the usual menu for Chinese restaurants, but for something different order the ooey, gooey spareribs ($6.95).

Spike's Pub and Subs (410-651-9124), 30264 Mt. Vernon Road. This is the local bar, but it does make a variety of good (and filling) subs, and the prices can't be beat ($3–5).

Westover
Flannery's Inn (410-651-5900), 8380 Crisfield Highway. Located within the Great Hope Golf Course, Flannery's is the acknowledged local BBQ spot. Rolls ($4.50) or 6-inch subs ($6.50) can be filled with pulled pork, chopped chicken, ham, open-pit beef, or smoked turkey BBQ.

CRABS **Side Street Seafood Market and Restaurant** (410-968-2442), 204 South 10th Street, Crisfield. Open for lunch and dinner. My choice for steamed crabs (market

price) in Crisfield. The open upper deck lets the Tangier Sound breezes cool you off as you pull tasty morsels from the shell. The downstairs market will pack up a variety of fresh seafood to take home.

COFFEE BARS **Allegro Coffee and Tea Salon** (410-651-4520), 11775 Somerset Avenue, Suite 6A, Princess Anne. Monday through Friday 9–5:30. In addition to serving the usual coffees and teas, this is also a pleasant little restaurant. An assortment of fresh soups ($2.50) changes daily, and the focaccia bread sandwiches ($5) are just right for a light lunch. Cakes, pies, and pastries round out the menu.

SNACKS AND GOODIES **Ice Cream Gallery** (410-968-0809), 5 Goodsell Alley, Crisfield. Monday through Sunday 11–9:30. The Gallery's deck overlooking Tangier Sound is the place to enjoy the sunset after a meal at one of the local restaurants.

Sno Biz/Shave Ice (410-651-4548), 12100 Carol Lane, Princess Anne. Closed Sunday. Good for a cool, sweet treat on a hot day.

SOFT-SHELL CRABS TO GO **Southern Connection Seafood** (410-968-3367), 7th Street, Crisfield. In addition to packaging live or frozen soft-shell crabs for you to travel with, these friendly folks will take you on a tour of the factory to learn more about crabs.

✳ Selective Shopping
ART GALLERIES
Crisfield
♿ **Burton Avenue Gallery** (410-986-2787), 26430 Burton Avenue.

The outlet for the artwork of members of the local Somerset County Arts Council.

Just Ducky (410-968-1614), 113 Richardson Avenue. Shop owner and artist Linda English was born in Crisfield, and the local scenery is the subject of her paintings. Other artists and decoy carvers are also featured, notably Wes Bratcher, who received his first carving knife from Steve Ward.

SPECIAL SHOPS & **Tropical Chesapeake** (410-968-3622), 712 Broadway, Crisfield. Handmade pottery, local and Caribbean artwork and clothing, copper hangings, and a plethora of other items.

OUTLETS **Carvel Hall** (410-968-0500), MD 413, Crisfield. Charlie Biddle Sr. fashioned oyster knives and tongs in his Crisfield blacksmith shop during the late 1800s. Carvel Hall, the company that grew out of his enterprise, still manufactures its own cutlery and seafood tools, so not only will you be purchasing a locally made item, but you will get it at a discount price.

PICK-YOUR-OWN PRODUCE FARMS **Vassey's Orchards** (410-957-1454), Rehobeth Road, Rehobeth. Beginning in July you can pick squash, tomatoes, peaches, apples, and pumpkins during their respective seasons.

✳ Special Events

April: **Annual Daffodil Show** (410-651-9636), Princess Anne. More than 400 blooms and arrangements are on display at the Peninsula Bank.

May: **Annual 1800s Festival** (410-651-0351), Fairmont Academy, Upper Fairmont. 1800s classroom, old-fashioned spelling bee, food, crafts, and music. **Annual Soft Shell Spring Fair** (410-968-1125), Crisfield. Food, crafts, entertainment, and lots of crab.

July: **Annual J. Millard Tawes Crab and Clam Bake** (410-968-2500), Somers Cove Marina, Crisfield. All-you-can-eat crabs, clams, fish, corn, and more. Tickets must be purchased in advance. **Somerset County Fair** (410-651-2341), Civic Center, Princess Anne.

September: **Annual National Hard Crab Derby and Fair** (410-968-2500), Somers Cove Marina, Crisfield. Lots of fun with crab races, boat-racing and -docking contests, crab-picking contests, arts and crafts, much seafood, and live entertainment. **Annual Skipjack Races** (410-784-2203), Deal Island Harbor. Food, entertainment, and children's activities in addition to boat races.

October: **Olde Princess Anne Days** (461-651-2238), Princess Anne. Historic homes and gardens tours, Revolutionary War encampment, period crafts, music, and kids' activities. **Annual Native American Heritage Festival and Powwow** (410-623-8329), Bending Water Park Living Village, Marion.

SMITH ISLAND

Defining the western edge of Tangier Sound and existing in the heart of the Chesapeake Bay—12 miles from Crisfield—is a world unto itself, tiny Smith Island (see map on page 66). Eight miles long and 4 miles wide, its highest point is only a few feet above high tide; much of the acreage is marshland. The island was sighted by Captain John Smith and settled by Cornish fishermen in the 1600s, and some of the island's inhabitants retain the Elizabethan accents and idioms of their ancestors. Most still make their living from the waters of the bay, heading out early in the morning from the island's many marshy channels. Crab-shedding shanties built upon stilts rise near the water's edge, resulting in its unofficial title: "soft-shell crab capital of the world."

The island is actually a conglomeration of islands separated by creeks, canals, marshes, and inlets. The towns of **Ewell** and **Rhodes Point** are connected by a roadway, but tiny **Tylerton** can be reached only by boat.

Visitors are usually day-trippers who ferry over to Ewell to stay on the island for a few hours, have a meal, and take a quick walking tour or guided minibus tour.

The best way to really appreciate the island's uniqueness, however, is to spend the night. After other tourists have gone, overnight visitors can share unhurried conversations with residents, take a walk along the waterfront, or just enjoy the sunset spread a reddish glow across the marshlands. Spring—when the blossoms of pomegranate, fig, pear, and mimosa trees color the scenery and perfume the air—is a great time to visit. Be sure to look in the stores for fig preserves and pomegranate jellies made by island residents in their homes.

GUIDANCE The **Smith Island Visitor's Center** (410-425-3351), 20846 Caleb Jones Road, Ewell, 21824, provides information once you are on the island. Before going, you might want to contact **Somerset County Tourism** (410-651-2968; 1-800-521-9189) at 11440 Ocean Highway, Princess Anne, 21853.

If you want to really understand the history and the people of the island before you arrive, read the book *An Island Out of Time*. Author Tom Horton spent three years on Smith Island, and his book is an eloquent and sensitive study.

GETTING THERE The *Captain Tyler* (410-425-2771) leaves from the Somers

Cove Marina for a lightly narrated cruise at 12:30 daily, arrives at Smith Island about 1:10, and leaves at 4 sharp.

The *Captain Jason* (410-425-4471; 410-425-5931) departs the Crisfield city dock and follows the same schedule. More of a working boat than a tourist boat, it is the one many of the islanders use. Expect to share space with furniture, dog food, cases of paper towels, and other items. The gossip you overhear makes up for the lack of narration.

The *Island Belle II* (410-968-1118) is the island's mail boat and follows the same schedule as the other two. Hauling passengers as well as the mail, it leaves from the Crisfield city dock.

GETTING AROUND Bicycles and golf carts may be rented at the ice cream stand beside the **Bayside Inn,** 4065 Smith Island Road, Ewell.

PUBLIC REST ROOMS Public comfort stations are found inside the Smith Island Visitor's Center.

✳ To See

MUSEUMS ⟨ **Smith Island Visitor's Center Cultural Museum** (410-425-3351) 20846 Caleb Jones Road, Ewell. Small admission charge. Open daily noon–4, April through November. Sometimes open during the off-season. Murals, interactive displays, full-sized workboats, and occasional live interpreters make this the first place to stop to learn more about your Smith Island visit. The timeline puts things in perspective and shows how the vagaries of the seafood harvest have affected the islanders.

✳ To Do

BICYCLING Bicycles may be rented at the ice cream stand beside the **Bayside Inn**, 4065 Smith Island Road, Ewell. In addition to riding around Ewell, take the 1-mile road through salt marshes and over a wooden bridge to Rhodes Point.

WALKING TOURS The best way to experience Smith Island is by foot, and a small brochure available from the visitors center (see *Guidance*) in Ewell describes the sites you will see in the island's three small towns.

✳ Lodging

MOTELS AND HOTELS Smith Island Motel and Waterman's Rest (410-425-3321), 4025 Smith Island Road, Ewell, 21824. April 15 through October 15. A basic motel with eight rooms that share baths. The Waterman's Rest is a small cottage available to those who wish an extended stay on the island.

BED & BREAKFASTS ✐ **Ewell Tide Inn** (410-425-2141; 1-888-699-2141; www.smithisland.net), 4063 Tyler Road, Ewell, 21824. Certainly the nicest accommodations in Ewell, with four rooms that share two baths. The porch and long front yard overlook the water. Husband and wife Captain Steve Eades and Theresa Siejack welcome children and provide bikes for island exploration. $75.

Inn of Silent Music (410-425-3541; www.innofsilentmusic.com), 2955 Tylerton Road, Tylerton, 21866. The only place to stay in Tylerton and accessible only by the *Captain Jason* (see *Getting There*). Hosts Sherryl Lindberg and LeRoy Friesen offer four rooms with private baths. The entire house overlooks the bay, but the upstairs Drum Point Room has the best water views. Canoes, bicycles, and charter boats are available for sight-seeing. The seafood dinners ($15) Sherryl offers have become legend among former guests. $105–125.

✳ Where to Eat

EATING OUT

Ewell

Bayside Inn (410-425-2771), 4065 Smith Island Road. The Bayside Inn has picture windows overlooking the town dock and is the place most tourists eat lunch. The all-you-can-eat dinner ($12.95) is most popular and includes items such as crab soup, crabcakes, ham, coleslaw, corn pudding, stewed tomatoes, and applesauce custard pie. Other lunches and dinners (starting at $5.95) are also available.

Ruke's Seafood Deck (410-425-2311), 20840 Caleb Jones Road. Be adventurous and pass up the tourist environment of the Bayside Inn in favor of Ruke's, the local restaurant of choice. If you don't mind the rather dull and dingy decor of this grocery/general store, you can dine on sandwiches, french fries, or crabcakes made from local crabs ($7.95) on a screened porch overlooking the marsh. Better yet, sit inside with everyone else and overhear conversations about who is dating who at the high school, how the seafood harvest is going, or the latest prank played by one islander on another.

✳ Selective Shopping

SPECIAL SHOPS

Ewell

&. **Smith Island Visitor's Center Cultural Museum** (see *Guidance*). The museum's gift shop stocks a number of locally made items and handicrafts.

Bayside Gifts (410-425-2771), 4065 Smith Island Road. The shop, a part of the **Bayside Inn** (see *Eating Out*), has a nautical theme with decoys, gifts, and books on Smith Island and the bay area.

SALISBURY

Salisbury has been the economic and cultural center of the lower Eastern Shore since its establishment in 1732. Large boats coming up the Wicomico River from the bay were the first to bring trade to the city. Because Salisbury is at the intersection of several railroads, rail lines later figured prominently. Finally, easy access via modern highways brought more commerce to the city. Agriculture has always been important to the area, but today's city owes much to Frank Perdue, whose poultry business is a dominant economic engine.

Devastating fires in 1860 and 1868 almost destroyed the town. As a result, much of Salisbury looks like other modern American cities, with undistinguished strip malls, convenience stores, and fast-food shops. However, pockets of loveliness still remain, such as the main downtown area (now a pedestrian mall), the campus of Salisbury University, and the historic district of Newtown with six blocks of magnificent Victorian homes. The park along the South Prong Wicomico River is a quiet place within the city and contains the well-managed Salisbury Zoological Park.

The arts and cultural offerings are sophisticated in this metropolitan area of 70,000 inhabitants. Salisbury has its own symphony orchestra, a minor league baseball team, and a number of museums, while presentations at Salisbury University range from local stage productions to international guest lecturers.

GUIDANCE A modern and spacious welcome center operated by the **Wicomico County Convention and Visitors Bureau** (410-548-4914; 1-800-332-8687; www.wicomicotourism.org), 8480 Ocean Highway, Delmar, 21875, is located north of Salisbury on US 13. This is more than just a place to obtain information. It is located next to an attractive, large pond and within the greenery of **Leonard's Mill Park,** which has public rest rooms, picnic facilities, and canoe-launching capabilities.

GETTING THERE *By air:* The **Salisbury/Ocean City Airport** (410-548-4827), 5485 Airport Terminal Road, is the second largest airport in the state, averaging close to 150,000 passengers a year. It is currently serviced by regularly scheduled flights via US Airways (1-800-428-4322).

Salisbury Area

By car: **US 50** and **US 13** intersect in Salisbury and provide access to all points north, south, east, and west. Traffic becomes heavy on US 50 during the summer months as vacationers head to and from Ocean City.

By bus: **Carolina Trailways** (410-749-4121) has a station at 350 Cypress Street, Salisbury. **Greyhound** (1-800-229-9424) also has information on bus service to the lower Eastern Shore.

GETTING AROUND *By taxi:* **Delmarva Cab** (410-219-3677); **Ideal Cab** (410-742-3200); **Salisbury Taxi** (410-749-3500).

By bus: The local bus service, **Wicomico/Shore Transit** (410-548-4865), reaches into every sector of the city and the university. Additional routes make it possible to ride to a number of outlying areas such as Princess Anne, Mount Vernon, Crisfield, Berlin, Ocean City, and Cambridge.

MEDICAL EMERGENCY **Peninsula Regional Medical Center** (410-546-6400), 100 East Carroll Street, Salisbury.

✳ To See

COLLEGES **Salisbury University** (410-543-6161; 1-888-543-0184), Camden and West College Avenues, Salisbury. Tours of the 125-acre campus, which has been declared a national arboretum and called the most beautiful in Maryland, begin every Monday, Wednesday, and Friday at 1:30 at the Admissions House. The campus contains more than 2,100 plant species, pieces of outdoor art, and notable works of architecture. The university is home to the Salisbury Symphony

ALONG THE SALISBURY URBAN GREENWAY

Salisbury

© The Countryman Press

Orchestra, SU Theatre, and several galleries, and has a range of lectures and activities open to the public.

MUSEUMS

Salisbury

Ward Museum of Wildlife Art (410-742-4988), 909 South Schumaker Drive. Open daily. Adults $7, students $3, seniors $5. The $5.5 million Ward Museum, named for decoy carvers Lem and Steve Ward, opened in 1992. Its 4,000 objects interpret the history and development of decoy carving, from early Native American pieces to the present day. An excellent display shows how specialized decoys were developed for the different North American flyways, while another examines various Eastern Shore hunting methods. The re-creation of Lem and Steve Ward's workshop is an accurate portrayal of their Crisfield business. Do not miss the Championship Gallery, which contains winners from past Ward carving competitions held annually in Ocean City. The detail, beauty, and artistry of these pieces is nothing short of spectacular. One of Elmer Crowell's decoys sold for $319,000. The museum's building is a work of art in itself.

Also see **Ward Brothers' Workshop** under *To See—Historic Sites* in "Tangier Sound Area.")

✂ **Excel Interactive Science Museum** (410-546-2168; www.excel.org), The Centre at Salisbury (see *Selective Shopping—Malls*). A couple of small rooms located inside the mall provide interactive activities for kids. Free Internet access.

HISTORIC HOMES Poplar Hill Mansion (410-749-1776), 117 East Elizabeth Street, Salisbury. Guided tours Sunday 1–4. The oldest house in Salisbury (circa 1805) is the logical starting or stopping point for a walking tour of the **Newtown Historic District** (see *To Do—Walking Tours*). Even if you can't get inside to enjoy the period antiques and original brass hardware on the woodwork, the transitional Georgian-style building—with bull's-eye windows, dentil molding, and a second-story Palladian window—is worth walking by.

HISTORIC SITES Pemberton Historical Park (410-860-2447), Pemberton Drive, Salisbury. Small entrance fees are charged for the house and museum. A short drive from downtown Salisbury, this county-operated park includes the home of Isaac and Anne Handy, built in 1741. The Flemish-bond brickwork house still contains the original interior wood paneling. Guided tours are given on Sunday from May through September, but call to make sure someone is there. Handy was a ship-

PEMBERTON HISTORICAL PARK

owner and captain, merchant, farmer, and justice of the peace, and raised grains, tobacco, and flax on his plantation. The park also includes a re-created 18th-century barn with more than 3,000 items of local history, a few picnic tables, and almost 5 miles of nature trails that wind onto Bell Island in the Wicomico River. Side-by-side gardens compare 18th-century crops with those of today. Special events range from canoe trips to maple sugaring demonstrations to living-history weekends.

ZOO ✥ ♿ **Salisbury Zoological Park** (410-548-3188), 750 South Park Drive, Salisbury. Open daily—and parking and admission are free! The Salisbury zoo is one of the prettiest in the Mid-Atlantic region, set within an old pine forest and beside the South Prong Wicomico River. Even though it has 400 examples of 100 species found within the Western Hemisphere, it is not overwhelming like some zoos. Expect to devote a couple of hours to observing animals such as American alligators, Central American black-handed spider monkeys, jaguars, capybaras, and the only bear native to South America, the endangered spectacled bear from the Andes Mountains. The pathways are nearly level, so walking is easy and accessible to everyone. Do not miss this place.

✳ To Do

BICYCLING
Salisbury
The **Wicomico County Convention and Visitors Bureau** (see *Guidance*) has developed an excellent set of maps and descriptions that detail dozens of rides from a few miles to over 100 miles. Short ones are within the city, while others reach to Ocean City, Assateague Island, and Crisfield. A local favorite makes use of the Upper Ferry across the Wicomico River.

The **Salisbury Bicycle Club** (P.O. Box 3512, Salisbury, 21802) and **Salisbury University Bicycle Club** (Campus Box 3046, Salisbury, 21801) welcome guest riders on their outings.

BIRDING
Salisbury
The **Ward Museum of Wildlife Art** (see *To See—Museums*), 909 South Schumaker Drive, and **Salisbury Zoological Park** (see *To See—Zoo*), 750 South Park Drive, are both located along the Salisbury Urban Greenway next to the South Prong Wicomico River. Cedar waxwings, hummingbirds, woodpeckers, and nuthatches are often seen in the zoo. Schumaker Pond in front of the museum attracts ducks, wigeon, and swans. Scarlet tanagers often breed on site.

A BISON IN THE SALISBURY ZOO

COMING INTO WHITEHAVEN ON THE WHITEHAVEN FERRY

Open meadows, woodlands, and stream banks attract a variety of bird life to **Pemberton Historical Park** (see *To See—Historic Sites*).

BOAT EXCURSIONS 🛥 **Whitehaven B&B** (410-873-3294; 1-888-205-5921), 23844-48 River Street, Whitehaven. U.S. Coast Guard–licensed Captain Mark Herrett, the son of B&B hosts Maryen and Carlton Herrett (see *Lodging—Bed & Breakfasts*), runs charter trips on the Wicomico River. Refreshments are provided during the sunset cruise to the river's expansive mouth.

FERRIES The **Whitehaven Ferry** (410-873-2862), off MD 352 in Whitehaven, lays claims to being the oldest ferry in continuous operation in the United States. (A ferry in New Jersey is older but has not been in continuous use.) Connected to a fixed line, the ferry's journey across the Wicomico River lasts less than 5 minutes, but offers some of the most free fun you can have on the Eastern Shore. Operates year-round during daylight hours. The **Upper Ferry** (410-749-2892), off MD 349 in Upper Ferry, crosses

the Wicomico River less than 10 miles west of Salisbury. Like the Whitehaven Ferry (see above), it, too, is free and has the same schedule.

GOLF Horse Bridge (410-543-4446), 32418 Mt. Hermon Road, Salisbury. Open year-round. Ponds, waste bunkers, and drainage ditches make this a challenging course.

Woodcreek Golf Links (410-896-3000; www.golflinks.com), 9080 Executive Club Drive, Delmar. Opened to the public in 2001, it has town houses for sale around the links.

HIKING Pemberton Historical Park (see *To See—Historic Sites*), Pemberton Drive, Salisbury. The park has almost 5 miles of trails that wind through bottomland forests along the Wicomico River, and deliver you to Bell Island and the site of docks that were once used to load the plantation's crops onto ships.

SWIMMING Cherry Beach is a 0.3-mile-long beach along the Nanticoke River in the small town of Sharptown. Access is free, and there are picnic tables and a playground.

TENNIS A long list of courts located in and around Salisbury may be obtained by contacting the **Wicomico County Department of Recreation and Parks** (410-548-4900), 500 Glen Avenue, Salisbury, 21804.

WALKING TOURS A brochure describing a **Walking Tour of Downtown Salisbury** is available from the Wicomico County Convention and Visitors Bureau (see *Guidance*). Fires in the late 1800s destroyed much of the city, so most of the architecture reflects a later period. The Masonic Temple stands next to the Victorian Court House. The old firehouse and the Brewington Building are two other standouts. Many of the buildings line the Pedestrian Plaza.

The **Newtown Walking Tour** pamphlet is also available from the bureau. The neighborhood of Newtown was built after the fires and has now become the oldest part of town. The Victorian homes found here are magnificent and well taken care of. So many of them would make great B&Bs, but ordinances prohibit such an enterprise. The best time to visit is during the October **Newtown Festival** (see *Special Events*) when many of the homes are open to tours.

✳ Lodging

MOTELS AND HOTELS
Salisbury, 21801
Ramada Inn (410-546-4400; 1-888-800-7617), 300 South Salisbury Boulevard. About as centrally located as you can get, the Ramada is in the downtown district and has the area's only heated indoor pool. Its spacious rooms overlook the River Walk Park and pedestrian plaza. Complimentary Salisbury Airport Shuttle.

Sleep Inn (410-572-5516), 406 Punkin Court, 21804. On US Business 13 and convenient to US 50. Free continental breakfast and local calls. $90–125.

🐾 **Best Western** (410-546-1300), 1735 North Salisbury Boulevard. On US Business 13 and close to the mall and movie theater. Free exercise room, continental breakfast, and local calls. Pets permitted for extra fee. $120–140. The rates drop by almost 50 percent in the off-season.

🐾 **Comfort Inn** (410-543-4666), 2701 North Salisbury Boulevard. Free continental breakfast, pets permitted, and some two-bedroom suites. $90–140.

BED & BREAKFASTS ✿ **Whitehaven B&B** (410-873-2194; 1-888-205-5921; www.whitehaven.com), 23844–48 River Street, Whitehaven, 21856. Maryen and Carlton Herrett have restored the two side-by-side 1800s homes of the Whitehaven B&B, to which they welcome you with a glass of wine and friendly conversation. The six rooms have antique furnishings, some share a private bath, and all overlook the marshes and waters of the Wicomico River. I had a quiet walk around town (all of Whitehaven is on the National Register of Historic Places), took the Whitehaven Ferry (see *To Do—Ferries*) across the river, and read a book on the screened porch as the sun set. It is impossible to find a quieter place in the Salisbury area to spend the night. Next visit, I intend make use of the front-yard hammock under a large maple tree. $90–100. (Also see *To Do—Boat Excursions.*)

CAMPING 🐾 **Roaring Point Campground** (410-873-2553), Nanticoke

Wharf Road, Nanticoke, 21840. April 1 through November 1. There are lots of amenities at this campground, which sits next to the wide mouth of the Nanticoke River: boat rentals, a sandy beach, horseshoes, hayrides, basketball, a coin laundry, and live country music on some weekends. Crabs, rockfish, flounder, perch, and more are caught from the 35-foot pier. Pets permitted on leash.

❦ **Woodlawn Family Camping** (410-896-2979), 1209 Walnut Street, Delmar, 21875. March 15 through October 31. One of the smallest, but lowest-cost, private campgrounds on the Eastern Shore. Free showers. Pets permitted on leash.

✳ Where to Eat

DINING OUT ❧ **Legends** (410-749-7717), 213 West Main Street, City Center, downtown Salisbury. Irish owner-chef Damion Heaney has created a spot where you can dine on gourmet meals at a reasonable price; some dinners start at $12. The seafood is notable.

EATING OUT

Salisbury

❧ **Cactus Taverna** (410-548-1254), 2420 North Salisbury Boulevard. This restaurant is the end store of a small strip mall, so there is not a lot of atmosphere, but the quality of the Mexican, South American, and Mediterranean dishes makes up for it. The shrimp Cancún with raspberry sauce ($15.95) is a house favorite, as is the lamb shank roasted in a Spanish red sauce ($14.95). The huge plate of paella ($14.95) I ordered brought back delectable memories of travels to Spain. Lots of appetizers,

vegetarian selections, Mexican specialties, and a children's menu could keep you coming back often. Low-key live entertainment some evenings.

❧ **Brew River Restaurant and Bar** (410-677-6757), 502 West Main Street. The atmosphere and food remind me of an Applebee's or TGI Friday's. The scenery is nice, as the restaurant sits at the end of River Walk Park on the Wicomico River; lots of seating on the outside deck. BBQ ribs (half rack, $14.95) are a favorite. The seafood selection is extensive; shrimp (from $14.99), scallops ($15.99), flounder (from $15.99), crab (market price), and a seafood medley ($22.99). Children's menu.

Flannery's Cajun Café (410-546-2570), 327 East Main Street. The flavor of New Orleans. Jambalaya, red beans, slow-cooked ribs, chicken, muffaletta, and alligator. Dinner $11–23.

Goin' Nuts Café (410-860-1164), 947 Mt. Hermon Road. As the name implies, the atmosphere makes this a fun place to eat. More than 20 sandwiches to choose from ($4–7.95). Entrées are also extensive: vegetable stir fry ($11.95), curried honey shrimp ($15.95), and Thai-seasoned seafood ($16.95). A signature item is the City Slicker Chicken—mozzarella and prosciutto on chicken breast simmered in a garlic cream sauce ($14.95).

Dayton's (410-548-2272), 909 Snow Hill Drive. The breakfast place of choice; low-cost meals. $3–12.

Lombardi's (410-749-0522), 315 Civic Avenue, Twilley Centre. Offers a typical Italian menu of pasta, strombolis, and subs. The pizza is the best item, as it is cooked in a stone oven.

The cannolis come from Little Italy in Baltimore. $3.50–15.

Hebron
Hebron Diner (410-749-9955), 201 South Main Street. Hearty country cooking. $4–15.

Pittsville
Pittsville Dinette (410-835-2541), 34200 Old Ocean City Road. Plain, but good, traditional Eastern Shore food. $4–$14.

CRABS ⚓ **Waterman's Cove** (410-546-1400), 925 Snow Hill Road, Salisbury. Owned and operated by a local waterman, so you know the seafood is fresh. Steamed crabs (market price) are available by the dozen; fried soft-shell crabs are served at lunch ($7.95) and dinner ($14.95). The poached flounder Piccata in lemon butter with crabmeat and capers melts in your mouth (lunch $7.95, dinner $15.95).

&. **The Red Roost** (410-546-5443; www.redroost.com), 2670 Clara Road, Whitehaven. Although it does not sit right on the water, the Red Roost is a classic Eastern Shore crab house. The roof is tin, long wooden tables are covered in brown paper tablecloths, and bushel baskets serve as lamp shades. The all-you-can-eat steamed crab special (market price) brings the locals in by droves, but another favorite, which I tried and really enjoyed, is the chicken cordon bleu ($16.95) with lump crabmeat. The Sampler ($17.99) gives you about everything: crab, shrimp, snow crab, and chicken. Portions are large and desserts are homemade. Be sure to pick up a pamphlet to learn the restaurant's colorful history.

TAKE-OUT Downtown Deli (410-749-0611), Plaza Gallery Building, downtown Salisbury. Fresh-baked breads, breakfast and lunch sandwiches, coffee, and special desserts.

COFFEE BARS Aesop's Table (410-546-4471), 124 North Division Street, Salisbury. Open weekdays 8–3. Inside this antiques dealer's shop is a small coffee bar that also serves light fare.

SNACKS AND GOODIES Scoops (410-548-989), Camden Avenue across from the university, Salisbury. Old-fashioned shakes, sundaes, and other ice cream concoctions.

✳ **Entertainment**
FILM Hoyts Cinema Centre (410-543-0902), 2312 North Salisbury Boulevard, Salisbury, shows first-run movies.

MUSIC Making use of performance facilities at Salisbury University in Salisbury, the **Salisbury Symphony Orchestra** (410-548-5587) has a full set of concerts scheduled each year.

THEATERS Although the **SU Theatre** (410-543-6000) is affiliated with Salisbury University in Salisbury, the cast of most productions is composed of students, faculty, and community members.

SPORTS The **Delmarva Shorebirds** (410-219-3112), 6400 Hobbs Road, Perdue Stadium, Salisbury, are the Class A affiliates of the Baltimore Orioles. Thanks to the wealth of poultry king Frank Perdue, the stadium they play in is one of the plushest you will find of any minor league team. Admission cost, though, is still a pittance compared to that in the majors. A great way to spend a summer evening.

✳ Selective Shopping

ANTIQUES

Salisbury

Holly Ridge (410-742-4392), 1411 South Salisbury Boulevard. A large selection of 18th- and 19th-century items.

Market Street Antiques and Collectibles Center (410-749-4112), 150 West Market Street. Almost 90 dealers under one roof.

Parker Place (410-860-1263), 234 West Main Street. Three floors of antiques.

Other shops in town include **All Manor of Things** (410-546-4471), 12 North Division Street; **Anne's Tiques** (410-543-0880), 2825 North Salisbury Boulevard; and **Sweet Nothings** (410-219-3322), 1918 North Salisbury Boulevard.

ART GALLERIES

Salisbury

The **Atrium Gallery** and the **University Gallery** at Salisbury University (see *To See—Colleges*) feature the works of students and professors, and traveling exhibits.

Art Institute and Gallery (410-546-4748), 212 West Main Street Gallery Building on Downtown Plaza. Changing exhibits of original works by local and regional artists. Sponsors classes, field trips, and free film programs. As an interesting aside, the walls outside the gallery are adorned with old photos of Salisbury.

Salisbury Art and Framing (410-742-9522; www.artcafe.net/salisart), 213 North Salisbury Boulevard. A mix of paintings, pottery, decorative art, and handmade jewelry.

BOOKSTORES Market Street Books (410-219-3210), 146 West Market Street, Salisbury. A great collection of used and out-of-print books of interest to adults and children.

CRAFTS Chesapeake East Handmade Ceramics (410-546-1534; 1-800-320-7829; www.chesapeakeeast. com), 501 West Main Street, Salisbury. Dana Simson creates original and bright designs, which she incorporates onto ceramic bowls, plates, pitchers, vases, drawer pulls, and more. A multitalented artist, she creates stationery items, decor products, and gift books, and writes the award-winning children's "Legendbook" series. I thought this would be just another pottery shop, but Ms. Simson's works are refreshingly new and different. Also, ask for the brochure that describes the building's extraordinary past.

SPECIAL SHOPS

Salisbury

Country House and Country Village (410-749-1959; www.thecountryhouse.com), 805 East Main Street. Claims to be "The Largest Country Store in the East." With 23,000 square feet of display space for ever-changing merchandise, they may be right.

The New Card and Gift Shop (410-860-5171), 1210 Nanticoke Road. Look for hand-painted glass by local artist Suzy Hayman.

OUTLETS Salisbury Pewter (410-546-1188; 1-800-824-1469), North Salisbury Boulevard—US 13, Salisbury. Monday through Saturday, and sometimes on Sunday. A small glass window lets you watch crafters at work before you purchase pewter items at factory prices.

MALLS The Centre at Salisbury (410-548-1600), 2300 North Salisbury Boulevard, Salisbury. Contains many of the usual national chains found in most malls.

FARMER'S MARKET Salisbury. Located at Civic and Glen Avenues. Saturday 8–1, April through November.

PICK-YOUR-OWN PRODUCE FARMS Peach Blossom Farm (410-742-6545), 27616 Little Lane, Salisbury. A retail stand, and pick-your-own cantaloupes and watermelons.

Strawberry Fields Forever (410-835-8586), 4820 Powell School Road, Parsonsburg. Strawberries for the picking from mid-May through mid-June.

Garden of Eden Orchards (410-546-0081), 4380 Upper Ferry Road, Eden. Retail stand and pick-your-own fruits.

Catalpa Grove Farms (410-546-0006), 8398 Riggin Road, Mardela Springs. A wide variety of pick-your-own fruits and vegetables.

✳ Special Events

Contact the **Wicomico County Convention and Visitors Bureau** (see *Guidance*) for more information on all of these events.

May: **Salisbury Festival,** Salisbury. Entertainment, triathlon, carnival, children's activities, and lots of food.

June: **Seaside Memorial Horse Show,** Equestrian Center, Winterplace Park, Salisbury.

July: **Sunday Night Concerts,** City Park, Salisbury. Free concerts by the Community Band each Sunday evening in July.

August: **Great North American Turtle Races,** Cedar Hill Park, Bivalve.

September: **Pemberton Colonial Fair,** Pemberton Historical Park, Pemberton. Music, games, sports, crafts, demonstrations, food, and other activities of the 18th century.

October: During the **Newtown Festival** visitors can tour the magnificent Victorian homes in Salisbury's historic district. Includes music, crafts, and walking tours. **Chesapeake Wildlife Showcase,** Ward Museum of Wildlife Art (see *To See—Museums*), Salisbury. Auctions and sales of antique wildlife decoys.

November: **Salisbury Kennel Club Dog Show,** Salisbury. Competition and judging.

CAMBRIDGE AND VICINITY

C ambridge's location on the southern bank of the wide Choptank River makes its setting one of the prettiest on the Eastern Shore. Author James Michener has praised its maritime heritage, shaded streets, and lovingly cared-for homes. A walk down High Street (with a brochure from the Dorchester County Department of Tourism, see *Guidance*) brings you past one beautiful Victorian home after another, while the public park and wharf at street's end gives a sweeping vista of the river.

Despite Cambridge's waterfront location, agriculture was the area's first important business. By the mid-1800s lumber and flour mills were established, which in turn led to the building of ships to transport goods. The late 1800s saw a rise in oyster harvesting. Local lore claims skipjacks were so tightly packed in Cambridge Creek Harbor that you could walk completely across it on their decks.

Seafood and other packing houses came to the fore in the early 1900s and, despite some decline, still dot Cambridge's landscape. Visitors of today find a community that is waking up to its appeal to the outside world. Museums, boat trips, and outdoor adventures on the water and land are bringing in increasing numbers of tourists. The opening of the Hyatt Regency Chesapeake Bay Golf Resort Spa and Marina in 2002 provided Cambridge with the area's first destination resort.

COMMUNITIES **Church Creek** received its name from Trinity Church, the oldest Episcopal church in continuous use in the United States. The community is believed to have been in existence as early as the late 1600s.

On the banks of the Nanticoke River, **Vienna** was settled by 1669. Once a thriving port, its size diminished as main roadways passed it by. A brochure available from the **Visitor Center at Sailwinds Park** (see *Guidance*) describes a walking tour of the now quiet town.

Hurlock began as a railroad station and is now the second largest town in Dorchester County. The train station has been restored and hosts occasional train trips.

Taylors Island is a traditional waterman's village. Marinas, docks, and activity around the water are the reasons to visit.

Hooper Island, another waterman's settlement, is actually three islands and is even more removed from the mainstream than is Taylors Island. The community quietly goes about harvesting and processing thousands of pounds of catch from the bay annually.

A pamphlet available from the **Dorchester County Department of Tourism** (see *Guidance*) points out the historic aspects of **East New Market,** a town whose four entrances are each marked by a church. The entire town is on the National Register of Historic Places.

GUIDANCE & Overlooking the Choptank River beside US 50, the **Visitor Center at Sailwinds Park** and the **Dorchester County Department of Tourism** (410-228-1000; 1-800-522-8687; www.tourdorchester.org), 2 Rose Hill Place, Cambridge, 21613, have one of the most scenic settings of any welcome center in the state. A gigantic Teflon-coated fiberglass sail makes the spot even more dramatic, while a whimsical outdoor sculpture provides additional charm. There's also a short boardwalk trail to the river and a handicapped-accessible playground.

GETTING THERE *By car:* **US 50** bisects the region with a north–south orientation.

By air: You can fly your own plane into **Cambridge Dorchester Airport** (410-228-4571), 5223 Bucktown Road, Cambridge. Otherwise, the closest commercial airport is **Salisbury/Ocean City Airport** in Salisbury (see *Getting There* in "Salisbury").

By bus: **Carolina Trailways** (410-289-9307) makes a stop at the Sunburst Mobil Station in Cambridge (410-228-4626) at US 50 and Bucktown Road.

By water: If you own or rent a boat, the Choptank River provides easy access from the Chesapeake Bay. A number of marinas in Cambridge have transient slips.

GETTING AROUND Other than **US 50,** which nearly becomes bumper-to-bumper with Ocean City traffic on summer weekends, the roadways in this area are lightly traveled and provide pleasant, unhurried driving experiences.

THE OUTDOOR SCULPTURE AT SAILWINDS PARK AND VISITOR CENTER ON THE CHOPTANK RIVER

By taxi: **Moxey's Taxi** (410-221-0689); **Streeter's Taxi** (410-228-8791).

By bus: The **Dorchester city bus** (410-221-1910) routes also include part of the surrounding countryside. If you wish to go farther afield, **Wicomico/Shore Transit** (410-548-4865) can take you to most places on the lower Eastern Shore, including Salisbury and Ocean City.

PUBLIC REST ROOMS Rest rooms available to anyone are at the Visitor Center at Sailwinds Park (see *Guidance*) and in the Police Department on Academy Street in Cambridge.

MEDICAL EMERGENCY Dorchester General Hospital (410-228-5511), 300 Bryn Street, Cambridge.

✷ To See
MUSEUMS
Cambridge
Brannock Maritime Museum (410-228-6938), 215 Talbot Avenue. Friday

and Saturday 10–4, Sunday 1:30–4. (If nobody is there, ring the doorbell.) Donations accepted. It is the guided tour by founder and curator Earl Brannock (also see *Lodging—Cottages*) that makes this small museum stand out. There is much to see—old photos of Chesapeake Bay steamboats, information on bay activity during the two world wars, dozens of boat models, the compass from Admiral Byrd's yacht, shipwright's tools, displays about the oyster navy—and Mr. Brannock has a story about each one.

DISCOVER DORCHESTER
Pick up a copy of *Discover Dorchester.* It gives not only some practical information about the area but also detailed descriptions of water trails for canoeists and kayakers, and routes for bicycling.

The **Dorchester County Historical Society** (410-228-7953), 912 LaGrange Avenue, oversees the **Meredith House, Nield Museum and Herb Garden,** and **Goldsborough Stable** within a small complex along a residential street. Thursday, Friday, and Saturday 10–3. Items in each building reflect the history of the area and include Native American artifacts, a McCormick reaper, and household items from the 18th, 19th, and 20th centuries.

Richardson Maritime Museum (410-221-1871), 401 High Street. Wednesday, Saturday, and Sunday 1–4. Dedicated to the boatbuilders of the Eastern Shore, exhibits include dozens of wooden scale models (some are spectacular in detail), a mural depicting Cambridge in the early 1900s, and boatbuilding implements. Of particular interest are the works of local master builder Jim Richardson. All of this is housed in what is believed to be the oldest bank building in town.

Dorchester Heritage Museum (410-228-5530), 1904 Horn Point Road. Saturday and Sunday 1–4:30, April 15 through October 30. The collection of local history items in the museum began when a teacher asked students to bring in items that pertained to their grandparents. It is now housed in a former airplane hangar a few miles west of town, and the number of items has grown to include watermen's tools (the eel fishing implements are interesting), airplane engines, and Native American artifacts.

HISTORIC CHURCHES Bazzel Church, Bestpitch Ferry Road, about 1 mile south of Greenbrier Road (which is about 12 miles south of Cambridge). This small wooden structure is where Harriet Tubman's family worshiped in the mid-1800s.

St. Mary, Star of the Sea, on MD 335 on the way to Hooper Island. The second oldest Catholic church on Maryland's Eastern Shore.

Old Trinity Church (410-228-2940), 1716 Taylors Island Road, Church Creek. Built in the late 1600s, this is the oldest Episcopal church in continuous use in the United States. The floor tiles, altar table, and exterior brick walls are original.

OTHER SITES—WINDMILL Spocott Windmill, MD 343, 7 miles west of Cambridge (no phone). Daily 9–5. Free admission. No, you are not in Holland! Taking on a different kind of project, master boatbuilder James B. Richardson designed and crafted the fully operating English-style post windmill, which can be turned in any direction to face prevailing winds. This is such a novelty that you have to stop by. Even if a docent is not present, you can still look inside at gears and millstones. Also on site is the **Tenant House** of Adeline and Columbus Wheatly, who worked on Spocott Farm from 1880 to 1930, and a historic one-room schoolhouse.

THE SPOCOTT WINDMILL CAN BE ROTATED TO FACE ANY DIRECTION.

GUIDED TOURS

Cambridge

Harriet Tubman Museum (410-228-0401), 424 Race Street. The museum, with African and Jamaican artifacts, is open Monday through Friday 9–5. Tours must be arranged in advance and are available to just a few individuals at a time. The museum has a brochure describing a self-guided driving tour, but the excellent narrated van tours take you to many nearby sites to relate the story of Harriet Tubman, who led more than 300 slaves to freedom along the Underground Railroad. The site of her childhood, the place she first stood up to her slave masters, and churches used as stops on the railroad are included. Such an inspiring person and story should not be missed. The tour also provides insight and background on African American experiences around the Dorchester area. Just gaining a different perspective on what went on in the town's historic homes makes the tour worthwhile.

Brooks Barrel Co. (410-228-0790; 1-800-398-2766; www.brooksbarrel.com), 5228 Bucktown Road. Call in advance to schedule your $5 tour (children over 12 are $3; under 12 are free). One of the few remaining slack cooperages in the country. The barrels were originally designed as meat and seafood shipping containers and are not watertight, which allows runoff from melting ice to escape. Today, most of the barrels are used for decorative purposes. This interesting tour, often provided by company president Ken Knox, shows the entire barrel-making process, still done on equipment from around the turn of the 20th century. You can purchase products at reduced prices after the tour.

SCENIC DRIVES A marked route, the **Cambridge Scenic Drive,** is 1.5 miles long and takes you from High Street to Maple Avenue along the Choptank River. Some of the residential homes along the tree-shaded streets are nearly as beautiful as the water views.

✳ To Do

BICYCLING The **Dorchester County Department of Tourism** (see *Guidance*) in Cambridge prints a map pamphlet with more than 100 miles of cycle routes within the immediate area. The scenery is great, and the flat terrain, paved roads, and light traffic are bonuses. Places to eat are identified on the maps.

Located close to the Blackwater National Wildlife Refuge (see *Green Space—Wildlife Refuges*), **Loblolly Landings and Lodge** (410-397-3033; see *Lodging—Lodges*) rents bicycles for only $10 a day.

BIRDING According to the *Birdwatcher's Guide to Delmarva*, **Blackwater National Wildlife Refuge** (see *Green Space—Wildlife Refuges*), 12 miles south of Cambridge, is the best place on the Eastern Shore to see bald eagles; it has the largest nesting population on the East Coast north of Florida. There is also the possibility of seeing golden eagles and scores of other bird species.

The **LeCompte Wildlife Management Area** (410-820-7098) near Vienna rewards visitors with species most often found in upland forests and shrubby areas. Also be on the lookout for the endangered Delmarva fox squirrel.

The **Municipal Basin** on the Choptank River in Cambridge is a great place to watch visiting waterfowl from fall to early spring.

BOAT EXCURSIONS

Cambridge
Nathan of Dorchester (410-228-7141; www.skipjack-nathan.org.), docked at Long Wharf at the foot of High Street. Cruise times vary; call for schedule. The skipjack was built and is sailed by volunteers whose enthusiasm surpasses that found on many commercial boat rides. Learn a thorough history of the bay, skipjacks, oystering, charts, crabs, and boatbuilding. Observe the raising and lowering of the sail, and rake for oysters. *The* boat trip to take if you have time for only one.

Cambridge Lady (410-221-0776), Trenton Street Dock on Cambridge Creek. Operates from May 15 through October 31; call for daily schedule. Narrated sight-seeing cruises on the Choptank, Trappe Creek, and Tred Avon Rivers on a classic

THE *NATHAN OF DORCHESTER* IN CAMBRIDGE

yacht-style wood passenger boat. Also has an extensive schedule of theme cruises.

Hurlock
Dorothy Megan (410-943-4775), 6304 Suicide Bridge Road. Call for schedule. Sight-seeing and lunch cruises aboard an authentic early-20th-century paddle wheeler.

BOAT RENTALS ***Miss Florida Point*** (410-376-0342; www.floridapoint.com/houseboat.htm), 4710 Ravenwood Road, Vienna. Owned by the folks at **Florida Point Hunting and Fishing Lodge** (see *Lodging—Lodges*), the 41-foot powered catamaran is offered for overnight, weekend, or weekly rentals. Cooking galley, satellite TV, air-conditioning, full bathroom, and more mean you can cruise in comfort.

FISHING No license is required to fish from **Long Wharf** at the end of High Street in Cambridge.

THE SKIPJACK WAY OF LIFE
Skipjacks became so popular because they were one of the easiest boats to build, and many a waterman spent his off-season building a boat of his own. By tradition, the owner of the boat received one-third of the catch, and the crew would have to split the rest, with the captain receiving two shares. So the captain came out way ahead if he was also the boat's owner.

CHARTER FISHING Among the many charter boats in the area are ***Joint Venture*** (410-228-7837), 311 Nathan Avenue, Cambridge; ***Sassy Lady Charter*** (410-397-3578), 2513 Old House Point, Fishing Creek; ***Double AA*** (410-310-3231), 6311 Suicide Bridge Road, Hurlock; and **Sawyer Charters** (410-397-3743), 1345 Hooper Island Road, Church Creek.

FISHING THE CHOPTANK RIVER FROM LONG WHARF IN CAMBRIDGE

GOLF See *Lodging—Resort.*

KAYAKING AND CANOEING A guide to canoe and kayak launches, boat ramps, and facilities is available from the Dorchester County Department of Tourism (see *Guidance*). An excellent map identifies hundreds of miles of paddleable waterways.

Muddy Marsh Outfitters (410-228-2770), 2527 Southside Avenue, Cambridge. Provides guided and unguided tours on the region's pristine creeks, marshes, and bays. Some of the most popular trips are those on Big and Little Blackwater Creeks. Rentals also available.

With access to the Blackwater National Wildlife Refuge (see *Green Space—Wildlife Refuges*), **Loblolly Landings and Lodge** (410-397-3033; see *Lodging—Lodges*) in Church Creek rents canoes and kayaks by the day and half day.

SWIMMING 🛶 **Dorchester County Public Pool** (410-221-8535), Virginia Avenue, Cambridge. Memorial Day through Labor Day.

TENNIS James Busick Tennis Courts, Glasgow Street, Cambridge. **Secretary Park,** Linden Avenue, Secretary. Public tennis courts.

✳ Green Space

GARDENS Harriet Tubman Memorial Garden, US 50, Cambridge. Interpretive signs, landscaped gardens, and a mural are a tribute to the Underground Railroad's "Moses of Her People."

PARKS Great Marsh Park (410-228-2040), Somerset Street, Cambridge.

There are picnic tables, short walking paths, a playground, fishing, and a boat ramp on a bit of land jutting into the Choptank River.

WILDLIFE REFUGES Blackwater National Wildlife Refuge (410-228-2677; blackwater.fws.gov), 2145 Key Wallace Drive, about 12 miles south of Cambridge. Just about every Marylander knows that the refuge in late fall and early winter is the place to observe hundreds, even thousands, of migratory waterfowl, especially Canada geese. An important resting and wintering area for birds that travel the Great Atlantic Flyway from Canada to the Gulf of Mexico, the 23,000-acre area is composed primarily of tidal marshes, evergreen and deciduous forests, freshwater ponds and impoundments, and some cropland.

Taking the 5-mile scenic **Wildlife Drive,** walking the two short but rewarding trails, bird-watching, and paddling upon multiple miles of flatwater are the favored activities here.

WALKS See *Wildlife Refuges.*

✳ Lodging

LODGES 🏠🐾 **Loblolly Landings and Lodge** (410-397-3033; www.loblollylandingsbandb.com), 2142 Liners Road, Church Creek, 21622. You could spend an entire vacation and never leave this 170-acre property. Trails wander through the pine forest, a stocked pond awaits anglers, and a creek provides paddlers access to Blackwater National Wildlife Refuge (see *Green Space—Wildlife Refuges*). Bring your own canoe, kayak, or bicycle, or rent one at a low cost. Or be sedentary in the comfort of the great room, with its impressive

90-ton stone fireplace, and watch bald eagles, turkey, owls, and deer wander in front of the picture windows. The lodge has three rooms that share two baths ($80) as well as a detached whirlpool suite ($175). Pets are welcome to stay in your room. Hosts Len and Marlene Slavin make sure you do not leave hungry from breakfast. A bunk-room ($20, no breakfast) lets you take advantage of the area without hurting your wallet.

🐾🏠 Florida Point Hunting and Fishing Lodge (410-376-0342; www.Floridapoint.com), 4710 Ravenwood Road, Vienna, 21869. The 1.5-mile gravel driveway through cultivated fields immediately lets you know that you will be spending the night in a quiet, secluded spot on the Chicamacomico River. As the lodge's name suggests, Jerry and Melanie Gore primarily cater to hunters and anglers (there is a large choice of packages), but they also welcome other guests to their **Cape Chalet Lodge,** rental cabins, and even a houseboat. A swimming pool, boat ramp, dog kennels, country breakfast, and packed lunch all make the $80 rate a great deal.

RESORT ⚓ Hyatt Regency (410-901-1234), 2800 Ocean Gateway, Cambridge, 21613. The Hyatt is the area's first destination resort, and is being touted as an economic savior. On 342 acres beside the Choptank River are 400 rooms, a golf course, a 150-slip marina with boat rentals and cruises, a European-style spa, six restaurants, and indoor and outdoor pools with slides, a river ride, and waterfalls. Many different package rates available.

Cambridge, 21613

Cambridge House (410-221-7700; www.cambridgehousebandb.com), 112 High Street. All rooms in this grand Queen Anne–style sea captain's mansion feature period decor, fireplaces, and private baths. The Dorchester and Garret Rooms open onto the back porch overlooking the Victorian gardens. The Garden Room caught my fancy with its poster bed and original 1847 bathtub, sink, and curved wood walls. A full breakfast, with sweet breads, is cooked to order. A short walk from the river and town wharf. $120.

Glasgow Inn B&B (410-228-0575), 1500 Hambrooks Boulevard. Glasgow was built in 1760 as the home of William Vans Murray, statesman, ambassador, and friend of George Washington, John Adams, and James Madison. He is believed to have set the stage for the Louisiana Purchase. The B&B offers seven rooms (two with shared bath, $100; the other five with private bath, $150), six fireplaces, and a Christian atmosphere.

Hurlock 21643

North Fork B&B (410-943-4706; 1-800-N-FORK-BB), 6505 Palmers Mill Road. Andrea Dowbekin and Frank Feltz welcome guests to their quiet 7-acre retreat on Marshyhope Creek. The main house has a suite ($140) and rooms with private bath ($120). The creek-view room is the one to ask for. A separate guest house has three rooms; you may rent one or all ($180–240). The second night in any room is about half off. Free use of rowboat and other facilities.

Vienna, 21869

🌸 The Tavern House B&B (410-

376-3347), 111 Water Street. The Tavern House is one of the oldest structures on the Eastern Shore, predating 1800 and overlooking the Nanticoke River. Harvey and Elise Altergott have restored its Colonial countenance. A somewhat plain exterior disguises the simple elegance of the interior. Numerous fireplaces, carved woodwork, authentic colors, and white lime, sand, and hair plaster evoke yesteryear. Rooms, with shared baths, are in period decor. The best part of my stay, though, were the great conversations with Harvey and Elise during evening refreshments and breakfast. $75.

COTTAGES Commodore's Cottage (410-228-6398; 1-800-228-6398), 215 Glenburn Avenue, Cambridge, 21613. Shirley and Earl Brannock have created their own 3-acre compound in a residential section of town. Encircling Shirley's prizewinning garden are the Brannocks' home, the Carriage House (living room, kitchen, and bedroom, $85), the Commodore's Cottage (living room, kitchen, and two bedrooms, $95), and the **Brannock Maritime Museum** (see *To See—Museums*). It's like having your own home, but with a generous continental breakfast delivered to you each morning.

✳ Where to Eat

DINING OUT

Cambridge
🦐 ♂ **The Cator House** (410-221-7517), 411 Muse Street. Cambridge native Jane Adams spent more than a decade working in the restaurant business before opening her own restaurant in 2001. She has created a fine dining establishment, but at eating-out prices. Everything is prepared fresh and arranged in eye-pleasing patterns with colorful garnishes.

The crab balls (six for $6) are crispy, but moist and tasty inside, while the house salad, which comes with each meal, is a mixture of 12 organically grown greens.

Menu items change, but some always remain, such as the coconut shrimp ($14.95) served with a pineapple sauce and the 14-ounce New York strip steak ($17.95) with onions sautéed in brandy. If offered as a special, the rockfish stuffed with a generous portion of crab imperial ($19.95) is my recommendation. The Amaretto cup ($3.95), a sponge cake soaked with vanilla and Amaretto cream and topped with crushed almonds, is mouthwatering.

Modern furnishings blend well with the older character of the house. The Cator House's dining experience is hard to match in this part of the Eastern Shore—do not miss it. There are even light-fare offerings and a kid's menu.

Canvasback Restaurant and Irish Pub (410-221-5177), 420 Race Street. Tony and Marion Thomas have taken an old storefront and turned it into one of the region's best dining experiences. Lunch is a casual affair, with sandwiches, salads, pasta, and pizza. Dinner entrées change frequently and are clever variations on familiar themes. Undeniably good are the fried pecan-coated soft-shell crab served with whiskey-lemon butter ($24.95). Then there is lobster ravioli ($17.95) and chicken scaloppini stuffed with crabmeat and cheese ($22.50).

Hurlock
Suicide Bridge Restaurant (410-

943-4689; www.suicidebridge.com),
6304 Suicide Bridge Road. The
region's special-occasion restaurant, it
has picture windows and a deck overlooking Cabin Creek. Nautical charts
on the tabletops, wood paneling, and
a stone fireplace add to the chimerical
atmosphere. A local native, owner
Dave Hickerson has been in the
seafood business for close to two
decades, so dishes such as Chesapeake rockfish ($15.95) and crab
imperial ($19.95) reflect his experi-
ence. Daily specials are an extra
value. The restaurant's name reflects
true incidents; ask for the explanation.

EATING OUT

Cambridge

✐ **Snappers** (410-228-0112), 112
Commerce Street. Southwest (quesadillas from $4.95) and Jamaican
(jerked chicken, tuna, or ribs from
$6.95) cuisine are the specialties, but
you can also get crabcakes (market
price) and other seafood (from
$13.95). The homemade vegetable
beef crab soup ($3.95) is a nice varia-
tion on the usual Eastern Shore crab
soup. Large picture windows provide
a view of Cambridge Creek Harbor.
Becomes a busy local watering hole
on summer and weekend evenings.

✐ **Blue Heron** (410-221-0222),
Woods Road. Owners, and natives of
the area, Guy and Jennifer Edgar
have retained some of the recipes of
former owner Becky Spicer while
developing some of their own. Adding
a different feel to the usual seafood
house are Guy's mounted trophies of
deer, ducks, and swordfish. Sandwiches (from $4.95), seafood ($12.95–
18.95), chicken and steaks ($8.95–
15.95), and homemade desserts. All
entrées come with moist corn bread, a

vanishing Eastern Shore tradition.
There is also a fresh seafood counter
for take-out.

Cambridge Diner (410-228-8898),
2924 Old US 50. Open 24 hours
every day. Good diner food, with
a menu that is seven pages long.
Breakfast starts at $3 and sandwiches
at $3. Entrées ($6.50–21.95) include
Italian specialties, seafood, steaks,
chops, and just about everything else
in between.

CRABS ✐ **Portside** (410-228-9007),
210 Trenton Street, Cambridge. A
characteristically casual seafood
restaurant with wooden tables and
vinyl-covered booths. The outside
deck is beside Cambridge Creek.
Steamed crabs (market price) are, of
course, a favorite. The shrimp scampi
with pasta ($15.95) I sampled was hot
and spicy, while my companion liked
the teriyaki tuna steak ($14.95). Sand-
wiches (from $5.95), salads (from
$6.50), and a host of calorie-laden
appetizers (from $4).

COFFEE BAR The Place on Race
(410-228-0833), 421 Race Street,
Cambridge. An espresso bar that also
serves sandwiches, soups, and pas-
tries at a former soda fountain.
Shares space with the **Lilyfield
Gallery** (see *Selective Shopping—
Art Galleries*).

**SNACKS AND GOODIES Something
Special for Everyone** (410-228-
7599), 125 Washington Street, Cambridge. Snowballs (syrup-flavored
ice) are available in this small gift
shop.

✳ Entertainment

Sailwinds Park in Dorchester is the

site of concerts, plays, festivals, carnivals, community events, and more. Contact the **Dorchester County Department of Tourism** (see *Guidance*) for a schedule of events.

✳ Selective Shopping

ANTIQUES

Cambridge
Heirloom Antiques Gallery (410-228-8445), 419 Academy Street. A cooperative for several dealers of furniture, pottery, clocks, jewelry, and other antique items.

Packing House Antiques (410-221-8544), 411 Dorchester Avenue. More than 135 dealers under one roof.

ART GALLERIES

Cambridge
Dorchester Art Center (410-228-7782), 120 High Street. Ever-changing gallery exhibits of local artists and craftspersons. Paintings, pottery, baskets, quilts, sculptures, books, and more for sale in the gift shop. Sponsors concerts, plays, and lectures.

Break of Dawn Gallery (1-888-775-2850), 513 Race Street. The studio-gallery of native Eastern Shore artist Dawn M. Tarr, whose works feature local scenes, wildlife, and flowers.

Lilyfield Gallery (410-228-0833), 421 Race Street. The works of numerous local artists and craftspersons share space with the **Place on Race Café** (see *Where to Eat—Coffee Bars*). A "meet the artist" event is held Friday evenings.

SPECIAL SHOPS

Cambridge
Joie de Vivre (410-228-7000), 410 Race Street. Artist-owner Joy Staniforth has assembled an impressive

diversity of her own works and that of other local and international artists. Joy mostly works with textiles, but you will also find jewelry, wall hangings, and stained glass. Not just another run-of-the-mill store; there are some unique and distinctive items here.

Bay Country Shop (410-221-0700; 1-800-467-2046), 2709 Ocean Gateway (US 50). A nice mix of quality clothing, books, gifts, and artwork by local and regional artists and craftspersons. The wildlife decoys, boat models, and paintings are worth seeing, even if you don't intend to purchase anything.

Craig's Drug Store (410-228-3322), 409 Race Street. Of interest because it has been serving the community since 1867.

Taylors Island
Taylors Island General Store (410-221-2911), Taylors Island Road. This dimly lit local institution has a lot of Eastern Shore character. It is part grocery store, hardware store, flea market, bar, and restaurant, but mostly it is a community meeting place where the politics and gossip of the day are discussed. Good crab sandwiches for eat-in or take-out.

✳ Special Events

February: **National Outdoor Show** (410-397-8535), Golden Hill. Muskrat skinning, trap setting, oyster shucking, exhibits, and competitions.

April: **Nanticoke River Shad Festival and Kayak Adventure Paddle** (302-875-1650), Vienna. Old-fashioned river festival and paddle course.

May: **Blackwater Wildlife Refuge Spring Fling** (410-221-1874; see *Green Space—Wildlife Refuges*), about 12 miles south of Cambridge.

Guided walks, canoe trips, bus and bike tours, storytelling, and kids' activities in celebration of International Migratory Bird Day. **Antique Aircraft Fly-In** (410-228-5530), Cambridge. Antique planes from across the country arrive for judging and exhibits at the Dorchester Heritage Museum (see *To See— Museums*).

July: **Bay Country Festival** (410-228-1000), Cambridge. A 4-day July 4 celebration at Sailwinds Park (see *Entertainment*) on the Choptank River. **Annual Power Boat Regatta** (410-228-0291). Races and information booth. Great Marsh Park (see *Green Space—Parks*), Cambridge.

September: **Nause-Waiwah Band of Indians Native American Festival** (410-376-3889), Sailwinds Park (see *Entertainment*), Cambridge. **Dorchester Arts Showcase** (410-228-7782), High Street, Cambridge.

December: **Christmas Garden of Trains** (410-22-4220), all month in the Cambridge Rescue Company fire hall, Cambridge. **River Lights on the Choptank** (410-228-1000), Cambridge. All month. Light displays, carriage rides, and free performances.

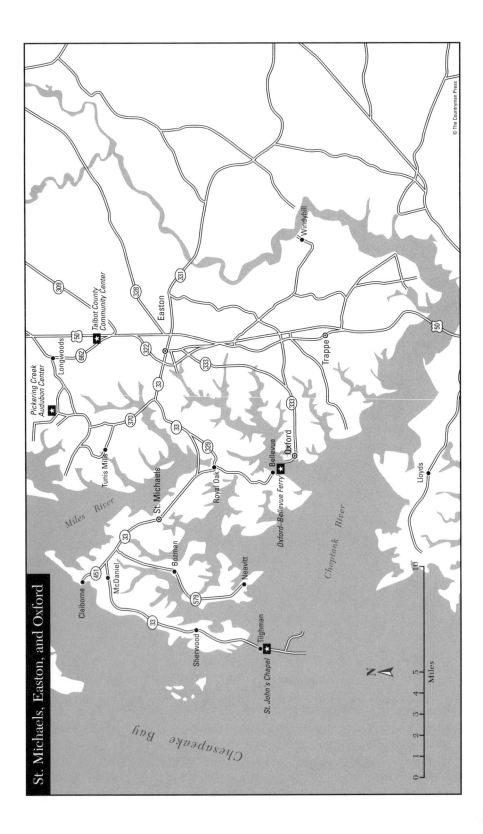

St. Michaels, Easton, and Oxford

ST. MICHAELS, EASTON, AND OXFORD

My wife, a native Annapolitan, can remember in the not-too-distant past when St. Michaels was a quiet Eastern Shore waterman's village with just a couple of stores and restaurants. Then recreational boaters on the Chesapeake Bay started sailing up the Miles River and discovered the pleasures of eating steamed crabs at the Crab Claw Restaurant. Other establishments soon followed, and St. Michaels is now a trendy destination with dozens of upscale shops, boutiques, B&Bs, antiques stores, numerous festivals focusing on boating and/or the bay, and some of the finest restaurants in Maryland. The Chesapeake Bay Maritime Museum, with exhibits indoors and out, has become a must-see stop.

Many visitors still come by water, but the automobile traffic is also so great that driving the few blocks of the business district is a slow proposition on nice weekends throughout the year.

All of this activity in St. Michaels has begun to spill over into Easton, just a few miles away. Entrepreneurs have recently opened quality boutiques and galleries, and innovative chefs are creating an abundance of delicious dining choices for townspeople and the increasing numbers of tourists. Retirees and other emigrants are coming here to live and creating a lively atmosphere for the arts, as evidenced by the restoration of the historic Avalon Theater and the quality of works to be found in the Academy Art Museum.

Easton had its beginnings in 1682 when the Third Haven Friends Meeting House (now the oldest religious frame structure in the United States) was erected. Organized as a town in 1788, its significance grew so quickly after the Revolutionary War that it was dubbed the "Capital of the Eastern Shore." In ensuing years it was home to the first newspaper, first bank, first gas plant, and first steam-

THE TOWN THAT FOOLED THE BRITISH

On August 10, 1813, residents of St. Michaels learned that British barges planned to attack the town. They tricked the naval forces by hanging lanterns in the masts of ships and in the tops of trees (and blacking out any other lights), causing the cannons to overshoot the town. The ruse was so effective that only one house was hit by a cannonball.

boat connections to Baltimore. A walking tour (with a brochure available from Talbot County Office of Tourism; see *Guidance*) takes in several buildings dating back to the 1800s.

Bordered on three sides by water, Oxford was once Maryland's largest port, with tobacco and slaves from the West Indies being two of the most important commodities exchanged by companies based in England. The Revolutionary War, and the increasing importance of Baltimore as a port, struck a blow to the town. After the Civil War, oystering, crabbing, and fish processing and packing became the mainstays of commerce, but the town has never regained its busy prominence.

Which is probably fine with its citizens of today, and is certainly okay with travelers who find a quiet village with tree-lined streets, a few shops, several restaurants and lodging choices, and the Oxford–Bellevue Ferry across the Tred Avon River.

A side trip not to be overlooked is the short drive from St. Michaels to Tilghman Island. A slender strip of land surrounded by water, the island is home to the largest remaining commercial fleet of skipjacks in the world sailing the water for oysters, crabs, and other seafood. Sportfishermen come here for charter boats, while other visitors come for the quiet scenery and good restaurants.

GUIDANCE The **Talbot County Office of Tourism** (410-770-8000; www.talbgov.org), 11 North Washington Street, 21601, is in the courthouse in downtown Easton. A **Visitors Welcome Center** is at 11 South Harrison Street in Easton.

There is a small information shed with brochures at the corner of North Talbot and Mill Streets in **St. Michaels,** and a booth with brochures at the entrance to **Tilghman Island.**

GETTING THERE *By air:* The closest airports with commercial service would be either **Baltimore/Washington International** (1-800-I-FLY-BWI) near Baltimore, or the **Salisbury/Ocean City Airport** (410-548-4827) in Salisbury.

By car: The **Bay Bridge** near Annapolis provides access from the west. **US 50** is the main route through the area; **MD 33** takes you to St. Michaels and Tilghman Island. **MD 322** and **MD 333** lead to Oxford.

By bus: **Trailways** services its station (410-822-5045) at 9543 Ocean Gateway (US 50) in Easton.

GETTING AROUND *By taxi:* **Bay Country** (410-770-9030) and **Scotty's** (410-822-1475), both in Easton.

PARKING Parking in St. Michaels is free on the street, but good luck in finding a spot on the weekends. A **free town parking lot** is located on the corner of North Talbot and Mill Streets.

PUBLIC REST ROOMS In **Oxford,** you can find rest rooms at the Oxford–Bellevue Ferry dock, at the parking lot near the end of The Strand, in the public library on North Morris Street, in Causeway Park located on Oxford Road (MD 333), and in the town hall.

ington Street, Easton. Part of the Shore Health System.

✳ To See

MUSEUMS

Oxford

Oxford Museum (410-226-0191), Market and Morris Streets. The museum was moving at press time, so call for its new location and hours. Among the many items of local history is the oldest known log canoe still in existence, the "Glide," built in 1864. Also look for original papers on indentured servants, and photos of students from the nearby Maryland Military and Naval Academy who revolted against the strict discipline of the late 1800s.

Easton

Historical Society Museum (410-822-0773; www.hstc.org), 25 South Washington Street. Tuesday through Friday 11–3; Saturday 10–4. Guided house tours ($5) are given Tuesday through Saturday at 11:30 and 1:30. The museum contains more than 40,000 artifacts, documents, and photographs pertaining to local history. The items pertaining to the history of African Americans, the original deeds of property transfers, and an unusual portrait of Richard Hughlett caught my attention.

The guided "Tour of Three Centuries" takes you through the Federal-period Neall House (circa 1810), Joseph's Cottage (circa 1790), and The Ending of Controversie—a reconstruction from the 1600s. The garden, with 100 boxwoods, is a quiet spot and open to anyone.

St. Michaels

✐ **Chesapeake Bay Maritime Museum** (410-745-2916; www.cbmm.org), Mill Street. Open until 6 in summer, 5 in spring and fall, and 4 in winter. $6.50 adults, $3 children, or $18 family rate. Possibly the finest maritime museum in the Mid-Atlantic; expect to devote a couple of hours. With some open-air displays, the story is told of the bay, the life of the watermen, and the region's history of fishing and hunting. The short film about oystering is very interesting, and don't overlook the opportunity to walk through the restored 1879 **Hooper Straight Lighthouse.** Several hands-on activities for the kids, and the museum store is a great stop, too (see *Selective Shopping—Bookstores*).

St. Mary's Square Museum (410-745-9561), Mullberry Street. Saturday and Sunday 10–4, April through October. A small museum that showcases the St. Michaels of the 1800s.

HISTORIC CHURCHES

Easton

Third Haven Meeting House (410-822-0293), 405 South Washington Street. Built in 1682 by the Religious Society of Friends (Quakers), this is the oldest frame religious building in continuous use in the United States. You are welcome to walk the grounds (no pets, please) and go into the building, which has no heat, electricity, or water. The wooden shutters are closed to separate men and women for business meetings, but the sexes worship together. The adjacent brick building was built in 1880 and is used in the winter.

Christ Church (410-822-2677), 111 South Harrison Street. This early-English-style church was built in the 1840s and features a tower and spire.

Tilghman Island

St. John's Chapel. Constructed in 1891 of lumber transported by skipjack from North Carolina.

THIRD HAVEN MEETING HOUSE

✳ To Do

BICYCLING The **Talbot County Office of Tourism** (see *Guidance*) has maps of lightly traveled routes perfect for cycling.

St. Michaels

Tour de Shore (410-745-9011; 1-866-745-9011; www.biketds.com), 114 Conner Street. These folks will set you up with an Eastern Shore tour and provide the bikes, other gear, and road support. Call for their daily schedule.

St. Michaels Marina (410-745-2400; www.stmichaelsmarina.com), 305 Mulberry Street; the **Aqua Center at St. Michaels Harbour Inn** (see *Lodging—Motels and Hotels*); and **Wheel Doctor** (410-745-6676; www.wheeldrbicycle.com), 1013 South Talbot Street, rent bikes for the day. For a small charge Wheel Doctor will deliver the bike to you.

Tilghman Island

Tilghman Island Marina (410-886-2500; www.TilghmanMarina.com), 6140 Mariners Court. Bicycle, kayak, and boat rentals by the hour, half day, or day.

BIRDING See **Pickering Creek Audubon Center** under *Hiking*.

BOAT EXCURSIONS

St. Michaels

&. ***Express Royale*** (410-886-2643; www.cruisinthebay.com), Maritime Museum dock. Call for reservations, as schedule and fees vary. Two-hour environmental tours and 90-minute champagne sunset tours.

&. ***Patriot*** (410-745-3100; www.patriotcruises.com), Maritime Museum dock. Rates vary. Cruises at 11, 12:30, 2:30, and 4. One-hour narrated tours of St. Michaels area and the Miles River.

❀ **The Harbor Shuttle** (410-745-9148), town dock at Mulberry Street. The boat leaves every 30 minutes. A 25-minute overview of St. Michaels Harbor. $5 adults; $2 children; pets free.

Also see *Sailing*.

FERRY Oxford–Bellevue Ferry (410-745-9023; www.oxfordmd.com/obf). Closed December, January, and February; $5.50 one way; $9 round trip. The ferry makes it easy to complete a circular driving tour of Easton, Oxford, and St. Michaels by making a crossing of the Tred Avon River about every 20 minutes—as traffic demands. Established in 1863, it is the oldest privately owned ferry in the United States. You are permitted to get out of your car and enjoy the scenery as you traverse the wide expanse of the river.

BOAT RENTALS

Tilghman Island

Deep Reef (410-886-2545), Knapps Narrows. Rents row-, motor-, and sailboats by the full and half day. Also offers sailing lessons.

Tilghman Island Marina (see *Bicycling*). Bicycle, kayak, and boat rentals by the hour, half day, or day.

BOWLING Easton Bowling Center (410-822-3426), Easton Plaza.

FAMILY ACTIVITIES ✍ **Talbot County Community Center** (410-770-

8050), 10028 Ocean Gateway (US 50), Easton. The spot to go for in-line and ice skating, and to try your hand at curling.

✍ **Big Mario's Sport Center** (410-822-7345), 4313 Ocean Gateway (US 50), Trappe. Miniature golf, batting cages, driving range, and putting green.

FISHING On Tilghman Island, **Captains Buddy Harrison and Buddy Harrison Jr.** (410-886-2121) are continuing the traditions of their ancestors of more than 100 years ago by being a one-stop shop for anglers. The **Harrison House** furnishes the lodging, while **Harrison's Restaurant** provides the sustenance. The Harrisons offer the largest sportfishing fleet on the bay and accommodate groups large or small. The Harrison House lounge is the place to gather for evening drinks and entertainment. The Harrisons' good fishing reputation ranges far beyond the Eastern Shore. Many package deals available.

A VIEW FROM THE OXFORD–BELLEVUE FERRY

THE *LADY PATTY* ON TILGHMAN ISLAND

In search of rockfish, Spanish mackerel, croaker, bluefish, sea trout, and more, many other charter and headboats operate out of Tilghman Island and St. Michaels. The **Talbot County Office of Tourism** (see *Guidance*) in Easton can supply you with a list of competent captains.

GOLF
Easton
Hog Neck (410-822-6079), 10142 Old Cordova Road. *Golf Digest* rated this par-72 course as one of the top 25 public courses in the country.

Easton Club (410-820-9100; 1-800-277-9800; www.eastonclub.com), 28449 Clubhouse Road. The par-72 course has over 6,700 yards and great water views.

St. Michaels
Harbourtowne Golf Resort and Conference Center (see *Lodging— Resorts*). With views of the Chesapeake Bay, this Pete Dye–designed course offers ponds, walls, railroad ties, and protected greens.

HIKING Pickering Creek Audubon Center (410-822-4903; www.pickeringcreek.com), 11450 Audubon Lane, Easton. The center's nature trail begins in a hardwood forest, crosses several bogs, and ends next to a demonstration garden. You can walk the gravel road back to your car instead of retracing your steps on the trail. This is an easy round-trip walk to possibly see hawks, warblers, woodpeckers, owls, thrushes, and bluebirds.

Also see *Green Space—Nature Preserves* for more information about the center.

SAILING
St. Michaels
Sirius (410-745-6203), docked at St. Michaels Marina on Mulberry Street. This 36-foot sailing catamaran takes passengers on 2-hour cruises on the Miles River from April through October. Daily departures, but call for the varying schedule and fees.

Tilghman Island
Lady Patty (410-886-2215; 1-800-690-5080; www.sailladypatty.com),

Knapps Narrows Marina. Champagne sunset cruises; call for schedule. The 2-hour sunset sails on this 35-foot bronze and teak Bay Ketch are not billed as ecotours, but I learned more about the bay, pound nets, ospreys, and environmental issues than on most nature-oriented boat trips I've taken. The champagne, the sunset, and Captain Mike Richards's tales of the *Lady Patty's* engaging history will remain in my mind for a long time. $30.

Rebecca T. Ruark (410-886-2176 or 410-829-3976), Dogwood Harbor. Built in 1886, this is the oldest skipjack to still be sailing. Captain Wade Murphy, with more than 40 years of oystering experience, gives 2-hour cruises on which you can hoist the sail, steer the boat, dredge for oysters, or throw a line. Walk-ons accepted, but it is best to make a reservation. $30 adults; $15 children.

HORSEBACK RIDING County Comfort Farm (410-745-3160), 23720 St. Michaels Road, St. Michaels. Indoor and outdoor arenas, and 70 acres for trail rides with experienced guides and horses.

KAYAKING AND CANOEING Tuckahoe Creek near Tuckahoe State Park (see *Green Space—Parks* in "Around the Bay Bridge and Kent Island") in Queen Anne has well over 10 miles of water bordered by farmlands and forested swamps. The book *Hiking, Cycling, and Canoeing in Maryland* by Bryan Mac Kay gives an excellent description of the route and what to watch for.

Tidewater Kayaks (410-820-5086), 975 Port Street, Easton. Kayaking the slow-moving streams of the Eastern Shore is one of the best ways to enjoy and come to know the area. Tidewater rents kayaks for the day or longer, and will even deliver a kayak to your location. Guided tours are also available.

Aqua Center at St. Michaels Harbour Inn and Marina (see *Lodging—Motels and Hotels*), St. Michaels. Rents canoes and kayaks by the hour or day.

Tilghman Island Marina (see *Bicycling*), Tilghman Island. Bicycle, kayak, and boat rentals by the hour, half day, or day.

SPECIAL CLASSES Sign up for a flight lesson at Easton Airport (410-822-8560) with **Easton Aviation** (410-822-8181), Easton.

✳ Green Space

PARKS See *Parks* in "Around the Bay Bridge and Kent Island."

NATURE PRESERVES 🐾 **Pickering Creek Audubon Center** (see *To Do—Hiking*), Easton. Open daily. Free admission. There's a lot to do on the 400 acres of forests, marshes, wetlands, and shoreline. Hiking on several nature trails, a canoe launch onto the creek, 150 species of birds to watch, a tool museum, and a wonderful Children's Imagination Garden. Canoe trips, bird-watching walks, lectures, and other programs are offered on a scheduled basis (some fees may apply). This is an oasis in an area where very little land is open to the public for outdoor pursuits.

WALKS See *Nature Preserves.*

✳ Lodging

RESORTS 🐾 **Harbourtowne Golf Resort and Conference Center**

(410-745-9066; 1-800-446-9066; www.habourtowne.com), MD 33 at Martingham Drive, St. Michaels, 21663. More than 100 standard motel-type rooms at the water's edge of the Chesapeake Bay, each with private balcony and some with fireplaces or wood-burning stoves. The draws here are the views, bicycling, an outdoor pool, several restaurants, a Pete Dye–designed golf course, and the 153 acres of open space. Very family-friendly; breakfast buffet included. $189 and up.

MOTELS AND HOTELS St. Michaels Harbour Inn and Marina (410-745-9001; 1-800-955-9001; www.harbourinn.com), 101 North Harbor Road, St. Michaels, 21663. Luxury waterfront suites and rooms, many with spas and extra features. Outside pool and waterfront spa. $210–475.

INNS

Oxford, 21654

✍ **Robert Morris Inn** (410-226-5111; www.robertmorrisinn.com), Morris Street. April through November; weekends only, December through March. Within view of the Tred Avon River, the inn was built in the early 1700s by ship's carpenters. The 16 rooms have elegant country furnishings such as four-poster beds. Private baths. Some have side water-view balconies. $130–220. James Michener proclaimed the restaurant's crabcakes to be a 9.2 on a scale of 10. About a half block away is the inn's **Sandaway Lodge,** with a small private beach. Some rooms have waterfront porches. $200–290.

✍ **Oxford Inn** (410-226-5220; www.oxfordmd.com/oxfordinn), 506 South Morris Street. Sue and Rick Schmitt receive rave reviews from their former guests. Most of the 11 rooms have private bath and pleasing furnishings. The third-floor Tavern Hall Room has four window seats with views of Town Creek, yet the lower-cost Chesapeake Room on the second floor provides the same view. $90–150.

Easton, 21601

✍ **Tidewater Inn** (410-822-1300; 1-800-237-8775; www.tidewaterinn.com), 101 East Dover Street. The Tidewater is in the heart of town and, although built in 1949, reflects the Eastern Shore's earlier period. Mahogany doors, 18th-century reproductions, and open fireplaces. A favorite place for gentlemen sport hunters, it has a rustic elegance about it. Pay the few extra dollars to stay away from the smaller rooms, as most of the rooms are ample sized and decorated nicely. The inn's restaurant (see *Dining Out*) is renowned for its seafood. $150–295.

Royal Oak, 21662

✍ **The Oaks** (410-745-5053; www.the-oaks.com), MD 329 at Acorn Lane. Built in 1748, The Oaks retains

BLACK-EYED SUSANS, MARYLAND STATE FLOWER.

its original exterior appearance but has been remodeled with modern amenities on the inside. Rooms look onto either Oak Creek or the formal gardens. Room 27 has its own deck near the water and a fireplace. $175–300. Across the road is the **Annex,** built in a former schoolhouse. Rooms are a bit more sparse, but you can enjoy everything else the inn offers. $85.

St. Michaels, 21663
Five Gables Inn and Spa (410-745-0100; 1-877-466-0100; www.five-gables.com), 209 North Talbot Street. All of the rooms have private bath, whirlpool tubs, and gas log fireplaces. Besides being in the middle of town and close to all the activity, the inn offers another enticement: a spa with herbal bath treatments, massages, facials, and body polishes. The setting is elegant, yet quite casual. Many different packages available. $215–325; about $100 less during the week.

The Inn at Perry Cabin (410-745-2200; 1-800 722-2949; www.perrycabin.com), 308 Watkins Lane. A part of the worldwide chain of exclusive Orient-Express properties, The Inn at Perry Cabin became even more exclusive and luxurious with a $15 million renovation and expansion in 2002. The 19th-century mansion now has 82 rooms and suites on 25 acres, and more lavish amenities than ever. The stay is magnificent and the food world-class, but it is not a place for those who must ask how much. Rates, from $265 to over $850, are quoted once you have made your reservation.

✒ **Wades Point Inn** (410-745-2500; 1-888-923-3466; www.wadespoint.com), Wades Point Road. Chickens in the yard let you know that you will be staying in country comfort. Located

on 120 acres, the inn was built in 1819 on a point of land jutting into the bay. Water-view rooms, screened porches overlooking the water, balconies, and a 1-mile trail let you enjoy the setting. Children welcome, but no facilities for very young infants. $125–230.

Tilghman Island, 21671
Tilghman Island Inn (410-886-2141; 1-800-866-2141; www.tilghman-islandinn.com), Coopertown Road. April 1 through November 1. Spacious and modern rooms and suites with views of the Narrows. Continental breakfast included, and excellent restaurant on premises (see *Dining Out*). $130–175.

BED & BREAKFASTS
Oxford, 21654
The 1876 House (410-226-5496), 110 North Morris Street. Furnished in Queen Anne decor, this B&B also features 10-foot ceilings and wide-planked pine floors. All the rooms have a private bath. Continental breakfast in the formal dining room. Complimentary transportation from local marinas or Easton Airport. $110.

🐾 **Combsberry** (410-226-5353; www.combsberry.com), 4837 Evergreen Road. A half-mile tree-lined driveway brings you into the 10-acre estate of Combsberry, built in 1730 along Island Creek. Luxury, quiet, and beauty are the emphases. The Waterfront Room in the Manor House has the best view, while the Garden Room looks onto the Victorian Gardens, which are lit at night. Four luxury cottages (the Oxford Cottage is pet-friendly, with a fenced-in area) provide privacy but still let you interact with other guests on the grounds or during breakfast served by innkeepers Cathy Magrogan and Donna Smith. The house's architecture, the luxurious furnishings, the perfectly cared-for grounds, the hammock on the lawn, and the creek make for a grand place to stay. $250–395; rates drop $100 from December through March.

Easton, 21601

The Bishop's House (410-820-7290; 1-800-223-7290; www.bishopshouse. com), 214 Goldsborough Street. This 1860s Victorian home is romantically furnished in period pieces and is located within the town's historic district. Sit on the wraparound porch and watch the world go by. All rooms have private bath. Bicycle rentals for guests. $110–120.

St. Michaels, 21663

Barrett's B&B Inn and Tea Room (410-745-3322; www.barrettbb.com), 210 North Talbot Street. Jim and Lin Barrett are purveyors of romantic getaways in a late-1860s Colonial home. The Cozy Rooms have a fireplace, private bath, and queen bed covered with a comforter and handmade quilt. In addition to those amenities, the Romantic Rooms have a double Jacuzzi tub in front of the fireplace, as well as candles and fresh flowers. Barrett's is in the center of town, so walking anywhere is easy. Many different package deals are available. Jim has some remarkable stories about interesting items he's found left behind by some guests. $200–260. (Also see **Barrett's Tea Room** under *Where to Eat—Coffee Bars*.)

Two Swan Inn (410-745-2929), foot of Carpenter Street. Right at the water's edge, with a small lawn in front. Built in 1790, it retains the original pine floors, and all rooms

have private bath. The first-floor front room overlooks the water, and upon the walls are official duck stamp prints. The upstairs room on the left has an heirloom bed from the DuPont family and a sunrise view. $165.

Victoriana Inn (410-745-3368; 1-888-316-1282; www.victorianainn. com), 205 Cherry Street. Within sight of the Maritime Museum (see *To See—Museums*), the Ionic-columned porch of this 1865 home overlooks the excitement of the harbor. The Tilghman Room and the Junior Suite also have views onto the water. A parlor and sunporch are nice spots for quiet conversation or reading. Complimentary wine, tea, and hors d'oeuvres in the afternoon. $189–299.

Kemp House Inn (410-745-2243), 412 South Talbot Street. Carved mantels, beaded baseboards, and a central-hall staircase hark back to 1807 when the Federal-style Kemp House was built. The rooms are decorated with period pieces such as four-poster rope beds and Queen Anne tables. Close to the center of activity in town. $90–120.

The Parsonage Inn (410-745-5519; 1-800-394-5519), 210 North Talbot Street. On the main street in town, the Parsonage Inn was built in 1883 and the furnishings in its eight guests rooms reflect the period. Hosts Bill and Char Wilhelm serve up breakfasts of stuffed French toast, egg casseroles, and Belgian waffles. $125–195.

Bay Cottage (410-745-9369; 1-888-558-8008; www.baycottage.com), 24640 Yacht Club Road. Close to town, but on secluded property, the cottage has six guest rooms and is located on a quiet point of land with water views. $185–285.

Tilghman Island, 21671
Chesapeake Wood Duck Inn (410-886-2070; 1-800-956-2070; www.woodduckinn.com), Gibsontown Road at Dogwood Harbor. Constructed in the 1890s, the inn has been a boardinghouse, bordello, and waterman's family residence. Kim and Jeff Bushey have been operating the B&B since 2000. Many original items remain, such as the wood floors, but their personal touch is evident in many small things: fresh flowers, scented towels, and original artwork by Jeff's mother (see **L'Atelier** under *Selective Shopping—Crafts* in "Around the Bay Bridge and Kent Island"). The green-themed Shirley G Room overlooks the harbor. I stayed in the Narrows, also with a harbor view, as Kim feels it is the most masculine-feeling room in the house. Kim's breakfasts are always a delectable adventure. Be prepared for crab, sweet corn, and spinach pie; an egg puff with asparagus, apples, raspberry *coulis,* and key lime mustard sauce; or banana bread French toast with peach and cinnamon cream. $149–229.

Lazyjack Inn (410-886-2215; 1-800-690-5080; www.lazyjackinn.com), 5907 Tilghman Island Road. Two suites and two rooms with views of Dogwood Harbor or the inn's gardens. The front porch lets you watch the sailing fleet leave in the morning and return at sunset. $155–230.

🐾 **Black Walnut Point Inn** (410-886-2452; www.tilghmanisland.com/blackwalnut), Black Walnut Road. At the very southern tip of Tilghman Island, the inn is located within a 57-acre wildlife refuge and bordered on three sides by water. All of the rooms in the main house have

water views, while a baby grand piano fits in with the downstairs decor. For privacy, I liked the Choptank North Cottage, which lets you stay in bed and watch the sunrise. Hammocks in the yard, a swimming pool, and tennis courts. $120–150.

COTTAGES
St. Michaels, 21663
🐾 🐾 **Cygnet House** (410-745-2929), 201 Carpenter Street. Run by the folks at Two Swan Inn (see *Bed & Breakfasts*), the cottage has two and a half bedrooms. There is nothing fancy here, the furnishings are simple, but there is a fireplace and it's a good arrangement if you have children, pets, or a group of up to six. The rate starts at $150 for two and goes up to $325 for six; the rate drops the longer you stay.

🐾 **Harris Cove Cottages** (410-745-9701; www.bednboat.com), 8080 Bozman-Neavitt Road. April through October. This "village" of six cottages has 400 feet of waterfront on Harris Creek. With the feel of a family campground, there is a fishing pier, boating activities for the kids, and boats for rent. The cottages can accommodate two adults and two children. $160–190.

CAMPING See *Parks* in "Around the Bay Bridge and Kent Island."

✳ Where to Eat
DINING OUT
Oxford
Latitude 38 (410-226-5303), 26342 Oxford Road. The distinct dishes make this a local favorite. The appetizer to try is the polenta-fried soft-shell crab with melon salsa and

prosciutto-wrapped greens ($9.95). Where else can you have grilled wahoo on white bean hummus served with jicama and nectarine salad and roasted jalapeño corn mole ($20.95)? Other meat, seafood, and chicken dishes are just as unique. Bistro atmosphere with a small fireplace.

Easton
Out of the Fire (410-770-4777; www.outofthefire.com), 22 Goldsborough Street. Several Easton restaurants are introducing new cooking styles, and owner-chef Amy Haines is helping lead the way. Her Mediterranean-influenced menu changes seasonally; desserts change daily as well. My appetizer of California champagne grapes and blue cheese complemented a medley of lettuce greens ($7). There were so many vegetables in the risotto primavera ($14) that it had a different taste with each bite. Chocolate hazelnut gelato ($4) ended the meal perfectly. Other dishes include Caribbean spiced pork ($17), wild mushroom penne ($16), and pizzas (from $11) cooked in a wood-burning stone oven. Bright murals and works of local artists make this a fun place. Currently my favorite Easton restaurant.

The Inn at Easton (410-822-4910; www.theinnateaston.com), 28 South Harrison Street. Wednesday through Sunday 5:30–9:30. Another innovative restaurant to appear on the Easton scene. Culinary Institute of America graduate Andrew Evens spent several years working in Australian restaurants before coming to Easton. His signature appetizer, Three Treasures of the Bay, includes a crabcake with tomato confit and tarter sauce, oyster poached in white truffle cream with Sevruga caviar, and teriyaki-glazed fish. The slowed-cooked lamb sirloin with Dijon herb crust is representative of the entrées ($15–29). You can also choose a prix fixe dinner for $49 on Friday and Saturday.

General Tanuki's Restaurant (410-819-0707; www.generaltanuki.com), 25 Goldsborough Street. Lunch 11–2; dinner 5–9. Closed Tuesday. Further evidence that Easton is experiencing a rise in good eating, General Tanuki's brings the foods of the Pacific Rim to town. $10–25.

✍ **Tidewater Inn** (410-822-1300), 101 East Dover Street. Open for breakfast, lunch, and dinner. The Tidewater has been known for its traditional Eastern Shore snapper turtle soup ($7) and crabcakes ($27.50) for more than 50 years. Other seafood, meat, and poultry dishes are also well prepared. Choose from elegant surroundings in the dining room or rustic appeal in the lounge. (Also see *Lodging—Inns*.)

St. Michaels
Madison's West End (410-745-0299), 106 North Talbot Street. Lunch 12–3; dinner starts at 6. Kenny and Terye Knopp decided to give their restaurant a Caribbean twist after a trip to the islands, and the bright colors, bowls of fresh vegetables on the six tables, and original artwork bring to mind many of the small restaurants I have visited on St. Barts and Martinique. Kenny is not afraid to cook a little differently so, breaking from tradition, his crabcakes (market price) contain mushrooms, peppers, rum, key lime juice, and orange zest. My chicken Marsala ($18.95) was the most delicious meal I had in St. Michaels. Try the curry shrimp with mango chutney and almonds ($10.95) for lunch. As an added bonus, Kenny may break out the acoustic guitar at any moment and serenade you with his own songs.

Bistro St. Michaels (410-745-9111), 403 South Talbot Street. Open for dinner Thursday through Monday. Chef David Stein, a graduate of the Baltimore Culinary Institute, combines a bit of Paris with the Eastern Shore. In a true bistro atmosphere, you can start with jicama, cucumber, watermelon, and fresh mint inside a mango soup ($5). The pork chop *au poivre* with cheddar-stuffed potatoes and sweet and sour plum sauce ($23) is representative of the entrées. Other main dishes range from $21 to $30.

208 Talbot (410-745-3838), 208 North Talbot Street. Open for dinner 5–9 on Sunday, Wednesday, and Thursday; 5–10 Friday and Saturday. Casually elegant atmosphere; coat and tie welcome but not necessary. Paul Milne graduated first in his class at the Culinary Institute of America and has been winning awards since. He uses fresh seafood and local produce to make baked oysters, sauté of snail, peppered rockfish, and grilled salmon. $20–35. Saturday-night dinner is prix fixe for $50.

Tilghman Island
Tilghman Island Inn (410-886-2141), Coopertown Road. The picture windows and outside deck provide views of Knapps Narrows. Executive chef David McCallum's dishes have been winning awards and accolades for the inn (see *Lodging—Inns*) since the late 1980s. The black-eyed pea-cakes with tomato salsa ($6.95) is one of his signature appetizers. The rock-fish Norfolk ($27.50) I had was a thick fillet smothered by crab, prosciutto, sherry, and succotash. Pasta, paella, beef, duck, and more are served with similar flair. $18.50–29.50.

EATING OUT
St. Michaels
Town Dock Restaurant (410-745-5577; 1-800-884-0103; www.town-

THE HOOPER STRAIGHT LIGHTHOUSE AT THE CHESAPEAKE BAY MARITIME MUSEUM dock.com), 125 Mulberry Street. Yes, you can get steamed crabs (market price) here, but chef Michael Rork is known for much more. The crab bisque ($4.95) or oysters Rockefeller ($7.95) should be your appetizer—I had both. Choosing among the potato-crusted rockfish sautéed with shrimp and green tomato piccalilli ($20.95), roasted free-range chicken ($17.95), and southern-style shrimp with grits and andouille sausage ($19.95) is tough. A complimentary chocolate-covered strawberry comes with all meals. Inside seats and outside deck overlook the harbor.

The Tavern on Talbot (410-745-9343), 409 South Talbot Street. Jeannie Willis and Shelly Cover spent several years at the Inn at Perry Cabin (see *Lodging—Inns*) before taking over The Tavern on Talbot. They kept some of the former owner's recipes and added a few of their own. The menu ranges from chicken fingers with potato chips and a pickle spear ($7) to sautéed lobster Florentine ($22). My Maryland crab soup ($4) had just the right amount of spices, and the linguine with fresh tomato and crabmeat ($12) was topped with a lemon butter sauce that was creamy, yet light. Judging from what other guests were enjoying, the rockfish and chips ($12) and châteaubriand filet mignon ($20) are also menu highlights. Several lunch items, such as a BBQ sandwich ($6) with coleslaw, are available at dinner.

Tilghman Island
Bay Hundred (410-886-2126), 6178 Tilghman Island Road. Breakfast, lunch, and dinner. The picture windows look out upon the boat activity of Knapps Narrows. Mussels Aegean ($6.95) and clam picante ($6.95) are

chef Brian Bennett's signature appetizers. Sandwiches, beef, chicken, and seafood fresh from the bay. $5.95–21.95. Ask about the history of the restaurant's name.

So Neat Café (410-886-2143), Black Walnut Road. A small shop with specialty omelets, French toast, Belgian waffles, and quiches for breakfast and lunch. The Baltimore omelet with crab, asparagus, and hollandaise sauce ($8.95) starts the day deliciously.

CRABS
St. Michaels
☙ **St. Michaels Crab House** (410-745-3737; www.stmichaelscrabhouse.com), 305 Mulberry Street. Owner-chef Eric Rosen turns out a crab dip ($6.95) that is a superb, melt-in-your-mouth appetizer, while his crab balls ($.95 each) are, refreshingly, broiled and not fried. Steamed crabs (market price) are available by the dozen or half dozen. I have sampled several different entrées here and was well satisfied with all of them ($9.95–18.95). The 1830s former oyster-shucking house on the waterfront makes this an appropriate setting for the restaurant.

☙ **The Crab Claw** (410-745-2900), on the waterfront. Open daily 11–10, March through November. This place could almost be credited with turning St. Michaels into a tourist town—and establishing what an Eastern Shore crab house should look like. Pleasure boaters and sailors have been pulling up to its dock since 1965 to feast upon bushels of fresh-steamed crabs (market price) on the outside deck. Oysters on the half shell ($6.95) and steamed cherrystone clams ($8.95) are also popular. Other seafood entrées start at $13.95.

TAKEOUT

Easton

Captain's Ketch Seafood (410-820-7177; 1-800-318-4749; www.captains-ketch.com), 36 Glebe Road. Fresh seafood packed for take-home, travel, or shipment.

At Home Chef (410-820-0666), 314 North Aurora Street. Sean and Tracy Connolly make such good bread that several local restaurants serve it instead of baking their own.

Railway Market (410-822-4852), 108 Marlboro Road. A gourmet supermarket with organic produce, fresh breads and pastries, sushi bar, juices, and espresso.

St. Michaels

Gourmet by the Bay (410-745-6260), 415 South Talbot Street. This small store is about a block from the main shopping area, so many people never stop by to taste the wonderful fresh breads, pâtés, mousses, and fresh fudges. The flavors of the homemade ice cream by the pint remind you of what ice cream is supposed to be. Sidney and Jim Trond will also make you a picnic basket filled with seasonally available items.

COFFEE BARS

Easton

🐾 **Coffee East** (410-819-6711), 5 Goldsborough Street. Coffees, teas, shakes, pastries, candies, salads, and sandwiches. A small shop with just a few seats that does a brisk breakfast and lunch business. The "Andrew" sandwich ($5.29) I enjoyed had low-fat ham, cucumbers, red peppers, and mango chutney. They are pet-friendly and even give free doggy treats. Internet access also.

St. Michaels

Blue Crab Coffee Co. (410-745-4155), 211 North Talbot Street. Full-service espresso bar and other specialty coffees. Pastries and desserts.

Barrett's Tea Room. "Tea for Two" with scones and pastries served daily 2–5. Espresso bar and other drinks. (Also see **Barrett's B&B Inn** under *Lodging—Bed & Breakfasts.*)

SNACKS AND GOODIES

Easton

Old Towne Creamery (410-820-5223), 9B Goldsborough Street. Ice cream, frozen yogurt, shakes, sundaes, and Italian ices.

St. Michaels

St. Michaels Candy Co. (410-745-6060; 1-888-570-5060; www.candyis-dandy.com), 216 South Talbot Street. Maryland handmade chocolates and truffles, cookies, jelly beans, and gourmet-candy gift baskets.

Justine's (410-745-5416), 101 Talbot Street. Ice cream and yogurt.

✳ Entertainment

FILM **Tred Avon Movies** (410-822-5566), Tred Avon Square, Easton. First-run movies.

Also see *Theaters* for vintage and non-mainstream films.

THEATERS **Avalon Theater** (410-822-0345), Dover and Harrison Streets, Easton. A wide range of plays, symphonies, variety shows, musicals, dance, movies, and arts is presented within this historic art deco theater. Worth a peek inside even if you are not attending a function.

✳ Selective Shopping

ANTIQUES

Easton
There are so many antiques shops in Easton that it would be impossible to list them all in this book. A small guide available from the **Easton Business Management Authority** (410-822-0065; www.eastonmd.org), 14 South Harrison Street, describes what more than a dozen dealers offer.

Tharpe Antiques (410-822-0773), 30 South Washington Street. A consignment shop operated in the late-1800s Mary Jenkins House by the Talbot County Historical Society.

St. Michaels
Canton Row (410-745-2440), 216-C Talbot Street. Antiques of every shape and form from more than a dozen dealers.

Pennywhistle (410-745-9771), 408 South Talbot Street. In business for more than two decades.

ART GALLERIES

Easton
Academy Art Museum (410-822-2787), 106 South Street. Small admission fee. By far one of the best local arts councils in Maryland. They sponsor lecture series, dances, music, theater events, and a host of classes for children and adults. In addition to national touring exhibits, the museum offers changing displays that showcase the talents of local artists—and the quality is above what you often find through an arts council.

Troika Gallery (410-770-9190; www.troikagallery.com), 218 North Washington Street. Laura Era, Dorothy F. Newland, and Jennifer Heyd Wharton present their works and those of other artists.

✑ **South Street Art Gallery** (410-770-8350), 5 South Street. Works of local and national artists—and a children's gallery room.

St. Michaels
Hidden Artisans' Studio (410-745-4125), 123 South Freemont and Canton Streets. A studio where craftspersons and artists make and sell their work. The quality of items you will find here, especially the sculpture, paintings, and textiles, is superior to what you will find in any gift shop. I was impressed. As a bonus, you never know what work of art you may get to witness being created.

BOOKSTORES

Easton
News Center (410-822-7212), 218 North Talbot Street. Newspapers, magazines, and the area's largest bookstore.

St. Michaels
Chesapeake Bay Maritime Museum Store. One of the best and largest collections of maritime and local books and authors to be found on the Eastern Shore. There are also quality selections of children's toys,

WINDOW-SHOPPING IN ST. MICHAELS

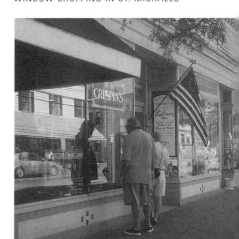

nautical items, and artwork. (Also see *To See—Museums.*)

USED BOOKS **Janet Fanto** (410-763-9030), 13 North Harrison Street, Easton. Used books and antiques.

Unicorn Book Shop (410-476-3838), US 50, Trappe. Rare and secondhand books bought and sold. Maps, too.

CRAFTS **Wood That Works** (410-745-0650; www.woodthatworks.net), 400 South Talbot Street, St. Michaels. Whimsical, funny, and well-handcrafted wooden waterfowl planters, birdhouses, mailboxes, and life-sized "silent server" figures.

SPECIAL SHOPS
Oxford
Silent Poetry (410-226-5120), 201 Tilghman Street. Mixed in with usual gift-shop items are authentic boat models and half hulls, wood carvings, and original works of art and Chesapeake Bay photographs.

Oxford Mews Emporium (410-820-8222), 105 South Morris Street. Gourmet foods, original art, clothes, boating supplies, books about the bay, and best-sellers. I'll let you decide how to categorize this store.

Easton
Vintage Chic (410-822-2317), 12 North Washington Street. Very interesting shop with ethnic art, memorabilia, furniture, clothing, and international artifacts.

✿ **Cracker Jacks** (410-822-7716), 7 South Washington Street. Children's books and some engaging toys.

St. Michaels
Flamingo Flats (410-745-2053; 1-800-HOT-8841), 100 Talbot Street. More than 900 hot sauces, 600 mus-

tards, 200 BBQ sauces, 75 salsas, 50 kinds of olives, and 800 cookbooks. Throw in cigars, pastas, Maryland souvenirs, Haitian art, and 300 flamingos in hundreds of different poses and you have a one-of-a-kind store.

Chesapeake Trading Co. (410-745-9797), 102 South Talbot Street. A few books, a few CDs, clothing, and an espresso bar.

Captain's Wheel (410-745-6763), 110 North Talbot Street. Gifts with a nautical theme.

Galerie Française (410-745-6329), 211 North Talbot Street. A bit unexpected on the Eastern Shore—vintage French posters and antique furniture from Provence.

The Mind's Eye (410-745-2023), 210 South Talbot Street. A great collection of unique, playful, and useful "things" from more than 200 American craftspersons. A fun store just to walk through.

✿ **Calico Gallery** (410-745-5370), 212 South Talbot Street. Be sure to go upstairs for some interesting children's toys.

🐾 **Flyin' Fred's** (410-745-9601), 202 North Talbot Street. Gifts for pets and animal lovers. They welcome your dog and will give it a free treat. I like their motto, "Come spoil man's best friend."

FARMER'S MARKETS **Easton Farmer's Market** (410-822-0065), North Harrison Street. Open on Saturday and Wednesday afternoon during the season (which varies from year to year).

✴ Special Events

May: **Historic Homes and Gardens Tours** (410-770-8000), St. Michaels.

Mid-Atlantic Maritime Arts Festival (410-820-8606), St. Michaels. Model ships, crafts, food, carvings, and music.

June: **Eastern Shore Chamber Music Festival** (410-819-0380). Various venues throughout the area. **Boat Bumm's International Cardboard Boat Races** (410-820-4104), Oxford. Build a boat and enter the race or just see which boats stay afloat.

July: **Talbot County Fair** (410-822-8007), Talbot County Fairgrounds, Easton. **Antique and Classic Boat Festival** (410-745-2916), St. Michaels. A rendezvous of more than 100 antique boats and automobiles.

August: **Crab Days** (410-745-2916), St. Michaels. Possibly the largest celebration of the blue crab on the Eastern Shore. Crab races, crabbing demonstrations, and lots of crab to eat.

October: **Arts Marketplace** (410-822-2787), Easton. **Tilghman Island Day** (410-866-2677), Tilghman Island. Boat races, oyster-shucking and crab-picking contests, music, and food.

November: **Waterfowl Festival** (410-822-4567), Easton. Attracts close to 20,000 visitors. Wildlife arts, duck-calling contests, music, lots of kids' activities, demonstrations. Proceeds benefit Atlantic Flyway migratory bird projects. **Festival of Trees** (410-819-FEST), held at the Tidewater Inn (see *Lodging*) and the Academy Art Museum (see *Selective Shopping— Art Galleries*), Easton. **Oyster Fest** (410-745-2916), St. Michaels. Learn how oysters are caught, shucked, and eaten.

AROUND THE BAY BRIDGE AND KENT ISLAND

T he completion of the Bay Bridge, which connects Annapolis with Kent Island, in 1952 opened the Eastern Shore to a rush of travelers and new residents (sometimes referred to as "come here-ers" by older Eastern Shore citizens). In a way, history was just repeating itself, as the island had been in the vanguard several centuries before.

A narrow strip of land that juts far into the waters of the upper Chesapeake Bay, Kent Island was the first place to be settled on the Eastern Shore. Soon after William Claiborne established a fort on its western edge in 1631, the fertile soils of the island were being used to raise tobacco, the most important cash crop of the day. Additional settlers pushed their way inland, establishing large plantations that, around the time of the American Revolution, began to switch over to grain crops and dairy farming. When steam-powered boats made the rapid transit of goods possible, oystering, crabbing, and other commercial fishing became viable occupational choices.

Even today there are several large packing houses clustered around Kent Narrows, and watermen still ply the bay and inlets, capturing large amounts of blue crabs and soft-shell clams. (It is said that the clams grow three times faster in the bay than they do in the North Atlantic.) With its access to the large populations of Annapolis, Baltimore, and Washington, D.C., the area has become a center of activity for pleasure sailors and sportfishermen.

COMMUNITIES Little is left of the early days on the main part of Kent Island. The communities have been swallowed by modern-day America, and about all that is visible from US 50/301 are strip malls, restaurants, and motels. However, get off the four-lane and you will discover little gems, such as **Stevensville.** Developing out of couple of farms owned by James and Charles Stevens in 1850, the town began to grow, as it was the center of the steamboat trade of the late 1800s. The arrival of the railroad made the town thrive even more, but growth came to an end when rail service stopped in the mid-1900s and the main highway bypassed the town.

Today, Stevensville is a small town worthy of a short and easy walking tour. Many of its older buildings are in remarkably good shape, and its historic district was placed on the National Register in 1986. An artists' colony began to develop in

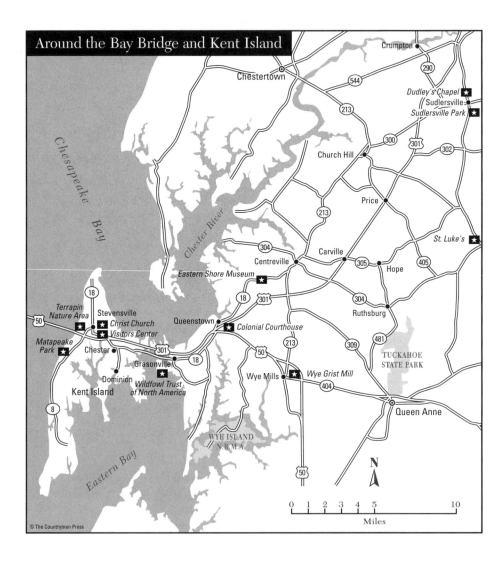

Around the Bay Bridge and Kent Island

Crumpton
Chestertown
290
544
213
Dudley's Chapel ★
Sudlersville ★
Sudlersville Park ★
300
301
302
Church Hill
Chesapeake Bay
Chester River
Price
213
St. Luke's ★
304
Carville
Centreville
305
405
Eastern Shore Museum
Hope
18
304
Ruthsburg
Terrapin Nature Area ★
18
50
Stevensville ★
Christ Church ★
Queenstown
Colonial Courthouse ★
Visitors Center ★
301
481
TUCKAHOE STATE PARK
Matapeake Park ★
Chester
18
309
213
50
Grasonville ★
Dominion
Wildfowl Trust of North America ★
Wye Mills ★
Wye Grist Mill
Kent Island
404
Queen Anne
8
WYE ISLAND N.R.M.A.
Eastern Bay
50

N

0 1 2 3 4 5   10
Miles

© The Countryman Press

the 1990s, and numerous studio-galleries and a couple of nice restaurants have opened and blended in well with the town's character.

Within **Queenstown** is the oldest continuously used courthouse in the state. As with Stevensville, this small village is worth a visit to walk through its historic streets.

A mill has been operating at **Wye Mills** from at least the late 1600s, making it the Eastern Shore's (and maybe even Maryland's) oldest frame gristmill. A small community consisting of blacksmiths, farmers, merchants, and schools, shops, and churches grew up around the mill.

As settlers moved farther inland from the bay, citizens needed a more centrally located county seat, so the legislature moved it from Queenstown to **Centreville** in 1782. A walking tour (brochure available from Queen Anne's County Department of Business and Tourism, see *Guidance*) takes you by many of the buildings still standing from those early days. Styles range from early Federal to late Victorian, providing an architectural view of the town's development. The main business district is along Commerce and Liberty Streets, and it is here that you will find one of the best independently owned bookshops on the Eastern Shore and an agreeable meal at a good café. A nice diversion from the city streets is the Nature Walk along the south bank of the Corsica River.

Church Hill is home to St. Luke's Episcopal Church and the Church Hill Theatre, a cultural treasure for the Upper Eastern Shore.

Many people know **Sudlersville** for it famous son, baseball great Jimmy Foxx. He hit 58 home runs in 1932 while playing for the Philadelphia Athletics, and the town erected a life-sized bronze statue of the Baseball Hall of Fame member in 1997.

GUIDANCE ✔ The **Queen Anne's County Department of Business and Tourism** (410-604-2100; 1-888-400-RSVP; www.qac.org), 425 Piney Narrows Road, Chester, 21619, has a visitors center just a few miles east of the Bay Bridge and is accessed from US 50 Exit 41. Also known as the **Chesapeake Exploration Center,** it has interactive displays and a lookout tower providing views of the bay and inlets.

GETTING THERE *By car:* **US 50/301** crosses the bay just east of Annapolis, making this route the gateway to the Eastern Shore. For travelers from Philadelphia, New York, and other points in the Northeast, US 301 is the most efficient and easy route into the area.

By air: The nearest airport with scheduled flights is **Baltimore/Washington International** (1-800-I-FLY-BWI) between Baltimore and Annapolis.

By bus: **Carolina Trailways** (410-749-4121) makes several stops along the US 301 corridor. **Greyhound** (1-800-229-9424) crosses the Bay Bridge and makes one stop in Stevensville. **Annapolis Transit** provides commuter service to Annapolis, Baltimore, and Washington, D.C. Contact **Queen Anne's County Department of Business and Tourism** (see *Guidance*) for a copy of the very complicated schedule.

GETTING AROUND *By car:* Within a few miles of crossing the Bay Bridge, US 50/301 splits. **US 301** heads to the northeast on its way to Wilmington, Delaware, and passes through the dairy farms and croplands of Queen Anne's and Kent Counties. (**MD 213** is a smaller, less traveled route that turns to the west toward Chestertown.) **US 50** drops to the south and then turns to the east, providing the quickest route to Salisbury and the Ocean City area.

By bus: **County Ride** (410-758-2357), 104 Powell Street, Centreville, 21617, has routes throughout Kent Island and connections with Grasonville, Queenstown, and Centreville.

By taxi: **Dart Cab** (410-643-2466).

PUBLIC REST ROOMS Public rest rooms may be found at Queen Anne's County Department of Business and Tourism (see *Guidance*) in Chester; Prime Outlets (see *Selective Shopping—Outlets*) in Queenstown; and at the Matapeake Trail and Pier (see *Green Space—Parks*) in Stevensville.

MEDICAL EMERGENCY Around Kent Island, the closest hospital is in Annapolis: **Anne Arundel Medical Center** (410-481-1000), 2000 Medical Parkway. For emergencies in the northern part of this area, go to **Kent and Queen Anne's Hospital** (410-778-3300), 100 Brown Street in Chestertown.

✳ To See

MUSEUMS Museum of Eastern Shore Life (410-822-6109), 126 Dulin Clark Road, Centreville. Saturday and Sunday 1–4, April through October. Free admission. A collection of tools, implements, and other items from bygone times.

HISTORIC SITES Colonial Courthouse (410-827-7646), MD 18 and Del Rhodes Avenue, Queenstown. The first courthouse built in Queen Anne's County, the circa-1708 structure was restored in the late 1900s using most of the original studs, diagonal braces, and doorjambs and headers. A simple one-room wooden building, it is furnished with authentic reproductions. Interestingly, the gavel is made from one of the building's original beams. The attached brick building was added as a kitchen sometime in the mid-1800s; it is now used for administrative offices. Check with office personnel for a tour of the courthouse.

HISTORIC CHURCHES Christ Church (410-643-5921), 117 East Main Street, Stevensville. This Gothic church, with its steep slate roof and stone foundation, was constructed—using wooden pegs instead of nails—in 1880. The oldest established congregation in the state, founded in 1631, worshiped here until it moved to a location south of US 50.

St. Luke's Episcopal Church (410-556-6644), 401 Main Street, Church Hill, was constructed in 1732 and is believed to be the oldest intact brick church in the state. In an example of how important tobacco was in colonial days, the congregation did not pay for the church with money, but with 140,000 pounds of tobacco.

Dudley's Chapel (410-827-4810), Benton Corner Road, Sudlersville. Constructed in the late 1700s, this brick structure is the oldest Methodist church still standing in the United States. The first Native American Methodist minister, Freeborn Garrettson, preached here.

OTHER SITES **Wye Grist Mill** (410-827-6909), just a few hundred feet south of the MD 662/MD 213 intersection, Wye Mills. Open weekends from mid-April through early November; sometimes during the week. With flour being shipped to Europe, South America, and the West Indies, the late 1700s were the halcyon days for wheat on the Eastern Shore. The Wye Grist Mill is a bit of that time still in existence. A small museum contains many items from the miller's trade, and when all of the gears, millstone, and wheel are in motion, you will be amazed at how little water is required to operate it.

✳ To Do

BICYCLING See *Green Space—Walks.*

BOAT EXCURSIONS **B & B Yacht Charters** (410-643-1529), 206 Holly Court, Stevensville. The 40-foot sloop *Captiva* takes passengers onto the Chesapeake Bay for 3-hour ($35–45) and 6-hour ($40–55) sailing cruises. Also weekend and weeklong chartered trips.

✐ **Grabacrab Charters** (410-758-1837), 433 Kent Narrows Way at Harris Crab House, Grasonville. This is an outing for as many as 26 passengers, and designed for the whole family, with crabbing for the kids. The cruise includes a feast of crab dip, shrimp, corn, and crabs. Advance reservations required.

BOAT RENTALS **Island Boat Rentals** (410-827-4777), at the Jetty Restaurant off US 50 Exit 42, Stevensville. Half-day, full-day, and weekly rentals of 16-foot skiffs with outboard motors.

Schnaitman's Boat Rental (410-827-7663), 12518 Wye Landing Lane, Wye Mills. Full-day rentals of 16-foot

Orrell's Maryland Beaten Biscuits (410-827-6244; 410-822-2065; www.beatenbiscuits.com), about 1.5 miles south of Wye Mills on MD 622—watch for the sign. There is no storefront here; just knock on the kitchen door. Open Tuesday and Wednesday; call ahead to arrange a quick tour. The phrase "a throwback from another time" has never been as appropriate as when describing this place. Beaten-biscuit making is at least 300 years old, dating from when leavening was hard to come by. The dough was beaten with a hammer—for at least 30 minutes—to get it to rise. Using a rolling machine to take the place of beating, the Orrell family has been selling the biscuits since the 1930s. After being rolled, five women (several have been with Orrell's for decades), sitting around an old vinyl table, hand-form each biscuit. Cooked in an oven—not a commercial one, but like the one you have in your kitchen—they are crunchy, but chewy inside. A place with a lot of character that should not be missed.

wooden rowboats for fishing and crabbing along the Wye East River.

FISHING

Stevensville

ᵭ **Matapeake Pier** (410-974-2149), about 3 miles south of US 50 on MD 8. The 900-foot handicapped-accessible pier is open for public fishing 24 hours a day.

Pocomoke Pier, located at the southern end of MD 8. Open for fishing and crabbing from sunrise to sunset from May through October.

Chester

Island Queen (410-827-7737). This 65-foot headboat takes anglers on a first-come, first-served basis and leaves daily from the Captain Meredith Seafood Restaurant in Kent Narrows at 7 AM and 3 PM, April through December. Can accommodate more than 100 passengers.

Also contact the **Queen Anne's County Department of Business and Tourism** (see *Guidance*) for a listing of other licensed charter-boat captains.

GOLF Blue Heron (410-643-5721), 101 Queen's Colony High Road, Stevensville. Operated by Queen Anne's County Parks and Recreation, and open 7 AM to dusk, the course is open to the public on a first-come, first-served basis.

Queenstown Harbor Links (410-821-6611; 1-800-827-5257), 310 Links Lane, Queenstown. Two courses. The 18 holes on the River Course are often within view of the Chester River, while the scenery along the other 18-hole course centers upon a series of lakes.

HIKING See *Green Space—Walks* and *Parks.*

KAYAKING AND CANOEING The Choptank and Tuckahoe Rivers Water Trail is a 60-mile route that runs along the narrow, cypress-tree-lined Tuckahoe River and the more open waters of the Choptank River. An excellent guide to this trip—which provides not only route descriptions but also access points, interpretive information, and cultural aspects along the way—may be obtained from the Old Hartford Town Maritime Center (410-241-8662; www.riverheritage.org), 10215 River Landing Road, Denton, 21629.

TENNIS Public courts can be found in **Mowbray Park** on MD 8 south of Stevensville, **Grasonville Park** on Perry's Corner Road in Grasonville, **Roundtop Park** on Roundtop Road in Chester Harbor, and **Love Point Park** on Old Love Point Road in Stevensville.

✳ Green Space

BEACHES See **Matapeake Trail and Pier** under *Parks.*

NATURE PRESERVES ✐ **Horsehead Wetlands Center** (410-827-6694; www.wildfowltrust.org), 600 Discovery Lane—US 50 and 301 Exit 43B or Exit 44A, Grasonville. Open 9–5. Small admission fee. The 500-acre headquarters of the Wildfowl Trust of North America. I have always been rewarded with something during my walks on the 4 miles of trails: trumpeter swans coming in for a landing on one of the ponds, an osprey swooping down to grasp a fish in its talons, a black snake warming itself in

A VIEW OF BENNETS POINT FROM FERRY POINT ON WYE ISLAND

the sun. There are also canoeing opportunities, kids' exhibits and programs, an enclosed aviary, and special events.

Wye Island Natural Resource Management Area (410-827-7577), 632 Wye Island Road, Queenstown. Open sunrise to sunset. When Wye Island was threatened with development, many people objected. To prevent future such attempts and to preserve the nature of the locale, the state purchased most of it in the mid-1970s. Because of the foresight of others, a visit here gives you the chance to explore an island that has been used for agricultural purposes for three centuries.

The Department of Natural Resources administers the approximately 2,450 acres and still manages them for agricultural uses. There are about 30 miles of shoreline, while virgin stands of timber serve as habitat for the endangered Delmarva fox squirrel.

Three short pathways wander through fields, meadows, and woodlands to views of the Chesapeake Bay. If you feel like exploring beyond the trails, you are also permitted to walk the grassy buffer strips between cultivated fields and woodlands.

& **Adkins Arboretum** (410-634-2847; www.bluecrab.org), 12610 Eveland Road, Ridgely. Daily 9–5. Many arboretums are artificially created places, but much of the Adkins Arboretum, a part of Tuckahoe State Park (see *Parks*), has been left in its natural state. Walking trails, many with informational signs, and service roads wind through the 400 acres of wooded swamps, upland forest, created meadows, and ornamental plantings. The visitors center has maps and information about guided tours. Service roads and some trails could easily be negotiated in a wheelchair.

PARKS

Stevensville
🐾 & **Matapeake Trail and Pier** (410-758-0835; www.qac.org), on MD 8 south of US 50 Exit 37. Open dawn

to dusk. A small area on the bay operated by Queen Anne's County Parks and Recreation. There is a free public beach, boat ramp, picnic area, fishing pier, and two short pathways—one of them designated as a dog trail.

& **Terrapin Nature Area** (410-758-0835), 191 Log Canoe Circle. Open dawn to dusk. A nearly level trail winds through meadows, wetlands, and forest on its way to tidal pools and an isolated sandy beach along the bay with a view of the Bay Bridge. A nice place to escape to, and especially quiet during the week. Also a small picnic area and portable restroom facilities.

Queen Anne
Tuckahoe State Park (410-820-1668), 13070 Crouse Mill Road. About 20 miles east of Wye Mills, and bordered by tranquil wooded swamplands, Tuckahoe Creek forms the dividing line between Queen Anne's and Caroline Counties. Just as it has done with many of its other streams and rivers, the state has wisely protected much of this riparian habitat

by establishing 3,700-acre Tuckahoe State Park.

Within this tract is a 35-site campground with modern facilities, a 60-acre lake providing fishing and canoeing opportunities (canoe rentals available), a ball field, an archery range, and two picnic areas. Naturalists programs are available through the spring and summer. All of this is centered in the northern section of the park, which leaves the southern portion—where several pathways wander—undeveloped and natural.

Denton
& **Martinak State Park** (410-820-1688), 137 Deep Shore Road. Mid-March through mid-November. Most people come to Martinak to take advantage of the boating on the Choptank River and Watts Creek. The 60-site campground has flush toilets and a dump station.

WALKS

Stevensville–Kent Narrows
& **Cross Island Trail** (410-758-

TUCKAHOE LAKE IN TUCKAHOE STATE PARK

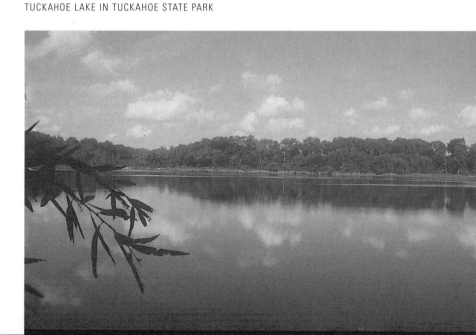

0835). Open dawn to dusk. Completed in 2001, this is one of the nicest things to happen to Kent Island in years. The paved pathway, open to walkers, cyclists, skaters, and wheelchairs, is nearly 6 miles long. Starting at the Terrapin Nature Area (see *Parks*) next to the bay, it passes through farmland, small forested areas, meadows, marshes, and beside US 50 before crossing Cox Creek on a bridge to come to an end at the Chesapeake Exploration Center (see *Guidance*) in Kent Narrows. This is a great resource that is being incorporated into the American Discovery Trail, which crosses the United States from the Atlantic to the Pacific.

✴ Lodging

MOTELS AND HOTELS ✍ **Sleep Inn** (410-827-5555), 101 VFW Avenue, Grasonville 21638. Agreeable rooms with refrigerators, ironing boards, and oversized showers. Continental breakfast, free local calls, and a free scoop of ice cream in the evening. $80–130.

INNS ✍ **Kent Manor Inn and Restaurant** (410-643-7716; 1-800-820-4511; www.kentmanor.com), 500 Kent Manor Drive, Stevensville, 21666. This country manor house (circa 1820) has been added onto, providing the inn with 24 guest rooms. It would be hard to tell which are original, as each room has been constructed and decorated in keeping with the feel of country elegance.

All rooms have a private bath and many feature a fireplace with an Italian marble mantel. The inn's 226 acres invite investigation by the provided bikes and paddleboats, or along the quiet lanes. Many special events

and packages available. The restaurant (see *Dining Out*) has a fabulous reputation. $170–235.

BED & BREAKFASTS
Chester, 21619
Chester Peake (410-604-0588), 101 Swan Cove Lane—US 50 and 301 Exit 41. There is a lot of bustle near the Chester Peake—a four-lane highway, a full-service marina and boatyard, the Queen Anne's County Visitors Center—but all of this fades away once you step inside the door. The three guest rooms, each with a private bath, and the large common room look westward onto the quiet of the Chester River. Hosts Janice and Bill Costello encourage you to sit on the deck or sunbathe on their small private beach. A stocked kitchen lets you choose your own continental breakfast. $125.

Grasonville, 21638
Land's End Manor on the Bay (410-827-6284), 232 Prospect Bay Drive. The twists and turns you have to make while driving to this B&B make it a place you have to really want to get to. With 17 acres bordered on three sides by water, it truly is at land's end. There are only two large guest rooms (a third smaller one is used for overflow); the Swan Room was my favorite with its down bed and view of the water.

The wood throughout the manor house, which was once a private hunting lodge, adds richness to each room, while the elliptical staircase and eight working fireplaces hark back to another era. Bicycles, a canoe, pedal boat, and rowboat are available for guest use, as is a swimming pool. Of course, you could just sit in the stone-floored sunroom and watch the daylight play upon the water, or become mesmerized by the fireplace flames in the great room. $125–175.

Queenstown, 21658

Stillwater Inn (410-827-9362), 7109 2nd Avenue. This Victorian inn was built in 1904 as the home and offices of Dr. Wilmer Adams, became a vestry of the Wye Parish in 1907, and started providing overnight lodging to hunters and fishermen in 1939. Kevin and Linda Vasbinder have operated their B&B—which has its original pine floors—since 1992, offering two rooms decorated with antiques, lace curtains, and sleigh and canopy beds. Full breakfast. $125.

& **Queenstown Inn** (410-827-3396; www.queenstowninn.com), 7109 Main Street. Located on a quiet residential street, the inn offers five rooms, each with its own decorating theme, and all with a private bath, air-conditioning, and ceiling fans. Two rooms have private entrances. Guests often gather on the screened porch with its view of the flower gardens. $125–145.

CAMPING See *Parks.*

✳ Where to Eat

DINING OUT Kent Manor Inn and Restaurant (410-643-5757), 500 Kent Manor Drive, Stevensville. Open for lunch and dinner. Within the setting of four Victorian dining rooms with working fireplaces, chef Dennis Shakan and staff offer the area's finest dining. Forgoing other delicious appetizers, start your meal with the Elizabethan scampi ($9), bacon-wrapped shrimp brushed with horseradish and vermouth concassé. You could order crabcakes (market price), lamb ($28), or chicken ($19) for dinner, but here is a chance to have something differ-

ent—like spice-crusted ostrich tenderloin on a sweet-potato pancake ($27). How often can you try tomato-crusted wild boar with jicama slaw and mango chutney ($28)? A signature entrée is the two quails ($23). One is stuffed with black rice, apricots, and cherry, the other with a sourdough stuffing of raspberries, blackberries, and blueberries, and served with apple cream sauce. All I can say is yum! (Also see *Lodging—Inns.*)

EATING OUT

Stevensville

Hemingway's (410-643-2711), Pier One Road (US 50/301) Exit 37. After many years of working with the Clyde's Corporation of Restaurants, Bianna Arentz took over the reins of this seafood restaurant with a commanding view of the bay and Bay Bridge. She grew up in Puerto Rico, and she summers in Spain—thus the restaurant's name. Bianna personally oversees the wine list, and she and the staff are continually trying new recipes. The gazpacho was fresh and tangy ($4.75), and I couldn't resist having mine topped with crabmeat (additional $1.25). Just as tasty was the seafood tortellini ($24) filled with shrimp, scallops, crabmeat, lobster, and cheeses, and served with saffron sauce. Many other good choices are here, such as the crab dip ($9) and venison scaloppini ($21). Downstairs is **Lola's** (see *Nightlife*), a bar and grill.

✐ & **Kentmorr Restaurant** (410-643-2263), 910 Kentmorr Road—US 50/301 Exit 37, south 5 miles on MD 8. Casual dining with a deck and picture windows overlooking the Chesapeake Bay and Kentmorr Harbor Marina. The tuna salad with chunks of fresh fish ($5.99) filled me up for lunch. Dinner selections include flounder ($13.95), 8-ounce sirloin ($13.99), and fried Delmarva chicken ($8.99). All-you-can-eat crabs (market price) when available.

Matapeake Café and Deli (410-643-5330), 410 Love Point Road. A popular place with the artists and shop owners in historic Stevensville. Muffins, bagels, and "Samichies" for breakfast. Fresh soups (from $2.25), salads (from $5.75), and sandwiches for lunch. Sondra's Veggie sandwich ($4) is the healthy choice; the Avalanche ($6.25) with roast beef, turkey, ham, salami, pastrami, two cheeses, mayo, and Italian dressing is at the opposite end of the spectrum.

Grasonville

Annie's (410-827-7103), 500 Kent Narrows Way—US 50/301 Exit 42. At the Marina in Kent Narrows, Annie's serves steaks ($12.95 and up), seafood (from $9.95), and Italian dishes (crab fettuccine, $19.95).

Holly's (410-827-8711), US 50 and Jackson Creek Road. In business since 1955, Holly's serves home-cooked breakfasts, lunches, and dinners and is the kind of place that everyone ends up at eventually. The Shoreman's Breakfast ($5.50) contains pancakes, eggs, bacon, and sausage. The Shore Special ($18.95) is three pieces of fried chicken and a crab-cake. Sandwiches, soups, and homemade ice cream.

Centreville

✿ Café on the Square (410-758-0471), 144 North Commerce Street. Open Tuesday through Saturday 11–3 for lunch; dinner is served Tuesday through Thursday 5–9 and Friday and Saturday 5–10. A bowl of cream of crab soup ($4.95) is the best meal

starter, while the chicken Marsala ($13) is a good entrée choice. Other soups, salads, and sandwiches are available for lunch and dinner.

CRABS ✿ Harris Crab House (410-827-9500), 433 Kent Narrows Way—US 50/301 Exit 42, Grasonville. The Harris family has been purchasing seafood directly from watermen since 1941, and opened their oystering-paraphernalia-decorated restaurant in 1981. Because it is impossible to find seafood any fresher, it draws many people over the Bay Bridge to devour dozens of steamed and soft-shell crabs (market price), cooked in the Harris's own hand-tossed spices. The Seafood Basket, with five items and corn, is only $22.95. Rockfish stuffed with crab imperial is $20.95; other seafood, meat, and chicken entrées $12.95–21.95. The Harris family also works with the Chesapeake Bay Foundation and the Oyster Recovery Project to study ways to preserve the waters their restaurant overlooks.

SEAFOOD TAKE-OUT

Grasonville

Fisherman's Seafood (410-827-7323), 3036 Kent Narrows Way South. All items are cleaned and steamed or packed in ice at no extra charge.

Hunter's Seafood (410-827-8923), MD 18 and Station Lane. Steamed crabs by the dozen or the bushel. Hunter's also has a complete line of other seafood.

✳ Entertainment

NIGHTLIFE

Stevensville

Lola's. Open from the end of April

through October. This downstairs bar area of Hemingway's (see *Dining Out*) serves a full menu with a Caribbean flair. The fun spills outside on the sand when live bands entertain on Thursday through Sunday nights.

Verna's Island Inn (410-643-2466; 1-800-360-1202), 800 Main Street. DJs on Thursday and Friday; live music on Saturday, 9:30 PM–2 AM.

Grasonville
Fisherman's Crab Deck (410-827-6666), 3036 Kent Narrows Way South. Cocktails and live bands on the weekend.

THEATERS

Church Hill Theatre (410-758-1331), 103 Walnut Street, Church Hill. Music, plays, films, workshops, and other cultural events are presented inside this art deco theater by professional and amateur groups. Call for schedule.

✳ Selective Shopping
ANTIQUES Stevensville Antiques (410-643-8130), Historic Stevensville. Several dealers of antiques and other collectibles.

Chesapeake Antique Center (410-827-6640), US 301, Queenstown. Daily 10–5. The outlet for a number of dealers.

Dixon's Furniture (410-928-3006), Dudley Corner Road, Crumpton. In addition to having an almost incomprehensible amount of antiques, Dixon's holds auctions every Wednesday beginning at 9 AM.

ART GALLERIES Kent Island Federation of Art (410-643-7424), 405 Main Street, Historic Stevensville. Tuesday through Friday 1–4, and Sun-

day noon–4. In addition to featuring works of local artists in its gallery, the federation sponsors art sales, museum exhibits, and dinner-theater bus trips.

Queen Anne's County Arts Council (410-758-2520), 206 Commerce Street, Centreville. Changing displays of local artisans and craftspersons. Classes, workshops, concerts, lectures, and more.

BOOKSTORES Corsica Bookshop (410-758-1453), 101 South Commerce Street, Centreville. One of the finest independent bookstores on the Eastern Shore.

CRAFTS

Historic Stevensville
L'Atelier (410-643-4336), 104 Cockey Lane. Maureen Bannon, the mother of Jeff Bushey at the Chesapeake Wood Duck Inn on Tilghman Island (see *Lodging—Bed & Breakfasts* in "St. Michaels, Easton, and Oxford"), was the driving force behind this collective. Her works, and those of fellow artists Sally Clark, Bonnie Howell, and Beth Kosterich, have distinctive styles recognizable from that often found in other galleries.

Cheers Pottery (410-643-9774). A working pottery studio and gallery.

The Glassburg (410-643-5021). Stroll in and watch stained glass being made and displayed in the studio-gallery.

Paul Reed Smith Guitars (410-758-5366; 1-800-723-9096), 380 Log Canoe Circle. The manufacturing home for the well-known brand of electric guitars. Factory tours are given by reservation on Tuesday, Wednesday, and Thursday at 1:30.

SPECIAL SHOPS ✐ **Ye Olde Church House** (410-643-6227), 426 Love Point Road, Stevensville. Friday, Saturday, and Sunday 10–6. More than just an antiques shop located in a former church. Owner Janet Denny also offers 18th-century crafts items such as hand-spun yarn, handmade soap, herbal vinegars, and dried-flower arrangements. There are also some sheep and goats for children to feed.

OUTLETS **Prime Outlets** (410-827-8699), at the split of US 50 and 301 North, Queenstown. Outlets for Bass, Liz Claiborne, Brooks Brothers, Bugle Boy, Dockers, Geoffrey Beene, Lenox, and other nationally recognized brands.

PICK-YOUR-OWN PRODUCE FARMS
✐ **Kent Fort Farm** (410-643-1650), 10 miles south of US 50 via MD 8 to Kent Point Road, Stevensville. Mid-April through October, Tuesday through Sunday. Berries, fruit, and pumpkins. Also the site of the annual **Peach Festival** in August, with a petting zoo, hay- and pony-cart rides, face painting, and homemade peach ice cream.

Erickson's Farm (410-758-1655), 171 Strawberry Lane, Centreville. U-pick strawberries in-season.

G. H. Godfrey Farms (410-438-3501), 130 Blueberry Lane, Sudlersville. Strawberries (mid-May through Mid-June) and blueberries (late June through late July).

✳ Special Events

March: **Annual Artists of the Chesapeake Art Auction** (410-758-2520), Chesapeake College, Wye Mills.

April: **Tuckahoe Easter Egg Hunt** (410-820-1668), Tuckahoe State Park (see *Green Space—Parks*), Queen Anne. The Eastern Shore's largest Easter egg hunt. **Spring Festival** (410-758-1419), Centreville. Tractor pulls and other activities; also quilting, weaving, chair caning, and other crafts.

May: **Annual Open-Judged Art Show** (410-643-7424), Stevensville. **Annual Bay Bridge Walk** (1-877-BAY-SPAN). The one day of the year when people are permitted to walk across the 4.3-mile span. Strollers and wheelchairs allowed. A big event on both sides of the bay that attracts close to 50,000 people. My wife was the first person to walk across the bridge and back during the first bridge walk several decades ago. **Waterfowl Weekend** (410-643-7226), Horsehead Wetlands Center (see *Green Space—Nature Preserves*), Grasonville. Carving competition, exhibits, food, and vendors inside the 500-acre preserve. **Kent Island Days** (410-643-5969), Stevensville. Commemorating the 1631 founding of the island's settlement with historic displays, entertainment, food, crafts, and an 18th-century encampment.

June: **Waterman's Festival** (410-604-2100), Grasonville. Celebrates the waterman's livelihood with docking and anchor-throwing contests, crab races, children's activities, food, and entertainment. **Annual Tuckahoe Triathlon** (410-820-1668), Tuckahoe State Park (see *Green Space—Parks*). A 10-mile bike ride, 2-mile run, and 1-mile canoe course. **Wheat Harvest Fair** (410-822-1910), Wye Mills. A festival celebrating the ways of the past. Oxcart rides, blacksmiths, woodworkers, candle makers, etc. Colonial and Civil War reenactments.

July: **Annual Fireman's Carnival** (410-604-0650), Kent Island.

August: **Queen Anne's County Fair** (410-758-0267), Centreville. Annual **Peach Festival** (410-643-1650) at Kent Fort Farm in Stevensville (see *Selective Shopping—Pick-Your-Own Produce Farms*).

September: **Annual Rockfish Tournament**, 410-643-8530, Kentmorr Harbor Marina, Stevensville. **Wetlands Fest** (410-827-6694), Horsehead Wetlands Center (see *Green Space—Nature Preserves*), Grasonville. Games, exhibits, live-animal programs, hiking, and bird-watching.

October: **Holiday Lighted Boat Parade** (410-643-4101), Kent Narrows.

CHESTERTOWN AND ROCK HALL

The word *quaint* is found so often in travel books that I resist using it. However, in the case of Chestertown I must break my hesitancy. For *quaint* is certainly the right word to describe a place with an Italianate-style courthouse, a hotel that has managed to hang on to its early-20th-century attractiveness, and one after another of stately and well-maintained Victorian homes. The downtown has not been abandoned, turned over to national chain stores, or relegated to parking buildings. Rather, you will find small, independently owned shops, businesses, and restaurants lining laid-brick sidewalks.

There are so many buildings of historical and architectural significance that it takes six columns of a walking-tour brochure (available from the Kent County Office of Tourism Development—see *Guidance*) to briefly describe them. The town is also home to a college, but not one of those huge universities that takes over the character of a place. Washington College has barely more than 1,000 students and blends in so well because much of its campus is a maintained arboretum.

The Chester River does not figure in economic importance, as it did several centuries ago when Chestertown was a Royal Port of Entry and later the center of an agricultural and seafood area shipping its wares by steamboat. Although watermen still pursue catches within its waters, it is now a stream of pleasure for recreational boaters and sailors—or just plain beautiful scenery when viewed from the town dock or the riverside Wilmer Park.

Rock Hall is one of the few places on the Eastern Shore that has been able to hit a balance in preserving its traditional watermen's way of life while providing the amenities and attractions travelers want and need. If fact, you can observe this balance every day during the summer when visitors gather in Rock Hall Harbor about 5 PM to watch the watermen unload their daily catches. Less than an hour later, the crowd moves over to P. E. Pruitt's dock to witness the charter boats bring in the sportfishermen's trophies of the day.

A small watermen's museum provides a glimpse of what it once took to survive this rugged occupation, while a drugstore is a reminder of what many small towns in America were like in the early 1900s.

As befits a town bordered on three sides by water, Rock Hall has numerous marinas catering to recreational boaters, dozens of charter-boat captains, and

Chestertown and Rock Hall

sailing-excursion operators. The many waterfront restaurants serve up the fresh catches of the day.

COMMUNITIES **Betterton** was a thriving beach resort in the days of steamboat travel. Although visitors are now far fewer in number, its small beach remains the only place in the Chesapeake Bay that you can swim without fear of brushing up against a sea nettle (jellyfish).

The site of a silver mine before the War of 1812, **Galena** is a small crossroads town with a number of antiques shops and stores. Its dogwood-tree-lined streets come aglow with pink and white blossoms in the spring.

GUIDANCE The **Kent County Office of Tourism Development** (410-778-0416) has a visitors center on the third floor of 400 High Street, Chestertown, 21620.

GETTING THERE *By car:* **US 301** crosses in a north–south direction in the eastern part of the area, while the smaller **MD 213** swings to the west to pass through Chestertown.

By air: The nearest and largest airport with scheduled flights is **Baltimore/Washington International** (1-800-I-FLY-BWI), located between Baltimore and Annapolis.

By bus: **Carolina Trailways** (410-749-4121) makes a couple of stops along the US 301 corridor.

By water: If you have your own boat, the Chesapeake Bay, of course, is the way to get to the area; the Chester and Sassafras Rivers give you access to inland waters.

GETTING AROUND *By car:* **US 301** and **MD 213** are the major thoroughfares. However, **MD 298** parallels MD 213 several miles to the north, has much less traffic, and passes through some beautiful countryside. **MD 20** is the major link between Chestertown and Rock Hall.

By trolley: The **Rock Hall Trolley** (866-RHTROLY; www.rockhalltrolleys.com) makes a complete tour of Rock Hall, covering the town from one end to the other and making nearly 20 stops. It's a fun ride, as its passengers are a good mix of locals and visitors. Ride all day for $2. Weekdays it operates 3–10 PM, Saturday 9 AM–10 PM, and Sunday 9 AM–7 PM.

PARKING There are four lots in Chestertown, all accessed from Cannon Street, in which you can park for free 7 days a week. The meters along the streets have a 2-hour limit but are free after 4 and on Saturday and Sunday.

PUBLIC REST ROOMS The public is free to use the rest rooms in the Chestertown's library on High Street, the courthouse on Cross Street, and the town hall at the corner of Cross Street and Maple Avenue.

MEDICAL EMERGENCY **Kent and Queen Anne's Hospital** (410-778-3300), 100 Brown Street, Chestertown.

✳ To See

COLLEGES Washington College (1-800-422-1782; www.washcoll.edu), 300 Washington Avenue, Chestertown. Washington College was founded in 1782, making it the first college chartered after the founding of the United States, the oldest in Maryland, and the 10th oldest in the country. It is named after George Washington, who visited the institution in 1784. A walk on campus takes you through the **Virginia Gent Decker Arboretum** (see *Green Space—Arboretums*) and by several buildings dating from the early 1800s. Lectures, exhibits, and other entertainment are presented in the **Gibson Performing Arts Center** (see *Entertainment—Music*).

MUSEUMS

Chestertown
Geddes-Piper House (410-778-3499; www.kentcounty.com/historicalsociety), 101 Church Alley. Small admission fee; children under 10 free. Saturday and Sunday 1–4, May through October. The only 18th-century home in Chestertown open to the public on a regular basis. Guided tours bring you to each room of the house to appreciate the slate fireplaces, original kitchen utensils in the basement, and changing exhibits reflecting the region's history. The Victorian room with a number of quilts, the children's room with a dollhouse, and the fan collection make for interesting examinations.

Rock Hall
Waterman's Museum (410-778-6697), 20880 Rock Hall Avenue. Free admission. If the museum is not open, you may obtain the key from the Haven Harbor Marina's Ditty Bag shop store next door. Exhibits on oystering, crabbing, and fishing, with carvings and with a reproduction of a shanty house. It's a small museum, but that makes it easy to see everything; many items donated by local watermen.

Tolchester Beach Revisited (410-778-5347), Oyster Court. Saturday and Sunday 11–3. A small museum put together by Bill Betts, containing memorabilia from the Tolchester Beach Amusement Park, which was a popular resort from 1877 to the mid-1900s.

HISTORIC CHURCHES St. Paul's Episcopal Church, 7579 Sandy Bottom Road, accessed from MD 20 between Chestertown and Rock Hall. The parish was established in 1693. The present building, with a semicircular apse and Flemish-bond brickwork, dates from 1713, making it one of the oldest continuously used churches in the state. Wander around the 19-acre churchyard shaded by boxwood trees and you will find the final resting place of actress Tallulah Bankhead.

Emmanuel Episcopal Church, Cross Street and Park Row, Chestertown. Built in 1767, the large, two-story nave measures 66 feet by 44 feet. Also take note of the Tiffany window on the south wall, and the bell tower, which was added in 1905.

Shrewsbury Episcopal Church, MD 213, Kennedyville. Completed in 1832, this building was constructed using bricks from one of the earlier churches built on this site in 1722. The churchyard dates from the Revolutionary War and contains the graves of veterans from all U.S. wars. Of particular note is the grave of Revolutionary War hero Brigadier General John Cadawalader.

SCENIC DRIVES **Chesapeake Farms** (410-778-8400), 7319 Remington Drive (off MD 20 between Chestertown and Rock Hall), Chestertown. Open during daylight hours, February 1 through October 10. Free admission. A brochure, available in the farm office or the tourism office (see *Guidance*) is keyed to different signed stops along the way on this 3,300-acre farm. From it you will learn how the ponds, fields, hedgerows, and forests are designed to develop, evaluate, and demonstrate agricultural and wildlife management techniques. It should easily take less than an hour if you stop to read everything (you must stay in your car), but it is still a worthwhile drive if you just want to enjoy the scenery.

Also see **Eastern Neck Wildlife Refuge** under *Green Space—Nature Preserves*.

✳ To Do

BICYCLING Maps of a number of bicycle tours in Chestertown using lightly traveled roads are available from the **Kent County Office of Tourism Development** (see *Guidance*).

Swan Haven Rentals (410-639-2527), 20950 Rock Hall Avenue, Rock Hall. In addition to renting floatable transportation devices, they will also provide you with a bike for an hour or a day. (Also see *Boat Rentals*.)

BOAT CHARTERS

Rock Hall

Gratitude Yachting Center (410-639-7111; www.gratitudeyachting. com), 5990 Lawton Avenue. Boats of varying shapes and sizes are available for charter by the day or week. Since you are your own captain and crew, you must provide some evidence of your sailing proficiency.

Southern Cross Charters (410-778-4460), Great Oak Landing Marina, Great Oak. You don't need to know a thing about sailing, as Southern Cross provides a captain for you on their 41-foot ketch. Sit back and enjoy the ride, but expect to pay several hundred dollars for the privilege of being inactive.

BOAT RENTALS **Chester River Boat Rental** (410-778-2240), US 213 south of town, Chestertown. Rentals of outboard motorboats, aquacycles, and pedal boats.

Swan Haven Rentals (410-639-2527), 20950 Rock Hall Avenue, Rock Hall. If it floats, these folks seem to have it for rent: Kayaks, canoes, jonboats, daysailers, Windsurfers, and more.

FISHING CHARTERS

Rock Hall

As seems natural for an area close to so much water, there are many captains who take sportfishermen out onto the bay and local rivers. Among the many are **Captain Marc Van Pelt** and **Captain Bob Ritchie** (410-639-7936; www.fishfearus.com); **Captain Larry Simns** (410-639-2966; www.dawnii. com); and **Captain Greg Jetton** (410-639-7127; www.GregJetton.com).

The Kent County Office of Tourism Development (see *Guidance*) can provide a listing of many other Coast Guard–certified charter operators. The amount of fishing time and fees vary greatly, so be sure to check specifically how long your trip is, what is provided, and the total costs.

HORSEBACK RIDING *∂* **Crimson Stables** (410-778-7304), Morgnec Road, Chestertown. Trail rides, pony rides, and hayrides.

KAYAKING AND CANOEING

Rock Hall

∂ **Chester River Kayak Adventures** (410-639-2001; www.crkayakadventures.com), 5758 Main Street. These folks not only provide kayak lessons but also lead guided tours upon the local waters for individuals or groups. The half-day tour is $50, or $40 for children older than 10; the full-day tour is $90, or $75 for children older than 10; and the sunset trip is $40, or $32 for children older than 10. It would be wise to make reservations to ensure your time and place.

Kayak/Canoe, LLC (410-639-9000), 6039 Rock Hall Road. Kayak lessons for individuals or groups, and guided kayak and canoe tours. Most of the trips are a half day and set out in early morning and/or early afternoon at a cost of about $50 a person. Walk-ins accepted as schedule permits.

SAILING *Kathryn* (410-639-9902), docked at Rock Hall Harbor at the foot of Bayside and Caroline Avenues, Rock Hall. Captains Bruce and Kathy Meeks take passengers onto the bay on their 43-foot ketch. The 2-hour sail ($25) leaves at 10 AM; the 3-hour cruise ($35) sets sail at 1:30 PM.

SAILING LESSONS

Rock Hall

Maryland School of Sailing and Seamanship (410-639-7030; www.mdschool.com), 21035 Spring Cove Marina. From Basic Sailing through Ocean Touring Courses, the school can turn any landlubber into an old salt in just a few lessons. Students can become certified by the American Sailing Association. All classes last at least a few days; fees vary. You may take your classes on the bay or travel to exotic locations, such as the Caribbean, with the school.

Sailing Emporium (410-778-1342), 21144 Green Lane. One-day classes provide you with basic sailing instruction and knowledge.

SWIMMING *∂* The swimming pool in a small county-operated park in Millington is open to the public from Memorial Day through Labor Day.

TENNIS Public courts in Worton are available on a first-come, first-served basis in Worton Park.

✳ Green Space

ARBORETUMS **Virginia Gent Decker Arboretum** (410-778-7726; 1-800-422-1782, extension 7726), Washington College campus, Chestertown. The arboretum was established in 1996 and is based upon the model found at George Washington's Mount Vernon. Building upon the existing trees and shrubs, the college is continually adding to their number and diversity. Although many of the plants are marked by identifying labels, your experience will be enhanced if you pick up an arboretum brochure in Dunning Hall off Campus Avenue.

Eastern Neck National Wildlife Refuge (410-639-7056), 1730 Eastern Neck Road, Rock Hall. Open year-round. From October through mid-March, thousands of migratory waterfowl winter in the Chesapeake Bay region, many of them on this 2,285-acre refuge. The most common species that have been documented here include as many as 20,000 Canada geese, more than 7,000 tundra swans, over 15,000 canvasback ducks, and an assortment of thousands of others, such as mallards, wigeon, pintails, and buffleheads. Seen throughout much of the year are great blue herons, great and snowy egrets, turkey vultures, ospreys, and bald eagles. In addition, close to 250 other species—ranging from common bluebirds and chickadees to rarely observed peregrine falcons and American woodcocks—have been identified.

Why else should you come here? How about a couple of short trails where you might see white-tailed deer, diamondback terrapins, muskrats, beavers, red foxes, eastern gray squirrels, and the endangered Delmarva fox squirrel? Or sift your hands through mounds of huge shells of oysters shucked by Native Americans more than a millennium ago. Then again, you could come to the refuge just for the quiet beauty of a typical Chesapeake Bay landscape of marshes, croplands, loblolly forests, and grass fields surrounded by sun-speckled water.

Getting to Eastern Neck National Wildlife Refuge can be an enjoyable outing in itself—the Maryland government considers the drive to be so picturesque that it has designated it a **State Scenic Route**. The island may be reached by leaving MD 213 in Chestertown and driving southward on MD 20 for nearly 13 miles to Rock Hall. Turn left on MD 445 and cross the bridge onto the island 6 miles later.

A BOARDWALK STRETCHES OVER THE MARSH AT EASTERN NECK NWR.

BEACHES Rock Hall's small beach has great sunsets framed by the Bay Bridge to the southwest.

A 3.2-acre sandy beach in **Betterton** is the only swimming area on all of the Chesapeake Bay side of the Eastern Shore that is free of stinging jellyfish. There is also a fishing jetty, boat ramp, and bathhouse. Lifeguards are on duty on Saturday and Sunday during the usual swimming season, but even then the number of people is rather light.

NATURE PRESERVES Sassafras River Natural Resource Management Area (410-778-1984), on MD 448 about 3 miles north of Kennedyville. Open sunrise to sunset. This area contains close to 1,000 acres of farmland, marshes, forests, beaches, and tidal pools whose access is limited to those on foot, bicycle, or horseback. Expect to see lots of waterfowl, deer, beaver, and maybe a bald eagle. The adjoining Turner's Creek is a recreation area with a public boat ramp, fishing, and picnic facilities. If time permits, do not miss the historic tree grove and farm museum.

PARKS Wilmer Park is Chestertown's waterfront park on the Chester River and is just one block from the historic district.

✳ Lodging

MOTELS AND HOTELS The Imperial Hotel (410-778-500; 1-800-295-0014; www.imperialchestertown.com), 208 High Street, Chestertown, 21620. Built in 1903, the Imperial has been renovated to give it modern amenities but retain its earlier charm. Its double verandas—one on the first floor, the other on the second—are inviting

spots to sit and watch the world go by. All of the deluxe guest rooms ($135) have a private bath and are decorated with period furnishings. The Parlor Suite ($200) occupies the entire third floor and has its own veranda. (Also see *Dining Out*.)

INNS

Rock Hall, 21661

✍ **Tallulah's** (410-639-2596; www.tallulahsonmain.com), 5750 Main Street. Hosts Barry E. Barr and Jim Messersmith have refurbished this historic building, which has been a hotel, inn, or boardinghouse for decades. A great spot for families or those having an extended stay in the area. Each efficiency room (named for significant things in Tallulah Bankhead's life) has a private bath, fully equipped kitchen, and television. Suites include a bedroom, living room, and kitchen. The cedar deck on the second floor is a nice place to lounge and enjoy the breezes coming off the bay. $125–135.

The Inn at Osprey Point (410-639-2194; www.ospreypoint), 20786 Rock Hall Avenue. It almost looks like a modern-day hotel when you drive up, but each of the seven guest rooms is nicely decorated. Some overlook the water and marina, while others have a view of the woods. $135–170. The inn's restaurant (see *Dining Out*) draws people from many miles around.

Georgetown, 21930

Kitty Knight House (410-648-5200; www.kittyknight.com), 14028 Augustine Herman Highway (US 301). In 1813, when the British were torching many Eastern Shore towns, Kitty Knight convinced them to spare the two houses (one was the home of an invalid friend) that now make up the inn and restaurant (see *Dining Out*). Purchased and renovated by Joe and Jo Ann Thompson, owners of the largest thoroughbred standards farm in the country, the house has 11 guest rooms. Some overlook the activity of the harbor on the Sassafras River; all have a private baths. Room 1 ($160) is the largest, has its original pine floors, and a private deck. Room 5 may be smaller, but it still has a water view and is only $95. Breakfast in the restaurant is included. $95–160.

BED & BREAKFASTS

Betterton, 21610

🦞 ⚓ **Lantern Inn** (410-348-5809, 1-800-499-7265) 115 Ericsson Avenue. Just one block from Betterton Beach (see *Green Space—Beaches*). Built in 1904 as a hotel when Betterton was a resort destination, the Lantern has been an inn or boardinghouse ever since. There are 13 rooms, some with private bath. Room 15 is bright and overlooks the backyard; Room 9 on the third floor has rich wood furniture; and Room 5 is referred to as the Cinderella Room for its feminine furnishings. Room 1 is the deal—it is large with lots of space and a view of the street. Children over 10 welcome; younger children are accepted on an individual basis after conference with parents. $75–90.

Chestertown, 21620

🦞 **Widow's Walk** (410-778-6455; 1-888-778-6455; www.chestertown/widow), 402 High Street. Built around 1877, the Victorian Widow's Walk is named for the lookout on its roof on which fishermen's wives would stand looking for their husbands to come home from the bay or sea. Innkeepers Bob and Sue Lathroum have made the home a genial

place to stay by placing family treasures among the antique furnishings. All three suites ($125) have a sitting area and private bath; the two upstairs rooms ($100) share a bath. Its central location makes it easy to walk just about anywhere in Chestertown.

Hill's Inn (410-778-1926) Washington Avenue. Mike and Marta Girone purchased a 200-year-old stained-glass window from a church in England and said they would buy the first house it fit into. A search across the United States brought them to this American Gothic Victorian home. In addition to mounting the window, they replastered, put up period reproductions of wallpaper, and restored the original flooring. Four guest rooms with antique furnishings were completed when I visited (I liked the Stam Room, whose windows looked onto Washington Street), and they had plans to open two more to guests. $100–120.

Pratt-Perry House (410-718-2734; www.prattperryhouse.com), 224 Washington Avenue. My taste in art must be the same as innkeeper Carolyn Perry's. The furnishings she purchased on her world travels fit in well with the atmosphere of the Victorian home, and the classically beautiful artwork on the walls is reason enough to visit here. The bed in the Dean Jones Room was made for an English nobleman, and the table is a replica of the one in Winston Churchill's birth room. The wonderfully stocked library, gardens, full breakfast, and afternoon hors d'oeuvres add to the graciousness of a stay. $100–150. There is a two-bedroom accommodation for families with responsible children.

Parker House (410-778-9041; www.chestertown.com/parker), 108

Spring Street. Within easy walking distance of downtown and Washington College. Private bath in each guest room—which is appropriate, as this was the first house to have an indoor bathroom in Chestertown. The Gemini II Room has its own screened porch. $110–125.

✒ **Lauretum Inn** (410-778-3236; 1-800-742-3236), 945 High Street. Constructed in 1881 and listed on the National Register of Historic Places, Lauretum sits on a 6-acre tree-covered knoll on the outskirts of town. Rooms with semiprivate baths ($75), some with private bath ($115), and a couple of suites ($130–140). Well-behaved children are welcome, and those under 10 are free.

✤ **April Inn** (410-778-5540), 407 Campus Avenue. Built in the mid-1900s, the home is furnished in 19th-century antiques. Within a quiet residential neighborhood, it has some of the lowest B&B rates in the area. $65–85.

🐾 ✒ **Claddaugh Farm** (410-778-4894; www.claddaughbb.com), 160 Claddaugh Lane. Children and outdoor pets are welcome at this late-19th-century farmhouse about 2 miles south of Chestertown. Three of the rooms have queen-sized beds (two with sleigh beds) and private baths. The two rooms on the third floor share a bath between them. $85–95.

Great Oak Manor (410-778-5943; 1-800-504-3098; www.greatoak.com), 10568 Cliff Road. Constructed in the 1930s, this manor house has the mien of an older Georgian mansion surrounded by 12 acres. Lots of common areas, a wonderful library with many good books, a grand staircase, and a private beach on the Chesapeake Bay. All guest rooms have a private bath

and are appropriately decorated by hosts Don and Dianne Cantor. Free bicycle use and passes to the adjacent nine-hole golf course. $125–235.

Rock Hall, 21611
✒ **Moonlight Bay and Marina** (410-639-2660), 6002 Lawton Avenue. Each of the five rooms in the Main Inn has a view of the Chesapeake Bay and private bath. The Garden Moon Room ($120) and Blue Moon Room ($135) are the ones that caught my fancy. The West Wing, built in 1997, is even closer to the water and offers five rooms ($155) decorated in a Victorian Queen Anne style, each with its own whirlpool tub. Rooms 8 and 9 have the most spectacular views. Private beach and afternoon high tea included.

COTTAGES **Bayview Beach House** (410-639-2596), 5783 Beach Road, Rock Hall, 21611. Nothing fancy here—modern furniture in a mid-1900s-style small cottage. But it can accommodate four adults, has spectacular views of Chesapeake Bay sunsets, and is across the street from Rock Hall Beach. Available for $185 a night or $880 a week.

✳ **Where to Eat**
DINING OUT

Chestertown
Blue Heron Café (410-778-0188), 236 Cannon Street. Open for lunch and dinner, Monday through Saturday. After running restaurants in New York and California and the Byard House for the DuPont family in Chesapeake City, Paul Hanley opened his own place in Chestertown. Building upon local seafood and produce, his recipes let the tastes come

through while leaving your mouth feeling refreshed and clean. The shrimp quesadilla ($9.50) is a good appetizer for dinner but is large enough to be served as a lunch entrée. The lump crab frittata ($9.25) is also great for lunch, but if you come here for dinner, do not overlook the cioppino ($23). This stew is packed with lobster, mussels, clams, shrimp, crab, and finfish in an herb and tomato broth. Meat entrées include veal sweetbreads ($20) and grilled duck breast ($19).

Imperial Hotel (410-778-5000), 208 High Street. Open for lunch and dinner. Quality food in turn-of-the-20th-century elegance. Start with the chilled avocado soup ($7) or Thai-fried soft-shell crab ($12) and move on to the mushroom phyllo ($16) or the pecan and peanut encrusted rack of lamb ($28). (Also see *Lodging—Motels and Hotels.*)

Harbor House Restaurant (410-778-0669), Buck Neck Road at Worton Harbor. Dinner only; closed Monday. Out in the boonies, a cinderblock building and a gravel parking lot cluttered with old boats mask some of the Eastern Shore's finest dining. The owner is a graduate of the Culinary Institute of America, a former owner of Kitty Knight House in Georgetown, and a gregarious and resourceful chef.

Meals begin with baked breads ranging from dinner rolls to cranberry bread to chocolate bread. The crab imperial ($28) is by far the most delicious, and different, that I've had. Huge lumps of crab are baked atop a flavorful and light sauce. The menu changes daily, but representative entrées include filet mignon ($22.50), rubbed spareribs ($19), and scallops

($20) served with a crispy casino and bacon topping. The crabcakes ($23) are all crab with just a light seasoning. Once you've had the homemade *tiramisu* ($5), you will never again order what The Olive Garden serves up as authentic *tiramisu*. Wednesday is Mystery Dinner night and could be anything. After you eat, you pay what you think it's worth.

Call for reservations a few days ahead (ask for directions), and dishes on the menu will be named after you the evening you dine.

Georgetown

Kitty Knight House (410-648-5200), 14028 Augustine Herman Highway (US 301). One of big draws here is the commanding view of the Sassafras River. Chef Michael Dilks used to own the Colonel's Choice in Aberdeen, and his menu is traditional Eastern Shore—crabcakes ($20.95), fried jumbo shrimp ($15.95), and oyster-stuffed chicken breast ($12.95). The dish I really enjoyed was the shrimp and crab penne in basil cream with sun-dried tomatoes ($17.95). Luncheon entrées include crab salad ($10.95), Reuben grill ($8.95), and a sassafras burger with onions, peppers, mushrooms, and melted mozzarella ($6.25). (Also see *Lodging—Inns.*)

Live music on the awning-covered deck Friday and Saturday nights, with more laid-back acoustic music presented Sunday afternoon. As an added bonus to those traveling by water, the kitchen will make up and deliver food baskets to boats tied at the dock.

Rock Hall

Osprey Point Restaurant (410-639-2762), 20786 Rock Hall Avenue. A warm and romantic colonial atmosphere seems like the right setting for the restaurant's traditional dishes, enhanced for modern palates. Oysters Osprey ($9.95) with prosciutto, crab, spinach, and sherry sauce is the signature appetizer. The filet of beef ($22) is topped with a Madeira–wild mushroom demiglaze. Duck breast ($19), rockfish with a bourbon–maple butter sauce ($20), and crabcakes ($21) are other entrée choices. (See also **Inn at Osprey Point** under *Lodging—Inns.*)

EATING OUT

Chestertown
✎ **Black-eyed Susan** (410-778-1214), Washington Street. Lunch and dinner. Has something for everyone. Home cooking with chicken potpie ($7) or liver and onions ($8.95). Specialty dishes include peanut-crusted lamb chops ($18.95) and onion-roasted rockfish ($16.95). For something different, try the snapper soup ($5.95) with creamed sherry or the honey-touched alligator ($7.95). Sandwiches, southwestern dishes, and kid's menu are also available.

La Ruota (410-778-9989), 323 High Street. Using recipes taught to him by his Sicilian mother, chef Sal Evola changes his menu nightly depending on what is fresh and available. The night I was there he was featuring Scaloppini alla Toscano ($20), veal with peas and served in a vermouth sauce, and Spaghetti alla Siciliana ($17) with tomato, baby shrimp, and toasted bread crumbs. Every once in a while, Sal emerges from the kitchen to serenade diners with contemporary Italian songs.

Bayside Bagels (410-778-1101), 4 Washington Square. Monday through Saturday 7–2, Sunday 8–noon. A great place to grab a quick bite. Breakfast bagels (from $1.69), bagels and cream cheeses (from $1.45), and lunch bagels (from $3.49).

Ellen's (410-810-1992), 205 Spring Avenue. Open 6 AM–2 PM Monday through Wednesday and Saturday; 6 AM–8 PM on Tuesday and Friday; 6 AM–1 PM on Sunday. The local breakfast spot. Ham and cheese omelet with homefries is only $3.05, while two pancakes are just $1.75. Lunch is sandwiches from $1.80, and dinner is home-cooked items such as pork chops ($6.95) and fried chicken ($5.95).

Rock Hall
Swan Point Inn (410-639-2500), Coleman Road and Rock Hall Avenue. Open for lunch and dinner. There is no doubt the appetizer to have is the Angels on Horseback ($8.95)—broiled bacon-wrapped shrimp laced with horseradish and served with homemade dipping sauce. Three choices of veal entrées (from $16.95), several other meat dishes (up to $22.95), and local seafood (from $15.95) prepared a variety of ways are included in the dinner menu.

Bay Wolf (410-778-6855), Rock Hall Avenue. Open for lunch and dinner. It is unexpected to run into an Austrian/Eastern Shore restaurant in tiny Rock Hall. Dine like you are in the Alps with Wiener schnitzel ($16.95), Schweinsbraten ($16.95), and apple strudel ($3.95). Or return to the Chesapeake Bay with more local dishes such as crab-imperial-stuffed flounder ($17.95) or the broiled seafood combo ($24.95) with a whole lobster, crabcake, shrimp, and scallops.

Ford's Seafood Restaurant (410-639-2032), 6262 Rock Hall Road. After many years in the wholesale business shipping clams and operating an oyster-shucking house, Nevitte and Sharon Ford open their restaurant on the approach into town. Part restaurant and part sports bar. The menu contains sandwiches (from $4), soups (from $3), and full dinners. The seafood is caught daily and includes rockfish ($15.95), flounder ($15.95), and a sampler ($17.95) with a crab-cake, a fish fillet, and fried oysters. Live entertainment on Friday and Saturday evenings. The recipes for the crabcakes ($18.95), crab imperial ($14.95), and crab bisque ($5) are Sharon's.

Millington
Dutch Family Deli (410-778-0507), intersection of US 301 and MD 291. Open 24 hours. An alternative to McDonald's, Hardees, and other fast-food/road-food restaurants. They serve a quick, real breakfast (not on a biscuit) starting at $3.99; lunch is your choice of burgers ($2.99) and other sandwiches. Dinner is home-cooked ham, chicken, steak, or seafood, $6–12.

CRABS **Waterman's Crab House** (410-639-2261), at the foot of Sharp Street, Rock Hall. Recreational boaters come here to enjoy mounds of steamed blue crabs by the dozen the bushel (market price). Tuesday and Thursday nights feature all-you-can-eat crabs (market price). Waterman's is also known for its full rack of ribs ($15.99) and ice cream drinks, such as the Polar Bear ($5.50): ice cream, Kahlúa, and vodka. Live entertainment on the waterfront deck on Friday and Saturday nights and Sunday afternoon.

TAKE-OUT **Chestertown Natural Foods** (410-778-1677), 214 Cannon Street, Chestertown. One of the few natural-foods and -products stores on the Eastern Shore.

J & J Seafood (410-639-2325), MD 20, Rock Hall. The crabs, clams, and other seafood are purchased fresh directly from the watermen. J & J will even steam your crabs for you.

COFFEE BARS **Play It Again Sam** (410-778-2688), 108 South Cross Street, Chestertown. What a deal. All espresso drinks, none of which costs more than $2.75, are made with double shots. Teas, sandwiches, and lots of baked goodies are other reasons to visit.

SNACKS AND GOODIES **Durding's Store** (410-778-7957), Main and Sharp Streets, Rock Hall. Enjoy a myriad of ice cream concoctions while you sit at the marble counter in this authentic 1930s shop. The stainless-steel fountain is original. In step with modern times, Durding's also offers fat-free, sugar-free ice creams.

✳ Entertainment
FILM
Chestertown
Chester Theatres (410-778-2227), Washington Square. First-run movies.

Washington College (410-778-7849). The college's many different clubs, disciplines, and the Office of Campus Events sponsor several film series, festivals, and programs throughout the year, many of them with topics not found anywhere other than a college campus.

MUSIC **Gibson Performing Arts Center** (410-778-7849), Washington College campus, Chestertown. Concerts, plays, lectures, and more are presented.

NIGHTLIFE Andy's (410-778-6779), 337½ High Street, Chestertown. Andy's is a popular nightspot with live entertainment that serves a light fare of soups ($3), salads (from $3), and entrées such as the beef burrito ($5.75).

P. E. Pruitts (410-639-7454), Bayside Avenue, Rock Hall. In addition to having crowds show up for their weekend waterside live entertainment, they also have a full menu of local dishes and New Orleans–style seafood.

Also see **Waterman's Crab House** under *Where to Eat—Crabs.*

✳ Selective Shopping

ANTIQUES

Chestertown
Blue Heron (410-778-8118), 204 High Street. Antiques, collectibles, and furniture.

Chestertown Antique and Furniture Center (410-778-5777), 1 mile south of town on MD 213. Old and new furniture sold under the same roof.

Galena
Firehouse Antique Center (410-648-5639), Main Street. A multidealer shop.

ART GALLERIES

Chestertown
Washington College's Tawes Gallery (410-778-7849), Washington College campus. Ever-changing exhibits of local and student artists, and some nationally touring programs.

Chester River Artworks (410-778-

6300), Radcliffe Mill at intersection of MD 20 and MD 291. Open 11–2; closed Monday. Changing exhibits of local and regional works. Classes on every type of arts and crafts.

Kent County Arts Council (410-778-3831), Spring Avenue. The gallery for the local arts council. Also classroom space for those who want to learn arts and crafts.

Rock Hall
Rueben Rodney Gallery (410-639-2494), 5761 Main Street. Presents works of local artists in acrylics, pottery, watercolors, photography, woodcraft, and other artists' works.

BOOKSTORES

Chestertown
The Compleat Bookseller (410-778-1480), 301 High Street. There are so few bookstores on the Eastern Shore that walking into this one is a pleasure. Although the shop is small, the choice of books is extensive, and the employees are true book lovers.

Chestertown Used Bookstore (410-778-5777), 1 mile south of town on MD 213. Located inside the Chestertown Antique and Furniture Center (see *Antiques*), it claims to have more than 80,000 used books.

FARMER'S MARKETS **Chestertown Farmer's Market.** In Fountain Park on Saturday 9–noon, April through December.

✳ Special Events

May: **Annual Chestertown Tea Party** (410-778-0416), Chestertown. Celebrates May 23, 1774, when local residents boarded the *Geddes* and dumped its load of tea into the Chester River.

June: **Chestertown Annual Garden Tour** (410-778-0416), Chestertown. **Rockfish Tournament** (41-639-7611), Rock Hall.

July: **July 4th Sassafras Boat Parade** (410-648-5510), Georgetown Harbor, Georgetown. Fireworks and a parade of decorated boats. **Kent County Fair** (410-778-1661), Kent Agricultural Center, Tolchester.

August: **Betterton Beach Day and Parade** (410-348-5239), Betterton.

September: **Annual Chestertown Jazz Festival** (410-348-5528). Jazz from early afternoon to early evening in Wilmer Park on the waterfront, Chestertown. Also at the same time and place is **Art in the Park,** the sale of works by artists and craftspersons. **Rock Hall Fall Fest** (410-778-0416), Rock Hall. Arts and crafts, music, local foods, a Kid's Kourt of children's activities, oyster-shucking contest, and boat show. **Candlelight Walking Tour** (410-778-3499), Chestertown. An annual peek into many of the town's historic homes.

October: **Chester River Wildlife Exhibition and Sale** (410-778-0416), Chestertown. Decoy carving, duck- and goose-calling contests, retrieving contests, live raptor exhibit, entertainment, food, and nature and wildlife films and slide programs.

At the Head of the Bay

PENNSYLVANIA

222

Chrome

Covered Bridge

Fair Hill

273

Newark

Oakwood

Rising Sun

273

Zoo

213

FAIR HILL
N.R.M.A.

Conowingo Dam

1

222

276

274

272

Pleasant Hill

Cherry Hill

95

College Green

Covered Bridge

316 279

Paw Paw
Museum

Welcome
Center

Bayview

Upper Bay Museum &
Cecil Community
College Cultural Center

Elkton

40

Port Deposit

95

Historical Society
of Cecil County &
Elkton Arts Center

40

North East

213

301

Charlestown

Chesapeake &
Delaware Canal
Museum

Perryville

272

Chesapeake
City

C & D Canal

301

Rodgers
Tavern

Northeast River

Elk River

ELK NECK
STATE PARK

95

Chesapeake
Bay

310

301

40

Bohemia River

301

Crystal Beach

282

Earleville

213

282

DELAWARE

Cecilton

301

N

Sassafras River

Mt. Harmon
Plantation

0 1 2 3 4 5   10
Miles

© The Countryman Press

ED.

AT THE HEAD OF THE BAY—
CHESAPEAKE CITY, ELKTON,
AND NORTH EAST

I t is said that life on the Eastern Shore is determined by the water around it. At the head of the bay, where the Eastern Shore meets mainland Maryland, the land itself is defined by water.

Along its western edge is the wide Susquehanna River, delivering the water it has collected during its long journey from humble beginnings near Coopers-town, New York. At its mouth, where it empties into the bay, are the Susquehan-na Flats, shallow waters that attract nearly 90 percent of the waterfowl traveling the Atlantic Flyway. The unique style and heritage of the hunters attracted to these flats more than 100 years ago are preserved in the Upper Bay Museum in North East.

The Chesapeake Bay rings the area with miles of shoreline, while the land at the southern edge is cut by not just one, but three, waterways: the Sassafras and Bohemia Rivers and the Chesapeake & Delaware Canal (C&D).

As early as the mid-1600s, Augustine Herman proposed a canal that would reduce water travel by nearly 300 miles between Philadelphia and Baltimore. More than a century passed before surveys were done, and it was not until 1829 that the canal was completed. Today, it is the third busiest canal in the world, permitting oceangoing vessels easy passage to the bay, as well as providing scores of pleasure boaters a protected and scenic passage along the Intracoastal Water-way.

As for the land in the area, the Kentucky bluegrass has nothing on this gently rolling, coastal plain. Some of the largest and most prestigious horse farms in the country have produced a succession of thoroughbred and standardbred champi-ons. Even if the names Kelso, Northern Dancer, Bet Twice, and Two Punch mean nothing to you, you can still enjoy a ride through the countryside. Miles of wooden fences wrap around acres of lush, green fields, accented by the flying manes and rippled haunches of galloping future champions.

COMMUNITIES The history and fortunes of **Chesapeake City** are tied to the C&D Canal. As construction on the canal progressed, the town sprang up as a place to house workers and supply needed materials. For a while, the canal actu-ally supplied the construction material for the town, as many of its buildings were built from the lumber of dismantled "Susquehanna Arks" that had come across the Chesapeake Bay but were too large to pass through the locks. Chesapeake City's importance as a port faded once the federal government purchased the canal, widened and deepened it, and removed the locks in the early 20th century. Its growth was even more stunted when the construction of the arched bridge on MD 213, which soars 135 feet above the canal, enabled traffic to bypass the town.

Yet it is still one of the most picturesque spots in the area. Many of its buildings date from the early 1800s, and a walking-tour brochure available from Cecil County Tourism (see *Guidance*) provides insight into them. The view of traffic upon the wide waters of the canal makes for a stunning backdrop from the small but active "downtown" area. The Chesapeake and Delaware Canal Museum provides an accounting of the canal's and town's history, while several good restaurants and an abundance of B&Bs are reason enough to visit.

The origin of **North East** (its motto is, "not just a direction . . . it's a destination") is also tied to water. In this case, it is the Northeast River, which supplied the needs of several early mills and an ironworks. Most of its buildings are from the late 1800s and early 1900s, and many of them still stand in the busy business district—along with antiques stores, restaurants serving regional foods, and interesting shops—on Main Street.

Built upon a narrow strip of land between the Susquehanna River and towering cliffs, the entire town of **Port Deposit** is on the National Register of Historic Places. Many of its buildings are constructed from granite quarried from the cliffs; their history is revealed in a walking-tour brochure available from the Paw Paw Museum in town or from Cecil County Tourism (see *Guidance*).

Perryville gained importance in colonial days, as it sits on the eastern shore of the Susquehanna River and became a stopover for travelers taking the ferry across the river. George Washington was just one of the many people passing through here on their way to Philadelphia or Baltimore.

Elkton, with a population of close to 10,000, is the economic hub of the area. Some of its earliest structures remain to remind you of the past, although they have become mixed in with the office buildings, storefronts, and strip malls of modern America. The local historical society and art gallery are definitely worth stopping for.

GUIDANCE **Cecil County Tourism** (410-996-6290; 1-800-CECIL-95; www.see-cecil.org), 1 Seahawk Drive, Suite 114, North East, 21901.

GETTING THERE *By car:* I-95 is the main route into the region, providing easy access from Baltimore and the rest of Maryland, and from Delaware and Philadelphia. **MD 213** is the quickest roadway for those arriving from the southern portion of the Eastern Shore.

By air: **Baltimore/Washington International** (1-800-I-FLY-BWI), located between Baltimore and Annapolis, is about an hour's drive to the southwest of the Chesapeake City area. Located to the northeast, **Philadelphia International Airport** (215-937-5400) is also about an hour's drive away.

By bus: **Greyhound** (1-800-229-9424) has a station and makes stops in Elkton.

By train: **MARC** (1-800-325-RAIL), the commuter train from Baltimore, makes its final stop at Perryville on its northeastern run.

By water: If you own a boat or are chartering one, the Chesapeake Bay is the obvious way to come from mainland Maryland. Also, the Chesapeake & Delaware Canal is a part of the Intracoastal Waterway and provides access from the Delaware River and other points to the east.

GETTING AROUND *By car:* **I-95** is the way to get around quickly, but using **US 40** will give you a chance to see more of the towns along the way. Lightly traveled **US 222** and **US 1** run through the more rural northern portions of the area, while **MD 213** takes you into the southern region to the C&D Canal and Sassafras River. You can have a scenic drive and get to know this latter area intimately by purchasing the $5 **Historic Driving Tour** audiotape and map from a number of shops or from Cecil County Tourism (see *Guidance*).

By taxi: **Cox's Cab** (410-287-2797) and **Joe's Taxi** (410-287-2697) are headquartered in North East. **Maryland Cab** (410-378-4300) operates out of Port Deposit.

PARKING Municipal parking lots in North East are located off Main Street between West Street and Wallace Avenue.

PUBLIC REST ROOMS In **Chesapeake City,** a public rest room is located beside the Franklin Hall building on Bohemia Avenue.

In **North East,** rest rooms may be found in the North East Community Park off Walnut Street at the southern end of town.

MEDICAL EMERGENCY **Union Hospital of Cecil County** (410-328-4000), 106 Bow Street, Elkton, is a full-service facility with an emergency room.

✳ To See

COVERED BRIDGES Spanning a waterway within the Fair Hill Natural Resources Management Area (see *Green Space—Parks*) in Fair Hill is the **Big Elk Creek Covered Bridge.** An interesting tidbit: Construction cost for the bridge in the 1860s was $1,165; its 1992 renovation came in at an amazing $152,000.

About 3 miles north of North East on MD 272 is the 1860 **Gilpin Falls Covered Bridge.** The arches of this 119-foot bridge—the longest covered bridge still standing in the state—are

THE BIG ELK CREEK COVERED BRIDGE

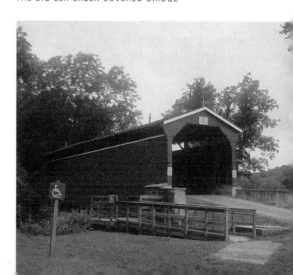

made from single timbers that were gradually warped into shape by balancing them on a pivot and pulling down on each end with cables and restraints.

MUSEUMS Chesapeake and Delaware Canal Museum (410-885-5621), 2nd Street and Bethel Road, Chesapeake City. Monday through Saturday. Free admission. Exhibits, displays, and models provide a glimpse into the canal's past. One of the models is of the James Adams Floating Theater, which worked the C&D Canal and was the inspiration for the musical *Showboat*. (Yes, *Showboat* took place on the Mississippi, but it was this boat that piqued the composer's imagination.) A computer screen shows the location of ships—in real time—as they travel the canal. Also on museum grounds is a replica of the Bethel Bridge Lighthouse—and sweeping vistas of the canal.

Historical Society of Cecil County (410-398-1790; www.cchistory.org), 135 East Main Street, Elkton. Monday noon–4 PM; Tuesday 6–8 PM; Thursday 10 AM–4 PM; and the fourth Saturday of each month 10 AM–2 PM. Free admission, but donations accepted. Housed in a former bank building (circa 1830), the society maintains exhibits relating to colonial furnishings, Victorian dollhouses, a country store, an early-American kitchen, military items, and a log house.

Upper Bay Museum (410-287-2675), Walnut Street at the North East Community Park, North East. Saturday and Sunday 11–3, but hours and days have been variable. Housed within two large buildings, the museum has a collection of materials reflecting the history of commercial and recreational hunting and fishing on the upper Chesapeake Bay. The size of the decoy collection is impressive when you realize the museum is sponsored and maintained by the local Cecil-Harford Hunters Association. The punt guns, sculling oars, and sink boxes (ask if you don't know what these are—they're interesting) sketch a vivid picture of the heady age of bay waterfowl hunting.

Paw Paw Museum (410-738-3086), 98 North Main Street, Port Deposit. Open 1–5 on the second and fourth Sunday of the month, May through October. Items relating to the history of Port Deposit include letters from Civil War soldiers and

THE SUSQUEHANNA RIVER AS SEEN FROM RODGERS TAVERN IN PERRYVILLE

HISTORIC HOMES

Mount Harmon Plantation (410-275-8819), Mount Harmon Road (off Grove Neck Road—MD 282), Earleville. Tuesday and Thursday 10–3 and Sunday 1–4, May through September. Small admission fee. In 1963, Mrs. Harry Clark Boden IV purchased the early-1700s tobacco plantation home of her ancestors. She had it restored (which included installing beautifully hand-painted Chinese wallpaper) and furnished with American, English, Irish, and Scottish antiques of the period.

A 2-mile, tree-lined drive brings you to the three-story, five-bay brick manor house. Tour guides point out the Italian marble fireplaces (the screens kept sparks and fire off ladies' dresses), the master-of-the-hunt chair, and the wooden panels along the staircase. The furnishings and artwork are some of the nicest I've seen. Make sure you see the portrait of Lady Arabella Stuart. It reminds me of a modern holograph: The image changes depending on the angle it is viewed from—but it was painted in the 1500s! (Also quite remarkable are the extraordinarily ornate bathrooms installed in the mid-1900s.) Tours also take in the plantation kitchen and the tobacco prize house. A "prize" is a large wooden screw used to compress tobacco into half its volume for more efficient shipment.

Afterward, you are free to wander around the plantation's 200 acres, enjoying the formal boxwood and wisteria gardens, or following maintained pathways along fields, forests, and creeks (ask for a trail brochure). The entire plantation is a nature preserve that protects several rare species of plants.

An example of historic preservation at its best.

photographs of the town in the 19th and 20th centuries. Ask for the story about the signature quilt, which came into being as punishment for "acting up in church."

HISTORIC SITES Rodgers Tavern (410-642-6066), 259 Broad Street, Perryville. Hours vary; call for times. George Washington, Marquis de Lafayette, Thomas Jefferson, and James Madison are just a few of the luminaries to make a stop at Rodgers Tavern. Built in the early 17th century, it served passengers using the ferry to get across the wide mouth of the Susquehanna River. Guided tours take you through the lightly furnished basement tavern, first-floor parlor and office, and second-floor sleeping accommodations. George Washington truly did sleep here! The view from the lawn is spectacular.

GUIDED TOURS Chesapeake Horse Country Tours (410-885-2797; 1-800-466-1402; www.uniglobehilltravel.com), 200 Bohemia Avenue, Chesapeake City. Offered for two to seven people by reservation from Monday through Saturday.

THE BOHEMIA STABLES OF WOODSTOCK FARM NEAR CHESAPEAKE CITY

Wayne Hill has put together a tour that provides an overview of life, in his words, "at the peak of the Chesapeake." After a walking tour of Chesapeake City, a guided van trip explores Maryland's largest land preserve, which encompasses many of the horse farms in the area. In addition to enjoying the scenery, you will learn of the DuPont family's role in reviving the horse industry here, travel through their Bohemia Stables Farm, and make a stop at the grave of Kelso, a champion stallion who was Horse of the Year an unprecedented five times. Upon his gravestone are the words, "Where he gallops, the earth sings."

ZOO ✎ **The Zoo at Plumpton Park** (410-658-6850; www.plumptonparkzoo. org), 1416 Telegraph Road (MD 273), Rising Sun. Daily 1–5, March 2 through September 30; Thursday through Monday 10–4, October 1 through March 1, weather permitting. Adults $6.75; children 2–12, $3.50; seniors over 60, $5.75. This small zoo had its beginnings as a haven for injured animals. Since then, it has accepted exotic and endangered species confiscated by U.S. Customs, and animals no longer wanted or on loan from other zoos. Because of this, there is no real theme to the park, but you do get the chance to see more than 250 animals from around the world. There are also picnic facilities, a children's playground, and a nature trail.

✳ To Do

AUTO RACING Cecil County Dragway (410-287-9105), 1573 Theodore Road, Rising Sun. From March through November you can listen to the roar of engines as various vehicles head down the quarter-mile track in Federal Mogul Points, rocket, and street races.

BOAT RENTALS Elk River Outfitters (866-LQIDFUN), 145 River Road, Elkton. Located at Locust Point Marina, a short distance north of Chesapeake City. Canoes, kayaks, day-fishing boats, and Sunfish sailboats available for rent for $20 (half day) or $40 (full day).

THINGS TO LOOK FORWARD TO
Principio Iron Works (410-642-2358), Perryville, and **Elk Landing** (410-620-6400; www.elklanding.org), Elkton, are being developed as historic sites. The Iron Works were most active before the Revolutionary War, but production continued into the 1900s. Although not in the best of shape, the manor house, furnace, and some outbuildings remain.

At the confluence of Little Elk and Big Elk Creeks, Elk Landing played a role in the colonies' earliest transportation corridor. There are big plans for both of these places, including living-history demonstrations. Check with **Cecil County Tourism** (see *Guidance*) to find out what is available while you are in the area.

THE MANOR HOUSE AT PRINCIPIO IRONWORKS

GOLF

North East and Rising Sun
Chesapeake Bay Golf Club North East (410-287-0200), 1500 Chesapeake Club Drive, and **Chesapeake Bay Golf Club Rising Sun** (410-658-4343). These two 18-hole courses are under the same management and are only 6 miles apart. The North East course is a bit more rolling and wooded than the Rising Sun course. Discounts are given if you play both of them. The food at **Blue Heron Restaurant** (at the North East course) is of higher quality than that found at many other golf clubs.

Elkton
Brantwood (410-398-8848), 1190 Augustine Herman Highway (MD 213). Championship 18-hole course with clubhouse and pro shop.
Elkton Club at Patriot's Glen (410-

392-9552; 1-800-616-1776; www.patriotsglen.com), 300 Patriots. One of the newest courses in the area, it has a par 72.

HIKING **Elk Neck State Park** (410-287-5333), 4395 Turkey Point Road, North East. (Also see *Green Space— Parks.*) Upland forests just a short distance away from the shorelines of the Chesapeake Bay and Elk River provide some of the most diverse environments found in a park on the Eastern Shore, and the best way to explore them is via the park's pathways.

The easy 1.5-mile **Red Trail** passes through a forest of beech, tulip poplar, and red, white, and chestnut oak. A dike along the 1-mile **Green Trail** overlooks a small lake and a marsh. The 2-mile **Black Trail** provides access to the shoreline of the Elk River, where you can take a swim (at your own risk—no guards). The white-blazed **Thackery Swamp Self-Guiding Nature Trail** is only 0.75 mile long, with an interpretive booklet available at the camper registration office.

The trail I enjoy most is the 2-mile **Blue Trail,** which passes through field and forest on its way to the **Turkey Point Lighthouse** and a

EARLY MORNING AT TURKEY POINT LIGHTHOUSE

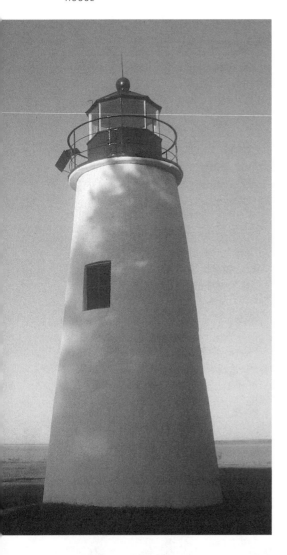

100-foot-high cliff overlooking the Chesapeake Bay and Elk River. There is absolutely no better way to greet a new dawn than to be sitting on one of the benches next to the lighthouse and watching the source of Earth's warmth rise inch by inch into the eastern sky.

Also see **Fair Hill Natural Resources Management Area** under *Green Space—Parks.*

HORSEBACK RIDING Fair Hill Stables (410-620-3883; www.fairwinds-stables.com), accessed from Entrance 3 in Fair Hill State Park on MD 273, Fair Hill. Operated by Ted and JoAnn Dawson, hosts of Tailwinds Farm (see *Lodging—Bed & Breakfasts*). Guided 1-hour trail rides ($25; $20 for children 8–12) through the woods and fields of Fair Hill Natural Resources Management Area (see *Green Space—Parks*). Pony rides (only $2) every Saturday and Sunday, noon–3. The Dawsons also offer riding lessons, and carriage and hayrides.

SUMMER CAMPS ✎ Sandy Hill Camp (410-287-5554; www.Sandy-HillCamp.com), 3380 Turkey Point Road, North East. June through August. This residential camp for boys and girls 8–16 years of age is located on 216 acres overlooking the Chesapeake Bay. There are weekend and weeklong sessions of equestrian activities, sailing, sports, English for international travel, a counselor in training program, and traditional camp activities. Eight campers and two counselors share a rustic cabin.

✳ Green Space

BEACHES Crystal Beach (410-275-8083), Earleville. Admission fee. A small, sandy public beach located along the Elk River at the end of MD 282.

PARKS Fair Hill Natural Resources Management Area (410-398-1246), 376 Fair Hill Drive, Elkton. Open sunrise to sunset. At 5,613 acres, this is one of the largest pieces of public land on the Eastern Shore. Approximately 40 miles of trails open to hikers, bicyclists, and horseback riders wander through its wood and fields and across its many water runs. A very popular place for the local equestrian community. Facilities include the Fair Hill Training Center for racehorses and a turf course, where steeplechase and flat races are held.

Elk Neck State Park (410-287-5333), 4395 Turkey Point Road, North East. In addition to a network of hiking trails (see *To Do—Hiking*), the state park offers picnic areas, a boat launch (bring your own vessel or rent one), fishing, a naturalist program, rental cabins, and a campground with bathhouses (see *To Do—Camping*). Bordered by the Elk River and the Chesapeake Bay, it is a place of grand sunrises and sunsets.

WALKS The shoreline **Riverwalk** in Port Deposit is a part of the proposed Lower Susquehanna Heritage Greenway, which will include multiple miles of trail along both sides of the Susquehanna River.

✳ Lodging

MOTELS AND HOTELS ✿ Crystal Inn (410-287-7100; 1-800-631-3803), 1 Center Drive (MD 272 at I-95 Exit 100), North East, 21901. Spacious rooms, each with microwave, refrigerator, and free local calls. Indoor pool, whirlpool, spa, fitness room, and deluxe continental breakfast. A short drive to North East, Elk Neck State Park (see *Green Space—Parks*), Elkton, and outlet shopping. One of the more pleasant motels I've stayed in. Pets permitted with deposit. $79–99.

BED & BREAKFASTS
Chesapeake City, 21915
✇ ♿ **Blue Max Inn** (410-885-2781; www.bluemaxinn.com), 300 Bohemia Avenue. Less than two blocks from the waterfront and main business area. The large porch invites guests to just sit and watch small-town life unfold as they listen to the sounds of the grand player piano coming from the living room. There are seven guest rooms; I liked the rich blue color of the Randall Room with its own balcony. The Lindsey Room on the first floor is handicapped accessible. Resident owners Wayne and Wendy Mercer serve a large breakfast in the solarium or the fireside dining room—and then provide afternoon tea and cookies. Children 10 and over welcome. $110–185.

If you are wondering about the name, it comes from a former occupant, Jack Hunter, who wrote *The Blue Max*. A best-seller, the book was adapted as a major motion picture.

✇ **Inn at the Canal** (410-885-5995; www.innatthecanal.com), 104 Bohemia Avenue. Emigrating from the Philadelphia area, Mary and Al Ioppolo opened their B&B, the first such establishment in Cecil County, in the late 1980s. They greet you upon arrival to their 1870s home with refreshments, and serve a full breakfast in the morning. Each of the six guest rooms has its own decorating theme and private bath. Far from minding the few wooden steps I had to go down to get to the bathroom in my room, I felt that it just added another historical and unique aspect to my stay. My after-dinner lounging was done on the front porch, watching the boats on the C&D Canal. Children over 10 may be welcome; call to make arrangements. $100–150.

&. **Ship Watch Inn** (410-885-5300), 410 1st Street. All eight suites have private whirlpool baths and a private balcony in this 1920s waterfront inn. Room 5 is the largest, but my choice would be Room 6 because you can see the water without even having to sit up in bed. Room 2 is handicapped accessible. A nice touch is the binoculars to watch the boats on the canal. $115–150.

North East, 21901

♂ **Tailwinds Farm** (410-658-8187; www.fairwindsstables.com), 41 Tailwinds Lane. Children over 8 are welcome. This has the feel of what B&Bs started out as. You share the Victorian farmhouse with a family—Ted and JoAnn Dawson and their children. Of two guest rooms, I liked the Blue Room with its bed in a recessed alcove. A good place to relax and enjoy the quiet beauty of a 50-acre working farm. You may bring your own horses and stable them overnight in the 17-stall barn. The Dawsons also own the **Fair Hill Stables** (see *To Do—Horseback Riding*). In fact, some of their horses were featured in Oprah Winfrey's film, *Beloved*—and JoAnn has been an actress in such films as *Twelve Monkeys* and *The Sixth Sense*. $75.

North Bay (410-287-5948), 9 Sunset Drive. Four contemporary, antiques-accented guest rooms (one with pri-

vate bath) on the headwaters of the bay. The Captain's and Harbor Rooms have their own water views. $65–95. The hosts also offer cruises on their 50-foot yacht.

Elkton, 21921

Long Creek View (410-885-2012; www.magpage.com/~lcv), 1702 Augustine Herman Highway (MD 213). Two rooms with private baths in a quiet retreat within its own woodlands. Gardens and a nature trail. $85–110.

Elk Mills, 21920

&. **Elk Forge B&B Inn and Retreat** (410-392-9007; 1-877-ELK-FORGE; www.elkforge), 807 Elk Mills Road. An intriguing place whose core is a centuries-old home, but whose additions, while modern, provide very pleasant and interesting guest rooms (each with a private bath). Harry and LeAnn Lenderman engaged artists Jeanette Robison and Vitale Sem to paint pictures in each room. Robison created one in a 1920s art deco style and painted angels floating on clouds in one of the hallways. Sem's works are more classical, such as the stunning action scene depicting George Washington at the Battle of Brandywine.

The solarium, which overlooks the yard and woodlands and contains a stained-glass window from a Pennsylvania church, is so big that a large water fountain is dwarfed inside it. LeAnn's breakfasts, served in the solarium, have portions to match the size of the room. The many miles of pathways within Fair Hill Natural Resources Management Area (see *Green Space—Parks*) can be accessed directly from the side yard.

LeAnn also operates a spa within Elk Forge that is just one more reason to stay in this most relaxing, inviting, and unique B&B. There are many thoughtful amenities for business travelers, too. $115–185.

COTTAGES **The Old Wharf Cottage** (410-885-5040; 1-877-582-4049; www.bayardhouse.com), 10 Bohemia Avenue, Chesapeake City, 21915. You cannot get any closer to the water than in this small cottage administered by the Bayard House next door. At the very edge of the land, it has served as an icehouse, tailor shop, and cargo-storage place. It is in the center of activity in town, so expect to have many passersby. $150; discounted rates for multiple-night stays.

VACATION RENTALS **Liquid Fun** (1-866-LQIDFUN; www.liquidfun.com), 145 River Road, Elkton, 21921. Liquid Fun is the umbrella name used to cover a number of businesses, including a marina, river outfitters (see *To Do—Boat Rentals*), and vacation rentals on the Elk River and the C&D Canal. All of the rental houses have nice views, and each has its own special amenities. One house sleeps two, four of the houses sleep six, and the one on the canal can accommodate four. Weekly rentals are $900–1,500.

Elk Neck State Park (1-888-432-2267), 4395 Turkey Point Road, North East, 21901. Rental cabins are available from the first weekend in May through the second weekend in October. Some are equipped with electricity, refrigerator, stove, and running water; others are more rustic with just electricity. Both types make use of a central bathhouse and are popular, so make reservations as soon as possible. (Also see To Do—Hiking and Green Space—Parks.)

Sinking Springs Herb Farm (410-392-2389; www.cecilcounty.com/Sink-Spring/), 234 Blair Shore Road (enter from 843 Elk Forest Road), Elkton, 21921. A visit to the Sinking Springs Herb Farm is like stepping into a chapter of Jethro Kloss's *Back to Eden.* There is a little bit of New Age mixed in with a lot of just good old country living. Ann and Bill Stubbs's Wellness Retreats focus on stress, health issues, nutrition, and gardening, and include yoga, massage therapy, regression hypnosis, and more. You do not have to participate in a retreat to enjoy a stay in the small and rustic, but cozy, **Garden Cottage B&B** ($95) or to make arrangements for family-style lunch with Ann and Bill in their 1700s home. The quiche, bread, and vegetables (all with fresh herbs) I had were a welcome taste of delicious home-cooked food after I'd been on the road for a long time.

Within a couple of outbuildings are a gift shop offering the Stubbs's herbs and dried-flower arrangements, and the studio of painter Carol Mangano. Walking trails wander around the herb and flower gardens and throughout the farm's 130 acres. Be sure to stop and pay homage to the huge sycamore tree next to the house. It was already full grown when Shakespeare was but a teenager.

CAMPING Riverside Ponderosa Pines (410-642-3431), 1435 Carpenter's Point Road, Perryville, 21903; **Riverview** (410-642-6200), 1200 Frenchtown Road, Perryville, 21903; and **Woodlands** (410-398-4414), 265 Starkey Lane, Elkton, 21921, cater primarily to those with RVs.

🐾 For a more rustic experience, check into the campground at **Elk Neck State Park** (see *To Do—Hiking*). Pets on a leash are permitted in certain sites.

✳ Where to Eat

DINING OUT

Chesapeake City
Bayard House (410-885-5040; www.bayardhouse.com), 11 Bohemia Avenue. Open for lunch and dinner. Some of the most pleasurable dining in the area is found in this structure, built decades before the construction of the C&D Canal. Once a private home, it has been a restaurant or tavern since 1829. Restored in 1985, its ambience, quality of food, and sweeping water vista make it a favorite "special-occasion" restaurant.

The award-winning Maryland crab soup ($5.75) is spicy without being hot, and is full of crab. One of the most popular entrées, the Anaheim peppers ($25) are stuffed with lobster, crabmeat, and shrimp and baked with green chile salsa and cheddar cheese. It is simply luscious. Even side dishes are prepared with thought. The au gratin potatoes are made rich and creamy by adding sour cream, cheddar cheese, chives, and smoked bacon.

Other entrées include salmon with watercress and artichokes ($23) and broiled crabcakes ($25). Especially indulgent are the twin filets mignons ($26), one topped with a crabcake, the other with a lobster cake. If with a group, try the petits fours ($4.75) for dessert. Each of you will get to try a variety of flavors, textures, and tastes.

Chesapeake Inn (410-885-2040; www.chesapeakeinn.com), 605 2nd Street. Open for lunch and dinner. Upscale waterfront dining with a bit of a Mediterranean flavor to the menu. Popular items are the crab ravioli ($19) and the shellfish Sicilian ($25) with five different types of shellfish. I made a full lunch out of the seafood quesadilla ($13).

Elkton
Fair Hill Inn (410-398-4187), at the intersection of MD 213 and MD 273 north of Elkton. Open for lunch and dinner. Anthony Grazianof and son Peter have been offering Eastern Shore fare with a bit of a French-Italian twist for more than two decades inside this mid-1700s inn. Although the inn was restored, many original items remain, such as the huge stone fireplace and the original pass-through.

The pasta, garlic, and wilted greens ($13.95) reminded me of dishes my Italian-descent mother used to make. My dinner companion enjoyed his jumbo shrimp served in curry cream sauce ($19.95). We split the flavorful appetizer of crabmeat-stuffed mushroom caps ($7.50). Other meat, poultry, seafood, and pasta entrées range $13.95–27.95.

The dining area is actually four rooms, so you never feel like you are in a crowd. For an even more romantic setting, order the Classic for Two dinner and have your seafood Beatrice ($58), châteaubriand ($56), or rack of lamb ($58) prepared tableside.

North East

Windows on Main (410-287-3512), 101 South Main Street. Open for lunch and dinner. After operating the **Tavern on Main** (410-287-8761) for a number of years, Barbara and Ed Landis opened this restaurant next door to offer customers a bit more refined dining. It is a comfortable place with heavy wood tables, and books scattered about for you to leaf through. The two tables in the window alcoves are the coveted seats. The lunch sandwiches and soups ($3.25–5.95) are offered at dinner. The 24-ounce porterhouse steak ($18.95) doused in a Jack Daniels pepper-and-mushroom sauce was moist and tasty, but so large that I left with more than half of it in a doggy bag. The folks at the next table enjoyed their rockfish with crab imperial ($18.95) and fish-and-chips ($11.95). Other entrées $10.95–19.95.

Port Deposit

Union Hotel (410-378-3503), 1282 Susquehanna Road. Open for lunch and dinner. Closed Monday. The hotel was built of hemlock logs around 1783 to cater to the needs of travelers on the Susquehanna Canal. Janet Dooling has been overseeing the restaurant a little over 20 years, serving soups, salads, sandwiches, and light entrées for lunch. I was here with three others, and we all agreed on the watercress and spinach quiche ($7.95). Dinner is a bit more formal and hearty. Sambuca shrimp and scallops ($18.95) is popular, as is the grilled rack of lamb ($22.95). A couple of dishes reflect the hotel's earlier days: Sautéed veal liver with bacon and onions ($17.95) and maple-mustard pork loin ($16.95).

Chesapeake City

Yacht Club Restaurant (410-885-2267), 225 Bohemia Avenue. Open for lunch and dinner. Chef Gary Klunk has no formal training, yet most of the Yacht Club's savory offerings are his recipes. It was hard deciding which appetizer to try: the escargot ($6.95) over a pastry puff, sautéed spinach, and hazelnut butter, or the crab and corn chowder ($4.95). The gazpacho with lump crab ($4.95) I settled on did not disappoint. The chicken Chesapeake ($14.95) was rubbed in Old Bay seasoning and topped with crabmeat in a luscious cream sauce—a nice variation on an old standard. Sandwiches (from $6.95) are served at lunch, and seafood ($14.95–22.95), meat (up to $19.95), and pasta dishes (around $13.95) at dinner.

I liked the waiters' attentive but non-intrusive service, as well as the old photos of Chesapeake City on the walls. Gary and co-owner Cheri Wilson did such a good job of renovating that you would never imagine you are eating in a former hardware store. As a nice touch, you are treated to a horse-drawn carriage ride if you leave your car at the public parking lot under the MD 213 bridge on Friday, Saturday, or Sunday night.

North East

Pier One (410-287-65990, 1 North Main Street. Pam and Vinny Cirino have been operating this popular diner-style place since the late 1990s. Like most diners, it has an extensive menu of sandwiches, pastas, meats, and seafoods. $10.95–20.95.

CRABS *Woody's Crab House* (410-287-3541), 29 South Main Street,

North East. Open for lunch and dinner. A classic Maryland crab house with brown paper tablecloths and a concrete floor (on which you are expected to throw the shells from the complimentary peanuts served with every meal). Steamed crabs in Woody's own spice blend (market price) are the obvious choice, but people also come here for the steamed sack of 50 shrimp ($15.95) or big bucket of littleneck clams ($15.95). My dining mate and I couldn't decide, so we ordered the Net Buster ($27.95), with enough lobster, crabcake, crab imperial, two varieties of shrimp, clams, and fresh fish to satisfy us both. A crowded, noisy, and fun atmosphere.

COFFEE BARS Beans, Leaves, Etc. (410-287-8033), 33 South Main Street, North East. Coffees, teas, and gourmet foods.

SNACKS AND GOODIES Canal Creamery (410-885-3314), 9 Bohemia Avenue, Chesapeake City. With outdoor seating right on the waterfront, this is the best spot for homemade ice cream on a hot afternoon or as an after-dinner treat. Also serves light lunch and dinner items.

✳ Entertainment
THEATERS
North East
Cecil Community College Cultural Center (410-287-1037), I-95 Exit 100. Dance, music, and theatrical productions are presented here. The local Covered Bridge Theatre Company does at least three presentations annually, two of which are musicals.

✳ Selective Shopping
ANTIQUES
Chesapeake City
Antique Turtle (410-274-2450), 3rd Street and Bohemia Avenue. Its logo is "The odd, old, and curious."

North East
5 and 10 Antique Market (410-287-6565), 115 South Main Street. Eighty dealers housed within a former hotel (which was also a five-and-dime store). **North Chesapeake Antique Mall** (410-287-3938), 2288 Pulaski Highway. Another multidealer shop, this one is on US 40 north of town.

ART GALLERIES
Chesapeake City
McKeown Gallery on the Canal (410-885-3653), 19A Bohemia Avenue. Geraldine McKeown displays and sells her own works and those of other local and regional artists and craftspersons.
Neil's Artwork (410-885-5094), 226 George Street. Neil's works focus on the scenery of the upper Chesapeake Bay.

Elkton
Elkton Arts Center (410-392-5740; www.CecilCountyArtsCouncil.org), 135 East Main Street. The home of the extremely active Cecil County Arts Council. Their calendar of events includes changing exhibits of regional artists and craftspersons, classes, concerts, dance recitals, readings, lectures, and more.

North East
Chesapeake Gallery and Frame Shop (410-287-5300), 17 South Main Street. Primarily a frame shop, but it does feature the works of some very competent local artists.

BOOKSTORES Charing Cross Books (410-287-2002), 112 South Main Street, North East. A small store that also carries greeting cards and gift items.

USED BOOKS Bookseller's Antiques (410-287-8652), 35 South Main Street, North East. Used books and old papers.

CRAFTS England's Colony on the Bay (410-287-5575), 505 South Main Street, North East. There are many touristy items in here, but be sure to stop in to take a look at the decoys and birds carved by local artisans.

SPECIAL SHOPS

Chesapeake City
Back Creek General Store (410-885-5377), 100 Bohemia Avenue. It is worth it to step into this shop, which has been restored to its 1800s makeup with original shelving and glass cabinets.

Back to Nature (410-885-3148), 108 Bohemia Avenue. Gifts and other items with a nature theme.

North East
Day Basket Factory (410-287-6100; www.daybasketfactory.com), 714 South Main Street. Although no longer owned by the Day family, the factory is still making baskets in the same manner it has done for more than 125 years. Each piece of local white oak is split and woven by hand into utilitarian and ornamental baskets. If the craftspersons are at work, ask to take a quick tour, and you will see why these baskets, which have only copper and brass fittings—not steel—put those marketed by Longaberger to shame. Day baskets are also guaranteed for life.

OUTLET Prime Outlets (410-378-9399), I-95 Exit 93, Perryville. Includes the outlet shops of Nike, L'eggs, Carole Little, Van Heusen, OshKosh B'Gosh, Book Cellar, and more than 35 other nationally known names.

PICK-YOUR-OWN PRODUCE FARMS
Elkton
✿ **Milburn Orchards** (410-398-1349; www.milburnorchards.com), 1945 Appleton Road (MD 316). The orchards have been in the Milburn family for more than 100 years, and the Milburns have learned a few things about growing and marketing produce. Their U-pick selections include cherries in early summer, peaches in midsummer, and apples in early fall. Lots of fun kid's activities throughout the season with a playground, petting zoo, and barnyard animals. Hayrides, crafts shows, corn maze, and other activities in the fall. The farm market (open July 5 through the last Saturday in January) sells not only produce but also some delicious home-baked goodies.

Walnut Springs Farm (410-398-3451), Blue Ball Road. U-pick fruits and seasonal events.

✳ Special Events

April: **Grandma's Attic and Spring Festival** (410-378-9136), Port Deposit. Yard and bake sales, crafts, and food on Main Street. **Red Heart American Indian Festival** (410-885-2800), Fair Hill Fairgrounds, Fair Hill.

May: **Spring Fling** (410-642-6066), Rodgers Tavern, 259 Broad Street, Perryville. Entertainment, crafts, food, and exhibits. **Highland Gathering** (410-885-2005), Fair Hill Race

Track, Fair Hill. A gathering of the clans for dance, piping, drumming, sheep dog demonstrations, and food.

June and July: **Summer Music in the Park** (410-392-5740), Pell Gardens, Chesapeake City. Free outdoor concerts ranging from bluegrass to rock 'n' roll. Sunday evening at 6 PM.

June: **Annual Mid-Atlantic Chevelle Show** (410-879-7893), Community Park, North East. Scores of Chevelles from 1964 to 1987. **Canal Day** (410-885-3132), Chesapeake City. A street festival with arts, crafts, food, and music.

July: **Cecil County Fair** (410-398-8544), Fair Hill Fairgrounds, Fair Hill.

August: **Susquehanna River Festival** (410-378-4133), Port Deposit. Entertainment and a crab feast.

September: **Annual Juried Exhibition** (410-392-5740), Elkton Arts Center, 135 East Main Street, Elkton. Works by regional artists. **Yesterdays**

(410-287-5801). North East celebrates its heritage with street entertainment, demonstrations, children's activities, crafts, music, and a evening ghost walk. **Port Deposit Heritage Day** (410-378-4480). Port Deposit commemorates its history with crafters, demonstrations, children's activities, performing arts, and tours of some of its historic homes and buildings.

October: **Annual Upper Bay Rockfish Tournament** (410-392-3833), Community Park, North East. **Harvest Fall Festival** (410-287-5333), Elk Neck State Park, 4395 Turkey Point Road, North East. Lots of fun for the kids with pumpkin painting, hayrides, scarecrow making, piñatas, and a costume parade. **Festival in the Country** (410-755-6065), Fair Hill Natural Resources Management Area, 376 Fair Hill Drive, Fair Hill. International-level equestrian championships and dog agility trials.

Central Maryland

HARFORD COUNTY—HAVRE DE
GRACE, ABERDEEN, AND BEL AIR

NORTH OF BALTIMORE—OWINGS
MILLS, HUNT VALLEY, WESTMIN-
STER, AND TANEYTOWN

BALTIMORE

WEST OF BALTIMORE—ELLICOTT
CITY AND COLUMBIA

ANNAPOLIS AND VICINITY

Central Maryland

HARFORD COUNTY—HAVRE DE GRACE, ABERDEEN, AND BEL AIR

Harford County is a place of transition. Its southern portion lies on the Coastal Plain, with the low, flat type of terrain and access to the Chesapeake Bay most often associated with the Eastern Shore. Yet north of I-95, the land rises quickly to the Piedmont Plateau, a landscape of rolling hills and deep gorges created by swiftly moving streams and waterfalls.

Water used to play a more important part in citizens' livelihoods than it does today. During the 1800s, the Susquehanna & Tidewater Canal carried timber, wheat, coal, and other products from Wrightsville, Pennsylvania, to Havre de Grace, but use of the canal declined with the coming of the railroads. Some of the best waterfowl hunting in the world was along the Susquehanna Flats, where the Susquehanna River meets the Chesapeake Bay. Many local residents became commercial hunters, and many more catered to the thousands of sport hunters who flocked to the area. The decline in waterfowl population and needed strict regulations brought that way of life to an end in the 1960s.

Like all metropolitan areas, Baltimore is ever-expanding, and Harford County started becoming one of its bedroom communities around the 1970s. In fact, a large percentage of the population is now employed in the Baltimore metro area or is engaged in meeting the needs of those who are. It only takes a short drive on a country road to see how quickly living in housing developments is becoming the norm.

Yet a quick drive, especially into the northern and eastern reaches of the county, will also reveal that much of the beauty of the land survives. Susquehanna and Rocks State Parks preserve thousands of acres along waterways, and large farms still provide large, pleasing-to-the-eye, open spaces.

Havre de Grace's location next to the water would have, by itself, ensured that it was the county's most scenic town. But it has also managed to become a 21st-century travel destination without damaging its earlier architecture and small-town atmosphere. Elegant Victorian homes line Union Avenue, waterfront parks abound, and independent businesses—not national chains—still occupy the downtown area.

Havre de Grace has dubbed itself the "Decoy Capital of the World," and its Decoy Museum goes a long way in substantiating that claim. The Susquehanna Museum chronicles the days when the town was the southern terminus for the

PENNSYLVANIA

Whiteford
Fiore Winery
136
623
1
Eden Mill
Park
Pylesville
23
543
136
165
24
ROCKS
STATE
PARK
440
1
161
SUSQUEHANNA
STATE PARK
Jarrettsville
1
Ladew Topiary Gardens
152
23
Churchville
155
165
22
Havre de Grace
HARFORD COUNTY
BALTIMORE COUNTY
Fallston
Bel Air 543
136
Welcome
Center
40
Aberdeen
83
24
Jervale Mill &
Jericho Covered Bridge
Kingsville
7
ABERDEEN
PROVING
GROUNDS
1
Edgewood
695
Baltimore

CECIL COUNTY

Susquehanna River

Bush River

Chesapeake Bay

N

0 1 2 3 4 5   10
Miles

© The Countryman Press

Susquehanna & Tidewater Canal, while the Maritime Museum tells the story of
the waters around the town. A favorite activity of residents and visitors alike is
the simple joy of walking The Promenade, a boardwalk along the shoreline.

COMMUNITIES **Aberdeen** was originally called Hall's Cross Roads but was
renamed when the Wilmington & Baltimore Railroad's first station manager
asked that it be changed to the name of his hometown in Scotland. It was an
important transshipment center but truly began to grow after the establishment
of the military's Aberdeen Proving Grounds in 1917. Aberdeen's most well-
known site celebrates the town's favorite son, baseball legend Cal Ripken Jr.

Bel Air is the county seat, which, in addition to its administrative functions, primarily serves as a retail hub for the thousands of homes and housing developments that began to ring around it in the late 1900s. The nearby community
college has an active Center for Cultural Arts, and the Ma and Pa Railroad Trail
provides a pleasant diversion from urban activity.

GUIDANCE The **Discover Harford County Tourism Council** (410-575-7278; 1-800-597-2649; www.harfordmd.com) has a visitors center located in a downtown location at 3 West Bel Air Avenue, Aberdeen, 21001.

Information specific to the Havre de Grace area may be obtained through the **Havre de Grace Tourism Commission** (410-939-8810; 1-800-851-7756; www.hdg-tourism.com), 712 Giles Street, Havre de Grace, 21708.

A state visitors center, the **Maryland House Travel Center** (410-272-0176), is on I-95 between Exits 80 and 85, and can provide information on the local area as well as the entire state.

GETTING THERE *By car:* **I-95** is the main route into the region, providing easy access from Baltimore and the rest of Maryland, and from Delaware and Philadelphia.

By air: **Baltimore/Washington International Airport** (1-800-I-FLY-BWI), located between Baltimore and Annapolis, is less than an hour's drive to the southwest. Located to the northeast, **Philadelphia International Airport** (215-937-5400) is a bit more than an hour's drive away.

By bus: **Greyhound** (1-800-229-9429) has a station and makes stops in Aberdeen.

By train: As a part of its Washington, D.C.–New York route, **AMTRAK** (1-800-USA-RAIL) has a station in Aberdeen and makes a stop there. **MARC** (1-800-325-RAIL), the **commuter train** from Baltimore, makes stops in Edgewood and Aberdeen.

By water: If you own a boat, or are chartering one, the Chesapeake Bay is the obvious way to arrive. Also, the Chesapeake & Delaware Canal is a part of the Intracoastal Waterway and provides access from the Delaware River and other points to the east.

GETTING AROUND *By car:* **I-95** is the way to get around quickly. **US 40** is also a four-lane highway, but it has a tendency to bring you by the faded parts of the county. **US 1** runs through the more rural, central portions of the area, while **MD 136** in the very northern part of the county is a designated **State Scenic Byway.**

By bus: **Harford County Transportation Services** (410-612-1621) has several bus routes that operate in towns along the I-95/US 40 corridor, and one that runs into Bel Air.

By taxi: In Havre de Grace, you can call **DP Cab** (410-939-1133), **Montville Taxi** (410-939-0900), or **Poole's Taxi** (410-939-2506). **Victory Cabs** (410-272-0880), **Dollar Cab** (410-273-6099), and **Aberdeen Cab** (410-272-3200) operate out of Aberdeen.

PARKING In Havre de Grace, parking lots are located near the water at the foot of Franklin Street, in town at the corner of North Union and Pennington Avenues, and at the Havre de Grace Yacht Basin next to Millard E. Tydings Memorial Park.

PUBLIC REST ROOMS In Havre de Grace, you can find public rest rooms in Millard E. Tydings Memorial Park along the southern end of The Promenade, and in small Hutchins Memorial Park at the foot of Congress Avenue near the center of town.

MEDICAL EMERGENCY Harford Memorial Hospital (410-843-5000), 501 South Union Street, Havre de Grace.

Upper Chesapeake Medical Center (410-643-1000), 500 Upper Chesapeake Drive, Bel Air.

✳ To See

COLLEGES Harford Community College (410-836-4000; www.harford.cc.md. us), 401 Thomas Run Road, Bel Air. Most community colleges go about their business of providing an education but are not known for their cultural arts offerings to the local community. Not the case here. The **Center for Cultural Arts** is very active in presenting concerts, plays, musicals, dance theater, and a changing gallery of works of art.

COVERED BRIDGES See **Jerusalem Mill** under *Historic Sites*.

MUSEUMS

Havre de Grace

Havre de Grace Decoy Museum (410-939-3739; www.decoymuseum.com), 215 Giles Street. Open daily 11–4. Small admission fee. The excellence and quantity of decoys here rivals that of the larger Ward Museum of Wildlife Art in Salisbury on the Eastern Shore (see *To See—Museums* in "Salisbury"). The exhibits include working decoys (hand-carved and factory-produced), decorative decoys, and those made by local, but nationally known, craftspersons. Do not overlook the superb diorama of a decoy carver's shop or the upstairs picture windows' sweeping view of the bay.

Susquehanna Museum of Havre de Grace (410-939-5780), Erie and Conesto Streets. Saturday and Sunday 1–5, May through October. Small admission fee. The Susquehanna & Tidewater Canal provided a water transportation system between Philadelphia and Baltimore from the early 1800s to 1900. Although much has changed at this site, which was the canal's southern terminus, you can still get a feel for the early days by walking along a short section of the towpath and across the pivot bridge. Volunteers take visitors into the lock house furnished with Victorian-period reproductions. The 1782 survey map of the town also helps bring things into perspective.

Havre de Grace Maritime Museum (410-939-4800), 100 Lafayette Street. One of the newest cultural assets in Havre de Grace, the Maritime Museum preserves the heritage of the area with artifacts, photographs, and memorabilia. It is also home to the **Chesapeake Wooden Boat Builders School** (see *To Do—Boatbuilding School*).

Steppingstone Museum (410-939-2299), 461 Quaker Bottom Road (accessed from I-95 Exit 89). A stone farmhouse and several outbuildings preserve and demonstrate the 1880–1920 rural lifestyle and crafts of the region. (Also see *To Do—Special Classes*.)

Aberdeen

U.S. Army Ordnance Museum (410-278-3602), Maryland and Aberdeen Boulevards, on the Aberdeen Proving Grounds. Open daily 10–4:45; the outside exhibits are open during daylight hours. Free admission. An amazingly extensive collection of military hardware that is sure to be of interest to military-history students. Inside are technological breakthroughs that made history, such as body armor, the Gatling gun, and a V-2 rocket. Many items are the last ones of their kind. The outside 225-acre lot contains more than 200 tanks and vehicles from around the world, dating from World War I to the present.

✂ **The Ripken Museum** (410-273-2525), 3 West Bel Air Avenue. Open daily during the summer; Friday through Monday, Labor Day through Memorial Day. Small admission fee. Although small, the Ripken Museum paints a good picture of the lives of the Baltimore Orioles' most famous family of players, Cal, Cal Jr., and Billy Ripken. Lots of memorabilia, and the interactive trivia game is a lot of fun. *Note:* The museum is scheduled to move into much larger quarters sometime in the near future. Call for the latest information.

Bel Air

Hays House Museum (410-838-1213; www.harfordhistory.net), 324 Kenmore Avenue. Sunday 1–4. Donations accepted. Currently the repository for the Historical Society of Harford County's collection of artifacts, furniture, and other items. The house still has its original staircase, mantels, woodwork, and shutters.

TANKS ON DISPLAY AT THE U.S. ARMY ORDNANCE MUSEUM

HISTORIC SITES Rock Run Grist Mill, in Susquehanna State Park (also see *To Do—Hiking*), north of Havre de Grace. Located next to the Susquehanna River, the Rock Run Grist Mill was built by John Stump in 1794. It still works, and grinding demonstrations are presented on a scheduled basis. The building to the left of the parking area is the Jersey Toll House, built for the toll collector of the Susquehanna River Bridge, which was destroyed by ice floes in 1856. It is now the information center for the park. To get a better understanding of the mill and its heyday, pick up the historic walking-tour brochure from the information center. On the easy 45-minute journey you will learn how the mill operated, and pass by the springhouse, the miller's home, and the stone Rock Run House.

Jerusalem Mill (410-877-3560; www.JerusalemMill.org), 2813 Jerusalem Road (off MD 152), Kingsville. The Friends of Jerusalem Mills have restored the 18th-century mill and several other buildings that were a part of a Quaker settlement that prospered for two centuries. A small museum, and living-history demonstrations presented from time to time, provide background information. The circa-1865 **Jericho Covered Bridge** is nearby and was an important part of the community.

HISTORIC CHURCHES
Churchville
Calvary and Cokesbury United Methodist Churches (410-734-6920), 1321 Calvary Road. The oldest continuously operating original Methodist church on Maryland's western shore, it still has many of its 1821 features—including the slave gallery.

LIGHTHOUSE Concord Point Lighthouse (410-939-0768), Concord and Lafayette Streets, Havre de Grace. Saturday and Sunday 1–5, April through October. No admission fee; donations accepted. Built of nearby Port Deposit

ROCK RUN GRIST MILL

granite in 1827, this is one of the oldest continuously operating lighthouses in the United States, and possibly the oldest in Maryland. Other than its electric light, it has been restored, with lighthouse-keeper furnishings and other accoutrements, to appear as it did in the 19th century.

Being at the end of The Promenade (see *Green Space—Walks*) and overlooking the point where the Susquehanna River meets the Chesapeake Bay, this is a great spot to sit, walk, or picnic even if the lighthouse is not open.

✳ To Do

AIR RIDES UltraFlight UltraFun (410-688-1027; 1-877-367-2359; www.forafly.com), 309-U St. Johns Street, Havre de Grace. Short introductory lessons and hour-long flights on an ultralight float aircraft. The trips start out by skimming across the water before taking you up for a bird's-eye view of the Susquehanna River and the Chesapeake Bay. In fact, with such a small amount of machinery and materials keeping you aloft, this is probably the closest you can get to feeling like a bird.

BICYCLING See *Kayaking and Canoeing.*

BOAT EXCURSIONS Skipjack *Martha Lewis* (410-939-4078; 1-800-406-0766), at the Concord Point Lighthouse, Concord and Lafayette Streets, Havre de Grace. The *Martha Lewis,* owned by the Chesapeake Heritage Conservancy and one of the last remaining oyster dredge boats, offers 75-minute Discovery Cruises to the public. Cruises depart at noon, 1:30 PM, and 3 PM on Saturday and Sunday, April through October. Reservations are not needed, but be mindful that the sailboat is limited to only 28–30 passengers.

BOATBUILDING SCHOOL Chesapeake Wooden Boat Builders School (410-939-4800), 100 Lafayette

CONCORD POINT LIGHTHOUSE

SKIPJACK *MARTHA LEWIS* MOORED IN HAVRE DE GRACE

Street, Havre de Grace. Located within the Havre de Grace Maritime Museum (see *To See—Museums*). Here is a chance to learn a true craft whose product is just as useful and beautiful today as it was in decades past. Classes include antique canoe repair and restoration, model-ship building, and basic wooden-boat building. There are always a number of boats in various stages of construction, so stop by to see the process even if you are just visiting the museum.

BOWLING Bowl Harford Lanes (410-272-3555), 20 Custis Street, Aberdeen.

GOLF Bulle Rock (410-939-8887; 1-888-285-5375), 320 Bleinheim Lane, Havre de Grace. Bulle Rock is a Pete Dye course that opened in the late 1990s to favorable reviews from numerous golfing magazines.

Beechtree (410-297-9700; 1-877-233-2487; www.beechtreegolf.com), 811 South Stepney Road, Aberdeen. Designed by Tom Doak to make use of the natural lay of the land. The front nine are played in rolling, open meadows, and the back nine wander through woodlands.

MINIATURE GOLF 🎨 Churchville Golf and Baseball (410-879-5357; www.churchvillegolf.com), 3040 Churchville Road, Churchville. Batting cages and miniature golf.

HIKING A 20-mile section of the 190-mile **Mason-Dixon Trail System,** which branches off the **Appalachian Trail (AT)** in Cumberland County, Pennsylvania, passes through Harford County and Susquehanna State Park (see below). Some of it follows roadways, yet it is a scenic hike with a number of views of the Susquehanna River. More information may be obtained by writing 719 Oakburne Road, West Chester, PA 19382.

As it comes through the county, the Mason-Dixon Trail System shares its footpath with a portion of the **Lower Susquehanna Heritage Greenway,** a proposed system of trails that will include multiple miles of pathways along both sides of the Susquehanna River. Approximately 10 miles of the trail that run from Havre de Grace to Susquehanna State Park (see below) have been marked and are easy to follow. The Lower Susquehanna Heritage Greenway, Inc. (410-475-2182; www. marylandhistoricaltrust.net/ha-lsusq.html), 4948 Conowingo Road, Darlington, MD 21304, can provide maps and up-to-date information.

Susquehanna State Park (410-557-7994), north of Havre de Grace along the Susquehanna River on Stafford and Rock Run Roads. The waters of the Susquehanna River rise in Otsego County, New York, and flow for more than 400 miles to empty into the head of the Chesapeake Bay, close to where the river separates central Maryland from the Eastern Shore. Protecting a portion of the river's drainage just before it meets the bay is 3,600-acre Susquehanna State Park.

A network of approximately 15 miles of pathways enables you to explore this varied topography of riverside vegetation, heavy forest cover, lightly flowing brooks, rock outcrops with grandstand views of the river, and interesting history (see **Rock Run Grist Mill** under *To See—Historic Sites*). In addition, the park offers a campground with rest rooms and hot showers, a picnic area, boat-launch facility, and evening interpretive programs.

Rocks State Park (410-557-7994), 3318 Rocks Chrome Hill Road, Jarretsville. Deer Creek has cut a gorge into the Piedmont Plateau, creating a rugged scenery of large boulders, interesting rock formations, and steep cliffs. The park's trail system winds through the irregular landscape, going down to the creek and up to the heights. Don't miss the route to the **King and Queen's Seat.** These rock outcrops, close to 200 feet above the creek, look down onto some pretty dramatic views.

THE SUSQUEHANNA RIVER AS VIEWED FROM SUSQUEHANNA RIVER STATE PARK

Located nearby, and administered by the state park, are **Hidden Valley Natural Area** with additional trails, and **Falling Branch,** the state's second highest vertical waterfall.

Also see *Green Space—Parks* and *Walks.*

KAYAKING AND CANOEING Moon River Tours/Starkk Moon Kayaks (410-939-9500; www.moonrivertours. com), 500 Warren Street, Havre de Grace. Half-day, day, weekend, and weekly rentals in addition to guided trips that not only take you on the water but also include a bit of instruction along the way. Bicycles rentals, too.

SAILING BaySail (410-939-2869; www.baysail.net), 100 Bourbon Street, Tidewater Marina, Havre de Grace. BaySail is a one-stop sailing shop. Their school, which offers courses for beginners on up to bareboat-charter certification, is certified by the American Sailing Association. Once you gain a bit of proficiency, you can set out on your own cruise with a charter boat rented by the half day, day, or week— or buy a boat of your own from Bay-Sail. If you don't have the time to gain the needed expertise, just ask them to include a captain with your charter boat.

SPECIAL CLASSES Steppingstone Museum (410-939-2299), 461 Quaker Bottom Road (accessed from I-95 Exit 89), Havre de Grace. The museum sponsors historical crafts workshops in early spring, usually in May. (Also see *To See—Museums.*)

SWIMMING Deer Creek passes through **Rocks State Park** (see *Hik-*

ing) in Jarretsville, within the deep gorge it has cut into the land, and is a popular swimming and tubing stream. Be aware that you are on your own; there are no lifeguards.

TENNIS Courts open to the public are located in a number of the parks operated by the Harford County Department of Parks and Recreation. Among the many are **Francis Silver Park** on Shuresville Road, **Churchville Recreation Complex, Forest Hill Recreation Complex,** and **Norrisville Recreation Complex.** More information may be obtained by calling 410-638-3572.

✳ Green Space

PARKS 🐾 ♿ **Eden Mill Park and Nature Center** (410-836-3050; www.edenmill.org), 1617 Eden Mill Road, Pylesville. The Nature Center, located in an old mill building, is one of the most impressive I have seen in a county-operated park. Lots of good displays for the kids and a very active volunteer group that presents programs on a wide variety of topics. The park's trail system is well thought out. In just 2 miles, it can take hikers through a variety of environments along Deer Creek, into small meadows, and over a low ridge. There are also several public canoe-launch sites; one is handicapped accessible.

WALKS The Promenade in Havre de Grace is a half-mile boardwalk along the waterfront with interpretive signs explaining the natural and human history of the area. Because it starts at **Millard E. Tydings Memorial Park,** goes by the **Decoy** and **Maritime Museums,** and ends at the **Concord Point Lighthouse,** it is a

GARDENS

✐ **Ladew Topiary Gardens** (410-557-9570; www.LadewGardens.com), 3535 Jarretsville Pike, Monkton. Monday through Friday 10–4, Saturday and Sunday 10:30–5, mid-April through October 31. Admission to the gardens and nature walk is $8 adults, $7 seniors/students, and $2 children. Admission for the gardens, nature walk, and a guided tour of the house is $12 adults, $11 senior/students, and $4 children.

Expect to spend several hours to appreciate all that is here. In fact, bring your lunch or eat in the **Ladew Café** and devote a half day to walking, relaxing, and enjoying the gardens' 22 acres and house.

Between 1929 and 1971, Henry S. Ladew developed 15 gardens, each with a different theme, form, and color. Among them are the **Woodland Garden** (the first to bloom in spring), the **Berry Garden** (designed to be bright and colorful in winter and to provide forage for birds), and the **Yellow Garden** (with its variety of yellow blossoms throughout the season). I found that as I walked from one to the other, the landscaping created angles of vegetation that were pleasing to the eye and drew me along in anticipation of what was around the next bend.

The centerpiece, of course, is the **Topiary Garden** with its sculpted unicorn, seahorses, Churchill's top hat and victory sign, birds in flight, and more. Very young children will enjoy the animal sculptures, while older teens will appreciate the work and talent that went into creating them.

The **Manor House** is also a tribute to Ladew's vision. It was nothing more than a farmhouse when he purchased it in 1929. It is now a place of such architectural character and lavishness, tempered with an eye toward quality, that one of its rooms, the **Oval Library,** is included in the book *100 Most Beautiful Rooms in America.*

FANCIFUL SHRUBBERY AT LADEW TOPIARY GARDENS IN MONKTON

convenient way to see the sites without having to drive. Looking out upon the Chesapeake Bay, it as also a great place to be for sunrise and sunset. This is surely one of the nicest gifts the citizens of Havre de Grace have given themselves and visitors to enhance the quality of town life.

The Ma and Pa Trail in Bel Air follows an easy, nearly level old railroad grade through the town of Bel Air and out into the countryside. Several miles are usable now; when completed it will total 7 miles in length.

✳ Lodging

MOTELS AND HOTELS

Edgewood, 21040

⌇ & **Comfort Inn** (410-679-0770; 1-800-221-2222), 1700 Van Bibber Road (accessed from I-95 Exit 77). Within easy driving distance of many area attractions. Lots of extras, including complimentary deluxe continental breakfast, HBO, in-room coffeemakers, and an outdoor pool. Children 18 and under stay free. $69–109.

🐾 **Best Western** (410-679-9700), 1709 Edgewood Road (accessed from I-95 Exit 77). Operated by the same management corporation as the Comfort Inn, it offers the same amenities but also has an exercise room and permits small pets (with an additional deposit). $69–99.

INNS

Havre de Grace, 21078

⌇ **Vandiver Inn** (410-939-5200; 1-800-245-1665; www.vandiverinn.com), 301 South Union Avenue. Built in 1886 by Murray Vandiver as a wedding gift to his wife, Annie. The opulence of the house reflects his political career, which included serving in the

Maryland House of Delegates, as state treasurer, as mayor of Havre de Grace, and an appointment to the IRS by President Cleveland. The chandelier and stained glass in the parlor are original, as are many items in the nine large guest rooms. The two houses next door to the inn have eight rooms available to guests. Children over the age of six are welcome. The inn was for sale when I visited, so call for its current status. $85–185.

🌹 **Crazy Swede** (410-939-5440; www.crazyswederestaurant.com), 400 North Union Avenue. The Crazy Swede offers 10 suites in three different houses. All come with a private bath, continental breakfast in the room, and 20 percent off meals purchased in the **Crazy Swede Restaurant** (see *Dining Out*). Some suites have full kitchens and/or Jacuzzi. The size of the rooms and their elegant furnishings are a good deal for the price. $95–135.

BED & BREAKFASTS

Havre de Grace, 21078

Currier House (410-939-7886; 1-800-827-2889; www.currier-bb.com), 800 South Market Street. In 1996, Jane Currier Belbot opened a B&B in the 1760 house that has been in her family since 1861. I truly felt more like I was visiting someone's home than I did in any other establishment in Harford County. The house is decorated with heirlooms, family furniture, original Currier and Ives lithographs, and photos of ancestors and the glory days of Havre de Grace. All four guests rooms have a private bath, and two of them have balconies overlooking a grand magnolia tree, the Concord Point Lighthouse, and the bay. I was especially taken by the milieu of the Crawford Room's cedar-wood-lined bathroom. The full watermen's breakfast includes oysters and Maryland stewed tomatoes (in-season). $95–115.

La Clé D'or (410-939-9562; 1-888-HUG-GUEST), 226 North Union Avenue. This place should have a motto something like, "Live in opulence for a while without spending a fortune." The 1868 home is loaded with gorgeous antiques and has 17 Strauss crystal chandeliers. The guest rooms are decorated with their own theme. Breakfast is served on a variety of fine china accompanied by gold utensils, the brick-walled garden is entered through a wrought-iron gate, and the outdoor whirlpool Jacuzzi is large enough to handle a party of 10. Refreshments and a cookie jar are always available. $110–125.

Spencer Silver Mansion (410-939-1097; 1-800-780-1485; www.spencersilvermansion.com), 200 South Union Avenue. Children welcome. One of the most beautifully restored Victorian mansions I've seen. Guests rooms are lavishly furnished

with oak and mahogany antiques of the period; a stone two-story carriage house is available for those wishing privacy. $70–140.

CAMPING See **Susquehanna State Park** under *To Do—Hiking.*

✳ Where to Eat

DINING OUT

Havre de Grace

MacGregor's (410-939-3003; 1-800-300-6319), 331 St. John Street. Open for lunch and dinner. Seafood is the definite specialty of this restaurant, which has a casually elegant atmosphere. Crabcakes (market price), stuffed flounder ($19.95), and the shrimp and chicken stir fry ($16.95) make use of the local catch. The older portion of the restaurant is inside a former bank building, while the newer glass-enclosed section provides memorable views of the Susquehanna River. The tavern serves light fare and has live entertainment on the weekends.

Note to film and history buffs: The

MacGregor name comes from owner Daniel Lee, a direct descendent of Rob Roy MacGregor.

Tidewater Grill (410-939-3313), 300 Franklin Street. Open for lunch and dinner. The dining room and two outside decks overlook the Susquehanna River. Seafood, much of it mixed with pasta, occupies at least half of the menu, with chicken, beef, and chops making up the rest of the entrées. Meat lovers will enjoy the American Mixed Grille with a petite filet, breast of chicken, loin lamb chop, and "An Do We" sausage ($24.95). $14.50–24.95.

Crazy Swede Restaurant (410-939-5440; www.crazyswederestaurant. com), 400 North Union Avenue. Within the old 1893 Chesapeake Hotel building (where Al Capone once dined), you will find a refined preparation of seafood, poultry, beef, and pasta served in a casual atmosphere. My crab dip appetizer ($9.75) was remarkably creamy, while the shrimp stuffed with crabmeat and topped with the restaurant's own imperial sauce ($21.95) was even richer and creamier. Entrées $14.95–24.95.

The Crazy Swede also operates an inn with a number of suites available (see *Lodging—Inns*). The moniker, by the way, comes from a former owner, who named it after "that crazy Swede chef" he once employed.

EATING OUT

Havre de Grace
✴ **The Bayou Restaurant** (410-939-3565), 927 Pulaski Highway (US 40). Open for lunch and dinner. You know that family-owned restaurant near you that has been around for decades and that everyone in town patronizes from

time to time? Well, this is Havre de Grace's version. Expect friendly service and honest home cooking. All of the soups, breads, and pies are made from scratch. The seafood combo ($15.95) of flounder, crabcake, oysters, shrimp, and scallops is available broiled or fried. A filling, healthful, and low-cost entrée is the vegetarian fettuccine ($6.95). Many choices of beef, veal, poultry, and other seafood entrées fill the menu ($6.50–24.95). Lunch buffet ($5.95) Tuesday through Friday.

Aberdeen
The New Ideal Diner (410-272-1880), US 40. Open for breakfast (served all day), lunch, and dinner. Established in 1931. The present structure is the restaurant's fourth dining car in the same location. The gleaming stainless-steel and green-enamel striped car was manufactured by Jerry O'Mahony, Inc., and transported to the site in four sections in 1952. A very popular local favorite, it is always crowded for breakfast and lunch. Dinner selections include seafood, meats, and pasta. $6.45–18.95.

✴ **Olive Tree** (410-575-7773), 1005 Beards Hill Road. Open for lunch and dinner. Since the pasta is made fresh before your eyes inside the glass "pasta booth," it only makes sense to order a dish containing one of its many forms. Choose a pasta entrée by itself or accompanied with crab, chicken, or beef. $8–18.

✴ **Japan House** (410-272-7878), 984 Beards Hill Road. Open for lunch and dinner. Fresh sushi and sashimi ($3–9) are what bring diners in. Items from the *teppanyaki* grill, such as salmon ($13.95) and sesame chicken ($11.95), are also popular.

Edgewood

☙ **Vitali's** (410-671-6370), 1709 Edgewood Road (accessed from I-95 Exit 77). Open for breakfast, lunch, and dinner. The atmosphere and quality of food is nicer than what you usually find in a restaurant next to a motel. Seafood, chicken, beef, and veal entrées are prepared with an Italian slant. The pasta dishes, with plenty to choose from, are among the most flavorful offerings. $9.95–19.95.

COFFEE BARS Java by the Bay (410-939-0227), 118 North Washington Street, Havre de Grace. Coffees and teas by the cup or the pound. Lots of goodies to choose from, such as a bagel, muffin, or Danish, to go with your drink.

SNACKS AND GOODIES

Havre de Grace

Bomboy's (410-939-2924; www.bomboyscandy.com), 329 Market Street. Closed Monday. The chocolate candies created at Bomboy's, available by the piece or the pound, are made fresh daily using old family recipes. Fresh fudge and sugar-free chocolates are also available. If candy is not your fancy, **Bomboy's Homemade Ice Cream** is directly across the street.

Ritz (410-939-5858), 100 North Washington Street. With the atmosphere of a coffeehouse, Ritz serves desserts, pastries, beverages, and Edy's ice cream. There is also a good selection of sugar-free treats.

Ice Dreams (410-939-1525), 209 North Washington Street. Within an old stone house, you can order hand-dipped Hershey's ice cream and all of the things you can do with it, such as shakes, sundaes, and malts. There is also a complete restaurant menu of crabcakes, sandwiches, and full dinners.

✳ Entertainment

FILM Beards Hill Movies 7 (410-272-6770), 963 Beards Hill Road, Aberdeen, is the place to see movies in and around town.

The Campus Hills Cinema 7 (410-836-2111), Campus Hill Shopping Center, and the **Tollgate Movies 7** (410-838-7077), 615 Baltimore Pike, both in Bel Air, both show first-run movies.

✳ Selective Shopping

ANTIQUES There are so many antiques shops clustered along St. John Street, North Union Avenue, and North Washington Street in Havre de Grace that the area has come to be known as **Antique Row.**

Memory Makers (410-877-0450), 1804 Harford Road, Fallston. Tuesday through Sunday 11–6. Antique wood furniture and porcelains and china are found in abundance here.

Spenceola Antique Center (410-803-0011), 1445 Rockspring Road, Bel Air. Over 22,000 square feet of display space and more than 150 dealers showing their wares. You should be able to find just about anything you want, if you can just wade through that much merchandise.

ART GALLERIES The **Picture Show Art Gallery** (410-939-0738), 301 St. John Street, Havre de Grace. Features Chesapeake Bay sculpture and artwork.

USED BOOKSTORES

Havre de Grace

Washington Street Books (410-939-

6215), 131 North Washington Street. Wednesday through Monday noon–6. More than 35,000 used, rare, and out-of-print books. A small selection of new books.

Courtyard Book Shop (410-939-5150), 313 St. John Street. Open every day. A selection of used and antiquarian books.

SPECIAL SHOPS National 5 and 10 (410-939-2737), 232 North Washington Street, Havre de Grace. Like the five-and-dimes of yore, National sells toys, clothing, housewares, hardware, and souvenirs.

FARMER'S MARKETS Havre de Grace Farmer's Market. 9–noon, May through October, you can find seasonal offerings at the market on Pennington Avenue.

Bel Air Farmer's Market. Produce stands are set up at the Harford Mall, MD 24 and US 1, on Sunday 10–2, April through October.

Edgewood Farmer's Market. You can purchase the bounty of the seasons in Edgewood in the lot across from the MARC station on Thursday 3:30–7 PM, June through October.

PICK-YOUR-OWN PRODUCE FARMS
🌱 **Applewood Farm** (410-836-1140), 4425 Prospect Road, Whiteford. You can pick your own pumpkins, gourds, and mums during September and October. Special events during the year include a petting zoo, hayrides, a maze, and train displays.

WINERIES
Fiore Winery (410-879-4007; www.fiorewinery.com), 3026 Whiteford Road (MD 136), Pylesville. Open for tours and tastings Wednesday

through Saturday 10–5, and noon–5 Sunday. Vintner Mike Fiore was born in Calabria, Italy, and grew up in a family whose experience in wine making goes back more than 400 years. Coming to this sloping hillside in northern Harford County, he planted his first grapes in 1977. Besides the tour and the tastings, you are also permitted to enjoy the scenery and the vineyards. Fiore sponsors several annual fun events, such as its well-attended jazz and arts festival.

✴ **Special Events**
May: **Annual Decoy and Wildlife Art Festival** (410-939-3739). For 3 days in May, Havre de Grace hosts one of the largest and longest-running festivals to honor decoy carving and other forms of wildlife art. **ArtQuest** (410-638-5974), Bel Air. Food and live entertainment accompany the works of local professional and amateur artists.

June: **Annual Evening of Wine and Jazz** (410-939-5780), Susquehanna Museum (see *To See—Museums*), Havre de Grace. **Scottish Festival** (410-939-2299), Steppingstone Museum (see *To See—Museums* and *To Do—Special Classes*), Havre de Grace. A full day of pipe-band music, sheep herding and shearing, spinning and weaving, and lots of Scottish food and fashions. **Harford County Farm Fair** (410-838-8663), Bel Air.

August: **Annual Arts and Crafts Show** (410-939-9342), Millard E. Tydings Memorial Park, Havre de Grace. For more than four decades, the local chapter of Soroptimist International has been sponsoring this 2-day event. Arts, crafts, food, demonstrations, and music. **Antique Street Fest** (410-939-9397), Franklin Street,

Havre de Grace. **Annual Corn Festival** (410-939-7946; www.cacofhdg.com), Havre de Grace. Games, rides, food, and entertainment.

September: **Annual Duck Fair** (410-939-3739), Havre de Grace. Wildlife artists and carvers, retriever demon-strations, and many children's activities.

December: **Candlelight Tour** (410-939-3947), Havre de Grace. A yearly event in which businesses, churches, B&Bs, and historic homes open their doors to visitors.

North of Baltimore

NORTH OF BALTIMORE—
OWINGS MILLS, HUNT VALLEY,
WESTMINSTER, AND TANEYTOWN

B altimore's neighbors to the north, especially those within 15 miles or so of the I-695 beltway, are becoming ensnared in the city's sprawl. Long strings of strip malls, fast-food restaurants, and convenience stores meld into one another. It's hard to tell where some towns, such as Pikesville, Owings Mills, Towson, Lutherville, and Timonium, begin or end.

This does not mean you should overlook these places in your quest to explore the best that Maryland has to offer. Just off the beltway in Towson is Hampton, the first property to be accepted into the National Park Service system on architectural, and not necessarily historic, merit in 1948. The Fire Museum of Maryland in Lutherville, with more than 60 vehicles dating from the early 1800s, has one of the largest collections of its kind in the country. The last remaining serpentine grasslands in the state, Soldier's Delight National Environmental Area, are located just outside of Owings Mills, while more than one-fourth of all of Maryland's horse farms occupy large amounts of acreage between I-83 and MD 140/MD 30.

Also providing quick escapes from the density of Baltimore are Oregon Ridge, a regional park whose pathways provide impressive views of Hunt Valley, and the North Central Railroad Trail with a level route stretching for 20 miles from the Pennsylvania border to Cockeysville. More than 100 miles of trails snake around the varied terrain of 17,000-acre Gunpowder Falls State Park.

Farther afield, and a bit to the west, Carroll County has more land devoted to agricultural purposes than any other county in the state. A drive on just about any of its two-lane roadways yields a scenery of rolling meadows freckled by grazing cattle and poultry farms. All of those open fields means the county is also the least forested, but places like Piney Run and Hashawha Parks help preserve large stands of mature trees for present and future generations.

Substantial population growth in the last few decades has not robbed the communities of their small-town personalities. On the outskirts of Westminster, the county seat, MD 140 is lined with big-box discount stores and shopping centers, yet the historic district around Main Street remains packed with structures from the 1800s, many mom-and-pop businesses, and a 1920s art deco theater— home of the local arts council.

Nearby Taneytown, most scenically reached via MD 832 instead of MD 140, is the county's oldest town. George Washington visited the Adam Good Tavern in 1791, when a sign above it read, "A damn Good Inn, entertainment for man and beast." Undoubtedly much more upscale, the Antrim 1844 Inn takes in today's travelers.

Mount Airy has always been a place along America's busiest transportation routes. First, it was the Old National Pike in the early 1700s, then the Baltimore and Ohio Railroad in the 1800s, and US 40 in the early 1900s. High-speed motorists on I-70 now tend to zip by, missing its antiques shops and nearby wineries.

An interesting chapter in Sykesville's history is Betsy Syke's wedlock to Napoleon Bonaparte's brother, Jerome. Napoleon was against the marriage and refused to allow Betsy to enter France, and she never saw Jerome again. The town is one of the many old railroad towns in Maryland that thrived when the trains came through, but withered away once they left. The train station now houses a restaurant whose live folk and jazz entertainment attracts many locals and Baltimorians on the weekend.

Uniontown has no such commercial establishments; its claim to fame is its historic district with a diversity of 18th-, 19th-, and 20th-century structures. An easy walking tour of 20 minutes will take you past an abundance of architectural delights decorated by cupolas, cornices, dormers, and hipped roofs.

GUIDANCE **The Carroll County Visitor Center** (410-848-1388; 1-800-272-1933) shares space with the Historical Society of Carroll County and is located at 210 East Main Street, Westminster, 21157.

Information may also be obtained from the **Carroll County Office of Tourism** (410-386-2983; www.carr.org/tourism), 224 North Center Street, Room 100, Westminster, 21157.

The Baltimore County Conference and Visitor's Bureau (410-296-4886; 1-888-STAY-N-DO; www.visitbacomd.com) is located in the Towson Mall, Lutherville, 21094, and at 118 Shawan Road, Hunt Valley Mall, Hunt Valley, 21030.

GETTING THERE *By car:* **I-83** heads directly north of Baltimore after it branches off the beltway (**I-695**) at Exit 24 near Lutherville. The largest percentage of listings and attractions in this section are located in Carroll County, which may be reached by taking **I-795** from Baltimore and then continuing along **MD 140.**

By air: **Baltimore/Washington International Airport** (1-800-I-FLY-BWI), located between Baltimore and Annapolis, is about an hour's drive to the southeast.

GETTING AROUND *By car:* Traffic along any of the roads within 15 miles of the **Baltimore Beltway (I-695)** is extremely heavy during the morning and evening rush hours. There are not any good alternatives, so just turn on the radio and accept it. During the middle of the day, **I-83** becomes a fairly rapid way to head directly north into Baltimore County.

The situation is much better in Carroll County. **MD 140** is a good four-lane highway that becomes a two-lane country road north of Westminster. Other roads are lightly traveled during the middle part of the day.

By rail: The **Central Light Rail Line** (410-832-1200, extension 3990), the commuter train service out of Baltimore, basically parallels I-83 and makes stops at Lutherville, Timonium Business Park, and Timonium. Trains run about every 15 minutes and operate until 11 PM; 7 PM on Sunday. The **MARC** rail service (1-800-325-RAIL) makes stops in Owings Mills and Hunt Valley.

By taxi: One phone number—410-486-4000—puts you in contact with taxicabs based in Owings Mills, Reistertown, and Pikesville. Near Towson you can call **Jimmy's** (410-837-7200), and in Overlea contact **Overlea Cab** (410-665-1300).

PARKING In Westminster, parking meters are free after 3 PM and all day Saturday and Sunday.

MEDICAL EMERGENCY **St. Joseph Medical Center** (410-337-1226), 7601 Osler Drive, Towson.

Northwest Hospital Center (410-521-2200), 5401 Old Court Road, Randallstown.

Carroll County General Hospital (410-848-3000), 200 Memorial Avenue, Westminster.

✳ To See

COLLEGES **Western Maryland College** (410-848-7000), Westminster. A liberal arts college, Western Maryland has been educating students for more than 135 years. It could also be considered the cultural engine for the area with its **Esther Prangley Rice Gallery** (see *Selective Shopping—Art Galleries*) and various vocal and instrumental groups, lectures open to the public, and its sponsorship of **Common Ground on the Hill** (see *Entertainment—Music*) and **Theatre on the Hill** (see *Entertainment—Theaters*).

MUSEUMS

Westminster
Historical Society of Carroll County (410-848-6494; www.carr.org/hscc), 210 East Main Street. The society's Shriver-Weybright Exhibition Gallery displays items from its permanent collection illustrating the history of the county. The exhibits are constantly changing, so there will probably be something new each time you visit.

Union Mills Homestead (410-848-2288), 3311 Littlestown Pike (about 7 miles north of Westminster on MD 97). Tuesday through Friday 10–4, and Saturday and Sunday noon–4, June 1 through September 1. Small admission fee. Because all of the furniture and artifacts in this 1797 clapboard farmhouse belonged to the Shriver family, visitors get a true picture of what life was like when the Shrivers lived here. Things that caught my eye were the letter to David Shriver from Thomas Jefferson, the 1863 Steinway piano, and an original "Wanted"

UNION MILLS HOMESTEAD

poster for runaway slaves. The gristmill, built with bricks made on the property, still works. Guided tours are given of the house and mill.

Sykesville
Gate House Museum of History (410-549-5150), 7283 Cooper Drive. Wednesday and Sunday 1–6; Friday 6–8 PM. Donations accepted. A small collection of objects from the town's history.

Union Bridge
Western Maryland Railway Historical Society (410-775-0150), Union Bridge Station (MD 75). Sunday 1–4. Housed in the 1902 station is a collection of artifacts and memorabilia from the 125-year history of the Western Maryland Railroad.

Freeland
♿ **Morris Meadows Historic Preservation Museum** (410-329-6636), Freeland Road. Associated with the Morris Meadows Campground (see *Lodging— Camping*); you may need to go to the campground to get someone to open the museum. Old tractors, dolls, farm machinery, and displays of a schoolhouse, general store, kitchen, and gristmill. The sheer volume of items becomes even more impressive when you realize it is the private collection of Clive and Virginia Morris.

Lutherville
🐶 ♿ **Fire Museum of Maryland** (410-321-7500; www.firemuseummd.org), 1301 York Road (accessed from I-695 Exit 26B North). Tuesday through Saturday 11–4, June through August; Saturday only, September through May. Adults $6; seniors and firefighters $5; children 3–18 get in for $4. Presents the history of firefighting from the colonial days to the present. Children especially enjoy sitting in the 1938 fire-engine driver's seat.

✎ & **Carroll County Farm Museum** (410-876-2667; 1-800-654-4645), 500 South Center Street, Westminster. April through October. Small admission fee. Was I ever mistaken when I thought all I would see was a few old farm implements! This 140-acre complex does contain a few of those, but it provides a much broader picture of 1800s farm life with its completely furnished farmhouse, wagon shed, kitchen, smokehouse, and springhouse. Artisans within the living-history center practice the crafts of yesteryear that would have supplied the farm with many of its necessary items. Be sure to walk over to the barnyard full of chickens, cows, turkeys, pigs, horses, goats, and lambs. Bring a picnic lunch and plan to spend a few hours. This is one of the best re-created farms I have ever seen—especially in light of the small amount of change it costs to get in.

HISTORIC HOMES Hampton National Historic Site (410-823-1309), 535 Hampton Lane (just a few moments' drive from I-695 Exit 27B), Towson. Open daily 9–5. Small admission fee. Hampton was the largest house in the country when constructed in the late 1700s. Guided tours take you through this grand house, which is furnished almost exclusively with items that belonged to the six generations of the Ridgely family. Afterward, walk over the rest of the grounds to the family cemetery, slave quarters, dairy house, and gardens.

GUIDED TOURS The Carroll County Visitor Center (see *Guidance*), 210 East Main Street, Westminster, has put together a number of walking-tour brochures for Westminster, Uniontown, and other nearby sites. For a fun time, pick up the one for the **ghost walk** through Westminster. There are also driving-tour pamphlets to the Civil War sites and one that takes you to places important to the birth of American Methodism.

HAMPTON NATIONAL HISTORIC SITE

✴ To Do

BICYCLING Liberty Bike Shop
(410-549-9258; www.libertybikeshop. com), 1912 Liberty Road, Eldersburg. If you are riding around in the area and your bike develops a problem, these folks have a complete center that services all makes and models.

CIVIL WAR The rolling terrain of this area north of Baltimore saw a lot of troop movement and battle activity during the Civil War, especially when Robert E. Lee was trying to gain a foothold in Northern territory. That movement was, of course, halted at Gettysburg in the summer of 1863. Brochures available from the **Carroll County Visitor Center** (see *Guidance*) map out a couple of driving tours to the site of a cavalry skirmish that took place in Westminster and other places that played a part in the Gettysburg drama.

FAMILY ACTIVITIES ⊘ Cascade Lake (410-374-9111), 3000 Snydersburg Road, Hampstead. Open 10–7; the season is usually from around Memorial Day through close to Labor Day. This 6-acre spring-fed lake has a gently sloping sandy bottom and a large roped-off swimming area watched over by certified lifeguards. The kiddie area has a number of fun things to do and is well guarded. There are several water slides, floating rafts, and a high dive platform. Within the 25-acre property are fishing and boating areas (boat rentals), picnic tables, a playground, and a hiking trail. Popular with local families.

GOLF

Westminster
Wakefield Valley (410-876-6662; www.wakefieldvalley.com), 1000 Fenby Farm Road. Three 9-hole courses make up Wakefield Valley's 27 holes. The Green Course has long par

---

ROAD BIKING CARROLL COUNTY

A packet of brochures available from the **Carroll County Visitor Center** (see *Guidance*) details 10 rides throughout the county. Conceived by a group of local cyclists, the outings range from 8 miles to 33 miles and take in scenic farmlands, lightly traveled country roads, and small towns. Three are designed to bring you past ice cream shops, some go by historic sites, and others enable you to leave the bike for a while and take to a hiking trail. All of the rides are circular, so you always return to the starting point, where you are permitted to park your car.

I like the 15-mile **Westminster South route,** which not only delivers me to **Hoffman's Ice Cream Shop** but also enables an exploration of the **Carroll County Farm Museum** (see sidebar on page 191). Then there is the 30-mile **Taneytown tour** with lots of great scenery and diversions. Open meadows are often dotted with deer, small Pipe Creek bubbles beside the road, and the public pool in Taneytown Memorial Park beckons when the asphalt begins to release the heat it has soaked up on a sunny day.

5s, and the White Course covers hilly terrain. Combined, the courses have the second highest slope rating in the state.

Western Maryland College Golf Course (410-848-7667; www.greenterrorgolf.com). This nine-hole course was built on the college campus in 1935 by students and faculty and is one of the oldest courses in the county. Open to the public; students, faculty, and staff play for free.

Finksburg
River Downs Golfers Club (410-526-2000; www.riverdowns.com), 1900 River Downs Drive. A par-72 Arthur Hills–designed course on very rolling, wooded countryside.

White Hall
Greystone (410-887-1945), 2115 White Hall Road, less than 10 minutes from I-83 Exit 31. An abundance of tall trees and other vegetation, ponds, and wetlands add a challenge to this Joe Lee–designed course.

Timonium
Longview (410-887-7735), 1 Cardigan Road. A scenic and open course that is considered to be friendly to beginning golfers. Fees are lower here than at many other courses in the area.

MINIATURE GOLF ✏ **Four Seasons Sports Complex** (410-239-3366), 2710 Hampstead–Mexico Road, Hampstead. There are fast-pitch baseball and slow-pitch softball batting cages in addition to the 18-hole Play-A-Round Miniature Golf Course.

HIKING Gunpowder Falls State Park (410-592-2897), 2813 Jerusalem Road, Kingsville. Cool, shaded spots by a small swimming hole. Wildflower

and pine fragrances wafting through the air. Owl hoots breaking the stillness of early evening. Muskrat and raccoon paw prints stamped into soft mud. Hazy silhouettes of deer foraging in the morning mist.

These are not descriptions of things you must travel to western Maryland to enjoy, but rather some of the delights to be found in Gunpowder Falls State Park, located a short drive from Baltimore. More than 100 miles of trails wander through the parks 17,000 acres, which are divided among four areas that are separated from each other. *50 Hikes in Maryland* (Backcountry Guides) describes a hike in each area.

Soldier's Delight National Environmental Area (410-461-5005), 5100 Deer Park Road, Owings Mills. Looking at the types of vegetation in Maryland today, it may be hard to imagine that grasslands once spread across tens of thousands of acres of this landscape. Prior to colonial settlement, much of Baltimore and Harford Counties, and adjacent counties in Pennsylvania, was covered by open spaces not unlike the prairies found in the Midwest. At 2,000 acres, Soldier's Delight preserves the largest remaining serpentine grasslands in the state. A network of trails lets you explore the area to enjoy the open scenery and wide skyscape, and to find interesting plants and flowers such as the sandplain gerardia and fringed gentian.

HORSEBACK RIDING Brochures and maps available from the **Carroll County Department of Enterprise and Recreation Services** (410-386-2103; 1-888-302-8978), 225 North

Northern Central Railroad Trail (administered by Gunpowder Falls State Park; see above). The northernmost parking area for this trail is on MD 108 at Freeland, and the southern terminus is on Ashland Road in the Ashland Village housing development off MD 45 in Hunt Valley. The Rails-to-Trails Conservancy, the association generally recognized as spearheading the nationwide movement to convert abandoned railroad rights-of-way into trails, was formally organized in 1986. Nearly a decade before that, though, the state of Maryland, Baltimore County, and a group of local citizens were already laying the groundwork for the Northern Central Railroad Trail.

From 1838 to 1972, the Northern Central Railroad connected Baltimore with York, Pennsylvania, providing a major link for small communities along the way. Union troops made use of the railroad during the Civil War, and Abraham Lincoln traveled it on his way to deliver his famous Gettysburg Address. The construction of the interstates—and the resulting increase in truck and automobile transportation—marked the railroad's decline. Floods from Hurricane Agnes in 1972 dealt the final blow by washing out trestles and miles of track.

Never far from civilization, yet with long stretches of detachment from the humanized world, this 20-mile route is a great place to introduce someone to the joys of outdoor walking, without subjecting them to the rigors, and fear, of a harsh or isolated terrain. The pathway is level, and road crossings are fairly frequent if the need for help should happen to arise. In addition, public rest rooms are situated at seven sites, with drinking water available beside three of the road crossings. The historic aspects of the railroad are an added bonus. This is a multiuse trail, also open to bicyclists and equestrians, so always walk to the right and avoid walking two abreast. Pets must be on a leash.

Center Street, Room 100, Westminster, 21157, point out the many miles of trails and locations in the county available to equestrians.

SKIING, CROSS-COUNTRY See *Green Space—Parks.*

TENNIS Six of the parks in Carroll County have courts that are open to the public. Call 410-386-2103 for locations and availability.

✳ Green Space

PARKS 🐾 ♂ ♿ Hashawha Environmental Center (410-848-9040), 300 John Owings Road, Westminster. Open sunrise to sunset. So much land is devoted to agricultural purposes (and lately housing developments) that Carroll County is the least forested county in the state. Knowing that may help you to appreciate even more so the woodlands that the pathways of Hashawha wander through. The trails are open to hikers, bikers, and cross-country skiers; one is handicapped accessible. **Bear Branch Nature Center** (410-848-2517), inside the park, has a number of interpretive displays and sponsors a variety of outings and programs on and off site.

🐾 ✇ ♿ **Piney Run Park** (410-795-3274), 30 Martz Road, Sykesville. April 1 through October 31, 6 AM–sunset. Small vehicle entrance fee. From November through March visitors may park outside the gate, hike the trails, fish from the banks, and visit the nature center.

In addition to fishing and boating opportunities on the 300-acre lake, there is a network of trails on the surrounding 500 acres. One of the trails is open to mountain bikers and another to equestrians; all trails are open for cross-country skiing in winter. If your time is short, follow the **Field Trail,** as it will lead you into a variety of environments in only 0.7 mile. Canoes, sailboats, rowboats, kayaks, and electric-powered fishing boats are available for rent during the season.

The nature center has several small exhibits and offers a host of programs for children and adults. Pets on leashes are permitted.

🐾 **Oregon Ridge** (410-887-1815), 13555 Beaver Dam Road, Cockeysville. Oregon Ridge is an excellent model of a county or regional park that has been able to meet many of the diverse recreational needs of a growing local population, yet still keep the vast majority of the land undisturbed. Within the park's 1,036 acres are tennis courts, picnic areas, a dinner theater and lodge, an outdoor stage (the summer home for the Baltimore Symphony Orchestra), a swimming lake and sandy beach, and a bathhouse and snack bar. A network of marked pathways meanders through the undeveloped part of the park, rising to the main forested ridgeline and descending into a narrow creek valley. The nature center, with exhibits relating to local natural and human history, sponsors one of the best and most active interpretive programs available anywhere in Maryland—pick up a schedule and take

PINEY RUN PARK

part in an activity. Pets permitted on leashes.

✳ Lodging

INNS Westminster Inn (410-876-2893), 5 South Center Street, Westminster, 21157. Here's a twist: This is an old schoolhouse that has been turned into an inn with luxury rooms (each with a Jacuzzi) and a complete fitness club. Close to the center of town. $100–200.

Bowling Brook (410-848-0353), 6000 Middleburg Road, Middleburg, 21757. Located on 225 acres just a short drive from Westminster. This late-1800s Victorian house has gone through many design changes throughout the years, but it still offers eight guest rooms, each with a private bath and television. Bowling Brook is the Westminster Inn's (see above) sister business, and guests have free use of the Westminster's fitness club. $110–175.

✎ ♿ **Antrim 1844** (410-756-6812; 1-800-858-1844; www.antrim1844.com), 30 Trevanion Road, Taneytown,

21787. It is almost hard to grasp that small Taneytown contains one of the most celebrated inns in all of America. The constant attention to details, lavish furnishings, and impeccable service are rarely found in such a perfect combination. The 22 guest rooms and suites are furnished with canopy featherbeds, fireplaces and/or Jacuzzis (my room had a pedestal Jacuzzi, a bidet, and a private balcony), and antiques appropriate to the inn's antebellum history.

Everything has been arranged to be pleasing to the eye, even the 23 acres of grounds. The gardens are reminiscent of those found in European estates, the croquet lawn is perfectly manicured, and the swimming pool and its gazebo are surrounded by hedgerows. The quality of the restaurant's meals (see *Dining Out*) matches that of the inn. $210–375.

BED & BREAKFASTS Yellow Turtle Inn (410-635-3000), 111 Springdale Avenue, New Windsor, 21776. Several

ONE OF MANY RELAXING SPOTS ON THE 23 ACRES OF ANTRIM 1844

years ago, Joan Bradford had a dream about opening an inn. She became convinced it was her destiny when, a few days later, someone else said they, too, had had a dream about her and an inn—and the inn looked exactly the same in both dreams.

Sitting on 3 acres, the 1800s house is decorated in an amazing amount of Victorian furnishings and items. Each guest room is unique: The Windsor Vineyard Room has a curved wall, there is a mural in the Mary Cole Room, and the Queen's Chambers has a bed constructed of tree branches.

The grounds include a swimming pool and an interesting seven-circuit meditation labyrinth. If a full-body massage and herbal tea are not enough to relax you, the view of the 100-acre preserved farmland from the wraparound porch surely will. $105–165.

✿ ♿ **Wood's Gain** (410-775-0308; www.woodsgainbnb.com), 421 Mc-Kinstry's Mill Road, Linwood, 21791. Open weekends September through June and daily July through August. The 1866 brick house, with five fireplaces and four stairways, is the oldest structure in tiny Linwood village. Beverly and Steve Kerkam have expertly restored the house while adding modern fixtures and amenities. All guest rooms have a private bath. The Keeping Room, in the oldest section of the home, is fully handicapped accessible. I thought the decor in the Grandmother's Room, which had belonged to both sets of grandparents, was a loving tribute to family. However, I enjoyed an evening in the Summer Kitchen, a detached two-room cottage with a sitting room, fireplace, and whirlpool tub.

Guests often gather around the old upright piano and phonograph in the parlor, or sit in the rose garden or on the porch to watch the evening unfold. Supervised children 7 and older are welcome. $85–140.

✿ **Americana B&B** (410-549-5763; www.americanabnb.com), 2400 Constantine Drive, Eldersburg, 21784. The Americana's location next to miles of trails around Liberty Reservoir could not be any better. Host Randi Wetzel is familiar with all of them, and has directed hikers, mountain bikers, and bird-watchers to many hours of pleasure. Those of you who travel with your horse will be happy to know that there are even accommodations for your equine companion and that guided trail rides can be arranged.

The Americana is a modern home set on 10 acres of rolling land. The two guest suites have private baths and a lot of room to spread out. Breakfast is served in the sunroom overlooking the pastures—and Randi's "cowboy" cookies are always available. Supervised children 10 and older welcome. $90–130.

CAMPING ✿ **Ramblin' Pines Campground** (410-795-5161; 1-800-550-8733), 801 Hoods Mill Road (3 miles from I-70 Exit 76), Woodbine, 21797. As much a destination resort as it is a campground. Besides RV (with full hookups) and tent sites, there's a swimming pool, a playground, a miniature-golf course, hiking trails, and planned activities such as hayrides, bingo, and live entertainment. Sites are somewhat close together, but the property is rambling and spread out. Cabins and trailers available for rent.

Morris Meadows (410-329-6636; 1-800-643-7056), 1523 Freeland Road,

Freeland, 21053. Located just a couple of minutes' drive from I-83 Exit 36. The campground is on land that has been in the Morris family since 1793; the original deed, written on goatskin, is on display in the registration lobby. This is a mini family resort with tent and RV sites, rental cabins, a swimming pool, miniature golf, fishing, and the most extensive list of planned activities (April through October) I've ever seen in a commercial campground. (Also see **Morris Meadows Historic Preservation Museum** under *To See—Museums*.)

✳ Where to Eat

DINING OUT ✿ ✐ **Paradiso Ristorante** (410-876-1421), 20 Distillery Drive, Westminster. Open for lunch and dinner. Salvatore and June Romeo serve traditional Italian dishes in what was once the dryer house for a distillery. The large windows allow the sun to light the attractive atmosphere. The cheese tortellini rose ($12.50) with mushrooms, sun-dried tomatoes, and prosciutto is a taste I will always remember. My dining partner raved about her veal medallions sautéed in cognac sauce with mushrooms and spinach ($17.50). The service, setting, and quality make the prices a bargain. Other entrées $9.50–19.00.

⌖ **Antrim 1844's Smokehouse Restaurant** (410-756-6812; 1-800-858-1844), Taneytown. Open for dinner. Reservations are mandatory. *the* place to go to really celebrate a special occasion. The six-course prix fixe ($62 per person) dinner is determined each evening by renowned chef Michael Gettier from a menu of regional cuisine accented with a French flair. Hors d'oeuvres delivered

to you in the parlor by a butler, a wine list with more than 1,000 selections, large fireplaces, and a warm-hued brick floor complement the experience. (Also see *Lodging—Inns*.)

✿ **Rudy's 2900** (410-833-5777; www.rudys2900.com), 2900 Baltimore Boulevard, Finksburg. There are only about five dozen Certified Master Chefs and Master Pastry Chefs. Rudy Speckamp is one of them, and the prices you pay here (entrées are $16.95–28.95) are a bargain to sample what a master can do with continental and contemporary cuisine. Many of the dishes are even heart healthy, such as the seafood brochette ($18.95) and the veal scaloppini with artichoke, mushrooms, and capers ($18.95). There is also a menu of moderately priced items like game sausage with onions and greens ($9.95), and salmon with warm onion torte ($11.95).

EATING OUT

Westminster

Johanssons (410-876-0101), 4 West Main Street. Open for lunch and dinner. Johanssons makes its own beers, and the aroma of the brewing process spreads throughout the restaurant. The Honest Ale was to my liking, flavorful but not heavy.

Lunch, with sandwiches and salads, also includes English pub items like fish-and-chips ($8.95), shepherd's pie ($9.95), and bratwurst and mashed potatoes ($8.95). I decided on something a little lighter—the vegetable turnover ($7.95); the shell would do any pastry chef proud. Various forms of seafood, meats, and chicken are offered for dinner. $15.95–22.95. Ask for a window seat to watch the traffic go by on MD 27.

The Down Under Bar and Grill

downstairs is a festive place with billiard tables, a game room, and live entertainment on the weekend.

❦ **Harry's Main Street Grille** (410-848-7080), 65 West Main Street. Harry's has a full lunch and dinner menu, but its real claim to fame are the Coney Island–style hot dogs ($1.75) covered with chili, mustard, and onions. Soups, salads, and other sandwiches are served for lunch.

I stopped by for dinner, as the grille is also known for its baby back ribs that are marinated for 7 days, simmered for hours, and char-grilled with Harry's BBQ sauce. The half rack ($8.95) filled me up, but you could also order a full rack ($14.95). Other options for dinner are pastas, seafood, beef, and 8-ounce burgers. $4.95–15.95.

❦ ❦ **Baugher's** (410-848-7413), 289 West Main Street Extension (junction of MD 31 and MD 32). Open for breakfast, lunch, and dinner. You know this place—it has vinyl chairs and Formica tabletops, serves home-cooking-style food, and attracts everybody in town.

The prices on the breakfast plates ($1.85–3.40) and lunch sandwiches ($1.50–5.30) may make you think you have entered a time warp. And where else can you get four pieces of fried chicken, two vegetables, a roll, and a beverage for only $6.90? Similar entrées run $4.50–11.50. Save room for homemade ice cream or a slice of pie.

Ma Baugher began selling pies and other baked goods to supplement a meager income during the Depression. The operation today includes more than 1,000 acres of farmland, a packing house, fields of produce (see

Selective Shopping—Pick-Your-Own Produce Farms), a farm stand, and the restaurant.

Sofia's (410-840-1919), 32 West Main Street. Open for lunch and dinner; closed Sunday. A pleasant place that, in addition to a usual menu of sandwiches and entrées with meat, serves a number of healthy vegetable dishes. Try the veggie brochette ($6) appetizer or the veggie kabobs ($9) for dinner. Entrées $7–18.

Taneytown
Bart's Place (410-756-6001), 465 East Baltimore Street. Open for breakfast, lunch, and dinner. Bart is the host of *Cooking with Bart* on a Baltimore cable channel, so you know you're getting good food from a practiced chef. Sandwiches, salads, and dishes using regionally available seafood and poultry. Entrées $4.95–16.95.

Mount Airy
Brick Ridge (301-829-8191; www.brickridge.com), 6212 Ridge Road. Hours vary slightly each day, but it is open for lunch on Friday and Saturday, and for dinner Tuesday through Sunday. Sunday brunch 11–2. The menu changes often at the Brick Ridge, as the culinary team strives to provide contemporary cuisine from every state in America. A sample of a dinner menu includes filé gumbo ($4.95), horseradish-encrusted beef ($18.95), and Porterman's pie ($13.95), a slight variation on shepherd's pie.

The restaurant's building began its life in the late 1800s as a school for children from the ages of 6 to 20 years.

CRABS Gary and Dell's Crab House (410-346-7652), 2820

Littlestown Pike, Westminster. Like all crab houses, Gary and Dell's serves steamed crabs by the dozen (market price), but the real deal here is the all-you-can-eat crab special for only $21.95. And you are permitted to eat for 3 hours if you wish! Sandwiches, other seafood, and meats round out the menu. $4–25.95.

Tangier Crab House (410-549-1161), 1945 Liberty Road, Eldersburg. Sandwiches, crabcakes, and seafood platters are available inside the restaurant ($6.75–27.95), but a large portion of the business is the take-out seafood. Live or steamed crabs are available by the dozen, and half and full bushels. You can also purchase crabmeat and fresh fish by the pound.

COFFEE BAR Irish Moon Coffee Shop (410-756-6556), corner of MD 194 and MD 140, Taneytown. Coffee, food, and live Irish entertainment on the weekends.

TAKE-OUT Giulianova Groceria (410-876-7425), 11 East Main Street, Westminster. The grocery part of the store carries everything you could want to make your own Italian meal. If you don't feel like cooking, you can always order a hoagie, hot entrée, or Italian-style soup to go. Don't miss getting a cannoli for dessert—the pastry shell is not stuffed until you order it.

MICROBREWERY Johanssons (410-876-0101), 4 West Main Street, Westminster. Johanssons brews its own beers within its historic 1800s restaurant (see *Eating Out*). There are always at least five different brews to choose from at any time.

SNACKS AND GOODIES

Westminster

Baugher's (410-848-7413), 289 West Main Street Extension (junction of MD 31 and MD 32). Baugher's makes homemade pies (47 different kinds) and ice cream (20 flavors), both available for eat-in or take-out. Ask them to heat a piece of pie and top it with ice cream and you will be in sweets heaven. (Also see *Eating Out*.)

Heinz Bakery (410-848-0808), 42 West Main Street. This family-owned bakery, turning out pastries and breads, has been a downtown mainstay for many years.

Treat Shop (410-848-0028), 400 North Center Street. Open daily. The Treat Shop has been making fresh candy and fudge daily in Westminster for close to 50 years. It is almost impossible to walk by without being drawn in by all of the delicious creations displayed in the window.

Hoffman's Home Made Ice Cream (410-857-0824), 934 Washington Road. Open until 10 PM every day. Jeff, Linda, and Lori Hoffman are using the same recipes that their grandfather used when he started making ice cream in 1947. There are at least 30 different flavors available daily.

Eldersburg

Lee's Gourmet Ice Cream (410-795-5600), 2021 Liberty Road. Baltimore's gourmet ice cream is now available in Eldersburg.

✴ Entertainment

FILM Carrolltown Movies 6 (410-795-7744), 6405 West Hemlock Road, Eldersburg. Each theater has digital sound and rocking chairs.

Loews Theatre Valley Center 9 (410-363-4194), 9616 Reisterstown Road, and **General Cinema** (443-394-0060), 10100 Mill Run Circle. Both are in Owings Mills and show first-run movies.

Hoyts Hunt Valley Cinema (410-329-9800), 11511 McCormick Road, Hunt Valley. Mainstream films.

MUSIC **Common Ground on the Hill** (410-857-2771), Western Maryland College campus, Westminster (see also *To See—Colleges*). The organization takes its name from its mission, which is to promote learning experiences for artists, musicians, and craftspersons while searching for a common ground among ethnic, gender, and racial groups. Sponsors workshops and the annual **American Music and Arts Festival** during the summer.

THEATER ♪ **Theatre on the Hill** (410-857-2448), Western Maryland College Campus, Westminster (also see *To See—Colleges*). This professional theater company presents a number of productions—musicals, dramas, comedies, and children's shows—throughout the summer months.

✳ Selective Shopping

ANTIQUES

Westminster
Locust Wines and Antiques (410-876-8680), 10 East Main Street. The store combines two of the owner's passions—antiques and estate jewelry—with a selection of fine wines.

Patricia Keener (410-876-1130), 10 East Main Street. Ms. Keener displays 18th- and 19th-century furni-

ture, paintings, Oriental rugs, and estate jewelry inside an early-19th-century building.

Sykesville
Sykesville Antiques (410-795-7600), 7566 Main Street. Antiques, art, and vintage and salvage items.

Mount Airy
♿ **Shops of Yesteryear** (301-829-0330), 102 Center Street. An antiques marketplace in which more than 90 dealers show their wares.

ART GALLERIES

Westminster
♿ **Carroll County Arts Council Gallery** (410-848-7272; www.carr.org/arts), 91 West Main Street. Within a refurbished 1928 art deco movie house, this is much more than just an art gallery displaying changing exhibits. The theater is the setting for films, concerts, lectures, theatrical productions, and recitals. Classes in all of the various arts are available. The council also publishes the very complete *Discover the Arts in Carroll County* booklet, which provides information on countywide activities and classes throughout the year.

Ain't That a Frame (410-876-3096), 31 West Main Street. An art gallery, antiques shop, and custom framing store.

Esther Prangley Rice Gallery (410-857-2595), Peterson Hall, Western Maryland College campus (also see *To See—Colleges*). The gallery is the site of changing exhibits in a variety of media from students, professors, and local and national artists. There is also the continuous display of the Albert and Eva Blum Collection of Art from Five Continents.

BOOKSTORES Locust Books (410-876-1620), 9 East Main Street, Westminster. In addition to best-sellers and classics, Locust is a great resource for books concerning the local area and all of Maryland.

Whistlestop Bookstore (301-829-9601), 8 South Main Street, Mount Airy. Used and new books.

GENEALOGY BOOKSTORE Willow Bend Books (410-876-6101; www.WillowBendBooks.com), 65 East Main Street, Westminster. Willow Bend is the largest genealogy bookstore in the world. Its thousands of titles provide history and genealogy information on all 50 states and Canada. It has become the number three tourist attraction in Carroll County and a must-stop for anyone interested in the subject. Check out the web site if you are unable to make it to the store, as the majority of the company's sales are through mail order.

CRAFTS Carousel Stained Glass (410 876-6106), 732 Cindy Lane, Westminster. Roger Lewis has been a stained-glass artist for more than 30 years, and his works are installed in churches, mausoleums, and hundreds of homes. Most pieces are custom-designed. He also does carved and etched glass and restorations.

SPECIAL SHOPS

Westminster

Gypsy's Tea Room (410-857-9818), 13 Liberty Street, Suite B. Afternoon tea with scones by reservation Wednesday through Saturday 11–4.

Pennsylvania Dutch Farmer's Market (410-876-8100), intersection of MD 140 and MD 97. This is not so much a farmer's market as it is a mini mall selling country crafts, furniture, souvenirs, and gift items. There are fresh seafood and meat shops and—by far the main reason to visit—delicious home-baked Amish and Mennonite breads, pies, and other goodies.

FARMER'S MARKETS & Westminster Farmer's Market. A farmer's market operates from mid-June through early September in the Agricultural Center at 702 Smith Avenue on Saturday 8–1; additional farm

SerrvInternational Gift Shop (410-635-8711), 500 Main Street (MD 31), New Windsor. This nonprofit organization, started by the Church of the Brethren in the late 1940s, buys crafts at fair prices from more than 30 countries and the United States. These purchases help to provide a small bit of security for what would otherwise be hundreds of underprivileged people. The items here are not only of high quality but would be hard to find anywhere else. Textiles, pottery, furniture, candles, musical instruments, wood carvings, jewelry, and much more. If you're going to buy a gift or something for yourself, why not get it here and put money into the hands of a person instead of a faceless multinational corporation? A highly recommended stop; the peaceful setting on a knoll overlooking the countryside will do your soul some good, too. Mail-order catalogs available.

products can be found at the Sherwood Square parking lot (MD 27 and Distillery Drive), 8–noon on Saturday, from early June through late October. Both are handicapped accessible.

Sykesville Farmer's Market. Just a bit more than 5 miles from I-70 Exit 80 is the Sykesville Farmer's Market on Main Street at Baldwin Station. It's open for more months than any other in the area—from early June through late November, Wednesday 3–6.

Eldersburg Farmer's Market. Timed so that you may pick up fresh vegetables and fruits for the weekend, the farmer's market next to Carrolltown Center is open 3–7 on Friday from early June through late October.

PICK-YOUR-OWN PRODUCE FARMS

✧ **Baugher's** (410-848-5541), corner of MD 140 and Baugher Road, Westminster. The season begins in late May with strawberries and peas. Cherries come in late June and early July. Pumpkins can be picked on Saturday and Sunday in October, when hayrides will take you to and from the patch. The kids will enjoy the variety of animals in the petting zoo, which is open throughout the season. (Also see *Eating Out*).

✧ **Shady Hill Farm and Orchard** (410-875-0572), 2001 New Windsor Road (MD 31), New Windsor. A variety of apples become ripe from mid-September through October. The orchard has 600 dwarf and semi-dwarf trees, so it's a perfect outing for young children. There are also free hayrides on Sundays for pick-your-own customers.

Manchester

Cygnus Wine Cellars (410-374-6395; www.cygnuswinecellars), 3130 Long Lane. Tours, tastings, and sales on Saturday and Sunday noon–5. Sparkling and red and white table wines.

Mount Airy

The three wineries of Mount Airy are so close to each other that you could almost walk from one to the other—which is what you may want to do after tasting all they have to offer.

Berrywine Plantations Linganore Winecellars (410-795-6432), 13601 Glissans Mill Road. Weekdays 10–5, Saturday 10–6, and Sunday noon–6. A selection of more than 25 wines; lots of special annual events.

Elk Run Vineyards (410-775-2513), 15113 Liberty Road (MD 26). Wednesday through Friday noon–4, Saturday 10–5, and Sunday 1–5. Best known for its ice wine, champagne, and summer concerts.

Loew Vineyards (301-831-5464), 14001 Liberty Road (MD 26). Tours,

BAUGHER'S RESTAURANT AND PRODUCE STAND IN WESTMINSTER

tastings, and sales Saturday 10–5 and Sunday 1–5. Estate-bottled wines.

Sparks
Basignani Winery (410-472-0703; www.basignani.com), 15722 Fall Road. Wednesday through Saturday 11:30–5:30 and Sunday noon–6. Bertero Basignani was an amateur wine maker for 15 years before establishing his own winery in 1986. His low-key operation employs traditional cellar methods and produces about 5,000 gallons of wine a year from grapes that are estate grown and bottled.

Parkton
Woodhall Wine Cellars (410-357-8644; www.woodhallwinecellars.com), 17912 York Road. Tours, tastings, and sales are available Tuesday through Sunday noon–5. Woodhall was started by three amateur wine makers in 1983 and moved to its present scenic location next to the Gunpowder River in 1995. The largest percentage of grapes come from outside sources.

Hydes
Boordy Vineyards (410-592-5015; www.boordy.com), 12820 Long Green Pike. Open for tastings and sales Monday through Saturday 10–5; Sunday 1–5. Tours are given on the hour daily 1–4. Boordy is Maryland's oldest winery, having been established in 1945. The vines you see today were planted in the 1960s, and the winery began bottling the grapes in the 1980s. The 19th-century fieldstone barn is a pleasant atmosphere for tastings and serves as the focal point for the winery's many annual events.

✳ Special Events
Year-round: **An Evening of Poetry, Music, and Art** (410-848-7272). Sponsored by the Carroll County Arts Council Gallery (see *Selective Shopping—Art Galleries*) in Westminster on the first Thursday of each month.

March: **Maple Sugarin' Festival** (410-848-9040), Hashawha Environmental Center (see *Green Space—Parks*), Westminster. A day of maple syrup demonstrations, taste testing, kid's activities, and country crafts. **Annual Toy Show and Sale** (410-

BOORDY VINEYARDS IN HYDES

756-2430), Taneytown. New and antique farm and collectible toys for sale. **Annual Music Show** (410-848-9080), Westminster High School, Westminster. A full day of gospel music featuring nationally known talent.

April: **Annual Street Cars of Desire and Spring Fling** (410-751-1750), Taneytown. A streetcar show, flea market, crafts show, musical-entertainment venue, and food festival all wrapped up in a 1-day event.

May: **Annual Barbershop Quartet Extravaganza** (410-795-5050), Westminster High School, Westminster.

June: **Annual Strawberry Festival** (410-984-2448), Sykesville. Celebrates the ripening of the berry with food, crafts, kids' games and entertainment, and hayrides. **Art in the Park** (410-848-7272), Westminster. An annual outdoor festival of performing and visual arts. **Fiddlers' Convention** (410-876-2667), Carroll County Farm Museum (see sidebar on page 191), Westminster. A competition of bluegrass musicians with awards, crafts, and farmhouse tours.

July: **Carroll County 4-H and FFA Fair** (410-386-2760), Carroll County Agricultural Center, Westminster. **Annual Ice Cream Sundae Social** (410-848-2288), Union Mills Homestead (see *To See—Museums*), Westminster. Lots of fun for the kids, with face painting, pony rides, a clown, and tours of the mill.

August: **Annual Car Show** (410-756-2705), Taneytown. A gathering of antique, rod, and custom cars and trucks. There is also lots of food, music, raffles, and games.

August through September: **Maryland State Fair** (410-252-0200), State Fair Grounds, Timonium.

September: **Maryland Wine Festival** (410-876-2667; 1-800-654-4645), Carroll County Farm Museum (see sidebar on page 191), Westminster. The largest celebration of the fruit of the vine in the state. Thousands attend for the tastings, wine seminars, crafts, food, and strolling entertainers.

October: **Fall Festival** (410-795-3322), Sykesville. A banquet of arts, crafts, food, and entertainment in a small-town atmosphere. **Fall Harvest Days** (410-876-2667), Carroll County Farm Museum (see sidebar on page 191), Westminster. Bring the kids and yourself for scarecrow making, wagon rides, puppet shows, country food and crafts, and—the best of all—the milk mustache contest.

November: **Random House Book Fair** (410-386-8155), Community College, Westminster. Book signings by authors, silent auctions of signed and first-edition books, workshops, and children's stories.

December: **Festival of Wreaths** (410-848-7272), Westminster. The annual display and silent auction of more than 100 handmade theme wreaths that benefits the Carroll County Arts Council Gallery (see *Selective Shopping—Art Galleries*).

Baltimore

BALTIMORE

Baltimore grew from a small tobacco-producing community to a major shipping center in less than 100 years. By the mid-1700s, it was exporting flour, grains, iron, tobacco, and produce, and importing sugar, molasses, rum, slaves, and manufactured goods. It came into true prominence during the Revolutionary War, when members of the Continental Congress met in the city for two months after signing the Declaration of Independence.

Privateers, sailing in sleek clipper ships built in the city's harbors, took advantage of the turmoil to prey upon British merchant ships. Within a few years, they had made off with booty estimated at more than 1 million English pounds. They infuriated the British once more by resuming the practice during the War of 1812. Detained upon an English ship, Francis Scott Key watched Great Britain's forces exact revenge by bombarding the harbor area throughout the early morning of September 14, 1804. When the sun's first rays illuminated the large flag flying over Fort McHenry, signifying that the fort and city had held, Key was inspired to write what would become the U.S. national anthem.

It was primarily settlers from Germany and the British Isles, along with their African slaves, who first shaped the city, but soon immigrants from other parts of the world began to arrive. Italians, Russians, Ukrainians, Poles, and Lithuanians poured in, attracted by Baltimore's flourishing shipbuilding and shipping industries, transportation services, and cannery factories. In the last few decades, the majority of newcomers have been Hispanic, Caribbean, and Near Eastern in origin. The many cultural backgrounds are celebrated with a series of ethnic festivals throughout the summer months.

Just as the city's population is composed of diverse groups of people, so too are its neighborhoods. Many still reflect the origins of their inhabitants, while others possess a personality and atmosphere all their own.

Inner Harbor was the focus of an intense revitalization program that began in the late 1970s. What was once a place of decaying factories and warehouses is now a vibrant showplace attracting thousands daily. Water taxis cross the water, taking commuters and visitors all around the harbor. There is almost always some kind of outside entertainment going on, and the Harborplace pavilions are full of shops and restaurants. The strikingly triangular-shaped National Aquarium of Baltimore is topped by glass pyramids and contains more than 10,000 species

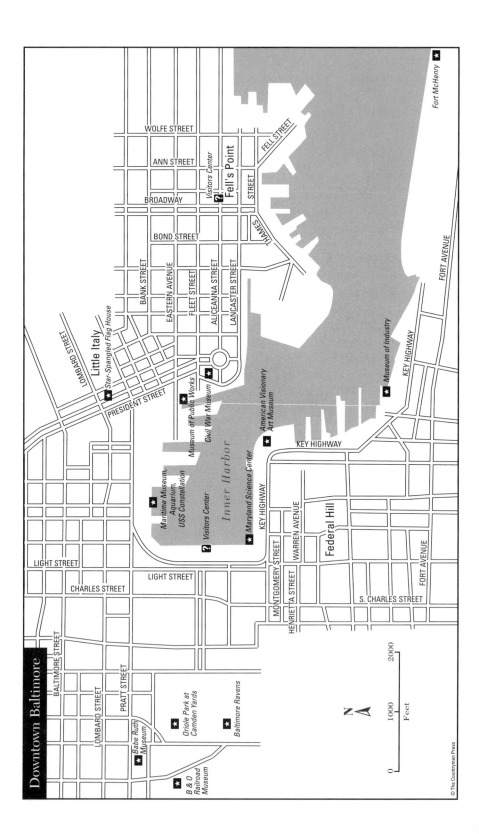

Downtown Baltimore

WOLFE STREET
ANN STREET
BROADWAY
BOND STREET

Visitors Center
Fell's Point

FELL STREET

STREET

BANK STREET
EASTERN AVENUE
FLEET STREET
ALICEANNA STREET
LANCASTER STREET

THAMES

LOMBARD STREET
Little Italy
Star-Spangled Flag House
PRESIDENT STREET

Museum of Public Works
Civil War Museum

American Visionary
Art Museum

Inner Harbor

KEY HIGHWAY

Maritime Museum,
Aquarium,
USS Constellation
Visitors Center
Maryland Science Center

Museum of Industry

KEY HIGHWAY

FORT AVENUE

LIGHT STREET
CHARLES STREET
LIGHT STREET

KEY HIGHWAY
MONTGOMERY STREET
WARREN AVENUE
Federal Hill
HENRIETTA STREET
S. CHARLES STREET
FORT AVENUE

BALTIMORE STREET

PRATT STREET
LOMBARD STREET

Babe Ruth
Museum
Oriole Park at
Camden Yards
Baltimore Ravens
B & O
Railroad
Museum

Fort McHenry

N

2000
1000
0
Feet

© The Countryman Press

of marine life. Tours of the USS *Constellation,* the last all-sail vessel built by the
U.S. Navy, and other historic ships tie into the harbor's past seafaring life.

Along the eastern edge of Inner Harbor is the Power Plant, a huge brick building the city obtained from the Baltimore Gas and Electric Company in 1977. It now houses a large Barnes & Noble bookstore, an ESPN Zone restaurant, and a Hard Rock Café, and has proven to be a magnet for the harbor area. Reflected in the water are the soaring, modern high-rise, steel and glass structures of a number of national hotel and motel chains.

I'm convinced you gain weight just by breathing in the aromas that waft through the 12 blocks of Little Italy. Dozens of restaurants, some quite formal and others very casual, line the streets and employ and expand the culinary arts that have made Italian food a world favorite. Take a walk through the neighborhood and you may feel like you've been transported to the old country. Good-natured, accent-flavored arguments arise from the games of bocce ball.

Fell's Point was established as a shipbuilding center in 1730, making it Baltimore's first port and one of the country's oldest waterfront communities. It soon developed a rough and rowdy reputation as sailors came ashore for rest and relaxation. Many of the rather seedy buildings were condemned to make way for an interstate in the late 1960s. However, locals banded together, defeated the idea, and embarked upon a revitalization program. Their efforts have been more or less successful, as the best way to describe the area would be "shabby chic." Hip restaurants, live theaters, and upscale lodging spots are interspersed among coffeehouses and shops that sport bohemian atmospheres. By the way, so that you won't be marked as an outsider, you need to pronounce *Thames* (Street) just as it is spelled, not as they say it in London.

Jubilant citizens went to one of the highest points in their city to mark Maryland's ratification of the U.S. Constitution in 1788 with celebrations and fireworks. Referred to as Federal Hill ever after, a park upon the promontory provides one of the best views of the city. The area was settled by blue-collar workers and still retains much of that feel, as many of the homes are two-story row houses. The Baltimore Museum of Industry, the innovative American Visionary Art Museum, an assortment of antiques shops, and a variety of restaurants are reasons to visit.

Mount Vernon, laid out in 1831, was once the most in-vogue address in town. The movers and shakers of Baltimore's politics and businesses took up residence in many of the largest homes and row houses. With their money came an array of cultural diversions, including the Walters Art Museum, Peabody Conservatory of Music, Lyric Opera House, and, later, Joseph Meyerhoff Symphony Hall. Charles Street, known as "Restaurant Row," is packed with culinary offerings from what seems like every nation in the world. The street also leads to the neighborhood's central point, the Washington Monument. A climb up the 228 steps will help work off some of the calories consumed for lunch. Baltimoreans claim that the structure, which was conceived in 1809 and completed in 1829, is the first one that was dedicated to the Father of Our Country. However, the citizens of Boonsboro, Maryland, completed their Washington Monument in 1827 and assert that theirs was the first.

GUIDANCE Information about all of Baltimore may be obtained from the **Baltimore Area Convention and Visitors Association** (410-659-7300; 1-800-343-3468; www.baltimore.org) at 100 Light Street, 12th Floor, Baltimore, 21202. Located on the waterfront in Inner Harbor is the **Baltimore Area Visitor Center** (1-877-BALTIMORE), 451 Light Street, Baltimore, 21202.

The **Fell's Point Visitor Center** (410-675-6750; www.preservationsociety.com/visitorcenter.html) at 808 South Ann Street, Baltimore, 21213 is open daily 10–4.

The **Mount Vernon Cultural District, Inc.** (410-605-0462; www.mvcd.org), at 217 North Charles Street, 21201, does a good job in highlighting what many people think is the city's cultural center.

The *Destination Planning Guide* will help you plan your trip, while *Discover Baltimore* is a guide to the city's African-American attractions. Both publications may be obtained from the **Baltimore Area Convention and Visitors Association** or the **Baltimore Area Visitor Center.**

The *City Paper,* available free from newspaper boxes, provides a lot of art, dining, and entertainment information as well as an alternative view of the city.

GETTING THERE *By car:* Like the spokes on a pinwheel, interstate highways come into Baltimore from many different directions. **I-95** is the major East Coast highway that runs from Florida to Maine and is the way people driving from the northeast (e.g., Philadelphia, Pennsylvania, and New York City) or the southwest (e.g., Washington, D.C., and Richmond, Virginia) will probably arrive. (The **Baltimore–Washington Beltway** is a slightly more scenic alternate from D.C.)

I-83 comes in from due north and ends near Inner Harbor. Travelers from the west (e.g., Frederick, Maryland, and Pittsburgh, Pennsylvania) will find that **I-70** is the most direct route. **I-795** connects the suburbs of the northwest with the city, while **I-97** is the fastest way from Annapolis and the Eastern Shore.

By air: **Baltimore/Washington International Airport** (1-800-I-FLY-BWI) is just about 10 miles south of Baltimore and has interstate, MARC and AMTRAK (see *By train,* below), and limousine connections with the city.

By bus: **Trailways** (703-691-3052) and **Greyhound** (1-800-229-9429) will deliver you to the Baltimore Travel Plaza (410-633-6389) in the eastern part of the city at the intersection of I-95 and O'Donnell Street. There is also a Greyhound terminal at 210 West Fayette Street, a few blocks north of Inner Harbor.

By train: **AMTRAK** (1-800-USA-RAIL) at Penn Station (410-231-2222), at the intersection of I-83 and North Charles Street, is close to the University of Baltimore and has received a major face-lift in the last few years.

MARC (1-800-325-RAIL) provides commuter rail service between Washington, D.C., and Baltimore on weekdays.

GETTING AROUND *By car:* **I-695** (Baltimore Beltway) encircles the city, giving access to each of its neighborhoods and suburbs. Going into Mount Vernon, Inner Harbor, and Federal Hill, Charles Street completely intersects the city in a north–south direction. **US 40** goes through the city in a west-to-east orientation.

Like all big cities, Baltimore has a traffic problem during rush hours, but it is surprisingly easy to get around during other times of the day. This is especially true in the downtown/Inner Harbor area—as long as you pay attention to the many one-way streets. Luckily, street and directional signs are plentiful and well placed.

By bus, by subway, and by rail: The **Mass Transit Authority** (MTA) (410-539-5000; 1-800-543-9809) operates bus, subway (closed Sunday), and rail lines that reach into every nook and cranny of the city, and many nearby areas and counties, making it possible to leave your hotel, go to dinner, and then attend the theater without having to drive. Maps and timetables may be obtained at the visitors center in Inner Harbor (see *Guidance*) or by calling MTA. A daily pass is available that is good on any MTA system; exact fare is required to ride the bus.

By taxi: The companies servicing the city are **Yellow** and **Checker Cab** (410-685-1212); **Diamond Cab** (410-947-3333); **Arrow Cab** (410-484-4111); and **Royal Cab** (410-327-0330).

By water: Among the most fun, and certainly most scenic, ways to reach many sites along Baltimore's waterfronts are the water shuttles and taxis. Coming to each stop at about 15-minute intervals (40 minutes off-season), they will take you to Inner Harbor, Fells Point, Canton, Federal Hill, and Fort McHenry. You also get ever-changing views of the city from the water, something many visitors miss. **Ed Kane's Water Taxi** (410-563-3901; 1-800-658-8947; www.thewater-taxi.com) is the city's original water service ($5 adults; $3 children 10 and under for an all-day, unlimited-use pass). **Seaport Taxi** (410-675-2900) offers an all-day pass ($4 adults, $2 children).

THE FUN (AND FASTEST) WAY TO GET AROUND INNER HARBOR

Mount Vernon

Lyric Opera House

Penn Station

MOUNT ROYAL AVENUE

Joseph Meyerhoff
Symphony Hall

CATHEDRAL STREET

BIDDLE STREET

CHASE STREET

GUILFORD AVENUE

JONES FALLS EXPRESSWAY

N

0   500   1000

Feet

READ STREET

FALLSWAY

Eubie Blake
National Museum
and Antique Row

Mount
Vernon Place
United methodist
Washington Church
Monument

Center
Stage

MONUMENT STREET

Maryland Historical
Society

Contemporary
Museum

Walters Art Museum

CENTRE STREET

Peabody Conservatory

FRANKLIN STREET

Basilica of the
National Shrine
of the Assumption

MULBERRY STREET

SARATOGA STREET

Mount Vernon
Cultural District, Inc.

ST. PAUL STREET

LEXINGTON STREET

LIBERTY STREET

CHARLES STREET

CALVERT STREET

Greyhound Terminal

FAYETEE STREET

GAY STREET

BALTIMORE STREET

PACA STREET

EUTAW STREET

HOWARD STREET

HOPKINS PLACE

WATER STREET

LOMBARD STREET

© The Countryman Press

PUBLIC REST ROOMS In the downtown/Inner Harbor area, rest rooms may be found in the Pratt Street and Light Street Pavilions.

MEDICAL EMERGENCY Baltimore has more than a dozen hospitals with emergency rooms. Among them are:

Downtown/Inner Harbor
University of Maryland Medical Center (410-328-6722), 22 South Greene Street. The state's largest hospital. On the corner of Baltimore and Greene Streets, about seven blocks west of Inner Harbor. **Mercy Hospital** (410-332-9477), 301 St. Paul Place—at the corner of Saratoga and Light Streets. About seven blocks north of Inner Harbor. **Church Home Hospital** (410-522-8505), 100 North Broadway. On the corner of Fayette Street and Broadway about 1.5 miles northeast of Inner Harbor. **Johns Hopkins Hospital** (410-955-2280), 600 North Wolfe Street. Located near the intersection of Orleans Street and Broadway about 2 miles northeast of Inner Harbor.

Mount Vernon
Maryland General Hospital (410-225-8100), 827 Linden Avenue. On the western edge of Mount Vernon next to Madison Street.

Northern part of the city
Good Samaritan Hospital (410-532-4040), 5601 Loch Raven Boulevard. About 3 miles south of I-695 Exit 29.

Northwestern part of the city (Park Heights)
Sinai Hospital (410-601-8800), 2401 Belvedere Avenue. Accessed from I-83 Exit 10.

✳ To See
MUSEUMS

Downtown/Inner Harbor
Baltimore Civil War Museum (410-385-5188; www.mdhas.org), 601 President Street. Open daily; small admission fee. Inside the old President Street Depot, which served rail customers from the mid-1800s to the mid-1900s, the Maryland Historical Society presents the role Baltimore played in the Civil War and the Underground Railroad. It is a small museum; an available cassette will take you on a 10-minute guided tour if your time is limited.

✔ **Baltimore Museum of Public Works** (410-396-5565), 751 Eastern Avenue. Tuesday through Sunday 10–4. Small admission fee. Many people complain about paying taxes; here's a fun place to discover what some of those funds accomplish. The museum takes you behind the scenes with displays and interactive exhibits about roads, bridges, sewage treatment, creating clean water, and waste disposal. You and the kids will enjoy negotiating the outdoor maze created from pipes and drains.

✔ ♿ **Maryland Science Center, Davis Planetarium, and IMAX Movie Theater** (410-685-5225; www.mdsci.org), 601 Light Street. Open daily. Adults

& **National Aquarium in Baltimore** (410-576-3800; www.aqua.org), 501 East Pratt Street, downtown/Inner Harbor. Open 9–8 daily in July and August; 10–5 Saturday through Thursday and 10–8 Friday from November through February; 9–5 Saturday through Thursday and 9–8 Friday from March through June, and September through October. Adults $14; seniors $10.50; children up to 17 are $7.50.

I admit to being somewhat of a skinflint when it comes to paying admission charges, but I would urge you to pay whatever they are asking to experience the National Aquarium. I've never been anywhere that does a better job of displaying the underwater world with live specimens and then explaining it with vivid exhibits.

A gently sloping walkway takes you along one tank after another, letting you linger as long as you want to observe the more than 10,000 creatures housed in the seven-story structure. There are sharks, dolphins, sea horses, frogs, eels, piranhas, stingrays, and turtles. The kids will love the touch tank and the dolphin show within the 1.2-million-gallon water-tank theater.

Be aware that baby strollers are not permitted and that long lines can form early in the day, especially during the summer months and in the fall when school classrooms fill the aquarium with hundreds of kids. Allow a minimum of 2 to 3 hours to experience it all. I felt rushed when I spent more than 3 hours there—and that was before the aquarium had completed an expansion that nearly doubled its size.

$11.50; seniors $10; children 4–12 are $8.50; IMAX is an extra fee. There is much to keep you and the children involved and learning for hours. Three floors with hundreds of interactive exhibits and hands-on displays relating to the bay, mathematics, energy, space, and other scientific discoveries. Pay whatever it costs to see a movie in the five-story IMAX theater, especially if the presentation is in 3-D. The IMAX 3-D films pull the images off the screen and put you in the middle of the action—the experience is unforgettable.

*& **Babe Ruth Museum and Birthplace** (410-727-1539), 216 Emory Street. The Sultan of Swat's home place also houses the **Orioles and Maryland Baseball Museums.**

& **B&O Railroad Museum** (410-752-2490; www.borail.org), 901 West Pratt Street (10 blocks from Inner Harbor). Open daily 10–5. Adults $7; seniors $6; children 3–12 are $5. Free parking. The huge 1844 brick and glass roundhouse is a familiar landmark to Baltimoreans. You don't have to be a train buff to appreciate the spectacular 40-acre collection of locomotives, railcars, models, and artifacts. The kids' (and your) imaginations will bring the glory days back to life when you actually get to board some of the engines and walk through the cars.

Great Blacks in Wax Museum (410-563-3404), 1601–3 East North Avenue (about 3 miles north of Inner Harbor). Closed Monday. Adults $6; seniors and students $5.75; children 12–17 are $4.25; children 2–11 are $3.75. The country's first-and-only wax museum of African American history has more than 100 life-sized figures. A replica of a slave ship is also featured.

Federal Hill

✑ **Baltimore Museum of Industry** (410-727-4808; www.thebmi.org), 1415 Key Highway (between Federal Hill proper and Fort McHenry). Closed Monday. Hands-on exhibits revisit the Industrial Revolution's impact on Baltimore, the bay, and the rest of Maryland.

American Visionary Art Museum (410-244-1900), 800 Key Highway. Closed Monday. The museum showcases the talents of innovative, self-taught artists, so the works you see here are almost always different, often unique, and probably found nowhere else.

Mount Vernon

🦐 �& **Walters Art Museum** (410-547-9000; thewalters.org), 600 North Charles Street. Closed Monday. Small admission fee. The Walters contains 55 centuries of art that is displayed in a manageable way. With just one or two visits you can experience much of its Egyptian, Roman, Greek, Etruscan, and ancient Near East collection. A recent renovation has made the exhibit spaces flow into one another, enhancing what each has to offer. The cost of admission is a bargain when compared to that of other art museums—many of which are not even close to being on par with the Walters.

�& **Baltimore Museum of Art** (410-396-7100; www.artbma.org), North Charles and 31st Streets (3 miles north of Inner Harbor), Uptown. Opens at 11 AM Wednesday through Sunday. Adults $6; seniors and students $4; children 18 and under are free. No charge on Thursday. Everything about the museum requires a superlative: As the state's largest art museum, it houses more than 100,000 objects that range from the ancient to the contemporary. The museum has one of the broadest Andy Warhol and other modern artists' collections; multiple galleries devoted to European masters such as Raphael and Rodin; art of Africa, Asia, the Americas, and Oceania; an American wing with paintings, furniture, and more from the 1700s to the present; and one of the country's most expansive outdoor sculpture gardens.

The Cone Sisters' collection of more than 500 works of art is considered to be one of the most important in the world. Because of them, you are able to appreciate the talents of Matisse, Picasso, Gauguin, van Gogh, Renoir, Cézanne, and others. Even the building is a work of art, having been designed by John Russell Pope, designer of the National Gallery of Art in Washington, D.C.

THE *USS CONSTELLATION* IN INNER HARBOR

Maryland Historical Society (410-685-3750; www.mdhs.org), 201 West Monument Street. Closed Monday. Small admission fee. The original manuscript of the "Star-Spangled Banner" is probably the most famous of the 5 million objects in the society's collection. You will also find furniture, costumes, uniforms, and more that relate to the state's past. The gift shop has many handmade items.

Eubie Blake National Museum and Cultural Center (410-225-3130; www.eubieblake.org), 847 Howard Street. Honors the life and music of this jazz great and Baltimore native. Also highlights others, such as Cab Calloway and Billie Holiday, who were also from Baltimore. Changing exhibits focus on many aspects pertinent to the city's African American community.

Contemporary Museum (410-783-5720; www.contemporary.org), 100 East Centre Street. Changing exhibits of contemporary art in a variety of media.

HISTORIC SHIPS

Downtown/Inner Harbor
USS *Constellation* (410-539-1797; www.constellation.org), Pier 1, Pratt Street. Handheld audio devices take you on a guided tour of the 1854 *Constellation,* the last all-sail vessel built by the U.S. Navy. I liked learning about the history and operation of the ship, but most amazing was the number of levels below the main deck.

Baltimore Maritime Museum (410-396-3453; www.baltimoremaritimemuseum.com), Pier 3, Pratt Street. Open daily. Adults $6; seniors $5; children 5–12 are $3. There are no real walls to this museum as it consists of three ships docked about a block from each other. The U.S. submarine *Torsk* was the last ship to sink an enemy boat in World War II; the *Taney* is the only ship still afloat that was in Pearl Harbor, and the *Chesapeake* served as a lightship for more than 29 years. Tickets also give you admission to the **Sevenfoot Knoll Lighthouse,** the oldest screw-pile lighthouse in the state.

HISTORIC HOMES

Little Italy
The Star-Spangled Banner Flag House (410-837-1793), 844 East Pratt Street. Tuesday through Saturday 10–4. Free parking. Small admission fee. The 1793 home, furnished in Federal-period antiques, was the home of Mary Pickersgill, who sewed by hand the flag that inspired Francis Scott Key's famous poem (see **Fort McHenry** under *Historic Sites*). The museum next door chronicles the War of 1812.

SAVE A FEW DOLLARS

The Mini-Seaport Day Pass (1-877-NH-CPORT; www.natlhistoricseaport.org) provides a combined discounted admission to the *Constellation,* the historic ships and lighthouse of the **Baltimore Maritime Museum** (see opposite page) and all-day transportation on the **Seaport Taxi** (see *Getting Around—By water*). Adults $15.50; seniors $13; children 6–14 are $8.50. The pass may be purchased at the *Constellation,* Pier 3 Ticket Booth, or at the Inner Harbor Kiosk. There is a more expensive pass that provides admittance to additional sites, but you would be hard-pressed to see everything in a day.

Uptown

Evergreen House (410-516-0341), 4545 North Charles Street. Open daily to 4 PM; tours offered on the hour. Adults $6, seniors $5, students $3. Surrounded by 26 acres, the Italianate Evergreen House was built in 1840, and its 48 rooms are filled with decorative arts, antiques, and Tiffany glass. The house and grounds have been restored to reflect the time when Ambassador John Garrett's family resided here, from 1878 to 1942.

Homewood House (410-516-5589) 3400 North Charles Street. Open to 4 PM; tours on the hour. Closed Monday. Adults $6, seniors $5, students $3. The Federal-architecture 1801 house was a wedding gift from Charles Carroll to his son and is now on the campus of Johns Hopkins University. Many of the pieces in the home belonged to the Carroll family. Be sure to visit the brick outhouse, which has graffiti from when the house served as a boys' school.

HISTORIC SITES ♿ **Fort McHenry** (410-962-4290), East Fort Avenue. Open

SEVENFOOT KNOLL LIGHTHOUSE IN INNER HARBOR

daily; small admission fee. After witnessing 25 hours of vehement bombardment by the British, the flag flying over this fort on the morning of September 14, 1814, inspired Francis Scott Key to pen the "Star-Spangled Banner." Star-shaped Fort McHenry has been restored to its pre–Civil War appearance with cannons, barracks, and jail cells. Be sure to watch the presentation in the visitors center, and remember that the place is a great spot to watch ships going in and out of the harbor.

HISTORIC CHURCHES

Mount Vernon
Basilica of the National Shrine of the Assumption (410-727-3564), Cathedral and Mulberry Streets. The 1821 basilica was the first Roman Catholic cathedral built in America and was designed by Benjamin Henry Latrobe, the architect of the U.S. Capitol. Many consider it to be one of the best neoclassical structures in the world. Guided tours are provided after the Sunday 10:45 Mass.

Mount Vernon Place United Methodist Church (410-685-5290), 10 East Mount Vernon Place. The ornately carved interior of the 1874 church contains an organ with 3,287 pipes and a labyrinth nearly a mile long. The green serpentine and gray stone church is on the site where Francis Scott Key died in 1843.

GUIDED TOURS African American Cultural Tours (410-727-0755) and **Renaissance Productions and Tours** (410-728-3837) conduct tours highlighting contributions, landmarks, institutions, and individuals of significance to African Americans.

ZOO 🐾 ♿ **Baltimore Zoo** (410 366-LION; www.baltimorezoo.org), Druid Hill Park, Uptown (accessible from I-83 Exit 7). Open daily. Free parking. Adults $10; seniors and children 2–15 are $6. Opened in 1867, it is the third oldest zoo in the country and is home to more than 2,000 animals from all seven conti-

FORT McHENRY

nents. There are the exotic species such as polar bears, lions, and leopards, as well as the locally familiar turtles, barnyard animals, and owls. This is a very child-friendly place, as most of the exhibits are arranged so that even the smallest of visitors can see the animals. Lots of special events for children, too.

✳ To Do

BALLOONING HiFlyer (410-727-8120; www.portdiscovery.com), downtown/Inner Harbor. An attraction of Port Discovery (see *Family Activities*), the HiFlyer is a helium balloon with an enclosed gondola that rises 450 feet above Inner Harbor for the most spectacular view you could possibly get of the city. Don't worry, you won't float away. The balloon is tethered to a steel cable.

BICYCLING Bicycle trails wend their way through the green landscape of **Herring Run Park** (see *Green Space—Parks*).

✎ **Light Street Cycles** (410-685-2234), 1015 Light Street, Federal Hill. A bicycle may just be the best way to tour the downtown/Inner Harbor/Federal Hill area, and these folks will rent you one for an hour or a day.

BIRDING See *Nature Preserves*.

BOAT EXCURSIONS

Inner Harbor

Clipper City (410-539-6277; www.sailingship.com), docked between the Light Street Pavilion and the Science Center. The 158-foot, two-masted schooner takes 2-hour sailing tours of the harbor daily at noon and 3 PM from April through November. Adults $12; children

LESSER FLAMINGOS IN THE BALTIMORE ZOO

under 10 years are $2. There are also special-theme and Sunday-brunch cruises.

Harbor Cruises (410-727-3113; 1-800-695-BOAT; www.harborcruises.com), 301 Light Street (close to the Light Street Pavilion). Offers daily lunch, dinner, sight-seeing, and evening cruises on three different boats. Departure times, costs, and itineraries vary widely, so call to obtain the latest information.

Minnie V (410-685-0295; www.living-classrooms.org), docked next to the *Constellation* pier. Adults $12; children under 12 years of age are $3. If you want to take the least commercially oriented boat trip and truly learn about the harbor, the sailing skipjack *Minnie V* is the way to go. The 90-minute walk-on excursions depart Saturday, Sunday, and holidays at 10:30 AM, 1 PM, and 3 PM from May through September. Limit of 24 passengers.

Discovery Channel Ducks (410-727-DUCK), Adults $19.95; children 3–12 are $10.95. A most interesting way to see the waterfront area. These 1945 army DUKWs have been converted into passenger vehicles. As they are amphibious, part of your 80-minute tour is on the water, while the

ALONG THE WATERFRONT PROMENADE IN INNER HARBOR

other portion takes you to sites along waterfront roadways.

BOAT RENTALS

Downtown/Inner Harbor
🚣 **Trident Electric Boat Rentals** (410-539-1837), located between the World Trade Center and the National Aquarium. Boats of various shapes and sizes are available for rent so that you can explore the harbor on your own.

FAMILY ACTIVITIES 🚣 ♿ **Port Discovery** (410-727-8120; www.portdiscovery.com), 35 Market Place, downtown/Inner Harbor. Open daily. Adults $10; children 3–12 are $7.50. The kids will just think they're having fun deciphering hieroglyphics, piecing together clues, or crossing the rope bridge, but Walt Disney's Imagineers designed the activities for children 6 to 12 years old to teach goal setting, problem solving, and creative thinking. Allow 1 to 2 hours.

Also see *Ballooning* and *To See— Zoos*.

GOLF There are five courses within the municipal boundary of Baltimore. Information on all five may be obtained by calling 410-444-4933 or visiting www.bmbcgolf.com.

FISHING Captain Don Marani (410-342-2004; www.captdonscharters.com), 1001 Fell Street, Fell's Point. From June through December, Captain Don heads into the bay from Henderson's Wharf Marina in search of rockfish, bluefish, croaker, spot, and more. Charters are full day ($360), half day ($300), and evening ($290).

HORSE RACING ♿ **Pimlico Race Course** (410-542-9400), Hayward and Winner Avenues, Mount Washington (northwestern part of the city). Pimlico is home to the second jewel in thoroughbred racing's Triple Crown, the Preakness Stake. The Preakness is run annually on the third weekend in May, but you can attend other races here throughout the warmer months of the year.

WALKING TOURS Frederick Douglass Walking Tour (410-675-6750), 808 South Ann Street, Fell's Point. Sponsored by the Preservation Society, the guided walk travels to sites that enslaved Africans, free blacks, runaways, and Frederick Douglass called home. The society also sponsors a general-history **Fell's Point Walking Tour.**

The Mount Vernon Cultural District, Inc. (see *Guidance*), Mount Vernon, has several brochures describing different walks throughout the neighborhood, taking in the cultural, historic, and retail aspects of each.

✳ Green Space

GARDENS Sherwood Park (410-323-7982), Stratford Road, Guilford (northeastern part of the city). Open dawn to dusk daily. Free admission. It is small, but loaded with azaleas, boxwoods, cherries, dogwoods, magnolias, and wisterias. The most spectacular time to visit is late April through early May, when the 80,000 tulips are in bloom.

NATURE PRESERVES ♿ Clyburn Arboretum (410-396-0180), 4915 Greenspring Avenue, Mount Washington (northwestern part of the city). Grounds open 6 AM–9 PM daily; mansion and museum open 8 AM–3 PM Monday through Friday. Free admission. Signs identify hundreds of plants and trees throughout the 170 acres. There are marked trails, a garden of senses for the physically impaired, and a number of flower gardens. The 1888 Clyburn Mansion contains a commendable nature museum.

This is one of the Baltimore Bird Club's favorite sites. Great horned owls are year-round residents, and a variety of thrushes and warblers pass through during migrations. Come here in midspring and you'll see (or at least hear) sparrows, scarlet tanagers, finches, and yellow-bellied sapsuckers.

PARKS 🐾 Druid Hill Park (410-396-6101), Druid Park Lake Drive, Hampden (accessed from I-83 Exits 7 and 8). One of the largest urban parks in America, Druid Hill was set aside as public space in 1688. Tennis courts, a public swimming pool, and lots of picnic tables. The main draws are the large amount of open ground on which to wander and several points overlooking various parts of the city. Pets permitted on a leash.

🐾 Herring Run Park (410-396-6101), Belair-Edison (northeastern part of the city). A linear urban park along the waters of Herring Run. A few picnic tables and several streamside trails make this green space a neighborhood escape. Parking is available at Sinclair Lane and Harford and Belair Roads. Pets permitted on a leash.

🐾 Gwynns Falls–Leakin Parks (410-396-6101), Edmonson Village (western part of the city). Officially they are separate parks, but they are side-by-side and their pathways connect. All together they provide more than 1,200 acres of preserved land within the city limits. One trail follows the route of an old millrace along Gwynns Falls, while others wind through the deep cleft created by Dead Run. Pets permitted on a leash.

WALKS The Waterfront Promenade in the downtown/Inner Harbor area runs for more than 7 miles, tak-

PIER 5 HOTEL IN INNER HARBOR

ing in the best that the waterfront has to offer. By starting at one end, you could walk through Canton, Little Italy, Inner Harbor, and Federal Hill, and end up at Fort McHenry.

✳ Lodging

RESORTS 🌹 🐾 **Gramercy Mansion B&B** (410-486-2405; 1-800-553-3404; www.gramercymansion.com), 1400 Greenspring Road, Stevenson, 21153. It calls itself a B&B, but with a swimming pool, a tennis court, formal and herb gardens, an organic farm, and trails winding through its 45 acres, I call it a resort. Guest rooms in the antiques-furnished, fireplace-rich 1902 Tudor-style mansion house range from spacious three-room suites with whirlpool tubs and private sunporches to basic rooms with shared bath. The basic "back-hall" rooms are a real deal, as they are less than half the cost of other rooms. I didn't feel like I was missing a thing because all amenities were still available to me. $75–295.

MOTELS AND HOTELS

Downtown/Inner Harbor, 21202
🐾 ♿ **Pier 5 Hotel** (410-539-2000; www.harbormagic.com), 711 Eastern Avenue. The Pier 5 is one of Baltimore's few boutique hotels—its art deco style is a splash of colors—and it is the only Inner Harbor hotel situated right next to the water. This permits you to walk to all of Inner Harbor's attractions without having to cross any busy streets.

The staff is gracious and very attentive to your needs, but the more than 60 spacious rooms let you attain large-hotel anonymity if you wish. Some rooms have water views, while others have views of the city; my room had both, as it overlooked the harbor and National Aquarium. Terry-cloth robes permitted me to lounge in comfort, while nightly turn-down service let me know someone cared. Parking fee. $250–325; many packages available. (Also see **McCormick & Schmick's** under *Dining Out*).

Baltimore Marriott Waterfront

(410-385-3000; www.marriotthotels. com), 700 Aliceanna Street. The Marriott is one of Inner Harbor's newest hotels, and most of its more than 700 rooms on 32 floors have views of the water. Indoor pool, exercise room. $279–309.

♂ ♿ **Harbor Court Hotel** (410-234-0550; www.harborcourt.com), 550 Light Street. The Harbor Court is a modern hotel with a feel from another era. The grand staircase sweeps up from the oak-paneled lobby, while a concierge staff caters to your needs. Most rooms are elegantly appointed and overlook the harbor. The fitness facilities are extensive. Child care available. Parking fee. $270–500.

Hyatt Regency (410-528-1234; 1-800-233-1234; www.baltimore.hyatt. com), 300 Light Street. The gleaming glass and steel Hyatt towers over Inner Harbor, reflecting the water, sky, and surrounding buildings. Amenities include an extensive health club, a recreation deck with jogging track, a putting green, tennis courts, and almost 500 guest rooms with great views. Concierge service. Parking fee. $250–300.

♂ ♿ **Renaissance Harborplace** (410-547-1200; 1-800-HOTELS-1; www.renaissancehotels.com), 202 East Pratt Street. Another towering steel and glass structure overlooking the harbor, the Renaissance has more than 600 rooms (some without a water view). Connected to the Gallery Mall, it has a swimming pool and exercise room. Children under 18 stay free in the same room with parent. Parking fee. $239–319; some suites are available ranging $600–3,500.

Sheraton Inner Harbor (410-962-8300; www.sheraton.com/innerharbor), 300 South Charles Street. Its location is perfect for families with dedicated sports fans and other members who would rather shop or see the sites. It is located just one block from Inner Harbor, two blocks from the Orioles' Camden Yards, and a few more blocks from the Ravens' Stadium. Some rooms have water views; amenities include pool and fitness room. Free on-site parking. $255–325.

🐾 ♿ **Tremont Plaza Hotel** (410-685-7777; www.tremontsuitehotels. com), 222 St. Paul Place. Located about halfway between Inner Harbor and Mount Vernon. Italian marble and mahogany add a touch of distinction to the lobby. All of the more than 200 guest accommodations are suites with separate living and sleeping rooms and fully equipped kitchens. Parking fee; pets permitted with extra fee. $159–179.

Note: Many more hotels and motels are located near the Baltimore/Washington International Airport and almost every exit along the I-695 beltway. Among the lower-cost national chains are **Days Inn** (1-800-544-8313; www.daysinn.com); **Comfort Inn** (1-800-228-5150; www.comfortinn.com); **Red Roof Inn** (1-800-RED-ROOF; www.redroof.com; **Courtyard by Marriott** (1-888-236-2427; www.courtyard.com); and **Microtel** (410-865-7500; www. microtelinn.com). The **Homestead Village Guest Studios** (410-691-2500), 939 International Drive, with low-cost studio efficiencies, is close to the airport.

INNS

Fell's Point, 21231
🐾 ♂ ♿ **The Admiral Fell Inn** (410-522-7380; www.AdmiralFell.com),

888 South Broadway. The European-style Admiral Fell Inn's main building originally served as a seamen's hostel. Today, guests sip complimentary coffee or tea next to the lobby's fireplace or retire to rooms decorated with Federal-period furnishings. My room had a canopy pencil-post bed and overlooked the fading VOTE AGAINST PROHIBITION sign painted on the building next door. Specialty rooms and suites have deep dormers, original wood floors, Jacuzzis, and balconies. A complimentary house breakfast is served in the inn's noted restaurant (see **Hamilton's** under *Dining Out*). Dogs permitted with extra fee; free parking nearby. $215–399.

🐾 ✒ ♿ **Inn at Henderson's Point** (410-522-7777; 1-800-292-4667; www.hendersonswharf.com), 1000 Fell Street. The inn was originally constructed in 1893 as a tobacco warehouse. Many of the large guest rooms retain the original 3-foot-thick brick walls, providing them a warm radiance. Some rooms overlook the water, others face the cobblestoned inner courtyard. Continental breakfast included. A good value when compared to the hotels in Inner Harbor. $149–209.

BED & BREAKFASTS

Fell's Point, 21231

🐾 **Ann Street B&B** (410-342-5883), 804 South Ann Street. Joanne and Andrew Mazurek were active in revitalizing Fell's Point when it was on the skids several decades ago. The B&B is the same row house Andrew grew up in, and they have restored the luster of the original hardwood floors and staircase, and maintained all 12 fireplaces. Only three guest rooms ensure an intimate stay, and the meticulously maintained garden (which the upstairs back room overlooks) is the place to relax after a meal at one of Fell's Point's many restaurants. $100–110.

✒ ♿ **Celie's** (410-522-2323; 1-800-432-0184), 1714 Thames Street. There are seven guest rooms in this large row house (long and narrow like most of Baltimore's row houses). Some have fireplaces, others whirlpool tubs; all have a TV and VCR. The ground-floor room has its own private courtyard and is handicapped accessible. Walk up the steps to the roof deck for a small view of the harbor. Children over 10 are welcome. $132–242.

Federal Hill, 21230

Scarborough Fair (410-837-0010; www.scarborough-fair.com), 1 East Montgomery Street. This is the place to stay if you want to be close to Inner Harbor (it is only two blocks away) but don't want the impersonal service (or higher prices) of a hotel. Ellen and Ashley Scarborough offer six period- and/or reproduction-furnished guest rooms in their 1801 home; each has a private bath and four have working fireplaces. Refreshments and treats available, and the Scarboroughs promise you will not go away hungry from breakfast. Free off-street parking. $139–179.

Mount Vernon, 21201

Aunt Rebecca's B&B (410-625-1007; www.auntrebeccasbnb.com), 106 East Preston Street. Within their 1870s brownstone town house, Becky and Joe Pitta offer three large (12-foot ceilings) guest rooms furnished in Victorian style. Each room has individually controlled air-conditioning, and the bathrooms retain the original claw-foot tubs for relaxing soaks. Off-street parking available. $95–140.

🖉 **Abercrombie Badger B&B** (410-244-7227; 1-888-9BADGER; www.badger-inn.com), 58 West Biddle Street. This 1880s row house is conveniently located in Mount Vernon, close to many of Baltimore's cultural offerings. The 12 guest rooms have private baths, while guests meet and greet each other in the parlor on the first floor. Well-mannered children over 10 are welcome. $115–155; single guests may have a smaller room for $90.

Bolton Hill, 21217

🖉 **Mr. Mole B&B** (410-728-1179; www.MrMoleBB.com), 1601 Bolton Street. Mr. Mole is just a few blocks away from its companion B&B, Abercrombie Badger. There are five guest rooms decorated with 18th- and 19th-century English-style antiques in the mid-1800s row house. Three are suites. Well-mannered children over 10 are welcome; be sure you understand the cancellation and check-in and check-out policy. $119–175.

✳ Where to Eat

DINING OUT

Downtown/Inner Harbor

McCormick and Schmick's (410-234-1300), 711 Eastern Avenue (in the **Pier 5 Hotel;** see *Lodging–Hotels and Motels*) at Inner Harbor. Open for lunch and dinner daily. Walls of dark wood, stained glass, and a mahogany bar embellish the view of the harbor. This Portland, Oregon–based chain came to Baltimore in 1998 with a changing menu featuring more than 30 varieties of fish from both of America's oceans. There can be as many as

10 different appetizers on the half shell ($7–13), and the menu tells you where the fish came from that day. Wanting to stay somewhat local, I had the mackerel, from New Jersey, grilled with tomatoes and capers ($13.60). Entrées $13–30.

♿ **Charleston** (410-332-7373; www.charlestonrestaurant.com), 1000 Lancaster Street (between Inner Harbor and Fell's Point). Open for dinner 5:30–10 Monday through Saturday. Reservations strongly advised. Considered by many to be one of Baltimore's finest dining experiences. Chef Cindy Wolf prepares a daily changing selection of American cuisine with bits of southern and French influences. Recent menus have included sautéed salmon with cucumber and watercress *coulis* ($24) and veal tenderloin with lobster and fresh asparagus ($32). A prix fixe menu of five courses is $57; the eight-course menu is $75.

Purple Orchid (410-837-0080), 729 East Pratt Street (on the corner of Pratt and President Streets). Open for lunch 11:30–2:30 Monday through Friday. Dinner is served 5:30–10:30 Monday through Friday, and 5–11:30 Saturday and Sunday. Known for its sushi and French and Oriental seafood. The oven-roasted rockfish with flying-fish roe ($21) is popular, as are the spicy sweet prawns in an orange and plum sauce ($21). Angus beef, veal, and fowl are also available ($14–24).

Little Italy

Da Mimmo Ristorante (410-727-6876; www.damimmo.com), 217 South High Street. Open for lunch Monday through Friday; dinner daily. Reservations strongly advised. Low lights, candles on the table, and a tuxedoed wait staff in a 200-year-old building—the idyllic setting to savor Chef Mimmo's irreproachable preparations. The *pasta fagioli* ($6) was like my mother's, while the taste of the *gnocchi alla Napolitana* ($16) almost made me believe my Italian grandfather had come back to life. An order of veal chops ($20–24) could serve a small army, as could the filet mignon alla Rossini ($28). As a bonus, Da Mimmo is the only restaurant in Little Italy with its own parking lot.

& **Dalesio's** (410-539-1965), 829 Eastern Avenue. Dalesio's forte is northern Italian cuisine, which, by its nature, has a bit of a French character to it. The *frutti di mare all Mediterranea* ($18) is shrimp and scallops with mushrooms in a creamy Marsala sauce. Not quite as heavy is the *capellini al Carciofi* ($16), with artichoke hearts, tomatoes, and a touch of Chianti. Veal, chicken, and duck dishes $16–24.

La Scala (410-783-9209; www.lascaladining.com), 1012 Eastern Avenue. Italian cooking that is inspired by the whole country and not just one region. The prices on the pasta dishes, such as the *capellini al pomodoro* ($11.95), are great deals ranging $11.95–17.95. Chicken, veal, beef, and seafood entrées are only slightly higher.

Fell's Point

& **Hamilton's** (410-522-2195), 888 South Broadway. Open for lunch Monday through Friday, dinner Monday through Saturday, brunch Sunday. Fine dining inside the historic **Admiral Fell Inn** (see *Lodging—Inns*). Featured on *Best Of* on the Food Network. The seasonal menu includes local seafood (crabcakes and their accompaniment are exceptional—

$32), Black Angus steaks ($28), and peppercorn-encrusted veal chops ($27). Desserts are always delectable. The banana caramel cheesecake ($8) is gently fried in a flour tortilla, and my taste buds savored each spoonful of the warm red wine strawberry soup with ice cream ($7).

& **The Black Olive** (410-276-7141; 1-877-916-5483; www.theblackolive. com), 814 South Bond Street. Open for dinner daily. Dimitris, Pauline, and Stellos Spiliadis use only organic produce, milk products, flour, and sugar in their Greek restaurant. The fish offerings, such as arctic char, sea bream, and Dover sole, arrive fresh from around the world, and are filleted tableside. Lamb, veal, and several vegetarian selections are also prepared with care. Entrées $24–48.

& **Kali's Court** (410-276-4700; www.kaliscourt.com), 1606 Thames Street. Open for lunch and dinner daily. Like The Black Olive (see above), Kali's offers fish from around the world. Many dishes, like the Australian swordfish ($22.95) and the bouillabaisse ($27.50), are cooked in a brick oven for a bit of a different taste. Appetizers range from the brick-oven oysters ($8.95) to an ounce of beluga caviar served with minced egg ($52).

& **Pierpoint** (410-675-2080; www. pierpointrestaurant.com), 1822 Aliceanna Street. Open for lunch Tuesday through Friday, dinner Tuesday through Sunday. Chef-owner Nancy Longo has been attracting customers into her small space since the late 1980s. The smoked crabcakes (market price) established her reputation as someone who does things differently. The BBQ duck egg rolls ($8.50), corn-fried oysters ($22), and

Maryland-style cioppino ($23) are just a few other examples.

Federal Hill

♿ **Corks** (410-752-3810; www.corks-restaurant.com), 1026 South Charles Street. Open for lunch and dinner, but hours vary each day; closed Monday. Reservations strongly recommended. An outstanding wine list paired with an ever-changing discriminating menu served inside a Baltimore row house. The veal, fish, beef, and fowl are almost always prepared a bit differently each time you visit. Entrées $20–30.

Mount Vernon

♿ **Tio Pepe** (410-539-4675), 10 East Franklin Street. Open for lunch Monday through Friday; dinner daily; hours vary slightly each day. Jacket and tie required; reservations strongly recommended. The dining rooms in which Tio Pepe serves its authentic Spanish food are in one of Baltimore's famous row houses. Black bean is the soup to go with ($4.75). The veal chops in black truffle sauce are truly decadent, while the paella for two ($43) could probably feed four. Other entrées $16–29.95.

EATING OUT

Downtown/Inner Harbor

♿ **ESPN Zone** (410-685-3776), 601 East Pratt Street (in the Power Plant). Open for lunch and dinner. Home run, three-pointer, touchdown, goal! More than 220 video monitors (they are even in restroom stalls) ensure that you will never miss a moment of action of any game, in any sport, being played at any moment in history.

ESPN, the sports network, has gone into the restaurant business, although the food is almost secondary to fans glued to the monitors or having fun in 10,000 square feet of interactive and electronic sports games. Appetizers, soups, sandwiches. Pasta (such as Cajun fettuccine), beef (like a 10-ounce filet), and seafood entrées (salmon) range $10–22.

♿ **Hard Rock Café** (410-347-7625; www.hardrock.com), 601 East Pratt Street (in the Power Plant). The Baltimore location of the international café chain serves traditional American food (burgers, steak, and pasta) amid a profusion of rock 'n' roll memorabilia. Entrées $8–20.

♿ **City Lights** (410-244-8813), 301 Light Street (in the Light Street Pavilion at Inner Harbor). Open for lunch and dinner daily. Seafood with a view of the water. Flambéed scallops ($16.95), fried fisherman's platter ($23.95), and roasted chicken ($14.95) are representative of the menu. Live entertainment on the weekend.

Attman's (410-563-2666; www.attmans.com), 1019 East Lombard Street. In the same location and serving a taste of New York deli sandwiches since 1915. Reubens ($5.95), pastrami ($4.95), kosher hot dogs

THE HARD ROCK CAFÉ IN INNER HARBOR

($2.49), cream cheese and lox on a bagel ($5.75), liverwurst ($4.49), and more. Combination sandwiches $4.95–9.95. They even have rice and bread puddings ($1.95) for dessert.

Marconi's (410-727-9522), 106 West Saratoga Street (between downtown and Mount Vernon). Marconi's has been in the same townhouse location since 1920, and is possibly the longest-running restaurant in Baltimore. The traditional American menu has stayed much the same, too. Italian fare, seafood, and meats. For something different, dine on the broiled sweetbreads with mushrooms. Most entrées are $14–25.

Little Italy

🍴 **Chiapparelli's** (410-837-0309; www.chiapparellis.com), 237 South High Street. Serving southern Italian cooking since the 1940s. Many people come just for the house salad (served with each entrée), which is topped by Chiapparelli's dressing of garlic, oregano, Parmesan cheese, eggs, and *pepperoncini*. Pastas, chicken, veal, beef, and seafood dishes available $13–28.

Fell's Point

The Nile Café (410-327-0005), 811 South Broadway. Open for lunch and dinner daily. There are just a few small tables in this spot, which prepares dishes with hummus, pita bread, feta cheese, lamb, and other items used in Middle Eastern foods. You can also choose from nearly 30 kinds of pizzas. Entrées $7.95–17.95.

Federal Hill

🍴 ♿ **Mother's Federal Hill Grille** (410-244-86860, 1113 South Charles Street. Open for breakfast, lunch, and dinner daily. Brothers Dave and Adam Rather took an old bakery and turned it into a local gathering spot. Crabcakes ($20.95) and other seafood are favorites, but don't overlook the ribs ($14.95), tuna wrap ($9.95), or Mediterranean pasta ($9.95). A number of bottled microbrews and homemade ice cream are other reasons people like Mother's.

Blue Agave (410-576-3938; www.blueagaverestaurant.com), 1032 Light Street. Michael Marx brought authentic food from the heart of Mexico and Baja peninsula to Federal Hill several years ago. Don't look for bland fajitas or chimichangas. Instead, try the mahimahi Veracruzana ($16.50) with sauce made from tomatoes, poblano chile, lime, olive, garlic, and oregano. Or maybe the quail stuffed with *huitlacoche* (often called Mexico's truffle), and served with green chile and sautéed spaghetti squash ($18).

♿ **Bandaloops** (410-727-1335), 1024 South Charles Street. A restaurant and tavern setting. The crab and artichoke in garlic Parmesan cream sauce ($7.50) is *the* appetizer. Salads and sandwiches are available, but try the rack of lamb topped with mango chutney ($18.50) or shrimp and garlic string bean stir-fry ($15.25).

♿ **One World Café** (410-234-0235), 904 South Charles Street. Open for breakfast, lunch, and dinner daily. Organic vegetarian fare and a few seafood dishes. Repeat customers often go for the cheese and bean burrito. Coffee, teas, and delicious treats. Most entrées are less than $10.

Mount Vernon

♿ **Sascha's 527** (410-539-8880), 527 North Charles Street. Closed Sunday. Sascha's has grown from a lunch-delivery-only service to serving cafeteria style for lunch and employing a wait staff at dinner. With a hip and upbeat personality and world-inspired dishes, it has some of the most refreshing foods I've encountered. How about potato pancakes, caviar, and smoked salmon ($8) for lunch? Instead of french fries (which are also available), get the portobello fries with peach ketchup and gingered soy ($4.50). Big sandwiches, a host of salads and veggie offerings, daily plate specials, and designer *pizettes* will make you want to come back again. Entrées $6.50–14.50.

Donna's Café and Coffee Bar (410-385-0180), 2 West Madison Street at Charles Street. Popular with the local bohemian crowd, Donna's is most often thought of for gourmet coffees ($2–4) and rich desserts ($1–7). Also served are pizzas, salads, a wonderful variety of sandwiches, and full dishes (after 5 PM). Entrées $6.50–12.95.

Women's Industrial Exchange (410-685-4388), 333 North Charles Street. Open for breakfast and lunch 9–3 Monday through Friday. You'll spend money to eat out anyway, so let it do some good at this nonprofit group (see *Selective Shopping—Special Shops*). The prices are very reasonable; the most expensive breakfast is $3. Lunch is salad and sandwiches (they're famous for chicken salad): $3.25–6.95. Finish the meal with a slice of sweet-potato pie ($1.95).

Uptown

Gertrude's (410-889-3399; www.johnshields.com), 10 Art Museum Drive. Open for lunch and dinner Tuesday through Sunday. The setting could certainly not be any more aesthetically pleasing, as Gertrude's is located inside the Balti-

more Museum of Art. However, many people come just for the flavorful Chesapeake-style food. Lots of seafood dishes, such as herb-encrusted rockfish (market price), crabmeat quiche ($10.95), and gumbo with six different seafoods and andouille sausage ($16.50). There are also "platters from the land" and several veggie offerings. The *panini* smothered in peppers, onion, field greens, caponata, and fresh mozzarella ($7.95) I had was an outstanding blend of tastes.

CRABS Obrycki's (410-732-6399; www.obryckis.com), 1727 East Pratt Street, Fell's Point. Open for lunch and dinner; closed during the winter. A classic crab house with crabs (market price) steamed in Obrycki's own spice mix, crabcakes ($24.95—rumored to be Oprah Winfrey's favorites), crab soup ($5.50), and other seafood and entrées ranging $7–28.95. If you like what you ordered, they have a mail-order business that ships worldwide.

Bo Brooks (410-558-0202; www.bobrooks.com), 2701 Boston Street (inside the Baltimore Marine Center), Canton. There have been several owners since Mr. Brooks began his business in the 1940s, but steamed crabs (market price) have remained a constant. The latest corporate owner has expanded and updated the menu to include a crab puff ($9.95), other seafood ($16.95–28.95), and sandwiches ($6.95–9.95).

TAKE-OUT Viccino (410-576-0266), 1315 North Charles Street, Mount Vernon. It is only a carry-out, but you'll get some of the city's best pizza. Try the pizza Viccino and you may never want another kind. Salads, pasta, and huge calzones. $6–16.

COFFEE BARS

Fell's Point

Funk's Democratic Coffee Spot (410-276-FUNK), 1818 Eastern Avenue. The name says it—a funky little spot with books to read and board games to play.

The Daily Grind (410-558-0399), 1726 Thames Street. A local hot spot that attracts the bohemian/shabby chic local crowd. At times it is next to impossible to get in, but the coffee is good enough that you should try.

Mount Washington (northwestern part of the city)

Stone Mill Bakery (410-234-0235), 1609 Sulgrave Avenue. Good coffee, sandwiches, and breads baked daily.

MICROBREWERIES

⚓ ♿ **Capital City Brewing Company** (410-539-PINT), 301 South Light Street (in the Light Street Pavilion in Inner Harbor). Open for lunch and dinner until 2 AM daily. A clamorous and bustling place with decor befitting a microbrewery. Overlooks the harbor. The menu recommends the beer to complement each entrée. The Pale Rider Ale is suggested for the stuffed shrimp platter ($19.95), and the Amber Waves Ale for the brew master's chicken breast ($12.95). Other entrées and sandwiches $7–23.

SNACKS AND GOODIES **Cheesecake Factory** (410-234-3990), 201 East Pratt Street (inside the Pratt Street Pavilion), downtown/Inner Harbor. Yes, this national chain has a full menu, but the desserts are the real reason to visit. The thick slices of

cheesecake ($5.75–6.95) are available in more than 30 varieties. The espresso drinks ($2–4.50) are a good complement.

Vaccaro's (410-685-4905), 222 Albemarle Street, Little Italy. Some of the best Italian sweets to be found in the eastern United States. The *tiramisu* melts in your mouth, the cream in the éclairs is surely rich enough to clog your arteries after two bites, and the cannolis are stuffed to order. To really indulge, have your pastry topped with a dip of gelati.

Maggie Moo's Ice Cream (410-276-4556), 821 South Broadway, Fell's Point. The ice cream is made fresh daily in the shop.

✳ Entertainment

FILM ♿ **Charles Theater** (410-727-3456), 1711 North Charles Street, Charles Village (a few blocks north of Penn Station). This neighborhood theater is the place to go to see the foreign, art, independent, and documentary films that never seem to make it to the cineplexes.

♿ **The Senator** (410-435-8338), 5904 York Road, Homeland (northern part of the city). The 1939 Senator shows first-run movies in its opulent art deco atmosphere and has been named one of the top movie theaters in the country.

MUSIC

Mount Vernon

♿ **Baltimore Opera Company** (410-494-2712; www.baltimoreopera. com), Lyric Opera House, 140 West Mount Royal Avenue. The opera has been producing hits for more than 50 years, and features international singers and conductors. Operas are performed in the original language with projected English subtitles.

♿ Baltimore Symphony Orchestra

(410-783-8000; www.baltimoresymphony.org), Joseph Meyerhoff Symphony Hall, 1212 Cathedral Street. A wide variety of classical, pops, and family entertainment is presented throughout the year in the near-perfect symphony hall.

♿ Peabody Conservatory of Music

(410-659-8124), 1 East Mount Vernon Place. Operas, symphonies, and recitals performed by student and guest artists. Many of the performances are free.

NIGHTLIFE

Downtown/Inner Harbor

Have a Nice Day Café (410-385-8669), 34 Market Place. Thursday through Saturday. Claims to be "Baltimore's Grooviest 70s and 80s Nightclub."

Howl at the Moon (410-783-5111), 34 Market Place. Claims to be the "World's Best Dueling Piano Rock-and-Roll" bar.

Improv Comedy Club (410-727-8500), 6 Market Place. The Baltimore location of the nationally known comedy club that has given many professional comedians their start. Reservations suggested.

Fell's Point

The Horse You Came In On Saloon (410-327-8111), 1626 Thames Street. It says it was established in 1775, which would make it the country's oldest saloon. The saloon has a bit of an English pub atmosphere. Local live music is presented nightly.

Latin Place (410-522-6700; www.latinplace.com), 509 Broadway. Closed Monday. Learn the merengue or salsa as you dance the night away to Latin and international music.

Belair-Edison (northeastern part of the city)

♿ **Café Tattoo** (410-325-7427), 4825 Belair Road. Open 4 PM–2 AM Tuesday through Saturday. Live jazz and blues in the bar downstairs, which serves an extensive list of imported and microbrews. Tattoo parlor upstairs.

THEATERS ♿ **The Vagabond Players** (410-563-9135), 806 South Broadway, Fell's Point. All of the actors and stagehands are volunteers, but this does not stop them from presenting professional-caliber theater. Productions have included *Prelude to a Kiss*, *Inherit the Wind*, and *Blood Brothers*.

CenterStage (410-685-3200; www.centerstage.org), 700 North Calvert Street, Mount Vernon. The **State Theater of Maryland** mounts productions ranging from Broadway hits to works by new artists. Previous presentations have included *A Raisin in the Sun*, *Three Tall Women*, and *The Pajama Game*. The season usually runs from October through June.

♿ **Theater Hopkins** (410-516-7159), The Merrick Barn at Johns Hopkins University, Uptown. An ever-changing and entertaining schedule of major American, British, and Irish plays is presented in the 1804 brick barn.

SPORTS ⚾ ♿ **Oriole Park at Camden Yards** (410-685-9800; www.theorioles.com), 333 West Camden Street (about six blocks west of Inner Harbor). The American League Baltimore Orioles have been playing in Baltimore since 1954 and in Camden Yards since it was built in the early 1990s. All of the seats in the stadium provide a clear view of the action and, amazingly in this day and age, bleacher seats are still a bargain.

♫ ⓕ **Baltimore Ravens** (410-986-5225; www.ravenszone.com), Hamburg Street (a couple of blocks south of Camden Yards). The Browns changed their name to the Ravens to honor Edgar Allan Poe when they moved from Cleveland to Baltimore in the mid-1990s. Their new stadium is a luxurious place compared to the old Memorial Stadium—and ticket prices reflect the cost to build it.

ⓕ **Baltimore Arena** (410-347-2020; www.baltimorearena.com), 201 West Baltimore Street. Home for the Baltimore Blast (410-732-5278; www.baltimoreblast.com), members of the Major Indoor Soccer League.

Baltimore Bayhawks (410-666-0200; www.baltimorebayhawks.com). Major league lacrosse is played in the Ravens Stadium.

Baltimore Burn (410-768-1383; www.baltimoreburn.com), CCBC Dundalk Field at 7200 Sollers Point Road. This Women's Professional Football team started playing in spring 2001.

✳ **Selective Shopping**

ANTIQUES

Fell's Point
There are close to 30 antiques dealers within a few blocks of each other in Fell's Point, so just about everything imaginable is available. I found artwork, lamps, furniture, handcrafted pieces from around the world, architectural items, memorabilia, and more. A map and brochure of the shops is available from the **Fell's Point Antique Dealers' Association** (410-675-4776). The association can also supply information about the **Antique Market** held on the second Sunday of every month from April through October.

Federal Hill
Antique Center at Federal Hill (410-625-0182), 1220 Key Highway. Open daily. More than 25 dealers display their wares in room settings instead of the usual large warehouse atmosphere.

Mount Vernon
The 700 and 800 blocks of Howard Street are known as Baltimore's **Antique Row.** There are close to 40 shops that, very appropriately, are located in somewhat revitalized antique buildings. A brochure available from the Mount Vernon Cultural District, Inc. (see *Guidance*), describes what each shop has to offer.

ART GALLERIES

Fell's Point
Art Gallery of Fell's Point (410-327-1272), 1716 Thames Street. Open daily. A cooperative of more than 40 artists working in a variety of media.

Conrad-Miller Studios and Gallery (410-563-3190), 2007 Fleet Street. Step inside to watch Melvin Miller create his latest maritime scene, or Nancy Conrad paint one of her many floral works. The works of other local artists are also featured in the gallery.

Federal Hill
Tradestone Gallery (410-752-8085; www.tradestonegallery), 803 Light Street. Closed Monday. Offers paintings of Russian artists and other items—such as nesting dolls and painted eggs—of Russian origin.

Montage Gallery (410-752-1125;

THE SHOPS OF FELL'S POINT

www.montagegallery.com), 925 South Charles Street. Tuesday through Saturday. Monthly exhibits of artwork from recognized and new regional, national, and international artists.

BOOKSTORES

Downtown/Inner Harbor
Barnes & Noble (410-385-1709), 601 East Pratt Street (in the Power Plant). Yes, this is the chain store, but its location in Inner Harbor makes it very convenient. It is also one of the largest and busiest in the chain.

Fell's Point
Mystery Loves Company (410-276-6708; 1-800-538-0042), 1730 Fleet Street. Closed Monday. The name says it all. The little shop is packed with mystery books, old and new. Among them you may find first editions or author-signed copies.

Adrian's Book Café (410-732-1048), 714 South Broadway. Open daily. The new magazines and books are primarily located on the first floor; used books and the café—which serves many vegetarian items—are on the second floor.

Mount Vernon
Drusilla's Books (410-225-0277) 817 Howard Street. Tuesday through Saturday. A place to bring back childhood reading memories, as Drusilla's specializes in children's and illustrated books, both old and rare.

SPECIAL SHOPS

Federal Hill
Global Village Market (410-230-3540), 700 Light Street. Much like Ten Thousand Villages (see below) in Fell's Point, this shop carries fairly traded handicrafts from around the world.

Fell's Point
Ten Thousand Villages (410-342-5568; www.villages.com), 1621 Thames Street. This is the local outlet for the international nonprofit organization by the same name that purchases fairly traded handicrafts from around the world. A number of unique items.

Menvu (410-558-1212; www.menvuonline.com), 1716 Fleet Street. Specializes in African musical instruments, jewelry, batiks, and stone and wood carvings.

Mount Vernon

Women's Industrial Exchange (410-685-4388), 333 North Charles Street. The nonprofit exchange was established in 1880 to benefit financially ailing women by providing a place to sell their handcrafted goods. The purpose is still the same, except some of the items are now produced by men. The quality items you find here may not be available anywhere else—and the money you spend helps others.

FARMER'S MARKETS Baltimore Farmer's Market (410-752-8632), Saratoga Street (between Holiday and Gay Streets), downtown/Inner Harbor. You will find thousands of people shopping for fresh produce 8–noon on Sunday mornings from June through December. Lots of parking space underneath I-83.

32nd Street Farmer's Market (410-889-8095; www.32ndstreetmarket. org), 400 block of East 32nd Street, Charles Village. This place almost becomes a street fair every Saturday from 7 to noon throughout the year, as people come out to eat goodies and watch the entertainment in addition to buying produce.

✳ Special Events

April: **Waterfront Festival** (1-877-BALTIMORE), Inner Harbor. A celebration of the waterfront with entertainment, maritime exhibits, sailing races, seafood cooking, and a children's crafts and adventure area.

May: **Film Festival** (1-877-BALTI-MORE), various locations. A week of lectures, screenings, and events that highlight the city's contributions to the movies. **The Preakness Celebration** (410-837-3030) is held in different places. The running of the Preakness race is preceded by a week of events including a parade, a hot-air balloon race, the Pee Wee Preakness, boat races, and a concert.

July: **Artscape** (1-877-BALTI-MORE), Mount Royal (in the northern part of the city). Thought to be the largest arts festival in the country.

July and August: **Little Italy Open-Air Film Festival** (1-877-BALTIMORE), Little Italy. If you saw *Cinema Paradiso,* you will love this festival, which projects movies onto an outdoor screen every Friday at 9 PM.

August: **Annual Hip Hop and Comedy Music Crab Fest** (410-484-5600); various sites around the city. Features DJs and comedy acts from Baltimore and New York. **Hispanic Festival** (410-558-8419), Patterson Park, downtown. A celebration of Hispanic heritage.

September: **Book Festival** (1-877-BALTIMORE), various locations in Mount Vernon. The annual event includes author readings and signings, children's writers and storytellers, and book vendors. **Ukrainian Festival and Carnival** (410-682-3800), Patterson Park, downtown. Dances, songs, and Ukrainian Easter eggs and crafts.

October: **Annual Fun Festival** (410-675-6750; www.preservationsociety. com), Fell's Point. Food, drink, dancing, and a plethora of local bands. **Annual Maryland Craft**

KIDS CAN PADDLE A SEA MONSTER TO EXPLORE INNER HARBOR.

Beer Festival (410-377-5523; www. federalhillevents.com), Federal Hill. Food, crafts, and retail vendors, and a chance to sample two selections from every microbrewery in the state.

November and December: **Zoo Lights** (410-366-LION; www.baltimorezoo.org), Baltimore Zoo (see *To See—Zoos*). Annual display of more than 750,000 lights. Active and passive light sculptures and displays.

West of Baltimore

© The Countryman Press

WEST OF BALTIMORE—ELLICOTT CITY AND COLUMBIA

Three Quaker brothers, John, Andrew, and Joseph Ellicott, traveled from their Pennsylvania home and settled along the banks of the Patapsco River in the 1770s. Deeper and stronger than it is today, the river provided the power needed for the brothers' mill to grind wheat produced by local farmers. The town, known as Ellicott City (first called Ellicott Mills), that grew up around their business soon became the largest flour-milling center in the American colonies. Although it gave life to the settlement, the Patapsco River has been a harsh benefactor, periodically flooding nearly the entire town. Markers on the railroad bridge show the dates of the floods and how high the water has reached.

The country's first railroad terminal was built in Ellicott City in 1831, to service the first 13 miles of track laid in America. Soon afterward, Andrew Jackson became the first president to ride a train, taking it from the city into Baltimore. The station is now a museum, providing insight into the past.

In fact, much of the town, now bypassed by four-lane US 40, is like a museum. Buildings within the historic district have been well preserved. Some of today's restaurants were former mills, and shops along Main Street are filled with antiques that would have suited the town's glory days. Tongue Row, a small specialty-shop area off Main Street, was once owned by Ann Tonge as rental property. Local tradition says the spelling of its name changed because so many "millers' wives would lean out of windows to gossip with each other."

Columbia's birth as one of America's first planned communities in 1966 was conceived and directed by developer James Rouse. He envisioned a city that would give residents a sense of belonging by having a variety of houses set up in small communities, with each clustered around its own neighborhood social center. The city would provide a large portion of its own jobs, shopping, health care, education, cultural resources and activities, and recreation. Commercial and industrial development would be balanced by permanently designated parks and green spaces.

For the most part, his dream has retained its original ideas. Columbia is now a city of about 100,000 residents (with average family income well over $80,000), living in a number of designated villages. Cultural venues abound, from art classes and exhibits at several community centers and in the African Art Museum of Maryland to the city's own orchestra, a professional theater troupe, and an endless procession of festivals, celebrations, and free concerts and movies. More than 5,300 acres (well over one-third of the city's land) have been set aside for parks, playgrounds, and natural areas, and close to 88 miles of walking and biking trails provide alternatives to getting around by automobile.

COMMUNITIES The Patapsco River was a major means of transportation during our nation's early history, and trade vessels would ply its waters to the bustling port town of **Elkridge.** Now much shallower—due to erosion and siltation—the river is no longer a busy thoroughfare but a quiet waterway protected by long and narrow Patapsco Valley State Park. The town's fortunes have followed those of the river, and despite some recent housing development around it, its stately Victorian homes give it an air of a slow-moving small town.

Savage grew up around its namesake textile mill that operated from the early 1800s to the mid-1900s. Many of the modest mill workers' homes are still occupied by today's residents. The mill has been converted to a major antiques, specialty-shop, and artisans' workshops attraction.

GUIDANCE The entrance to the **Howard County Tourism Council, Inc.** (410-313-1900; 1-800-288-TRIP; www.VisitHowardCounty.com), is a side door on the ground floor of the Ellicott City Post Office at 8267 Main Street, Ellicott City, 21043.

Maryland **welcome centers** are located on I-95 between Exits 35 and 38. The phone number for the one near Savage is 301-490-1333. You may contact the other, near Laurel, by calling 301-490-2444.

GETTING THERE *By car:* **I-70** cuts across the northern portion of this part of Maryland. It arrives from Baltimore in the east and Frederick in the west. **I-95** and **US 1** run along the area's eastern section, as they connect Baltimore with Washington, D.C.

By air: **Baltimore/Washington International Airport** (1-800-I-FLY-BWI) is about a 20-minute drive from the eastern part of this region.

By rail: **AMTRAK** (1-800-USA-RAIL) makes stops in Baltimore and Washington, D.C. Local buses and **MARC** commuter trains (see *Getting Around*) can then deliver you to several points in the Ellicott City–Columbia area.

GETTING AROUND *By car:* **I-70** runs east–west along the north, while **I-95** and **US 1** run north to south in the eastern part of this region. Four-lane **US 29** is the quickest route between Columbia and Ellicott City. **MD 144** is only a two-lane road, but it goes through some of the smaller towns.

By bus: **Howard Transit Service** (410-313-1919) makes multiple stops in Columbia, Ellicott City, the BWI airport terminal, the MARC/AMTRAK station, and along the US 1 corridor. **MTA** (1-800-543-9809) has buses that will take you into Baltimore and Washington, D.C., on a scheduled basis.

By rail: The **MARC** commuter trains (1-800-325-RAIL) make stops in Savage, Jessup, Dorsey, and St. Denis as they run between Baltimore and Washington, D.C.

By taxi: **Howard County Yellow Cab** (410-381-1818).

PARKING In Ellicott City, parking is free in the municipal lots on the corner of Ellicott Mills Drive and Main Street, on Courthouse Drive above the main part of the city, and in the Oella Lot located across the Patapsco River. Some of the spaces in the lot behind the post office are free; other spaces have meters. Check the signage for the on-street parking meters, as some have 1-hour limits and others have 2-hour limits.

MEDICAL EMERGENCY **Howard County General Hospital** (410-740-7890), 5755 Cedar Lane, Columbia.

✳ To See

MUSEUMS

Columbia

African Art Museum of Maryland (410-730-7105; www.africanartmuseum. org), 5430 Vantage Point Road (inside Historic Oakland). Tuesday through Friday 10–4, Sunday noon–4. Small admission fee. Within its small quarters, the museum presents permanent and changing exhibits of masks, sculptures, textiles, musical instruments, jewelry, baskets, and items of everyday life from the entire African continent. I was especially impressed by the intricacy of work on the gold weights made by the-lost wax method (which may or may not be on display when you arrive).

✐ **Howard County Center of African American Culture** (410-715-1921), 5434 Vantage Point Road. Tuesday through Friday noon–5, Saturday noon–4. Small admission fee. A dining room, kitchen, and living room are furnished to represent the 19th-century lifestyle of county African Americans. Other exhibits include sports and military memorabilia, hands-on exhibits for children, and an extensive collection of early and contemporary African American artwork, inventions, and musical recordings.

Ellicott City

✐ **Ellicott City B&O Railroad Station Museum** (410-461-1944), 2711 Maryland Avenue. Hours vary. Small admission fee. The oldest railroad terminal in America, it was built circa 1830 to accommodate freight service and expanded for passengers in 1856. Amazingly, almost 50 percent of all of the supplies and soldiers that participated in the entire Civil War passed through the town on the railroad.

Exhibits chronicle its history, but there is much more to see and experience here. Living-history demonstrations are presented on an irregular basis, and the HO model layout of the railroad from Baltimore to Ellicott City is elaborate and detailed. Be sure to spend time learning about Owney, the mascot of the Railway Mail Service. A stray dog who was adopted by postal workers, he rode the trains on top of mailbags. At each stop workers would attach tags to commemorate his visit. He collected more than 1,000 and traveled to far-flung places in the world such as China and Japan.

Firehouse Museum (410-313-2600), Main Street and Church Road. Sunday 1–4 in the summer, by appointment other times. Donations accepted. The firehouse was built on an incline above the town to give the firemen "a running start."

Artifacts include a horse-drawn hose cart, the original fire-alarm bell that was loud enough to be heard across town, and a whimsical display of toy fire equipment.

HISTORIC SITES

Ellicott City

Thomas Isaac's Log Cabin (410-461-1945), Main Street and Ellicott Mills Drive. Saturday 11–4, Sunday noon–4. Donations accepted. Living historians relate the story of the National Road and what life was like in the late 1700s. The cabin is the oldest surviving structure in the city.

&. **Patapsco Female Institute Historic Park** (410-465-8500), 3961 Sarah's Lane. Sunday 1–4. Guided tours are given at 1:30 and 3. Small admission fee. On a hilltop overlooking Ellicott City, the institute opened in 1837 as a finishing school for young women. It was one of the first places in America to teach math and science to women. The building was used for various venues after the school closed in 1891 but eventually fell into ruin.

It is now the site of what is believed to be one of the few stabilized ruins in the country, and elevated walkways lead visitors through the building's shell to imagine what the living quarters, classrooms, and kitchen would have looked like.

Next door, **Mt. Ida,** the 1828 home of William Ellicott, serves as the park's visitors center.

Savage

Bollman Truss Railroad Bridge, 8600 Foundry Street (next to **Historic Savage Mill;** see *Selective Shopping—Special Shops*). This style of wrought-iron and cast-iron semisuspension bridge was once used throughout the United States and Europe. This B&O Railroad bridge from the 1860s is the last of its kind left in the world.

HISTORIC CHURCHES St. Paul's Catholic Church, St. Paul Street, Ellicott City. The 1830s church was the site of Babe Ruth's first wedding in 1914.

OTHER SITES St. Joseph Cupertino Franciscan Friary Companions of St. Anthony (410-531-2800), 12300 Folly Quarter Road, Ellicott City. Originally, this was the 18th-century country estate of Charles Carroll, the last surviving signer of the Declaration of Independence. Folly Quarter is now the site of a Franciscan friary and chapel dedicated to St. Anthony, Patron Saint of the Lost. The public is welcome, and I enjoy visiting the extensive grounds, taking a quiet walk on the meditative nature trails, and appreciating the architecture of the chapel and other buildings.

✳ To Do

BALLOONING Friendship Hot Air Balloon Company (410-442-5566), 12465 Barnard Way, West Friendship. Sunrise and sunset flights over Central Maryland.

BICYCLING Columbia Association Welcome Center (410-715-3000), 10221 Wincopin Circle, Columbia. The association publishes "A Path Runs Through It," a map of the 80

HIKING

⚘ **Patapsco Valley State Park** (410-461-5005), 8020 Baltimore National Pike (US 40), Ellicott City. Surprisingly detached from the signs of civilization surrounding it, this is park is an exquisitely beautiful area with trails beside tumbling streams and along quiet hillsides. The park is more than 40 miles long and is developed in several separate sections.

The 5-mile **Switchback Trail** (a favorite with mountain bikers) and its numerous side routes in the McKeldin area lead into a wonderfully isolated valley in which the river rolls down picturesque **South Branch Rapids.** Trails in the **Daniels Dam** area (off Old Frederick Road in Ellicott City) provide easy miles of walking to discover the ruins of a former river town. About 3 miles of trails wind along the hillside and connect the campground (see *Lodging— Campgrounds*) to the river in the Hollofield area.

Within the Hilton and Avalon–Orange Grove areas are easy trails along the river that are favorites with families with small children, while the routes that wind onto the hillside attract mountain bikers. **Buzzard Rocks** overlooks the river, and **Cascade Falls** tumbles down the hillside. Be aware that the hillside trails in these areas may have few signs, meager markers, rugged terrain, and rough footing.

CASCADE FALLS

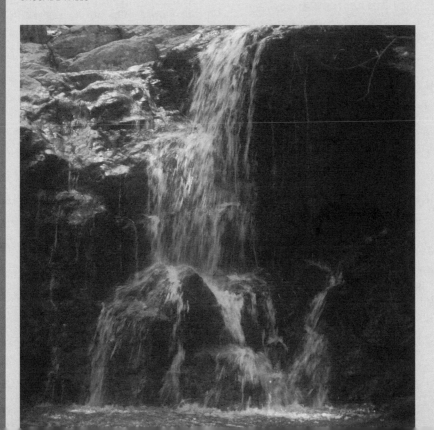

miles of biking and hiking trails that wind through natural areas and connect the city's villages with each other. Some of those miles pass through parklands, while many are roadway or sidewalk connectors.

Also see **Patapsco Valley State Park** sidebar on page 241.

BOAT RENTALS Columbia Association Welcome Center (410-715-3000), 10221 Wincopin Circle, Columbia. The center rents a variety of small boats during the summer months, enabling visitors to explore the 25 acres of Lake Kittamaqundi. (Also see *Bicycling.*)
Centennial Park (410-313-7268), MD 108, Ellicott City. Visitors can rent small boats from May through August and enjoy the park's 52-acre lake.

FAMILY ACTIVITIES *♪* **Rounding 3rd Family Entertainment Center** (410-796-0800; www.roundingthird. baweb.com), 6600 Amberton Drive, Elkridge. Miniature golf, go-carts, batting cages, and an arcade.

GOLF The Timbers at Troy (410-313-GOLF; www.timbersgolf.com), 6100 Marshalee Drive, Elkridge. The par-72 course has over 6,650 yards from the back tees, and is bordered by streams and mature woodlands.
Waverly Woods (410-313-9182), 2100 Warwick Way, Marriottsville. The Arthur Hill–designed course follows the natural contours of the land with minimal bunkering. Five sets of tees range from 4,808 yards to 7,024 yards.
Willow Springs (410-442-7700; www.willowspringsgolfcourse.com), 12980 Livestock Road, West Friend-

ship. Opened in the 1990s and designed by Al Janis. Walk-ons are welcomed and will be accommodated as soon as possible.

Also see **Turf Valley Resort and Conference Center** under *Lodging—Resorts*.

MINIATURE GOLF See *Family Activities.*

WALKING TOURS Columbia Association Welcome Center (410-715-3000), 10221 Wincopin Circle, Columbia. The association publishes a pamphlet describing the sites to be seen along Lake Kittamaqundi. Most interesting are the outdoor sculptures, especially that of Pierre du Fayet. (Also see *Bicycling.*)

✽ Green Space

GARDENS Mill Stone Park, Ellicott Mills Drive, Ellicott City. Millstones rescued from the Patapsco River are bordered by a small garden maintained by local volunteers.

PARKS See **Patapsco Valley State Park** sidebar on page 241.

✽ Lodging

RESORTS Turf Valley Resort and Conference Center (410-465-1500; www.turfvalley.com), 2700 Turf Valley Road, Ellicott City, 21042. The 1,000-acre resort has three 18-hole golf courses to choose from, two restaurants, more than 200 hotel rooms, several golf villas, swimming pools, and a full European spa. Most amenities require an additional fee, but many packages are available. $150 and up.

MOTELS AND HOTELS

Columbia, 21045

Hampton Inn (410-997-8555; www.hamptoninn.com), 8880 Columbia 100 Parkway. Indoor pool, fitness center, and complimentary deluxe continental breakfast. The common areas are large and nicely furnished. $99–150.

Sheraton (410-730-3900; 1-800-325-3535; www.sheraton-columbia. com), 10207 Wincopin Circle, 21044. Overlooks 25-acre Lake Kittamaqundi in Columbia's Town Center. Fitness room, pool, and in-room coffee. $99–199.

Staybridge Suites (410-964-9494; 1-800-238-8000), 8844 Columbia 100 Parkway. Designed for extended-stay business travelers, the studio, one-bedroom, and two-bedroom/two-bath suites also appeal to families with children. Complimentary breakfast. $125–155.

Elkridge, 21075

Best Western (410-796-3300; 1-800-528-1234), 6755 Dorsey Road (accessed from I-95 Exit 43). Just a few minutes away from Baltimore/Washington International Airport. Fitness center, indoor pool, sauna, and free morning newspaper. $89–109.

Ellicott City, 21043

Residence Inn by Marriott (410-997-7200; 1-800-331-3131; www.residenceinn.com), 4950 Beaver Run. Most of the guest accommodations are like small apartments. One or two bedrooms, kitchen, and a separate sitting room. Small pets permitted with a substantial deposit. $150 and up.

Forest Motel (410-465-2090; 1-877-606-6424), 10021 Baltimore National Pike (US 40). A simple but clean motel on the main highway with only

25 rooms. Reminiscent of the 1950s and 1960s. Pool. $60–70.

Jessup, 20794

Holiday Inn (410-799-7500), 7900 Washington Boulevard. Characteristic Holiday Inn rooms with in-room coffee and pay-per-view movies. Swimming pool and coin laundry. $130–175.

Super 8 (410-796-0400), 8094 Washington Boulevard. Nothing fancy, but one of the lowest rates in a high-rate area. $75–99.

BED & BREAKFASTS Clarksville Inn (410-531-5332; 866-806-7920), 11746 MD 108, Clarksville, 21029. The 5,000-square-foot 1985 California contemporary home has lots of wood inside and large picture windows to look onto the hillside forest. Six decks and a teahouse enable you to get even closer to the trees. The inn markets itself to extended-stay corporate travelers but also accepts guests for single nights if possible. The seven suites have private baths, desk and chair, and satellite TV. $100–225.

Peralynna Manor at Rose Hill (410-715-4602; 1-877-PERALYNNA; www.howardcounty.com/hotel/peralynna.htm), 10605 Clarksville Pike, Columbia, 21044. Like Clarksville Inn (see above), Peralynna Manor caters primarily to extended-stay corporate travelers but also accepts guests for single nights if possible. And what a place to stay. The 14,000-square-foot contemporary manor, located next to a 1,100-acre farm, has a great room bigger than my entire home. Guest suites are large, have private balconies, and are packed with amenities geared for those on business trips. Exercise equipment, hot tub, and food provided to make your own breakfast. $150.

Wayside Inn (410-461-4636; www. waysideinnmd.com), 4344 Columbia Road, Ellicott City, 21042. The field-stone inn was built in the late 1700s as a plantation manor, and local lore claims it was visited by George Washington and John Quincy Adams. The two suites have private baths; the other two guest rooms share a bath. My choice would be the Ellicott Room with fireplace, sleigh bed, and view of the landscaped backyard. $95–135.

CAMPING 🏕 ♿ **Patapsco Valley State Park** (410-461-5005; call 1-888-432-CAMP for reservations), 8020 Baltimore National Pike (US 40), Ellicott City, 24102. More than 70 RV and tent sites are available in the Hollofield area of the park next door to Ellicott City. A special loop is reserved for those with pets. The season usually runs from late March through late October.

Ramblin' Pines (410-795-5161), 801 Hoods Mill Road, Woodbine, 21797. More than 150 RV sites and about 20 tent sites. A dump station, showers, a pool, and miniature golf; facilities limited in winter. Short nature trails wind through the 45 acres.

✳ Where to Eat

DINING OUT ♿ **Tersiguel's** (410-465-4004; www.tersiguels.com), 8293 Main Street, Ellicott City. Open for lunch Monday through Saturday 11:30–2:30; lunch Sunday 10:30–2:30; dinner Monday through Thursday, and Sunday, 5–9; dinner Friday through Saturday 5–10. Dinner reservations recommended. French coun-

---

🦞 🍽 ♿ **Il Giardino Ristorante** (410-461-1122), 8809 Baltimore National Pike (US 40), Ellicott City. Open for dinner daily. Momma Mia, I thought I had died and gone to Italian restaurant heaven! The chef is from northern Italy and received her classical training throughout Europe. The seafood is obtained locally, and local produce is turned into sumptuous sauces. The traditional dishes—lasagna ($13.95), eggplant parmigiana ($13.95), and ravioli ($14.95)— are all great, but be adventurous, as there are so many things you won't find as well prepared elsewhere.

The house salad with house dressing was full of fresh romaine, and the minestrone ($3.75) could have come straight out of my Italian mother's pot. But even she couldn't have turned out the crêpes filled with spinach, ricotta, sausage, egg, and nutmeg ($16.95) and served with béchamel sauce and fresh tomatoes. My dining companion proclaimed the wine-sautéed veal with green peppers, onions, and mushrooms ($17.95) to be the most tender she had ever had.

They know how to do desserts here, too. The *tiramisu* ($3.50) is authentic—not heavy like that found in other places. And even the wait staff is talented. Our Italian-born waitress made the biscotti ($3.95) fresh at home before coming to work.

Friendly service, pleasant atmosphere, and very reasonable prices.

try fare based upon Fernand and Odette Tersiguel's original home in Brittany. Served in the 1800s home of Ellicott City's first mayor.

The hors d'oeuvres menu takes up a full page; saumon fumé ($9.95) is a local favorite. Lamb, steak, duck, chicken, pork, and seafood entrées are well presented. Entrées $23.95–35.95. Daily specials and prix fixe menu also available.

&. **Elkridge Furnace Inn** (410-379-9336; www.elkridgefurnaceinn.com), 5745 Furnace Avenue, Elkridge. Open for lunch Tuesday through Friday 11:30–2; open for dinner Tuesday through Friday 5–9, Saturday 5–10; open Sunday 2–8. Dinner reservations recommended. Meals can be peaceful and relaxing in this 1700s country manor home and restaurant on the banks of the Patapsco River. Chef-owner Dan Wecker changes his French-cuisine menu almost every month. Appetizers have included *ravioli d'escargot* ($9); entrées might range from vegetarian "paella" ($17) to *fruits de mer Romesco* ($28) and *filet de boeuf Cabernet* ($29).

EATING OUT

Columbia

✒ &. **Clyde's** (410-730-2828; www.clydes.com), 10221 Wincopin Circle. Open for lunch and dinner daily. Picture windows overlook Columbia's Lake Kittamaqundi, and the Victorian bar is decorated with circus and travel posters. Sandwiches and light entrées for lunch ($5.95–11.95). I liked the vegetable frittata ($7.95). Dinner entrées are a bit heavier, with pork chops ($14.95), BBQ platter ($13.95), and pan-roasted halibut ($15.95) being some of the favorites. Extensive wine list.

&. **P. F. Chang's China Bistro** (410-730-5344), 10300 Little Patuxent Parkway (in The Mall in Columbia). Open daily for lunch and dinner. Possibly the most impressive things about this chain are the huge sculptures at its restaurants' entrances. They are interpretations of 11th-century B.C. sculptures unearthed in China in the 20th century.

The menu draws from major regions of the country. The beef à la Szechwan is twice-cooked with celery and carrots ($11.95); the Mu Shu pork is served with *hoisin* sauce and thin pancakes ($8.95); and lemon-pepper shrimp is stir-fried with chives and bean sprouts ($12.95). Other entrées $6.95–13.95.

❀ &. **The Mango Grove** (410-884-3426), 6365B Dobbin Road. Open for lunch and dinner; closed Tuesday. Authentic southern Indian vegetarian food served in a plain interior at amazingly low prices. The wait staff will be happy to explain if you do not know what *samosas, dosas,* and curries are. The most expensive dinner entrée is less than $10.

&. **La Madeleine French Bakery and Café** (410-872-4900), 6211 Columbia Crossing. Open for breakfast, lunch, and dinner daily. This national chain sends each new café manager to France to learn the country's ways. Breakfast is light baked goods, lunch is sandwiches and pizza, and dinner has many choices like goat-cheese ravioli and pasta Française. Dinner entrées $6–13.

Ellicott City

The Trolley Stop (410-465-8546), 6 Oella Avenue. Open for breakfast, lunch, and dinner. Yes, the trolley did stop at this tavern constructed in 1833, and the brick walls and exposed beams hark back to the building's earliest days. Lots of soups (the Maryland crab—$3.95—has a definite homemade taste), salads, and sandwiches ($4.95–8.95) for lunch. A few entrées are also served for lunch, with more on the dinner menu. The chicken *riggie* with artichoke and shallots ($10.95) is a standout. Other entrées $10.95–15.95.

✐ ⬧ **Crab Shanty** (410-465-9660), 3410 Plumtree Drive. Fresh seafood in its many forms makes up the bulk of the menu, with a few meat items. If you are on a tight budget, go for the deep-fried shrimp ($12.95); if money is no object, then the two New Zealand lobster tails are for you ($46.50). Most entrées range $12.95–25.95.

Almost every item in the decor has a story, which is related on the back of the menu.

⬧ **La Palapa** (410-465-0070), 8307 Main Street. Open daily for lunch and dinner. The fajitas, chimichangas, enchiladas, and tacos are joined on the menu with house specialties such as chile *verde* ($12.95); chicken mole ($13.95); trout grilled with tomatoes, onion, capers, olives, and wine ($13.95); and a *muy delicioso* vegetarian burrito ($10.95). Live music on the weekend. Most entrées are $5.95–16.95.

Jessup

⬧ **Frank's 24-Hour Diner** (410-799-8198), 7395 Cedar Avenue and US 1. Nothing fancy here; the name describes it well. Breakfast is always available, so it is the place for when you feel the need for eggs, pancakes, bacon, or sausage. Lunch and dinner

are the usual sandwiches and diner entrées. Meat loaf is a specialty. Dinner entrées $7–13.

⬧ **Log Cabin** (410-799-9874), 8126 Washington Boulevard. Monday through Friday 6 AM–7 PM. The same family has owned the restaurant for about a half century. Come here if you are familiar with chitterlings, pig's feet, maws, and fried eggplant. Better yet, come here if you don't know about them and learn why the restaurant has such a loyal following. By the way, be sure to order the extremely cheesy macaroni and cheese as a side dish. Entrées $6–10.

COFFEE BARS Kirinyaga Coffee and Specialties (410-203-2743), 8381 Merryman Street, Ellicott City. Also see **Old Mill Bakery Café** under *Snacks and Goodies.*

SNACKS AND GOODIES Old Mill Bakery Café (410-465-2253), 4 Frederick Road, Ellicott City. The espressos, cappuccinos, and lattes are superb complements to the many goodies. The éclairs, Danishes, rolls, muffins, and cookies are baked in-house. The gourmet pastries are made by "various chef friends" who bake for Washington, D.C., embassies and hotels.

✳ Entertainment

FILM

Columbia

Marvelous Movies and More at the Slayton House Gallery (410-730-3987), Wilde Lake Village Green. A series of classic movies from the 1920s through the 1950s is presented throughout the year. Most of the films are unavailable in video, and a discussion and dessert bar are held after each showing. A most interesting way to spend an evening.

Loews Columbia Palace (410-730-4600), 8805 Centre Park Drive, and **Snowden Square Stadium** (410-872-0670), 9141 Commerce Center Drive, are the area's first-run movie houses.

MUSIC
Columbia
Columbia Orchestra (410-381-2004; www.ColumbiaOrchestra.org). The orchestra began life as a small chamber music group in 1978 but grew quickly to include well over 50 members. It now presents a season of full orchestral works, and numerous small "candlelight concerts" at various area venues.

Sundays at Three (410-381-3240), Christ Episcopal Church (corner of Oakland Mills and Dobbin Roads). Chamber music concerts presented in an intimate setting on selected Sunday afternoons. The audience is invited to mingle with the guest artists after the performances.

THEATERS
Columbia
❦ **Rep Stage** (410-772-4900), 10901 Little Patuxent Parkway, Howard Community College. The theater offers professional productions at low ticket prices; the troupe has received a multitude of Helen Hayes awards and nominations. Past performances have included O'Neill's *A Moon for the Misbegotten* and Albee's *Three Tall Women.*

Toby's (410-730-8311; 1-800-88-TOBYS; www.tobysdinnertheatre. com), 5900 Symphony Woods Road. Toby's is a dinner theater "in the

round" that has presented productions such as the *Wizard of Oz, It's a Wonderful Life,* and *Joseph and the Amazing Technicolor Dreamcoat.* Performances are accompanied by live music.

Also see **Howard County Arts Council** and **Slayton House Gallery** under *Selective Shopping— Art Galleries.*

✳ Selective Shopping
ANTIQUES
Columbia
Mimi's Antiques (410-381-6862; 1-888-368-6862; www.mimisantiques. com), 8763 Carriage Hills Drive. Specializes in 18th-and 19th-century porcelains, furniture, and paintings.

Ellicott City
Ellicott City's Country Store (410-465-4482), 8180 Main Street. Open daily. There are four floors of antiques within the historic Walker-Chandler Building, believed to be the country's first duplex.

Taylor's Antique Mall (410-465-4444), 8197 Main Street. Open daily. Four floors of possible hidden treasures.

Ballindullagh Barn Antiques (410-988-8002), 2410 Woodstream Court. European pine and hardwood furniture from the 18th century.

Wagon Wheel Antiques (410-465-7910), 8061 Tiber Alley. Be sure to go upstairs to see the 1850s Easton's Funeral Hearse that owner Ed Growl has restored.

Elkridge
Flea Market World (410-796-1025), 6675 Amberton Drive. Saturday and Sunday 8–4. More than 300 vendors under one roof.

Columbia

Slayton House Gallery (410-730-3987), Wilde Lake Village Green. The nonprofit organization provides space for classes, and theatrical and musical performances. Its two galleries have changing exhibits from local artists working in various media.

Ellicott City

Howard County Arts Council (410-313-ARTS; www.hocarts.org), 8510 High Ridge Road. The county's arts council offers a gallery for changing exhibits of local and regional artists. Its **Black Box Theatre** provides a venue for emerging groups, and theatrical and musical productions. A great place to not only catch locals "in the act" but also to see works not found anywhere else.

Margaret Smith Gallery (410-461-0870; 1-888-227-8670; www.margaret-smithgallery.com), 8090 Main Street. Works of local artists, and an affiliate for animation art from Disney, Warner Brothers, and other studios.

BOOKSTORES Daedalus Books (410-309-2370), 9645 Gerwig Lane, Columbia. Warehouse outlet with most books at least 50 percent off.

USED BOOKS Gramp's Attic Books (410-750-9235), 8304 Main Street, Ellicott City. Used, old, and rare books in many different categories.

SPECIAL SHOPS ✍ Forget-Me-Not Factory (410-465-7355), 8044 Main Street, Ellicott City. The building once served as an opera house and vaudeville theater, and is believed to be where John Wilkes Booth gave his theatrical debut. It is now filled with items such as fairy crowns, bubble wands, wind banners, toys, and other whimsical things of interest to both children and adults. Ask them to let you see where the hillside bedrock was incorporated into the structure when it was originally built as the Patapsco Hotel.

Historic Savage Mill (1-800-788-MILL; www.savagemill.com), 8600 Foundry Street, Savage. One of the most interesting venues for a shopping center you will ever visit. The mill operated as a weaving business from 1822 to 1947, and its 200,000 square feet are now home to more than 50 specialty shops (primarily antiques or art shops) with more than 250 dealers. Part of the amusement in visiting here is negotiating the maze of convoluted great rooms, halls, and stairways to discover a nearly hidden treasure store or an artist painting a life-sized portrait. The **Bollman Truss Railroad Bridge** is next to the mill (see *To See—Historic Sites*).

Stillridge Herb Farm (410-465-8348), 10370 Old Frederick Road (MD 99), Woodstock. This is a pick-your-own place, but instead of fruits and vegetables you pick flowers and herbs. Walking between the rows, you can choose strawflowers, zinnias, celosias, basil, chives, sage, and much more. The gift shop is full of items that incorporate the farm's harvest.

PICK-YOUR-OWN PRODUCE FARMS Tridelphia Lake View Farm (410-489-4460), 15155 Tridelphia Mill Road, Glenelg. Pick your own vegetables from mid-July through September.

✍ ♿ **Larriland Farm** (410-442-2605; 301-854-6110), 2415 Woodbine Road (MD 94), Woodbine. The Moore family invites people to pick a very wide variety of fruits and vegetables from mid-spring into fall. October activities include hayrides and a straw maze. Choose and cut your own tree at Christmastime.

✳ Special Events

March: **Annual Teddy Bear and Doll Show and Sale** (301-498-6871), Historic Savage Mill (see *Selective Shopping—Special Shops*).

March or April: **Easter Egg Hunt and Bonnet Contest** (410-465-8500), Patapsco Female Institute Historic Park (see *To See—Historic Sites*), Ellicott City.

April through August: **Ghost Tours** (410-313-1900), Ellicott City. The first Friday and Saturday of each month. Guides tell true tales of hauntings in the city.

May: **Maryland Sheep and Wool Festival** (410-531-3647), Fairgrounds, West Friendship. Nationally known festival with sheep-dog demonstrations, shearing, spinning and weaving, arts and crafts, and more than 1,000 woolly animals. **Wine in the Woods** (410-313-PARK), Merriweather Post Pavilion, Columbia. Samples of Maryland's

wines, foods, and arts and crafts.

June: **Columbia Festival of the Arts** (410-715-3044), various locations in Columbia. A 2-week celebration with entertainers, children's activities, and many works of arts and crafts.

June through September: **Summer Lakefront Festival** (410-715-3000), Columbia. Music, movies, and other events every night of the week.

August: **Howard County Fair** (410-442-1022), fairgrounds, West Friendship.

September through November: **Ghost Tours** (410-313-1900), Ellicott City. Every Friday and Saturday of each month. Guides tell true tales of hauntings in the city.

September: **Annual Heritage Day** (410-465-8500), Patapsco Female Institute Historic Park (see *To See— Historic Sites*), Ellicott City. Relive the Victorian days when the institute was in its prime. Family games, lectures, music, and dance. **Maryland State Quarter Horse Show** (410-747-0363), fairgrounds, West Friendship. **Annual Farm Heritage Days** (410-531-2569), Mt. Pleasant Farm, Woodstock. Vintage farm equipment, antique cars and trucks, wagon rides, music, and crafts.

Annapolis and Vicinity

ANNAPOLIS AND VICINITY

Annapolis has come to be a special place for me. It is where my wife was born and raised, and we have spent many a blithe hour or day revisiting the places of her memories. She has brought me to the woods where she and her friends would ride bikes and transport themselves to their imaginary worlds of cowboys and Indians, knights in shining armor, and the jungles of Tarzan. I have seen her favorite swimming hole, the high school she graduated from, her old family home, and the preferred haunts of her teenage years.

Although the town she grew up in has changed—former cow fields are now shopping malls, housing developments have replaced woodlands, and four-lane highways reach into previously isolated locales—much has remained the same.

The waterfront has been the focal point of activity since 1649 when a group of Puritans wandered northward from Virginia in search of religious tolerance. Within a year, their settlement along the Severn River was part of the new Anne Arundel County, named for the wife of Cecil Calvert, second Lord Baltimore. Around 1695, the town became the capital of the Maryland colony and was renamed Annapolis in honor of Princess Anne, heiress in the British monarchy.

The protected harbor soon enabled the city to become a major international shipping center, with goods flowing to and from England, Africa's west coast, and the West Indies. Prosperous merchants built their Georgian-style town houses just a block or two from the water. A stroll in the area (see *Green Space—Walks*) will take you through what the federal government proclaims is "the greatest concentration of 18th-century homes anywhere in America." All four of Maryland's signers of the Declaration of Independence lived here, and three of their homes are open for public tours.

The merchants of today occupy the same storefronts as their predecessors. Except for a few changes for modern serviceability, the buildings look as they did centuries ago, while the streets they line are as narrow as they were in horse-and-buggy days. The plaque dedicated to Kunta Kinte was placed at the waterfront in 1981 and commemorates the day that Alex Haley's ancestor arrived in America aboard a slave ship.

The U.S. Naval Academy was established in the mid-1800s, and its presence almost overshadows everything else in Annapolis. Much of the life in the city revolves around the academy's calendar, and the town becomes loaded with

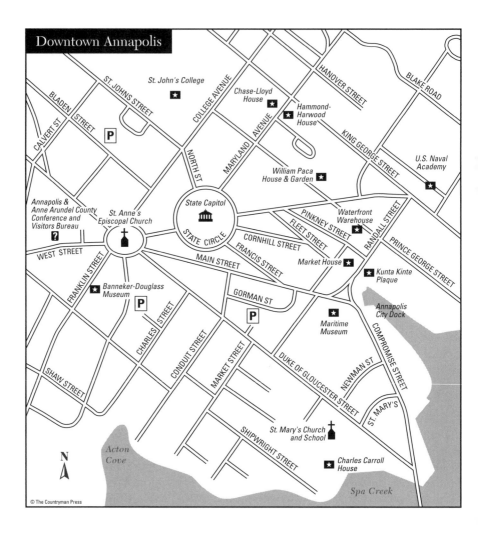

Downtown Annapolis

proud parents in late May when midshipmen graduate to become fully commissioned naval officers. There are no professional sports teams in Annapolis, but that doesn't matter, as the academy's football, lacrosse, soccer, and other athletic endeavors provide a full roster for spectators year-round. The academy, and St. John's College—one of the country's oldest—create an atmosphere of culture, sophistication, and artistic endeavor often found lacking in towns of similar size.

The City Dock is no longer crowded with warehouses of goods waiting to be sent to foreign lands. Yet the Naval Academy, recreational boaters, and sailing schools keep the harbor so busy that the town has been dubbed the "Sailing Capital of the United States." One of the most pleasant, and absolutely free, things to do in Annapolis is to walk down Main Street and watch the glow of a morning or evening sun light up the water to highlight the scores of sailboats wending their way in and out of the harbor.

COMMUNITIES The **Eastport** neighborhood of Annapolis developed as a farming and maritime community around the time of the Civil War, and is now a vibrant residential and dining spot.

The area around **Spa Creek** is a quick walk or water-taxi ride from the City Dock and is full of marinas and popular restaurants.

Highland Beach began as the state's first incorporated African American settlement when the son of Frederick Douglass subdivided 44 acres south of Annapolis. Many of the families that live on this beautiful stretch of land along the Chesapeake Bay are descendants of the original homeowners.

Arnold, Severna Park, Pasadena, Glen Burnie, Linthicum, and other neighborhoods strung along MD 2 serve as bedroom communities for the Washington, D.C./Baltimore/Annapolis metro area.

The southern portion of Anne Arundel County belies its proximity to such a large population center. Here the small towns of **Galesville, Deale,** and **Shady Side** still go about the business of harvesting the fruits of the Chesapeake Bay. This is the place to go if you want to catch a glimpse of the way life used to be along the bay but don't have time to visit the Eastern Shore.

GUIDANCE Information may be obtained by contacting or stopping by the **Annapolis and Anne Arundel County Conference and Visitors Bureau** (410-280-0445; www.visit-annapolis.org), 26 West Street, Annapolis, 21401. The adjacent parking garage offers 1-hour free parking.

There is also a **Visitors Information Booth** open seasonally in the harbormaster's office on the City Dock.

Inside Annapolis Magazine, available free from newspaper-type boxes, is published bimonthly with articles about life in and around the city. The free *What's Up* magazine features much of the same type of information.

ANNAPOLIS ROW HOUSES

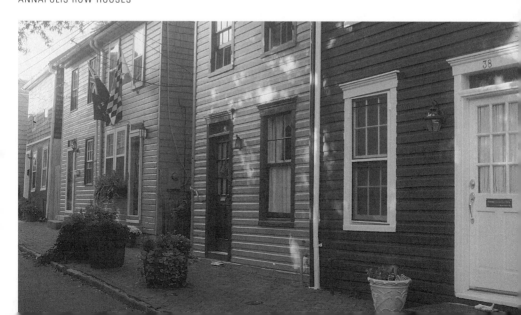

GETTING THERE *By car:* **US 50/301** is the main four-lane highway access to Annapolis and connects the city with Washington, D.C., and the Eastern Shore. **I-97** comes southward from Baltimore and connects with US 50/301 just west of Annapolis.

By air: The **Baltimore/Washington International Airport** (1-800-I-FLY-BWI) is located in the northwestern part of Anne Arundel County and is less than a 30-minute drive from Annapolis. Interstate highways, rail, bus, taxi, and limousine services can transport you just about anywhere you wish to go from the airport.

By bus: **Greyhound** (1-800-231-2222; www.greyhound.com) stops in Annapolis at the Department of Transportation at 308 Chinquapin Round Road seven times a day, 7 days a week. The **Maryland Mass Transit Administration** (410-539-5000; 1-800-543-9809; www.mtamaryland.com) operates both rail and bus routes that permit you to travel to Annapolis and northern Anne Arundel County from Baltimore, Washington, D.C., and the Eastern Shore without having to drive a car.

By rail: See *By bus.*

GETTING AROUND *By car:* The streets within the Annapolis downtown/City Dock area were created in the 17th century for horse-and-buggy travel and have not changed much since then. There are many narrow, one-way streets and traffic circles, so pay attention to the signs and avoid the short rush times in the mornings and evenings. Traffic is tolerable the rest of the day.

The **Governor Ritchie Highway (MD 2)** is the local route between Annapolis and Baltimore, but you will probably make better time using **US 50** and then **I-97**. MD 2 is known as **Solomons Island Road** as it travels south of Annapolis. It is an efficient and scenic way to get into the southern portion of Anne Arundel County.

By bus: **Annapolis Transit** (410-263-7964) serves the city and much of the surrounding area with regular bus routes that have more than 150 stops.

By taxi: **Annapolis Cab** (410-268-0022; 410-268-1323), **Yellow Checker** (410-268-3737), **Neet-N-Kleen** (410-320-3374), and **Reliable Cab** (410-268-4714).

By water: Although it does not provide quite the extensive service that its counterparts in Baltimore do, **Jiffy Water Taxi** (410-263-0033) is still a fun and efficient way to get around to many of the waterfront areas—and to do some sight-seeing along the way.

PARKING In Annapolis, parking meters are in effect from 10 AM to 7:30 PM daily and have only a 2-hour time limit. You are permitted to park free on residential streets, but again the limit is only 2 hours. This rule is strictly enforced.

In the downtown area, the **Gotts Court Garage** off Calvert Street or Northwest Street, and the **Hillman Garage** off Main Street, provide free parking for the first hour. Fees imposed hourly after that. Be sure to get your ticket stamped for a discount if you make a purchase at a participating **"Park and Shop"** store.

You can avoid the headache of parking downtown by leaving your car at the

Navy—Marine Corps Memorial Stadium and taking a shuttle into the historic district. Parking is about $5, and the shuttle is about $1 (it is free on the way back).

PUBLIC REST ROOMS In Annapolis, public rest rooms are located in the Harbor Masters Building at the City Dock, in the State House on State Circle, and in the Annapolis and Anne Arundel County Conference and Visitors Bureau at 26 West Street.

MEDICAL EMERGENCY Anne Arundel Medical Center (410-481-1000), 2001 Medical Parkway (off Jennifer Road), Annapolis.

North Arundel Hospital (410-787-4000), 301 Hospital Drive, Glen Burnie.

✳ To See

COLLEGES St. John's College (410-263-2371; www.sjca.edu), 60 College Avenue, Annapolis. In a city filled with historic sites, St. John's is one of the most historic. It traces its origins all the way back to 1696 with the founding of King William's School. McDowell Hall was built in the mid-1700s for the colonial governor and housed the entire college when given to the school in the 1800s. The exhibits in Mitchell Art Gallery (see *Selective Shopping—Art Galleries*) are open to the public. Known today for its fine liberal arts education, the school has an unusual curriculum that features the study of "great books of the ages."

Also see **U.S. Naval Academy** under *To See—Guided Tours.*

MUSEUMS

Annapolis
& **Banneker-Douglass Museum** (410-216-6180), 84 Franklin Street. Tuesday through Friday 10–3, Saturday noon–4. Free admission; donations accepted. The small museum maintains a collection of artifacts and photographs relevant to black life in Maryland, along with African and African American art, documents, and rare books. The former Mount Moriah African Methodist Episcopal Church, which houses the museum, is a Victorian-Gothic structure worthy of being named a National Historic Landmark in 1973.

Waterfront Warehouse (410-267-7619; www.annapolis.org), 4 Pinkney Street. Exhibits within the 1800s warehouse focus upon Maryland's early tobacco trade with Great Britain.

Eastport neighborhood of Annapolis
Annapolis Maritime Museum (410-268-1802; www.annapolismaritimemuseum.org), Second Street and Bayshore Drive. Saturday 11–4. The exhibits detail the cultural and maritime history of the Eastport neighborhood.

Galesville
Hartage Nautical Museum (410-268-1837), Hartage Boat Yard, Church Lane. Open daily. Free admission. The models, photos, and artifacts in the private museum commemorate the more than 150 years of boat designing and building that have taken place in the small Chesapeake Bay town.

THE FREDERICK DOUGLASS MUSEUM AND CULTURAL CENTER, HIGHLAND BEACH

HISTORIC HOMES

Annapolis

♿ **Hammond-Harwood House** (410-269-1714; www.hammondharwood-house.org), 19 Maryland Avenue. Open daily; last tour begins at 3. Small admission fee. The carved entranceway, large and elegant formal rooms, and grand scale of Matthias Hammond's 1774 home are a testament to his wealth and architect William Buckland's talent. Guided tours take guests throughout the house, furnished with 18th- and 19th-century decorative arts and Peale family portraits. Be sure to go into the gardens to enjoy the boxwoods and to appreciate the house's design and 15-inch-thick walls.

Chase-Lloyd House (410-263-2723), 22 Maryland Avenue. March through December, Monday through Saturday. Small admission fee. Guided tours of the 1769 Georgian mansion of Samuel Chase, a signer of the Declaration of Independence.

William Paca House and Garden (410-263-5553; www.annapolis.org), 186 Prince George Street. Open daily, but hours are limited in January and February. House and garden admission is $7 for adults, $3.50 children 6–8. Fees are less to visit either just the house or just the garden. The restored 1760s Georgian Mansion of William Paca, a signer of the Declaration of Independence, contains period furnishings. The garden, laid out around 1770, is one of the most relaxing places in the downtown area.

♿ **Charles Carroll House** (410-269-1737; www.carrollhouse.com), 107 Duke of Gloucester Street. Open daily June 1 through September 1. The waterfront home of Charles Carroll, the only Catholic and last surviving signer of the Declaration of Independence, was built in several stages over the course of 100 years. The partially restored home has little furniture but does retain its original flooring and many drawings from the days when George Washington and General Lafayette were regular visitors.

Highland Beach

Frederick Douglass Museum and Cultural Center (410-295-7233), 3200 Wayman Avenue. Small admission fee. Many places that are open only by appointment have been left out of this book, but abolitionist/orator/publisher Frederick Douglass is such an important and inspiring figure in our nation's history that it would have been a disservice to ignore this small home and museum. Douglass's former summer home overlooks a small beach along the bay (with a grand view of the water), and contains a number of items that belonged to him. The impressive woodwork in the modest home is original, while displays and exhibits provide insight into the man, the experiences of other African Americans, and a bit of history on the local community.

Linthicum

Benson-Hammond House (410-768-9518), 7101 Aviation Boulevard. Tuesday through Saturday 11–3. Small admission fee. The Anne Arundel County Historical Society saved this farmhouse from destruction by the expansion of the Baltimore/Washington International Airport in the mid-1970s. Made of clay bricks from the farm, the original four rooms were constructed in the 1820s. Some of the floors are still original, and the period furnishings reflect the period when the Hammond family occupied the house, from the 1880s to the 1940s.

HISTORIC SITES Historic London Town and Gardens (410-222-1919; www.historiclondontown.com), 839 Londontown Road, Edgewater. Open daily. Admission fee about $5 adults; children 7–12 are about $3. Established along the South River in 1863, London Town was a major tobacco exporting center by the early 1700s. William Brown—carpenter, ferry master, and tavern keeper—built his large brick home around 1760. He used convict labor to operate a tavern and inn in part of the house, and a guided tour takes visitors through the restored home, which reflects those days. Ongoing archaeological digs are uncovering more of the history of the town, and future plans call for reconstructed buildings and living-history demonstrations. A walk through the extensive gardens, filled with tree peonies, daylilies, cherry trees, bloodroot, trillium, and many shrubs, takes you down to the banks of Almshouse Creek and is the way I like to relax and end my visits here.

HISTORIC LONDON TOWN

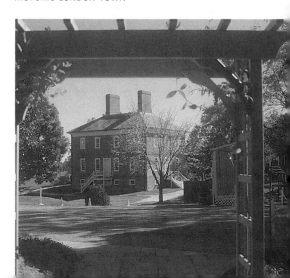

HISTORIC CHURCHES

Annapolis

Asbury Methodist Church, (410-268-9500), 87 West Street. This 1888

Gothic Revival church stands on the site of an earlier 1803 church, which was home to one of the earliest African American congregations in Annapolis.

St. Anne's Episcopal Church (410-267-9333), Church Circle. The present structure, built in the late 1800s, is the third church to stand on this site. The stained-glass window by Tiffany and Company won first prize for ecclesiastical art in the 1893 World's Fair, and the silver communion service presented to the congregation by King William III in 1695 is still in use.

St. Mary's Church (410-263-2396), Duke of Gloucester Street. The Victorian Gothic church dates from the 1860s. Be sure to go inside the rib-vaulted interior to view the wonderfully hand-carved altar screen.

GUIDED TOURS

Annapolis
Maryland State House (410-974-3400), 91 State Circle. Free guided tours of the country's oldest continuously used statehouse are given every day at 11 AM and 3 PM. (Adults must show photo ID.) The only statehouse to also serve as the nation's capital, it was built between 1772 and 1779 and occupies the highest point in the city. The tour takes you into the Old Senate Chamber where Congress ratified the Treaty of Paris, giving America its independence from Great Britain.

✎ **Discover Annapolis Minibus Tours** (410-626-6000; www.discover-annapolis.com) depart from the Annapolis and Anne Arundel County Conference and Visitors Bureau at 26 West Street. Adults $12; children 11–15 are $6; children 10 and under are $3; preschoolers are free. The 1-hour narrated tour of the city in air-conditioned/heated buses runs daily between April and November and on most weekends from December through March.

&. **U.S. Naval Academy** (410-263-6933; www.usna.edu or www.navyonline.com), 52 King George Street (entrance is at Gate 1), Annapolis. The grounds and visitors center are open to the public from 9 to 5 (9 to 4, January through February); the chapel and crypt close at 4. Several tours are given daily, but times vary with the season. The first tour always begins at 10; be aware that it is quite tight to get everything in before closing time if you take the 3 PM tour. Adults $6; seniors $5; children in 1st to 12th grade are $4. (Adults must show photo ID.) The 338-acre academy along the banks of the Severn River was established in 1845 and is the undergraduate college of the United States Navy. There is much to see here, and the best way to do it is to take one of the guided tours that originate at the Armel-Leftwich Visitor Center. You will walk through 33-acre Bancroft Hall to see a typical midshipman's dorm room, the Tripoli Monument (oldest military statue in the United States), Memorial Hall, the Academy Museum, chapel, and the crypt of Revolutionary War hero John Paul Jones. If you are here around noon on weekdays during the school year, you will witness the formation of all midshipmen as they march off to lunch.

✳ To Do

BICYCLING

Annapolis

Annapolis has been called one of the most walker-friendly cities in the country, but it has not forgotten bicyclists. A 38-mile system of designated bike routes along city streets and grade-separated trails lets you explore on two wheels instead of four. The **City Planning and Zoning Department** (410-263-7961) can provide more information. All buses in the city have racks that will hold two bikes; there is no additional charge for this service.

The Baltimore and Annapolis Trail is a paved pathway that follows the route of an old railroad bed close to Governor Ritchie Highway (MD 2) for more than 13 miles. Although it does pass by busy streets, housing developments, and a mall or two, it can be a nice ride, especially along the least-developed 3 miles closest to Annapolis. The trail begins near the Baltimore/Washington International Airport (where it connects with another paved

---

Annapolis Tours' Three Centuries Tour of Annapolis (410-263-5401; www. annapolis-tours.com), 48 Maryland Avenue. Twice daily, April through October; once only on Saturday from November through March. Adults $9, students $3. I enjoyed following the colonial-garbed guide, taking in the many historical sites in the city and the U.S. Naval Academy. However, I was most entertained by the guide's explanations of phrases we use in our everyday conversations:

Put your best foot forward: Colonial women enjoyed looking at men's well-developed calves, so a man would stand with one foot in front of the other, which accentuated his calf muscle.

Mind your P's and Q's: Tavern revelers would run a tab and, in order not to come up short of money, a barmaid had to keep track of who had drunk how many pints and quarts.

Crack a smile: Beeswax was used as a facial cosmetic, which you would crack if your smile was too large. Also the origin of "Mind your own beeswax."

Not playing with a full deck: The king put a tax on playing cards, but it only applied to the ace of spades. So people would purchase a deck without that card.

Straitlaced: Respectable ladies would keep their bodices tightly laced. On the other hand, a female who wanted to show a bit of her bosom would not pull the laces quite so tight. She soon became known as a "loose" woman.

Putting on the dog: Affluent members of society would have slippers made out of the family dog's hide and fur after it died.

trail encircling the airport) and ends on MD 2 just as it enters Annapolis. More information and a map may be obtained from the **Anne Arundel County Department of Recreation and Parks** (410-222-6244).

Also see **Quiet Waters Park** and **Truxton Park** under *Green Space—Parks*.

BOAT EXCURSIONS

Annapolis

Watermark Cruises (410-268-7601; www.watermarkcruises.com), slip 20 at the City Dock. Narrated tours of 40 minutes (adults $7; children 3–11 are $4) and 90 minutes (adults $14; children 3–11 are $7) are provided from March through December. Days and times vary throughout the season, so call for the latest information.

⚓ **Schooner *Woodwind*** (410-263-7837), 80 Compromise Street (at the Marriott Hotel). Closed Monday. Times and rates vary. Most cruises are around $25–30 for adults and $15 for children under 12. The 74-foot sailboat, beautiful with its mahogany woodwork and chrome trim, offers daily sailing cruises. Most of the trips last about 2 hours and take in Annapolis harbor, the Naval Academy, and a portion of the Severn River. You can be passive or take a turn at the wheel or hoist the four sails.

BOAT RENTALS Eastport Electric Boat Company (410-263-5060), 326 First Street, Suite 32-B (inside the Marriott Hotel), Annapolis. Quiet and easy-to-use 18- and 21-foot electric-powered boats are rented by the day.

South River Boat Rentals (410-956-9729), located at Pier 7 Marina, Edgewater. Hourly, daily, overnight, and weekly rentals of a variety of motor- and sailboats. No experience needed. Rates range from $30 an hour up to $400 per day.

Also see **Quiet Waters Park** under *Green Space—Parks*.

FAMILY ACTIVITIES ⚓ ♿ **Horizon Organic Dairy** (410-923-7600; www.horizonorganicfarm.com), 100 Dairy Lane (off MD 175), Gambrills.

A HAYRIDE AT HORIZON ORGANIC DAIRY IN GAMBRILLS

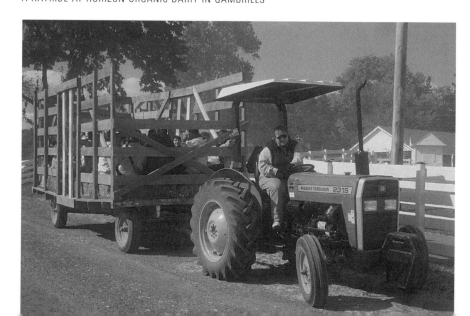

Children love this place. Displays, exhibits, and live-animal demonstrations teach the benefits of organic farming. There are also picnic facilities, wagon rides, trails on the 875 acres, an organic marketplace, and a very kid-friendly staff.

FISHING Charter fishing excursions are offered by a number of outfitters in the Annapolis area. Among the many are:

Bounty Hunter (1-800-322-4039; www.bountyhuntercharter.com), 7 Belevedere Court, Annapolis. Captain Glenn James takes groups of 6 to 49 onto the water on the 55-foot *Bounty Hunter.*

Captain Clyde's Charters (410-974-4314; www.captclydes.com), 1058 Deep Creek Avenue, Arnold. More than 20 years of fishing and cruising experience.

Mallard **Charters** (410-798-1119), 3742 Bay Drive, Edgewater. Groups of up to six can go along with Captain Steve Vierkorn on his 42-foot *Mallard.*

GOLF **Dwight D. Eisenhower Golf Course** (410-571-0973), Generals Highway (MD 178), Crownsville. You will need to reserve your tee time at this public course.

South River Golf Links (1-800-767-4837), 3451 Solomons Island Road, Edgewater. The closest course to Annapolis is set amid a dense forest with dramatic elevation changes on the links.

⚓ **Severna Park Golf Center** (410-647-8618), 1257 Governor Ritchie Highway, Arnold. A nine-hole course and a driving range with sheltered and heated tees. Miniature golf and batting cages for the kids.

MINIATURE GOLF See **Severna Park Golf Center** under *Golf.*

KAYAKING AND CANOEING **Amphibious Horizons** (410-267-8742; 1-888-I-LUV-SUN; www.amphibioushorizons.com), 600 Quiet Waters Park Road, Annapolis. Not only will the staff here rent you a kayak and instruct you on how to use it, but they can also arrange guided kayaking tours of Annapolis harbor or set up camping and B&B kayaking trips throughout the Chesapeake Bay region.

SAILING **Sunsail Sailing Vacations** (1-800-327-2276; www.sunsail.com), 980 Awald Road, Suite 302, Annapolis. The largest charter-boat company in the world, with operations as far flung as Turkey and Tahiti, offers bareboat and crewed charters on which you choose the time, pace, and destination.

Rogue-Sail, Inc. (410-798-6235; www.annearundelcounty.com), 3776 Colliers Drive, Edgewater. Contact these folks to set up a captained sailing trip of your own choosing aboard the 36-foot *Sea Diva.* You decide on the length and destination of the trip, and they take care of the details and the sailing.

SAILING LESSONS
Annapolis
⚓ **Annapolis Sailing School** (410-267-7205; 1-800-638-9192; www.annapolissailing.com), 601 Sixth Street. One of the most well-respected institutions of sailing knowledge, Annapolis Sailing is also the oldest and largest sailing school in the country. Courses of various duration are designed for basic, cruising, and advanced sailing, and for those

interested in preparing for a bareboat charter or coastal navigation and piloting. There are also classes for children 5–15 years aboard 12- to 14-foot sailing dinghies.

AYS Charters and Sailing School (410-267-9151), 7416 Edgewood Road. Charter trips (captained or bareboat) and sailing instructions on 28- to 42-foot sailboats. Chartercertification courses are offered every weekend.

Womanship, Inc. (410-267-6661; www.womanship.com), 137 Conduit Street. Sailing instruction taught by and for women. Their courses are for novice to advanced sailors. I like their motto, "Nobody yells!"

Annapolis Powerboat School (410-267-7205; www.annapolispowerboat. com), 601 6th Street. Several different hands-on, on-the-water classes are offered. One of the most popular is the 5-day instruction course, which cruises around the bay, enabling you to spend evenings at various waterfront inns.

SKATING Dahlgren Hall Ice Rink (410-293-2350; www.dahlgrenhall. com), U.S. Naval Academy, 52 King George Street (entrance is at Gate 1), Annapolis. Open daily. Adults $4.50, children $4, skate rental $2.50. The season usually begins by mid-October. Also see **Quiet Waters Park** under *Green Space—Parks.*

SWIMMING See *Tennis* and **Truxton Park** under *Green Space—Parks.*

TENNIS The **Anne Arundel County Recreation and Parks Department** (410-222-7300), 1 Harry S. Truman Parkway, oversees more than 30 regional parks with tennis courts open

to the public on a first-come, first-served basis, and four parks with swimming available to the general public. Contact them for more information.

Also see **Truxton Park** under *Green Space—Parks.*

WALKING TOURS Annapolis boasts more than 35 homes and sites of historical significance within a few blocks of each other in the downtown/City Dock area of the city. These sites are described in the *Annapolis and Anne Arundel County Visitors Guide,* which is available from the Annapolis and Anne Arundel County Conference and Visitors Bureau (see *Guidance*). Pick up a copy and take an easy stroll into the city's past.

✳ Green Space

BEACHES See **Sandy Point State Park** sidebar opposite.

GARDENS ♿ **Helen Avalynne Tawes Garden** (410-260-8189), next to the Tawes State Office Building on Taylor Avenue, Annapolis. Open daily dawn to dusk. Expect to see a number of state employees escaping bureaucratic headaches when you walk through this 6-acre park. One of the nicest free city botanical gardens on the East Coast, it has sections representing Eastern Shore habitats, mountain forestland, and streamside environments. An abundance of birds and small wildlife make their home in the garden.

PARKS

Annapolis

🦆 ♿ **Quiet Waters Park** (410-223-1777), 600 Quiet Waters Park Road. Open 7 AM to dusk; closed Tuesday. This 336-acre park is easily accessed from Bay Ridge Road in the Eastport neighborhood of the city and has been called the finest county-operated park in the state. It is bordered by Harness Creek and the South River, so much of the recreational emphasis is on water sports, with a variety of boats for rent from spring through fall. There are also more than 6 miles of hiking/biking trails through wetlands and shoreline, picnic facilities, a visitor center (with two art galleries), a large playground, and even an outdoor ice rink open during the colder months. A great place to make a quick escape from the city traffic and noise.

✍ **Truxton Park** (410-263-7958), Hilltop Lane. Only 77 acres in size, the park is a city playground with tennis and basketball courts, a swimming pool, bike routes, and picnic facilities. Small fee for swimming.

Pasadena
Downs Memorial Park (410-222-6230), Johns Down Loop. Small parking fee. A small shoreline park that offers biking opportunities, picnicking, interpretive programs, and outdoor concerts.

WALKS ✍ **Smithsonian Environmental Research Center** (410-798-4424), 647 Contees Wharf Road, Edgewater. An easy pathway works its way to a re-created Piscataway Indian village, by dairy-farm implements and exhibits about tobacco plantations, and across a marsh. A great escape spot from noisy highways and cities.

✳ Lodging

Annapolis Accommodations, Inc. (410-280-0900; 1-800-715-1000; www.stayannapolis.com), 41 Maryland Avenue, Annapolis, 21401. Represents hotels, motels, inns, and B&Bs in and around Annapolis and will make recommendations and reservations based upon your needs.

MOTELS AND HOTELS
Downtown, 21401
🐾 ♿ **Loews Annapolis Hotel** (410-263-7777; 1-800-23-LOEWS; www.

✍ ♿ **Sandy Point State Park** (410-757-1841), 800 Revell Highway (off US 50/301), Annapolis. Open year-round for day use. Less than 10 miles northeast of Annapolis, the park's beaches (guarded from Memorial Day through Labor Day) are considered among the finest along the Chesapeake Bay and are favored by local families. Rowboats and motorboats are available for rent, and close to 5 miles of trails course through woodland and marsh. The varied habitat makes for good bird-watching and, being on the Atlantic Flyway, attracts a large number of migratory waterfowl. Some facilities are handicapped accessible.

Of the more than 4,600 miles of shoreline around the bay, less than 2 percent is accessible to the public; the rest is privately owned—a fact that is almost impossible to accept. Maybe we should utter a word of thanks that the state was wise enough to preserve the open land of Sandy Point in the 1950s.

loewsannapolis.com), 126 West Street. One of the closest hotels to the waterfront and the City Dock. Large, luxurious rooms and an attentive staff have enabled the Loews Annapolis to be designated a AAA four-diamond hotel for more than a decade. The common areas are bright and airy. Pets permitted. $100–250.

✿ ⭑ **Annapolis Marriott Waterfront Hotel** (410-268-7555; 1-800-336-0072; www.annapolismarriott. com), 80 Compromise Street. The Annapolis location of this national chain is the city's only downtown hotel to be located directly on the water. Pets permitted. $240–375.

Note: Many more hotels and motels are located near the Baltimore/Washington International Airport and along many state roads between Annapolis and Baltimore. Among the lower-cost national chains are **Days Inn** (1-800-544-8313; www.daysinn.com); **Courtyard by Marriott** (1-888-236-2427; www.courtyard.com); and **Microtel** (410-865-7500; www.microtelinn. com). **The Comfort Suites** (410-691-1275; 1-800-228-5150) at 815 Elkridge Landing Road in Linthicum is within a couple of minutes' drive of the airport. $119–199.

INNS

Downtown, 21401
⭑ **Gibson's Lodgings** (410-268-5555; 1-877-330-0057; www.avmcyber.com/gibson), 110 Prince George Street. Features a variety of guest rooms in two historic homes and another structure built in 1988. Close to most of the downtown/City Dock attractions. $89–169.

Scotlaur Inn (410-268-5665; www.scotlaurinn.com), 165 Main Street. Wallpaper, quilts on metal

beds, throw rugs, and windows looking onto the bustle of Main Street give the 10 rooms above **Chick and Ruth's Deli** (see *Eating Out*) the feel of a neighborhood hotel or tourist home from the turn of the 20th century. Central heating and air-conditioning. $80–150.

Historic Inns of Annapolis (410-263-2641; 1-800-847-8882; www. annapolisinns.com.), 58 State Capital Circle. The Historic Inns are actually three inns operated under the same management group. The **Governor Calvert House,** facing the State Capitol, was built in 1727 for the colonial governor. The **Robert Johnson House,** also facing the capitol building, was constructed as a private residence in 1765. The **Maryland Inn** (also see **King of France Tavern** under *Nightlife*), on State Circle, is the only one of the three that was originally built to cater to travelers. The **Treaty of Paris** restaurant (see *Dining Out*) downstairs has been serving patrons for more than 200 years. Each inn offers a wide variety of accommodations, with many different amenities. $159–249.

BED & BREAKFASTS

Downtown, 21401
⚓ **Flag House Inn** (410-280-2721; 1-800-437-4825; www.flaghouseinn. com), 26 Randall Street. The location couldn't be any better. The City Dock and the main Naval Academy gate are only one block away, and the B&B has private off-street parking. All six guest rooms in the restored 1870 Victorian home have a private bath, TV, and air-conditioning. There were so many things I enjoyed about my stay here: The two-sided fireplace that heated the living and dining rooms; the front

porch to lazily sit on and watch the rest of Annapolis hurry by; and Charlotte and Bill Schmickle's large English breakfast. The guests I shared breakfast with came from many corners of the globe. Children over 10 welcome. $120–250.

Randall House (410-263-4970), 30 Randall Street. Just a couple of doors down from the Flag House Inn (see above), the Randall House shares the same great location. Each guest room in the mid-1800s house has a private bath; the back room has a deck overlooking the garden. $140–160.

✎ **Chez Amis** (410-263-6632; 1-888-224-6455; www.chezamis.com), 85 East Street. Chez Amis was a corner grocery store when the 20th century began and, as the B&B home of Don and Mickie Deline, retains the original Georgia pine floors, tin ceiling, and an oak display counter. All rooms have private bath, TV, and down comforters on the brass beds. Children over 10 welcome. $115–140.

The Annapolis Inn (410-295-5200; www.annapolisinn.com), 144 Prince George Street. Alex DeVivo and Joseph Lespier have turned the home of Thomas Jefferson's physician into the modern personification of pampering and luxury. Crystal chandeliers, etched-glass shower and pocket doors, sumptuous furniture, cedar guest closets, and a heatable tumbled marble bathroom floor are just a few of the niceties. Yet they have kept much of the old, such as original crown moldings and medallions, and the horsehair plaster on the walls. $310–475.

Two-O-One (410-268-8053; www.201bb.com), 201 Prince George Street. All of the guest quarters in this Georgian home have four-poster beds and are elegantly furnished, but I am particularly smitten by the Crow's Nest Suite on the third floor. There is just something about the large tiles and woodwork in the bathroom that provides a rich and sensuous experience. The large gardens are a nice respite from the noise of the city. Off-street parking. $150–200.

THE MARYLAND INN IN ANNAPOLIS

Prince George Inn (410-263-6418; www.princegeorgeinn.com), 232 Prince George Street. In the 1980s, the 1884 Victorian Prince George Inn was the first B&B to be licensed within the city of Annapolis. Like most of the row houses in Annapolis and Baltimore it is longer and taller than it is wide, which is reflected in the shape of its rooms. Guest rooms are furnished with antiques and a TV. $140–180.

William Page Inn (410-626-1506; 1-800-364-4160; www.williampageinn. com), 8 Martin Street. Native Annapolitan Robert Zuchelli has been operating his B&B for more than 15 years and is one of the most composed hosts I have met. He personally redesigned and refurbished the 1908 home and has created a place of soothing elegance. The home is on a quiet cross street that creates the illusion of being in a much smaller town. Off-street parking. $125–270.

55 East (410-295-0202; www.annearundelcounty.com/hotel/55east.htm), 55 East Street. Matt and Tricia Herban have renovated their 1864 home (originally a grocery store) and decorated it with fabulous heirlooms and furnishings, such as Matt's grandfather's Las Cruces desk and spectacular pieces from China in the sitting room. However, what I remember most from my visit are the luscious corn and pecan waffles served at breakfast. All three guest rooms have a private bath and sitting area. $140–150.

Gatehouse B&B (410-280-0024; 1-888-254-7576), 249 Hanover Street. The Georgian-style B&B home of Carol and Jim Woller overlooks the Naval Academy and is furnished in period reproductions. Most rooms

have a private bath; all come with fresh flowers to brighten the day, and soft robes for comfortable lounging. Breakfasts are wonderful variations on old standards, such as cream cheese and ice cream French toast or Italian-style quiche. $180–285.

Georgian House (410-263-5618; 1-800-557-2068; www.georgianhouse. com), 170 Duke of Gloucester Street. Innkeeper Sandy Mayer's breakfasts of fresh breads and hot entrées are reason enough to stay here. There is also her masterful decorating of the guest rooms and common areas of the 1747 home. $160–185.

The Doll's House (410-626-2028; www.annapolis.net/dollshouse), 161 Green Street. Built in 1901, this late-Victorian home is one block from the City Dock. All three guest accommodations are suites with a private bath and furnished in "Victorian whimsy." $125–140.

❦ ⚘ The Barn on Howard's Cove (410-571-9511; www.bnb.com/howards-cove.html), 500 Wilson Road. Just minutes away, but seemingly a world apart, from the activity of downtown, Libbie and Graham Gutsche have been quietly operating their B&B for two decades. You would never know the house, with two guest suites—each with private bath and entrance—was the barn for a mid-1800s farm. Porches, decks, and large windows overlook a quiet cove of the Severn River. Canoes and a kayak are available to explore the waterway, and a full breakfast will give you the energy to do so. Children welcome. $125.

❦ ❀ Meadow Gardens (410-224-2729; www.bnbweb.com/meadowgardens/index), 504 Wilson Road. There is only one guest suite in this modern home B&B operated by the daughter of the folks at the adjacent Barn on Howard's Cove (see above). This means you will not only have her undivided attention, but also have access to the boats and water at the Barn, as well as a swimming pool and hot tub. The sunroom, where an ample breakfast is often served, overlooks the 6.5 acres of gardens and meadows. Pets welcome. $95.

Eastport neighborhood of Annapolis, 21403

The Inn at Spa Creek (410-263-8866; www.innatspacreek.com), 417 Severn Avenue. This very contemporary home was a bachelor's party house until Rick and Jeanne Brown made it a B&B in the late 1990s. The open floor plan, flowing from one room to the next, still lends itself to socializing—which fits in which the milieu of the neighborhood. Jeanne says that she lives in the "Key West of Annapolis." I like the huge windows that let you look out on the action. $125–165.

Captain's Cottage (410-263-0955; 1-800-508-0009; www.captainscottage. net), 519 Burnside Street. In a quiet, residential neighborhood, hosts Captain Ken Kloostra and Andie McCullars entertain just one set of guests at a time. The two-bedroom suite has its own entrance and private living room and bath, and is decorated with quilts and antiques. The three-sided porch is the spot to relax after walking down to the harbor for a day of sight-seeing. Andie is the publisher of *Inside Annapolis Magazine*, so she is full of information about the area. $150.

VACATION RENTALS Leisure Management, LLC (410-224-3257; www.leisuremanagementllc.com),

2007 Tidewater Colony Drive, #1A, Annapolis, 21401. If you will be in the area with a large group or family for an extended period, you might consider contacting these folks, who operate a four-bedroom, two-and-a-half-bath modern house in the Eastport neighborhood. A group of eight can rent the entire house for $1,350 for a 3-day weekend. Weekly and monthly rentals also available.

CAMPING ☀ **Capital KOA** (410-923-2771), 768 Cecil Avenue, Millersville, 21108. Late March through November 1. This is the closest campground to Annapolis, and one of the closest to Washington, D.C. Free daily shuttle to D.C. Transit. Expect the many amenities found in this national chain: pool, dump station, playground. Pets permitted.

☀ **Duncan's Family Campground** (410-741-9558; 1-800-222-2086), 5381 Sands Road, Lothian, 20711. Open year-round; limited facilities in winter. Located in the southern part of Anne Arundel County, close to the bay and Patuxent River Park. Free transportation to Washington, D.C., metro services. Pool, miniature golf, tent sites. Small pets permitted.

✳ Where to Eat

DINING OUT

Annapolis

Piccola Roma (410-268-7898), 200 Main Street. Silvana Recine left her homeland more than 30 years ago, but her cooking shows that her Roman roots remain strong. All of the dishes served here are from her recipes, with many adapted to make use of local products. I started my meal with the crab, prosciutto, and artichoke in a cream sauce ($10.50).

The salmon with orzo, sun-dried tomatoes, and zucchini baked in parchment paper ($23.50) may be the most succulent fish I've had. Pasta dishes range from $16–21; other selections are $17–29. In true Romanesque style, salad is served after the entrée. Save room for the ever-changing selection of desserts.

The wait staff is friendly, knowledgeable about the extensive wine list, and attentive. When time allows, Silvana mingles with her guests. Without a doubt, this is currently my favorite Annapolis restaurant.

Treaty of Paris (410-216-6340), Church Circle and Main Street (inside the **Maryland Inn;** see *Lodging—Inns*). Nouveau French cuisine served within the gracefully restored inn. A lunch buffet is available, but you will certainly enjoy the food—and appreciate the kitchen's abilities—more if you order from the menu. Entrées $18–27. (Also see **King of France Tavern** under *Nightlife.*)

Yin Yankee Café (410-268-8703; www.yinyankee.com), 105 Main Street. Brings the foods of the Pacific Rim to Annapolis's City Dock area. Lots of seafood and vegetable dishes. Expect to pay about $25–30 per person for a meal.

🍴 ♿ **Les Folies** (410-573-0970), 2552 Riva Road. It sometimes seems like you have to take out a second mortgage to enjoy a meal at a good French restaurant. Not at Les Folies. Manager Alain Matrat and chef Jean-Claude Galan, both born in France, provide a Parisian atmosphere and quality food at rational prices. The recipes of the ever-evolving menu reflect distinct regions of France: Paris, Gascony, Provence, Alsace, Lyon, and others. Expect an appetizer of crabmeat custard with lobster sauce ($8.95) on one visit, and garlic sausage over lentil salad ($6.50) on another. The fish and pasta dishes are some of the most popular entrées, and, of course, you cannot leave with having one of the special desserts. My second-favorite Annapolis dining spot. Entrées $14–24.

Northwood's (410-268-2609), 609 Melvin Avenue. Open daily for dinner only. The place that couples come to when they are looking for a romantic spot. The menu has a definite Mediterranean flavor, so start the meal with a *zuppa de pesce* ($4.95–7.95) and continue with a seafood bisque ($22.95). Entrées range $19–23; a four-course prix fixe dinner is usually available for about $30.

Eastport neighborhood of Annapolis

Carrol's Creek (410-263-8102; www.carrolscreek.com), 410 Severn Avenue. Steaks and other meats are available at this waterfront restaurant, but it would be a mistake not to go for the seafood. The cream of crab soup ($6.25) is thick and rich, but you might also want to try the curried zucchini and shrimp soup ($5.25). The crabcakes (market price) are delicious, as is the rockfish served over Parmesan polenta ($21). Most entrées run $14–28.

EATING OUT

Annapolis

McGarvey's Saloon and Oyster Bar (410-263-5700; www.mcgarveyssaloon.com), 8 Market Space. Open for lunch and dinner Monday through Saturday; Sunday brunch at 10. The festive, publike atmosphere and location at the City Dock has made McGarvey's a popular eatery since it opened in 1975. Obviously, oysters prepared many different ways are a specialty, but there is also light fare ($3.95–7.95), sandwiches ($6.95–10.95), and a few entrées such as filet mignon ($22.95). The rich wood and brick interior created a pleasant place to enjoy the filet béarnaise sandwich ($10.95) I ordered.

Buddy's Crabs and Ribs (410-626-1100; www.buddysonline.com), 100 Main Street. Open for lunch and dinner daily. A typical crab house, and close to the City Dock. Many people choose the buffet bar (lunch $8.95; dinner $14.95), but you will probably be more satisfied with ordering from the menu. Entrées $8.99–37.99.

49 West Coffeehouse (410-626-9796), 49 West Street. Open daily for breakfast, lunch, and dinner. I thought long and hard on how to describe this place to you. I came up with: It is a funky-chic place that appeals to the sophisticated beatnik/vegetarian meat-eater/yuppie/coffee lover in all of us. The interior is a funky blend of an old brick wall on one side, a 1950s dropped acoustic tile ceiling above, and a plaster wall covered in artwork for sale on the other side.

The menu is as varied. Baked goods, a Belgian waffle ($5.95), quiche ($7.25), and egg dishes ($4.95) for breakfast. Sandwiches range from melted ham and cheese ($7) to vegetarian burgers with soy cheese ($7.50). Entrées served after 6 PM include crab scampi over pasta ($14.95) and honey-garlic pork ($15.95). Everything is well prepared.

Galway Bay (410-263-8333; www.galwaybayannapolis.com), 61–63 Maryland Avenue. Open daily for lunch and dinner. Authentic Irish food prepared according to the recipes of owner Michael Galway, who left his native Kilkenny in south-

east Ireland in 1986. My potato and leek soup ($3.95) served with hearty baked bread was creamy and tasty, while the seafood pie, crammed with salmon, shrimp, crabmeat, scallops, and clams ($9.95), was a nice variation on the traditional shepherd's pie ($8.95). Steak, chicken, and other seafood ($13.95–17.95) prepared the Irish way are also available. Bread pudding, rhubarb and strawberry tart, and Irish whiskey cake are just a few of the desserts ($2.95–4.95).

Chick and Ruth's Deli (410-269-6737; www.Chickandruths.com), 165 Main Street. Open daily for breakfast, lunch, and dinner. Chick and Ruth have been gone for some time now, but their family continues to serve up solid deli and diner food. A long menu complete with 16 kinds of omelets ensures that this is the place to start your day. As an added bonus, you can join the staff as they recite the Pledge of Allegiance each morning. Entrées $4–15.

Annapolis Gourmet (410-263-6115), 116 Annapolis Street. The Leano family has been in the deli business for more than 65 years, so they know a thing or two about making sandwiches, soups, and salads. The chicken salad has become a local tradition. Entrées $4–12.

Middleton Tavern (410-263-3323; www.middletontavern.com), 2 Market Space. Open daily for lunch and dinner. Traditional American/Maryland cuisine inside the historic tavern on the City Dock. Many seafood items from the raw bar and appetizer menu. Pasta, sandwiches, meats, and seafood entrées. Broiled rockfish with lemon butter ($27.95) is a house specialty. Other entrées are $16.95–33.95.

Eastport neighborhood of Annapolis

The Main Ingredient Café (410-626-0388; www.souptonutsinc.com), 914 Bay Bridge Road (at Georgetown Plaza). Open for breakfast, lunch, and dinner. It is in a strip mall, but the sunlight and bright decor can help you overlook that fact. The food will, too; there is a light touch on everything, even the fried onion rings ($2.99) and the BBQ beef brisket sandwich ($6.99). Lots of healthy items like a salmon burger ($8.99), chicken gyro ($6.99), and three-bean chili ($3.99). Heartier appetites might go for the fish-and-chips ($8.99), meat loaf ($7.99), or white pizza ($7.50).

Rocco's Pizzeria (410-263-9444), 954 Bay Ridge Road. Open daily. A good choice for pizza or subs for take-out (or eat-in at a few tables).

Jalapeños (410-266-7580; www.jalapenosonline.com), 85 Forest Drive. Open for lunch Monday through Friday; dinner daily. Gonzalo Fernandez and Alberto Serranco serve up foods from Spain and Mexico, and you can choose items from either or both countries in one meal. A house favorite is the *Gambas alajillo*—shrimp sautéed in olive oil, garlic, tomatoes, and dry sherry. Paella, enchiladas, and other entrées $9.95–19.95.

CRABS ☙ **Cantler's Riverside Inn** (410-757-1311; www.cantlers.com), 458 Forest Beach Road, near Annapolis. Open daily for lunch and dinner. Cantler's own boats bring the seafood in daily, so you know it is

CHICK AND RUTH'S DELI IS A LOCAL INSTITUTION

fresh. Many B&B owners directed me to this scenic Mill Creek spot when I inquired about the best place in Annapolis for steamed hard-shell crabs (market price). There are also many types of fresh fish and meat entrées to choose from. $8.95–20.95.

Mike's Bar and Crab House (410-956-2784; www.mikescrabhouse.com), 3030 Old Riva Road, Edgewater. On the South River waterfront, Mike's serves steamed crabs by the dozen or by the bushel (market price). Other seafood available for lunch and dinner ($15.95–24.95). Takes on a festive atmosphere on the outside deck every day during the summer, and has live music on Friday night.

Skipper's Pier (410-867-7110; www.skipperspier.com), 6158 Drum Point Road, Deale. A favorite with recreational Chesapeake Bay boaters who come here to enjoy steamed crabs (market price) on the waterfront. Light-fare and full-entrée choices are also available. $7.95–19.95.

COFFEE BARS

Annapolis

The Pony Espresso (410-280-6160), 33½ West Street. Baked goods and specialty coffees just across the street from the Annapolis and Anne Arundel County Conference and Visitors Bureau (see *Guidance*).

Seattle Coffee Company (410-263-9747), 71 Maryland Avenue. Enjoy a cappuccino as you sit on the window couch watching the rest of Annapolis walk by.

Also see **49 West Coffeehouse** under *Eating Out*.

Annapolis

✐ **Fudge Kitchen** (1-800-898-9701), 112 Main Street. They make all of their items—fudge, cookies, peanut brittle, lemonade, and more—from scratch, and you can watch them do it.

✐ **Storm Brothers Ice Cream Factory** (410-263-3376), 130 Dock Street. A wide variety of flavors in a family-owned business at the waterfront.

Great Harvest Bread Co. (410-268-4662; www.greatharvest.com), 208 Ridgely Avenue. Closed Sunday and Monday. The owners and employees are up and working early in the morning to deliver more than a dozen types of baked goodies (the caramel-chip scones are great!) by 7 AM and at least two dozen varieties of bread by 9 AM. (Not all are available each day.) Great Harvest grinds its own wheat fresh every day.

Severna Park

Atlanta Bread Company (410-315-7887), 551 Governor Ritchie Highway. Specialty breads, coffee, muffins, cookies, and Danish.

✱ Entertainment

DANCE ♿ **Ballet Theatre of Maryland** (410-263-8289; www.btmballet.org) 801 Chase Street, Annapolis. The professional troupe's season usually runs from October into April and consists of at least four different programs. The ballet has been presenting live music along with its dance performances during a few of its presentations over the last few seasons.

FILM

Annapolis

Apex Annapolis Theatres (410-224-1145), 2474 Solomons Island Road;

Annapolis Mall XI (410-571-2796), Annapolis Mall; and **Eastport Cinemas I and II** (410-268-1431), 1027 Bay Ridge, all show first-run movies.

The Annapolis Cinema Grill (410-2MOVIES), Forest Plaza, is the place to head if you miss a flick on its first time around. The price is lower, and you can have lunch or dinner with the movie.

MUSIC
Annapolis
Annapolis Opera (410-267-8135; www.annapolisopera.com), Maryland Hall for Arts, 801 Chase Street. The season runs from September into April. There are usually two or three full operas (with electronic English subtitles) and several other concerts during the season. *La Bohème* and *Don Giovanni* are a couple of past productions.

Annapolis Symphony Orchestra (410-269-1132; www.mdhallarts.org/ASO.html), 801 Chase Street. The city's professional music organization offers classical, pops, family, and chamber music presentations throughout the year.

NIGHTLIFE
Annapolis
Rams Head Tavern and Fordham Brewing Company (410-268-4545; www.ramsheadtavern.com), 33 West Street. Open daily. You can enjoy a good meal, a Fordham microbrew, and a nationally known act all in the same location. Past performers have included Arlo Guthrie, Livingston Taylor, Richie Havens, Jose Feliciano, Spyro Gyra, and Leon Redbone. Dinner/show combos are available.

King of France Tavern (410-216-6340), inside the **Maryland Inn** (see *Lodging—Inns*). The live music presented each weekend usually falls within the jazz or big-band genre.

THEATERS
Annapolis
Annapolis Summer Garden Theatre (410-268-9212; www.summergarden.com), 143 Compromise Street. Comedies and musicals are presented in an outdoor setting Thursday through Sunday in the evening from Memorial Day through Labor Day.

Colonial Players (410-263-0533), 108 East Street. This acting troupe's season usually runs from September into April. This is a great place to see theatrical works that are well known but not presented that often on stage. A recent season included *The Trip to Bountiful, Hay Fever,* and *To Gillian on Her 37th Birthday.*

& **Chesapeake Music Hall** (410-626-7515; 1-800-406-0306; www.chesapeakemusichall.com), 339 Busch's Frontage Road. The area's only dinner theater presents a buffet and musical play, drama, or comedy on Thursday, Friday, and Saturday night, and matinees on Sunday. Look for Broadway-style standards such as *Oklahoma!* and *Damn Yankees.*

✳ Selective Shopping
ANTIQUES
Annapolis
Bon Vivant (410-263-9651; www.bonvivantantiques.com), 104 Annapolis Street. Furniture, glassware, dolls, toys, plus designer pieces by local artists.

Hobson's Choice Antiques (410-280-2206), 58 Maryland Avenue.

Closed Tuesday. Chinese porcelain, silver, 18th- and 19th-century furniture, along with nautical items and Lionel trains.

Antiquity Perfection (410-216-9067), 69 Maryland Avenue. Closed Wednesday. A multidealer shop with two floors of furniture, toys, books, glassware, and other collectibles.

ART GALLERIES

Annapolis/Downtown/City Dock

♪ **Mitchell Art Gallery** (410-626-2556; www.sjca.edu/main.html), 60 College Avenue. Closed Monday. St. John's College's art gallery (see also *To See—Colleges*) features changing exhibits of high-quality works in a variety of media. Also sponsors tours, lectures, and children's programs.

Annapolis Marine Art Gallery (410-263-4100; www.annapolis-marineart.com), 110 Dock Street. Open daily. Befitting the Sailing Capital of the World, the gallery presents only marine art—paintings, graphics, ship models, scrimshaw, and more—produced by living artists.

La Petite Galerie (410-258-2425), 39 Maryland Avenue. Closed Monday and Tuesday. Works by Chinese, French-Russian, American, and local artists.

Carl Patty Studio (410-268-6550; 1-888-476-9866), 55 Maryland Avenue. Open daily. Stop in to watch Mr. Patty work on his latest watercolor creation. Guest artists also work in the studio from time to time.

Maria's Picture Place (410-263-8282), 45 Maryland Avenue. Maria's lays claim to having the largest selection of Annapolis scenes anywhere.

Dawson Gallery (410-269-1299), 44

Maryland Avenue. Monday through Saturday and some Sundays. Most commercial galleries emphasize works by contemporary artists, but you will find the paintings of 19th- and early-20th-century American and European artists in the Dawson Gallery.

Aurora Gallery (410-263-9150), 67 Maryland Avenue. Changing exhibits by local and regional artisans in a variety of styles and media.

Maryland Federation of Art Gallery on the Circle (410-268-4566), 18 State Street. Closed Monday. The exhibits in all media by local and regional artists change monthly in the nonprofit organization's gallery. A good place to catch rising or promising artists early in their career.

McBride Gallery (410-267-7077; www.mcbridegallery.org), 215 Main Street. Open daily. The city's largest gallery contains seven rooms of landscapes, wildlife paintings, and nautical scenes.

ArtFX (410-990-4540), 45 West Street. Closed Monday. A cooperative venture of approximately 25 artists, so you will find items in just about every medium possible. You can meet a new featured artist on the first Sunday of every month 6–9 PM.

BOOKSTORES ♿ **U.S. Naval Institute Bookstore** (410-295-3754; www.usni.org), Preble Hall, U.S. Naval Academy, 52 King George Street (entrance is at Gate 1), Annapolis. The number of books pertaining to seamanship and naval history, American and worldwide, is just short of phenomenal.

USED BOOKS Briarwood Bookshop (410-268-1440), 66 Maryland Avenue, Annapolis. Closed Wednesday. A wide selection of used, out-of-print, rare, and old books. These folks also do expert repairs on books that may have seen better days.

CRAFTS

Annapolis/Downtown/City Dock

League of Maryland Craftsmen (410-626-1277), 216 Main Street. Closed Tuesday. This outlet for the statewide organization is where you will find the output of some of the state's finest artists and craftspersons. Works are done in watercolor, oils, glass, pottery, metal, and textiles.

✍ **Annapolis Pottery** (410-268-6153), 40 State Street. Owners Bill and Genevieve McWilliams, along with other potters, so enjoy sharing their craft with others that they have installed benches inside their studio so that you can watch them create various items. They are happy to converse with you and are especially friendly to inquisitive children.

MALLS

Annapolis

Annapolis Harbour Center (410-266-5857; www.lernerenterprises.com), US 50 Exit 22. Contains a Barnes & Noble bookstore, other national chains, and a multiplex.

Westfield Shoppingtown Annapolis (410-266-5432; www.shoppingtown.com), 2002 Annapolis Mall. Located 4 miles from downtown.

Hanover

Arundel Mills (410-540-5110; www.millscorp.com), at the intersection of I-295 and MD 100 (near the Baltimore/Washington International Airport). The area's largest mall attracts shoppers from Baltimore, Annapolis, and Washington, D.C.

SPECIAL SHOPS

Annapolis

Historic Annapolis Foundation Museum Store (410-268-5576; 1-800-639-9153), 77 Main Street. This little shop gets my vote as the best place to obtain mementos of your visit to the area. In addition to pottery, jewelry, glassware, and books, the store offers many items that relate to the history of Annapolis.

Annapolis Treasure Company (410-263-7074), 161 Main Street. A full line of nautical gifts such as ship models, brass bells, lanterns, and nautical jewelry.

Soiree (410-990-1077; www.Soiree-Gifts.com), 196 Main Street. Gifts for the home imported and inspired by France and its national sense of style.

Plat du Jour (410-269-1499; www.platdujour.com), 210 Main Street. You would have to travel to Italy or France to find the selection of linens, glassware, ceramics, and artwork that you may purchase here.

FARMER'S MARKETS Anne Arundel County Farmer's Market (410-570-3646), Riva Road and Harry S. Truman Parkway, Annapolis. April through early December. Usually on Saturday 7–noon and Thursday 3–6. Days and hours may change late in the season.

Deale Farmer's Market (410-570-3646), Deale–Churchton Road, Deale. Produce dealers bring their wares to the Cedar Grove Methodist Church parking lot in the southern part of Anne Arundel County on Thursday 4–7, July through October.

Piney Orchard Farmer's Market (410-672-4273), Stream Valley Road (off MD 170), Odenton. Wednesday 2–6:30, June through October.

Severna Park Farmer's Market (410-841-5770), MD 2 and Jones Station Road, Severna Park. Look for fresh fruits and vegetables on Saturday 8–noon from mid-April through late November.

PICK-YOUR-OWN PRODUCE FARMS

Mt. Airy U-Pick (410-798-0838), 832 Mt. Airy Road, Davidsonville. Planters Jim and Tim Hopkins request that you call first before heading out to choose your own strawberries from mid-May through mid-June.

✴ Special Events

April: **Maritime Heritage Festival** (410-268-7676; www.aaaccc.org), Annapolis City Dock. Crafts, entertainment, historic homes and sites tours, lots of boats and maritime-history displays. **County Fair Craft Show** (410-923-3400; www.aacountyfair.org), fairgrounds, Crownsville. More than 100 artists and craftspersons show their wares. **The Great Kite Fly** (410-626-2530; www.shca. edu), St. John's College (see *To See—Colleges*), Annapolis. Kite-flying contests, ballets, and stunts.

May: **Annual Bay Bridge Walk** (1-877-BAY-SPAN). The one day out of the year that the public is permitted to walk the 4.3-mile US 50/301 bridge across the bay.

June through August: **Concerts at Banneker-Douglass Museum** (410-366-5008), Annapolis (see *To See—Museums*). Free live concerts on Thursday night by young musicians from the Heifetz International Music Institute.

August: **Rotary Crab Feast** (410-841-2841; www.annapolisrotary.com), Annapolis. Thought to be the largest crab feast in the world. So many people attend that it is held in the U.S. Navy–Marine Corps Stadium. **Kunta Kinte Celebration** (410-349-0338; www.kuntakinte.org), Annapolis. A 2-day celebration of African American history, arts, and entertainment. Children's tent and ethnic foods.

September: **Anne Arundel County Fair** (410-923-3400; www.aacountyfair.org), fairgrounds, Crownsville. **Annual Maryland Seafood Festival** (410-268-7862; www.mdseafoodfestival.com), Sandy Point State Park (see sidebar on page 263), Annapolis. Arts and crafts, petting zoo, beach golf, and lots of other family-oriented

⚓ **Maryland Renaissance Festival** (410-266-7304; 1-800-296-7304; www.rennfest.com), on Crownsville Road in Crownsville. Held every weekend from late August through late October. Adults $14.95; seniors $13; children 7–15 are $5.95; special prices for multiday visits. Go back in time to 16th-century England and watch knights in armor joust on horseback, eat a turkey leg so big that it would have choked even King Henry, and watch comedies and tragedies unfold on 10 theatrical stages. The atmosphere of this festival is one of grand celebration. Visitors, as well as volunteers, show up in period dress and never break character for a moment. Many children's activities and much food and music from those merry old days.

activities in addition to mounds of Chesapeake Bay seafood prepared various ways. **USNA Artists Authors Fair** (410-263-6933; www.navyonline.com), U.S. Naval Academy (see *To See—U.S. Naval Academy*), Annapolis. Meet authors, craftspersons, and artists whose works pertain to the navy, Annapolis, and the Chesapeake Bay. **Deale Bluegrass Festival and Car Show** (410-867-6707), Herrington Harbor North Marina, Deale.

October: **United States Sailboat Show and United States Powerboat Show** (410-268-8828; www.usboat.com), Annapolis City Dock. These shows run back-to-back over two weekends and are the country's oldest and largest in-water boat shows. Attracts tens of thousands of vendors and enthusiasts from around the world. **Anne Arundel Scottish Highland Games** (410-849-2849), Anne Arundel Fairgrounds, Crownsville. A clans' gathering that includes dancing, piping, fiddling, sheep dog demonstrations, children's games, and livestock exhibitions. A variety of Scottish goods for sale, too. **Fall Crafts Festival** (410-923-3400; www.aacountyfair.org), fairgrounds, Crownsville. More than 100 crafters, entertainment, flower and pumpkin sales.

November: **Annapolis by Candlelight** (410-267-7619; www.annapolis.org), Annapolis. An annual self-guided tour of private homes and public sites in the city's historic district.

December: **Bed and Breakfast Holiday Tour** (410-268-7070), Annapolis. B&Bs in the heart of the city open their doors for guided tours. **Eastport Yacht Club Lights Parade** (410-263-0415), Annapolis Harbor. The state's oldest lighted boat parade usually has more than 70 lighted boats.

Capital Region

LAUREL, COLLEGE PARK, BOWIE,
AND UPPER MARLBORO

SILVER SPRING, BETHESDA,
ROCKVILLE, AND GAITHERSBURG

Capital Region

Mount Airy

West Friendship

Baltimore

Ellicot City

VIRGINIA

Poolesville

Germantown

Gaithersburg Olney

Sandy Spring

Seneca

Rockville

Burtonsville

Baltimore Washington International Airport

Odenton

Potomac River

Dulles International Airport

Potomac

Silver Spring

College Park

Beltsville

Laurel

Greenbelt

Glenn Dale

Crofton

Washington D.C.

Largo

Bowie

Ronald Reagan Washington International Airport

Upper Marlboro

N

0 2 4 6 8 10   20

Miles

Clinton

Patuxent River

Accokeek

© The Countryman Press

CAPITAL REGION

Getting a handle on just what is available, and where it is located, can be difficult in the Capital Region, that portion of Maryland around Washington, D.C. An ever-expanding population, spurred on by ever-increasing federal and state bureaucracies, has transformed the once agrarian landscape. It is now a place of sprawling housing developments, large business parks and office buildings, and scores of malls and other shopping centers. Town lines have blurred, and it is often hard to tell where one ends and another begins.

This can be a good thing for travelers and explorers, however. You are, of course, right next door to Washington, D.C., and can make quick forays into the city without having to pay its inflated lodging rates. You also don't have to drive very far to take in most of the Capital Region's museums, galleries, parks, restaurants, shopping areas, and other attractions.

Laurel, College Park, Bowie, and Upper Marlboro

The Laurel Museum
Laurel
195
97
29
Montpelier
Mansion
95
1
32
270
193
PATUXENT RESEARCH
REFUGE/NATIONAL
WILDLIFE VISITOR
CENTER
Beltsville
NASA/Goddard
Space Flight
Visitor Center
3
Greenbelt
Museum
Dorsey
Chapel
197
Belair Stable
College Park
Glenn Dale
Belair Mansion
Aviation Museum
564
Hyattsville
Lanham
193
Bowie
Riverdale
New Carrollton
50
301
Riversdale
Mansion Museum
50
193
Washington
Chevery
D.C.
Andover Hills
Mitchellville
214
202
Largo
214
Watkins Regional Park
495
Suitland
95
202
395
Upper Marlboro
4
495
95
4
Oxon Hill
Oxon Hill Manor
Surratt House
Museum
301
Clinton
His Lordship's
Kindness
Duvall Tool Museum
& Patuxent River Park
5
Merkle Wildlife Sanctuary
VIRGINIA
Fort
Washington
223
Fort Washington Park
Brandywine
Piscataway Park
Accokeek
Patuxent River
210
CEDARVILLE
STATE FOREST
Potomac River

N

0 1 2 3 4 5   10
Miles

5

301

© The Countryman Press

LAUREL, COLLEGE PARK, BOWIE, AND UPPER MARLBORO

L aurel was one of the area's first industrial centers. Early in the 1800s, members of a prominent Quaker family, the Snowdens, developed iron mines and furnaces, and operated grist- and cotton mills. The Laurel Museum helps preserve those times. By the early 1900s, most of these businesses had closed; but due to its proximity to Washington, D.C., the town's population has only continued to grow and is now dominated by shopping centers, restaurants, and other services associated with bedroom communities.

Life in College Park focuses upon the University of Maryland, and businesses clustered around the school reflect the liberal lifestyles of the 35,000 students. The university's Clarice Smith Performing Arts Center is a theatrical showplace that provides the town with a cultural event of some kind or another almost every day of the year.

Unbeknownst to many of the state's citizens, Bowie is Maryland's fifth largest municipal entity. It quickly grew as a transportation center around two railroad lines that junctioned here soon after the Civil War. Although the city has expanded to encompass 16 square miles, the old part of town has retained its early charms. A brochure detailing a self-guided tour of historic sites is available from the Prince George's County, Maryland, Conference and Visitor's Bureau, Inc. (see *Guidance*).

Although it is the county seat of Prince George County, the municipal boundary of Upper Marlboro is quite small. Once a thriving center of trade for the tobacco grown around it, the town lost some of its prominence when large-scale plantations began to fail and modern highways passed it by. Those roadways did, however, enable scores of housing developments to spring up on former agricultural lands.

For a region with such a dense population, the area has a surprising amount of land set aside for recreational and open-space use. Patuxent Research Refuge encompasses 13,000 acres; 6,000 acres along the Potomac River are preserved by Piscataway Park; and state and regional parks, forests, and preserves ensure that thousands of other acres will escape any future development.

GUIDANCE The **Prince George's County, Maryland, Conference and Visitor's Bureau, Inc.** (301-925-9574; www.visitprincegeorges.com), is located in a modern office building within a business park at 9200 Basil Court, Suite 101, Largo, 20774. There is ample free parking, but you may have to drive around the building to find an open space.

GETTING THERE *By car:* **US 50** cuts across the northern part of this region, arriving from Washington, D.C., in the west and continuing to the Eastern Shore in the east. The **Baltimore–Washington Parkway (I-195)** connects those two cities and provides access to the northwestern part of the region. **US 301** crosses the Potomac River on a toll bridge, arriving from Virginia's Northern Neck.

By air: **Ronald Reagan Washington National Airport** (703-417-8000; www.mwaa.com/national) in northern Virginia and **Baltimore/Washington International Airport** (1-800-I-FLY-BWI) between Baltimore and Washington are within a 30-minute drive. Both have bus and rail connections that can bring you into this region.

By rail: **AMTRAK** (1-800-USA-RAIL) makes a stop in New Carrollton during its New York–Washington, D.C., run.

GETTING AROUND *By car:* **I-495 (Capital Beltway), I-195, US 50, US 301,** and **MD 201** are four-lane highways, but expect heavy traffic on all of them throughout most of the daylight hours.

By bus: **MTA** (1-800-543-9809; www.mta.maryland.com) buses connect and make stops in all of the major cities and towns in the region. **The Prince George's County Bus System** (301-324-BUSS) provides service on a more local level, enabling you to visit most of the attractions listed in this region without having to drive to them.

By rail: **MARC** commuter rail service enables you to visit many of the towns in this area, as well as Baltimore and Washington, D.C., without the hassle of driving a car. **METRO** rail (202-637-7000) provides the same service from Capitol Heights, Cheverly, Landover, New Carrollton, College Park, and a few other sites. (Also see *By bus.*)

MEDICAL EMERGENCY A number of hospitals have the facilities to handle an emergency should one arise:

Greater Laurel Beltsville Hospital (301-497-7954), 7300 Van Dusen Street, Laurel.

Doctor's Community Hospital (301-552-8665), 8118 Good Luck Road, Lanham.

Prince George's Hospital Center (301-618-3750), 3001 Hospital Drive, Cheverly.

Southern Maryland Hospital Center (301-899-4500), 7503 Surratts Road, Clinton.

✳ To See

COLLEGES **University of Maryland** (301-314-9866; www.maryland.edu), College Park. The university began as an agricultural college in the mid-1800s; in

1988 it joined a statewide system that includes numerous other campuses with a total enrollment of more than 130,000 students. The school offers a full range of graduate and undergraduate courses, but possibly its most interesting facet for a visitor is the **Clarice Smith Performing Arts Center.** Opened in 2001, the $130 million, 318,000-square-foot center has performance halls, galleries, studios, and rehearsal rooms. See *Entertainment* for information on performances presented by the various art disciplines.

MUSEUMS Laurel Museum (301-7225-7975), Main and 9th Streets, Laurel. Wednesday 10–2. Free admission. The 1830 mill workers' house contains photographs, tools, personal belongings, and other items depicting the town as a thriving mill center in the early 1800s.

✈ **College Park Aviation Museum** (301-864-6029; www.pgparks.com), 1985 Corporal Frank Scott Drive, College Park. Open daily; small admission fee. The museum is adjacent to **College Park Airport,** the world's oldest continuously operating airport, and celebrates its many aviation firsts: the first American female passenger, the training of the first military pilots (by Wilbur Wright), the first U.S. Postal Air Mail service, and more.

There is a multitude of kid-friendly interactive exhibits and a number of historical aircraft—like the plane Gus McCloud flew over the North Pole. You are even permitted to sit in a Taylorcraft airplane. The upstairs contains changing exhibits and a balcony to view the aircraft from a different angle.

♿ **Greenbelt Museum** (301-507-6582), 10-B Crescent Road, Greenbelt. Sunday 1–5. Free admission. The small museum is actually one of the planned community's original houses (for more information on this community, see **Greenbelt Park** under *Green Space—Parks*). It lends insight into the lives of those who lived here when Greenbelt first opened during the Great Depression. The two bedrooms, bath, living room, and kitchen are decorated with the original furniture constructed specifically for the community. Within walking distance is the art deco–style community center, with friezes on the outside wall depicting the preamble to the Constitution and exhibits inside pertaining to life in Greenbelt.

♿ **Duvall Tool Museum** (301-627-6074), 16000 Croom Airport Road, Patuxent River Park (see *Green Space—Parks*), Upper Marlboro. Sunday 1–4. W. Henry Duvall scoured the countryside for more than 50 years, buying old farm, home, and hand tools used during the 1800s. His collection of 1,000 pieces is now housed in this museum.

Surratt House Museum (301-868-1121; www.surratt.org), 9118 Brandywine Road, Clinton. January 1 through mid-December, Thursday through Friday 11–3, and Saturday and Sunday noon–4. Small admission fee. Period-dressed guides present a balanced account of the role John and Mary Surratt played in Lincoln's assassination. Their middle-class home was a tavern, post office, inn, and safe house in southern Maryland's Confederate underground. John Wilkes Booth stopped here during his escape from Washington, D.C., to retrieve weapons and supplies, and the upstairs bedroom is furnished as it would have been at that time.

LEARNING HISTORY AT THE SURRATT HOUSE

The museum also sponsors a 12-hour bus trip, the John Wilkes Booth Escape Route Tour, which makes stops at significant sites on his flight through Maryland. Dates, times, and fees vary; call for the latest information.

HISTORIC HOMES **Montpelier Mansion** (301-953-1376; wwww.pgparks.com/places/artsfac.html), Muirkirk Road and MD 197, Laurel. Tours given on the hour Sunday through Thursday noon–3 (at 1 and 2 January through February); please note that this schedule has been known to change frequently. Small admission fee. Guided 60-minute tours take visitors through the late-1700s Georgian home of Thomas and Anne Ridgely Snowden. Furnished with period pieces based upon an 1831 inventory of their belongings. The dining room contains some original family pieces; also on display is the wedding dress of the Snowdens' granddaughter. If not discussed during your tour, ask your guide to show you the secret trapdoor and hidden stairway.

The **Montpelier Cultural Arts Center** (301-953-1993) is adjacent to the mansion. Free guided tours (daily 10–5) enable visitors to watch sculptors, painters, printmakers, and other craftspersons at work.

Riversdale Mansion (301-864-0420), 4811 Riverdale Road, Riverdale. Sunday noon–4. Small admission fee for a 60-minute guided tour. A National Historic Landmark, the five-part, stucco-covered plantation home of George Calvert, grandson of the fifth Lord Baltimore, has been restored and furnished to reflect the early 1800s. The mahogany handrail and some of the furnishings are original, and be sure to ask a docent to provide background on the scenic wallpaper in the study.

&. **Belair Mansion and Stable Museum** (301-809-3089), 12207 Tulip Grove Drive, Bowie. Days and times that this attraction is open seem to change constantly, but it has always been open on Sunday from 1 to 4. Small admission fee; stable museum is free. Self-guided tours of the 1700s five-part Georgian mansion take in many original pieces of furniture that help interpret its 300-year history.

The largest cucumber tree of its kind in the state (planted in 1820) is located on the terraced grounds leading down to the stables. From the 1930s to the 1950s, this was one of the premier racing stables in the country and was the home of Gallant Fox and Omaha, the only father-and-son horses to win the coveted Triple Crown. Individual stalls contain separate and distinct displays chronicling thoroughbred racing in America.

BELAIR STABLES IN BOWIE

His Lordship's Kindness (301-856-0358; www.somd.lib.md.us/lordship), 7606 Woodyard Road, Clinton. March through December, Friday 1–4 and Sunday noon–3. Small admission fee for self-guided tour. This National Historic Landmark was named by Colonel Henry Darnell in gratitude of the 7,000-acre land grant given to him by Lord Baltimore. The architecture and many features in the house are original; however, it is furnished as it would have been in the 1950s when the last owners, John and Sarah Walton, lived there.

SITES ALONG THE POTOMAC RIVER There is a succession of protected lands strung along the east bank of the Potomac River. They preserve and interpret bits of history, and provide spectacular views across the wide river to Washington, D.C., and Alexandria and Mount Vernon in Virginia. They can all be accessed from **MD 210,** and from north to south are:

HIS LORDSHIP'S KINDNESS

Oxon Hill

⚓ **Oxon Cove Park/Oxon Hill Farm** (301-839-1176; www.nps.gov), 6411 Oxon Hill Road. Free admission and parking. The 512-acre property is operated as a working farm of the late 1950s by the National Park Service. It is a great place for urban children to find out about country life. I've watched entire groups become amazed when a ranger reaches under a cow and squeezes some milk into a pail. Chickens, sheep, and donkeys wander around in pens next to fields of corn, sorghum, and wheat. The farmhouse, barn filled with historic agricultural equipment, and a visitors center help round out the story. The horses stabled here are the ones that pull the White House tree through the streets of Washington, D.C., at Christmastime.

Short hiking and biking trails wind into fields and woods, and down to the river. Great views of Alexandria, Virginia.

Fort Foote Park, Fort Foote Road. A small picnic area on the site of a pre–Civil War fort. A few of the old ramparts and guns remain. Nice views across the river.

Fort Washington

Fort Washington Park (301-763-4600; www.nps.gov/fowa), 13661 Fort Washington Road. Open daily. Small entrance fee per car. You can take a self-guided tour or a ranger-narrated walk (times and dates vary) of the early 1800s fort, built on the site of an earlier one destroyed by the British in the War of 1812. Cannons, ramparts, earthworks, and displays in the visitors center help interpret the fort's important history as the first line of defense of the nation's capital. As a journalist once remarked, "We know our country is safe as long as we see the garrison flag at Fort Washington." Impressive view of Washington, D.C.

LEARNING TO MILK A COW AT OXON HILL FARM

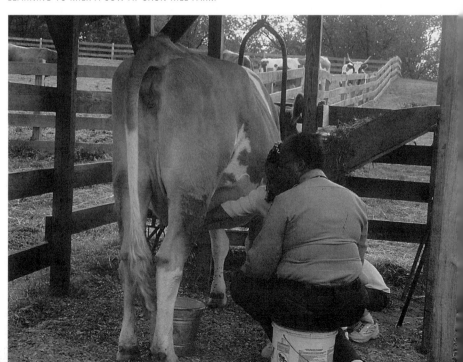

✒ **National Colonial Farm and Piscataway Park** (301-283-2113; www.nps. gov/pisc; www.accokeek.org), 3400 Bryan Point Road. Tuesday through Sunday, mid-March through mid-December; open on weekends the rest of the year. Small admission fee. The farm is operated by the nonprofit Accokeek Foundation as a living-history demonstration of a typical 1800s farm owned by a colonial family of modest means. Many of the plants and animals are heritage breeds—meaning they are no longer part of mainstream farming and are in danger of disappearing.

Self-guided tours (or guided tours on the weekends) take you by structures and gardens, all built and tended with period practices and implements. A ferryboat (a replica of an 1800s riverboat) crosses the Potomac to Mount Vernon, Virginia, on the weekends to provide insight into how the upper classes fared during colonial days. The foundation also sponsors an eco-farm, on which local volunteers work to create organic produce.

The colonial farm is within the 6-mile-long, 4,000-acre **Piscataway Park,** created by the National Park Service to protect the views of Mount Vernon. Numerous trails, some along the Potomac River, meander through the property and provide easy escapes from the modern world.

HISTORIC CHURCHES Dorsey Chapel (301-464-5291), 10704 Brookland Road, Glen Dale. Open the first and third Sunday of each month. Small admission fee. The small frame meetinghouse-style church was in use by the local African American community throughout most of the 1900s.

OTHER SITES ✒ **National Wildlife Visitor Center in Patuxent Research Refuge** (301-497-5580; www.fws.gov), 10901 Scarlet Tanager Loop, Laurel. (Also see the sidebar on page 291.) Open daily. Free admission. The National Wildlife Visitor Center is by far the largest and best facility of its kind that I have ever seen. The quality and quantity of its displays and exhibits outshine many museums for which you pay a fee to visit. Hands-on activities, multimedia presentations, and life-sized dioramas not only portray the natural drama of the refuge but also examine global environmental issues, different habitats around the world, and the behavior of a wide variety of animals. Be sure to allot a few hours to take it all in; what you learn here will add greatly to outings you happen to take anywhere in the natural world.

✒ ♿ **NASA/Goddard Space Flight Visitor Center** (301-286-8981; www.gsfc.nasa.gov), Explorer Road, Greenbelt. Open daily 9–4. Free

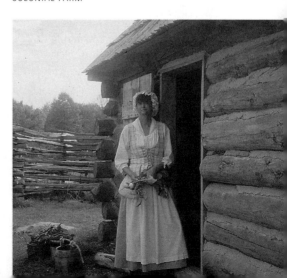

A COSTUMED DOCENT AT THE NATIONAL COLONIAL FARM

admission. Guided tours Monday through Saturday at 10:30 and 1:30, and Sunday at 11 and 2. Goddard is the center of all of NASA's space-flight tracking activities. There are many presentations, interactive displays, programs, and the opportunity to view the working areas of communications operations, satellite control, and spacecraft construction.

Paul E. Garber Facility (202-357-1400), 3904 Old Silver Hill Road, Suitland. Free, 3-hour guided tours given Monday through Friday at 10, and Saturday at 10 and 1. The facility is an artifact storage and restoration center for the Smithsonian's National Air and Space Museum. Besides taking you by more than 160 air-travel-related objects, tours include behind-the-scenes looks at restoration projects, some of which take years to complete.

GUIDED TOURS See **Surratt House Museum** under *Museums.*

SCENIC DRIVES ✈ **Chesapeake Bay Critical Area Driving Tour** (301-627-6074), 16000 Croom Airport Road, **Patuxent River Park** (see *Green Space—Parks*), Upper Marlboro. Open to automobiles Sunday 10–3; open to walkers and bicycles on Saturday. Originating at the entrance of the Jug Bay Natural Area of Patuxent River Park, the 4-mile, self-guided drive highlights the natural resources of the river and the Chesapeake Bay. Passing over wetlands on an elevated boardwalk, it provides tidal marshes, forests, a 40-foot observation tower with a grand view of the river, and glimpses of wildlife. I think this is one of the best and, since you are driving and not walking, easiest introductions to a variety of the state's environments.

✳ To Do

BICYCLING Washington, Baltimore, and Annapolis Trail (301-699-2407). The 5.6-mile trail follows an old railroad grade from Glen Dale to the Patuxent River.

Anacostia Trails (301-210-3788; www.anacostiatrails.org). A system of trails, multiple miles in length, is open to bikers and hikers along the Anacostia River and a number of its tributaries. Some trails are nicely isolated while others go through urban areas, but they all are pleasant alternatives to driving in this region.

Also see *To See—Scenic Drives; Hiking;* and the **Patuxent Research Refuge** sidebar on page 291.

FAMILY ACTIVITIES ✈ **Six Flags America Theme and Water Parks**

(301-249-1500; www.sixflags.com/america), Central Avenue, Largo. Open limited days April through May and September through October, and daily June through August. A 1-day ticket is about $35 to $40; the ticket grants admission to both parks. From humble beginnings as a small animal safari park, Six Flags America has grown to 140 acres (and still owns 300 acres on which to expand). Live shows, special small-children's rides in Looney Tunes Movie Town, and numerous roller coasters. The Wild One is 85 years old, the Superman has a 200-foot crest and reaches 70 miles an hour on its 1.5-mile track, and you ride facing the ground on the Batwing.

✈ **Watkins Regional Park** (301-249-9220), 301 Watkins Park Drive, Upper Marlboro. The 1,800-acre park provides a great variety of activities for the family. In addition to a small campground and several miles of nature trails, there are tennis courts, a miniature-golf course, and a miniature train that winds through woodlands and by the **Old Maryland Farm.** The farm is a petting zoo that provides the chance to visit livestock, participate in nature activities, and walk through organic gardens. Close to the farm is the **Chesapeake Carousel,** an early-1900s Dentzel carousel with hand-carved animals. All of these attractions are open on various days and times; contact the park office for details.

GOLF Henson Creek (301-567-4646), 7200 Sunnyside Lane, Fort Washington. The nine-hole course is open to the public with no advance tee times—first come, first served.

Paint Branch (301-935-0330), 4690 University Boulevard, College Park. Like Henson Creek (see above), Paint Branch is a nine-hole course with no advance tee times. Its links are short and flat, and have small greens.

Enterprise Golf Course (301-249-2040), 2802 Enterprise Road, Mitchellville. The par-72 course is constructed on the site of a former dairy farm and is open daily from 6:30 AM to dark.

Marlton Golf Club (301-856-7566), 9413 Midland Turnpike, Upper Marlboro. Open to the public with bentgrass fairways, water hazards, and many sand bunkers.

MINIATURE GOLF See **Watkins Regional Park** under *Family Activities.*

HIKING Cedarville State Forest (301-888-1410), MD 310 and Cedarville Road, Brandywine. Harboring some of Maryland's rare and endangered species such as the bald eagle, red-bellied woodpecker, and diamondback terrapin, **Zekiah Swamp** is the state's largest freshwater swamp. Stretching to the southwest for approximately 20 miles, from Cedarville State Forest to the Wicomico River, it is almost a mile wide in some places.

OLD MARYLAND FARM IN WATKINS REGIONAL PARK

Within the boundary of the state forest, miles of trails cross and parallel headwater streams, where the extra moisture enables the vegetation to become lush and thick. This provides a wonderful feeling of walking along a swamplike environment but without having your boots become mired in several inches of mud and ooze. In addition, the deep forest filters out much of the noise from the outside world, creating a quiet sense of isolation. Trails are also open to mountain bikers and equestrians. (Also see *Lodging—Campgrounds.*)

Also see **Oxon Cove Park/Oxon Hill Farm,** and **National Colonial Farm and Piscataway Park,** under *To See—Sites along the Potomac River; Bicycling;* **Merkle Wildlife Sanctuary** under *Nature Watching;* the **Patuxent Research Refuge** sidebar opposite; and *Green Space—Parks.*

KAYAKING AND CANOEING See **Patuxent River Park** under *Green Space—Parks.*

NATURE-WATCHING **Merkle Wildlife Sanctuary** (301-888-1410), 11704 Fenno Road, Upper Marlboro. The center opens at 10 daily; trails are open from sunrise to sunset. Rover and Fido must be left at home. Continuing the dream of Edgar Merkle, the 2,000-acre sanctuary provides habitat for Canada geese. Trails go by ponds, wetlands, upland and bottomland forest, cultivated fields, and creeks, which provide a variety of scenery as well as habitats for plants and animals. It takes a six-page pamphlet to catalog all of the birds observed here, while raccoons, rabbits, squirrels, skunks, foxes, and white-tailed deer have been spotted making quick dashes from field to

forest. A list of flowers blooming in just one month, July, contains nearly 100 species.

Exhibits in the visitors center focus on the goose and local human history. An observation deck with telescopes overlooks Merkle Pond, and an extensive schedule of interpretive programs is offered throughout the year.

RACING **Rosecroft** (301-567-4000; 1-877-818-WINS; www.rosecroft.com), 6336 Rosecroft Drive, Fort Washington. Admission $2. Free parking. Live harness racing every Thursday through Saturday starting at 7:20 PM.

✳ Green Space

PARKS **Greenbelt Park** (301-344-3948), 6565 Greenbelt Road (accessed from I-495 Exit 22), Greenbelt. It is ironic that a bureaucratic housing project ended up saving the natural environment of Greenbelt Park. The land was acquired in the 1930s by the federal government to be part of Greenbelt, one of a number of model towns within a belt of open space to be developed around the District of Columbia. Although some housing was constructed, the project never progressed as hoped, and the government sold the buildings to a local cooperative. Most of the remaining land became a component of the National Park Service in 1950.

Although the park is bordered by four-lane highways on three sides, its network of more than 8 miles of trails enables you to make a quick escape from urban landscapes to sweet gum trees, blueberry bushes, and small wetlands areas. The park also has a campground (see *Lodging—Camping*), and sponsors nature walks and evening programs.

Patuxent River Park (301-627-6074), 16000 Croom Airport Road, Upper Marlboro. Located along its namesake, the 6,000-acre park contains marshes, swamps, and forests with many miles of trails. Also available are fishing piers, canoe and kayak rentals, and a number of organized hikes, boat excursions, and special events. (Also see **Chesapeake Bay Critical Area Driving Tour** under *To See—Scenic Drives.*

Also see National Colonial Farmland Piscataway Park under *To See—Sites Along the Potomac River.*

THE BOARDWALK IN PISCATAWAY PARK IN ACCOKEEK MAKES A GREAT OUTDOOR CLASSROOM.

✳ Lodging

MOTELS AND HOTELS ♿ **Fairfield Inn** (301-572-7100), 4050 Powder Mill Road (accessed from I-95 Exit 29), Beltsville, 20705. Fairly low rates

for being this close to Washington, D.C., and having a swimming pool and exercise room. $89–$149.

🐾 ✂ **Comfort Suites** (301-206-2600;

🐾 ✂ **Patuxent Research Refuge** (301-497-5580; www.fws.gov) 10901 Scarlet Tanager Loop, Laurel. President Franklin D. Roosevelt established the refuge in 1936, and it has grown from an original 2,670 acres to nearly 13,000 acres. It supports a diversity of wildlife in a typical Maryland landscape of meadow, wetland, and forest habitats. Although the more than 200 species of birds that are known to be in the refuge at one time or another receive the greatest share of visitors' attention, deer, beavers, squirrels, muskrats, snakes, lizards, turtles, frogs, salamanders, raccoons, rabbits, and mice are also part of the environment.

The refuge is divided into three areas. The **North Tract** offers over 10 miles of roads and trails that are open to hikers, bikers, and horseback riders. The **Central Tract** contains offices and study sites, and is closed to the public. The **South Tract** is probably the most visited portion, with a network of scenic trails (open only to foot travel), two large lakes, and a visitors center (see **National Wildlife Visitor Center** under *To See—Other Sites*). Pets are permitted on the trails, but must be leashed. Sadly, for those who enjoy early-morning or early-evening strolls, when wildlife is most active, the South Tract is open to the public only from 10 to 5:30. (The North Tract has longer hours; check at the visitors center.)

1-800-628-7760), 14402 Laurel Place, Laurel, 20707. Surrounded by restaurants and shopping opportunities, and close to **Patuxent Research Refuge** (see the sidebar on page 291). Indoor pool and fitness center. Kids stay free in parent's room; small pets welcome with a deposit. $99–$249.

Marriott Inn and Conference Center (301-985-7300; www.marriott.com/confcenters/theinn.htm), University Boulevard and Adelphi Road, College Park, 20740. Original paintings and sculptures fill the spacious public areas and hallways, calling to mind an upscale resort more than a hotel interior. Within a few short blocks of the University of Maryland's **Clarice Smith Performing Arts Center** (see *To See—College*). Has its own fitness room, golf course, and jogging and walking trails. $139–249. (See also **The Garden Restaurant** under *Dining Out*.)

& **Hampton Inn** (301-809-1800; 1-800-HAMPTON), 15202 Major Lansdale Road, Bowie, 20716. All rooms have a large desk and chair, in addition to an iron and a hair dryer. Swimming pool. Close to **Six Flags America** (see *To Do—Family Activities*). $99–199.

& **Doubletree Club Hotel** (301-773-0700; 1-888-444-CLUB; www.clubhotels.com), 9100 Basil Court (accessed from I-495 Exit 17A), Largo, 20774. Large and comfortable lobby and other public areas, nicely appointed rooms, heated indoor pool, exercise facility and sauna. Within a few minutes' drive of **USAir Arena,** and downtown Washington, D.C. $99–199.

🐾 **Forest Hills Motel** (301-627-3969), 2901 Crain Highway, Upper Marlboro, 20774. Nothing fancy here—no swimming pool or fitness center—but they will let you take your pet into the room with you. $75–85.

& **Colony South Hotel and Conference Center** (301-856-4500; www.colonysouth.com), 7401 Surratts Road (accessed from I-495 Exit 7A), Clinton, 20735. With a Cape Cod–like exterior and lush wooden interior, this place feels more like a country lodge than a hotel that is less than 5 miles from Pennsylvania Avenue and downtown Washington, D.C. Rooms are quite large, there is a full-service fitness center with indoor pool, and free shuttle service is provided to and from Ronald Reagan Washington National Airport in Virginia and a METRO station. $149–229. (Also see **Wayfarer** under *Dining Out*.)

Best Western Potomac View (301-749-9400), 6400 Oxon Hill Road (accessed from I-495 Exit 3A), Oxon Hill 20745. Indoor pool, weight room, and oversized guest rooms. Very reasonable rates given its close proximity to the attractions of Washington, D.C. $99–149.

CAMPING 🐾 & **Cherry Hill Park** (301-937-7116; www.cherryhillpark.com), 9800 Cherry Hill Road, College Park, 20740. The closest RV campground to Washington, D.C., its 60 acres have a heated swimming pool, miniature golf, and modern facilities. A dog-walking service is offered, as well as guided tours of the nation's capital. METRO buses also make several stops a day to take visitors into Washington, D.C.

🐾 **Greenbelt Park** (301-344-3948), 6565 Greenbelt Road (accessed from I-495 Exit 22), Greenbelt, 20770. Just 12 miles from the downtown attractions of Washington, D.C. The setting of the

174 spaces is a bit more forested than those found in Cherry Hill Park (see above). Other than traffic noise from nearby four-lanes, this is usually a quiet, laid-back experience. Pets permitted. (Also see *Green Space—Parks*.)

Watkins Regional Park (park office—301-249-9220; campground 301-249-6900), 301 Watkins Park Drive, Upper Marlboro, 20774. Located next door to **Six Flags America** (see *To Do—Family Activities*), this small campground has just over 30 sites with a restroom/shower facility in the middle of it. Be aware that there are neither hookups nor a dump station for RVs.

✿ Cedarville State Forest (301-888-1410), MD 310 and Cedarville Road, Brandywine, 20613. The wooded camping area, with a central bathhouse, is open from late March through early December. A couple of sites are reserved for campers with pets. (Also see *To Do—Hiking*.)

Cosca Regional Park (301-868-1397), 11000 Thrift Road, Clinton 20735. A small campground with a central comfort station.

✳ Where to Eat

DINING OUT The Garden Restaurant (301-985-7300; www.marriott.com/confcenters/theinn.htm), University Boulevard and Adelphi Road, College Park. Open for breakfast, lunch, and dinner. The restaurant's small space inside the large **Marriott Inn and Conference Center** (see *Lodging—Motels and Hotels*) belies the quality of its slightly French-influenced foods. My wild mushroom vol-au-vents ($6) were in some of the crispiest pastry shells I've had, and my entrée of grilled lamb chops with herbes de

Provence ($22) was succulent. Duck ($20), filet mignon ($24), and seafood ($18–22) are also on the menu.

✍ Wayfarer (301-856-4500), 7401 Surratts Road. Inside the **Colony South Hotel** (see *Lodging—Motels and Hotels*), Clinton. Open for breakfast, lunch, and dinner. Consistent with the country-lodge feel of the hotel, the restaurant's decor includes a fireplace and beamed ceilings. The menu focuses on northern Italian dishes such as veal Piccata ($17.50), chicken Romana ($13.50), and penne with crabmeat and spinach (market price). A lunch buffet is offered Monday through Friday.

EATING OUT

Laurel
Café de Paris (301-490-8811), Laurel Lakes Center, 14252 Baltimore Avenue. Recalling a French bistro of the mid-1900s with wooden floors and posters on the wall, the café has a menu that is an ever-changing variation on French county cooking. The onion soup ($3.95) is good, as are the seafood offerings. Dinner entrées $19–25.

✍ Pasta Plus (301-498-5100), Central Plaza Shopping Center, 209 Gorman Avenue. The name as well as this restaurant's exterior do not do justice to its warm interior and quality of food. The pizzas ($7.95–14.95) have a great taste because they are cooked in a wood-burning stove, and most of the other dishes are delicious because the pasta and sauces are made fresh daily on the premises. Veal and seafood round out the menu. $9–20.

Beltsville
Kay's Diner (301-595-3042), 10973 Baltimore Avenue. Open 6 AM–5 PM. Closed Sunday. How can you go wrong when the average price of a

complete breakfast is less than $5? Most lunches, such as sandwiches, burgers, and a few entrées, will not cost you more than $7.

College Park

🍴 **94th Aero Squadron** (301-699-9400), 5420 Paint Branch Parkway. Open for lunch and dinner. Overlooking the College Park Airport (see **College Park Aviation Museum** under *To See—Museums*), the restaurant is built to resemble how a distressed French countryside farmhouse would have looked after experiencing the troubles of World War I. Lots of aviation memorabilia inside, and the wait staff is in period dress. Steaks ($17.95–28.95) are the specialty, with a few seafood ($17.95–23.95) and "farmhouse favorites" (meat loaf $12.95; pot roast $14.95) mixed in.

🍴 **R. J. Bentley's Filling Station** (301-277-8898), 7323 Baltimore Boulevard. Open for lunch and dinner. Located within in a 1920s gas station, Bentley's has been a favorite with University of Maryland students and alumni for several decades. Signed jerseys of university athletes who went on to become professionals adorn the walls.

The menu features what I call "bar food," lots of burgers and sandwiches ($5.95–8.95) with a few chicken, pasta, and steak dinner entrées ($8.95–18.95).

CRABS 🍴 **Captain Jerry's** (301-604-CRAB), 143 Bowie Road, Laurel. Open daily for lunch and dinner. The all-you-can-eat crabs (market price) are the way to go when available. If they're not, then try a soft-shell crab sandwich ($8.95) for lunch, or one of the many seafood entrées for dinner ($12.95–27.95). The crabcake dinner special ($16.95) is a deal.

Pop's Seafood and Carry Out (301-459-4141), 7437 Annapolis Road, Landover Hills. You come here for the hard- and soft-shell crabs (market price), not for the atmosphere; but Pop's has been serving to the locals for more than two decades.

COFFEE BARS **Year of the Rabbit Coffee Pub** (301-809-0979; www. ourbowie.com/yotr), Hilltop Plaza, 6700 Race Track Road, Bowie. Open daily. Nestled in an alleyway, the pub offers hot and cold coffees, a variety of beers and wines, pastries, and live regional entertainment Thursday through Sunday.

SNACKS AND GOODIES **Simple Pleasures Ice Café** (301-809-5880), 6948 Laurel-Bowie Road, Bowie. Closed Monday. Santamaria Perrin and Terri Russell, mother and daughter, offer homemade ice cream, cakes, sorbets, and gourmet coffees and teas. Sugar-free items also available.

✳ Entertainment

DANCE **School of Dance** (301-405-ARTS; www.claricesmithcenter. umd.edu), University of Maryland, College Park. The school sponsors performances throughout the school year, many of them by professional troupes, and several student presentations each semester. (Also see *Music* and *Theaters*.)

FILM All of the following show first-run movies:

Sony Theatres (301-937-0742), 4001 Powder Mill Road, Beltsville.

Showcase Market Place Cinema (301-464-1702), 3208 Superior Lane, Bowie.

AMC Academy (301-474-0077), 6198 Greenbelt Road, Greenbelt.

Old Greenbelt Theater (301-474-9744), 132 Centerway Road, Greenbelt.

P&G Laurel Towne Center (301-776-2500), 13314 Laurel Bowie Road, Laurel.

Laurel Lakes Cinema (301-490-8001), 929 Fairlawn Road, Laurel.

AMC Carrollton (301-459-6999), 7828 Riverdale Road, New Carrollton.

AMC Rivertown (301-389-9571), 6075 Oxon Hill Road, Oxon Hill.

Andrews Manor (301-736-6373), Andrews Manor Shopping Center, Suitland.

MUSIC **Maryland Presents** (301-405-ARTS; www.claricesmithcenter. umd.edu), University of Maryland, College Park. Maryland Presents is the theatrical arm of the **Clarice Smith Performing Arts Center,** which presents a wide range of programs throughout the year (also see *Dance* and *Theaters*). Performances include solo artists, full orchestras, quartets, popular music, Broadway and theatrical productions, and student and faculty recitals. Since all of the arts disciplines are housed in the center, artists from each discipline often work together on the productions.

THEATERS **University of Maryland Department of Theater** (301-405-ARTS; www.claricesmithcenter.umd. edu), University of Maryland, College Park. Performances have included many Broadway standards, such as *The Music Man,* along with newer works like George F. Walker's *Problem Child.* The productions include mem-

bers of the school's faculty, students, and local actors—professional and amateur. (Also see *Dance* and *Music.*)

&. **Publick Playhouse** (301-277-1710), 5445 Landover Road, Cheverly. Located just 10 minutes from downtown Washington, D.C., the playhouse—a converted 1940s movie theater—presents everything from jazz and gospel to modern dance, and from musical theater to historic drama.

SPORTS **University of Maryland Terrapins** (301-314-7070), College Park. The university's student teams provide action for spectators in basketball, baseball, soccer, lacrosse, swimming, and other sports.

Washington Redskins (301-276-6000), FedEx Field, Landover. The professional NFL team plays its home games in the 83,000-seat FedEx Field.

✍ **Bowie Baysox** (301-805-6000; 1-800-956-4004), Prince George's Stadium, 4101 North East Crain Highway, Bowie. Come watch a possible future Baltimore Oriole as the AA team plays its season from April through September.

Washington Power Lacrosse (301-324-1755), Capital Center, Largo. Professional indoor lacrosse.

✳ Selective Shopping

ART GALLERIES **Harmony Hall Regional Center** (301-203-6060), 10701 Livingston Road, Fort Washington. A converted elementary school provides arts classes and an exhibition gallery.

Also see **Montpelier Mansion** under *To See—Historic Homes.*

FARMER'S MARKETS **Main Street Farmer's Market** (301-262-6200),

Gallant Fox Lane and MD 197, Bowie. Start the week with fresh produce by stopping by on Sunday between 9 and 1 during the season of May through October.

Prince George's Plaza Farmer's Market (310-627-0977), MD 410, Hyattsville. Strawberries are some of the first things to appear when the season opens in May, while pumpkins close it out in November. Open Tuesday 3–6.

USDA Farmer's Market (301-504-1776; 1-800-384-8704), 5601 Sunnyside Avenue, Beltsville. This market should offer some of the best fruits and vegetables around, as it is adjacent to the Beltsville Agricultural Research Center. Open Thursday 10–2, June through September.

College Park Farmer's Market (301-262-8662), 5211 Calvert Road, College Park. Stands are temporary and quite informal, as everything is set up in a swimming-pool parking lot on Saturday from May through November. Things crank up at 7 AM and get pretty quiet by noon.

PICK-YOUR-OWN PRODUCE FARMS
Cherry Hill Orchard (301-292-4642), 12300 Gallahan Road, Clinton. The season starts in mid-May with red raspberries and continues well into the fall with other berries, fruits, and a very wide variety of vegetables.

Miller Farms (301-297-5878), 10140 Piscataway Road, Clinton. The strawberries are usually ripe by mid-May; return about a month later to choose and pick your own vegetables.

✿ **Robin Hill Farm Nursery** (301-888-1849), 15800 Croom Road, Brandywine. Bring the kids out to choose a pumpkin so that they can carve their own jack-o'-lantern.

✳ Special Events

February: **Annual Choreographers' Showcase** (301-405-ARTS), Clarice Smith Performing Arts Center (see *To See—Colleges*), College Park.

March: **Annual Jewelry, Mineral and Fossil Show and Sale** (301-297-4575), Fort Washington. Also includes the **Family Wildlife Art Festival** with performances, music, workshops, and kid's activities.

April: **Play Festival** (301-322-0444), Prince George's Community College, Largo. Annual presentation of new theatrical works and talent from the region.

May: **Spring Festival Horse Show** (301-952-7999), Upper Marlboro. A-rated hunter/jumper horse show. **Montpelier Spring Festival** (301-776-2805), Laurel. Arts and crafts, several stages presenting music and dance, pony rides, and kid's parade. **Harlem Renaissance Festival** (301-918-8418; www.prgeoharlemrenaissancefestival.org), Landover. Several stages of music, dance, poetry, and theater, with other activities for all ages. **Marlboro Day and Parade** (301-952-9575), Upper Marlboro. Parade, food, crafts, vendors, and entertainment.

June: **Main Street Antique, Arts and Craft Show** (301-725-7539), Laurel. Juried show featuring regional artists and antiques dealers. Appraisals and entertainment.

September: **County Fair** (301-579-2598), Equestrian Center, Upper Marlboro.

November through early January: **Winter Festival of Lights** (301-699-2545), Watkins Park, Upper Marlboro.

SILVER SPRING, BETHESDA, ROCKVILLE, AND GAITHERSBURG

Francis Preston Blair was out riding his horse in the mid-1800s when his mount became spooked, throwing him to the ground. With his face in the mud, he noticed he had landed next to a spring, whose mica deposits shone like silver in the bright sunshine. He purchased the land around the water source, built his home, and Silver Spring was born.

Although it is not an incorporated city, its downtown area was a major shopping point in the mid-1900s but lost favor as the 20th century came to a close. A $400 million revitalization program has reversed the trend, and shops, restaurants, and businesses have returned. The National Capital Trolley Museum is just a few miles away and chronicles the days before automobiles ruled the roadways.

Numerous research centers, such as the National Institutes of Health, National Naval Medical Center, National Cancer Institute, and software development and telecommunications firms make Bethesda the state's second largest employment center. The money generated by these enterprises has transformed the city into a sophisticated and trendy place. The shopping district is crowded with some of the most upscale stores—both locally owned and national chains—in the Washington, D.C., area.

Bethesda is also a great patron of the arts, recently having dedicated its Art in Public Spaces Discovery Trail. A stroll along urban streets and byways will reveal more than 40 indoor and outdoor works of art, and McCrillis Gardens and Gallery presents a changing array of exhibits. The written word is also valued here, evidenced in the number of new and used bookshops.

Rockville began with the establishment of Owen's Ordinary, an inn and tavern, around 1750. A few years later, in 1774, citizens gathered in another inn, Hungerford's Tavern, to discuss their outrage over Britain's blockade of Boston Harbor and called for a Maryland boycott of trade with England. From those early days, Rockville has become Maryland's second largest city in area, occupying more than 13 square miles.

Much of its history is preserved in the architecture of the downtown area and within the 1800s Beall-Dawson House, open for public tours. F. Scott Fitzgerald, his wife, Zelda, and other family members are buried in the cemetery of nearby St. Mary's Church. Those wishing to escape the urban environment can drive

Silver Spring, Bethesda, Rockville, and Gaithersburg

© The Countryman Press

just a few miles to Rock Creek Regional Park along the city's northern border, or Cabin John Regional Park to south.

Gaithersburg began as a small agrarian community known as Log Town in the mid-1700s. The arrival of the Baltimore & Ohio Railroad in 1873 allowed the farmers to reach a wider market and enabled travelers to escape the summer heat in Washington, D.C. These earlier days are recalled in the exhibits of the now restored B&O Railroad Station. The arrival of the interstates, specifically I-270, in the late 20th century put an end to the farming way of life, and the city now functions as a bedroom community for the Washington, D.C., metropolitan area.

COMMUNITIES Towns removed just a few miles from the I-270 corridor are also growing but so far have escaped rapid urbanization. **Sandy Spring** was settled by Quakers in 1725, and the Sandy Spring Museum documents its history.

Close to the Potomac River, **Poolesville** was settled in 1783 and retains much of its rural, farming roots. It is believed that **Clarksburg** can trace its roots back to a Native American trading post. Much of the green space that would have surrounded the small Indian settlement has been preserved by Little Bennett Regional Park.

GUIDANCE Contact the **Conference and Visitors Bureau of Montgomery County, Maryland, Inc.** (301-482-9702; 1-800-925-0880; www.cvbmontco. com), 12900 Middlebrook Road, Suite 1400, Germantown, 20874, for information, brochures, and other travel advice.

GETTING THERE *By car:* **I-270** makes an almost arrow-straight run through the middle of the region, and connects with **I-70** at Frederick to the northwest and with the **Capital Beltway (I-495),** which encircles Washington, D.C., to the southeast.

By air: This area is blessed with being serviced by three major airports. The two closest are **Ronald Reagan Washington National Airport** (703-417-8000; www.mwaa.com/national) and **Dulles International Airport** (703-572-2700) in northern Virginia. Located between Baltimore and Washington, D.C., is the **Baltimore/Washington International Airport** (1-800-I-FLY-BWI).

By rail: **AMTRAK** (1-800-872-7245) makes a stop at the Rockville Metro Station, which means you can arrive here by train from any other place that has AMTRAK connections.

By water: **White's Ferry** (301-349-5200), US 15. The only remaining ferry across the Potomac River permits you come into Maryland near Poolesville from US 15 just north of Leesburg, Virginia. Although the ferry is a utilitarian boat, the ride across the river can be a scenic and enjoyable one as you watch waterfowl and other birds wing their way above the water. You will also get a chance to look at the river and the Chesapeake & Ohio (C&O) Canal from the same perspective as the folks who took the ferry in the 1800s did.

It operates daily from 5 AM to 11 PM and costs about $3 one way; $5 round trip.

GETTING AROUND *By car:* **I-270** and **I-495 (Capital Beltway)** are the major limited-access highways. The interstates are extremely crowded and slow during morning and evening travel hours, and at lunchtime; automobile travel on local highways can be frustratingly slow at any time of day. Just accept it, go with the flow, and give yourself twice as much time as you think you need to get to your destination. Here's an **Insider's Tip:** It is not always true, but many times **MacArthur Boulevard** and **Clara Barton Parkway** along the Potomac River are blessedly free of traffic when other roadways are bumper-to-bumper.

By bus: The **METROBUS** (202-637-7000) system has routes on every major roadway in the region and can also transport you into Washington, D.C., and Baltimore.

Ride On (240-777-7433; www.rideonbus.com), the Montgomery County bus system, has more than 80 routes with thousands of stops. Its buses also connect with the METRO system to provide transportation throughout the Washington, D.C.–Baltimore area.

The **Bethesda Trolley** (301-656-0868; www.bethesdatransit.org) has a figure-8 route that takes the trolley through the downtown business and office area. It runs until midnight Monday through Thursday, and until 2 AM on Friday and Saturday.

By rail: The **METRO** (202-637-7000) subway rail system operates out of Washington, D.C., and makes 13 stops in this region. The line is just a bit east of the I-270 corridor it parallels.

By taxi: Among the many taxi companies operating in and around Silver Spring, Bethesda, Rockville, and Gaithersburg are **Montgomery Taxicab** (301-762-2001), **Action Taxi** (301-840-1222), **All-County Cab** (301-924-4344), and **Regency Cab** (301-990-9000).

&. **Taxi Plus** (301-984-1900) has wheelchair-accessible minivans.

MEDICAL EMERGENCY Suburban Hospital (301-896-1000), 8600 Old Georgetown Road, Bethesda.

Montgomery General Hospital (301-774-8882), 18101 Prince Phillip Drive, Olney (close to Rockville and Gaithersburg).

Shady Grove Adventist Hospital (301-279-6000), 9901 Medical Center Drive, Rockville.

Holy Cross Hospital (301-754-7000), 1500 Forest Glen Road, Silver Spring.

✳ To See

MUSEUMS Dennis and Philip Ratner Museum (301-897-1518; www.ratner-museum.com), 10001 Old Georgetown Road, Bethesda. Sunday 10–4:30. Free admission. Provides a visual depiction of the Hebrew Bible through sculpture, drawings, paintings, and other works of art—primarily those of Philip Ratner. Although this is a private museum based upon the scriptures of the Jewish faith, everyone is welcome, the atmosphere is low-key (in other words, no proselytizing like that found in some other religious museums), and the artwork is interesting and worthwhile.

Community Museum (301-258-6160; www.gaithersburghistorical.org), 5 South Summit Avenue, Gaithersburg. Thursday through Saturday 10–2. Donations accepted. Exhibits inside the restored 1884 B&O Railroad Station chronicle local rail history and the city's movement from a farming community to the present day. The outdoor rail yard has a number of locomotives and other railcars.

Sandy Spring Museum (301-774-0022; www.sandyspringmuseum.org), 17901 Bentley Road, Sandy Spring. Closed Tuesday and Friday. Much to see and do here. The **Farquhar Gallery** features changing traveling exhibits, a guided tour explains the museum's historical aspects and furnishings, and a stables and blacksmith shop reflect the life of earlier times. Musical concerts of various types presented throughout the year.

C&O CANAL NATIONAL HISTORICAL PARK

Around the turn of the 19th century, individual canals afforded access around waterfalls and rapids, providing an easy water route between a young America's eastern coastline and areas west of the Blue Ridge Mountains. Taking a cue from ideas expressed by George Washington and Thomas Jefferson, construction of the Chesapeake & Ohio Canal began on July 4, 1828.

Originally projected to extend 360 miles, the canal never lived up to its investors' dreams. Mounting costs, coupled with the other problems, caused financial backers to decide in 1850 that enough was enough, and that Cumberland was the farthest west the canal would be constructed—a distance of 184.5 miles.

Dry spells, floods, winter freezes, and competition from the B&O Railroad (which coincidentally began construction on the very same day) kept the canal from operating at a profit. A tremendous flood in 1924 destroyed so much of the infrastructure that the canal never reopened. Canal owners turned it over to the federal government for $2 million in 1938.

The canal was proclaimed a national monument in 1961 and named a national historical park in 1971. Today, the towpath is opened to hikers, bikers, and (except for a short section) horseback riders, and camping is permitted at designated sites. The park service has an abundance of informational handout sheets at its **Great Falls Visitor Center** (301-299-3613; www.nps.gov/choh), 11710 MacArthur Boulevard, Potomac, 20854. Exhibits within the center illustrate the history of the canal, while Mike High's book, *The C&O Canal Companion,* covers the subject in great detail.

Also see **C&O Canal** under *To Do—Hiking.*

⌀ **National Capital Trolley Museum** (301-384-6088; www.dctrolley.org), 1313 Bonifant Road, Silver Spring. Open year-round, but days and hours vary greatly. Small admission fee. Clickety-clack, clickety-clack. Take a ride on one of the electric trolley cars that serviced the area for nearly 100 years to relive the days of screeching wheels and swaying cars. The museum has interactive displays, a model streetcar layout, and dozens of vehicles that serviced the area "from Lincoln to Kennedy."

HISTORIC HOMES **Clara Barton National Historic Site** (301-492-6245), 5801 Oxford Road (off MacArthur Boulevard), Glen Echo. Open daily. Free admission and parking. Almost before artillery stopped firing and bullets ceased whistling through the air, Clara Barton was on the battlefield attending to the wounds of Civil War soldiers. Guided 1-hour tours take you through the home of this founder of the American Red Cross. The 1891 house, which was built along the lines of a Red Cross relief structure, contains many items that once belonged to Barton. Adjacent to **Glen Echo Park** (see the sidebar opposite).

Beall-Dawson House (301-340-2825; www.montgomeryhistory.org), 103 West Montgomery Avenue, Rockville. Small admission fee. Guided tours provide insight into early 1800s life. Many of the items in the house (such as the pianoforte and the interesting tin bathtub) belonged to the Beall family. Mr. Beall came and went often, so most of the time the house was inhabited and run by women and slaves. Rotating exhibits on the second floor focus on local Rockville history. Located on the lawn is the small **Stonestreet Museum of 19th-Century Medicine**. The Gothic Revival office was built for Dr. Stonestreet in 1852 and contains many items from his practice.

OTHER SITES **F. Scott Fitzgerald Burial Place** (301-428-9702), corner of Rockville Pike (MD 355) and Viers Mill Road, Rockville. In what could be interpreted as a summation of the human condition, Fitzgerald wrote in the *Great Gatsby*, "So we beat on, boats against the current, borne back ceaselessly into the past." These words are now engraved upon his St. Mary's Church cemetery tombstone, located at a busy highway intersection next to a METRO rail station. His wife, Zelda Sayre, lies next to him.

✳ To Do

BALLOONING **Fantasy Flights** (301-417-0000; www.airtravel.com/fantasy), 823 Quince Orchard Road, Gaithersburg. Sunrise and sunset hot-air balloon rides over the countryside.

BICYCLING **Capital Crescent Trail** (202-234-4874). The packed-surface rail-trail connects local communities from Georgetown in Washington, D.C., to Silver Spring—for a distance of about 11 miles. It does pass through heavily populated areas, but by making use of the C&O Canal, a country club, and a couple of parks, the trail ride can be a pleasant one. One of the highlights is the Delecarlia Tunnel, whose brick-faced portals are a testament to the masons' expertise.

Rock Creek Trail (301-495-2525). This mostly paved route follows Rock Creek for 21 miles from Lake Need-

⬧ **Glen Echo Park** (301-492-6282), 7300 MacArthur Boulevard, Glen Echo. Open daily. Free admission and parking. It almost feels as if you have walked into the middle of a *Twilight Zone* story. The bumper-car pavilion and the arcade still stand, and the horses of the carousel are freshly painted, but no one is there to operate the rides or entice you to play a game of ring toss.

The land was first developed in 1891 by the National Chautauqua Assembly as a center for the sciences, arts, languages, and literature. The Glen Echo Company, operators of trolleys in the Washington, D.C., area, purchased the land and operated the amusement park from 1899 to 1968. The federal government acquired it in 1971, and the park is now used, once again, as a place for cultural pursuits. Classes are conducted on nearly every type of art and craft imaginable; children's theater productions are presented throughout the year—The Puppet Company's are a favorite—and the dances (waltz, big-band, contra, square, and popular) in the Spanish Ballroom are attended by hundreds every weekend. The **Discovery Center Children's Museum** is geared for children ages 2–11.

I just enjoy coming here for an early-morning walk or a browse through the bookstore and gift shop, and to take a ride on the carousel when it happens to be operating (contact the office for times and dates). Ranger-conducted tours of the carousel are given at 2 PM on Sunday.

THE REFURBISHED CAROUSEL'S ROUND HOUSE

wood in Rockville to the heart of Washington, D.C. Most of the time it runs through the woods along the creek or passes through the recreation areas of neighborhood parks. Be careful at the many intersections with busy roadways.

Seneca Creek State Park (301-924-2127), Gaithersburg. The trailhead parking lot is at 14938 Schaeffer Road, accessed from MD 118 (Germantown Road) south of Gaithersburg. In an out-of-the-way section of Seneca Creek State Park, local citizens have cooperated with authorities and put in many volunteer hours constructing and maintaining a 10-mile network of trails. Hikers, mountain bikers, and horseback riders can freely visit over and over again, watching corn and soybean crops advance from tiny seed sprouts to tall mature plants. The variation from open land to wooded tracts ensures a variety of wildlife, and warblers, vireos, meadowlarks, woodpeckers, vultures and owls have all been seen visiting or living here.

Bicycle Tour of the African Ameri-can Community, Sandy Spring. Call 301-260-8860 to obtain a map that details this tour.

Also see C&O Canal National Historical Park sidebar on page 301.

BOAT EXCURSIONS ⚓ **C&O Canal,** Great Falls. The 1-hour rides originate at the Great Falls Visitor Center (see C&O Canal National Historical Park sidebar on page 301) and operate from April through October. Adults $8; seniors $6; children 4–14 are $5. Take a ride on the mule-drawn *Canal Clipper* boat. Rangers/naturalists and the mule driver dress in period costume, and the clip-clop of the mules along the towpath brings back the canal's former days.

Also see **Rock Creek Regional Park** under *Green Space—Parks.*

FAMILY ACTIVITIES See *Miniature Golf,* and **Dave and Buster's** under *Eating Out.*

GOLF Hampshire Greens (301-476-7999), 616 Firestone Drive, Ashton. Features bent grass all the way from

THE *CANAL CLIPPER* PREPARES TO LEAVE LOCK 20

the tee to the green on all 18 holes. Total distance from the tip tees is almost 7,000 feet.

Little Bennett Golf Course (301-253-1515), 25900 Prescott Road, Clarksburg. The par-72 course's hilly terrain offers a challenge as well as nice scenery.

Rattlewood Golf Course (301-607-9000), 13501 Penn Shop Road, Mount Airy. The excellent drainage on this par-72 course makes it the place to go when other courses are too wet to play on.

Trotter's Glen (301-570-4951), 16501 Batchellors Forest Road, Olney. Ed Ault designed the par-71 course.

Falls Road Golf Course (301-299-5156), 10800 Falls Road, Potomac. The weekend fee for playing the 18 holes situated around a lake is about $35.

White Oak Golf Course (301-593-6910), 10911 New Hampshire Avenue, Silver Spring. The course is only nine holes, but the low cost of a round and the par 32 make it a good choice for beginning or intermediate golfers.

MINIATURE GOLF ✍ **Bohrer Park** (301-258-6240), 506 South Frederick Avenue, Gaithersburg. The park's miniature-golf course is open May through October.

HIKING Seneca Creek State Park (301-924-2127). Seneca Creek State Park (also see *Bicycling*) provides enough easy trails to make for enjoyable morning or afternoon hikes. The 3.7-mile **Lake Shore Trail** encircles Clopper Lake, passing through fields of wildflowers. **Long Draught Trail** is 2.5 miles long and follows a stream

to a wetlands area and onto a laurel-covered hillside. The **Great Seneca** and **Mink Hollow Trails** are each 1.25 miles in length and traverse forested slopes and marshlands. The **Old Pond Trail,** only 0.33 mile long, passes by a pond in its last stages of succession. All of these pathways interconnect in some way or another.

C&O Canal, Great Falls (also see the C&O Canal National Historical Park sidebar on page 301). The area around Great Falls has an abundance of hiking trails. One side trail off the main towpath leads to the dramatic scenery of **Great Falls,** where the Potomac River rushes and churns over a series of drops within the narrow confines of the gorge it has etched out of the landscape.

Another outing, with only a few short ups and downs, brings you by reminders of gold-mining days and may enlighten you as to just how much wildlife can exist in proximity to large human population centers.

The **Billy Goat Trail** just might have the most awkward and exhausting 1-mile portion of trail in all of Maryland as it climbs over huge boulders and rock outcroppings along the northern bank of the Potomac River.

Also see *Bicycling* and *Parks.*

HORSEBACK RIDING Wheaton Regional Park (301-622-3311), Wheaton, **Rock Creek Regional Park** (301-589-9026), Rockville, and the **Maryland Horse Center** (301-948-8585), Gaithersburg, provide lessons, recreational riding, and some boarding services throughout the year.

You are also permitted to ride your own horse on the trails of many of the regional parks. Contact the **Mont-**

gomery County Department of Parks (301-495-2507), 9500 Brunett Avenue, Silver Spring, for the latest information.

Also see the **C&O Canal National Historical Park** sidebar on page 301, and **Seneca Creek State Park** under *Bicycling*.

KAYAKING AND CANOEING Canoes, rowboats, and some paddleboats are available for rent during the warmer months at **Black Hill** (in Boyds) and **Rock Creek** (in Rockville) **Regional Parks** (see *Green Space—Parks*). Most of the paddling is on small lakes or quiet creeks.

One of America's most scenic waterways, the **Potomac River** provides close to 30 miles—from White's Ferry to Great Falls Park—of delightful canoeing and kayaking for paddlers of all skill levels. Below the Great Falls Visitor Center (see the C&O Canal National Historical Park sidebar on page 301)at **Great Falls,** the river reaches its fall line and becomes narrow, swift, and dangerous for anyone but those who possess the most proficient of paddling skills. If you are an expert, however, that stretch of river will give you the thrill of your life, with narrow channels, 90-degree turns, and drops of 22 or more feet.

Anyone attempting to paddle the falls should go with someone who has made a successful run; paddlers are required to register with C&O Canal park rangers in the visitors center before beginning the trip. Have fun, this is a great thrill, but do not take it lightly, as many have lost their lives here.

Canoes for paddling the Potomac River are available for rent by the hour or day at the **White's Ferry store** (301-349-5200), White's Ferry.

They will also shuttle you and your canoe if you make reservations ahead of time.

NATURE WATCHING See *Green Space—Walks*.

SKATING Skate Park in Bohrer Park (310-258-6350), 506 South Frederick Avenue, Gaithersburg. Open daily; children under 10 must be accompanied by an adult. The 12,300-square-foot park is designed for in-line skating and skateboarding. The ramps and boxes are designed to suit all skill levels, while the ground surface is asphalt.

Cabin John Regional Park (301-365-2246), 10610 Westlake Drive, Rockville. The park's enclosed rink provides ice skating well into June.

Rubini Athletic Complex—Ice Skating Rink (301-649-2703), 1800 Glenallan Avenue, Wheaton. Located within Wheaton Regional Park.

SWIMMING The **Montgomery County Department of Recreation** (301-217-6880) operates six public outdoor pools (usually open Memorial Day through Labor Day) and three year-round indoor pools.

Water Park at Bohrer Park (301-258-6445), 510 South Frederick Avenue, Gaithersburg. Open Memorial Day through Labor Day. Small admission fee. The main pool has several different areas, and a double 250-foot water slide twists and turns into the splash pool.

✳ Green Space

GARDENS McCrillis Gardens and Gallery (301-365-5728), 6910 Greentree Road, Bethesda. Open daily from

10 to sunset. The time to visit is between April and mid-June when the 5 acres are ablaze with azaleas and rhododendrons. The gallery features changing exhibits from area artists.

Brookside Gardens (301-949-8230; www.mc-mncppc.org/parks/brookside), 1800 Glenallan Avenue, Wheaton. Open daily from sunrise to sunset. By far one of the most well-maintained, extensive, and prettiest free-admission gardens I have been privileged to visit. A dozen themed gardens, with plants that bloom from early spring into early winter, allow you to enjoy the beauty of the 50 acres. Sculpted ponds add variety to the scenery, as does the maturing forest around the gardens. This is a don't-miss place, and even if outside temperatures drop too low for you in winter, you can always visit the plants and flowers inside the two conservatories.

PARKS ♿ **Rock Hill Regional Park** (301-972-9396), 20930 Lake Ridge Drive, Boyds. Little Seneca Lake, at 505 acres, is the focal point of the park. You may bring your own electric-powered boat, or rent a canoe or rowboat (in season). Anglers come here for the largemouth bass, tiger muskie, crappie, catfish, and sunfish. A fishing pier is handicapped accessible. A system of more than 13 miles of trails (3 miles are paved and handicapped accessible) enable exploration of the surrounding fields and woodlands. Other features include playgrounds, volleyball courts, and afitness course.

Little Bennett Regional Park (301-972-9222; www.mncppc.org), 23701 Frederick Road, Clarksburg. Unlike many other parks located close to large population centers, Little Bennett Regional Park is not overdeveloped with swimming pools, amusement centers, skating rinks, basketball courts, and the like. It does offer a campground with hot showers and a camp store (see *Lodging—Camping*), horseshoe and volleyball areas, and a nature center; yet these facilities are concentrated on just a few acres of its southern edge off MD 355 (and are only available to campers).

The rest of the park has been—more or less—left in its natural state, and 14 miles of trails are available to lead visitors onto 3,700 acres of dense forests, open meadows, narrow hollows, low-rising ridgelines, and small stream valleys lush with vegetation.

Rock Creek Regional Park (301-762-1888), 15700 Needwood Lake Circle, Rockville. Located close to the center of Montgomery County, the park has two distinct sections:

The portion around Lake Needwood is quite developed, with an 18-hole golf course, archery range, picnic shelters, playground, a snack bar, and a boat shop that rents canoes, rowboats, and paddleboats in-season.

BROOKSIDE GARDENS IN WHEATON

There is even a pontoon boat that carries 25 people onto the lake for 20-minute cruises on weekends and holidays throughout the summer season.

In contrast, the section of the park near Lake Frank has been left in a more natural state. A well-designed network of trails goes beside a small pond, comes into contact with several streams and open areas, and swings around the lake. You may be privileged to watch some of the park's inhabitants—such as squirrels, rabbits, white-tailed deer, snakes, frogs, salamanders, raccoons, weasels, foxes, and beavers—go about their daily lives.

WALKS Woodend Nature Trail (301-652-9188; www.audubonnaturalist.org), 8940 Jones Mill Road, Chevy Chase. Woodend is the headquarters of the Audubon Naturalist Society of the Central Atlantic States. The 40-acre property was willed to the society in 1967, and a brochure keyed to stops along the trail describes the wonders of a nature preserve hidden within a major metropolitan area. The walk is easy and should take about 30 minutes. Free guided walks of the trail are given on the third Saturday of each month at 10, and bird-watching and other nature programs are provided on a scheduled basis. Be sure to visit the gift shop for a superb selection of natural-history books.

✳ Lodging

MOTELS AND HOTELS This area is nearly bereft of B&Bs but is awash with scores of hotels and motels. Any national chain you can think of will have one or more properties here.

Some of the standouts that I have stayed in or visited include:

Bethesda, 20814
Bethesda Court Hotel (301-656-2100), 7740 Wisconsin Avenue. This boutique hotel has imaginatively appointed rooms and serves a European-style afternoon tea. Exercise room. $125–175.

Gaithersburg, 20879
🐾 ⟁ **Holiday Inn** (301-948-8900; 1-800-HOLIDAY; www.holiday-inn.com), 2 Montgomery Village Avenue. The many amenities raise the rooms a notch above those typically found in a Holiday Inn. In-room iron and ironing boards, coffeemaker, free movie channel on the TV, data ports, and an unusually large amount of work space. Indoor pool and fitness center are also available. $89 and up.

⟁ **Springhill Suites by Marriott** (301-987-0900), 9715 Washingtonian Boulevard. All of the guest accommodations are spacious suites with a sofa bed in the outer room. Fitness center, heated pool, whirlpool, and complimentary continental breakfast. $89–150.

Rockville, 20850
🐾 ⟁ **Sleep Inn** (301-948-8000; 1-800-753-3746), 2 Research Court. One of the lowest-cost motels in the region, it has an outdoor swimming pool and free continental breakfast. $80–125.

Silver Spring, 20904
⟁ **Courtyard by Marriott** (301-680-8500), 12521 Prosperity Drive. Spacious rooms and nicely decorated public areas and landscaped courtyard. Pool, whirlpool, and exercise room. Some rooms have a coffeemaker, refrigerator, and microwave. $150 and up.

BED & BREAKFASTS Longwood Manor (301-774-1002; 1-866-774-1002; www.bbonline.com/md/longwood), 2900 DuBarry Lane, Brookeville, 20833. Once here, you realize that the modern housing development you drove through occupies land that once belonged to the manor house. Situated on 2 of the original 280 acres, the Mount Vernon–like house was the home of Thomas Moore, who had his friend Thomas Jefferson stay with him a number of times.

Hosts Bruce and Lynn Bartlett are proud of their home and love to share its history (ask about its Civil Defense days) and that of the surrounding area. The furnishings reflect its early-1800s origin, and guest accommodations include two suites and a room that can accommodate three people. I enjoyed sitting on the screened porch overlooking the grounds during my stay in the Brookmore Suite, and I look forward to returning in warmer weather to make use of the swimming pool surrounded by century-old trees. $95–155.

✒ ♿ **The Reynolds of Derwood B&B** (301-963-2216; www.reynolds-bed-breakfast.com), 16620 Bethayres Road, Derwood, 20855. Just 2 minutes from a METRO subway station, the modern home has two guest rooms, hot tubs, sauna, and putting green. Children are welcome; lots of toys and videos for them. $95.

♫🐾 **Park Crest House** (301-588-2845), 8101 Park Crest Drive, Silver Spring, 20910. The 1930s English Tudor brick home is one of closest B&Bs to Washington, D.C. (which makes its low rate even more of a deal). European antiques fill the one suite and one other guest room, and

terraced gardens descend to a neighborhood park. Pets permitted with prior approval. $80–90.

✒ **Davis Warner Inn** (301-408-3989; www.daviswarnerinn.com), 8114 Carroll Avenue, Takoma Park, 20912. Built in the mid-1800s, the 6,400-square-foot inn has four guest rooms. Three share a common bath, and one has its own Jacuzzi bath. The third floor has three bedrooms and is available for families with children under 16 (inquire about the rate). $75–125.

CAMPING Little Bennett Regional Park (301-972-9222; www.mncppc.org), 23701 Frederick Road, Clarksburg, 20871. The campground is located within one of the largest regional parks in the Washington, D.C., area (see *Green Space—Parks*) and provides access to miles of trails and 3,600 acres of woodlands. Close to 100 tent and RV sites with showers, dump station, and coin laundry.

Cabin John Regional Park, 7701 Tuckerman Lane, Rockville, 20850. Head to this park for rustic camping at its seven walk-in primitive sites. Water is not available from November through March. Permits must be obtained in advance by calling 301-495-2525.

Also see **Seneca Creek State Park** under *To Do—Bicycling* and *Hiking*.

✳ Where to Eat

DINING OUT ♿ **La Ferme** (301-986-5255), 7101 Brookeville Road, Chevy Chase. Closed for lunch on Saturday. The traditional French cuisine pairs with an ambience and decor inside an old farmhouse to transport you to the French countryside. Châteaubriand is a house specialty, but many diners

Old Angler's Inn (301-365-2425), 10801 MacArthur Boulevard, Potomac. Open for lunch and dinner daily. Reservations recommended for dinner, when semi-formal attire is expected. Old Angler's opened in 1860 to serve C&O Canal travelers and local estate owners. Its popularity with the movers and shakers of the federal government continues to this day, and it is very possible that the person at the next table will be a Washington, D.C., politico, an upper-echelon business executive, or a nationally known sports figure.

Olympia Reges has owned the inn for more than 50 years, and many of its recipes are hers. She does, however, let the kitchen staff be a bit adventurous at lunch, while the offerings at dinner are classic French. Sit on the patio in good weather, or use the spiral staircase to reach the second-floor dining area.

I practically melted into my chair when a bite of the crab porcupine with tarragon ($12.50) hit my taste buds. My dining mate smiled when she sampled her tuna carpaccio ($10). We both smiled as we dined on roasted guinea hen with rosemary sauce ($26) and the bourride of seafood medley ($28). Other items on the menu sounded equally enticing and ranged $20–32. The menu changes seasonally, so there will always be something new and exciting.

OLD ANGLER'S INN

claim the fricassee of lobster is the restaurant's pièce de résistance. Prices are very reasonable for a French restaurant. Entrées run $18–28.

EATING OUT

Gaithersburg

O'Donnell's (301-519-1650; www.odonnellsrestaurants.com), 311 Kentlands Boulevard. Open daily for lunch and dinner. Fresh fish is brought in daily. Most dishes are prepared as founder Tim O'Donnell prepared them when he founded his restaurants in 1922. Raw bar, crabcakes, steaks, pasta, and chicken. The broiled rockfish with corn, crab aioli, fried green tomatoes, and rice ($18.95) was tasty and nicely presented. And, oh those rum buns they serve with each meal! They alone make a visit here worth your time. Entrées $13.95–34.95.

Summit Station Restaurant and Brewery (301-519-9400; www.summit-station.com), 227 East Diamond Avenue. Open daily for lunch and dinner. Located in Historic Olde Town. The menu is contemporary American with offerings such as crabcakes (market price), marinated strip steak ($17.95), and pan-seared salmon ($14.95). A variety of their own ales are available throughout the year, with stouts and porters brewed seasonally.

North Bethesda

Dave and Buster's (301-230-5151; www.daveandbusters.com), 11301 Rockville Pike. Open daily for lunch and dinner. Much like the ESPN Zone restaurant in Baltimore, food is almost secondary to entertainment at Dave and Buster's. The business occupies 60,000 square feet on the

third floor of the White Flint Mall, and most of it is devoted to video games, billiard tables, and simulated horse and car racing and golf games. Lunch is busy, but evenings truly attract the crowds—families and singles alike.

The six-page menu is full of salads, sandwiches, seafood, steaks, chicken, and pasta. The Jack Daniels BBQ Cheeseburger ($7.25) is popular for lunch; expect dinner entrées to be around $15–20. I enjoyed the chicken tortilla soup ($4.50).

Poolesville

Meadowlark Inn (301-428-8900), 19611 Fisher Avenue. Open daily for lunch and dinner. The family-owned restaurant is known for its large portions and country cooking. You will find the usual chicken and beef items, along with crabcakes and other traditional Maryland dishes. It is hard to resist filling up on the warm homemade bread before your meal arrives. Entrées $10–20.

Rockville

Wurzburg-Haus Restaurant (301-330-0402), 7236 Muncaster Mill Road (inside Red Mill Shopping Center). Open daily for lunch and dinner. The background music and decor fit right in with the robust German cuisine. Dishes like the potato pancakes or the sauerbraten will keep your digestive juices busy for many hours after you have finished eating. The imported beers and wines have been selected to complement the food. Entrées $9–15.

Silver Spring

Crisfield Seafood Restaurant (301-589-1306), 8012 Georgia Avenue. Open for lunch and dinner; closed Monday. A local tradition for more than a half century, the decor is, of course, nautical and the atmosphere relaxed. Seafood dishes include crab-stuffed flounder and fried oysters. The creamy seafood bisque is the way to start your meal. Entrées $12–20.

Wheaton

✏ Anchor Inn Seafood Restaurant (301-933-1814), 2509 University Boulevard. Open daily for lunch and dinner. Family-friendly. Clam chowder and baked crab imperial are favorites here. However, do not overlook the meats: The filet mignon with béarnaise sauce is so tender, you almost don't need a knife to cut it. A complete meal (minus drink and dessert) will run you somewhere between $10 and $20.

✷ Entertainment

FILM The Cineplex Odeon (301-469-6601), 7101 Democracy Boulevard, Bethesda, presents first-run movies.

Montgomery Village Theatres (301-948-9200, 19236 Montgomery Village Avenue, and **Loews Cineplex** (301-948-0906), 9811 Washington Boulevard, are the places to see the blockbusters in Gaithersburg.

The Olney 9 Cinemas (301-774-0018), 18167 Town Center Drive, Olney, is located in a shopping center north of Rockville and Gaithersburg.

AMC City Place 10 (301-585-3738), 8661 Colesville Road, and **Apex Aspen Hill Cinemas** (301-460-3010), 13279 Connecticut Avenue, in Silver Spring, are usually among the first theaters in the area to show Hollywood's most highly advertised films.

MUSIC See **Sandy Spring Museum**

under *To See—Museums*, **Strathmore Hall** under *Selective Shopping—Art Galleries,* and **Imagination Stage** under *Theaters.*

NIGHTLIFE Rock Bottom Brewery (301-652-1311), 7900 Norfolk Avenue, Bethesda. Open daily. A full restaurant menu of pizzas, steaks, and meats are served alongside the microbrewer's own offerings of lagers, ales, and stouts. Pool tables attract people during the week, and crowds pour in for the live music on the weekends.

Hollywood Ballroom (301-622-5494; www.HollywoodBallroom.com), 2126–38.Industrial Parkway, Silver Spring. Singles and couples show up every Wednesday and Thursday through Sunday to practice and participate in new and old dance steps on the 7,200-square-foot floating maple dance floor.

THEATERS The Olney Theatre Center (301-924-4485; www.olney-theatre.org), 2001 Olney–Sandy Spring Road, Olney. One of the two state theaters of Maryland, the Olney is located on 14 acres and has presentations throughout the year. Besides staging 20th-century American classics, it also produces experimental and alternative plays. Recent productions have included *Grease!*, *Candida*, and *Bye Bye Birdie.*

✏ Imagination Stage (301-881-5106), 11301 Rockville Pike (at White Flint Mall), Rockville. The **Bethesda Academy of Performing Arts** produces plays, musicals, and other theatrical events for children throughout the year. Free or very low-cost admission.

✴ Selective Shopping

ANTIQUES

Brookeville
Lessig's Pleasant Valley (301-924-2293), 21000 Georgia Avenue. Usually open daily. Furniture, china, and collectibles.

Gaithersburg
Julia's Room (301-869-1410) 9001-A Warfield Road. Thursday through Sunday. Carol Bills specializes in English and Belgian furniture, silver, and china.

Kensington
You could easily spend a full day enjoying the architecture and investigating the treasures to be found in the five-block **Antique Row** in Old Town Kensington. Among the many places to browse are:

Prevention of Blindness Society Antique Shop (301-942-4707), 3716 Howard Avenue. All of the money generated from the shop helps the nonprofit society offer free visual screening and testing, eyeglasses, and other services to those who would go without. Shop here and do a good turn all at the same time.

⚘ **Aunt Betty's General Store** (301-946-9646; www.AuntBettysGeneral-Store.com), 3730 Howard Avenue. The interior still has its original pressed-tin ceiling and wood flooring. A great gift shop, especially for kids' items such as old-fashioned toys, Hardy Boys and Nancy Drew books, dolls, and a number of handmade items. The friendly staff will take the time to point out and explain items without any hint of pushing you toward making a purchase.

Pritchard's (301-942-1661), 3748 Howard Avenue. Stained glass, art deco items, and Mission arts and crafts.

Doll Shop (301-946-4242), 3758 Howard Avenue. Antique and collectible dolls and toys.

Kensington Antique Center (301-942-4440), 3760 Howard Avenue. More than 10 dealers in one building.

Antique Scientific Instruments (301-384-1394), 3760 Howard Avenue. Almost a museum, as it is filled with old-time weather, navigation, and timepieces.

Olney
The Briars Antiques (301-774-3596), 4121 Briars Road. Thursday through Sunday. Two floors of furniture, china, silver, and crystal. An admirable selection of Victorian jewelry.

ART GALLERIES
Kensington Gallery (301-946-6577), 3766 Howard Avenue, Kensington. Changing exhibits and displays from local artists.

Strathmore Hall (301-530-0540; www.strathmore.org), 10701 Rockville Pike (MD 355), North Bethesda. A dozen major exhibits focusing on artists of the area are presented throughout the year in the early-1900s mansion. Classes on various art disciplines are also provided, along with a series of classical, jazz, and popular music programs.

Gudelsky Gallery (301-649-4454; www.mcadmd.org), 10500 Georgia Avenue, Silver Spring. Located at the Maryland College of Art and Design. One goes to the Gudelsky to see tomorrow's art luminaries today. Although there are exhibits by professional artists, some of the most interesting are those from the college's students and faculty.

Also see **McCrillis Gardens and Gallery** under *Green Space—Gardens*.

BOOKSTORES The chain stores, such as **Barnes & Noble, B. Dalton Bookseller, Tower Books, Waldenbooks,** and **Borders** are well represented in Kensington, Bethesda, Gaithersburg, and Rockville.

Bethesda

⚘ **Bookoo Books for Kids** (301-652-2794), 4945 Elm Street. Jam-packed with children's books. Also stocks games, science-project kits, and toys not often found elsewhere.

Olssons Book and Records (301-652-6399), 7647 Old Georgetown Road. This local chain is known for its extensive selection and active community events such as author signings and talks.

Mystery Bookshop (301-657-2665), 7700 Old Georgetown Road. Located inside an office building. Books of intrigue, mystery, and who-dun-it are stacked all the way to the ceiling. Some are used, most are new; and if you don't feel like reading, there is an extensive selection of audio- and videotapes.

Also see **Woodend Nature Trail** under *Green Space—Walks*.

USED BOOKS Second Story Books (301-656-0170; www.secondstorybooks.com), 4836 Bethesda Avenue, Bethesda. With more than 86,000 titles in stock, you are sure to find something to your liking.

All Books Considered (301-929-0036), 10408 Montgomery Avenue, Kensington. Located at one end of Antique Row, it has an extensive collection of used and rare books.

Bonifant Books, Records & CDs

(301-946-1526), 11240 Georgia Avenue, Wheaton. Trade in the books you have read for used records and CDs.

SPECIAL SHOPS G Street Fabrics (301-231-8998), 11854 Rockville Pike, Rockville. Open daily. The store is known and visited by people from around the country who prize its wide selection of materials and sewing items.

FARMER'S MARKETS Gaithersburg Farmer's Market (301-590-2823). Be at the corner of East Cedar and South Frederick Avenues Thursday 2–6, June through November, to make your choice from the offerings.

Silver Spring Farmer's Market (301-590-2823). The Fenton Street Village Parking Lot 3 is the site of crates and boxes full of the bounty of the land for sale Saturday 7–1, June through October.

Rockville Farmer's Market (301-309-3335). You will find the market open at the Rockville Town Center, Wednesday 11–2 and Saturday 9–1, June through October.

PICK-YOUR-OWN PRODUCE FARMS

Germantown

⚘ **Butler's Orchards** (301-972-3299), 22200 Davis Mill Road. A variety of berries is available for picking from late spring through early fall. Call to find out what is in-season when you get ready to go. Butler's also has a pumpkin festival each weekend in October with hayrides, a petting zoo, and entertainment.

⚘ **Phillips Farm** (301-540-2364), 13710 Schaeffer Road. Jean Phillips invites people to the farm from mid-summer into autumn to pick hot pep-

pers, nonhybrid varieties of tomatoes, and flowers. Free hayrides to the pumpkin patch during October.

Poolesville
☙ **Homestead Farm** (301-977-3761), 15600 Sugarland Road. Fruits and vegetables available throughout the entire growing and harvesting season. Hayrides every weekend in October, and you can return in December to cut your own Christmas tree.

Silver Spring
☙ **Beacraft's Farm** (301-236-4545), 14722 New Hampshire Avenue (MD 650). Pick strawberries in May and return to choose a pumpkin in October. Weekends in October are quite festive with a corn maze, a pumpkin patch, and games for the kids.

✳ Special Events

February: **Annual East Coast Jazz Festival** (301-933-1822), DoubleTree Hotel, Rockville. Concerts, exhibitors, workshops, and competitions.

March: **Gem and Mineral Show** (301-926-7190), fairgrounds, Gaithersburg. An annual exhibit of minerals, gemstones, and fossils. Demonstrations, workshops, and sales from screened and certified reputable dealers.

April: **Annual Sugarloaf Crafts Festival** (1-800-210-9900), fairgrounds, Gaithersburg. A major festival that attracts more than 500 artisans and craftspersons from around the country. **Steam and Gas Show and Civil War Medical Seminar** (301-670-4661), Agricultural History Farm Park, Derwood. A celebration of tractors, trucks, cars, and riding lawn mowers. A kid's tractor pull and—somehow mixed in with all of this—a demonstration of medical

practices from the Civil War. **Literary Festival** (301-215-6660), various sites in downtown Bethesda. Annual event that features nearly 50 literary and cultural artists.

May: **Audubon Nature Fair** (301-652-9188), Woodend (see *Green Space—Walks*), 8940 Jones Mill Road, Chevy Chase. Annual event of juried arts and crafts, live animals, educational games, and entertainment.

June: **Annual Strawberry Festival** (301-774-0022), Sandy Spring Museum, Sandy Spring. Strawberries galore, plus crafts, music, and kid's games.

July: **Silver Screen Under the Stars** (301-565-7300), Georgia Avenue and Ellsworth Drive, Silver Spring. A 3-day event of food vendors and movies presented on a large outdoor screen.

August: **Montgomery County Fair** (301-926-3100), Agricultural Center, Gaithersburg. The largest county fair in Maryland.

September: **Shaker Forest Festival** (724-643-6627), Seneca Creek State Park (see *To Do—Bicycling* and *To Do—Hiking*), Gaithersburg. Hand-crafted folk, contemporary, and Shaker styles of furnishings. **Germantown Octoberfest** (240-777-6821), Town Center, Germantown. **Takoma Park Folk Festival** (301-589-3717), Takoma Park Middle School, Silver Spring. Six stages of music and dance, crafts, and children's activities.

October: **Antique and Classic Car Show** (301-309-3340), Civic Center Park, Rockville. Car show and automobile-related flea market. **F. Scott Fitzgerald Literary Conference** (301-309-9461), Montgomery College, Rockville. Workshops, discussions, and tours.

November: **Railroad-Transportation Artifacts Show and Sale** (703-536-2954), fairgrounds, Gaithersburg. More than 600 tables of railroad, steamship, bus, and airline memorabilia for sale.

December: **Winter Lights Festival** (301-258-6310), Seneca Creek State Park (see *To Do—Bicycling* and *To Do—Hiking*), Gaithersburg. A 3.5-mile drive through the holiday light show.

Southern Maryland

ALONG THE CHESAPEAKE SHORE—
CHESAPEAKE BEACH, NORTH
BEACH, PRINCE FREDERICK, AND
SOLOMONS

AT THE MOUTH OF THE
POTOMAC—ST. MARY'S CITY
AND LEONARDTOWN

ALONG THE POTOMAC SHORE—
LA PLATA, PORT TOBACCO, AND
WALDORF

SOUTHERN MARYLAND

A bit off the beaten path, and overshadowed by the Washington, D.C.–Baltimore metro area, southern Maryland is often ignored as a travel destination by Marylanders and visitors alike. Yet this is where the state had its beginnings when 140 European settlers arrived to found the Maryland colony in 1634. One of the best-preserved 17th-century town sites in the United States, Historic St. Mary's City is an 800-acre living-history museum on the site of the state's first capital.

History is around every curve in the road. St. Ignatius Church is one of the oldest active Catholic parishes in the country, having served worshipers for more than three centuries. The home of Dr. Samuel Mudd, the physician who treated the broken leg of President Lincoln's assassin, is here, in Waldorf. Several light-houses from bygone eras are preserved near the shorelines, while it is even possible to scuba dive to the only known World War II rubber-clad German U-boat found within America.

Southern Maryland's lifestyle and low-lying landscape are influenced by the waters of the Chesapeake Bay and those of the Patuxent and Potomac Rivers. Although some of the trappings of the 21st century—such as strip malls and planned communities—are making inroads into the area, many of the old ways remain. In search of flounder, crab, clams, and oysters, many watermen rise before dawn to venture onto the rivers and the bay. Oyster houses and seafood processing plants along the waterfronts provide employment for those who stay on land.

Numerous tiny towns dot the many miles of shorelines, which, in addition to providing scenic places to rest, can arrange charter excursions for those wanting to cast a line for rockfish or bass. The gently rolling terrain has attracted road bikers for decades, and the local tourist offices have responded by producing a brochure describing various circuit excursions. Finally, no journey into southern Maryland would be complete without a hike to the bay's western shore at Calvert Cliffs State Park to hunt for fossilized shark's teeth.

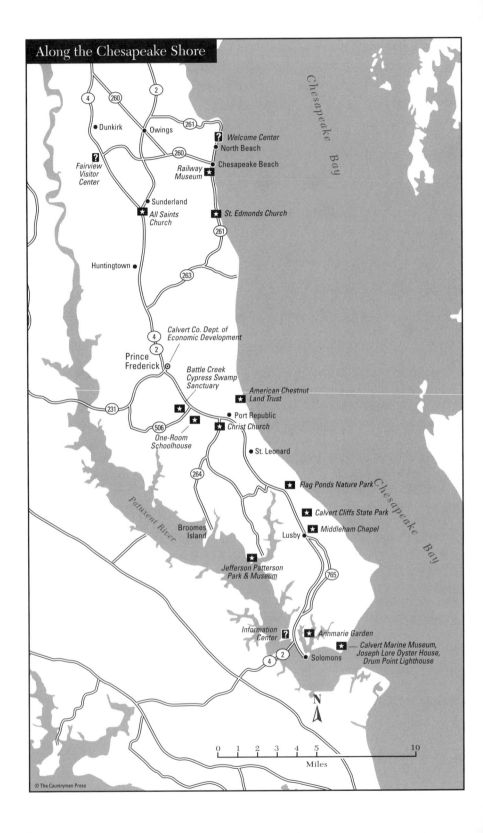

Along the Chesapeake Shore

Chesapeake Bay

260
4
2
261
● Dunkirk   ● Owings
260
? Welcome Center
● North Beach
? Fairview
Visitor
Center
Railway ★ ● Chesapeake Beach
Museum
● Sunderland
★ All Saints ★ St. Edmonds Church
Church
261
Huntingtown ●
263
4
2 Calvert Co. Dept. of
Economic Development
Prince
Frederick ◉
Battle Creek
Cypress Swamp
Sanctuary
American Chestnut
★ Land Trust
231
★ ● Port Republic
506 ★ ★ Christ Church
One-Room
Schoolhouse
● St. Leonard
264
★ Flag Ponds Nature Park

Chesapeake Bay

★ Calvert Cliffs State Park
Broomes
Island
Lusby ● ★ Middleham Chapel
Patuxent River
★ 765
Jefferson Patterson
Park & Museum

Information ?
Center ★ Annmarie Garden
4 2 ★ Calvert Marine Museum,
● Solomons   Joseph Lore Oyster House,
Drum Point Lighthouse

N

0 1 2 3 4 5   10
Miles

© The Countryman Press

ALONG THE CHESAPEAKE SHORE—CHESAPEAKE BEACH, NORTH BEACH, PRINCE FREDERICK, AND SOLOMONS

C hesapeake Beach began in 1900 as the dream of Colorado railroad baron Otto Mears. By laying railroad tracks from Washington, D.C., he hoped to entice people to visit his newly constructed resort town on the western shore of the Chesapeake Bay. For a while his dream was a reality, with scores of people flocking to the amusement park, casino, and hotel along the mile-long boardwalk. Fires, the Great Depression, and easy access to Ocean City on the Eastern Shore brought the dream to an end by the mid-1930s.

Gradually, though, the town has reemerged as a destination spot with a sandy beach, a water park, and several good restaurants.

Due to its proximity to Chesapeake Beach (in fact, it is hard to tell where one town ends and the other begins), the history of North Beach is a parallel of its neighbor: A rise in tourism in the early 1900s, a decline in the mid-1900s, and revitalization in the late 1900s. A brochure available from the North Beach Welcome Center (see *Guidance*) leads visitors along on a self-guided walking tour of the significant features of the waterfront town. Many people may not take the full tour, but it would be a mistake to overlook the town's boardwalk (now bordered by homes and B&Bs) and its free beach.

Prince Frederick has been the Calvert County seat since 1725, but little remains of its early days. The British burned it in 1814, and another fire in 1884 completed the job of destroying many other buildings. It remains the hub of county services, and has developed into the economic and shopping center of the region.

Solomons has emerged as the area's primary 21st-century destination spot. It was the scenery that first drew me, and many other people, to the small village, located as it is at the wide mouth of the Patuxent River where it meets the Chesapeake Bay. Once here, though, I found many reasons to linger: The excellent exhibits in the Calvert Marine Museum, the Riverwalk boardwalk (from which sunsets are nothing short of spectacular), charter fishing and other boat excursions, and an abundance of B&Bs and restaurants. Nearby, Annmarie Garden and Calvert Cliffs State Park satisfy the need to explore the natural world.

GUIDANCE The **Calvert County, Maryland, Department of Economic Development** (410-535-4583; 1-800-331-9771; www.co.cal.md.us./cced), Courthouse, Prince Frederick, 20678, is full of useful information, and its employees are well versed in what to see and do.

The **Solomons Information Center** (410-326-6027), MD 2/4, Solomons, 20688, sits underneath the Governor Thomas Johnson Memorial Bridge and is staffed by information specialists proud of the area in which they live.

Along the North Beach boardwalk is a small structure housing the **North Beach Welcome Center** (301-812-1046), 9032 Bay Avenue, North Beach, 20714.

At the very northern end of this area is the **Fairview Information Center** (410-257-5381), 8120 Southern Maryland Boulevard (MD 2), Owings, 20736.

GETTING THERE *By air:* The closest two airports with commercially scheduled flights are **Baltimore/Washington International** (1-800-I-FLY-BWI) near Annapolis and **Ronald Reagan Washington National Airport** (703-417-8000; www.mwaa.com/national), in northern Virginia.

By car: **MD 4** arrives in the region from the Washington, D.C., area, while **MD 2** comes in from the north—allowing access from **US 50/301** near Annapolis and the Eastern Shore. (MD 4 and MD 2 combine into one four-lane roadway north of Huntingtown.) The **Governor Thomas Johnson Memorial Bridge** crosses the Patuxent River at Solomons, bringing travelers into the region from St. Mary's County on **MD 2/4.**

By bus: **Calvert County Public Transportation** (410-535-1600; 301-855-1243) operates several commuter buses that could bring you from Washington, D.C., to connect with buses continuing on to local sites and towns.

By rail: **AMTRAK** (1-800-USA-RAIL) will deliver you to Washington, D.C. From there, you could take one of the commuter buses (see *By bus*, above) into the area.

By water: If you own a boat, or are chartering one, the Chesapeake Bay is the obvious way to arrive. There are many marinas along the shoreline to take care of your needs.

SOLOMONS HARBOR

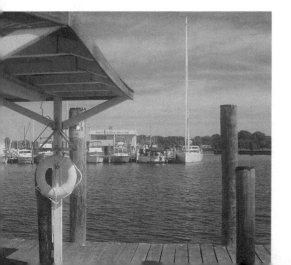

GETTING AROUND *By car:* Four-lane **MD 2/4** runs in a north–south direction through the center of this area. Traffic is only moderately heavy, even during rush hours. The smaller two-lane roadways that reach into the more isolated areas are lightly traveled and are great ways to see the local countryside without feeling harried. **MD 261** through Chesapeake Beach, and **MD 263** to Plum Point, are particularly scenic.

By bus: **Calvert County Public Transportation** (410-535-1600; 301-855-1243) has interconnecting bus routes that reach into nearly every corner of the region. You may have to take a couple of different buses, but you can get to wherever you wish from wherever you are. General fare is $1.50 or less.

By taxi: **Yellow Cab** (410-257-2202), Prince Frederick; **B&B Cab** (410-326-8200), Solomons; and **Calvert Taxi** in North Beach (410-257-2510) and Prince Frederick (410-535-6272).

PUBLIC REST ROOMS In **North Beach,** rest rooms (and shower facilities!) are located in the rear of the Welcome Center (see *Guidance*) on the boardwalk.

In **Solomons,** public rest rooms may be found along the boardwalk overlooking the Patuxent River and inside the Solomons Information Center (see *Guidance*).

MEDICAL EMERGENCY Calvert Memorial Hospital (410-535-4000), 100 Hospital Road (about a mile north of town), Prince Frederick.

Dunkirk Medical Center (410-286-7911), 10845 Town Center Boulevard, Dunkirk, and **Solomons Medical Center** (410-394-2800), 14090 Solomons Island Road, Solomons, have urgent-care facilities that can handle minor emergencies.

✳ To See

MUSEUMS ♿ **Railway Museum** (410-257-3892), 4155 Mears Avenue (off MD 261), Chesapeake Beach. Open 1–4 daily, May through September; October through April, weekends only, 1–4. Free parking and admission. Exhibits in the 1898 rail station focus on Chesapeake Beach's boardwalk, amusement park, and railroad history.

One Room Schoolhouse (410-856-0482), Broomes Island Road, Port Republic. Sunday 2–4, June through August. Free. The little building served the community for more than 100 years, and is now restored and filled with memorabilia.

THE RAILWAY MUSEUM IN CHESAPEAKE BEACH

✏ ♿ **Calvert Marine Museum** (410-326-2042; www.calvertmarinemuseum.com), 14200 Solomons Island Road, Solomons. Open daily 10–5. Small admission fee. It may be smaller in size, but the quality of exhibits and the experience you will have here will easily rival those found in the maritime museum in St. Michaels on the Eastern Shore. Life-sized boats, models, paintings, and wood carvings illustrate the life of the watermen, while fossilized remains and skeletal models of huge sea creatures vividly paint the natural history of the bay and its tributaries. More than 15 **aquariums** contain live specimens of the bay's colorful inhabitants. A **children's Discovery Room** has enough activities to keep even the most rambunctious kid interested and occupied. Outside exhibits include a re-created salt marsh, live river otters splashing about in a native habitat site, and a boat basin with vintage vessels.

Don't leave the museum without climbing through the hatch of the **Drum Point Lighthouse,** one of only three surviving Chesapeake Bay screw-pile, cottage-style lighthouses. Restored to its original appearance and furnished as it would have been in the early 1900s, it is a glimpse into the past.

One-hour cruises around Solomons Harbor and the Patuxent River aboard the *Wm. B. Tennison,* the only Coast Guard–licensed passenger-carrying log-hulled vessel on the bay, originate from the museum's dock (see *To Do—Boat Excursions.*)

The museum also sponsors shuttle-bus trips ($3; daily from June through August, weekends in May and September) to the **Cove Point Lighthouse,** the oldest continuously operating lighthouse in the state. Built in 1828, it marks one of the narrowest parts of the Chesapeake Bay and helps guide ships into the Patuxent River.

THE DRUM POINT LIGHTHOUSE AT CALVERT MARINE MUSEUM

Joseph C. Lore & Sons Oyster House (410-326-2878), 24430 Solomons Island Road, Solomons. Open daily 10–5, June through August; 10–5 Saturday and Sunday only in May and September. Free. The restored 1934 packing house chronicles the boom and decline of the area's seafood business. Tools, equipment, and boats illustrate the lifestyle of the watermen.

HISTORIC CHURCHES St. Edmonds United Methodist Church (410-535-2506), 3000 Dalrymple Road, Chesapeake Beach. The original church on this site was built of logs and served as a house of worship and a school for the African American community. It burned in 1893.

Patuxent United Methodist Church (410-535-9819), 3500 Solomons Island Road, Huntingtown. Built by its African American congregation, the original church on this site burned in 1893 and was replaced with the present structure.

Middleham Episcopal Chapel (410-326-4948), 10210 H. G. Trueman Road, Lusby. Built in 1784, this is the oldest religious structure in Calvert County. It is also the oldest cross-shaped church in the state. The bell is the oldest one in Maryland.

Christ Church (410-586-0565), 3100 Broomes Island Road, Port Republic. The present structure dates from 1772; be sure to take a walk through its garden of biblical plants.

All Saints Episcopal Church (410-257-6306), at the intersection of MD 4 and MD 2, Sunderland. The Flemish-bond brick church is based upon Georgian ecclesiastical architecture. The baptismal font was imported from England in the early 1700s.

OTHER SITES ✔ Jefferson Patterson Park and Museum (410-586-8500; www.jefpat.org), 10515 Mackall Road, St. Leonard. Wednesday through Sunday, April 15 through October 15, 10–5. Free admission. The museum part of the 544-acre park has a permanent exhibition, *12,000 Years in the Chesapeake,* a children's discovery room, and historical farm equipment. Several short trails (brochure available in the museum) go through fields and forest and down to the bank of the Patuxent River.

Chesapeake Biological Laboratory Visitor Center (410-26-7443; www.cbl. umces.edu), Charles Street, Solomons. Tuesday through Sunday 10–4, April through late December. Free. The small visitors center tells the story of the oldest state-supported marine laboratory on the East Coast. Its mission is to increase knowledge about the ecology and natural history of the bay. Free tours of the entire facility are available on Wednesday and Friday at 2, but you must make arrangements in advance.

GUIDED TOURS Solomons Walkabout (410-394-0775; www.solomonswalkabout.com), Solomons. Reservations required. Tours are given May 31 through October 31, Tuesday through Saturday 10:30–4 and Sunday after 2. Adult $7; seniors $5; student $3; children under 6 are free. Learn the historical and architectural aspects of Solomons Island during the 2-hour walking tour.

✳ To Do

BICYCLING The flat to gently rolling terrain of this region makes it an ideal place to explore by wheel and pedal powder. Most of the side roads are lightly traveled, while the main highway, MD 2/42, has moderately heavy traffic but is blessed with paved shoulders.

The Calvert County, Maryland, Department of Economic Development (see *Guidance*) can supply information on several popular and scenic circuit rides.

One of the rides is 37 miles long and passes by the beaches at **Chesapeake Beach, North Beach,** and **Breezy Point,** in addition to traversing lightly traveled roads close to the **Patuxent River.** Another, about 15 miles in length, offers the opportunity to get off the bike and do some walking in **Battle Creek Cypress Swamp Sanctuary, Flag Ponds Nature Park, Jefferson Patterson Park and Museum,** and **Calvert Cliffs State Park.** A third circuit ride is less than 3 miles long and takes in most of the small streets and attractions in **Solomons.**

4 X-Treem Sports (410-257-7858), 3865 Old Town Road (at Huntingtown Plaza), Huntingtown. These folks will repair your bike if you happen to run into trouble while touring. They, of course, will be happy to sell you a new one, too.

BOAT EXCURSIONS 🐾 ⌀ **Wm. B. Tennison** (410-326-2042), docked at the Calvert Marine Museum (see the sidebar on page 324), Solomons. Cruises on Wednesday at 2, May through October; there is an additional 12:30 PM cruise in July and August. Small admission fee. The lightly narrated 1-hour trips aboard this 1899, nine-log, chunk-built bugeye (the oldest licensed passenger-carrying vessel of its kind on the bay) take you along Back Creek and onto the wide mouth of the Patuxent River. It's a nice excursion that gives you a different perspective on the land you sail by. The pure white stucco of Our Lady of the Sea Catholic Church stands out impressively against the scenic background.

BOAT RENTALS Bill's Boat Rentals (410-586-3599), 9250 Broomes Island Road, Broomes Island. Bill's has just about any kind of boat you could want to rent—pontoon boats, sailboats, skiffs, and canoes.

Solomons Boat Rental (410-326-4060), Alexander Street and MD 2, Solomons. If sailboats, canoes, and pontoon boats are too slow for you, these folks rent 15- and 20-foot powerboats in hour, 4-hour, and 8-hour increments.

BOWLING Lord Calvert Bowl (410-535-3560), 2275 Solomons Island Road, Huntingtown, has 22 lanes.

FAMILY ACTIVITIES

Chesapeake Beach

⌀ **Chesapeake Beach Water Park** (410-257-1404; 301-855-3803), 4079 Gordon Stinnett Avenue. Open Memorial Day through the first day of school. Admission is by height: Guests 42 inches or taller are $14, those shorter (and seniors) are $12. County and town residents are admitted at a reduced rate. It may be small by the standards of water parks in major resort areas, but it still has enough features for a full day's worth of fun. Activity pool, kids' pool, seashell and other slides, and free use of tubes.

FISHING The middle part of the Chesapeake Bay is generally considered to have the best variety of fish species. Charter boats usually take sport anglers onto the water in April in search of rockfish, and in late May and early June for black drum and Atlantic croaker. Bottom fishing for spot, trout, and white perch takes place in July. Bluefish and Spanish mackerel make their appearance in August and are joined by schools of gray trout in September. The season is rounded out by the return of the rockfish in October.

This area of Maryland lays claim to having the largest charter-fishing fleet on the Chesapeake Bay. It is certainly true that there are so many charter boats and charter-boat associations that it is impossible to list them here. **The Calvert County, Maryland, Department of Economic Development** (see *Guidance*) can supply you with information on the associations and individual charter companies.

If you decide to go fishing on the spur of the moment, **Captain Mike Shaw** takes the *Elizabeth S.* (301-997-0852) out of Solomons twice a day. One trip starts at 7 AM, the other at 6 PM. He operates it as a headboat, meaning no reservations are required—just show up. Adults $30, children 12 and under $20.

Other headboats operate out of **Rod 'N Reel** (301-855-8450) in Chesapeake Beach and **Bunky's Charter Boats** (410-326-3241) in Solomons.

GOLF ♿ **Chesapeake Hills** (410-326-4653), H. G. Trueman Road, Lusby.

The par-72 course has tree-lined fairways, doglegs, and a varying terrain. The back nine have a number of water hazards.

♿ **Mellomar Golf Park** (410-286-8212), 6215 Scaggs Road, Owings. The nine-hole course has water hazards, sand traps, and bent-grass greens.

♿ **Twin Shields Golf Club** (410-257-7800; 301-855-8228), 2425 Roarty Road, Dunkirk. Roy and Ray Shields designed the par-70 course with rolling terrain and water hazards on seven of the holes.

HIKING **Flag Ponds Nature Park** (410-586-1477), Flag Ponds Parkway (MD 4), Lusby, is just a 10-minute drive north of Calvert Cliffs State Park (see sidebar on page xx) and worth visiting while you're in this area. A network of trails courses through a similar environment and can deliver you to another beach for more fossil hunting (see sidebar).

Also see the **American Chestnut Land Trust** sidebar on page 329.

KAYAKING AND CANOEING **Island Creek Outfitters** (410-286-0950), 40 Honeysuckle Lane, Owings. They will rent you a kayak by the hour or the day, and will arrange for an instructive class if you are a novice.

✳ Green Space

BEACHES

Chesapeake Beach
Bay Front Park (410-257-2330). There is no admission or parking fee for this small, sandy beach open daily during daylight hours.

♿ **Breezy Point Beach and Campground** (410-535-0259), Breezy Point Road (off MD 261 about 5 miles

⚓ **Calvert Cliffs State Park** (301-872-5688), MD 765 (off MD 4/2), Lusby. Open daily sunrise to sunset. Donation requested. Impressively rising to heights of more than 100 feet above the water, Calvert Cliffs was formed millions of years ago when southern Maryland was under a shallow sea. More than 600 species of sea creatures, such as whales, sea cows, porpoises, rays, sharks, seabirds (the size of small airplanes!) crocodiles, mollusks, and reptiles lived in the warm waters.

Since as far back as the 1600s, people have been coming to the base of the cliffs to see what new fossils they would yield. Whale ear bones and skulls, sea cow ribs, crocodile snouts (and fossilized dung), and even peccary scapulas and fossilized pinecones have been uncovered. But it is the thousands of fossilized shark's teeth, some from the extinct great white shark, that have made the cliffs famous and drawn generations of schoolchildren and other visitors to the area.

Today most of the cliffs' 30 miles are privately owned, so you and I are lucky that the state has set aside a short stretch of the shoreline. Here, we can walk to the water's edge, study the bay's ecology, search for small paleontological treasures hidden in the sand, or just sit peacefully on the beach. (For visitors' safety, walking on or below the crumbling cliffs is prohibited; and to keep the cliffs from deteriorating any faster, visitors are not permitted to dig for fossils on them.) A network of marked trails takes visitors into uplands forest, through freshwater and tidal marshlands, and beside slowly flowing creeks. It is about 2 miles (one way) to the beach.

CALVERT CLIFFS

south of town). Memorial Day through Labor Day. Adults $4; seniors and children under 12 are $2; children under 2 are free. This sandy beach on the Chesapeake Bay is about 2,600 feet long; nets protect the swimming area from jellyfish. Popular with the locals for swimming, picnicking, and crabbing from a 300-foot pier.

The campground (additional fee) has waterfront and water-view tent and RV sites with hookups. May 1 through October 1.

North Beach
✤ **North Beach Public Beach** (410-257-9618; 301-855-6681). Free. The beach and its bordering boardwalk measure just a bit more than a half mile in length. A fishing and crabbing pier is open 24 hours; the beach is

open 6 AM–10 PM. Public rest rooms and shower facilities are located in the rear of the welcome center (see *Guidance*). Since there are no large, rolling ocean waves, the beach is the perfect place to let the kids build a sand castle without fear of it (or them) getting washed away. This gets my vote as the best beach in Maryland after Ocean City.

Also see *To Do—Hiking* and the **Calvert Cliffs State Park** sidebar opposite.

GARDENS **Annmarie Garden** (410-326-4640), Dowell Road, Solomons. Open daily 10–4. Free. The combination sculpture and botanical garden lends itself to quiet contemplations of artwork and appreciation of the beauty found in nature. The 30 acres are

NATURE PRESERVE
American Chestnut Land Trust (410-586-1570), Scientists Cliffs Road, Port Republic. Open daily from dawn to dusk. Free. Concerned about the detrimental effects Calvert County was experiencing as a result of having the fastest population growth of any county in the Washington, D.C., area, a group of farsighted citizens banded together to form the nonprofit American Chestnut Land Trust. So far, the trust has been able to preserve almost 1,000 acres and has accepted the management of 350 acres owned by the state. Along with adjacent land held by The Nature Conservancy, 2,700 acres of fields, forests, marshes, swamps, and streams are no longer threatened by the modern world.

A network of pathways on these lands is open to the general public. Because they are not well known and are located off main roadways, the trails are blissfully underutilized. About the only other people you may see are trust members on a hike or a local neighbor out for a morning walk. Among the natural features are one of the state's largest living American chestnut trees and Maryland's only known community of sweet pinesap. Parkers Creek, a brackish tidal stream, flows through the last pristine salt marsh on the bay's western shore.

divided into display areas with individual works connected by an easy, level path through the woods. I thoroughly enjoy this place and urge you to visit; even the entrance gate and the rest rooms are works of art.

WALKS ✎ ♿ **Battle Creek Cypress Swamp Sanctuary** (410-535-5327), Grays Road, Prince Frederick. Closed Monday. Free. This is a favorite place of mine when I don't have a lot of time to spare but still have a strong urge to return to the natural world. A quarter-mile boardwalk snakes through the 100-acre sanctuary, allowing me to enjoy the abundant wildlife and stately bald cypress trees—which are at their northernmost natural limit here. Exhibits in the nature center explore the area's mysteries (what purpose do cypress knees serve?), and its natural and cultural history.

✳ Lodging

MOTELS AND HOTELS ♿ **Holiday Inn Select** (410-326-6311; 1-800-

ANNMARIE GARDEN

356-2009), 155 Holiday Drive, Solomons, 20688. More than 300 rooms on a 9-acre waterfront property. Health club, outdoor pool, and tennis and volleyball courts. Modern, clean, well kept, and a friendly staff. $119–199.

BED & BREAKFASTS
North Beach, 2014
Bay Views B&B (410-257-1000; 1-877-245-2223; www.Bayviewsbb.com), 9131 Atlantic Avenue. With its location directly on the boardwalk and sandy beach, you may think you are in an Ocean City B&B; but here things are quieter, crowds are fewer, and there is only one guest room and one suite—each with private bath and deck. $120–160.

Prince Frederick, 20679
❦ **The Cliff House** (410-535-4839), 156 Windcliff Road. The "Cliff" is right! The modern home is spectacularly perched on the edge of the same cliff face made famous by Calvert Cliffs State Park (see sidebar on page 328). The sunrises over the Chesapeake Bay are spectacular, and lounge chairs at water's edge let you enjoy the breezes. Owner Christine Ferrandino was raised in a German "pension" and she has a degree in hotel management, so she knows a bit about hospitality. Only one guest room and one suite ensure a quiet stay. $95–120.

Solomons, 20688
By-the-Bay (410-326-3428), 14374 Calvert Street. The waterfront Victorian structure was built around 1900 as a waterman's home, and hosts Joan and Tom Hogenson have restored and furnished it to reflect its early days. All guest rooms and the suite (private

entrance) have a private bath. The screened-in porch, yard hammock, and screened "water house" let you lazily watch the life of the harbor go by. $90–125.

&. **Back Creek Inn B&B** (410-326-2022; www.bbonline.com/md/backcreek), Alexander Lane and Calvert Street. Former navy wives Lin Cochran and Carol Pennock offer landscaped gardens and a goldfish pond, a hot tub, and water-view rooms in their 1880s waterfront home. All rooms have a private bath. The suites and cottage (with its own whirlpool) are additions that provide a bit more privacy with their own entrances. I was drawn to the Tansy Room, where you can watch the sun rise over the water in the fall. Free bike use for guests. $95–175.

Solomons Victorian Inn B&B (410-326-4811; www.solomonsvictorian-inn.com), 125 Charles Street. The 1906 Queen Anne Victorian home overlooks Solomons harbor. All guest rooms and suites have a private bath; my favorite was the third-floor Solomons Sunset Suite. Its nooks and lush woodwork made me feel like I was in the cabin of a sailboat. The Carriage House suites have great harbor views. Breakfast is a grand affair with dishes such as shrimp soufflé or a Brie tarragon croissant. $110–195.

Kathi's Cottage B&B (410-394-1939; www.kathiscottage.com), 250 C Street. You will feel like a member of Kathi's family, as there are only two simply furnished guest rooms; the long backyard leads to the water. Kathi always has fresh coffee and treats sitting out for you, but save room for the delightful breakfasts. She has been known to serve blueberry walnut pancakes, raspberry tortes,

frittatas, and a rich sour cream coffee cake. $95.

COTTAGES **The Cottages of Governors Run** (410-586-2346; 1-877-586-1793; www.BayCottages.com), 2847 Governors Run Road, Port Republic, 20676. Mid-March through October. The two cottages are on a low cliff overlooking the Chesapeake Bay, so great sunrises are assured. A small beach is only a minute's walk away. Sue and Steve Kullen have refurbished the 1940s vacation homes and stocked them with everything you need, including linens. One cottage sleeps four to six; the other is designed for two to four. Weekly rates are $750–950; weekend and 5-day rates are available.

CAMPING **Patuxent Camp Sites** (410-586-9880), 4770 Williams Wharf Road, St. Leonard, 20685. Open year-round, but limited sites and facilities in winter. Waterfront sites with hookups, dump stations, and hot showers in the bath facilities. The 100-foot pier is great for fishing or crabbing.

Also see **Breezy Point Beach and Campground** under *Green Space—Beaches*.

☀ Where to Eat
DINING OUT

Prince Frederick
🍴 &. **Old Field Inn** (410-535-1054), 485 Main Street. Open for dinner daily. The winding driveway that goes by manicured lawns delivers you to the 1890s Victorian home and its graciously furnished dining rooms. Seafood is featured prominently on the menu ($14.95–23.95), and the honey-nut shrimp is a standout.

THE NORTH BEACH BOARDWALK

Hand-cut steaks ($14.95–18.95) and juicy prime rib ($17.95) are local favorites. A nice place to spend a quiet, romantic evening.

Solomons

& DiGiovanni's Dock of the Bay
(410-394-6400; www.digiovannis-restaurant), 14556 Solomons Island Road. Open daily at 5 for dinner. Venetian Anna Maria DeGennaro brings the food of her homeland to this small restaurant overlooking the mouth of Back Creek. *Cacciucco all Livornese,* a mélange of six seafoods and shallots blended in a tomato sauce ($17.95), is the house specialty. The tasty black linguine with scallops in a pesto sauce ($20.95) was different from any pasta dish I've had. Other items based on Anna's recipes, as well as traditional Italian entrées, range from $13.95–24.95.

& Dry Dock Restaurant (410-326-4817), C Street in Zahniser's Marina. Open for dinner only 5:30–9; Sunday brunch 10–1. Great view of Solomons harbor. The menu changes daily and features seafood purchased fresh from local vendors. The day I dined, Chef Shana Murphy (who started here as a dishwasher before going to culinary school) prepared basil-crusted rock-fish with garlic- and parsley-tossed pasta ($23.95), jumbo lump crabcakes ($27.95), Cornish game hen ($24.95), and cinnamon-crusted oysters ($21.95). Lots of big chunks of meat in the crab soup ($4.50).

& Lighthouse Inn (410-326-2444), 14636 Patuxent Avenue. Crabcakes and other seafood are the specialties of the two-story restaurant whose huge windows overlook the Patuxent River. The bar, a one-third replica of a skipjack, was designed and built by local craftsperson "Pepper" Langley. $13–30.

White Sands

& Vera's White Sands Restaurant
(410-586-1182), 1200 White Sands Drive. Tuesday through Saturday 5–9 PM, Sunday 1–9 PM. Closed October through April. Live entertainment Thursday through Sunday. Vera's extraordinary personality, wardrobe, and decorating style have made this a must-see place for decades. Holding court under a reed and bamboo ceil-

ing, she wanders among guests bedecked in pearls, woven headband, and Polynesian-style dress, and sipping an endless glass of champagne.

Dinner entrées ($14.95–26.95) include beef, poultry, lamb, and seafood. The veal osso buco ($19.95) is simmered in a "provincial" sauce for hours, while the bouillabaisse ($18.95) has an abundance of seafood in a tomato sauce.

EATING OUT

Broomes Island

&. **Stoney's Seafood House** (410-586-1888), 3939 Oyster House Road. Open daily for lunch and dinner. The restaurant is next to the Patuxent River, and to get a real feel of being on the water, ask to be seated on the floating deck. Entrées are made with items purchased from Denton's Seafood next door, so everything is as fresh as it can get. The crabcakes (market price) have received accolades for years, while the Neptune's platter ($23.95) gives you a taste of several items. If you are here in the

right season, lunch on one of the soft-shell crab sandwiches ($8.95). Steamed crabs by the dozen (market price) are served if locally available. Stoney's has **another restaurant** (410-535-1888) in the Fox Run Shopping Center in Prince Frederick. The menu is the same, but I always miss the atmosphere of the place on the water.

Chesapeake Beach

&. **Wesley Stinnet's Restaurant** (410-257-6100), 8617 Bayside Road. Open daily for breakfast, lunch, and dinner. Stinnet's has been a local institution since it opened in 1936. Nothing fancy here—vinyl chairs and tables—but definitely the place to enjoy a good breakfast at a low price ($4–7). The photographs on the wall showing the changes in the boardwalk and towns of Chesapeake Beach and North Beach may be the most interesting thing about the restaurant.

North Beach

✔ &. **Thursday's** (410-286-8695), 9200 Bay Avenue. Open daily for

STONEY'S SEAFOOD HOUSE

lunch and dinner. Thursday's is a local watering hole that serves good, solid food. Appetizers ($4.95–7.95) and soups ($4.75) are made from scratch, and prime rib ($13.95) is hand cut and slow-roasted. A few seafood dishes ($10.95 to market price) and "south of the border" ($7.95–12.95) items are also on the menu. A dozen draft beers complement meals.

Solomons

&. **The CD Café** (410-326-3877), 14350 Solomons Island Road. Open daily for lunch 11:30–2:30; dinner 5:30–9. There is a reason people are willing to sometimes wait a long time to get seated at one of the less than a dozen tables: Owner-chefs Catherine File and Deborah Witmer create delicious, and for the most part healthful, dishes. The roasted vegetarian sandwich (with house salad; $8.95) I lunched on was full of sweet and flavorful red peppers. The pasta with sun-dried tomatoes, artichoke, feta, and garlic caper sauce ($13.95) I had the next evening was equally satisfying, while my dining mate almost wanted to lick the plate after finishing her honey-blackened salmon ($16.95). Other entrées $7.95–18.95. CD Café is, without a doubt, my choice for Solomons' best taste-bud experience.

&. **The Wharf** (410-326-3261), 14442 Solomons Island Road. Serves lunch and dinner daily in a casual waterfront atmosphere. A dock is available for those arriving by boat. The menu includes steaks ($12.95–15.95) and other entrées ($12.95–17.95), but since you are next to the Chesapeake Bay, go for one of the well-prepared seafood dishes. The she-crab soup (market price) may just be the best and creamiest you will find in all of Maryland, and the crab imperial ($19.95) is full of backfin crabmeat.

&. **Solomons Pier** (410-326-2424), 14575 Solomons Island Road. Open daily for lunch and dinner. Located on the pier built in 1919 on the Patuxent River (read about its colorful history on the menu's front cover), so it has a great view of its surroundings. Seafood is the specialty, with a variety

SUNSET AT THE SOLOMONS WATERFRONT

of crab dishes (market price), oysters (market price), and crab-imperial-stuffed flounder ($16.95). Chicken, steak, and pasta entrées available $9.95–20.95.

CRABS ♿ **Abner's Crab House** (410-257-3689 or 301-855-6705), 3748 Harbor Road, Chesapeake Beach. Open daily for lunch and dinner. Overlooks the marsh in Fishing Creek Park. Typical crab house with crab balls ($14.95), crabcakes ($14.95), and other fresh catches from the bay ($11.95–18.95). Daily specials and a raw bar.

TAKE-OUT **Dunkirk Seafood Market** (410-257-3000), Lyon's Creek Center (on MD 260), Dunkirk. Open daily. Live or steamed crabs, oysters, and a variety of fish that is available whole or filleted.

Captain Smith's Seafood Market (410-326-1134), MD 4/2, Solomons.

Live and steamed crabs, shrimp, seafood, and fresh crabmeat.

COFFEE BARS ♿ **One of a Kind Gallery and Espresso Bar** (410-257-7580), 3725 East Chesapeake Beach Road, Chesapeake Beach. The name says it all—coffee amid artwork.

SNACKS AND GOODIES ✑ **Old Town Candy** (410-286-7300), 9122 Bay Avenue, North Beach. Lots of things to satisfy the sweet tooth. Individual candy bars or items by the pound.

✳ Entertainment
FILM **Apex Theatres** (410-535-0776), Calvert Village Mall, Prince Frederick, shows first-run movies.

✳ Selective Shopping
ANTIQUES **Southern Maryland Antiques Center** (410-257-1677), 3176 Solomons Island Road (MD 4/2), Huntingtown. Thursday

---

MAKE YOUR OWN CRABCAKES

Many restaurants proclaim that their crabcakes are 100 percent meat—so that they won't be accused of using filler—but the traditional Maryland recipe included a few extra ingredients:

  1 cup seasoned bread crumbs (usually Old Bay seasoning)

  1 large egg

  ¼ cup mayonnaise

  ½ tsp. salt

  ¼ tsp. pepper

  1 tsp. Worcestershire sauce

  1 tsp. dry mustard

  1 lb. crabmeat

  butter or oil for frying

Mix bread crumbs, egg, mayonnaise, and seasonings together; then mix in crabmeat. Shape into 6 cakes. Cook in frying pan with a bit of oil until well browned on each side. Enjoy.

through Sunday. A multidealer center with items from furniture to china to folk art.

About a dozen antiqueS dealers, some with their own storefronts and others in a center with several other shops, are located on Bay, 7th, and Chesapeake Avenues in North Beach. All are within easy walking distance of each other.

Dodson's On Mill Creek (410-326-1369), 13690 Olivet Street, Lusby. English and nautical antiques.

Grandmother's Store Antique Center (410-326-3366), 13892 Dowell Road, Dowell. Open daily. Inside an old country store are nine rooms of antiques, books, and other items available from various vendors. Be sure to locate the **In the Country** shop to take a look at the "Lilamericans" figurines hand-sculpted by the owner-artist.

Island Trader Antiques (410-326-3582), 225 Lore Road, Solomons. Closed Wednesday. A mix of furniture, trunks, linens, and old advertising boxes.

The Chesapeake Marketplace (410-586-3725; 1-800-655-1081), 5015 St. Leonard Road, St. Leonard. Wednesday through Sunday 10–5. More than 80 shops gathered within a 5-acre, former lumberyard complex. The majority are antiques dealers; the others have local crafts, gift items, ceramics, and collectibles.

ART GALLERIES Calvert County Cultural Arts Council (410-535-0302), 246 Mirrimac Court, Prince Frederick. A small area displays the works of local council members.

BOOKSTORES Bay Books (410-535-9540), 541 Solomons Island Road North, Prince Frederick. Best-sellers and local interest.

SPECIAL SHOPS Coffee, Tea and Whimsey (410-286-0000), 9122B Bay Avenue, North Beach. You can sip on a cup of coffee while wandering through the gift items.

Main Street Contemporary Art (410-535-3334), 486 Main Street,

SEA GULL COVE GIFTS, SOLOMONS

Prince Frederick. Closed mid-February through April 1. The quality of pottery, jewelry, tile, blown glass, and other objets d'art is higher than that often found in similar shops.

Sea Gull Cove Gifts (410-326-7182), 14488 Solomons Island Road, Solomons. Many nautical and local theme items. Worth a stop to browse and see what is available.

✳ Special Events

February: **Sportfishing Show and Seminar** (301-262-5668), Solomons. Seminars on all bay species taught by experts. Equipment sales, free boat rides, face painting, and casting contests for all ages.

March: **Calvert Artists Showcase** (410-535-7005), Owings. Annual event celebrating the works of local artists. Moneys raised support local nonprofit organizations. **Fishing Flea Market** (410-326-2622), Solomons. Fishing equipment, raffles, and door prizes.

April: **Right of Way Hike** (410-257-3892), Chesapeake Beach. Annual exploration of the old Chesapeake Beach Railway route, by car and by foot. **Herb and Wildflower Sale** (410-535-5327), Battle Creek Cypress Swamp Sanctuary Nature Center (see *Green Space—Walks*), Prince Frederick. Annual sale of herbs, vegetable plants, and native wildflowers. **Celtic Festival of Southern Maryland** (410-257-9003), St. Leonard. Music, dance, bagpiping, children's games, competitions, storytelling, and all things Celtic.

May: **African American Family Community Day** (410-586-8500), St. Leonard. Annual celebration of music, African dancing, a fashion show, kid's activities, food, and wagon rides. **Annual Antique Car Show** (410-257-3892), Chesapeake Beach. More than 100 antique and classic cars.

August: **Calvert County Jousting Tournament** (410-535-1710), Port Republic. Oldest tournament in Maryland of the state's official sport. Crafts, country supper, and bazaar. **North Beach Bayfest** (301-855-6681), North Beach. Crafts, Maryland food, pony rides and other children's activities, music, and antique cars.

September: **Artsfest** (410-326-4640), Annmarie Garden (see *Green Space—Gardens*), Solomons. Juried arts and crafts show, with visual and performing arts. **War of 1812 Reenactment and 19th-Century Tavern Night** (410-586-8500), Jefferson Patterson Park and Museum (see *To See—Other Sites*), St. Leonard. Relive the Battle of St. Leonard during the War of 1812. Reenactors stage the land and water aspects of the skirmish. Re-creations of camp life, period crafts, and food. **Calvert County Fair** (410-535-0026), fairgrounds, Barstow.

November: **Bull/Oyster Roast** (410-326-3274), Lusby. All-you-can-eat fried, steamed, and raw oysters; oyster stew; open-pit beef; and side dishes.

December through early January: **Garden in Lights** (410-326-4640), Annmarie Garden (see *Green Space—Gardens*), Solomons.

December: **Solomons Christmas Walk** (410-326-1950; www.solomons.md.us), Solomons. Annual event with candlelit streets, art, entertainment, bell choirs and carolers, a puppet show, and a boat light parade.

At the Mouth of the Potomac

5 Hughesville
231
231

Charlotte Hall
New Market
St. Mary's County
? Chamber of
Commerce
Mechanicsville ●
236
Budds Creek ●
5
235

Chaptico ●
Christ
★ Episcopal
Church
Clements ●
234
242
243

St. Clement's Island ★
Potomac River
Museum
Colton's
Point
St. Clement's
Island

Prince Frederick ●

Port Republic ●

St. Leonard ●

264
2
4
Broomes
Island ●
Lusby ●
Sotterley
Plantation
Greenwell
★ State Park

Myrtle Point Park
Hollywood ● ★

Leonardtown
235
4
California ●
Solomons ●

Patuxent
★ Naval Air Station

ST. MARY'S
RIVER STATE
PARK
★ Naval Air Museum

246 Lexington Park
Great Mills ●
5
Callaway ●
Park Hall ●

244 Drayden
St. Mary's City
★
Trinity Church
5
235
Dameron ●
St. Inigoes ●
St. Ignatius
★ Church
Ridge ●

Piney Point ●
★
249
Piney Point
Lighthouse
Museum & Park
St. George
Island

Scotland ●
5

VIRGINIA

Potomac River
Breton Bay
St. Clement's Bay
Patuxent River
Chesapeake Bay
St. Mary's River

★ Point Lookout
State Park

N
↑

0 1 2 3 4 5   10
Miles

© The Countryman Press

AT THE MOUTH OF THE POTOMAC—ST. MARY'S CITY AND LEONARDTOWN

Maryland's deepest roots grow here, for this is where the colony that eventually became a state was born.

Maryland's story begins in November 1633. Imagine the courage, fortitude—and desperation—it must have taken for close to 200 British men, women, and children to leave all they had known to venture forth into unclear futures in an unknown land. Longing for a religious tolerance denied to them in their home country, they boarded the *Ark* and the *Dove* to face a four-month voyage across the Atlantic Ocean. Sailing into the mouth of the Potomac River, these seekers of a new life landed at St. Clement's Island in March 1634. A large wooden cross was erected in thanks, and they prayerfully celebrated the first Roman Catholic Mass in the English-speaking colonies.

Soon afterward, they moved to a more suitable site for a permanent settlement along the St. Mary's River. Their story, and that of the state's early days, is vividly portrayed and preserved for visitors to experience in 800-acre Historic St. Mary's City.

As to be expected on fertile land bordered by two rivers and the Chesapeake Bay, life in the colony developed around large plantations and seafood harvesting. To some degree, many things remain the same today. Yes, housing developments eat into farmland, and strip malls replace tobacco barns; but acres of open meadows still edge quiet country lanes, and new generations of watermen carry on the traditions of their grandparents. And like many American presidents, going all the way back to James Madison, visitors are lured here by the water, the scenery, and a slower pace of life. Montana may be known as Big Sky Country, but to stand on a southern Maryland shoreline surrounded by open fields and gaze to where water meets Earth's canopy is to be filled with a sense of immense space.

COMMUNITIES Leonardtown, despite being St. Mary's County seat since 1708, still has a population of only about 2,000 people. While retaining a small-town atmosphere—it has a central square bordered by local businesses and the courthouse—it has some of the best upscale restaurants and shops in the region.

The area around **Lexington Park** remained a quiet place until the middle of World War II, when a small naval station expanded into the 6,000-acre Patuxent

ST. CLEMENT'S ISLAND

Naval Air Station. The federal government developed a housing project outside the station for military personnel, and the city has continued to expand. It is now the economic center of the region, and shows all of the signs of rapid modernization, with shopping centers, restaurants, malls, and—modest by big-city standards—the heaviest traffic around.

California is basically a suburb of Lexington Park, and its stores and restaurants are the first things people see when they arrive from Solomon's across the MD 4/Governor Johnson Memorial Bridge.

Like a thin finger jutting into the expanse of water created by the confluence of the Potomac and St. Mary's Rivers, **St. George Island** is connected to the mainland by a two-lane bridge. The life you see here is representative of what you would find if you were to drive many of the region's country lanes to small communities at land's end.

Amish families from Pennsylvania began to move onto farmland around **Charlotte Hall** in the mid-1900s, and it is not an uncommon site to see a horse and buggy moving along at 18th-century speeds on some of the back roads.

GUIDANCE St. Mary's County Division of Tourism (301-475-4411; 1-800-327-9023; www.co.saint-marys.md.us./tourism), 23115 Leonard Hall Drive, Leonardtown, 20650.

The **St. Mary's County Chamber of Commerce** (301-884-5555; www.smc-chamber.com), 28290 Three Notch Road (MD 5), Mechanicsville, can also supply you with some information.

GETTING THERE *By car:* This is almost a you-have-to-want-to-get-here kind of place. **MD 5/235** is the main highway coming into the area from the north and provides access from Washington, D.C., and the interstates. The **MD 4/Governor Johnson Memorial Bridge** crosses the Patuxent River near California for those coming from Solomons and other points in Calvert County.

By air: The two airports that serve this area with scheduled commercial flights are **Baltimore/Washington International** (1-800-I-FLY-BWI) near Annapolis and **Ronald Reagan Washington National Airport** (703-417-8000) in northern Virginia.

By water: There are no scheduled boats bringing you into the region, but if you own or are renting one, there are scores of marinas to make your stay easier.

GETTING AROUND *By car:* **MD 235** is a four-lane highway that runs in a north–south direction through the region. **MD 5** parallels MD 235 a bit to the south, is primarily two-lane, and travels through smaller towns and scenic countryside.

By bus: The **St. Mary's Transit System** (301-475-5100) has bus routes that make it possible to get to just about anywhere in the area: Leonardtown, Lexington Park, California, Great Mills, Charlotte Hall, and points in between. Most fares are about $1, but some rural routes are up to $3; exact change required.

By taxi: **Friendly Cab** (301-863-8141) in Lexington Park and **Leonardtown Cab** (301-475-9157) in Leonardtown.

MEDICAL EMERGENCY **St. Mary's Hospital** (301-475-8981), 25500 Point Lookout Road, Leonardtown.

✳ To See

MUSEUMS ✦ **St. Clement's Island Potomac River Museum** (301-769-2222), 38370 Point Breeze Road, Colton's Point. Weekdays 9–5 and weekends noon–5 from late March through September; noon–4 Wednesday through Sunday from October through late March. Small admission fee; children 12 and under are free. The displays in the small museum do a good job of telling the story of Maryland's first English settlers. By the time I left here, I knew what prompted them to leave their homeland, and the difficulties they faced before and during their ocean voyage. A 20-foot mural celebrates their arrival on St. Clement's Island.

The museum sponsors boat tours to the 40-acre island on Saturday and Sunday at 12:30 from May through October. Adults $5; children 12 and are under $3. Now a state park, it has interpretive signs along short pathways that lead to the large cross erected in 1934 to celebrate the 300th anniversary of the settlers' arrival.

✦ **Patuxent River Naval Air Museum** (301-863-7418; www.paxmuseum.com), MD 235 (next to Gate One of the Patuxent River Naval Air Station), Lexington

ON DISPLAY AT THE PATUXENT RIVER NAVAL AIR MUSEUM

Park. Open 10–5; closed Monday. Free parking and admission. The only museum in the country dedicated to naval aviation research and testing. Outside are a number of historic aircraft such as an E-2B Hawkeye, F-14 Tomcat, and Grumman A-6 Intruder. The inside exhibits tell of the development of the ejection seat, flight helmet, and the amazingly portable helicopter.

HISTORIC HOMES Tudor Hall (301-475-2467), 41680 Tudor Place, Leonardtown. Monday through Friday 10–2. Donations accepted. The 1700s Georgian mansion is notable for its inset portico, a new style for its day. The home sat on a 1,000-acre farm and was once owned by members of the Francis Scott Key family. It is now the research repository for the St. Mary's Historical Society. The public is welcome to walk through the house with a member of the society.

HISTORIC SITES ♿ Sotterley Plantation (301-373-2280; 1-800-681-0850; www.sotterley.com), on MD 245, Hollywood. Grounds open all year (free), Tuesday through Sunday 10–4; guided house tours (small admission fee) given Tuesday through Sunday from May through October. Operates as a working plantation of the 1800s. The house's initial construction began in 1717, making it decades older than other famous homes such as Mount Vernon and Monticello. The extensive grounds sit next to the Patuxent River. One of the most interesting sites is the slave quarters of the Hillary Kane family, the only publicly accessible slave cabin in the state. (**Greenwell State Park** is just a couple of minutes' drive from here; see *To Do—Birding* and *To Do—Hiking*).

Old Jail Museum (301-475-2467), 41680 Tudor Place, Leonardtown. The museum is officially open Wednesday through Friday noon–4, but you may need to go to Tudor Hall (see *Historic Homes*) to find someone to open it for you. A few pieces of furniture and other artifacts depict what the jail would have looked like in the mid-1800s. The jailer's family residence was on the first floor, the small women's cell has a bunk in it, and the larger men's cell is on the top floor.

HISTORIC CHURCHES ♿ Christ Episcopal Church (301-884-3451), MD 238, Chaptico. Constructed in 1736. During the War of 1812, the British dug up graves in the yard and stabled their horses inside the church. Members of the Francis Scott Key family are buried here in a family vault.

Dent Chapel (301-884-8171), Old MD 5, Charlotte Hall. Constructed of granite with a brick belt in 1883, it may be one of the best Victorian Gothic structures in the state.

St. Francis Xavier Church (301-475-9885), MD 243, Compton. Constructed in 1731, less than 100 years after the first settlers arrived in the area, it is thought to be the oldest Catholic church in continuous use in English-speaking America.

Trinity Episcopal Church (301-862-4597), MD 5, Historic St. Mary's City. Constructed in 1829 with bricks that were salvaged from Maryland's first statehouse, which had been built in 1676.

⚓ ✎ Historic St. Mary's City (240-895-4990; 1-800-SMC-1634; www.stmaryscity.com), Rosecroft Road (off MD 5). Wednesday through Sunday from late June through mid-September; Tuesday through Saturday in spring and fall. Days and hours have changed year to year, so call for the latest schedule. Adults $7.50; students with ID $5.50; children 6–12 are $3.50.

One of the best-preserved archaeological sites in America and certainly the best representation of a 17th-century colonial town in Maryland. Schedule a minimum of a half day to take in everything on this 800-acre living-history site of Maryland's first permanent English settlement. Self-guided tours (with provided map/brochure) lead you to costumed interpreters (who are some of the best I've met in not breaking character) in the recon-

THE FULL-SIZED REPRODUCTION OF THE *DOVE*

structed **Woodland Indian settlement, Godiah Spray Plantation, Farthings's Ordinary, State House,** and, most spectacularly, a full-sized reproduction of the ***Dove,*** one of the ships that transported the settlers across the ocean.

Williamsburg in Virginia may be bigger, yet Historic St. Mary's is a much more manageable place to get a handle on the big picture—and its admission fee is much less.

St. Ignatius Church (310-872-5590), Villa Road (off MD 5), St. Inigoes. Constructed in 1785, it is believed to house the oldest active Catholic parish in the country.

LIGHTHOUSES ⚐ Piney Point Lighthouse and Museum (301-769-2222), MD 249 and Lighthouse Road, Piney Point. Grounds open daily sunrise to sunset; the museum is open noon–5 Friday through Monday from May through October.

Donations accepted. Built in 1836, the brick tower Piney Point Lighthouse was Maryland's first permanent lighthouse on the Potomac River and is the only accessible such structure on its original location in southern Maryland. The small museum, once the chief petty officer's garage, tells the story of its construction, operation, and the role of the Coast Guard.

Piney Point's beautiful scenery and cool breezes have made it a popular recreation spot for many U.S. presidents, beginning with James Madison. A small beach is available for swimming (no lifeguards). Be here as the glow of a rising or setting sun shimmers upon the broad expanse of water and you will understand why they came.

Also see *Green Space—Parks.*

OTHER SITES Naval Air Station (301-757-4814), Lexington Park. The world's premier research, development, testing, and evaluation center for naval aircraft covers 6,000 acres, much of it environmentally and culturally interesting. A pamphlet describing a self-guided tour is available at the entrance gate. *Please note:* The events of September 11, 2001 have changed many procedures at military installations, and the policy on public visitation is now much more strict; call for the latest information.

✳ To Do

AUTO RACING ♿ **Maryland International Raceway** (301-884-9833; www.mirdrag.com), MD 234, Budds Creek. Races take place on the weekends from March through October at the International Hot Rod Association (IHRA) quarter-mile drag-racing track.

BICYCLING More and more bicyclists are discovering the pleasures of riding the lightly traveled roadways of the area. The **St. Mary's County Division of Tourism** (see *Guidance*) can provide information on four popular circuit routes.

One trip is almost 26 miles long and

PINEY POINT LIGHTHOUSE AND MUSEUM

concentrates on the sites to be seen near **St. Clement's Bay** and the **Wicomico** and **Potomac Rivers.** Another is a ride of less than an hour that is more centered upon what may be seen along the **Patuxent River,** such as **Sotterley Plantation** (see *To See—Historic Sites*) and **Greenwell State Park** (see *Birding* and *Hiking*). A third journey is just over 40 miles. Its route includes the waterside along **St. George Island** and **Piney Point Lighthouse** (see *To See—Lighthouses*). The fourth ride, at 27.5 miles, is historically interesting, as it brings riders into **Historic St. Mary's City** (see sidebar on page 343) and **Point Lookout State Park** (see *Green Space—Parks*).

St. Mary's River State Park (301-872-5688), Camp Cosoma Road (off MD 5), Great Mills. You may not think of the flat land of southern Maryland as having much terrain for mountain bikers. However, the 9-mile single-track course, built with mountain bikes in mind, encircles a 250-acre lake and can be a good challenge and a nice ride. Also open to hikers.

Mike's Bikes (301-863-7887), 21310-C Great Mills Road (at Great Mills Shopping Center), Lexington Park. Closed Sunday. They sell skateboards, and also sell and service bicycles.

BIRDING 🐾 ♿ **Greenwell State Park** (301-373-9775; 301-373-2731), 25402 Rosedale Manor Lane, Hollywood. Open daily during daylight hours. Free; donations accepted. The many different environments of the park—riparian, wetlands, floodplain, field, and forest—are attractive to a wide variety of feathered creatures. Among the many seen here are great blue heron, bald eagle, osprey, Ameri-

can kestrel, a variety of hawks (primarily red-tailed), and the elusive Swainson's hawk. Barred, great horned, and eastern screech owls are sometimes heard in the early evening, while black vultures soar over the fields—which are home to a bird I see and hear less often than I used to, the bobwhite.

Point Lookout State Park (310-872-5688), MD 5, Scotland. Its location on the tip of land at the confluence of the Potomac River and Chesapeake Bay ensures the park as a great place to experience the migrations along the Great Atlantic Flyway. Watch for northern gannets, brown pelicans, and others.

BOAT EXCURSIONS See **St. Clement's Island Potomac River Museum** under *To See—Museums.*

FAMILY ACTIVITIES ⚜ **Bowles Farm Corn Maze** (301-475-2139; www.cornfieldmaze.com), Pincushion Road (off MD 234), Clements. Friday through Sunday from mid-September through October. Adults $8; children 6–11 are $6; children under 5 are free. A fun way to spend a morning or

NEGOTIATING THE BOWLES FARM CORN MAZE

afternoon. More than 3 miles of trails twist, turn, and befuddle as the maze takes you through 15 acres of tall, living cornstalks. After making your way through the labyrinth (some folks have had to be rescued!), you can reward the kids by wandering over to the petting zoo and/or picking out your Halloween pumpkin.

Also see *Miniature Golf*.

FISHING Fishing in the area starts in late April and continues through December. Charter boats, many providing very personal service by taking only six or fewer passengers, can take you onto the water for rockfish, flounder, sea trout, Spanish mackerel, black sea bass, and more. The **St. Mary's County Division of Tourism** (see *Guidance*) can supply you with a full list of contacts.

Some of the many well-respected captains in the area include:

Ridge
Captain Gary Sacks (301-872-5506; www.paxp.com/marcia), 48862 Curley's Road.

Captain Randy Powers (301-872-9321; www.shannoniv.com), 16518 Chesapeake Drive.

Park Hall
Captain Scott Russell (301-737-0255; www.captscotts.com), P.O. Box 331.

Captain Mike Gerek (301-863-2330; paxp.com/sandramarie), 18164 Point Lookout Road.

GOLF & **Wicomico Shores** (301-884-4601), Aviation Yacht Club Road (Wicomico Shores Subdivision), Chaptico. Open daily. The course is scenically located next to the Wicomi-

co River and has many wooded areas with lots of wildlife. The back tees measure 6,397 feet, and 72 is par.

& **Breton Bay Golf and County Club** (301-475-2300), 21935 Society Hill Road, Leonardtown. Open daily. The 18-hole course was designed by J. Porter Gibson and built in 1974. Fairways have Bermuda grass; the greens are planted with bent grass. Lakes and other water come into play.

MINIATURE GOLF ✏ **Hollywood Swing and Swat** (301-373-8858), Clarkes Landing Road, Hollywood. Open daily March through November. The 18-hole course is adjacent to a driving range and batting cages.

HIKING 🐾 & **Greenwell State Park** (301-373-9775; 301-373-2731), 25402 Rosedale Manor Lane, Hollywood. The 600-acre park is on land that was once a part of 4,000-acre Resurrection Manor. A patchwork of open fields, wetlands, and forests keeps the land looking much the way it would have in the 17th century, and about 6.5 miles of trails take visitors out to the far reaches. Most of the routes are easy and level, but if you don't have time to hike all of the pathways, I would urge you to at least take the one along the Patuxent River. It is a particularly pretty outing, and a portion of it is handicapped accessible. All but two of the trails are also open to bikers and equestrians; pets must be leashed.

Also see **St. Mary's River State Park** under *Bicycling*, and *Green Space—Parks*.

KAYAKING AND CANOEING Blue Wind (301-737-2713; www.bluewindsports.com), MD 235, California. The staff at Blue Wind can sell (new or used) or rent you a kayak, canoe, or sailing craft and provide instructions on how to safely use it.

SCUBA DIVING U-1105 Black Panther Historic Ship Preserve (301-769-2222), Piney Point. The World War II German Black Panther was the world's first stealth weapon, as its rubber coating made it invisible to sonar equipment. Captured near the end of the war, it was tested by the U.S. Navy and then intentionally sunk in about 100 feet of water in the Potomac River. Expert recreational divers are permitted to dive to the site after obtaining information from the Piney Point Lighthouse and Museum (see *To See—Lighthouses*).

✳ Green Space

BEACHES Myrtle Point Park (301-475-4572), Patuxent Boulevard, California. Free. The small beach and several short trails have a view onto the Patuxent River and its Governor Johnson Memorial Bridge. No lifeguards.

Elm's Beach (301-475-4572), Forest Road, Dameron. Free. A county-operated park, Elm's has a nice beach (access open year-round) on the Chesapeake Bay. The bay is so wide here that you could almost convince yourself that you are at an oceanside beach. No lifeguards.

🐾 **Greenwell State Park** (301-373-9775; 301-373-2731), 25402 Rosedale Manor Lane, Hollywood. Swimming is permitted from the park's small beach along the Patuxent River. Remember that you are swimming in a river, so there may be a strong current to contend with. No lifeguards.

Also see *To Do—Birding*, *To Do—Hiking*, and *Parks*.

PARKS 🐾 **Point Lookout State Park** (310-872-5688), MD 5, Scotland. Open daily sunrise to sunset. Free admission, except $3 for admission to the beach on weekends and holidays. The park's location at the mouth of the Potomac River made it a strategic defense point, and it served as a watch post during the Revolutionary War and the War of 1812. During the Civil War, it functioned as a military hospital and prison camp—in which more than 3,000 of the estimated 20,000 to 50,000 Confederate prisoners died from exposure, starvation, and diseases related to poor sanitation. The park's museum (the original photos of prisoners are vivid relics of the past) and nearby ruins of **Fort Lincoln** tell the story.

Also in the park are picnic areas, several short nature trails, and a swimming beach and picnic area. The 1830 **Point Lookout Lighthouse** sits at land's end and is open to the public

POINT LOOKOUT LIGHTHOUSE

THE REAR ENTRANCE OF THE BROME-HOWARD INN, ST. MARY'S CITY

only one day a year in November (see *Special Events*). (Also see *To Do—Birding* and *To Do—Hiking*.)

✳ Lodging

INNS Brome-Howard Inn (301-866-0656; www.bromehowardinn.com), 18281 Rosecroft Road, St. Mary's City, 20686. Roses on your bed and dresser welcome you to your room in the elegant 19th-century Brome-Howard Inn. All guest rooms and the suite have a private bath. Come here for beautiful St. Mary's River views, miles of hiking trails connecting with those of Historic St. Mary's City, free bicycle use, and the opportunity to enjoy a delicious dinner (see *Dining Out*). Ask how the house came to sit on this particular piece of land—it is an amazing story. $110–160.

BED & BREAKFASTS
Ridge, 20680

Bard's Field B&B (301-872-5989), 15671 Pratt Road. Host James Pratt grew up in this 1798 small Colonial manor home that overlooks Rawley

Bay on the Potomac River. He and his wife, Audrey, refurbished it and offer two large guest rooms that share a bath. The surrounding fields, gardens, and water make for a relaxing stay. Do not leave without having James take you into the basement. It is a virtual museum of items he has collected from days gone by—tools, drills, carpenter's planes, and more.

Scotland, 20687
🐚 **Hale House B&B** (301-872-4558), 49644 Potomac River Drive. The Hales designed and hand-built their impressive contemporary home, which sits at the very mouth of the Potomac River. Many of the interior walls are brick, and each wall facing the river is basically one big window. All rooms, including the two for guests (private baths and entrances), are spacious. A swimming pool overlooking the river and the 500-foot pier only add to the value of the low-cost rates. $85.

St. Michael's Manor (301-872-4025), 50200 St. Michael's Manor Way. There are only two guest rooms (with shared bath) in this brick 1805 home sitting alone on 10 waterfront acres, so it has a very homey feel. In addition to cooking a full country breakfast, Nancy and Captain Joseph Dick set out figs, apples, and fruits freshly picked from their garden. A canoe and a pedal boat are available for guest use; the hammock overlooking the water is for relaxing after a dip in the pool. $60–90.

COTTAGES **Longpoint Cottage** (301-872-0057), P.O. Box 505, Ridge, 20680. The small two-bedroom vacation cottage is modestly furnished, but this is not the real reason to stay here. Come to enjoy the 13 acres of grounds, with 1,800 feet of shoreline, a sandy beach, a pier, and wonderfully serene views of Smith Creek and the Potomac River. Seemingly isolated, it is only a pleasant stroll away from three restaurants, a yacht club, and fishing charter boats. $100.

CAMPING 🐾 **Take It Easy Campground** (301-994-0494; 1-877-994-0494), 25285 Take It Easy Ranch Road (off MD 249), Callaway, 20620. Open year-round. There are tent and RV sites with hookups and a dump station, a swimming pool, and a 7-acre fishing lake on the 200-acre property. Pets permitted.

🐾 **Dennis Point Marina and Campground** (301-994-2288; 1-800-974-2288), 46555 Dennis Point Way, Drayden, 20630. Waterfront camping, a short nature trail, a couple of small playgrounds for the kids, a tennis court, a swimming pool, laundry facilities, fishing, canoeing and kayaking, a store, and a restaurant. With all of these amenities, you may never have to leave.

Le Grande RV Sales & Camping

Resort (301-475-8550), MD 5 (south of Leonardtown), Leonardtown, 20650. There are a few tent sites, but the obvious clientele is the motorized crowd. Hookups, a dump station, and RV sales and service.

Seaside View Recreation Park & Campground (301-872-4141; www.seaside-view.com), 48593 Seaside View Road, Ridge, 20680. Tent and RV sites with hookups and a dump station. A restaurant and full-service marina on Jutland Creek are on the premises.

Camp Merryelande (1-800-382-1073; www.campmd.com), MD 249, St. George Island, 20674. Open year-round. Waterfront tent sites overlooking the broad mouth of the Potomac River. A beach and swimming area, crabbing and fishing pier, and laundry. Rental cottages (one to six bedrooms) complete with kitchen, linens, TV, and air-conditioning.

Also see **Point Lookout State Park** under *Green Space—Parks.*

✳ Where to Eat

DINING OUT **The Tavern At The Village** (301-863-3219; www.thetavernatthevillage.com), Wetstone Lane, Wildewood Retirement Community, California. Reservations strongly recommended. Lunch served Tuesday through Saturday 11–2; dinner, Wednesday through Saturday 5:30–9. Fine dining in a retirement community? Yes. The menu changes frequently and has included crabcakes, pan-fried trout, pork chops, spinach ravioli, and many vegetarian dishes. Entrées $15.95–27.95.

Nook and Monk's (301-475-3020), Washington Street, Leonardtown. Open for lunch and dinner Monday through Saturday; brunch, Sunday 11–2. Pleasant atmosphere complements the ever-changing menu. A staple is fried tomato with crabmeat; other entrées have included crabcakes, coconut-fried shrimp, and New York strip steak. $12.95–22.95.

& **Spinnakers** (301-872-4340; www.spinnakersrestaurant.com), Wynne Road, Point Lookout Marina (off MD 5), Ridge. Open daily for lunch and dinner; closed January through mid-February. The menu changes almost daily at this restaurant overlooking Smith Creek and the Potomac River. Appetizers have included escargots with sun-dried tomatoes and shallots ($6), and baked Brie topped with pear preserves ($6). The scallops with andouille sausage and crawfish ($18) is a taste of New Orleans, while the "fin and shellfish" in a tomato sauce ($17) has local products in it. Duck, lamb, beef, and daily fresh fish specials. $17–22; many items are offered as half dishes.

& **Brome-Howard Inn** (301-866-0656; www.bromehowardinn.com), 18281 Rosecroft Road, St. Mary's City. Open for dinner Thursday through Sunday from 5 PM; Sunday brunch 11–2. Reservations appreciated. The menu changes frequently in this gracious manor house, whose two dining rooms have fireplaces, splendid views, and an impeccable wait staff. I think the crabcakes with *rémoulade* sauce ($22.50) are some of the best I've had in southern Maryland. The folks at the table next to me praised their pork tenderloin with apple-cranberry rum sauce ($20.95) and fisherman's stew ($20.95). Entrées $13.95–23.95. (Also see *Lodging—Inns.*)

EATING OUT

California
Asahi Japanese Steak and Seafood House (301-866-9070), 2576 MacArthur Boulevard (at San Souci Plaza). Open daily for lunch and dinner. The quality of the freshly made sushi and fresh-cooked meals have made this a popular spot with personnel from the Patuxent Naval Air Station, who have dined in many parts of the world. $6.95–19.95.

CLARKE'S LANDING, HOLLYWOOD

Hollywood

♿ **Clarke's Landing** (301-373-8468), Clarkes Landing Road. Open daily for lunch and dinner; closed Monday, October through May. The restaurant overlooks the Patuxent River, so it stands to reason that the seafood is obtained fresh locally. Steamed and soft-shell crabs are a favorite, but Rusty Shriver (the former head chef of Stoney's in Calvert County) also prepares pastas, soups, and hand-cut steaks. Entrées are $8.95 to market price.

Leonardtown

♿ **Café des Artistes** (301-997-0500; www.cafedesartistes.ws), corner of Fenwick and Washington Streets. Lunch, Tuesday through Friday 11–2; dinner, Tuesday through Thursday 5–9, Saturday 5–9:30, and Sunday noon–8. Days and hours subject to change. Such a delightful place to find in a small town. All dishes are based upon the French chef's own recipes. The *croque monsieur* (grilled ham and Swiss, $6.95) brought back memories of my travels through the Pyrenees. I returned for dinner, and the filet mignon in a puff pastry and green peppercorn sauce ($20.95) transported me to Paris.

And—ooh, la la—the desserts. Be sinful and have the pastries stuffed with ice cream and covered by warm dark chocolate ($5.95). Lunch entrées $6.95–13.95; dinner entrées $16.95–20.95.

🍴 **Do Dah Deli** (301-997-1604), 22696 Washington Street. Good for a quick salad ($2.75–5.50) or deli sandwiches ($2.95–5.95). PB&J sandwiches ($1.95) for the kids.

Mechanicsville

♿ **Bert's 50's Diner** (301-884-3837),

29760 Three North Road (MD 5). Return to the middle of the 20th century, with lots of neon lights, memorabilia, and hand-dipped ice cream, malts, and milk shakes. Blue-plate specials include meat loaf, hot turkey sandwich, and country-fried steak. Burgers, subs, pizza, and fries. Most full meals will cost you less than $12.

Ridge

Courtney's (301-872-4403), Wynne Road. The fading cinder-block exterior and old 1950s paneled interior make this the kind of place you might pass up if you didn't know locals congregate here daily for breakfast, lunch, and dinner. The owner is a waterman, so the fish is fresh. His wife, Julia, from the Philippines, does the cooking and provides a bit of a twist to the usual southern Maryland fare. Crabcake dinner ($11.50), a variety of broiled fish ($11), chicken ($9.95), and T-bone steaks are a few of the entrées ($13.95); others are $8.95–14.95.

St. George Island

♿ **Evans Seafood** (301-994-2299), MD 249. Closed Monday. Obviously, seafood is the specialty. Local steamed crabs are offered in the summer, oysters (from Evans's own beds) appear in the fall, and shrimp, scallops, and clams are on the menu year-round. Stuffed ham, a true southern Maryland dish, makes its appearance around the Thanksgiving/Christmas season. Entrées $15–25.

CRABS ♿ **Still Anchors** (301-994-2288), Dennis Point Way (at Dennis Point Marina), Drayden. Open for lunch and dinner, April through October 1. There is a full menu here, but the real reason to come is to enjoy dozens of freshly steamed crabs (market price) in the outside waterfront dining area. Entrées less than $25.

TAKEOUT American Soft Shell Crab Company (301-872-4444), 49676 Freeman's Road, Dameron. Open daily 7–7, Memorial Day through Labor Day. Dale and Mary Scheible take the crabs right off the boat to deliver them fresh to you. Soft- and hard-shell crabs—live or steamed.

Crabknockers Seafood Market (301-475-7830), Leonardtown Center, Leonardtown. A convenient location to pick up crabs and other fresh seafood.

SNACKS AND GOODIES Wildewood Pastry Shop (301-862-4177), 23415 Three Notch Road (at Wildewood Shopping Center), California. Pastries, cookies, breads, and candies.

Sweet Surprises (301-863-2498), Millison Plaza, 1703-D Great Mills Road, Lexington Park. Gourmet chocolates and nostalgia candies, ice cream, cookies, and a large selection of sugar-free items.

✳ Selective Shopping

ANTIQUES

Leonardtown

&. **Antiques on the Square** (301-475-5826), 22725 Washington Street. A multidealer facility with many antiques and items often found in a flea market.

&. **Maryland Antiques Center** (301-475-1960; www.paxp.com/mac), MD 5 (about 0.3 mile south of the MD 243 intersection). More than 30 dealers are spread out over 10,000 feet of display area. In addition to the usual antique items, be on the lookout for quality used books, artware, and nautical instruments.

ART GALLERIES &. **North End Gallery** (301-475-3130; northendgallery.org), Fenwick Street, Leonardtown. A cooperative gallery by local artists working in a myriad of media, including one of the most modern—digital images. There is a feature exhibit and a reception each month.

BOOKSTORES Bay Books (301-862-1424), 23415 Three Notch Road, Wildewood Shopping Center, California. Open daily. This is it—the only

---

MAKE YOUR OWN MARYLAND STEAMED CRABS
1 large pot with perforated false bottom
1 cup vinegar
1 cup water
1 dozen live crabs
3 tbsp. salt
2½ tbsp. seafood seasoning (such as Old Bay)
Bring vinegar and water to a boil, add live crabs (do not cook dead crabs, which contain bacteria!), and sprinkle a mixture of salt and seasoning between each layer. Allow water to come to a boil; then let crabs steam for at least 30 minutes.

full-service bookstore for many miles around. They have large selections of local-interest titles, best-sellers, and children's books.

Bowes Books (301-863-6200), 21550 Great Mills Road, Lexington Park. A combination framing shop, game store, and bookstore.

CRAFTS & **Cecil's Old Mill** (301-994-1510), Indian Bridge Road, Great Mills. Open Thursday through Sunday, mid-March through October; daily November through December 24. An interesting place, in that 50 craftspersons create and sell their wares among the gears, cogs, and other machinery of the circa-1900 grist- and sawmill. Some of the items are—please forgive the pun—just run-of-the-mill, but much of what is displayed is high quality, different, and worth stopping by to see even if you don't intend to buy anything.

& **Toddy Hall Pottery** (301-994-0947), Cherryfield Road, Hollywood. Open by appointment. I have seen pieces made here by local craftspersons show up on Internet auction sites. They also stock sculptures, paintings, and prints from local artisans.

Olde Town Crafters (301-997-1644), Washington Street, Leonardtown. Open Tuesday through Saturday 10–5. Many locally made items of arts, crafts, and baked goods.

SPECIAL SHOPS & **Cecil's Country Store** (301-994-9622), Indian Peg Road, Great Mills. Across the street from Cecil's Old Mill (see *Crafts*), this place keeps the same hours. It is part antiques shop, part country store. What sets it apart is that many of the items are displayed inside old dairy cases and iceboxes.

FARMER'S MARKETS

Charlotte Hall
North St. Mary's Farmer's Market (301-475-4404), in the library parking lot at the intersection of MD 5 and MD 6. Closed Sunday. Fresh produce, along with many products produced by the local Amish community, are available throughout the daylight hours from May through October.

Farmer's Market and Auction (301-884-3966), MD 5. Open year-round. As much of a flea market as it is a produce stand, there are more than 150 vendors here on Wednesday and Saturday 8–5. Also a place to find Amish goods.

California
California Farmer's Market (301-475-4404), 22180 Three Notch Road (MD 235). Saturday 9–1. The season lasts from May through October.

✳ Special Events

March: **Maryland Day** (301-769-2222), St. Clement's Island Potomac River Museum (see *To See—Museums*), Colton's Point, and at Historic St. Mary's City (see sidebar on page 343). A commemoration of the founding of Maryland. Wreath laying, militia musters, and refreshments.

April: **Rod and Classic Spring Fling** (301-475-7285), Leonardtown. Car and truck show with antiques, food, and activities.

May: **Annual Spring Festival** (301-994-0525), fairgrounds, Leonardtown. Arts and crafts, classic cars, carnival rides, live entertainment, and antiques auction. **Lighthouse Days** (301-769-2222), Piney Point Lighthouse Museum and Park. Decoy carvers, kids' programs, exhibits, and live entertainment. **Annual Quilt and Needlework Show** (301-373-2280; www.sotterley.com), Sotterley Plantation (see *To See—Historic Sites*), Hollywood. Juried exhibition. **Annual Blue and Gray Days** (301-872-5688), Point Lookout State Park (see *Green Space—Parks*). Artillery demonstrations, infantry march, and other living-history activities. Tours of Fort Lincoln.

June: **Crab Festival** (301-475-6910), Governmental Center on MD 245 near Hollywood. Antique car show, crafts, and lots and lots of crabs prepared many ways.

September: **St. Mary's County Fair** (301-475-2256), fairgrounds, Leonardtown. **IHRA President's Cup Nationals** (301-449-RACE; mirdrag.com), Maryland International Raceway (MD 234 near Budds Creek). The largest motor-sports event in the state. More than 400 teams.

October: **Annual Blessing of the Fleet** (301-769-2222), St. Clement's Island Potomac River Museum (see *To See—Museums*), Colton's Point. Entertainment, arts and crafts, parade and fireworks, the Blessing of the Fleet, and boat rides to the island. **Grand Militia Muster** (301-862-0990; 1-800-762-1634; www.stmarys-city.org), Historic St. Mary's City. Believed to be the largest gathering of 17th-century reenactment units in the country. **Oyster Festival** (301-863-5015; www.usoysterfest.com), fairgrounds, Leonardtown. Carnival games and rides, arts and crafts, live entertainment, and the **National Oyster Cook-Off** and **National Shucking Championship.**

November: **Lighthouse Open House** (301-872-5688), Point Lookout Lighthouse, Point Lookout State Park, Scotland. The only day of the year visitors can tour the lighthouse. Exhibits about the site, legends, and history. **Unique Boutique** (301-475-2365), Hollywood Volunteer Fire Department Social Hall, Hollywood. An annual juried exhibit of arts and crafts. **Amish Quilt Auction** (301-884-4062), MD 236, Charlotte Hall. A chance to bid on a handmade quilt.

ALONG THE POTOMAC SHORE—
LA PLATA, PORT TOBACCO, AND
WALDORF

As in all of southern Maryland, water has played a major role in defining this area and its way of life. Along its eastern border is the state's longest stream, the Patuxent River, while the wide expanse of the Potomac River outlines the western edge.

Through the centuries, the Port Tobacco River has silted in and become much shallower than it once was. During the early days of colonial settlement, it was the area's most important waterway. Wide and deep enough to be navigated by oceangoing vessels, it enabled Port Tobacco to be Maryland's second largest port throughout most of the 17th and 18th centuries, and to remain an important shipment center well into the 19th century. The coming of the railroads brought about the town's decline, but a visit to Historic Port Tobacco can bring those days back.

If Port Tobacco was the loser, La Plata was the winner when the railroad arrived in 1872. Coming from Baltimore and reaching all the way to the Potomac, the tracks brought prosperity to the town, which really started out as not much more than a post office and general store. Within a few years, the county seat was moved from Port Tobacco to La Plata. The coming of US 301 changed the town again, as its downtown area—now a small place worth a short stroll through—was bypassed. Most of the commerce, primarily strip malls, chain-food restaurants, and convenience stores, is located on the four-lane.

The largest city in the area, Waldorf, also owes its existence to the railroads. But it was tobacco, and not county bureaucracy, that brought money into the municipal coffers. The city and surrounding countryside were discovered in the mid-1900s by people wishing to escape living in Washington, D.C., and it is now primarily a bedroom community for the metro area, with large shopping malls and other modern conveniences.

COMMUNITIES You need to eschew US 301 and drive the back roads if you really want to explore the area. Leaving the major highway in Waldorf and driving east on MD 5 can bring you to such out-of-the-way places as where Dr. Mudd, the physician who worked on John Wilkes Booth's broken leg, lived. He is buried close to his home place in St. Mary's Church cemetery in **Bryantown**. Branch off MD 5 at **Hughesville** and you can follow MD 231 to the Patuxent River and

Benedict. In addition to being the landing site for British troops that marched westward to burn Washington, D.C., during the War of 1812, the now sleepy community bustled for more than 250 years. Established as a port in 1683, it continued to attract freight and passengers traveling on steamboats into the mid-1900s.

GUIDANCE **Charles County Visitors Bureau** (301-645-0558; 1-800-SO-MD-FUN; www.explorecharlescomd.com), 200 Baltimore Street, La Plata, 20646.

The **Crain Memorial Welcome Center** (301-259-2500), US 301, Newburg, is a state-operated facility and can provide information on all of Maryland as well as local attractions. It is located 1 mile north of the Governor Nice Memorial Bridge over the Potomac River on US 301.

GETTING THERE *By car:* Four-lane **US 301** will bring you into the area from the north around Washington, D.C. It is also the main highway coming in from the south, connecting southern Maryland with Virginia via the Governor Nice Memorial Bridge (toll) across the Potomac River.

By air: The closest airport, **Ronald Reagan Washington National Airport** (703-417-8000) is across the Potomac River in northern Virginia, but it is only about a 30- to 45-minute drive away. In another direction, but just a few minutes' longer drive away, is **Baltimore/Washington International** (1-800-I-FLY-BWI) near Annapolis.

By bus: **Greyhound** (1-800-229-9429) stops in Waldorf on its route between Virginia and other points in Maryland.

By water: The **Charles County Visitors Bureau** (see *Guidance*) can supply you with a long list of marinas that will take care of you if you happen to arrive on your personal boat.

GETTING AROUND *By car:* Except for **US 301,** most of the roadways are lightly traveled.

By bus: The **Charles County Department of Community Services** (301-934-9305) administers six bus routes in the Waldorf and La Plata areas that are in operation Monday through Saturday.

By taxi: **B&J Community Cabs** (301-843-7302), **Cab of Waldorf** (301-638-0696), **Waldorf Cab** (301-843-5400), and **Yellow Cab** (301-645-4316) are all based in Waldorf.

MEDICAL EMERGENCY Civista Medical Hospital (301-609-4160), 701 East Charles Street, La Plata.

✷ To See

COLLEGES College of Southern Maryland (301-934-7828), 8730 Mitchell Road, La Plata. The college's **Fine Arts Center** has so many things going on that it has become the cultural hub of the area. The **Walter Grove II** and **Tony Hungerford Memorial Galleries** feature works by students and staff, and the theater offers musicals, dramas, dances, concerts, and lectures throughout much of the year.

HISTORIC HOMES & **Dr. Samuel A. Mudd House** (301-645-6970), Dr. Samuel Mudd Road (about 6 miles east of Waldorf via MD 5 and Poplar Hill–Beantown Road), Waldorf. Saturday and Sunday noon–4 and Wednesday 11–3, April through November. Small admission fee. Dr. Mudd became known to the world when he set the broken leg of John Wilkes Booth, Abraham Lincoln's assassin. This private home museum, which has been in the Mudd family since 1694, relates that story in a very personal way. Although some historians believe Mudd knew who Booth was, Mudd maintained his innocence throughout his 3½ years of imprisonment and unto his death.

There is a real sense of history here, as many items in the house are original. It is easy to imagine the events when you look at the couch Booth laid on, the room in which he was operated on, Mudd's medical instruments, and furniture Mudd made while in prison.

Port Tobacco

& **Historic Port Tobacco** (301-934-4313), Chapel Point Road (off MD 6). Saturday, Sunday, and Wednesday noon–4, April through October. Small admission fee. Just a short time after the first settlers arrived in the Maryland colony at St. Mary's City (see the introduction to "At the Mouth of the Potomac—St. Mary's City and Leonardtown"), Captain John Smith, founder of Jamestown, founded Port Tobacco. The town soon developed into the second largest port in the state but declined when the railroad arrived in the area in the 1870s.

Costumed docents lead guided tours of the Court House, providing background on the town and some of the sites still recognizable. Upstairs, the model of the town puts things into perspective.

& **Port Tobacco One-Room School House** (301-932-6064), 7215 Chapel Point Road. Saturday and Sunday noon–4, April through October; also Wednesday noon–4, July through August. Free. The school was built in 1876 to serve students in grades one through seven. The furnishings reflect its earliest days.

& **Thomas Stone National Historic Site** (301-392-1776), 6655 Rose Hill Road (between MD 6 and MD 225). Open daily 9–5 Memorial Day through Labor Day; Thursday through Sunday 9–5 the rest of the year. Free. Thomas Stone was a contributor to the Articles of Confederation and one of Maryland's four signers of the Declaration of Independence. Guided tours take you through the five-part mansion, constructed in the 1770s. The house was nearly destroyed by fire in 1977 but has been fully restored. The original kitchen survived, and some of the original furnishings are spread throughout the house.

A number of pleasant hiking trails wander through the property.

HISTORIC CHURCHES St. Mary's Catholic Church, Bryantown. The final resting place of Dr. Samuel Mudd (see *Historic Homes*).

Oldfields Chapel (301-934-1424), MD 231, Hughesville. The chapel and surrounding area were used as a campground by the British during the War of 1812. Two soldiers who died there are buried in the cemetery.

Christ Church (301-932-1051), 110 East Charles Street, La Plata. Replacing earlier church structures, this one was originally built in Port Tobacco in 1884. In 1904, it was dismantled and its numbered stones carried by oxcart to La Plata, where it was reassembled next to the courthouse.

St. Ignatius Church (301-934-8245), 8855 Chapel Point Road, Port Tobacco. Along with St. Ignatius Church in St. Mary's County (see *To See—Historic Churches* in "At the Mouth of the Potomac—St. Mary's City and Leonardtown"), this is the oldest Catholic parish in the country. Located on a small knoll overlooking the Port Tobacco River, it houses a Relic of the True Cross, brought by settlers across the Atlantic Ocean on the *Ark* and *Dove*.

* To Do

BICYCLING Less than 25 miles from the nation's capital, this region lures many bicyclists to its quiet country roads. The **Charles County Visitors Bureau** (see *Guidance*) can provide information on three of the most popular circuit rides.

One of the rides, the longest of the three at about 27 miles, is my favorite. It follows roadways close to the **Potomac River** and passes by several opportunities to get off the bike and take to the woods on hiking trails. Another, at 16.5 miles, encounters **Historic Port Tobacco** and the sites in downtown **La Plata**. The third one is about an hour's ride and skirts the eastern edge of **Zekiah Swamp**.

Mike's Bikes (301-870-6600; www.ridemikes.com), 2102 Crain Highway, and **Bike Doctor** (301-932-9980), 5051 Festival Way, both in Waldorf, can help you with repairs if you run into problems you can't fix yourself.

BOAT RENTALS See **Gilbert Run Park** and **Smallwood State Park** under *Green Space—Parks*.

BOWLING *♪* **AMC Lanes** (301-843-1494), 11920 Acton Lane, Waldorf. Automatic scoring and bumper bowling for the kids.

FISHING The **Potomac River** has earned a reputation as a world-class fishery, especially for largemouth bass and striped bass (known in Maryland and Virginia as rockfish). Although fishing is a year-round event in the area, spring and fall are the best times to cast for striped bass.

Also see **Myrtle Grove Wildlife Management Area** under *Hiking*.

GOLF **Swan Point Country and Yacht Club** (301-259-0047), 11550 Swan Point Boulevard, Issue. A semi-private waterfront community with an 18-hole course designed by Bob Cupp. Great views of the Potomac River as the course goes through marshes and woodlands.

White Plains Golf Course (301-645-1300; 301-843-2947), at the intersection of DeMarr Road and St. Charles Parkway (inside White Plains Regional Park), White Plains. The county-operated, tree-lined, 18-hole course is open daily.

HIKING

La Plata

Myrtle Grove Wildlife Management Area (301-743-5161), about 5 miles west of US 301 on MD 225. In an area of the state where large tracts of public land available for outdoor recreation are somewhat sparse, this 900-acre tract provides the opportunity to enjoy natural beauty away from the traffic, strip malls, liquor stores, and other modern-day distractions along US 301. The majority of the 5 miles or so of hiking opportunities follow the routes of service roadways, but there are also a few narrow pathways.

Once home to the Piscataway Indians, the terrain is that of a typical southern Maryland landscape, with gently rolling hills of fields and forest, and natural and created wetlands. Watch for signs of beaver, woodcock, quail, and turkey. You might want to consider bringing along tackle, as small Myrtle Grove Lake contains bluegill, pickerel, catfish, and largemouth bass.

Doncaster Forest (301-934-2282), 13 miles west of La Plata on MD 6. Hiking in this 1,400-acre forest is done on well-established, but sometimes unmaintained or unmarked, pathways most often used by hunters. Do not let that deter you, however. If you have a sense of adventure, you can take these routes, which add up to well over 10 miles, into forestlands and along some very pretty small streams.

Also see **Thomas Stone National Historic Site** under *To See—Historic Sites.*

KAYAKING AND CANOEING **Nanjemoy Creek** is a tidal waterway with high banks in some places that harbor nesting sites for bald eagles. In other spots, it passes through miles of scenic marshlands with great blue herons trolling for a meal. One put-in place is at the bridge over the creek on MD 6 near **Grayton;** another is the boat ramp at **Friendship Landing Park** (301-932-3470) off MD 425 between Ironsides and Graydon. The paddling is easy, the scenery great, and obstructions few.

SKATING ✔ **Skatepark** (301-645-1300), at the intersection of DeMarr Road and St. Charles Parkway (inside White Plains Regional Park), White Plains. Small fee. Designed by local skateboarders, in-line skaters, and bikers, the park has various-depth bowls, and lots of street elements such as rails, ledges, and banks.

✳ Green Space

BEACHES See **Purse State Park** under *Parks.*

PARKS
La Plata
Gilbert Run Park (301-932-1083), 1001 Radio Station Road (about 6 miles east of La Plata on MD 6). The 180-acre county-operated park offers fishing and boating (rentals in-season) on a 60-acre lake, picnic areas, a nature center, and about 4 miles of trails. Pick up a booklet at the office to learn about what you are seeing along the 1.5-mile self-guided nature route.

Marbury
Smallwood State Park (301-743-7613), 2750 Sweden Point Road.

SMALLWOOD RETREAT HOUSE IN SMALLWOOD STATE PARK

Open daily; $2 admission on weekends and holidays, May through September. Trails of about 4 miles in total length connect at several points to form a continuous loop and pass through hardwood forests and a number of spots of historical interest. The **Smallwood Retreat House** (open Sunday, May through September) is the restored 18th-century home of General William Smallwood, Revolutionary War figure and governor of Maryland. Nearby is a 19th-century tobacco barn.

Also in the park are boat rentals (in-season), a marina on Mattawoman Creek, and a picnic area. A small campground is usually open from April through October and has hookups, a central shower house, and a few small cabins for rent.

Purse State Park (contact is Smallwood State Park; see above), MD 224. Because it is so overused, I refrain from using the phrase "hidden gem." Until now, that is. There are no improvements here (although the state is talking about some), just a quarter-mile trail through the forest that delivers you onto an isolated Potomac River beach. Swim (no lifeguards), stroll, search for fossils and centuries'-old shark's teeth, or do whatever comes naturally. If you go during the week, it is a good possibility you may be the only person in the entire 90-acre park.

✳ Lodging

MOTELS AND HOTELS

Indian Head, 20640

☙ **Super 8** (301-753-8100; 1-800-8000), Indian Head Highway. Basic rooms and few amenities in the motel, but a low rate. Free continental breakfast. Pets permitted, but you must call the local number for permission. $55–75.

La Plata, 20646

☙ **Best Western** (301-934-4900), 6900 Crain Highway. Small pool and exercise room. Free continental breakfast. Small pets permitted with a deposit. $80–125.

Waldorf, 20603

& **Comfort Suites** (301-932-4400), 11765 Business Park Drive. All rooms are suites with irons and in-room coffee. Indoor pool. $79–129.

☙ **Days Inn** (301-932-9200), 11370 Days Court. In-room coffee and irons. Complimentary continental breakfast. Pets permitted. $75–155.

Holiday Inn (301-645-8200), 1 St. Patrick's Drive (adjacent to the mall). Exercise room, outdoor pool, coin laundry; irons and hair dryers in the rooms. $89–105.

Super 8 (301-932-8957), 3550 Crain Highway. Basic low-cost motel with basic rooms and some suites. Free continental breakfast, fitness room. $50–75.

ALONG THE BEACH IN PURSE STATE PARK

BED & BREAKFASTS Shady Oaks of Serenity (301-932-8864; 1-800-597-0924), 7490 Serenity Drive, Bryantown, 20617. Fresh flowers and fruit are placed in the one and only guest room (with its own bath and TV) in this modern Georgian Victorian home. The front porch and back deck overlook the property's 3 acres. $75.

Linden Farm B&B (301-934-9003), 8530 Mitchell Road, La Plata, 20646. Located on a 47-acre working horse farm, in which young horses are always in training, the 1783 house sits on a knoll with a commanding view. Stairs, banisters, fireplaces, floors, and even the door latches are original. The 90-foot porch overlooks the Port Tobacco valley, and miles of trails can take you into woodlands or down to Port Tobacco Creek.

Two of the guest rooms share a bath; the other has a private bath. Any one of them you choose will provide almost as a nice a view as that from the porch. Continental breakfast. $85–125.

CAMPING ⛺ Goose Bay Marina and Campground (301-934-3812), 9365 Goose Bay Lane, Welcome, 20693. The full-service marina, which sits on Goose Creek, an inlet of Port Tobacco River, also contains waterfront campsites, hookups, a swimming pool, and a camp store. Pets permitted.

Also see **Smallwood State Park** under *Green Space—Parks*.

✳ Where to Eat

DINING OUT 🦀 ✎ The Crossing at Casey Jones (301-932-6226), 417 East Charles Street, La Plata. Open for lunch 11–2:30, and dinner from 5

PM; closed Sunday. In an area awash with national chains, it is a pleasure to find this place. Chef Gary Fiek, a Culinary Institute of America graduate, ensures that everything is prepared fresh, seafood is purchased direct from suppliers, and meats are organic. His menu changes seasonally and in response to his travels throughout the world in search of new ideas.

Entrées have included mango-soy-glazed duck ($19.95), London broil topped with sherry-shiitake reduction ($18.95), and roasted salmon with sauce verge and lemon crème fraîche. I thought I had eaten crab in every form possible until chef Fiek served me his luscious crab and pesto dumplings with a hot tomato *coulis* accompanied by shrimp, pine nut salad, and toasted orzo ($21.95). All desserts are made on the premises with only natural ingredients. Entrées $15.95–29.95.

EATING OUT Tony's River House (301-274-4440), 7320 Benedict Avenue, Benedict. A local favorite that is situated almost on top of the Patuxent River. The knotty-pine walls give it a mid-1900s feel, and the menu features what could only be called Maryland/American fare. Crab-cakes (market price), pork chops ($14), and chicken Chesapeake ($17) are on always on the menu. There are also daily specials like the tasty snapper sandwich I had for lunch ($9). Most entrées $14–28.

✎ Robertson's Crab House (301-934-3300), 11455 Popes Creek Road, Newburg. Open daily for lunch and dinner. A family business for several decades, it sits on the very bank of the Potomac River. I really enjoyed the crabcakes ($19.95) here. Unlike many places that are afraid to add something, these had tiny bits of onion, celery, green pepper, and spices. A very nice change from the commonplace. Other seafood, meats, and entrées range from $5.95 to $22.95 and up to market price.

TAKEOUT **Randy's Ribs and BBQ** (301-274-3525), MD 5 and Gallant Green Road, Hughesville. Open daily from 10 AM. It is just a roadside stand, but anytime you drive by, there is a line of people waiting to place their order. Beef, pork, chicken, ribs, hot dogs, and a variety of platters are offered. The thing to get, however, is the BBQ sandwich. It may be the tastiest BBQ I've had in Maryland. By the way, do not make the mistake of ordering two—even if you are hungry. The size of one is almost large enough to feed two people. $3.95–10.95.

SNACKS AND GOODIES **Walls Bakery** (301-645-2833), 2805 Crain Highway (US 301), Waldorf. After rising early every morning since 1968 to create their baked goods, George and Christa Walls, to the dismay of many, retired in 2001. However, George found that he was still waking up at the same time each day, and felt he might as well continue baking.

We are the winners. The breads, cookies, and pies are always worth coming in for. However, it is the pastries, especially the giant éclairs, that cause people and tour-bus loads of passengers to detour miles out of their way. It is impossible to miss seeing this place as you drive along US 301—it is an old nightclub/casino shaped like a wigwam.

✴ Entertainment

FILM **Waldorf North** (301-843-9381), 3232 Crain Highway, Waldorf, shows first-run movies.

Also showing most films when they are newly released is the **St. Charles Town Cinema** (301-645-0818), 100 St. Charles Town Center.

NIGHTLIFE **Spurs** (301-843-9964; www.spursniteclub.com), US 301 and Mattawoman Beantown Road, Waldorf. There is a lot of movement happening on the 1,250-square-foot wooden floor, with line-dance, hand-dance, and West Coast swing lessons from Wednesday through Friday, and live entertainment on Friday and Saturday. Pool tables, dartboards, video games, and big crowds on the weekend.

THEATERS **Port Tobacco Players** (301-932-6819), 508 Charles Street, La Plata. Housed in an old 1940s movie theater. The Port Tobacco Players formed in 1947 as a way to raise funds for the restoration of Port Tobacco buildings. The troupe stages a half-dozen or so productions each year. Most presentations are American musicals and plays, and past ones have included *A Streetcar Named Desire, You Can't Take It with You,* and Rodgers and Hammerstein's *Cinderella.* Most shows take place on Friday and Saturday evening and Sunday afternoon.

Also see *To See—Colleges.*

✴ Selective Shopping

ANTIQUES **The Shops at Heritage Design** (301-932-7379), 3131 Old Washington Road, Waldorf. A multi-dealer shop.

Hughesville Bargain Barn (301-934-8580), Leonardtown Road, Hughesville. More than 140 shops crowd into two large barns selling antiques, collectibles, coins, and new and used furniture. Much of the stuff is what you would find in a flea market.

Nostalgia Nook (301-753-6940), 36 Mattingly Avenue, Indian Head. Open Saturday and Sunday 9–3. English period and country furniture, and glassware; will do appraisals.

ART GALLERIES Mattawoman Creek Art Center (301-743-5159), inside Smallwood State Park (see *Green Space—Parks*), Marbury. Friday through Sunday 11–4. Set off by itself with woodlands close by, and overlooking where Mattawoman Creek meets the Potomac River; I can't imagine a prettier setting for a gallery. The inside space is illuminated by natural light to accent the high quality of works by local, regional, national, and international artists. A real treasure in an out-of-the-way place.

Also see *To See—Colleges.*

BOOKSTORES Two national chains, **Borders** (301-705-6672), 3304-A Crain Highway, Waldorf, and **Waldenbooks** (301-645-0770), St. Charles Town Center, are located in shopping malls.

USED BOOKS Ellie's Paperback Shack (301-843-3676), 2700 Crain Highway, Waldorf. More than 30,000 used books for sale and trade.

FARMER'S MARKETS Indian Head Farmer's Market (301-743-5511), Mildred Rice Road. Produce arrives at the village green every Tuesday and Thursday from June through October and is available for purchase 9–1.

La Plata Farmer's Market (301-934-8345), corner of Charles Street and Washington Avenue. Produce and other items are displayed on stands in the courthouse parking lot on Wednesday 10–7 and Saturday from 8–3:30.

PICK-YOUR-OWN PRODUCE FARMS Hydromont Berry Farm (301-932-0872), 8020 Hawthorne Road, La Plata. Show up in May and pick all the strawberries you can right off the vine.

✳ Special Events

March: **Children's Spring Party and Easter Egg Hunt** (301-743-5574), Indian Head village green. Live entertainment, children's activities, and photos with the Easter Bunny.

April: **Annual Potomac River Clean Up** (301-932-3599). Volunteers beautify the Potomac and other area streams. **House and Garden Pilgrimage** (301-934-8819), various sites. Every third year, the local garden club sponsors a tour of the area's best homes and gardens. **Artfest** (301-932-5900), Indian Head. A day of music, visual arts, theater, and literature. Lots of entertainment.

May: **Charter Day Celebration** (301-6454-0558). Historic sites throughout the area provide free admission, costumed docent tours, and refreshments to mark the county's birthday.

May through September: **La Plata Summer Concert Series** (301-934-8421), La Plata Town Hall, La Plata.

A series of outdoor musical concerts presented each Friday evening 7–9.

June: **Annual Juried Art Show** (301-743-5159), Mattawoman Creek Art Center (see *Selective Shopping—Art Galleries*). Artists from Maryland, Virginia, and Washington, D.C., display juried works in a wide variety of media. **Cobb Island Day** (301-259-0160), Cobb Island Field. Crab races, corn-shucking contests, many kids' activities, crafts sales, and fire-engine and carriage rides.

August: **Durham Parish Festival** (301-743-7099), Christ Church, Nanjemoy. This event has taken place each year since 1847! Traditional southern Maryland ham and chicken dinner, children's games, lots of home-baked goodies, and crafts.

September: **Charles County Fair** (301-932-1234), fairgrounds, La Plata.

November: **Annual Holiday Art Show** (301-743-5159), Mattawoman Creek Art Center (see *Selective Shopping—Art Galleries*). Works by local member artists.

December: **Annual Holiday Festival and Craft Fair** (301-743-5574), Indian Head. Live entertainment, door prizes, crafts and children's crafts-making activities, a gingerbread-house contest, and an antique model-train display.

Frederick and the Catoctin Mountains Area

Frederick and the Catoctin Mountains

Waynesboro

PENNSYLVANIA

15

Sabillasville   Emmitsburg

National Shrine of Elizabeth Ann Seton

National Shrine
Grotto of Lourdes

CATOCTIN
MOUNTAIN
PARK

550   15

Roddy Road
Covered Bridge

194

77

Thurmont

76

CUNNINGHAM
FALLS STATE
PARK

Catoctin
Wildlife Preserve

77

Loy's Station
Covered Bridge

40

CITY OF
FREDERICK
MUNICIPAL
FOREST

Catoctin

Catoctin Iron Furnace

New Midway

17

Utica
Covered Bridge

Utica

Woodsboro

Appalachian Trail

GAMBRILL
STATE
PARK

Walkersville
Southern RR

194

550

70   Myersville

15

Walkersville

40

26

26

75

Middletown

Ceresville

GATHLAND
STATE
PARK

17

Frederick

New Market

Burkittsville

Monocacy
National Battlefield

Mount Airy

Jefferson

340   15

Ijamsville

70

Knoxville

Brunswick
RR Museum

Buckeystown

Urbana

80

Harpers Ferry
National
Historic Park

Brunswick

464   15

75

Claggetsville

Lilypons
Water Gardens

Damascus

28

85

Sugarloaf
Mountain

270

Tuscarora

Clarksburg

C&O Canal
National
Historic
Park

Dickerson

27

121

VIRGINIA

28

N

0 1 2 3 4 5   10
Miles

Potomac River

© The Countryman Press

FREDERICK AND THE CATOCTIN MOUNTAINS AREA

Up from the meadows rich with corn,
Clear in the cool September morn,
The clustered spires of Frederick stand,
Green-walled by the hills of Maryland.
—John Greenleaf Whittier, "The Ballad of Barbara Fritchie"

The words of Whittier's 1862 poem are just about as true today as they were then. There may be a fewer meadows of corn, but the clustered spires still point skyward, framed by lush, green hillsides.

It seems that cities are always discussing ways to attract people by saving their downtown areas and historic structures; Frederick has accomplished it. Other than Annapolis, which has done an admirable job of preserving its harbor area, Frederick is the most viable, vibrant, and historic-architecture-rich city in the state.

The Historical Society of Frederick County is housed in an 1820s Federal-style mansion; the Barbara Fritchie House—where the events Whittier wrote about occurred—is reconstructed with its original materials; and many of the Victorian town houses are still lived in by families and have not been turned into offices. Yet businesses thrive within the inner city without destroying it: With a minimum of changes, a complex of small shops in Everedy Square and Shab Row occupy what were once 18th- and 19th-century dwellings. Market Street and Patrick Street, the crossroads of the downtown area, are lined by renovated buildings with restaurants, antiques shops, and galleries that entice people to linger after normal business hours have expired.

The city's spirited arts and culture community has also fallen in line with protecting the old. The Delaplaine Visual Arts Education Center makes use of the renovated Mountain Mill, while the Weinberg Center for the Arts, where presentations of all forms are staged throughout the year, is in a lavish 1926 movie palace. And, of course, the steeples, spires, and towers of more than a dozen buildings provide the city with one of its most photographed scenes, its skyline.

Just northwest of Frederick are the Catoctin Mountains. The eastern rampart of the Blue Ridge Mountains, they stretch almost 40 miles from southern Pennsylvania, across Maryland, and into the northern portion of Virginia. Geologists believe the mountains once attained heights comparable to those of the Andes Mountains in South America, but the power of wind and water over the course of millions of years have eroded Catoctin into a much lower ridgeline. Today, the high point is only about 1,900 feet above sea level, while the lowest spot is a mere 500 feet. The mountain's numerous rock outcroppings are a bit more resistant to erosion, being composed of Catoctin greenstone that developed from lava flows 600 million years ago.

The mountain range's name is a derivation of *Kittocton*, from an Algonquian tribe that once lived near the Potomac River. Linguists believe the word translates to "land of the big mountain" or "land of the white-tailed deer." Native Americans and colonial hunters traipsed through the folded landscape in search of abundant wildlife.

Several parks in the Catoctin Mountains, and on South Mountain a bit farther to the west (see "The Great Valley and Blue Ridge Region" in part 6, "The Mountains of Western Maryland"), along with the Chesapeake & Ohio (C&O) Canal along the southern region, have made this area a mecca for hikers, bikers, kayakers, canoeists, anglers, and others looking to experience and play in the natural world.

THE MORTUARY CHAPEL AT THE NATIONAL SHRINE OF SAINT ELIZABETH ANN SETON IN EMMITSBURG

COMMUNITIES Emmitsburg has been attracting religious pilgrims ever since Father John Dubois founded Mount St. Mary's College, a Catholic 4-year college and seminary, in the early 1800s. One of those attracted was Elizabeth Ann Seton, who began the country's first parochial school in Baltimore before moving to Emmitsburg and establishing the Sisters of Mercy. About 150 years after her death, she was canonized as a saint, the first native-born American woman to be so recognized. A nearby spot on the side of the Catoctin Mountains, now the National Shrine Grotto of Lourdes, was one of her favorite places of meditation.

True to the translation of its name, **Thurmont** is the "Gateway to the

Mountains." Nestled on the edge of the Monocacy Valley at the base of the
Catoctin Mountains, it began attracting hunters, anglers, and other outdoor
types when the railroad arrived in the 1870s. The establishment of Catoctin
Mountain Park and Cunningham Falls State Parks in the mid-1900s further
enhanced its sylvan appeal. The television age has brought the little town worldwide fame, as it is used as a base camp by news agencies and journalists to keep
track of events taking place in nearby Camp David. It is quite common to turn
on the evening news and to see Cozy Country Inn or Mountain Gate Restaurant
used as a reporter's backdrop.

During one of his many trips to the area, George Washington declared **Middletown** to be "one of the prettiest valleys I've ever seen." The town and surrounding areas are experiencing a building explosion as more and more housing
developments take over former farmlands.

Despite interstates and malls growing up a few miles away, **Buckeystown** has
managed to retain the look and feel of a Victorian village. Its main street, Buckeystown Pike (MD 85), remains a two-lane roadway passing by many homes and
structures from the late 1800s. The town's few commercial enterprises include
the upscale Inn at Buckeystown and the Catoctin Inn.

GUIDANCE The **Tourism Council of Frederick County, Frederick Visitor
Center** (301-228-2888; 1-800-999-3613; www.visitfrederick.org), 19 East
Church Street, Frederick, 21701, is located in one of the city's historic town
houses. Signs point the way from every major road access into town.

Maryland state welcome centers, which can provide local and statewide
information, are located at mile marker 39 on I-70 near Myersville. The phone
number for the center for eastbound traffic is 301-293-2526; the westbound traffic center may be reached at 301-293-4161.

Another **state welcome center** (301-447-2553) is located 1 mile south of the
Pennsylvania border on US 15 near Emmitsburg.

GETTING THERE *By car:* All roads may lead to Rome, but almost as many
seem to converge on Frederick and this area of Maryland. **I-70** comes from
Baltimore in the east and Hagerstown in the west. **I-270** is the way most people drive here from the Washington, D.C., area. **US 15** arrives from Pennsylvania to the north, while **US 340** crosses the Potomac River from Virginia and
West Virginia.

By air: **Dulles International Airport** (703-572-2700) in northern Virginia is
the closest air facility to the area, especially if you are driving a rental car and
can cross the Potomac River at either Point of Rocks on US 15, Brunswick on
VA 287, or Harpers Ferry on US 340. Flying into **Ronald Reagan Washington
National Airport** (703-417-8000) enables you to take the MARC commuter
train (see *By rail*) into the area. Located a little more than an hour away,
between Baltimore and Washington, D.C., is the **Baltimore/Washington
International Airport** (1-800-I-FLY-BWI).

By bus: **Greyhound** (1-800-229-9424) has a terminal on East All Saints Street

Frederick

Frederick Academy of Visitation Convent ★

14TH ST.

15

7TH STREET

MOLTER AVENUE

★ Winchester Hall

ROSEMONT AVENUE

WEST SECOND STREET

WEST SECOND STREET

COURT STREET

NORTH MARKET STREET

MAXWELL AVENUE

CHAPEL ALLEY

5TH STREET

4TH STREET

3RD STREET

COLLEGE AVENUE

BENTZ STREET

Visitors Center

2ND STREET

FLEMING

Evangelical Reformed Church ?

Evangelical Lutheran Church

CHURCH ST. ★

★ Historical Society & Museum ★

EAST ST.

Carriage House & Slave Quarters of the Ross/Mathias Mansions

CARROLL PARKWAY

Trinity Chapel ★

EAST PATRICK STREET

★ Frederick Presbyterian Church

Dr. John Tyler's Home ★

City Hall & ★ Courthouse Square ALL SAINTS ST.

★ National Museum of Civil War Medicine

★ Community Mural Bridge

William Tyler Page Birthplace

WEST PATRICK STREET

CATOCTIN AVE.

JEFFERSON STREET

CARROLL STREET

WISNER ST.

FRANKLIN ST.

SOUTH STREET

CENTER STREET

MADISON ST.

BROADWAY ST.

SOUTH MARKET STREET

CLARK PL.

MT. OLIVET

N

© The Countryman Press

(301-663-3311). Unlike many bus terminals, it is not located in some out-of-the-way, decaying part of town but is just a block or two from many of downtown's best attractions and restaurants.

By rail: **MARC** (1-800-325-RAIL) has a commuter train that can bring you to a late-1800s Victorian station in Point of Rocks, to downtown Frederick, or to MD 355 close to many of the city's motels.

GETTING AROUND *By car:* The main roadways mentioned in *Getting There* will get you around quickly—except in rush hours—but use the smaller roads, such as **MD 77** and **MD 194** in the north or **MD 85** and **MD 17,** to take you on the more scenic routes.

By bus: The local bus system, **TransIT** (301-694-2065), operates throughout Frederick and its immediate vicinity. Routes also go to Thurmont, Emmitsburg, Brunswick, and Jefferson.

PARKING In Frederick, parking meters are in from 9–5 Monday through Saturday. I find the municipal parking decks, especially the one at 44 East Patrick Street, to be convenient for downtown explorations without running back to feed the 2-hour-limit meters. "Park and Shop" merchants will stamp your ticket to give you a discount. Stop by the Frederick Visitor Center (see *Guidance*) to have your parking ticket validated for 2 free hours in the Church Street parking deck.

PUBLIC REST ROOMS An information station and public rest rooms can be found next to Arlene's Antiques at 41 West Main Street in New Market.

MEDICAL EMERGENCY Frederick Memorial Hospital (301-698-3300), 200 West 7th Street, Frederick.

✳ To See

COVERED BRIDGES All three of the area's remaining covered bridges are located north of Frederick:

Situated off Old Frederick Road near Utica, the 110-foot, Burr Arch–design **Utica Covered Bridge** was originally constructed in 1850 over the Monocacy River. It was washed away in 1889, and local citizens salvaged its remains to reconstruct it over Fishing Creek in 1889.

Just south of the intersection of Old Frederick Road and MD 77 east of Thurmont is the **Loy's Station Covered Bridge,** built in the mid-1800s. Spanning Owen's Creek, the 90-foot bridge retains its original timbers. A small park with picnic tables and a playground enable you to enjoy the setting while giving the kids something to do.

Less than 2 miles north of Thurmont on Roddy Road (off US 15), 40-foot **Roddy Road Covered Bridge** was built in 1856. A small park is adjacent to the single-span Kingpost-design bridge.

MUSEUMS

Brunswick
✎ **Brunswick Railroad Museum** (301-834-7100; www.brunswickmuseum.org), 40 West Potomac Street. Friday through Sunday. Small admission fee. Railroad equipment, photographs, furnishings, toys, and other items tell of the town's early history. Of special interest to rail fans (and children) is the HO-model layout of the B&O line from Washington, D.C., to Brunswick. In the same building is the **C&O Canal Information Center** (see *To Do—Biking*).

Frederick
Historical Society of Frederick County (301-663-1188; www.fwp.net/hsfc), 24 East Church Street. Open daily. Small admission fee. Guided tours take you through an 1820s Federal-style mansion furnished with the society's collection of

historic memorabilia, such as Barbara Fritchie items (see *Historic Homes*), furnishings of the early 1800s, and a superior collection of tall-case clocks.

& **National Museum of Civil War Medicine** (301-695-1864; www.CivilWarMed.org), 48 East Patrick Street. Open daily. Adults $6.50; seniors $6; children older than 10 are $4.50; children 9 and younger are free. Some of the most realistic life-sized dioramas I've seen tell of the care and healing efforts during the Civil War. More than this, though, the reason to visit is the unfamiliar facts brought to light. Did you know: More than 2,000 women, disguised as men, served as soldiers? About 3,000 horses and mules perished during the Battle of Antietam? Most operations were done under anesthesia and not by "biting the bullet," as portrayed by Hollywood? Nearly two-thirds of the 62,000 soldiers who died did so from disease and not battle injuries?

Interesting items include the only surviving field stretcher (and a photo of it in use during the war) and a set of war letters from Union private P. Bradford.

HISTORIC CIVIL WAR DRIVING TOUR A brochure available from the **Tourism Council of Frederick County, Frederick Visitor Center** (see *Guidance*), gives directions to, and details of, various sites of significance to the Confederacy's 1862 Maryland Campaign. Battles occurred at Monocacy, Antietam, and South Mountain. Another pamphlet from the visitors center, or the **Central Maryland Heritage League** (301-371-7090), P.O. Box 721, Middletown, 21769, provides additional insight into the Battle of South Mountain. By the way, the drive is just as scenic as it is historic.

HISTORIC HOMES **Barbara Fritchie House and Museum** (301-698-0630), 154 West Patrick Street, Frederick. Monday, and Thursday through Sunday, April through September; Saturday and Sunday, October through November. Small admission fee.

MONOCACY NATIONAL BATTLEFIELD

CATOCTIN IRON FURNACE IN THURMONT

The story goes that 95-year-old Barbara Fritchie defiantly waved the Union flag from her window as Confederate general Stonewall Jackson's troops marched through town. John Greenleaf Whittier made her famous in his poem "The Ballad of Barbara Fritchie": "Shoot if you must, this old gray head, / But spare your country's flag, she said."

Did the event really happen? Who knows; does it really matter? It is a great piece of Americana, and the museum (reconstructed out of materials from the original house) is furnished with items from the Fritchie family.

Schifferstadt (301-663-3885), 1110 Rosemont Avenue, Frederick. Wednesday through Sunday, April through mid-December. Small admission fee. Built in 1756, the German Colonial home retains much of its original hardware and exposed oak beams. A period garden compliments the scene.

HISTORIC SITES & **Monocacy National Battlefield** (301-662-3515; www.nps.gov/mono/mo_visit.htm), 4801 Urbana Pike, Frederick. Open daily April through October; Wednesday through Sunday, November through March. Free. A small visitors center provides perspective on the site of the last Southern push into Union territory. Although Confederate general Jubal Early's troops won the battle on July 9, 1864, they were delayed long enough that Federal reinforcements arrived to block the way to Washington, D.C.

Ranger-conducted programs and tours are presented during the summer months, while an available pamphlet keyed to numbered sites along a driving-tour route lets you experience the battlefield any time of year. The **Worthington Farm Trail** consists of two connecting loops. One takes you onto **Brooks Hill** for a lesson in forest succession; the other is through bottomland to the site of the **Washington–McKinney Ford** on the Monocacy River. Each loop is about 2 miles in length.

Catoctin Iron Furnace, on MD 806 (off US 15), Thurmont. Administered by Cunningham Falls State Park (see *Green Space—Parks*). Open daily from 8 AM to sunset. Free. The iron furnace was in use from 1776 to 1903, making it one of the state's longest-running such enterprises. It has only been about a century since it ceased operating, so its ruins are in fairly good shape; even portions of the ironmaster's home are identifiable.

The furnace is also accessible via a footpath from the state park.

HISTORIC CHURCHES

Frederick

The spires and steeples of Frederick have given the town much of its identity and have been immortalized and praised in words by luminaries such as Dr. Oliver Wendell Holmes and John Greenleaf Whittier. Among the many are:

Trinity Chapel, 10 West Church Street. Its Colonial steeple was designed by Stephen Steiner and constructed in 1807, making it Frederick's oldest spire. The 10-bell chimes are still used by the tower's clock.

Evangelical Lutheran Church, 35 East Church Street. The present German Gothic structure was built in 1854, and its twin spires were among those Whittier referred to when he wrote the 1862 Barbara Fritchie poem that opens this chapter in 1862. The west tower contains a bell that was cast in England in 1771.

Evangelical Reformed Church, 15 West Church Street. The church's two open towers, built in 1848, add to the city's skyline.

Also see **National Shrine Grotto of Lourdes** and **National Shrine of Saint Elizabeth Ann Seton** under *Other Sites.*

MEMORIALS ♿ National Fallen Firefighters Memorial Park (301-447-1365;

AT THE NATIONAL SHRINE GROTTO OF LOURDES

www.firehero.org), 1682 South Seton Avenue, Emmitsburg. Located on the Federal Training Center grounds, the monument has certainly taken on more meaning and significance since the events of September 11, 2001.

OTHER SITES

Buckeystown

Lilypons Water Gardens (301-874-5133; 1-800-999-5459; www.lilypons.com), 6800 Lilypons Road. Open daily March through September; Monday through Saturday, October through February. Looking at it one way, this is just a commercial aquatic plant nursery that has been in operation since 1917. It can also be a nice outdoor experience, however. You are permitted to follow pathways beside acres of water gardens to enjoy the flowers, cattails, and resident and visiting frogs, dragonflies, red-winged blackbirds, geese, and herons. Be aware there is no shade, and walking during hot weather can be uncomfortable.

By the way, I lost my car key on one of my outings here. Please let me know if you find it. Thanks.

Emmitsburg

& **National Shrine Grotto of Lourdes** (301-447-5318; www.msmary.edu/grotto), 16300 Old Emmitsburg Road. Open daily. Free. A short, paved, rhododendron-lined pathway leads to the Western Hemisphere's oldest replica of the Grottos of Lourdes. The meditative, scenic beauty of the place makes a visit worthwhile, even if you happen to have no interest in the shrine, the artistic quality of the copper-relief Stations of the Cross, or mosaic scenes of the Mysteries of the Rosary along the pathway.

& **National Shrine of Saint Elizabeth Ann Seton** (301-447-6606; www.setonshrine.org), 333 South Seton Avenue. Open daily, except Monday, from November through April 1. Free admission. In 1975, Elizabeth Ann Seton was the first native-born American woman to be canonized a saint. Her relics lie in the basilica built in her honor in the 1990s. The adjoining museum traces her early life, the founding of the Sisters of Charity of St. Joseph's, and the establishment of the country's fist parochial school. The architecture and interior of the basilica alone are worth a stop.

Frederick

The **Community Bridge Mural,** on South Carroll Street between East Patrick and East All Saints Streets. If there is a more impressive work of public art in Maryland, I have yet to see it. Muralist William M. Cochran spent 5 years transforming what had been a plain concrete bridge. From a distance, it now appears as an old, ivy-covered stone bridge. Even when you're standing right next to it, your eyes are convinced that the stones and other items are truly three-dimensional. Cochran is also the painter of the equally impressive, and somehow calming, *Angels in Architecture* murals you find in the downtown district. More information about him, his work, and the bridge may be obtained from the Frederick Visitor Center (see *Guidance*).

Mount Olivet Cemetery (301-662-1164), 515 South Market Street. The final resting place for Francis Scott Key, Barbara Fritchie (see *To See—Historic*

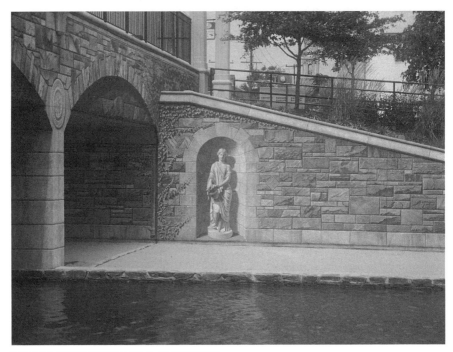

THE COMMUNITY BRIDGE MURAL IN FREDERICK

Homes), Thomas Johnson (see Children's Museum of Rose Hill Manor Park under *To Do—Family Activities*), and more than 800 Union and Confederate soldiers.

ZOOS

Thurmont

🦎 ♿ **Catoctin Wildlife Preserve and Zoo** (301-271-3180; www.cwpzoo.com), 13019 Catoctin Furnace Road (off US 15). Open daily April through October, weekends in March and November. Adults $9.95; children 2–12 are $6.95. The 30-acre zoo began as a small snake farm in 1933. Family owned since 1966, it now includes more than 300 animals from Australia and North and South America. Displays and enclosures are arranged to allow to you get as close as possible and still be safe.

✳ To Do

BICYCLING C&O Canal National Historical Park (see the sidebar on page 301 in "Silver Spring, Bethesda, Rockville, and Gaithersburg" in part 3, "Capital Region," for background history and information on the canal). Approximately 20 miles of the Chesapeake & Ohio Canal pass through this area, and some of the highlights are the impressive **Monocacy River Aqueduct,** the **Victorian Railroad Station** at Point of Rocks, and access to the **Railroad Museum** in the town of Brunswick.

Three designated campsites, with vault toilets and water (in-season), are available on a first-come, first-served basis.

There are also three public ramps from which you can launch a boat into the Potomac River. The **C&O Canal Visitor Center** in Brunswick (301-582-0813), 40 West Potomac Street, is located within the Brunswick Railroad Museum (see *To See—Museums*).

Also see **The Catoctin Trail** under *Hiking*, and **Gambrill State Park** under *Green Space—Parks*.

BIRDING See the sidebar on birding, page 405, in "The Great Valley and Blue Ridge Region" in part 6, "The Mountains of Western Maryland."

BREWERY TOUR Frederick Brewing Company (301-694-7899; 1-888-258-7434; www.fredbrew.com), 4607 Wedgewood Boulevard, Frederick. The brewer of Wild Goose, Blue Ridge, and Brimstone beer offers free tours and tastings on Saturday and Sunday at 1:30 PM.

FAMILY ACTIVITIES ✔ **The Children's Museum of Rose Hill Manor Park** (301-694-1650), 1611 North Market Street, Frederick. Open daily, April through October, weekends only in November. Costumed docents lead tours through the 1790s Georgian Colonial mansion of Thomas Johnson, Maryland's first governor. Hands-on exhibits invite children to help make a quilt or prepare beaten biscuits. Historic displays— and outbuildings such as the blacksmith shop, icehouse, and log cabin—help young ones gain an understanding of colonial life.

Also see *To See—Zoos,* and **Candlelight Ghost Tours** under *Walking Tours.*

FISHING See **Gambrill State Park**

and **Cunningham Falls State Park** under *Green Space—Parks.*

GOLF Clustered Spires (301-624-1295), 8415 Gas House Pike, Frederick. Open all year. The municipally owned course was designed by Ault-Clark and built in 1991. Look for water hazards on about half of the holes and heavily mounded fairways.

Whiskey Creek (301-694-2900; www.whiskeycreekgolf.com), 4804 Whiskey Court, Ijamsville. A dramatic course with 100-foot drops on some holes. Fees hover around $100 for weekend play.

& **Musket Ridge** (301-293-9930), 3555 Brethren Church Road, Myersville. The 150-acre course occupies the highest northern elevation in the Middletown Valley.

Maple Run (301-271-7870), 13610 Moser Road, Thurmont. The front nine of this family-owned course are in the open, with views of the Catoctin Mountains. The back nine are tree-lined, requiring shot-making accuracy.

& **Worthington Manor** (301-874-5400; www.worthingtonmanor.com), 8329 Fingerboard Road, Urbana. The 7,000-yard, daily-fee course has been the site of U.S. Open and U.S. Amateur Qualifiers. An Ault-Clark Signature Course, it sits in the shadow of Sugarloaf Mountain.

Glade Valley (301-898-5773), 10502 Glade Road, Walkersville. Gently rolling terrain, with views of the Catoctin Mountains, harbors the holes, which have numerous tricky sand traps.

MINIATURE GOLF ✔ & **Frederick Putt Putt** (301-694-0020; www.frederickputtputt.com), 192 Thomas Johnson Drive, Frederick. You can occupy the kids, and yourself, with two 18-hole courses, batting cages, and an arcade.

HIKING The Catoctin Trail. Public lands occupy much of the Catoctin Mountains northwest of Frederick, and in the late 1900s volunteers from the **Potomac Appalachian Trail Club** (703-242-0965), 118 Park Street Southeast, Vienna, VA 22180, built several miles of pathways to create the 26-mile Catoctin Trail. There are a few road crossings, but for the most part it provides a great sense of isolation. A series of extraordinary views and the opportunity to walk by **Cunningham Falls** (see Cunningham Falls State Park under *Green Space—Parks*) are other reasons to walk the trail. Backcountry camping is not permitted, but you can stay in either of Cunningham Falls State Park's campgrounds (see *Lodging—Camping*).

The trail begins in **Gambrill State Park** (see *Green Space—Parks*), where it soon rises to the ridgeline. Weaving around streams in the **City of Frederick Municipal Forest** (whose trails are also popular with mountain bikers), it enters Cunningham Falls State Park before coming to an end in **Catoctin Mountain Park** (see sidebar on page 383). *50 Hikes in Maryland* (Backcountry Guides) gives a detailed description of the entire route.

Sugarloaf Mountain (301-874-2024), 7901 Comus Road (off MD 109), Dickerson. Open sunrise to sunset. No fee. Sugarloaf Mountain is such a significant feature on the rolling lands of Maryland's piedmont that it is easily visible for miles

around. A *monadnock*—a residual hill or mountain that stands alone above a surrounding peneplain—Sugarloaf rises more than 800 feet above the farmland below. Its upper layer is composed primarily of quartzite, an extremely erosion-resistant material that was formed by compression about 500 million years ago. In contrast, the piedmont around it is believed to be mostly metamorphic rock, much more susceptible to the erosive effects of wind and water.

A nonprofit organization, Stronghold, Incorporated, has established a network of more than 13 miles on the mountain, with a roadway leading almost to the top. The quarter-mile **A. M. Thomas Trail** will take you to the summit for spectacular views of the lands to the south and west. The **Northern Peak Trail** leads to other vistas, while other trails wander around the mountainside and onto valley floors. Do not miss coming here.

&. **The Trail House** (301-694-8448), 17 South Market Street, Frederick. Thursday through Sunday. An outfitter for hiking, backpacking, cross-country skiing, and rock climbing. Also has an extensive offering of books on these activities and where to do them in the local area.

Also see *Green Space—Parks* and the sidebar on **Catoctin Mountain Park** on page 383. In addition, you'll find more hiking information under *To Do—Hiking* and in the Appalachian Trail sidebar on page 406 in "The Great Valley and Blue Ridge Region" in part 6, "The Mountains of Western Maryland."

KAYAKING AND CANOEING River

and Trail Outfitters (301-695-5177; 1-888-I-GO-PLAY; www.rivertrail. com), 604 Valley Road (off US 340), Knoxville. One of the most complete outfitters in the state, River and Trail can rent or sell you all the equipment you need to go kayaking, canoeing, rafting, tubing, biking, hiking and backpacking, and cross-country skiing. Better yet, take one of their guided trips and not only learn how to do the activity safely, but also become informed about the natural and human history of the areas you pass through.

Also see *Bicycling*.

TRAIN EXCURSIONS Walkersville Southern Railroad (301-898-0899; 1-877-363-9777; www.wsrr.org), 34 West Pennsylvania Avenue, Walkersville. The 1-hour, 15-minute excursions depart Saturday and Sunday at 11 AM, 1 PM, and 3 PM from May through October. Adults $7; children 3–12 are $3.50. Passing through the woodlands and farms north of Frederick, the train makes use of a route laid out just a few years after the Civil War. A highlight is the crossing of the reconstructed bridge over the Monocacy River.

WALKING TOURS

Frederick
Guided Walking Tours of Historic Frederick (301-228-2888; 301-845-7001). Tours originate at the Frederick Visitor Center (see *Guidance*) and begin 1:30 on Saturday and Sunday from April through December. Small tour fee. Certified guides lead the walks to learn of the city's architecture, history, and stories. If your guide neglects to tell you, ask what happened to the state representatives

who came to Frederick to discuss secession.

☙ **Candlelight Ghost Tours** (301-845-7001) depart from Brewer's Alley Restaurant at 124 North Market Street. Call for days and times. Adults $7; children 6–12 are $4. Period-costumed tour guides take you through dark streets and alleyways to relate paranormal happenings and stories based on historic fact. A fun way to spend 90 minutes of your evening.

✳ Green Space

PARKS

Frederick
Baker Park, Carroll Parkway and 2nd Street. The attractive 44-acre park, with Carroll Creek flowing along its southern edge, has a public swimming pool, tennis courts, and playgrounds to provide a respite from downtown noise and traffic. Also the site of many special events and outdoor concerts.

Gambrill State Park (301-271-7574), 8602 Gambrill Park Road. The park is a gift that a group of conservationists gave to themselves and other citizens of Maryland. After using private funds to purchase land around High Knob, the group donated the tract to the city of Frederick as a municipal park. In 1934, the city turned the 1,137 acres over to the state to develop as part of the state-park system.

Developed areas include picnic facilities, a campground with modern rest rooms and hot showers (see *Lodging—Camping*), a nature center, a ridgeline roadway with designated overlooks, and a small pond with largemouth bass, bluegills, and channel catfish. Nature walks and campfire programs are held throughout the summer season.

Encircling the top of the mountain is a trail system of about 10 miles that takes you through a predominantly oak and hickory forest, and out to a couple of Olympian views of the Monocacy Valley. Most of the pathways are also open to mountain biking.

Thurmont
Cunningham Falls State Park
(301-271-7574), 14039 Catoctin Hollow Road. There always seems to be confusion and misinformation when it comes to the height of a waterfall. A state brochure describes Cunningham Falls as a "78-foot cascading waterfall" and the highest in the state. Yet other official sources proclaim the "sparkling water tumbling from a 51-foot ledge" of Muddy Creek Falls in western Maryland to be "Maryland's highest waterfall."

For the most part, these incongruities don't matter to those who enjoy waterfalls, and you can find the narrow grotto that Cunningham Falls flows through in the northwestern corner of the park's 5,000 acres. The **Lower Trail** is the shortest and easiest pathway to it. Other trails wander onto the ridgelines and connect with those in **Catoctin Mountain Park** (see the sidebar opposite). **Hunting Creek Lake** has swimming and boating (paddleboat and rowboat rentals during the summer), and fishing in **Big Hunting** and **Little Hunting Creeks** is permitted with artificial flies and a catch-and-return trout policy. Anglers can also fish for bass, sunfish, catfish, crappie, and bluegills in the lake.

Also see *To Do—Hiking* in "The Great Valley and Blue Ridge Region" in part 6, The Mountains of Western Maryland."

CUNNINGHAM FALLS STATE PARK

Catoctin Mountain Park (301-663-9388; www.nps.gov/cato), 6602 Foxville Road, Thurmont. The federal government purchased land for Catoctin Mountain Park to demonstrate how worn-out lands could be rehabilitated. Earlier owners had clear-cut the forest or employed unsound farming practices. In 1954, 5,000 acres were deeded to Cunningham Falls State Park, while Catoctin Mountain Park retained 5,770 acres.

These lands have grown back to an eastern climax forest, much as they were in the 1700s. Barred owls, pileated woodpeckers, red-tailed hawks, and scores of other animals live in, or pass through, the park's woodlands. Close to 100 species of wildflowers, such as bloodroot, spring beauty, Dutchman's breeches, and nodding trillium, rise from the soil.

Catoctin Mountain Park has a visitors center, picnic areas, a campground (see *Lodging—Camping*), rental cabins, and a scenic drive with viewpoints. Well hidden from view, the U.S. presidential retreat, **Camp David,** is within the park. **Big Hunting Creek,** along MD 77, is known to anglers for the quality of its trout fishing, and the park has some of the most diverse interpretive offerings I have come across. Programs include cross-country skiing seminars, wildflower walks, and evening programs.

Approximately 15 miles of trail, including the northern portion of the **Catoctin Trail** (see *To Do—Hiking*), reach into every corner. My favorite outings are the 2.2-mile **Chimney Rock Trail,** from which there is an impressive view of the Monocacy Valley, and the short walk to the **Blue Ridge Summit Overlook** with views northward into Pennsylvania.

✳ Lodging
MOTELS AND HOTELS
Frederick, 21703
⟐ **Courtyard by Marriott** (301-631-9030; 1-800-321-2211; www.courtyard.com/wasfd), 5225 Westview Drive. May be reached from I-270 Exit 31B or I-70 Exit 54. Listed for its ease of access and location close to many attractions in and around Frederick. Many amenities to attract business travelers: work desk and chair, telephones with ports, in-room iron and coffee. Indoor pool and exercise room. $95–175.

Thurmont, 21788
⟐ **Cozy Country Inn** (301-271-4301; www.cozyvillage.com), 103 Frederick Road (MD 806). The inn is best known as the place the national and international press, as well as many dignitaries, stay while events take place at nearby Camp David in Catoctin Mountain Park (see the sidebar on page 383). There are the traditional motel rooms and cottages, but the standouts are the upscale rooms decorated to commemorate the styles of various past presidents.

The Carter Room reflects his penchant for hunting and fishing, the Eisenhower Room is decorated in Mamie's favorite colors, the Roosevelt Room has a bed similar to the one he was born in, and the Kennedy Room has the famous rocker. Other "presidential" rooms are similarly furnished; all are equipped with nice amenities. A bountiful continental breakfast is included. $60–140. (Also see **Cozy Restaurant** under *Eating Out*.)

Super 8 (301-271-7888; 1-877-678-9330), 300 Tippin Drive. The motel's amenities are few, but its proximity to Catoctin Mountain Park and Cunningham Falls State Park is the reason to stay. $59–89.

INNS Catoctin Inn and Conference Center (301-874-5555; 1-800-730-5550; www.catoctininn.com), 3619 Buckeystown Pike, Buckeystown, 21717. The inn has an accommodation for just about any type of traveler. If you enjoy the B&B atmosphere, stay in the 1780 manor house, where each antiques-filled room has its own character. The modern, motel-like rooms in the old stablehand quarters appeal to business travelers or to those who value their anonymity. The Smoke House, Summer Cottage, and Bucky's Cottage (with two-person whirlpool bath) ensure privacy for the romantically inclined. Breakfast is included with all rooms. $95–150.

Turning Point Inn (301-831-8233; www.turnigpointinn.com), 3406 Urbana Pike (at the intersection of MD 80 and MD 355 in Urbana), Frederick, 21704. The 1910 Edwardian home offers spacious rooms and cottages, all with private bath. Luxurious accommodations are one reason to stay. Another is the chance to dine in the award-winning restaurant (see *Dining Out*). Although it has the feel of being in the country, the inn is almost next door to a major upscale shopping mall. $125–150.

BED & BREAKFASTS
Buckeystown, 21717
The Inn at Buckeystown (301-874-5755; 1-800-272-1190; www.innat-buckeystown.com), 3521 Buckeystown Pike. Host Janet Wells has filled the 1897 Victorian mansion with period pieces to complement the three working fireplaces, grand chandeliers, and columned front porch. Everything speaks of the elegance and charm of the inn's earliest days.

Some of the rooms and suites have private baths; others share a bath. One of the most compelling reasons to stay here is to partake in one of the inn's prix fixe dinners (see *Dining Out*). The B&B rate, which includes breakfast, ranges $110–190. Rates with dinner for two included range $200–275.

Frederick, 21701
McCleery's Flat (301-620-2433; 1-800-774-7926; www.fwp.net/mc-cleerysflat), 121 East Patrick Street. The 1876 Empire-style town house is furnished with period antiques and reproductions. The three rooms and two suites have private baths. I stayed in the Franklin Room because I like the blue-and-white porcelain collection and large library, and the way the two brick fireplace flues come together to form an arch over the rice bed's canopy. The Grand Suite overlooks the backyard garden; the Secret Chamber was discovered during renovations. Host Jutta Terrell's breakfasts are what bring many guests for return visits. $110–135.

&. **Tyler Spite House** (301-831-4455), 112 West Church Street. Bill and Andrea Myer have filled their 1814 Federal-style home with historically significant antiques. The Thomas

Johnson room has his shaving mirror, and the chest of John Hanson (elected president by the Continental Congress in 1781) is in the room bearing his name. The parlor piano belonged to the Francis Scott Key family, and the Barbara Fritchie (see *To See— Historic Homes*) Room has her spinning wheel. Amazingly, the house also contains the desk on which Mac-Arthur signed the peace treaty in the Philippines. $125–175.

Hill House (301-682-4111), 12 West Third Street. Within Frederick's historic downtown area, Taylor and Damian Branson offer four guest rooms, each with private bath. The 1870 three-story Victorian town house is filled with original artwork and many heirloom documents, pieces of furniture, and other items. I enjoy staying in the Steeple Suite on the third floor, where small windows overlook the city's spires and spur thoughts of Whittier's Barbara Fritchie poem (see this chapter's introduction). Damian's years of catering and gourmet cooking are evident in the breakfast she will serve to you. $105–150.

HOSTEL American Youth Hostel (301-834-7652), 19123 Sandy Hook Road, Knoxville. The hostel is located along the **C&O Canal** and the **Appalachian Trail,** which means it is a place to meet some interesting travelers. You do not have to be a member of AYH or international hosteling organizations to stay. There are a couple of private rooms, but, for economy and companionship, most people stay in the bunk room, where you supply your own sleeping bag or linens. As with all such hostels, it is closed to patrons 9 AM–6 PM. $15–20.

VACATION RENTALS ❦ **Above All Else @ Windsong** (301-831-5083; www.windsongarabians.com), 1313A Old Annapolis Road, Mount Airy, 21771. The vacation home, with four bedrooms and three baths—and a corral so that you can bring your own horses—sits in a private corner of a large operating horse farm. $200 per couple; $75 each additional person. If you have a group and are staying for a week, the $1,000 charge for up to eight people is a real deal.

CAMPING

Brunswick, 21706
❦ **Brunswick Family Campground** (301-834-8050), adjacent to the C&O Canal. Open early April through early November. A municipal facility, it has trailer and tent sites, a playground area, and a bathhouse. The rates are some of the lowest you will find in the state. I like that you can walk out of your tent and onto the canal in just a few steps.

Frederick, 21701
❦ **Gambrill State Park** (see *Green Space—Parks*). The campground is located at the base of High Knob and provides access to the park's trail system. There are no hookups, and sites are quite primitive, but this makes a good, low-cost base from which to explore Frederick and the Catoctin Mountains area.

Thurmont, 21788
Catoctin Mountain Park (see sidebar on page 383). **Owens Creek Campground** sits high on the mountain and is usually open from mid-April through mid-November. There are flush toilets, but no showers. One of the prettiest settings of all of the area's campgrounds.

❦ **Crow's Nest Campground** (301-271-7632; 1-800-866-1959), 335 West Main Street. Open year-round. Swimming pool, children's playground, and trails that connect with those in **Catoctin Mountain Park** (see sidebar on page 383).

Cunningham Falls State Park (see *Green Space—Parks*). There are two campgrounds within the park. Just off US 15 are the 148 sites of the **Houck Area**. A little more isolated, and certainly quieter, are the 31 sites in the **Manor Area,** close to the falls and the lake. Be forewarned, the showers only have cold water.

Ole Mink Farms Recreation Resort (301-271-7012), 12806 Mink Farm Road. Open year-round. Many of the 90 sites are leased on a yearly basis to RV owners, but you can still enjoy the place in your tent or in one of the deluxe camping cabins. Swimming pool.

Also see **C&O Canal National Historical Park** under *To Do—Bicycling*.

✳ Where to Eat

DINING OUT

Buckeystown

The Inn at Buckeystown (301-874-5755; 1-800-272-1190; www.innat-buckeystown.com). Open for dinner Friday and Saturday only. Reservations are mandatory, as the chef prepares the five-course prix fixe meal based upon who and how many will be dining. The inn (see *Lodging—Bed & Breakfasts*) is elegant and the food superb, yet the atmosphere is anything but stuffy. Guests are often seated together at one big table, and as the courses (and BYOB bottles) flow one into the other, conversations become more amiable and animated.

Expect to be served lamb, duck, steak, pasta, or chicken (sometimes all in the same meal) prepared by a Culinary Institute of America–trained chef. An experience that will not soon be forgotten. The prix fixe meal is about $40 a person.

Frederick

🦞 ♬ ♿ **Turning Point Inn** (301-831-8233), 3406 Urbana Pike. Open for dinner; closed Monday. A special brunch is served Sunday 11:30–2. Host Charlie Seymour has guided the inn (see *Lodging—Inns*) to a plethora of awards from local, regional, national, and international authorities. This is a "special-occasion" restaurant with reasonable prices.

Try crab and Brie Wellington ($8.95) or lobster bisque ($6.95) before choosing from lamb, seafood, steaks, or pasta dishes for the main course. The inn is noted for a sophisticated wine list. $13.95–25.95.

The Province (301-663-1441; www. provrest.com), 129 North Market Street. Note the name is Province, not Provence. Yet the American fare has a decided European accent. The filet mignon is served with garlic cloves or Dijon sauce ($22), the lamb braised in wine ($18), and chicken roulade stuffed with smoked Gouda ($17). Attentive service and eye-pleasing presentations of the entrées ($16–25) add a touch of elegance to the overall experience.

Ijamsville

♬ ♿ **Gabriel's Inn** (301-865-5500), 4730 Ijamsville Road. Open for dinner from 3 PM Wednesday through Sunday. Traditional French cuisine served in a relaxed and casual atmosphere. Each meal is available French style (includes hors d'oeuvres, soup, entrée, vegetables, salad, cheese tray, and dessert) or American style (salad, entrée, and vegetables). American style $15.95–22.95; French style $17.95–29.95.

New Market

🍴 𝒮 ♿ **Mealey's** (301-865-5488; www.mealeysrestaurant.com), 8 Main Street. Open for lunch Friday and Saturday 11:30–2:30; dinner Monday through Saturday 5–9; dinner Sunday noon–8. Antiques fill the 1793 brick building, which has served as a general store and a hotel. The kitchen staff does an admirable job of preparing the typical American/Maryland fare. Prime rib is the specialty, but there are also many seafood choices. The atmosphere and quality of food and service are a special value, as many entrées are less than $20.

EATING OUT

Emmitsburg

Carriage House Inn (301-447-2366; www.carriagehouseinn.net), 200 South Seton Avenue. Open daily for lunch and dinner. With a colonial atmosphere inside and out, the inn serves what I call "upscale American" fare. Seafood, steaks, pork, chicken, and pasta all decently prepared and presented. Lots of tasty desserts, such as the chocolate mold with black raspberry ice cream inside. Entrées $12.95–30.95.

Frederick

🍴 𝒮 ♿ **Venutti's Ristorante** (301-668-2700; www.venuttis.com), 16 East Patrick Street. Open daily for lunch and dinner. The restored interior of the 1880s building, with brick walls and rich wood accents, gives Venutti's an upscale atmosphere, but entrée prices reflect an ownership willing to give value. Traditional Italian dishes of lasagna, veal Marsala, seafood Alfredo, and others cost less than $17.

𝒮 ♿ **Brewer's Alley** (301-631-0089) 124 North Market Street. Open daily for lunch and dinner; closed for a couple of hours between lunch and dinner on weekdays. Contemporary American pub fare and wood-fired pizzas complement the fresh brewed beer. The southwestern grilled chicken fajita ($8.25) went well with the ale I chose. Other sandwiches and entrées $7.95–15.95.

𝒮 ♿ **Jug Bridge Seafood** (301-228-2722; www.jugbridge.com), 909 Baltimore Road. Open for dinner daily; open for lunch Saturday and Sunday. Serving steamed crabs, crabcakes, crab imperial, and other seafood for

THE TOWN HOUSES OF FREDERICK

more than 50 years. Other entrées include steak and chicken, but it is hard to tell you exactly how they will be prepared, as the menu changes frequently to take advantage of seasonal items. $9–30.

La Paz Mexican Restaurant (301-694-8980), 18 Market Space. Open daily for lunch and dinner. The local Mexican restaurant serving the traditional dishes found in most American/Mexican establishments. Fajitas, burritos, quesadillas, tacos, and other entrées $6.50–13.50.

Old Town Saigon Vietnamese Restaurant (301-695-9688), 1003 West Patrick Street. Open daily for lunch and dinner. Good for those times when you wish for something from the East but don't want to spend a lot of time and money getting it. The freshly prepared entrées, such as ginger chicken and caramel shrimp, are $5.75–10.95.

Barbara Fritchie Restaurant (301-662-2500), US 40. Open for breakfast, lunch, and dinner. I have only had breakfast here—and certainly did enjoy it—so I can't advise you on the lunch and dinner entrées, but the menu features country-cooking items at fairly low prices. $5–12.95.

Thurmont

Cozy Restaurant (301-271-7373; www.cozyvillage), 105 Frederick Road (MD 806). Open daily for breakfast, lunch, and dinner. Established in 1929 by William Freeze and still owned by the Freeze family, the restaurant's fame parallels that of the adjacent inn (see Cozy Country Inn under *Lodging—Motels and Hotels*). Winston Churchill stopped by to play the jukebox, and Mamie Eisenhower was a frequent visitor to the pub. Dis-

play cases contain pictures, autographs, and other memorabilia from these and other famous diners.

Traditional country fare and Maryland seafood specialties are on the reasonably priced menu. The aroma of fresh-baked breads and desserts fills the air. During the growing season, the vegetables at the daily buffet were organically grown in Cozy's own garden. $8.99–15.99.

Mountain Gate (301-271-4373), 133 Frederick Road (MD 806). Open daily for breakfast, lunch, and dinner. Large buffets make this the place for hungry families looking for large quantities of country-cooked fare at low prices. Items from the menu include roast beef ($5.50), fried ham ($4.75), and a seafood platter ($12.95).

COFFEE BARS

Frederick

Mudd Puddle Coffee Café (301-620-4323), 124 South Carroll Street. Closed Sunday. Specialty coffees and gourmet sandwiches.

Frederick Coffee Company (301-698-0039), 100 North East Street. Live music on weekend evenings.

SNACKS AND GOODIES

Frederick

The Candy Kitchen (301-698-0442), 52 North Market Street. Producing handmade chocolates, truffles, fudges, and more since 1902.

McCutcheon's Apple Products (301-662-3261; www.mccutcheons.com), 13 South Wisner Street. The quality of McCutcheon's cider, preserves, apple butter, juices, relishes, and other jars of tasty victuals is such that Marylanders often give them as gifts.

Middletown

South Mountain Creamery (301-371-4388; www.southmountaincreamery.com), 8305 Bolivar Road. Call for business hours. The milk, yogurt, cheese, ice cream, and other products sold at the retail store, located on the farm, are not only the freshest you will find but are also grown completely organically.

Thurmont

Mom and Pop's Ice Cream Shop (301-271-7800), 19 Water Street. One of Mom and Pop's huge snowballs of shaved ice, available in almost 20 flavors, is the way to end a hike in nearby Catoctin Mountain Park.

✳ Entertainment

FILM

Frederick

West Ridge Cinema (301-698-9100), 1037 West Patrick Street. First-run films.

Hoyts Frederick Towne Mall Cinema (301-682-6400), US 40. One of the most expensive (tickets and goodies) first-run theaters I've ever been in.

Holiday Cinemas (301-694-0100), 100 Baughmans Lane. Shows films after they have been out awhile, at nicely reduced prices.

See **Weinberg Center for the Arts** under *Theaters* for classic films.

NIGHTLIFE **Oldies Music Legends**
(301-698-2600), 5311 Buckeystown Pike, Frederick. More than 5,500 square feet on which to ballroom dance. Call for days and times.

THEATERS

Frederick

✎ ♿ **Weinberg Center for the Arts**
(301-228-2828; www.weinbergcenter. org), 20 West Patrick Street. The renovated 1926 movie palace has developed into the arts and cultural center of the region. Traveling troupes and nationally and internationally known performers present plays, musicals, concerts, and dance throughout the year. The Weinberg also has a yearly series for families and one of classic movies.

Fredericktowne Players (301-694-6659; www.fredericktowneplayers. org), 306 East Patrick Street. The resident company for the Weinberg Center for the Arts (see above) presents at least four performances from September through July. Productions have included *The Seven-Year Itch, Run for Your Wife,* and *Joseph and the Amazing Technicolor Dreamcoat.*

Maryland Ensemble Theatre (301-694-4744; www.marylandensemble. org), 15 West Patrick Street. The multifaceted organization stages a number of performances during its season; most productions are new works by local talent. An added bonus is the comedy sessions presented after the Saturday-night performances. Works by regional artists are located in the lobby.

♿ **Way Off Broadway Dinner Theater** (301-662-6600; www.wayoff-broadway.com), Willowtree Plaza (US 40 west). A dinner buffet accompanies the presentations of musicals, comedies, and mysteries.

SPORTS **Frederick Keys Baseball**
(301-662-0013), 6201 New Design Road, Frederick. The Keys, Class A affiliates of the Baltimore Orioles, provide hometown action on the field of the Harry Grove Stadium from April through September. The stadium is also the site of profession-

al wrestling, concerts, and other events.

✳ Selective Shopping
ANTIQUES
Frederick
Antique Imports (301-662-6200; 1-800-662-2014), 125 East Street. A large selection of British furniture and accessories.

Emporium Antiques (301-662-7099; www.emporiumantiques.com), 112 East Patrick Street. Open daily. More than 100 dealers under one roof.

Cannon Hill Place (301-696-9304), 111 South Carroll Street. The 1700s stone granary houses antiques and collectibles.

Old Glory Antique Marketplace (301-662-9173), 5862 Urbana Pike. Open daily. Close to 110 dealers.

Middletown
Antiques in Middletown (301-371-7380), 100 North Church Street. A multidealer shop that is so eager to have you stop by that they offer everyone a free cup of coffee, whether or not you buy anything.

New Market
With more than 30 shops, the small town of New Market, a few miles east of Frederick, has dubbed itself the "Antiques Capital of Maryland." Sometimes, places with such a large number of dealers can be overwhelming, but many of the businesses are housed within historic homes and storefronts, giving you a chance to walk around, enjoy the scenery, and recharge before entering another establishment. All shops are open on the weekend; on other days, a flag flying on a storefront indicates it is

open. Information about the shops may be obtained from the **Tourism Council of Frederick County, Frederick Visitor Center** (see *Guidance*), or by logging on to www.newmarketmd.com.

ART GALLERIES
Frederick
&. **Delaplaine Visual Arts Education Center** (301-698-0656; www.delaplaine.org), 20 South Carroll Street. Open daily. A nonprofit organization, the center overlooks Carroll Creek and the *Community Bridge Mural.* The exhibit areas showcase local and regional talent, while the studio spaces are used for instruction and special events.

Museum Shop, LTD (301-695-0424; 1-888-678-0675), 20 North Market Street. Japanese woodcuts, handcrafted items, and original Whistler and Kornemann art.

Gallery Wear (301-662-7100), 116 East Patrick Street. Interesting blend of artist-made jewelry, clothing, ceramics, and furniture.

Thurmont
Her Studio Gallery (301-447-2866), 304 East Main Street. Friday through Sunday. Linda Postelle works with watercolors, acrylics, and painted furniture.

BOOKSTORES
Frederick
Book Center (301-663-1222), US 15 and West Seventh Street (at Frederick Shopping Center). A combination book/gift/café shop.

USED BOOKS &. **Market Street Books** (301-228-2127), 143 North Market Street, Frederick. Closed

Monday. A small selection of new books can be found among the many used volumes.

Quill and Brush (301-874-3200), 1137 Sugarloaf Mountain Road, Dickerson. A purveyor of signed, limited, and first editions of collectible books. All fields and genres are stocked, but they concentrate on literature and mysteries.

Wonder Book and Video (301-694-5955; www.wonderbk.com), 1306 West Patrick Street, Frederick. A retail outlet for the chain-store company that claims to have more than 1 million new, rare, and used books available through its Internet web site.

CRAFTS ✍ **I Made This!** (301-624-4030; www.imadethispottery.com), 10-B East Street, Frederick. Open daily. Paint your own pottery. A good rainy-day activity.

Catoctin Pottery (301-371-4274; www.catoctinpottery.com), 3205 Poffenberger Road, Jefferson. Closed Sunday. Susan Hanson's studio is located in a former gristmill where she creates her vivid pieces of ceramics, tableware, and lamps.

SPECIAL SHOPS

Frederick
The Shops at Everedy Square and Shab Row, corner of East and Church Streets. The 18th- and 19th-century dwellings that once housed wheelwrights, tinkers, and craftspersons are now a complex of small shops filled with everything from antiques to books to artworks and crafts supplies. As interesting for its history and architecture as it is for the shops.

✍ **Dancing Bear** (301-631-9300; www.dbeartoys.com), 200A North Market Street. Toys, gifts, and music

for the kids. I certainly no longer qualify as a kid, but I had a smile on my face as I looked through children's book written and illustrated by Maryland residents.

Hunting Creek Outfitters (301-668-4333), 29 North Market Street. An authorized Orvis dealer with fly-fishing rods and reels, accessories, and clothing.

Thurmont
Cozy Village, across from Cozy Country Inn and Restaurant (see *Lodging—Motels and Hotels,* and *Eating Out*), is an assemblage of cutesy little shops filled with handcrafted items, antiques, and gift ideas. Most of the shops are open until 5 daily.

FARMER'S MARKETS

Frederick
Everedy Square and Shab Row Farmer's Market (310-898-3183), Church and East Streets. Close to the antiques and shopping center of town, the market is open Thursday 3:30–6:30 during early June through late October.

Frederick County Fairgrounds Market (301-663-5895), fairgrounds. The area's largest selection of farmer's market items is open year-round 8–2 on Saturday.

West Frederick Farmer's Market (301-898-3183), 110 Baughman's Lane. Stands are set up in the Blue Cross/Blue Shield parking lot 10–1 on Saturday from early May through October.

PICK-YOUR-OWN PRODUCE FARMS
Maynes Tree Farm (301-662-4320), 3420 Buckeystown Pike, Buckeystown. The strawberries are ripe from mid-May through mid-June, and the pumpkins are ready to pick by

mid-September. Return during the holiday season to pick and/or cut your Christmas tree.

Glade-Link Farms (301-898-7131), MD 194, New Midway. The farm grows fruit, vegetables, and gourds, so you can come here from early spring through early fall and find something to take home.

Catoctin Mountain Orchard (301-271-2737; www.catoctinmountainorchard.com), 15036 North Franklinville Road, Thurmont. The blackberries, blueberries, and cherries all ripen about late June and can be picked into early July.

❋ Special Events

February: **Cabin Fever Festival** (301-898-5466; www.cabinfeverfestival.com), fairgrounds, Frederick. The annual event gets you outdoors for a midwinter arts and crafts show.

April: **Farm Museum Spring Festival** (301-694-1650), Rose Hill Manor Park, Frederick. Hayrides, pedal-tractor pull, petting zoo, and children's crafts.

June: **Festival of the Arts** (301-694-9632; www.frederickarts.org), Frederick. Juried arts market, children's activities, and live entertainment along Carroll Creek.

June through August: **Summer Concert Series** (301-694-2489), Baker Park, Frederick. Free outdoor concerts every Sunday evening feature local and regional acts. Expect to hear everything from New Age to country to jazz to urban music.

July: **Battle of Monocacy** (301-662-3515), Monocacy National Battlefield. Living-history portrayals of aspects of the battle.

August: **Country Peddler Show** (941-479-5005), fairgrounds. Annual event featuring folk artists from around the country. Crafts and folk art for sale.

Hunting and Fishing Show (301-865-3019), fairgrounds. An annual exposition of outdoor equipment. Classes, exhibits, and live animals.

September: The **Great Frederick (County) Fair** (301-663-5895), fairgrounds.

October: **Oktoberfest** (301-663-3885), Schifferstadt (see *To See— Historic Homes*), Frederick. Annual festival with German food, biergarten, and oompah bands. Children's events and juried arts and crafts show. **Maryland Mountain Festival** (301-898-5466; www.marylandmountainfestival.com), Lynfield Complex (north of Frederick). Juried arts and crafts. **Railroad Days** (301-834-7100), Brunswick Railroad Museum (see *To See—Museums*), Brunswick. Scenic bluegrass train excursions, and model-railroad exhibits and demonstrations.

The Mountains of Western Maryland

THE GREAT VALLEY AND BLUE
RIDGE REGION—HAGERSTOWN,
ANTIETAM, AND HANCOCK

THE ALLEGHENY PLATEAU—
ROCKY GAP, CUMBERLAND,
AND FROSTBURG

AROUND DEEP CREEK LAKE—
GRANTSVILLE, McHENRY,
THAYERSVILLE, AND OAKLAND

The Mountains of Western Maryland

© The Countryman Press

THE MOUNTAINS OF WESTERN MARYLAND

The mountains of Western Maryland are a world apart. Although they were the gateway through which early settlers passed on their way to America's early frontiers, they were the last area in Maryland to be settled. The construction of I-70, I-81, and I-68 has made them more accessible, yet things are still a little rough around the edges—and that is the allure.

Other than in Hagerstown and Cumberland, and their immediate vicinities, malls and supersized discount stores are few and far between; there are only a couple of large luxury resorts; home-style cooking is what you will find in many of the restaurants; and mom-and-pop enterprises are the norm. Two-lane roadways, which snake over heavily forested ridgelines and along swiftly moving mountain streams, connect one sparsely populated community with another.

Traveling along the interstates is more scenic than you would imagine. Valley floors resemble patchwork quilts, made up of cropland, fields of cattle, and meadows all tinted by nature's own hues. West of Hancock, the Allegheny Plateau continues into West Virginia, providing mile after mile of extended mountain vistas. This is Maryland's coalfield. While driving on country roadways, you may look into your rearview mirror to see the grille of an overloaded coal truck barreling down the mountain, just inches from your rear bumper.

Due to the access provided by the interstates, much of this is changing and "economic development" is on the rise. So the time to visit western Maryland is now, before it loses its rough edges, before its roadsides are littered with the parking lots of fast-food restaurants instead of being bordered by modest homesteads. Before other folks learn of the charms of the place and come flocking to an area just waiting to be discovered. Explore now, while public lands are not well visited and can provide rambles and wanderings in relative peace and quiet with few other wayfarers.

The Great Valley and Blue Ridge Region

PENNSYLVANIA

WEST VIRGINIA

VIRGINIA

Potomac River

Pen-Mar Park

Smithsburg
Cavetown

Appalachian Trail

Hagerstown

Cearfoss

Wilson

Williamsport

Clear Spring

Big Spring

Log House Museum

Indian Springs

Big Pool

FORT FREDERICK STATE PARK

Western Maryland Rail Trail

Hancock

Sideling Hill Visitor Center

C&O Canal National Historic Park (along Potomac)

Piney Grove

Little Orleans

GREENBRIER STATE PARK

Family Recreation Center

Boonsborough Museum of History

Crystal Grottoes

Keedysville

Antietam National Battlefield

Sharpsburg

Antietam

Boonsboro

WASHINGTON MONUMENT STATE PARK

GATHLAND STATE PARK

Gapland

Maryland Heights

Harpers Ferry

Sandy Hook

Brunswick

Frederick

C&O Canal National Historic Park (along Potomac)

Washington County Rural Heritage Museum

Roadhouse Museum

Train Room & Museum

Hager House & Museum

Miller House & Garden

Farmers Market

Visitors Center

Washington County Playhouse

Maryland Theater

Washington County Arts Council

Washington County Museum of Fine Arts

Washington County & Symphony

Municipal Stadium

Rose Hill Cemetery

City Park

BURHANS BLVD.

WALNUT ST.

PROSPECT ST.

SUMMIT AVE.

LOCUST STREET

MULBERRY STREET

POTOMAC STREET

MEMORIAL BLVD.

GUILFORD AVE.

N

Miles

0   1   2   3   4   5   10

© The Countryman Press

THE GREAT VALLEY AND BLUE RIDGE REGION—HAGERSTOWN, ANTIETAM, AND HANCOCK

A s I-70 rises onto the crest of South Mountain—a part of the Blue Ridge Mountains stretching from northern Georgia to central Pennsylvania—westbound travelers gaze upon the bounteous expanse of the Great Valley.

A miles-wide and relatively flat feature in an otherwise mountainous landscape, the valley extends from mid-Pennsylvania into southern Virginia and beyond. This natural travel conduit is what Jonathan Hager and other German settlers from Pennsylvania followed into the Maryland colony, arriving in the early 1700s to establish new lives on the fertile valley floor.

During the French and Indian War in 1755, British troops (including a young George Washington) under the command of General Braddock built a wagon road through Turners Gap on South Mountain, the valley's eastern barrier. In 1806, the route was designated part of the National Road (see "What's Where in Maryland") and became a major thoroughfare to the West.

Hagerstown began to grow where the two routes met, and its strategic location made it a contested site during the Civil War. Maryland was a free state, but there were many Confederate sympathizers in Hagerstown, and escaped slaves were often captured and returned to their Southern owners.

Confederate troops under the command of Robert E. Lee occupied the town prior to the Battle of Antietam in 1862, retreated after the conflict, and returned nine months later. Lee's push into Northern territory was once more thwarted, with most of the fighting this time taking place on South Mountain. Land on which these hostilities occurred has been preserved, and you can trace the events by visiting Antietam National Battlefield or walking the route of the Appalachian Trail along South Mountain.

The arrival of several railroad lines after the Civil War helped establish Hagerstown as the industrial center of the valley. The construction of I-81 (along the basic course Jonathan Hager followed) and I-70 (which parallels the route of the National Road) solidified its economic status and brought new people into the area. The downtown area, with a blend of old and new buildings, harbors a vibrant arts and cultural community, evident in the many museums, galleries, and theaters within a few blocks of each other. The Washington County Museum of Fine Arts is one of the best of its kind, and the Hager House and Museum preserve the city's former days.

On the western edge of the valley, Hancock began as a an early-1700s trading post close to where Native Americans forded the Potomac River. The settlement was later named for Revolutionary War figure Edward Joseph Hancock Jr. and, like Hagerstown, started to grow when the National Road, and later the Chesapeake & Ohio (C&O) Canal, reached the town. It, too, was fought over during the Civil War, with Stonewall Jackson laying siege to it as early as January 1862. Hancock lost much of its importance in the mid-1900s when I-70 bypassed it a bit to the north. Its narrow downtown area, however, has remained an active business district with antiques shops, a C&O Canal Visitor Center, and a number of places catering to canal bikers and hikers.

COMMUNITIES **Boonsboro** was established in 1792 by George and William Boone. Its position along the National Road brought it growth and prosperity, as it lay about halfway between Frederick and Hagerstown. There is now another spurt of growth as the population of the two cities migrate toward each other. A couple of museums (do not miss the Boonsborough Museum of History!), a commercial cavern, and a couple of the region's finest restaurants have begun to put the town on many a traveler's must-stop list.

Sleepy little **Williamsport** was once considered by George Washington as a potential site for the nation's capital, but its remoteness and inaccessibility caused him to look elsewhere. The town's fortunes grew once the C&O Canal reached it in 1834, yet declined when the waterway closed in the early 1900s. The canal and its history remain focal points, though, as people come to town to access the towpath or obtain information about it at the C&O Canal Visitor Center.

GUIDANCE The **Hagerstown/Washington County Convention and Visitors Bureau** (301-791-3246; 1-888-257-2600; www.marylandmemories.org) is located at Elizabeth Hager Center, 16 Public Square, Hagerstown, 21740, and can provide you with information if you are calling or writing when you are not in the area. The best place for guidance while in town is the bureau's **Welcome Center** at 6 North Potomac Street, Hagerstown.

GETTING THERE *By air:* By way of **Hagerstown Regional Airport** (240-313-2777; 1-800-428-4322), US Airways Express (1-800-428-4322) provides scheduled passenger commuter service to and from **Pittsburgh International Airport** (412-472-3525). Pan Am (1-800-359-7262) also makes it possible to fly into Hagerstown by taking its Clipper Connection from **Baltimore/Washington International Airport** (1-800-I-FLY-BWI).

By car: **I-81** comes into the region from Pennsylvania to the north, and West Virginia and Virginia to the south. **I-70** provides access from the east, while **I-68** (which terminates at I-70 in Hancock) is the way to arrive from the west.

By bus: **Greyhound** (1-800-231-2222) will drop you off at its local terminal (301-739-7420) located at 10527 Sharpsburg Pike in Hagerstown.

By rail: A **MARC** (1-800-325-RAIL) commuter train out of Washington, D.C., makes stops in Harpers Ferry, which is just across the Potomac River in West Virginia.

By bus: The local bus service, **County Commuter** (301-791-3047), has routes to
all points in Hagerstown and to a few of the nearby communities such as
Funkstown, Maugansville, Smithsburg, Long Meadow, and Williamsport.

By taxi: **Antietam Cab** (301-393-8811), **Antietam Transportation** (301-714-
2286), and **Turner Van Service** (301-733-7788) are based in Hagerstown. In
and around Hancock, you can call **Valley Cab** (301-678-7767).

MEDICAL EMERGENCY Washington County Hospital (301-790-8300), 2511
East Antietam Street, Hagerstown.

✳ To See
MUSEUMS

Boonsboro
Boonsborough Museum of History (301-432-6969), 113 North Main Street.
Sunday 1–5, May through September. Small admission fee. Doug Bast's late
father was a fanatical collector, and Doug has followed in his footsteps. Their
assortment of thousands of items is crammed into a two-story structure. It is
almost impossible to describe what is here, but it is, by far, one of the most
amazing personal museums I have ever seen. There are bullet carvings from the
Civil War, a preserved rose from Lincoln's coffin, a pike given to a slave by John
Brown, an original letter from Clara Barton, a cane carved by Geronimo, religious items dating from AD 800, and a clay lamp made in 1500 BC. Do not miss
this place!

Washington County Rural Heritage Museum (240-420-1712), 7313 Sharpsburg Pike (MD 65). Open Saturday and Sunday 1–4. Small admission fee. I
thought I would be visiting a typical farm museum with a few pieces of agricultural equipment. I found this museum, which depicts the struggles and achieve-
ments of farmers of the past, to be much more. There are grain reapers, potato
graders, and such, but there are also
sleighs, buggies, an original Conestoga
wagon, a replica of a country store,
the complete interior of the old
Keedysville post office—and a grain
harvester that is believed to have been
built in Eastern Europe nearly 1,000
years ago. Future plans include the
construction of a rural village.

THE LOG HOUSE MUSEUM IN CLEAR SPRING

Clear Spring
Log House Museum (301-842-
2553), 11 South Mill Street. Open by
appointment. Small admission fee. A
labor of love. Carl Brown restored this
1825 cabin with his own money during the late 1900s. Items of everyday

life from the 1800s and 1900s, many of them from the Brown family, fill the two-story cabin. The museum has received scant public funds, which makes it more remarkable that the spinning wheels, washing machines, a sled with sleigh bells, the medical instruments used by a local doctor, and a fireplace with wrought-iron cooking utensils have been preserved.

Hagerstown

& **Washington County Museum of Fine Arts** (301-739-5727; www.washco-museum.org), 91 Key Street (in Hagerstown City Park). Open Tuesday through Saturday 10–5, Sunday 1–6. Donations accepted. Certainly one of the most impressive free-admission, small-city galleries you will find anywhere. The permanent collection contains more than 7,000 pieces of noted American art, Old Masters, European works, decorative and folk arts, and items by regional and Maryland artists. In addition, the museum brings in some of the world's finest artwork for limited exhibitions. There is also at least one music concert a month. Steel baron William H. Singer donated the building that houses the museum, and its beauty alone makes a stop here worthwhile.

✑ **Roundhouse Museum** (301-739-4665), 300 South Burhans Boulevard. Open Friday through Sunday 1–5. Small admission fee. At one time, five railroad companies operated in the Hagerstown area, and more than 20 passenger trains a day came into the city. Inside are displays, items, and photographs from those days. The "HO"- and "O"-gauge model-train layouts are impressive, and children are permitted to operate the largest one, which depicts the roundhouse and nearby tracks. The museum sponsors a popular leaf-color train excursion each fall.

Hancock

Hancock Town Museum (301-678-6308), corner of High Street and Pennsylvania Avenue. Open 2–4 on the first and third Sunday from April through October. Donations accepted. Within a small basement area of a former school, the museum chronicles the town's history with photographs (seek out the original *Harper's* magazine prints), transportation exhibits, and an early tool collection. There is even an original letter from Henry Clay postmarked 1827. All in all, it is a great collection of items, especially for a place that charges no admission fee.

HISTORIC HOMES

Hagerstown

Miller House and Garden (301-797-8782; www.rootsweb.com/~mdwchs), 135 West Washington Street. April through December, Wednesday through Saturday 1–4 (December hours and days may vary). Small admission fee. The town house, built in various stages, is furnished as it would have been in 1825. The spiral staircase and furnishings reflect William Price's desire to let others know he was successful. The gardens are planted in period plants. One of the most interesting items is the original ledger of ransom for Hagerstown from Civil War Confederate general McCausland.

Hager House (301-739-8393), 110 Key Street (within Hagerstown City Park). Tuesday through Saturday 10–4 and Sunday 2–5. Small admission fee. Jonathan

HAGER HOUSE IN HAGERSTOWN

Hager arrived in frontier Maryland in 1739, built his house of uncut fieldstones (with 22-inch walls), married neighbor Elizabeth Kreshner, and set up a trading post in his home. The building is filled with period pieces, many of them Hager-family originals. (Ask the docent to explain the origin of "pop goes the weasel.") Period plants grow all around the house. The **Hager Museum** next door contains 18th- and 19th-century items found when the Hager House was restored in 1953. I find it amazing that so many of Hager's belongings still exist—such as his *Book of Sermons* (in German) and his waistcoat.

HISTORIC SITES

Big Pool
Fort Frederick State Park (301-842-2155), 11100 Fort Frederick Road. The park and the fort are open daily; other attractions have varying open dates and times. Free admission to the park; a small fee to enter the fort. The colony of Maryland constructed the fort in 1756 to protect its western frontier during the French and Indian War. It also saw action during the Revolutionary and Civil Wars. Restored to its earliest appearance, its stone walls enclose barracks, catwalks, and parade grounds. Costumed interpreters provide information on displays inside the barracks, and living-history demonstrations are presented on a scheduled basis. (A large reenactment with British, French, and Indian reenactors takes place each Memorial Day weekend.) A self-guided walking-tour brochure is available.

Also within the state park is a visitors center (with an excellent orientation film), a **Civilian Conservation Corps Museum,** seasonal boat rentals, a short nature

FORT FREDERICK

trail, and a small campground (see *Lodging—Camping*) scenically located on bottomland between the C&O Canal and the Potomac River.

Hagerstown

Rose Hill Cemetery (301-739-3630), 600 South Potomac Street. The cemetery, which still has plots available, is the final resting place for more than 2,000 Confederate soldiers killed during the Antietam and South Mountain battles. Less than 350 were able to be identified.

Beaver Creek Country School (301-797-8782), 9702 Beaver Creek Church Road. Sunday 2–5, April through September. The 1904 brick building, filled with desks, books, slates, and engaging wall charts, is the third school to stand on this site. The museum room contains artifacts of early rural life. Interestingly, across the street, the refined steeple and stained glass of the 1902 **Beaver Creek Christian Church,** laid out by the same architect who designed the school, stands in stark contrast to the simple lines and windows of the 1845 **St. Matthew's Lutheran Church** next door.

BEAVER CREEK COUNTRY SCHOOL

Sharpsburg

Antietam National Battlefield (301-432-5124). The visitors center is off MD 65 a few miles north of Sharpsburg. Open daily. Small admission fee. When Confederate general Robert E. Lee made his first push into Northern territories in September 1862, his troops clashed with Union soldiers on a battlefield that covered 30 square miles. More men were killed or wounded than on any other single day during the Civil War.

I was impressed with the way the park service had organized visitors' experiences when I first came here many years ago. It was the first Civil War battlefield I had ever visited, and I have never failed to learn something new on subsequent visits. A driving tour takes you by significant battle sites, rangers lead guided walks, and a couple of trails take the more inquisitive into hidden areas of the battlefield's 3,000 acres.

THE BURNSIDE BRIDGE AT ANTIETAM NATIONAL BATTLEFIELD

Antietam National Cemetery is off MD 34 in Sharpsburg. Grand old maple, oak, and Norway spruce trees provide shade for the graves set out in a circular fashion. It is mind-boggling to walk through here and realize that only a portion of those killed during the battle are buried here.

OTHER SITES

Throughout the area

Between 1819 and 1863, more than 30 **stone bridges** were constructed along Antietam and Conococheague Creeks and their tributaries. Many of these

SIDELING HILL

On Interstate 68 west of Hancock, the Washington County–Allegany County line, the interstate makes a long climb over 1,600-foot Sideling Hill. To reduce the length and grade of the ascent, workers spent more than 2 years making a cut 360 feet deep into the mountain's ridgeline (the deepest road cut in Maryland).

The passageway is a great place to learn about the geology of the mountains, so take a few minutes' break from driving to visit the **Sideling Hill Exhibit Center** (301-678-5442), accessed directly from the interstate. The four-story center offers exhibits, displays, and storyboards about many aspects of western Maryland. You will learn that the road cut reveals fossilized plants and seashells from 350 million years ago when the site was at the bottom of an ancient ocean. You can also see how the layers of sedimentary rock were folded as Africa collided with North America about 230 million years ago.

impressive and eye-pleasing structures still exist. Information on where they are located may be obtained from the **Hagerstown/Washington County Convention and Visitors Bureau** (see *Guidance*).

CAVERN TOUR ✐ **Crystal Grottoes Caverns** (301-432-6336), MD 34 about 1.5 miles west of Boonsboro. A 30-minute guided tour takes you through the 250-million-year-old caverns, believed to contain more formations per square foot than any other commercial cavern in the world. Triangular pyramids of calcite have formed eight-sided crystals rarely found anywhere else.

✳ To Do

BICYCLING Western Maryland Rail Trail (301-842-2155). The paved, and nearly flat, trail follows the route of the former Western Maryland Railroad. Still in the development stage, the completed portion begins about a half mile west of Fort Frederick State Park (see *To See—Historic Sites*) and continues westward for 19 miles into Hancock and beyond. A total of 25 miles will be available for riding when completed. The trail parallels the C&O Canal, which makes it possible to do round-trip rides without following the exact same course.

C&O Canal National Historical Park. The **C&O Canal Visitor Centers** in Williamsport (301-582-0813) and Hancock (301-678-5463) can provide you with much detailed information. (Also see the sidebar on page 301 in "Silver Spring, Bethesda, Rockville, and Gaithersburg" in part 3, "Capital Region," for background history and information on the canal.) Well over 50 miles of the canal pass through this area of Maryland, providing a grand opportunity for hours of easy riding and sight-seeing. Some of the highlights include access to the **Appalachian Trail** (see the sidebar on page 406) and **Maryland Heights** (see *Hiking*), the Big Pool area and **Fort Frederick State Park** (see *To See—Historic Sites*), and the rewa-

tered parts of the canal at Williamsport and Hancock. Spaced along the route are a dozen designated campsites, with vault toilets and water (in-season), that are available on a first-come, first-served basis. There are also numerous ramps from which you can launch a boat into the Potomac River.

Hancock
Potomac Outdoor Expeditions (301-678-6718). Amiable John Hess will rent you a canoe or bicycle and shuttle you to just about any point along the C&O Canal within 50 miles or so of Hancock. John has been doing this for so long that he is a true storehouse of knowledge, which he is willing to put to use for you if you ask for help in planning your trip. He will, if his schedule permits, also shuttle you if you wish to use your own bike or canoe.

C&O Bicycle (1-800-678-BIKE), located next to the C&O Canal. Bicycle rentals, sales, and service.

BOAT RENTALS See **Fort Frederick State Park** under *To See—Historic Sites,* and **Potomac Outdoor Expeditions** under *Bicycling.*

FAMILY ACTIVITIES ✐ **Family Recreation Park** (301-733-2333), 21036 National Pike, Boonsboro. Open daily

May through August; weekends in April, and September through October. You may not know what Water Wars is, but your kids do—and they probably can't wait to start propelling liquid-filled balloons into the air. This local hot spot also offers miniature golf, batting cages, attractions for very small children, and three go-cart tracks. The figure-8 is one of the most fun tracks I have ridden in many years. Also see *To See—Cavern Tour.*

GOLF

Hagerstown
Municipal Golf Course (301-733-8630), 2 South Cleveland Avenue. The nine-hole course was built in the 1930s by citizens who could not afford the fees of a private club. The entire grounds project a maturity and feel not found in newer courses.

Black Rock (240-313-2816; www.blackrockgolfcourse.com), 20025 Mount Aetna Road. Grand views of the mountains from the par-72, 6,878-yard course.

Yingling's Golf Center (301-790-2494), 20220 Jefferson Boulevard. The area's only par-3 course, it is an excellent choice for beginners or those wanting to brush up on their game. Also on the premises are a miniature-golf course and batting cages.

MINIATURE GOLF See **Family Recreation Park** under *Family Activities,* and **Yingling's Golf Center** under *Golf.*

HIKING Maryland Heights (304-535-6298), located off Sandy Hook Road across the Potomac River from

BIRDING—THE AUTUMN HAWK MIGRATION

Maryland's portion of the Appalachian Trail (see sidebar on page 406) has overlooks along South Mountain, which are great areas from which to watch the annual autumn hawk migration. Heated air from rays of the sun striking cliffs and rock outcroppings couples with warm air rising from the lowlands to create forceful drafts, or *thermals,* that the hawks use to soar upward. In addition, by gliding near the crest of the ridges, they take advantage of the northwesterly winds striking the Appalachians, providing more uplift.

Sometimes as early as mid-August, ospreys, American kestrels, and a few bald eagles begin the procession southward. The migration commences in earnest in the middle of September as broad-winged hawks take to the skies. Peak daily sightings of several thousand are not uncommon. In early October, peregrine falcons join the movement, while later in the month, one of the smallest hawks, the sharp-shinned, becomes the dominant migrant. Joining the procession are the larger, but fewer-in-number Cooper's hawks. Red-tailed hawks, northern harriers, and red-shouldered hawks zip by leaf-less trees in November. Soaring over an Appalachian Trail that could be covered by December snows, northern goshawks and golden eagles bring the migratory season to a close.

THE APPALACHIAN TRAIL

There may be no better introduction to backpacking and primitive camping than the Appalachian Trail through Maryland. Shelters and campsites are conveniently spaced so that you don't have to do marathon miles to find a place to spend the night, wildlife is abundant, and the trail crosses numerous roads where help may be available in case of an emergency. Even though the route has a good feeling of isolation, there are four places where it is possible to make use of modern restroom facilities—and one spot that offers free warm showers!

The gentle terrain and great scenery are what makes this the perfect place to bring the kids for overnight hikes or to break friends into the pleasures of backpacking without introducing them to the rigors of a more rugged topography. Other than a couple of climbs of less than 500 feet, the trail stays along the gently undulating crest of South Mountain for nearly the entire distance, neither losing nor gaining much in the way of elevation. On the rare occasions when winter cooperates by bringing in a blanket of snow deep enough to completely cover all of the rocks and boulders, the trail can be a great cross-country skiing or snowshoeing route.

In addition to its natural beauty, South Mountain has been the scene of numerous activities in American history. George Washington crossed the mountain a couple of decades before the colonies broke from England, the first National Road coursed its way over it, and skirmishes of the Civil War were waged on its heights.

The guidebook *50 Hikes in Maryland* (Backcountry Guides) gives a detailed description of the trail's 40-mile route through the state.

Harpers Ferry, West Virginia. A steep and strenuous circuit hike of 5 miles will take the hardy and adventurous past remnants of Civil War fortifications and out to a spectacular view of the confluence of the Shenandoah and Potomac Rivers. Thomas Jefferson proclaimed the vista to be "one of the most spectacular scenes in Nature, and worth a voyage across the Atlantic." Luckily, you only have to drive here and take a hike to enjoy it.

Also see **Antietam National Battlefield** under *To See—Historic Sites*, and *Bicycling*.

KAYAKING AND CANOEING Outdoor Excursions (1-800-77KAYAK; www.outdoorexcursions.com), P.O. Box 24, Osage Drive, Boonsboro. A one-stop shop for water-sports trips. They can teach you what you need to know and then will take you on guided kayaking, rafting, and tubing trips along the Potomac River. You can choose from day or weekend outings and a number of lesson packages. All instructors are certified by the American Canoe Association.

Also see **C&O Canal National Historical Park** and **Potomac Outdoor Expeditions** under *Bicycling*.

SKATING

Hagerstown

✎ **Hagerstown Ice and Sports Complex** (301-766-9122), 580 Security Road. Ice-skating lessons, rentals, and public sessions are available within the 35,000-square-foot structure.

✎ **Family Skating Center** (301-582-2020), 1733 Virginia Avenue, and **Starland Roller Rink** (301-739-9844), 800 Park Road, are both open to the public for roller-skating fun.

SKIING, CROSS-COUNTRY, AND SNOWSHOEING See the **Appalachian Trail** sidebar opposite.

SWIMMING Claude M. Potterfield Municipal Pool (301-733-2599), 730 Frederick Street, Hagerstown. Memorial Day through Labor Day.

TRAIN EXCURSIONS See **Roundhouse Museum** under *To See—Museums.*

WHITEWATER RAFTING See *Kayaking and Canoeing.*

✳ Green Space

PARKS

South Mountain at the Frederick and Washington County line

Five parks encompass most of the land along South Mountain's ridgeline and protect Maryland's 40 miles of the Appalachian Trail (see sidebar opposite). From south to north they are:

South Mountain State Park (301-791-4767), 21843 National Pike. It is hard to actually tell where this park is, as it was established to safeguard those lands along the mountain that were not already protected by the other parks. Be thankful the state appropriated the funds to purchase these additional acreages.

Gathland State Park (301-791-4767), Gapland Road (off MD 67). Open daily 8 AM to sunset. The park is the site of the only monument in the world to war correspondents. Planned and built by George Alfred "Gath" Townsend, a journalist and columnist from 1866 to 1910, it memorializes more than 150 reporters and artists who covered the Civil War from both sides of the conflict. The off-balance monument contains a large Moorish arch below three smaller ones of Roman design. Taking the time to look at and read the dozens of inscriptions and view the mythological figures could take up much of an afternoon. Picnic areas; also a small museum open on an irregular basis.

WAR CORRESPONDENTS MEMORIAL, GATHLAND STATE PARK

Washington Monument State Park (301-432-8065), accessed from US Alternate 40 east of Boonsboro. Open daily. Home of the original Washington Monument. Built by the citizens of nearby Boonsboro in 1827, the jug-shaped tower was the first structure to be completed in honor of America's first president. Be sure to ascend the inside staircase for a grand view of the rolling Maryland countryside to the west. There are also attractive picnic sites close to the monument.

Greenbrier State Park (301-791-4767), on US 40 about 9 miles east of Hagerstown. The focal point of the park is a 43-acre lake that provides swimming, fishing, and boating. Short hiking trails, a campground (see *Lodging—Camping*), and some great nature interpretive programs are other reasons to stop by.

Pen-Mar Park, in the town of Pen-Mar. Appearing to be not much more than a community picnic grounds today, this spot was an amazingly popular resort between 1890 and 1920. Seven hotels and close to 100 guest cottages were located nearby to cater to daily crowds of 5,000 or more drawn to an amusement park. Gas rationing during World War II forced the park to close in 1943. There is a splendid view of Hagerstown (Great) Valley to the west, and rest rooms and water are available in-season.

Hagerstown

✿ **City park,** located along Virginia Avenue in the city's South End. One of the state's prettiest municipal parks. Three man-made lakes are surrounded by 50 acres of open and forested areas, playgrounds, tennis courts and ball fields, and short walking trails. Within the park are the **Washington County Museum of Fine Arts** (see *To See—Museums*), **Hager House** (see *To See—Historic Homes*), and the restored **1912 Engine 202 Steam Locomotive and Caboose.**

✳ Lodging

MOTELS AND HOTELS ✿ **Four Points by Sheraton** (301-790-3010),

HAGERSTOWN CITY PARK

1910 Dual Highway (accessed from I-70 Exit 32), Hagerstown, 21740. Listed here because of its central location and proximity to many of the area's attractions. Exercise room, outside pool, and free continental breakfast. $75–125.

BED & BREAKFASTS
Hagerstown, 21740
Inn on Potomac (301-739-5679; www.innonpotomac.com), 400 North Potomac Street. By removing plastic shower stalls to expose original tile, refurnishing with a blend of antiques, and taking down walls that had turned the house into small rental apartments, Don Tollefson and Harold Walter have returned this home to its early-1900s beauty. When I tired of watching the daily bustle of Potomac Street from the Beige Suite, I closed the original wooden shutters and slid into the Jacuzzi tub. The walk-in bay in the Gold Room catches the morning sun, while the upstairs porch provides a grandstand view of holiday fireworks. The main downtown area is just a few minutes' walk away. $100–150.

If moments in the Jacuzzi are not relaxing enough, make an appointment for a facial or full-body massage with the **Potomac Studio Day Spa,** located within the inn.

Wingrove Manor (301-797-7769; www.wingrovemanor.com), 635 Oak Hill Avenue. The large manor home, with an inviting front porch, sits impressively atop its long, sloping lawn, fitting in perfectly with the other grand old homes of the neighborhood. A curved wood staircase leading to the four guest rooms, along with the fine furnishings and slate fireplace, exude elegance and add a touch of class to your stay. $100–140.

Bed & Breakfast at Lewrene Farm (301-582-1735; www.inns.com/midatl/mdhagers), 9738 Downsville Pike. Of the many B&Bs in which I have stayed, this one feels most like being invited into someone's home. The furnishings are not just antiques but are items from generations of Lewis and Irene Lehman's families. The couple spent many years on missions to Guatemala and Kenya, so the Colonial-style home is also filled with unique items—such as an intricately carved leather travel case and a hand-built marimba. Although you could wander around the working farm's 125 acres, enjoy the country breezes, or relax in the large parlor, the best use of your time would be getting to know this interesting couple who host not only B&B guests but also a succession of foreign exchange students. $68–95.

Hancock, 21750
Cohill Manor (301-678-7573), 5012 Western Pike. The five guest rooms (which share two and a half baths) are arranged in a circular pattern around the staircase in this 16-room home, whose original wing was built in the mid-1700s. Deborah and John Cohill (a great-grandson of an 1800s owner) have restored it to its original luster. The Cohills and their 16 acres that support goats, barnyard animals, and cats are popular with C&O Canal cyclists. Be sure to ask about the fire and the angel picture—it is a great story. $75–95.

Sharpsburg, 21782
Inn at Antietam (301-432-6601; 1-877-835-6011; www.innatantietam.com), 220 East Main Street. This Eastlake Victorian home, circa 1908, has been receiving accolades since its B&B inception in the 1980s. Charles

Van Metre and Bob Leblanc (memorabilia in the solarium chronicle their many years in the theater business) continue to run the inn with a touch a class. Each of the five guest suites has a private bath. I enjoyed the Rose Suite, with its antique four-poster bed and bright walk-in bay overlooking Sharpsburg's Main Street. The Smokehouse Suite is where hams and other meats were cured. Today, the stone fireplace remains the focal point of the sitting room, while guests bed down in an upstairs loft. Although somewhat out of character from the rest of the house, the Penthouse Suite's resemblance to a studio apartment and grandstand view of the surrounding mountains are a great use of the remodeled third-floor attic.

If a walk around the inn's 7 acres or an evening spent rocking on the wraparound porch are too relaxing, you can always exercise your mind by playing chess with the hand-carved Civil War set. $135–175.

Jacob Rohrbach Inn (301-432-5079; www.jacob-rohrbach.hypermart.net),

138 West Main Street. The 1800 Federal-period inn is named for the man who lost his life defending the property from horse thieves during the Civil War. The Clara Barton guest room is decorated with furniture made by host Paul Breitenbach's grandfather. I thought that the three small steps into the elevated bathroom in the Thomas Jackson Room added a bit of historic authenticity to my stay. The restored summer kitchen house was a great place to unwind. $109–119.

Piper House Bed & Breakfast (301-797-1862), P.O. Box 100 (within Antietam National Battlefield; see *To See—Historic Sites*). Every building has a history, but at the Piper House the stories almost come alive. During the Antietam battle, wounded soldiers died on the log house's first floor, while Confederate riflers on the second floor kept the Union military at bay.

Today, the house is surrounded by the peaceful fields of the national battlefield, and all three guest rooms have a private bath and are decorated in

INN AT ANTIETAM, SHARPSBURG

period antiques. Regina and Louis Clark are extremely knowledgeable about the events that occurred around their home, so this is the place to stay if you are serious about Civil War research. $95.

VACATION RENTALS Rustic Rentals (202-686-5339; 1-877-787-8425). They have four cabins (two in West Virginia and two in this area of Maryland) that are available for rent for the night, weekend, week, or month. Each is fully equipped and can accommodate 4–6 people.

CAMPING

Boonsboro, 21713
Greenbrier State Park (301-791-4767), on US 40 about 9 miles east of Hagerstown. Usually open early April through late October. The large campground has a dump station and flush toilets. Within the state park is a lake for swimming, fishing, and boating (with paddleboat and canoe rentals). (Also see *Green Space— Parks.*)

Big Pool, 21711
☀ Indian Springs Campground (301-842-3336), 10809 Big Pool Road. One of the lowest-cost commercial campgrounds in the state. Limited facilities in winter.

& Fort Frederick State Park (301-842-2155), 11100 Fort Frederick Road. April through October. Located adjacent to the Potomac River and the Big Pool area of the C&O Canal. Vault toilets and two handicapped-accessible sites. (Also see *To See— Historic Sites.*)

Gapland, 21779
☀ Maple Tree Campground (301-432-5585), 20716 Townsend Road.

THE PIPER HOUSE B&B IN SHARPSBURG

Open year-round. A nicely laid-back campground in which RVs and trailers are not permitted; there are only tent sites. Two camping tree houses accommodate up to six people—a fun and different way to enjoy the woods. Rates are some of the most reasonable you will find anywhere, and the campground backs up to the Appalachian Trail (see sidebar on page 406). Pets permitted on leash.

Hancock, 21750
☀ Happy Hills (301-678-7760), 12617 Seavolt Road. Open all year. The campground's 350 acres are within easy walking distance of the C&O Canal (see C&O Canal National Historic Park under *To Do—Bicycling*), which means you have access to many more miles of trails in addition to those in the campground. RV and tent sites, pool, miniature golf, and activities building. Camping cabins for rent. Pets on leash permitted.

Williamsport, 21795
☀ Antietam Hagerstown KOA (301-223-7571; 1-800-562-7607), 11579 Snug Harbor Lane. Open year-round. The campground's 24 acres are along scenic Conococheague Creek, and some of the sites are next to the

water. Canoe rentals, miniature golf, and many, many planned family activities.

McMahon's Mill (301-223-8778), Avis Mill Road (at mile 88.1 on the C&O Canal). The closest campground to **Antietam National Battlefield** (see *To See—Historic Sites*), it has tent and RV sites next to the Potomac River. Flush toilets and hot showers. Also on the premises are a restaurant and the small **Civil War Military and American Heritage Museum** (open Saturday and Sunday 12:30–2:30; $3 admission fee).

🐾 **Yogi Bear's Jellystone Park** (301-223-7117), 16519 Lappans Road. Open all year. Lots of things to do on the campground's 90 acres: pool, playground, basketball and volleyball courts, and miniature golf. Some sites have full hookups. Small camping cabins for rent.

✳ Where to Eat

DINING OUT

Boonsboro

Old South Mountain Inn (301-432-6155), 6132 Old National Pike. Open for lunch Saturday and Sunday, dinner Tuesday through Saturday. Reservations strongly recommended for dinner. The inn was established in 1732, so be sure to read about its eventful past on the back of the menu.

Complimentary cheese and crackers accompany every meal on the menu, which features Maryland dishes influenced by cuisines from around the world. Scallops Provençale ($21), chicken saltimbocca ($19), shrimp Mediterranean ($23), and a couple of vegetarian entrées are just a few of the savory surprises to be found in this restaurant sitting next to the Appalachian Trail. The wait staff is friendly and knowledgeable about the many wines available. Desserts are delectable—and huge.

Heather B's (301-432-5100), 1 South Main Street. Open for dinner at 4 Wednesday through Friday, and at noon Saturday and Sunday. Such an eclectic place to be found in tiny Boonsboro. The chef and the owner are influenced by foods from around the world, and you will find bits of New Zealand, Colombia, Ecuador, and many of the countries of Europe on the menu.

Start your meal with the Inebriated Brandied Mushrooms, and move on to pastas, seafood, or meats expertly presented and prepared with a taste found nowhere else in this area. The staff is attentive and friendly, the decor modern and uncluttered, all the beers are imported, and there is live guitar music on the weekends. One of western Maryland's finest dining experiences. Entrées $13.95–24.95.

Hagerstown

🍴 **Rocco's** (301-733-3724), 501 Liberty Street. Open for dinner Tuesday through Saturday 5–9 (hours and days have been known to change). Reservations recommended. Tucked within a residential neighborhood, Rocco's reputation is such that many of its customers drive more than 35 miles to enjoy its southern Italian dishes. Washington County's oldest continuously operating restaurant, it has been family owned since 1936. The interior's piazza-like appearance of stone brick walls and a Trevi Fountain mural furnishes a fitting atmosphere for a menu best known for its Italian wedding soup, lasagna, and eggplant parmigiana. $7.95–16.95.

The Rhubarb House (301-733-4399), 12 Public Square. Open 8 AM–3 PM for breakfast and lunch Monday through Friday; 5–10 PM for dinner Friday and Saturday. The lunch menu has a wide choice of salads, inventive sandwiches ($4.25–7.95), and soups (the $5.95 cream of seafood is flavorful). Homemade potato chips sprinkled with grated cheese are a house specialty. Seafood Alfredo ($19.95), and chicken and sautéed asparagus over pasta in a champagne cream sauce ($13.95) are standouts for dinner. Ask for the lower dining room if you want the quieter spot during lunch.

EATING OUT

Hagerstown
The Grille at Park Circle (301-797-9100), 325 Virginia Avenue. Open for lunch and dinner; closed Monday. Directly across from the city park. It may call itself a grill, but it is much more, with entrées like sautéed scallops and Italian sausage in a tomato cream sauce, and tenderloin smothered in a peppercorn sauce. The chef has labored over stoves in California, Washington, Italy, Australia, and Chile, and the menu show his experience. Most entrées are $11.95–16.95.

Ron's Deli (301-739-1090), 29 North Burhans Boulevard. Open for lunch and dinner Monday through Saturday. Good American deli food, with many sandwiches and a few seafood and meat entrées. Worth a stop for straightforward food and atmosphere. $4.95–15.95.

Schmankerl Stube (301-797-3354; www.schmankerlstube.com), 58 South Potomac Street. Open for lunch and dinner; closed Monday. From the dark sculpted wooden fixtures and beams, a portrait of King Ludwig II, music on the sound system, and original Bavarian wait-staff outfits, everything in the restaurant says, "Let's go

Roccoco (301-790-3331; www.roccoco.com), 20 West Washington Street, Hagerstown. Open for lunch Monday through Friday 11–3; dinner, Monday through Saturday 5–10. Cheryl Kenney and Pauli Santi opened their brasserie on the ground floor of an office building in 1998 and have built up a loyal and varied clientele. During lunch, I overheard conversations about a pending business deal, what it takes to be a good Christian, how New Age music improves a massage, and tourists' discussions about where to go next.

All items on the menu, which changes frequently to make use of seasonally available items, are made from scratch. I never thought I would so thoroughly enjoy grilled romaine lettuce served with a warm Caesar dressing ($7). Entrées are equally imaginative and have included shellfish stew ($29), potato-crusted crabcakes with saffron butter ($25), and shrimp scampi pizza ($14). Pastries are made fresh daily—the chocolate oblivion ($5) is aptly named.

Without a doubt, my current favorite Hagerstown restaurant. I never know what new wonder chef Santi will be serving.

to Bavaria!" Owner Charlie Sekula makes sure that the restaurant reflects his homeland, and the Kassler ripperl ($15.95), Wiener schnitzel ($19.95), and zwiebelrostbraten ($19.95) do a good job. Daily specials and an extensive selection of German brews.

The Plum (301-791-1717), 6 Rochester Place. Open for breakfast and lunch Monday through Friday 7:30–3. A gourmet deli serving hot and cold sandwiches ($4.50–5.50). Hartwick's Heap ($5.25) has enough meat to satisfy any carnivore, while Jen's Veggie Pita ($4.10) is for the artery conscious.

Hancock

🍴 **Weaver's Restaurant and Bakery** (301-678-6346), 77 West Main Street. A Hancock institution for more than 50 years, this is the kind of place that, if you were to come here often enough, you would eventually meet the town's entire population. The home-cooking menu features hot and cold sandwiches, country-cured ham, pork chops, and seafood. The peanut butter or red raspberry pies are hard to resist, as are the doughnuts, cakes, and other goodies you can take home. The most expensive entrée is $14.95.

Williamsport

Home Town Diner (301-223-4500), 2 East Potomac Street. Open daily. This is just a diner serving home-cooked food, but the local folks come here often for breakfast, lunch, and dinner. It is also frequented by C&O Canal bikers and hikers, who seem to favor the hamburger casserole. A full evening meal will cost you no more than $15, usually much less.

COFFEE BARS **Secret's** (301-678-6868), 42 West Main Street, Hancock.

Open daily. Sip a cup of coffee (many varieties from around the world) while browsing among baskets, sculptures, paintings, leather masks, and other artwork. Deli sandwiches also available.

SNACKS AND GOODIES
Hagerstown

Olympia Candy Kitchen (301-739-0221), 13154 Pennsylvania Avenue. The outlet for handmade chocolates produced in nearby Pennsylvania.

Big Dipper (301-797-5422), 1033 Virginia Avenue. Soft-serve and Hershey's ice cream available on cones or in shakes of 60 different flavors.

Sharpsburg

Nutter's Ice Cream (301-432-5809), 100 East Main Street. A pleasant place to stop after a hot afternoon's worth of exploring nearby Antietam National Battlefield (see To See—Historic Sites).

Also see **Weaver's Restaurant and Bakery** under Eating Out.

✳ Entertainment

FILM The two first-run movie theaters in the area are located in Hagerstown: **Valley Mall Movie** (301-582-1000), 17301 Valley Mall Road, and **Hagerstown Cinema** (301-797-4747), Leitersburg Pike.

MUSIC **Maryland Symphony Orchestra** (301-797-4000; www.mdsymphony.org), 21 South Potomac Street, Hagerstown. There are at least 10 full concerts in the orchestra's year-round schedule, and many smaller venues and outreach programs.

THEATERS
Hagerstown
Maryland Theater (301-790-2000), 21 South Potomac Street. The theater

has been a place for the performing arts since 1915. Home to the **Maryland Symphony Orchestra,** it also brings in national and international plays and musicals, events, and performers.

Potomac Players (301-797-8182), 31 South Potomac Street. The local community theater usually stages at least four productions each year, and has been doing so for decades.

Washington County Playhouse (301-739-7469), 44 North Potomac Street. Open Friday and Saturday evening, and Sunday afternoon. Year-round dinner theater with a huge buffet.

SPORTS 🐾 **Hagerstown Suns** (301-791-6266; www.hagerstownsuns.com), Municipal Stadium, 274 East Memorial Boulevard, Hagerstown. The Suns, affiliates of the San Francisco Giants, play in the Class A South Atlantic League and have some of the most loyal and colorful fans I have seen for a minor league baseball team. Almost more entertaining than the action on the field are the comments and antics of the spectators in the stands. A low-cost (tickets prices are a bargain) and enjoyable way to spend an evening watching America's favorite pastime. Who knows? You might even see a future star, like the fans who attended Willie Mays's first professional ball game here in 1950.

✳ Selective Shopping
ANTIQUES
Hagerstown
Country Village (301-790-0006), 20136 National Pike. A half-dozen small buildings clustered together and packed with interesting items.

Antique Crossroads (301-739-0858),

20150 National Pike. Closed Wednesday. More than 200 dealers display wares in separate booths and showcases.

Hancock
Hancock Antique Mall (301-678-5959), 266 North Pennsylvania Avenue. With more than 48,000 square feet of climate-controlled space and close to 400 dealers, just about anything imaginable might be found here. There are antiques of every shape and kind, handcrafted items, memorabilia, and lots of other stuff/junk/pieces.

ART GALLERIES **Washington County Arts Council** (301-791-3132; www.washcoartscouncil.org), 41 South Potomac Street, Hagerstown. Open daily. A renovated downtown storefront has been turned into a bright and airy place to showcase the best of local and regional persons working in all manner of arts and crafts. Definitely worth a stop to look around.

Also see **Washington County Museum of Fine Art** under *To See— Museums.*

BOOKSTORES **Black Bird Mysteries** (301-432-8781; www.blackbird-mysteries.com), Keedysville. The name describes it well.

Turn the Page (301-432-4588), 18 North Main Street, Boonsboro. Women's fiction author Nora Roberts has written more than 100 novels and sold more than 145 million books. Since this is her store, you should be able to find just about everything she has ever written—in addition to other best-sellers and local-interest titles.

Hagerstown

Wonder Book and Video (301-733-1888; www.wonderbk.com), 1701 Massey Boulevard (at Valley Plaza). Open daily. They claim to have more than 1 million used, new, and rare books.

Barnwood Books (301-790-0606), 103 South Potomac Street. Closed Sunday. Buys, sells, and trades used books, and specializes in estate and library purchases.

SPECIAL SHOPS

Clear Spring

Wilson's General Store (301-582-4718), 14921 Rufus Wilson Road. A throwback to another era, the store sells everything from livestock feed to denim jeans. It is like a museum, preserving the decades from when Rufus Wilson first opened it in 1847. Curved wood and glass display cases are filled with lye soap, ointments, elixirs, and spools of sewing thread. The ornately carved wooden and glass refrigerator still works, keeping meats and cheeses cold. After buying a stick of hard candy, you could sit by the old potbellied stove and play a game of checkers with the rough, hand-carved pieces. **Wilson's School,** Washington County's only remaining one-room schoolhouse, is adjacent to the store and will be opened by appointment.

Hagerstown

Homeplace (301-791-2756), 20519 Beaver Creek Road. The business, on a quiet country road east of town, started as a place to grow and sell herbs and everlasting plants. They still do this, but the shop, decorated and arranged in a very eye-pleasing manner, now contains books, baskets,

linens, crafts, and some great folk art and pottery from local and national artisans. Worth a short drive into the country just to browse.

✍ **The Train Room** (301-745-6681; www.the-train-room.com), 360 South Burhans Boulevard. Besides being a model-train store, the shop contains a **Lionel museum** (adults $2.50, children under 12 free) that is the remarkable collection of owner Charles Mozingo. More than 5,000 items include old transformers, a four-track layout, Lionel chemistry sets and microscopes, and many items made by Lionel for the World War II war effort.

Sharpsburg

Sharpsburg Arsenal (301-432-7700; www.sharpsburg-arsenal.com), 101 West Main Street. It looks like a museum, but every item of Civil War militaria is for sale, from bullets to weapons to clothing to medical items. Be aware that some of the pieces have been transferred from historic sites.

Smithsburg

Heart and Home (301-416-0091), 11622 Crystal Falls Drive. Specializing in log-cabin birdhouses, primitive dolls, and small garden items.

OUTLETS ♿ **Prime Outlet** (1-888-883-6288), I-70 Exit 29, Hagerstown. The local complex of this national developer of outlet malls contains places to purchase Adidas, Bose, Izod, Jockey, Maidenform, Corning Revere, and at least 80 other companies' merchandise at so-called reduced prices.

FARMER'S MARKETS

Hagerstown

City Farmer's Market (301-739-8577), 25 West Church Street. Open

Saturday year-round, 5–noon. This has been the area's gathering and gossiping spot since 1791. There are vegetables and fruits for sale, but the real draw is the opportunity to watch local residents meet, greet, and eat. There is no way you can leave here hungry, as there are baked goods, homemade chocolates, hot pretzels, fresh coffee, and a great breakfast stand to tempt you. Arts and crafts are available and become more dominant in the colder months.

Washington County Farmer's Market (301-733-4551), Prime Outlets parking lot (see *Outlets*). From May through October you can stop here on Wednesday 4–7 PM. Additionally, produce and other products are available on Saturday 10 AM–1 PM, June through September.

PICK-YOUR-OWN PRODUCE FARMS
Lewis Orchards (301-824-2811), 22550 Jefferson Boulevard, Cavetown. Head to the fields in mid-May to gather strawberries and return in mid-June to pick cherries.

✳ Special Events

March: **Flower and Garden Show** (301-790-2800), Hagerstown Community College. An annual event with more than 100 vendors and the chance to learn about plant care from personnel of the U.S. Botanical Garden and National Arboretum.

May: **Annual Sharpsburg Memorial Day Commemoration** (301-432-8410), Sharpsburg. The oldest continuous Memorial Day parade and celebration in the United States. It started after the Civil War to honor returning veterans.

Late May or early June: **Western Maryland Blues Fest** (301-791-3246), Hagerstown. Annual 3-day celebration of music, a street festival, and workshops with national and international blues luminaries.

June: **Cumberland Valley Artists' Exhibit** (301-739-5727), Hagerstown. Annual juried competition in all media.

July: **Maryland Symphony Orchestra's Annual Salute to Independence** (301-797-4000), Antietam National Battlefield (see *To See—Historic Sites*). Celebrate the nation's birthday with patriotic and light classical music accompanied by cannon fire and fireworks.

August: **60s Under the Stars** (301-791-3246), Hagerstown. An annual salute to 1960s rock 'n' roll with performances by many stars of those days. **Augustoberfest** (301-791-3246), Hagerstown. An annual celebration of the city's German heritage. **Washington County Agricultural Expo** (301-791-3246; 1-888-257-2600), Sharpsburg.

September: **Annual Sharpsburg Heritage Festival** (1-800-228-STAY), Sharpsburg. Guided walking tours, living-history demonstrations, period-music concerts, arts and crafts, and historical-topics workshops. **Annual Steam and Craft Show** (301-791-3246), Smithsburg. A lineup of old steam engines, gas-powered tractors, and arts-and-crafts vendors.

November: **Alsatia Mummers Parade** (301-739-2044), Hagerstown. An annual event with decades of history and tradition.

The Allegheny Plateau

© The Countryman Press

THE ALLEGHENY PLATEAU— ROCKY GAP, CUMBERLAND, AND FROSTBURG

West of Hancock, I-68 works its way over Sideling Hill (see the sidebar on page 403 in "The Great Valley and Blue Ridge Region") to rise onto the Allegheny Plateau. Once the floor of an ancient ocean, the land was raised to new heights when Africa collided with North America 250 million years ago. Through time, water and wind have cut valleys and eroded softer rock to leave behind higher ridgelines, yet the plateau has remained essentially a mountain tableland with only minor variations in elevation. The mountain streams and ridgelines beckon those in pursuit of outdoor adventure, while the slightly rolling landscape lends itself to agricultural purposes. Some of Maryland's most extensive farms line both sides of the interstate.

Like the more famous Cumberland Gap along the Virginia–Kentucky–Tennessee border, Rocky Gap has been used for centuries by humans as an access route through the mountains. Following the tracks made by game animals, Native Americans were the first to pass through. As settlers from the Old World began pushing into western Maryland, the course was enlarged into the Old Hancock Road, a wagon route connecting Hancock in the east with Fort Cumberland to the west.

The only thing many travelers know about Cumberland is that it is the small city in which winding I-68 takes you past one church steeple after another—all of which are at eye level because of the interstate's elevated route. To get off the four-lane and do a little exploring is to find a place rich in the history of America's westward expansion, yet with a forward-looking population ready to celebrate the life it enjoys today.

The settlement began in 1787, when General Edward Braddock (and a young George Washington) established Fort Cumberland (the Emmanuel Episcopal Church is built on its foundations) during the French and Indian War. Cumberland developed into a transportation center as all of the early-1800s modes of transportation converged upon it. People poured through town on the National Road (see "What's Where in Maryland") on their way to the western frontier, the B&O railroad arrived in 1842, and the town became the western terminus of the Chesapeake and Ohio (C&O) Canal in 1850.

Industrialization and coal mining brought unprecedented prosperity after the Civil War, and a walk along the opulent houses of Washington Street, now a

National Historic District, lets you see just how successful business leaders were. Railroading became a major employer around the turn of the 20th century, enabling more industries to establish themselves and bringing new wealth and refinement into the area. The Cumberland Academy of Music was so prestigious that it attracted luminaries such as George Gershwin. Many of the downtown's buildings date from this era, and a walking-tour brochure from the Allegany County Convention and Visitors Bureau (see *Guidance*) describes some of them.

When manufacturing jobs began to disappear and city shops began to lose business to malls and outlying areas, Cumberland was one of the first places in America to establish a pedestrian mall in 1980. It has taken a while, but downtown is once again filled with restaurants, businesses, antiques stores, and eclectic shops. The mall has become the spot for the annual Summer in the City events (see *Special Events*), a farmer's market, and a pleasant place to stroll and people-watch. It is just a few blocks from the C&O Canal Visitor Center and the Western Maryland Scenic Railroad Depot.

Like Cumberland, Frostburg owes much of its existence to the National Road. When stagecoach service began in 1818, an assemblage of taverns, houses, and businesses grew up around the stagecoach stop. The arrival of the railroad in the 1840s allowed the coal industry to develop, soon followed by the manufacture of bricks from the high-grade clays found in the area. The biggest employer today is Frostburg State University, established as a Normal School in 1898. Frostburg may not be the railroading center it once was, but rail enthusiasts still arrive by the thousands each year on their round-trip journey from Cumberland along the Western Maryland Scenic Railroad. Baseball pitching great Lefty Grove, voted the American League's Most Valuable Player in 1931, is buried in the Frostburg cemetery.

CANAL PLACE IN CUMBERLAND

COMMUNITIES **LaVale** was a sleepy village along US 40 until the expansion of malls and fast-food restaurants overtook many small towns in America. Two interstate exits can deliver you to the Country Club Mall and just about any national restaurant chain you can think of.

Mount Savage, like many of the small towns in the western part of this area, first developed as a coal-mining community. Around the turn of the 20th century, Andrew Ramsey came upon a way to produce a special colored, glazed brick. It soon received worldwide acclaim and was bought for its smooth, bright, and easily cleaned surface. Unfortunately, Ramsey never told anyone exactly what his process was, so his factory closed when he died.

The bituminous coal underlying the mountain lands along MD 36 gave rise to so many coal-mining communities that it is almost hard to tell where one community ends and another begins. These settlements, the largest of which is **Lonaconing,** were once so isolated from the outside world that the local speech still contains slight traces of an English accent.

GUIDANCE **The Allegany County Convention and Visitors Bureau** (301-777-5132; 1-800-425-2067; www.mdmountainside.com), 13 Canal Street, Suite 406, Cumberland, 21502, may be found on the ground floor of Canal Place, conveniently located next to the ticket office for the Western Maryland Scenic Railroad. If the volunteer staff, which is well trained and knowledgeable, can't answer one of your questions, ask them to contact one of the bureau's employees who work upstairs.

The early 1900's **Palace Theater** at 33 East Main Street in Frostburg now functions as a community auditorium and **tourism center.**

GETTING THERE *By car:* **I-68** is the major highway that will bring you into the area from the east or the west. **US 220** connects with the **Pennsylvania Turnpike** as it comes into the area from the north.

By air: US Airways Express (1-800-428-4322) provides scheduled passenger commuter service from the **Greater Cumberland Regional Airport** (304-738-0022), which has connections at the **Pittsburgh, Pennsylvania, International Airport** (412-472-3525).

By bus: **Greyhound** (1-800-231-2222) makes a stop at its local

THE NARROWS WEST OF CUMBERLAND

terminal (301-722-6226), at 37 Henderson Avenue, Cumberland, during an east–west run along I-68.

By rail: Cumberland is lucky enough to be one of the dwindling number of small cities in America that can still be reached by passenger-rail service. The **AMTRAK** (1-800-872-7245) station on Harrison Street receives passengers arriving from the west in the morning and those coming from the east in the evening.

GETTING AROUND *By car:* **I-68** is, of course, the fastest way to get around, but consider using **US 40,** which parallels it and will take you through rural areas and some of the smaller towns. It also is along the historic route of the **National Road** (see "What's Where in Maryland"). **US 220** and **MD 26** are two-lane roadways that will take you into the more isolated southern regions of this area.

By bus: **Allegany County Transit Division** (301-772-6360) operates 10 routes that can transport you to most of the cities and towns in the area.

By rail: See the **Western Maryland Scenic Railroad** sidebar on page 430.

By taxi: **Morgan Taxi** (301-722-2800) and **Yellow Cab** (301-722-4050) are both based in Cumberland.

MEDICAL EMERGENCY

Cumberland
Cumberland Memorial Hospital (301-777-4100), 600 Memorial Avenue.

Sacred Heart Hospital (301-759-5161), 900 Seton Drive.

✳ To See

MUSEUMS

Frostburg
&. **Thrasher Carriage Museum** (301-689-3380; www.thrashercarriagemuseum.com), 19 Depot Street (adjacent to the Western Maryland Scenic Railroad Depot). Open Tuesday through Sunday, May through September; daily in October; and Saturday and Sunday from November through December. Small admission fee.

Contains horse-drawn vehicles from almost every part of American life, including Theodore Roosevelt's inaugural parade carriage. Seek out the buckboard—the work the carpenter did with the wood is remarkable. Guides and interpretive signs provide detailed background.

Frostburg Museum (301-689-5903; www.frostmuseum.org), 69 Hill Street. Open Tuesday 1–4. Donations accepted. The volunteer-maintained museum is housed in the 1899 Hill Street School, and its exhibits preserve and portray the industrial and social past of the area.

HISTORIC HOMES History House (301-777-8678; historyhouse.allconet.org), 218 Washington Street, Cumberland. Open Tuesday through Sunday, June through October; Tuesday through Saturday, November through May. Guided

tours given on the hour; small admission fee. The Second Empire home was
built in 1867 for Judge Josiah Hance Gordon, president of the C&O Canal (and
a Southern sympathizer arrested during the Civil War). It was later purchased by
the West Milner Roberts Sr. family, who lived there until the 1950s. It is furnished with pieces reflecting their time of occupation. A few rooms contain
items of local historical interest.

After visiting the house, take a walk along the six blocks of Washington Street
listed on the National Register and you will glean a bit of information about
Cumberland's earlier days. History House reflects the obvious wealth of the Gordon and Roberts families, but their former home is quite simple and plain compared to the other, more extravagant houses along the street.

HISTORIC SITES & **George Washington's Headquarters** (301-777-5132),
Riverside Park on Greene Street, Cumberland. Most easily accessed by a 2-
minute walk from Canal Place: Simply cross the railroad tracks and use the
Esplanade over Wills Creek. Most places that are open by appointment only
have been excluded from this guidebook, but you can get a feel for history just
by walking around this small cabin and reading the interpretive signs. Local lore
(which some historians question) states that Washington used the structure when
he was aide-de-camp to General Braddock in the mid-1700s, and when he
returned as president in 1794. The Cresap Chapter of the Daughters of the
American Revolution has furnished the cabin with period replicas.

LaVale Toll Gate House (301-777-5132), Old US 40 in Upper LaVale. Open
1:30–4:30 Saturday and Sunday, May through October. The tollgate house was
built in the early 1800s and is now the only surviving such structure in the state.

GEORGE WASHINGTON'S HEADQUARTERS IN CUMBERLAND

Its seven-sided construction has windows facing all directions so that the gate-keeper could clearly see any approaching traffic. The antique furnishings reflect its earliest days; ask for the story behind the courting candle.

Just a few buildings and a small cemetery remain in **Oldtown** beside the C&O Canal to mark the site where the first settlement in Allegany County once stood. Thomas Cresap established a trading post in the 1740s next to the Potomac River and along the route of the Native American Warrior's Path. His son, Michael, was born in 1741, and his home—now a museum open on an irregular basis—is the only building from the early days that is still standing. (Michael was later engaged in battles with Native Americans along the Ohio River. Although Cresap was considered a hero by some, Chief Logan claimed he was the man who sparked the war by murdering, unprovoked, the chief's wife and all of his children.) Also on the site, and open on an irregular basis, is the **Lock House 70,** constructed when the C&O Canal was built in the mid-1800s.

HISTORIC CHURCHES Emmanuel Episcopal Church (301-777-3364), 16 Washington Street, Cumberland. Constructed in the mid-1800s with a commanding view of the town, the church is one of the earliest uses of the Greek Revival style in America. Louis Tiffany extensively remodeled its interior in the early 1900s. Among other things, he carved the High Altar, and three of the stained-glass windows are his. His original design sketches are on display in the church community room.

All of these things, however, are not the only reasons to visit. The church was built upon the foundations of the mid-1700s **Fort Cumberland.** Some of the earthworks, ammunition magazines, and fort tunnels still exist and are open for public visitation. To walk these narrow passageways is to perceive the ghosts of the soldiers who helped prepare the way for western Maryland's early settlers.

LaVALE TOLL GATE HOUSE

OTHER SITES & **C&O Canal National Historical Park Cumberland Visitors Center** (301-722-8226), 13 Canal Street (in the Western Maryland Railroad Station), Cumberland. Open daily 9–5. Free. Much more than just a visitors center, it has many exhibits pertaining to the history of the canal and the local area. Interactive displays with audiotapes let you become familiar with canal workers, such as lockkeeper Harvey Brant, who received $22.50 a week and was on call 24 hours a day. I found the exhibit, in which Mr. Sandblount describes growing up and working on a canal boat, to be both enlightening and entertaining. This is a great place, especially since it is free. Don't forget to take the short walk to the *Cumberland*, a full-scale canal-boat replica. (Also see **C&O National Historical Park** under *To Do—Bicycling* for information on the canal in this area.)

The visitors center is located in **Canal Place,** which is being developed as a performing arts/historic site incorporating several buildings and locations around the canal's western terminus.

Lonaconing Iron Furnace, in the town of Lonaconing. Built in 1837, it was America's first successful coal- and coke-fired furnace to produce pig iron. Most furnaces from these days are crumbling shells, but this one is nearly intact and worth a visit.

Dan's Rock, located on Dan's Rock Road, off MD 36 near Vale Summit. It is a twisting mountain road you must negotiate to reach Dan's Rock, but the view is definitely worth it. Just a few steps from the parking area is an Olympian view of Savage Mountain rising out of the depths of George's Creek Valley. The Allegheny Mountains of West Virginia recede far to the south, while farmlands stretch eastward along the Potomac River.

GUIDED TOURS See *To Do—Walking Tours.*

LONACONING IRON FURNACE

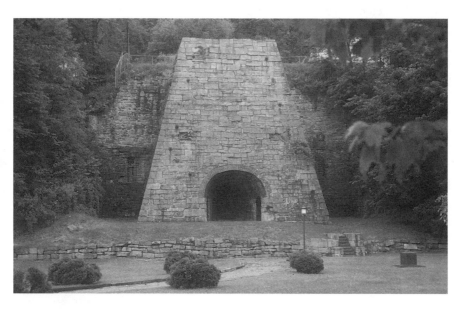

SOMETHING TO LOOK FORWARD TO—OR DO RIGHT NOW

The Allegheny Highlands Trail is a planned 214-mile bicycle route that will begin near Pittsburgh, Pennsylvania, and connect with the C&O Canal at Cumberland. When the trail is finished, you will be able to ride nearly 400 miles on a pathway devoid of road traffic or other similar hazards.

Actually, most of the trail is built, with only short sections still under construction. Many people have already ridden from Pittsburgh to Washington, D.C., by following back roads along the uncompleted portions.

Information on the route in Maryland is available from the **Allegheny Highlands Trail of Maryland** (301-777-2161; www.ahtmtrail.org), P.O. Box 28, Cumberland, 21501. Pennsylvania trail information may be obtained from the **Allegheny Trail Alliance** (www.atatrail.org), 419 College Avenue, Greensburg, PA 15601.

✳ To Do

BICYCLING C&O Canal National Historical Park. (Also see the sidebar on page 301 for background history and information on the canal.) More than 40 miles of the canal pass through this area of Maryland. The section is more isolated than any other portion, which enables you to ride and explore without the crowds often found elsewhere. Some of the highlights include access to **Oldtown** (see *To See—Historic Sites*), the **Green Ridge Hiking Trail** (see *Hiking*), and the **Paw Paw Tunnel** (see the sidebar opposite). About a dozen designated campsites (some free, some with a fee) are spaced along the route. Each has vault toilets and water (in-season) and is available on a first-come, first-served basis. There are also numerous ramps from which you could launch a boat into the Potomac River and paddle for several days while making use of the riverside campsites. The **C&O Canal Visitors Center** (see *To See—Other Sites*) in Cumberland can provide detailed information.

Cycles and Things (301-722-5496), 165 North Centre Street, Cumberland. Cycles and Things sells bikes, but they can also repair yours if you have a problem while in the area.

Green Ridge State Forest (301-478-3124), 28700 Headquarters Drive, NE, Flintstone. Multiple miles of trails and dirt roads are open to mountain biking. An exceptional ride, which has a variety of terrain (and may not be suited to beginners), is the 12-mile self-guided loop trail. The state-forest headquarters can provide you with a map of all the routes. (Also see *Lodging—Camping.*)

BIRDING ✐ ♿ Dan's Mountain State Park, (301-777-2139), Water Station Run Road (off MD 36), Lonaconing. The park's heavily wooded acres are habitat for those species that nest only in forests. Expect to find scarlet tanagers, ovenbirds, and yellow-throated vireos. (Also see *Green Space—Parks.*)

BOAT RENTALS See *Outdoor Adven-*

Paw Paw Tunnel, off MD 51 (at the Potomac River Bridge and the C&O Canal; see C&O Canal National Historical Park Cumberland Visitors Center under *To See—Other Sites*). Like so many other things associated with the canal, construction of the 3,118-foot tunnel faced difficulties and miscalculations from the onset. Intense friction among camps of Irish, English, and German laborers—in conjunction with a cholera epidemic—compounded the problems. Originally estimated to be built within 2 years at a cost of $33,500, it took 14 years and more than $600,000 to complete. Once finished, though, the tunnel—lined with close to 6 million bricks in layers of 7 to 11 deep—was used from 1850 to the canal's demise in 1924.

Break out the flashlights when you enter the tunnel, which is a little more than a half mile long. Even after its completion, the tunnel proved to be a source of contention. Although upstream boats were supposed to have the right-of-way in the narrow channel, some boat captains would refuse to yield. Local lore tells of an occasion where two barges stayed in place for several days because neither captain would give way. Canal workers finally built a fire to smoke them out.

The pathway is usually wet and slippery, so use the provided handrail. Some of the boards are the original lumber, and your hand can feel the grooves worn into it from years of towropes sliding across. Once through, you can take a break at a small picnic area. You have the choice of going back the way you came or taking the **Tunnel Hill Trail** over the ridgeline the tunnel goes through. The round-trip journey is about 3 miles.

ture, and **Rocky Gap State Park** under *Green Space—Parks.*

CARRIAGE RIDES See *Walking Tours.*

FISHING See **Rocky Gap State Park** under *Green Space—Parks.*

GOLF Rocky Gap State Park (301-784-8400; 1-800-724-0828; www.rockygapresort.com), 16701 Lakeview Road (accessed from I-68 Exit 50), Flintstone. The only Jack Nicklaus Signature Golf Course in Maryland. The front nine, carved out of the mountainous terrain and lined by trees, have quite dramatic elevation changes. The back nine course their

way over an open, rolling meadow. (Also see *Green Space—Parks.*)

Also see **Manhattan Centre Golf and Gallery** under *Selective Shopping—Special Shops.*

HIKING 🐾 Green Ridge Hiking Trail, Green Ridge State Forest (301-478-3124), 28700 Headquarters Drive, NE, Flintstone. This 18-mile trail is one of the best backpacking outings in Maryland at any time of year, but to get the most fun out of it, wait for a hot summer weekend. The majority of the hike is along one creek or another, each with miles of small ripples and cascades—and a profusion of swimming holes. Even if

TRAIN EXCURSION

Western Maryland Scenic Railroad (301-759-4400; 1-800-TRAIN-50; www.wmsr.com), 13 Canal Street Railway Station, Cumberland–Frostburg. From May through September, the diesel engine leaves Cumberland Wednesday through Thursday at 11:30 AM; the steam engine departs Friday through Sunday at 11:30 AM. In October, the diesel operates Monday through Wednesday, the steam from Thursday through Sunday. In November and December, there is only one departure (the steam engine) at 11:30 AM. Standard fare: adults $18, children $10. First class (includes lunch in the dining car): adults $30, children $15.

The 3-hour round-trip excursions (with a 90-minute layover in Frostburg) travel through some of western Maryland's prettiest scenery by negotiating the **Narrows,** climbing over 1,900-foot **Piney Mountain,** and passing through 914-foot **Brush Tunnel. Helmstedder's Curve** is such a long, tight horseshoe bend that even those sitting in the very rear passenger car can look across the way and see the engine. There is some taped narration along the way, but it would be nicer if it would describe more of what you are experiencing.

WESTERN MARYLAND SCENIC RAILROAD

you don't want to take a plunge, you still need to ford them well over 60 times; so wait until warm weather has raised the water temperature a few degrees.

Backcountry camping is permitted; obtain a permit (and pay the fee) at the forest headquarters just off I-68 Exit 64. A pamphlet for the **Pine Lick Hollow Segment** has information describing the natural and human history of the area. (The state forest is the habitat of the rarely seen large blazing star and Kate's mountain clover.) Pets must be on a leash and hunting is permitted during the season, so take proper precautions.

Headquarters personnel can also provide information on the more than 20 miles of other pathways in the forest. (Also see *Bicycling*.)

KAYAKING AND CANOEING See **C&O Canal National Historical Park** under *Bicycling*, and *Outdoor Adventure*.

OUTDOOR ADVENTURE Allegany Expeditions Inc. (301-722-5170; 1-800-819-5170; www.alleganyexpeditions.com), 10310 Columbus Avenue, NE, Cumberland. AEI can take care of you for just about any activity in the natural world that you can engage in during a visit to western Maryland. They can provide instructions or set up guided trips for climbing, caving and rappelling, paddling excursions, skiing, fishing, and backpacking. All of the required equipment can be rented or purchased.

Adventure Sports (301-689-0345), 113 Main Street, Frostburg. Adventure Sports provides all of the services

available through Allegany Expeditions (see above) but also offers instructions and guided trips for ice climbing, mountain biking, and even scuba diving.

SCUBA DIVING See **Adventure Sports** under *Outdoor Adventure*.

SKATING YMCA (301-777-YMCA), 601 Kelly Road, Cumberland. There may be others, but this is the only YMCA I know of that has an ice-skating rink as part of its facilities. Call for the days and times it is open to the public.

SWIMMING See **Rocky Gap State Park** under *Green Space—Parks*.

WALKING TOURS Westmar Tours (301-777-0293; www.wstme.com), 13 Canal Street, Cumberland. Costumed guides lead walking and riding tours (some in horse-drawn carriages) in historic Cumberland and surrounding areas. A great way to gain intimate knowledge of the region.

✳ Green Space

PARKS ♂ ♿ **Rocky Gap State Park** (301-784-8400; 1-800-724-0828; www.rockygapresort.com), 16701 Lakeview Road (accessed from I-68 Exit 50), Flintstone. As you descend westward on Martin Mountain on I-68, the first thing to catch your eye will be the dramatic setting of the park's massive 220-room resort lodge, built along the southern shore of Lake Habeeb. Below Evitt's Mountain's lush hillside, the manicured greens of a golf course (see *To Do—Golf*) stretch between the lodge and the four-lane highway.

(There is no doubt that this type of development adds another aspect and attraction to the state park, but there was much debate and protest in the local community, and throughout Maryland, about changing the natural character of the state park. Many people also questioned the propriety of the state's turning such a large amount of public land over to a private, profit-making corporation.)

Within the park are a campground (see *Lodging—Camping*), a camp store, laundry facilities, beaches with modern bathhouses, an outdoor pool, tennis courts, a snack bar, and boat rentals. The 243-acre Lake Habeeb attracts anglers with largemouth bass, panfish, and trout. A trail network brings hikers by the lake, up Evitt's Mountain to an old homesite, and down into scenic Rocky Gap Gorge. Thousands of visitors attend the park's annual music festivals (see *Special Events*) in August. Personnel at the park can arrange for you to participate in many of the state's **Nature**

Tourism (see "What's Where in Maryland") activities.

🐾 ♿ **Dan's Mountain State Park** (301-777-2139), Water Station Run Road (off MD 36), Lonaconing. Open daily during daylight hours. The 485 acres have the feel of a community park, as the local population comes here in significant numbers to enjoy the Olympic-sized swimming pool with water slide, and beautiful mountain scenery. There is a designated overlook, but the view from the children's playground is equally awe-inspiring.

✳ Lodging

RESORTS ♿ **Rocky Gap State Park** (301-784-8400; 1-800-724-0828; www.rockygapresort.com), 16701 Lakeview Road (accessed from I-68 Exit 50), Flintstone, 21530. The accommodations within the park's lodge are pretty much standard

DAN'S MOUNTAIN STATE PARK

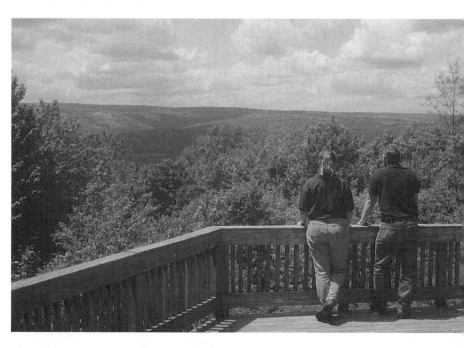

upscale hotel/motel-type rooms—but, oh, those views. I prefer a deluxe room (with a balcony and kitchenette) overlooking the lake and Evitt's Mountain, although there is certainly nothing wrong with the view of the emerald fairways of the golf course. Staying in any room gives you access to all of the park's facilities (see *Green Space—Parks*). $145–275.

Many package deals—golf, outdoor adventure, and honeymoon—are available. Also see *Camping*.

MOTELS AND HOTELS

Cumberland, 21502

🐾 ♿ **Holiday Inn** (301-724-8800; 1-800-HOLIDAY; cumberlandmdholidayinn.com), 100 South George Street. Talk about turning a negative into a positive! The hotel overlooks the noise and activity of a busy CSX rail-freight yard—which, admittedly, is not the most scenic of places. Recognizing the many railroad fans in the world, the manager mounted a video cam on the roof, pointed it toward the rail yard, and made the 24-hour action available on the hotel's web site. It has been receiving more than 1 million hits a year. Almost every day now there is someone making a reservation for one of the rooms with a rail-yard view, and special railroading events fill the entire facility.

The hotel also has an outdoor pool, a fitness room, and an on-site restaurant. $80–120.

Frostburg, 21532

Fallingers Hotel Gunter (301-689-6511), 11 West Main Street. Like many older, grand hotels, Fallingers now rents some rooms as residential apartments. However, the 14 remaining hotel rooms have been thoroughly renovated and reflect the property's glory days. Each is furnished differently with antiques and reproductions. The rooms are enjoyable enough, but wander around to appreciate the massive oak stairway in the lobby, the swing on the balcony where you can watch the rest of the world go by, and the stained-glass windows found on each stairway landing.

The basement is a small museum with items found during the renovation, plus the town's original jail and a replica of a coal mine. Rates range $65–90.

♿ **Hampton Inn** (301-689-1998), 11200 New George's Creek Road. A whirlpool, heated pool, and exercise room are available to work off the calories you consume during the free continental breakfast. All rooms have an iron and small refrigerator. $89–129.

FALLINGERS HOTEL GUNTER IN FROSTBURG

LaVale, 21502

&cube; **Best Western** (301-729-3300; 1-800-296-6006; www.bestwesternbraddock.com), 1268 National Highway. One of the most meticulously maintained mainstream motels in the state. Rooms are continually being renovated and updated, tanning beds and a sauna are in the exercise room, and the large inside pool adjoins an outside sundeck. Although the motel sits next to a crossroads area, the landscaping and natural brook add an unexpected gentle quality.

&cube; **Oak Tree Inn** (301-729-6700; www.lexres.com), 12310 Winchester Road. A well-maintained facility with a kitchenette in many rooms. Exercise center and coin laundry on the premises. Pets permitted. $75–85.

BED & BREAKFASTS &cube; **Shaw Mansion Inn** (301-463-3131; www.shaw-mansion-inn.com), 18311 Laurel Run Road, Barton, 21521. Close to Dan's Mountain State Park (see *Green*

Space—Parks) and Big Savage Hiking Trail (see *Hiking* note under *Lodging—Camping*).

I am partial to B&Bs in out-of-the-way rural settings, and this one is really to my liking. I enjoyed strolling across the 7-acre property to watch red-winged blackbirds fly by the pond and around the massive evergreen and maple trees growing in the front yard.

Ruth and Craig Marsh have restored the 1870 Victorian home, built of walnut trees grown on the property and brick made from the plantation's clay. The house is furnished with period antiques, and breakfast is served next to the large bay windows, which almost reach from the floor to the 13-foot ceilings. $95–125.

Inn at Walnut Bottom (301-777-0003; www.iwbinfo.com), 120 Greene Street, Cumberland, 21502. The inn's location in the heart of Cumberland made my explorations much easier, and host Grant Irvin's and Kirsten

SHAW MANSION INN IN BARTON

Hanson's knowledge of the area pointed me to many places I would have overlooked. The B&B is actually two adjacent town houses (circa 1820 and 1890) that have been joined together to provide 12 guest rooms and suites. Some share a bath, others have a private bath, and each is uniquely furnished with antiques and period reproductions.

The accommodations are attractive and breakfasts are legendary. Do not fail to schedule a massage during your stay. Kirsten is trained in afspaending, a type of massage developed in Denmark (her homeland) that is more relaxing than many other methods. $87–145.

The Castle B&B (301-264-4645; www.noomoon.com/castle), 15925 Mt. Savage Road, Mount Savage, 21545. The Castle started life in 1840 as a modest stone house, but near the beginning of the 20th century, nouveau riche owner Andrew Ramsey turned it into a replica of Scotland's Craig Castle. You get to enjoy large verandas and terraces of glazed tile, formal gardens, and a 16-foot stone wall (built by Italian masons) surrounding the property.

Six guest rooms (some with a private bath) range in rates $95–130.

CAMPING

Flintstone, 21530
Green Ridge State Forest (301-478-3124), 28700 Headquarters Drive, NE. Primitive campsites are designated along many of the roads that snake their way through the 43,000-acre forest. A permit (and payment of a fee) may be obtained in the state-forest headquarters. (Also see *To Do—Bicycling* and *Hiking*.)

☻ **Hidden Springs Campground** (814-767-9676), Pleasant Valley Road.

May through October. The campground's 58 acres are close to Rocky Gap State Park (see below and *Green Space—Parks*) and contain a swimming pool, playgrounds, miniature golf, and a stocked fishing pond.

☻ **Rocky Gap State Park,** (301-784-8400; 1-800-724-0828; www.rockygapresort.com), 16701 Lakeview Road (accessed from I-68 Exit 50). Nearly 300 sites are situated among the trees along the northern shore of Lake Habeeb. Hookups, bathhouses with hot showers, and access to all of the

THE CASTLE B&B IN MOUNT SAVAGE

park's facilities (see *Green Space— Parks,* and *Resorts*). Pets (on leashes) are permitted in two of the campground's loops.

Little Orleans, 21766

Little Orleans Campground (301-478-2325), 31661 Green Forest Drive, SE. Located less than a 5-minute walk from the C&O Canal (see C&O National Historical Park under *To Do—Bicycling*) and bordered on two sides by Green Ridge State Forest (see above). I would classify this almost as resort, as it contains RV and tent sites, a playground, a fishing pond, swimming pools, a game room, volleyball, basketball, and horseshoes—in addition to usual campground facilities.

✳ Where to Eat

DINING OUT ⅊ **Oxford House** (301-777-7101), 129 Baltimore Street (Downtown Pedestrian Mall), Cumberland. Open for lunch Monday through Friday 11–2:30; dinner, Monday through Friday 5–9:30. The schwitzerschnitzel ($17.95), rockfish Chesapeake ($19.95), scallops Provençale ($17.95), Delmonico *pizzaiola* ($21.95), and veal and crab served in a Cajun cream sauce ($18.95) are indications that the menu takes its cues from many parts of Europe and the United States. The furnishings and brick floor made me feel as if I were dining in a piazza.

⅊ **Lakeside Restaurant** (301-784-8444; www.rockygapresort.com), in Rocky Gap State Park (see *Green Space—Parks*), Flintstone. Open 6:30 AM–11 PM daily. I have found restaurants in many state parks to be so-so, but Lakeside is an exception. Dress may be casual, but the food has a

touch of class. Sesame-crusted shrimp and scallops ($8.25) and mozzarella *caprese* ($5.25) are my favorite appetizers. The pine nut dusted Allegheny trout ($18), and the shrimp, crayfish, scallops, and andouille sausage served over *paglia e fieno* (spinach and egg noodles) ($18.50) are testaments to the kitchen staff's expertise. Other chicken, steak, and vegetarian entrées range $15–28.

The view of Lake Habeeb and Evitt's Mountain adds to the overall experience.

🍴 ⅊ **Au Petit Paris** (301-689-8946; 1-800-207-0956; www.aupetitparis. com), 86 East Main Street, Frostburg. Open for dinner Tuesday through Saturday 6–9:30. Reservations recommended. Although this is the special-occasion restaurant for people from many miles around, the prices are amazingly low—and about half of what you would pay in a heavily populated area like Baltimore or Washington, D.C.

Louis and Jeanne St. Marie, and family, have been serving their delightful French cuisine since the mid-1950s. Seafood dishes are succulent, but do not overlook the veal and beef specialties. One of my favorite western Maryland fine dining experiences. $11–30.

EATING OUT

Cumberland

City Lights (301-722-9800), 59 Baltimore Street. Open daily 11 AM to closing. Having relocated from the shopping mall in LaVale, City Lights has become a favorite on the Downtown Pedestrian Mall. After having eaten a meal of stuffed mushrooms, Greek spinach salad, and walnut apple pork, customers of the two-story restaurant have a tendency to linger, socialize, and imbibe in selections from the bar. Friday and Saturday nights hop. The highest-priced entrée is $19.95.

🍴 ✍ **Bender's Family Restaurant** (301-724-6628), 204 Baltimore Street. Open 7 AM–3 PM daily. Painted plywood booths, vinyl chairs, and a listing counter are indications that people don't come here for the atmosphere. It is definitely not upscale, yet office workers, lawyers, and other professionals walk across the railroad tracks to eat here. The draw is honest home cooking at low prices. Breakfast is served all day, the pies are homemade, and the kids have their own lunch and breakfast menu. Proprietor Shirley Bender offers a light menu for those counting calories—a rarity for places such as this. You would be hard-pressed to spend more than $5 here.

Curtis's Famous Wieners (301-789-9707), 35 North Liberty Street. Open 7 AM–10 PM daily. A Cumberland tradition, it has been serving hot dogs, burgers, and hand-dipped milk shakes since 1918. A favorite of downtown office workers for lunch. Most meals will cost you less than $5.

✍ **When Pigs Fly** (301-722-7447; www.pigsonline.com), 18 Valley Street. Open for lunch and dinner; closed Sunday. Extensive beer selection in a pleasant bar area. Steaks, chicken, and seafood; but the main reason to dine here is the BBQ. It is available as pulled pork and ribs, beef, or chicken. Entrées $9.95–17.95.

The name? When the owners told their families they were going to open a restaurant, the skeptical relatives replied, "Yeah, sure. When pigs fly."

Uncle Tucker's 1819 BrewHouse (301-777-7005; www.edmasons.com), I-68 Exit 46. Under contract to build tollhouses along the National Pike, Jacob Hoblitzell built his own home in 1819. Used for many things, including a Civil War field hospital, the house eventually fell into disrepair. Now on the National Register after being restored—from its Georgia-pine floors to the horsehair plaster walls—by proprietor Ed Mason in the 1990s, Uncle Tucker's serves a widely varied menu. The Main Helper's Wood-Cooked Pizza, with basil, spinach, tomato, and artichoke hearts, proves a meal doesn't need meat to be tasty. The sauce used on the bruschetta appetizer is unique and flavorful. Other Italian dishes include homemade lasagna and cornmeal-crusted sea bass. A menu that changes often and a choice of the restaurant's own microbrews, including ales, lagers, and dark beers, keep the locals coming back. The upstairs is the quietest spot; the downstairs bar where the pizzas are made gets a little noisy, and many customers opt for the outside patio overlooking a trout stream. Entrées $4.95–14.95.

Two of Mason's other restaurants, **JB's Steak Cellar** (301-722-6060) and **Mason's Barn Family Restaurant** (301-722-6155) are next door.

Frostburg

🍴 ✍ **Princess Restaurant** (301-689-1968), 12 West Main Street. Open 6 AM–8 PM Monday through Saturday. I always take pleasure in finding places such as this—which are becoming increasingly harder to find. It is clean and well kept, but the atmosphere is nothing fancy; in fact, the place is somewhat reminiscent of a diner. Prices are so low that they have not been seen in other restaurants for years. The well-prepared food ranges from more than 40 different sandwiches to full dinners of meat loaf ($6.65), broiled haddock ($7.50), grilled pork chops ($8.45), and T-bone steaks ($9.75). The children's menu even includes an ice cream dessert in the cost of the meal.

Like his grandfather who started the business in this location in 1939 (a portion of the original tin ceiling is still in place), George W. Pappas ensures quality by doing things the old way, such as hand-forming hamburger patties, making gravies from scratch, and fresh-cutting potatoes for the homefries. Entrées $4.25–9.25.

Gandalf's (301-689-2010), 24 East Main Street. Open 5–10 PM; closed Sunday. Within a pub atmosphere, Gandalf's serves a surprisingly universal menu. The expected sandwiches are there, but you will also find dim sum ($5), a seafood sandwich ($5), and hummus ($6) and tofu vegetable ($6) subs. **Gandalf's Pub,** with microbrews and live entertainment, is located at 20 East Main Street and is open 5 PM–2 AM.

&. **Giuseppe's Italian Restaurant** (301-689-2220; www.giuseppes.net), 11 Bowery Street. Open daily for dinner. Good, traditional Italian fare, such as pizza, chicken cacciatore, shrimp scampi, lasagna, and baked ziti. Very reasonable prices—the most expensive entrée is less than $20; most are less than $15.

La Vale

&. **Gehauf's** (301-729-1746), 1268 National Highway (inside the Best Western hotel). Open daily for breakfast, lunch, and dinner. With lush plants adding a feeling of being out-doors, Gehauf's makes all of its soups, sauces, dressings, and baked goods from scratch. Seafood entrées are prominent, joined by traditional western Maryland dishes of turkey, ham, pork chops, and steak. Entrées $4.95–15.95.

⌁ **Penny's Diner** (301-729-6700), 12310 Winchester Road, SW. Open 24 hours. People who can actually remember the 1950s are getting to be fewer in number, so if you want to sample a slice of their life, head to Penny's. Shiny aluminum highlights the interior, the jukebox is filled with songs of the decade, and the black-and-white photos show a LaVale that no longer exists. Burgers, fries, and other sandwiches (hot and cold) are joined on the menu by meat loaf, liver and onions, and pot roast. Don't pass up the old-fashioned hand-dipped milk shakes topped by whipped cream and a cherry. Entrées $4.29–8.99.

SNACKS AND GOODIES

Cumberland

&. **Queen City Creamery and Deli** (301-697-4810), 108 Harrison Street. Open daily for breakfast, lunch, and dinner. They have breakfast items, deli sandwiches, and gourmet coffee, but the premium homemade ice cream is what entices me to stop in nearly every time I pass by.

⌁ **The Fruit Bowl** (301-777-2780), US 40 in the Narrows at the western end of town. Yeah, they sell fresh fruits and vegetables, but what you really want to stop for are the 800 bins filled with just about every kind of snack-bar-sized candy you can think of. Snickers, Milky Way, Reeses, 3 Musketeers, and dozens of others are available in bulk.

Flintstone
Alpine Pantry (301-478-3696), 21511 Flintstone Drive, NE, I-68 Exit 56. Open Monday through Friday 7:30 AM–5:30 PM, Saturday 7 AM–4 PM. A fun place in which to browse for fresh-baked pies, breads, cakes, and pastries in addition to meats, cheeses, and a vast assortment of bagged candies. The small sign on the door, "Thank you for shopping here modestly dressed and well covered," lets you know this is a Mennonite establishment.

Frostburg
McFarland Candies (301-689-6670; www.mcfarlandcandies.com), 22 Broadway. What a treat. The McFarland family has been making assorted chocolate candies in Frostburg since 1944. Enjoy a taste of the premium nut clusters, chewies, barks, cremes, jellies, and fudges. Ask, and they will take you on a tour of the kitchen to witness the art of homemade candy production.

✳ Entertainment
FILM AMC Country Club (301-729-6633), 1262 Vocke Road, LaVale. Shows first-run films.

Frostburg Cinema (301-689-1100), Frostburg Plaza, Frostburg. Also presents movies when they are first released.

See **Embassy Theatre** under *Theaters* for information on classic films.

THEATERS
Cumberland
ﾋ **Cumberland Theatre** (301-759-4990), 101–103 Johnson Street. Western Maryland's only professional theater presents at least six musical, drama, or other theatrical productions

during its season, which usually runs from April through December. The small auditorium provides an intimate setting.

ﾋ **Embassy Theatre** (301-722-4692; 1-877-722-4692), 49 Baltimore Street. Citizens' efforts saved this 1931 art deco movie house. Classic films, live music, dance, and theatrical productions are presented in the lovingly, and accurately, restored edifice.

✳ Selective Shopping
ANTIQUES
Cumberland
Historic Cumberland Antique Mall (301-777-2979), 113 Baltimore Street. Open daily. Antiques of various shapes and forms offered by a number of different vendors.

Yesteryear Antiques and Collectibles (301-722-7531), 60 Baltimore Street. There is the usual glassware, china, linens, and pottery found in shops such as this, but also stop by for vintage clothing, lingerie, and jewelry.

ART GALLERIES Allegany Arts Council (301-777-ARTS; www.alleganyartscouncil.org), 52 Baltimore Street, Cumberland. The gallery features works by local and regional artisans, and traveling exhibits. The council sponsors performing-arts events throughout the year.

BOOKSTORES Book Center (301-722-2284), 15–17 North Centre Street, Cumberland. The only non-chain bookshop for many miles around, it stocks a large selection of local history, railroad, and travel titles, along with children's books and games, newspapers, and magazines.

Cumberland

The Country Angel (301-722-5151), 444 North Centre Street. Open Tuesday through Friday 10–6, Saturday 10–3. In addition to her own handmade crafts, Betty Harvey offers a number of items from local and regional craftspersons. The surprising sculptures created from cardboard deserve special attention.

Snyder's Cut Crystal (301-777-8155), 422 North Centre Street. Associated with the once thriving glass industry in western Maryland, the Snyder family hand etches many of the items available in their store.

SPECIAL SHOPS

Cumberland

& **Fort Cumberland Emporium** (301-722-4500), 55 Baltimore Street. Open daily. A multivendor shop with handmade arts and crafts, antiques, jewelry, furniture, and more.

& **Manhattan Centre Golf and Gallery** (301-777-0021), 69 Baltimore Street. Do you think someone has combined their two passions into one business? The golf part offers complete sales, service, and lessons. The gallery has limited-edition prints and some nice original artwork.

Frostburg

Frostburg Shops by the Depot (301-689-3676), 20 Depot Street. Five of the 12 small shops are located in the 1840 Tunnel Hotel that once housed railroad workers and local coal miners. There is no doubt the shops exist to appeal to riders on the Western Maryland Scenic Railroad (see the sidebar on page 428), but you can find a few treasures, such as train

memorabilia and some not-so-tacky souvenirs.

OUTLETS & **Biederlack of America** (301-759-3633; www.biederlack.com), 11501 Bedford Road, NE, Cumberland. This is the manufacturing site of one of the world's premier producers of blankets and throws. The large showroom offers the products at outlet prices.

FARMER'S MARKETS Cumberland Downtown Farmer's Market (301-724-3320). The Downtown Pedestrian Mall becomes a beehive of activity with produce, fruits, and other items for sale 9:45–2 on Thursday and Saturday, June through October.

LaVale Country Club Mall Farmer's Market (301-724-3320). Part of the mall's parking lot becomes a farmer's market 9:30–2 on Tuesday from June through October.

Frostburg Farmer's Market (301-724-3320). Main Street is transformed into an open-air emporium 9:45–1 on Friday from June through October.

✳ Special Events

May: **Canalfest** (301-724-3655), Canal Place, Cumberland. A celebration of the C&O Canal's history, with period artisans, music, canal-boat-replica tours, and living-history demonstrations.

Late May through early September: **Summer in the City** (301-777-2787), Cumberland. A concert each Friday, Saturday, and Sunday featuring local and regional musicians.

June: **Heritage Days** (301-777-2878), Cumberland. The area's biggest street festival features entertainment, children's activities, a carnival, scenic railroad excursions, arts and crafts, and food demonstrations. **Schoolhouse Quilters Guild Quilt Show** (301-729-5464), Frostburg State University. Western Maryland's largest quilt show. Vendors, demonstrations, and raffles.

July: **Oldtown Celebration** (301-478-5548), Oldtown. Slide shows and reenactments along the C&O Canal. **Maryland Mountain Cruise** (301-724-3734), fairgrounds, Cumberland. A mixture of several activities: custom-car show, jousting demonstrations, games for all ages, and crafts. **Allegany County Fair** (301-729-1200), fairgrounds, Cumberland.

August: **Rocky Gap Music Festival** (1-888-ROCKY-GAP), Rocky Gap State Park (see *Green Space—Parks*), Flintstone. A major event that draws thousands of people to listen to some of the biggest names in contemporary country music. **Freedom Blues Fest/State Chili Cookoff/Micro-**

Brewers Beer (301-722-3621), Ali-Ghan Shrine Picnic Grounds, I-68 Exit 46. If the presentations by nationally known blues acts do not appeal to you, try some samples of the many types of chilis being prepared for judging and wash them down with several swigs of Maryland-produced ales and lagers.

September: **Street Rod Roundup** (301-777-7774), fairgrounds, Cumberland. More than 1,000 pre-1949 streetcars show up for exhibition and street jousting. **Cumberland Wine and Music Festival** (301-722-1760), Rocky Gap State Park (see *Green Space—Parks*), Flintstone. An annual event of wine tastings, fine food, and music that includes styles from jazz to reggae. **Cumberland Celtic Fest** (301-777-2800), Cumberland. The clans gather for live entertainment, dances, ethnic foods, and children's games.

October: **Railfest** (301-759-4400; 1-

EXTRA-SPECIAL SHOPS

There are two shops on the **Downtown Pedestrian Mall** that I certainly did not expect to find in a city as small as Cumberland. The quality and uniqueness of their products almost make them like small museums, so be sure to stop by, even if you have no intention of purchasing anything.

Bohemia Value (301-722-7300; www.bohemiavalue.com), 64 Baltimore Street. Open daily. Fania Knizhnik imports Czech Republic–style art glass, crystals, porcelain, chandeliers, and other items produced by the Bohemia process that dates from the 13th and 14th centuries. Among many other items are Russian religious icons, porcelain from St. Petersburg, and ceramics from Greece.

Jackie's II Gallery (301-724-5700), 105 Baltimore Street. Works of art from around the world. The items from Cuba, Belgium, and Africa are especially beguiling. I was taken by the metallic embossed cards, which depict everyday African life, and by the hand-spun, hand-dyed, woolen tapestries with African scenes handwoven into them.

800-TRAIN-50), Cumberland. The annual event focuses on western Maryland's railroad legacy with steam-train excursions (short and long ones), displays, entertainment, and activities designed to bring the children in on the fun. **Iron Rail Days** (301-264-3229), Mount Savage. Attended and participated in by much of the residential population. Look for a reenacted bank robbery and jail break, along with guided tours of local sites.

AROUND DEEP CREEK LAKE— GRANTSVILLE, McHENRY, THAYERVILLE, AND OAKLAND

Outdoor types have been coming here for centuries. Three Native American trails converged at a spot near Grantsville, enabling members of several tribes to use the area for hunting. In the early 1700s, Meshach Browning was one of the area's earliest settlers and known far and wide for his hunting skills. In his book, *Forty-Four Years of the Life of a Hunter,* he not only describes life on America's frontier but also estimates he killed "1,800 to 2,000 deer, 300 to 400 bears, about 50 panthers and catamounts, with scores of wolves and wildcats." Self-styled vagabonds Henry Ford, Harvey Firestone, Thomas Edison, and John Burroughs came to the area for some backcountry camping in 1918 and again in 1921.

Situated upon the elevated terrain of the Allegheny Plateau, Deep Creek Lake, Maryland's largest inland body of water, was formed in the 1920s when Deep Creek was dammed as part of a hydroelectric project to provide power to the residents of Pennsylvania. It covers 6 square miles with approximately 65 miles of shoreline, and has become a destination for those who enjoy motorboating, waterskiing, sailing, and fishing, as well as those who just appreciate its scenic beauty. Six other lakes attract boaters of all kinds, while sport anglers come in search of abundant game fish. The streams that feed these lakes—the Youghiogheny, Savage, Casselman, and North Branch Potomac Rivers; Deep, Muddy, and Herrington Creeks; Buffalo, Laurel, and Hoyes Runs; and others—are considered to be some of the country's best fly-fishing destinations, brimming with brook, rainbow, and brown trout. All of the state's record trout were caught in this area. These same waterways, especially the Youghiogheny, Savage, and North Branch Potomac Rivers, are legendary to kayakers and whitewater rafters.

Nearly 100,000 acres of state parks, state forests, wildlife management areas, and Wild and Scenic River lands are laced with scores of trails, ranging from easy to difficult. Most of the pathways are open to hiking, mountain biking, and cross-country skiing, with multiple miles also available to snowmobiles. There are hundreds of campsites, some in commercially developed campgrounds, others rustically situated in the state parks. Backcountry camping is permitted on thousands of acres of state-forest lands.

Maryland's only downhill skiing resort is located here, but it also takes advantage of every season by having a golf course, mountain biking and mountain boarding routes, and other outdoor activities available throughout the year.

COMMUNITIES Only two to three blocks wide and surrounded by farmland, **Grantsville** began as a small settlement clustered around Stanton's Mill, built in 1797. The 1818 Penn Alps and 1824 Casselman Inn were constructed to service travelers along the National Road, and are both still in use. The town developed into a destination center soon after Dr. Alta Shrock established a nonprofit organization in 1957 to study and promote the way of life in the Allegheny Highlands. The Penn Alps Restaurant and Spruce Forest Artisan Village are visible symbols of her efforts.

McHenry grew up after the establishment of Deep Creek Lake and is the commercial strip that greets people as they come into the lake area from the north. **Thayerville** is the business center at the southern end of the lake.

Oakland, with several (now defunct) grand hotels, was the area's vacation spot before the development of Deep Creek Lake. It is a modern town of 2,000 people, but its brick sidewalks, 1844 Queen Anne–style train station, Victorian homes, and farmer's market in a parklike setting festooned with native plants hark to a time past. The spring next to where George Washington camped is now along a 2.5-mile hiking/biking trail, and a paved route leads to a grandstand view of the town's many architecturally outstanding buildings.

Like Oakland, the stately hotels of **Deer Park** made it a Victorian vacation destination. Before it closed in 1929, the Deer Park Hotel's guests included Presidents Cleveland, Grant, and Harrison. The town is still somewhat famous for its commercially bottled Deer Park Spring Water.

Mountain Lake Park was established in 1881 as a Chautauqua-style summer resort with religious, educational, and recreational activities. A pamphlet available from the Garrett County Chamber of Commerce (see *Guidance*) will take you on a self-guided tour of its historic district.

Local legend says that **Accident** received its name in 1774 when two speculators, wanting to take advantage of Lord Baltimore's offer of land to settlers, surveyed the same acreage "by accident." Unto this day, it remains a small settlement of just a few hundred spread out on agricultural land.

Friendsville was the first settlement to be established in Garrett County. Although many travelers along I-68 see it as just an interstate exit, the small town sits next to the Youghiogheny River and is well known to whitewater rafters and kayakers.

GUIDANCE The **Garrett County Chamber of Commerce** (301-387-4286; www.garrettchamber.com), 15 Visitors Center Drive, McHenry, 21541, is located off US 219 just as you come into the commercial strip at the north end of Deep Creek Lake. In addition to the usual information, ask them for the pamphlets and brochures that have discount coupons in them.

The Lake Front is a free monthly magazine with news, events, and features on places around the lake. You can pick up one in many business establishments.

With a grand view of the Youghiogheny Lake, a **Maryland welcome center** (301-746-5979) is at mile marker 6 on I-68, east of Friendsville.

GETTING THERE *By car:* **I-68** will bring you into the area from the east or west, while **US 219** is the way to arrive from the north and south.

By air: There are scheduled flights to the airport in Morgantown, West Virginia, about 40 miles away, and the one in Cumberland, Maryland, about 50 miles away. Of course, you will save quite a few dollars by taking the numerous national and international airline companies that fly into **Pittsburgh, Pennsylvania, International Airport** (412-472-3525), just about a 2-hour drive from Deep Creek Lake.

By bus: **Greyhound** (1-800-229-9424) buses stop in Grantsville as they travel along I-68.

GETTING AROUND *By car:* If coming from the east, take **US 219** to Deep Creek Lake. If from the west, take **MD 42,** which will soon intersect with US 219.

MEDICAL EMERGENCY Garrett County Hospital (301-533-4000), 251 North 4th Street (on the corner of 4th Street and Memorial Drive), Oakland.

✳ To See

MUSEUMS Drane House (301-746-6346), Cemetery Road (off US 219), Accident. Open by appointment and on special days. Built around 1800 and believed to be the oldest structure in Garrett County, the log and frame home still has some of its original mud chinking. Items inside chronicle the town's history.

SPRUCE FOREST ARTISAN VILLAGE IN GRANTVILLE

Garrett County Historical Society (301-334-3226), Second Street, Oakland. Among the many items pertaining to the human history of the area are a period newspaper containing articles on Lincoln's assassination, glassware from the Glades and Oakland Hotels, and, what interested me the most, Meshach Browning's bear trap.

HISTORIC SITES The Oakland Train Station (301-334-2691), Oakland. A Queen Anne–style structure, it was built in 1884 to service the B&O Railroad's own resort. Be sure to walk by to appreciate the turret and other unique features.

OTHER SITES Spruce Forest Artisan Village (301-895-3332), 177 Casselman Road (US Alternate 40), Grantsville. Demonstrations of colonial and contemporary arts and crafts. Some of the best bird carvings, pottery, stained glass, and weaving you will find anywhere. Well worth a visit, especially since it is free.

LAKES Deep Creek Lake is the big draw to the area, but several other lakes have their own scenic and recreational attractions.

Youghiogheny River Lake (814-395-3166) spans the Mason-Dixon Line on the Maryland–Pennsylvania border. Powerboating and waterskiing are popular on the 16-mile body of water, and anglers come here for the variety of game and panfish, especially walleye and smallmouth bass. Picnic areas and three campgrounds (one in Maryland; see **Mill Run Recreation Area** under *Lodging—Camping*) are spaced around the lake. The access in Maryland is Mill Run Road, off MD 53 north of Friendsville.

DRANE HOUSE IN ACCIDENT

Savage River Reservoir (301-895-5759), accessed on Savage River Road from MD 135 at Bloomington, or from Big Run Road off New Germany Road. One of the most spectacular settings of any of the area's lakes. Big Savage Mountain, Mount Nebo, and other ridgelines rise dramatically and quickly from the water. Trout, bass, crappie, walleye, perch, and catfish are in abundance, while a fly-fishing catch-and-release site at the dam's tailwater often yields 6- and 7-pound trout. The tailwaters are a popular kayaking spot and have even been used by those training for the Olympics.

Broadford Lake (301-334-9222), in the town of Mountain Lake Park. Nongaso-line-powered watercraft are welcome, which means the 140-acre body of water is a great place to canoe, kayak, sailboard, and fish for the stocked trout, crappie, bass, and catfish. Boat rentals during the season.

Jennings Randolph Lake (304-355-2346) is more than 5 miles long and is located on the North Branch of the Potomac River, which separates Maryland from West Virginia. Scenically sandwiched in by high ridges, the lake is one of the area's least used for powerboating, waterskiing, and fishing. The fly-fishing tailwater area regularly yields brown, rainbow, and brook trout. Mount Zion Road, off MD 135, provides the only Maryland access to the lake (call 301-334-9180 for information). There is an inspiring view of the lake on Chestnut Grove Road, which is also off MD 135.

Also see **New Germany State Park** and **Herrington Manor State Park** under *Green Space—Parks.*

STONE BRIDGES Casselman River Bridge, on US Alternate 40 east of Penn Alps Restaurant (see *Eating Out*), Grantsville. An impressive example of the stonemason's art, the 80-foot Casselman River Bridge was the largest stone-arch bridge in the world when it was built in 1813. While standing on it, be sure to look across the road to its two modern successors, the US 40 and I-68 bridges.

CASSELMAN RIVER BRIDGE IN GRANTSVILLE

DEEP CREEK LAKE

✳ To Do

BICYCLING See **Swallow Falls/Herrington Manor Trail** and the text note under *Hiking,* and **New Germany State Park** and **Deep Creek Lake State Park** under *Green Space—Parks.*

BIRDING See *Green Space—Nature Preserves.*

BOAT RENTALS

Thayerville/Deep Creek Lake
Aquatic Personal Watercraft Center (301-387-8233; www.Aquatic-Center.com), 634 Deep Creek Drive. Open daily 9–8. I get annoyed when personal watercraft show up at quiet lakes, inlets, or rivers. At Deep Creek Lake, however, it seems that almost all the boaters, whether in a small or huge boat, are trying to see how fast their craft can go, so you might as well join in. I'll admit I did,

and I enjoyed it. Rentals by the hour or day.

Bill's Marine Service (301-387-5536), 20721 Garrett Highway (US 219). Little boats with less than 10 horsepower to monsters with 190 horsepower.

Silver Tree Marine (301-387-5855; www.silvertreecenter.com), 455 Glendale Road (on the way to Deep Creek Lake State Park; see *Green Space—Parks*). Rentals of inboard/outboard powerboats, pontoon boats, and personal watercraft by the hour, half day, day, and week.

McHenry/Deep Creek Lake
Deep Creek Outfitters (301-387-6977), 1899 Deep Creek Drive (off US 219). Hourly, daily, and weekly rentals of canoes as well as fishing, pontoon, and ski boats. Stop by in winter for cross-country ski equipment rentals.

Also see *Outdoor Outfitters.*

FAMILY ACTIVITIES
McHenry/Deep Creek Lake
🍦 **Smiley's FunZone** (301-387-5121; www.smileysfunzone.com), on US 219 across from the fairgrounds. There is enough here to keep the kids busy all day. There are batting cages (with slow-pitch softball or fast-pitch baseball), an old-time photo studio, arcade games, indoor laser tag, ice cream, pizza and other foods, and two go-cart tracks (one with a graded incline and the other with carts designed for kids as young as 4 years old). The bumper boats are a great way to get rid of some aggression, while the Smiley-designed miniature-golf course is different than any other you may have played on.

🍦 **Funland** (301-387-6168), Route 219 across from McHenry Plaza. Go-carts, a video arcade, miniature golf, bumper cars, and a "carousel for all ages." There is a free volleyball court and picnic tables to use while eating the burgers, pizza, or ice cream the kids insist on getting.

Swanton
🍦 **Discovery Center at Deep Creek Lake State Park** (301-387-5563), 898 State Park Road. Interactive displays about the geology, ecology, and human history of the area. (Also see *Green Space—Parks.*)

FISHING I have had the opportunity to go out with just two of many fly-fishing guides in the area:

A. J.'s Streamside Services (301-387-5465), 1951 North Glade Road, Swanton. A. J. Fleming is one of the very few professional guides to be certified by the Adventure Sports Institute—and one of the youngest. I had not been fishing since I was a preteen, yet within 10 minutes of being under A. J.'s tutelage on Big Run, I had a trout in my hands. Half-day, all-day, and overnight trips offered.

Streams and Dreams (301-387-6881; www.streams-and-dreams.net), 8214 Oakland–Sang Run Road, Oakland. Don Hershfeld, an aquatic ecologist, is also owner of a B&B (see *Lodging—Bed & Breakfasts*) on which a trout stream runs through the property. The Youghiogheny is a just a 2-minute walk away, and Don educated me quickly during that short stroll.

Other guides recommended by the

BIG RUN

Garrett County Chamber of Commerce (see *Guidance*) include:

Spring Creek Outfitters (301-387-2034; www.springcreekoutfitter.com), 578 Deep Creek Drive, McHenry/Deep Creek Lake. A fly shop and guide service that offers float, wading, and overnight horseback fishing trips.

Outdoor Adventures Unlimited (301-334-1266), 414 Maple Avenue, Oakland. Half-day and full-day lake and fly-fishing trips.

Also see *To See—Lakes*, and **New Germany State Park** and **Herrington Manor State Park** under *Green Space—Parks*.

ICE FISHING Ice fishing on **Deep Creek Lake** and **Savage River Reservoir** (see *To See—Lakes*) has become increasingly popular. Most anglers come in January and February in hopes of hooking yellow perch, walleye, northern pike, and a few other species.

GOLF **Golf Club at Wisp** (301-387-4911; www.golfwisp), 296 Marsh Hill Road, McHenry/Deep Creek Lake. The course has both open holes and tree-lined fairways, and shares some of the same land used by skiers in the winter (see *Skiing*).

Oakland Golf Club (301-334-3883), 433 North Bradley Lane, Oakland. April through October. Established in 1937, the par-72 course has a maturity that is lacking in newer courses.

MINIATURE GOLF ✔ **A & D Dairy Delite** (301-387-9293), US 219 and Glendale Road, Thayerville/Deep Creek Lake. An 18-hole course and goodies all in one spot.

Also see **Smiley's FunZone** and **Funland** under *Family Activities*.

HIKING The **Big Savage Hiking Trail** must be one of the best-kept outdoor secrets in Maryland. It offers a fine sense of isolation, relatively minor changes in elevation, several viewpoints (the one from **High Rock Firetower** is one of western Maryland's best), and an abundance of deer and other wildlife. The route traverses

THE POTOMAC IN MIDSUMMER

the crest of Big Savage Mountain for 17 miles. In addition, visitors may set up a backcountry camp wherever they wish—yet the trail shows very few signs of use. There are no worn-out areas from too many people camping in the same spot, fire rings are almost nonexistent, and the trail's treadway is narrow and shallow.

The required backcountry camping permit (and payment of a fee) may be obtained at the forest headquarters, accessible from I-68 Exit 22 or from the New Germany State Park office (see *Green Space—Parks*).

Try the **Swallow Falls/Herrington Manor Trail** for an easier trek. The 5.5-mile pathway follows the bed of a former logging railroad on its way from one state park to the other (see *Green Space—Parks*). It is also popular with mountain bikers and cross-country skiers.

Without a doubt, 4.5-mile **Lostland Run Trail,** west of Mountain Lake Park, is the showpiece of the **Potomac State Forest** (301-334-2038). Volunteers, members of the Maryland Conservation Corps, and personnel of the forest service have lavished much attention on the route, keeping it well maintained and building a number of bridges—both simple and complex.

The attention is well deserved, as the Lostland Run area is one of the most attractive in western Maryland. The hike begins in a hemlock grove, and soon comes into contact with three lively and gurgling mountain streams before it drops to the calmer waters of the Potomac River. Along the way are an abundance of wildflowers, numerous cascades, ripples, and waterfalls, and the possibility of seeing bobcats, opossums, deer, ground-hogs, weasels, minks, and black bears. An additional draw is backcountry camping in this beautiful setting. Because of the proximity of the forest service road, you also have the option of shuttling a car to make it a one-way hike.

Note: The **Garrett County Chamber of Commerce** (see *Guidance*) can provide you with information on the many other trails in this area that open up scores of miles for hiking, mountain biking, cross-country skiing, and snowmobiling.

Also see *Green Space—Parks*.

HORSEBACK RIDING Broken Bar Riding Stables (301-334-3114), Old Wilson Road (off MD 135, 9 miles east of Oakland), Swanton. There are 4-hour and 8-hour rides that originate at the stables on Saturday and Sunday. One-hour rides are given in Herrington Manor State Park on Monday and Tuesday, and at Deep Creek State Park on Thursday and Friday (for both parks, see *Green Space—Parks*). The stables also offers overnight camping trips in Potomac State Forest (301-334-2038).

KAYAKING AND CANOEING See **Savage River Reservoir** and **Broadford Lake** under *To See—Lakes, Outdoor Outfitters,* and *Whitewater Rafting.*

OUTDOOR OUTFITTERS High Mountain Sports (301-387-4199; www. highmountainsports.com), 21349 Garrett Highway (US 219 at Trader's Landing), Thayerville. A full-service store; if it has to do with the outdoors they can rent or sell you the equipment and teach you how to use it.

This includes mountain biking, hiking, kayaking, snow skiing, waterskiing, and guided mountain bike and kayaking tours.

SAILING Deep Creek Sailing School (301-387-4497; www.saildeepcreek.com), located in Deep Creek Yacht Club at Turkey Neck, Swanton. Low-cost group sailing lessons on small sailboats taught by U.S. Sailing–certified instructors.

SCUBA DIVING Breathe Deep Scuba (301-387-8035), Route 5, Box 4721, Mountain Lake Park. Provides air fills, equipment rentals, and diving instructions.

SKIING, CROSS-COUNTRY This area receives as much as 220 inches of snow, which can fall from November into April. **New Germany** and **Herrington Manor State Parks** (see *Green Space—Parks*) offer miles of wide, well-marked, and groomed trails. Ski rentals and warming lodges are available in both parks.

Many other miles of trails are located in the state forests; information is available from the **Garrett County Chamber of Commerce** (see *Guidance*).

Also see *Skiing, Downhill;* and *Hiking.*

SKIING, DOWNHILL ♂ Wisp Ski and Golf Resort (301-387-4911; www.gcnet.net/wisp), 290 Marsh Hill Road, McHenry/Deep Creek Lake. Maryland's only downhill skiing area has 22 trails totaling 14 miles. With an elevation over 3,000 feet and a 610-foot vertical drop, the resort also has facilities for ski boarding, cross-country skiing, and tubing. Night skiing is available. Like most such places, you can take lessons and buy or rent

equipment; children's lessons and programs also available.

Wisp's snowmaking system is considered to be one of the most efficient in the world, so even if Mother Nature does not supply the white powder, Wisp is capable of making plenty of its own.

SNOWMOBILING There are miles and miles of marked snowmobile trails throughout the state parks and forests. One of the most popular is the route along the crest of Meadow Mountain that runs from **Deep Creek Lake State Park** to **New Germany State Park** (see *Green Space—Parks*) and beyond. Another good choice is the 9.5-mile **Garrett State Forest Snowmobile System.**

Permits are required to ride some of the trails; information available from the **Garrett County Chamber of Commerce** (see *Guidance*).

SWIMMING Lifeguard-patrolled beaches are located at **Deep Creek Lake, Herrington Manor,** and **New Germany State Parks.** Many people swim in the Youghiogheny River at **Swallow Falls State Park;** be aware there are no lifeguards and the river can have a strong current. (Also see *Green Space—Parks.*)

WHITEWATER RAFTING Precision Rafting (301-746-5290; 1-800-477-3723; www.precisionrafting.com), Maple and Morris Streets, Friendsville. The premier company based in Maryland that runs the Upper Youghiogheny River's Class IV and V rapids. Kayaking lessons, family float trips, and runs in West Virginia and Kentucky, too.

✳ Green Space

NATURE PRESERVES Two tracts of land owned by The Nature Conservancy are situated in what are known as "frost pockets." The lower-lying swamplands are surrounded by high ridges, which trap cold air and create an environment more like Canada than Maryland. They are the location of some of America's southernmost occurrences of tamarack, wild calla, Canadian burnet, and insectivorous round-leaved sundew. Each has developed trails and is open daily during daylight hours. More background information may be obtained by contacting the Maryland Chapter of **The Nature Conservancy** (301-897-8570). The **Garrett County Chamber of Commerce** (see *Guidance*) can supply you with directions (which are quite lengthy) to both places.

State-rare breeding birds that have been seen in the 326-acre **Finzel Swamp** are the Virginia rail, sedge wren, alder flycatcher, and saw-whet owl. Others species spotted in the swamp have included the rose-breasted grosbeak, cedar waxwing, and whippoorwill.

More in West Virginia than Maryland, 1,600-acre **Cranesville Swamp** has a boardwalk that will take you by bogs, cranberries, and sphagnum moss. State-rare breeding birds found here include the golden-crowned kinglet, alder flycatcher, Nashville warbler.

PARKS

Grantsville
New Germany State Park (301-895-5453), 349 Headquarters Lane. The park is located off New Germany Road. In contrast to 3,900-acre Deep Creek Lake, New Germany's lake is all of 13 acres in size. It was formed in the early 1800s when John Swauger dammed Poplar Lick Run to obtain waterpower for a sawmill and gristmill. The lake is stocked with sportfish, and rowboat and canoe rentals are available during the summer season. Other attractions include rental cabins (open year-round) with modern amenities, a campground (see *Lodging—Camping*), and a sandy beach for swimming.

The park's trail system was designed with cross-country skiers (who come to the park in large numbers) in mind, so the routes are generally wide, and for the most part rise and fall at a moderate grade. A hike or mountain bike ride will not deliver you to any spectacular waterfalls nor open up any grand vistas but does provide the opportunity to meander through a quiet woodlands, surveying the different small parts of the forest that come together to make up the whole.

Oakland
Herrington Manor State Park (301-334-9180), 222 Herrington Lane—follow signs from US 219 in Thayerville on a convoluted route to the park. Like New Germany State Park, Herrington Manor's moderately easy trails are popular cross-country ski routes, and are groomed and tracked by park personnel. Ski rentals are available.

The park's blend of recreational opportunities makes use of many of the still-standing 1930s Civilian Conservation Corps constructions, such as rental cabins 1–10. (An exhibit in the park office profiles the corps.) **Herrington Lake,** at 53 acres, is stocked with trout, bass, crappie, bluegills, and catfish. Nongasoline-powered watercraft only; canoes and paddleboats are rented during the summer.

Swallow Falls State Park (see Herrington Manor State Park, above, for contact information). Follow signs from US 219 at Thayerville. A walk of less than 1.5 miles provides you with not just one, but four distinctly different waterfalls. **Muddy Creek Falls** is considered the highest in the state (although some claim Cunningham Falls near Frederick is). The area between **Lower Falls** and **Swallow Falls** on the Youghiogheny River is a popular swimming spot, while the sandy beach at **Toliver Falls** is another inviting place. An added attraction of the hike is a shaded 37-acre, 300-year-old hemlock and white pine forest.

The park also has a campground (see *Lodging—Camping*) and picnic facilities.

Swanton

Deep Creek Lake State Park (301-387-5563), 898 State Park Road. Although you are permitted to walk the shoreline around Deep Creek Lake, much of the land beyond has been turned into housing developments, private-home lots, or commercially operated enterprises. The Maryland General Assembly recognized the need for at least a bit of public land here, and after purchasing a mile of shoreline opened the park in 1959. Its 1,800 acres provide protected terrain for resident black bears, bobcats, wild turkeys, white-tailed deer, skunks, chipmunks, squirrels, raccoons, and numerous small mammals.

In addition to a swimming beach, amenities in the park include a campground (see *Lodging—Camping*), rowboat rentals, and a boat-launch facility. Stocked trout, walleye, bass, and yellow perch keep anglers busy. Ranger naturalists lead interpretive programs—sometimes throughout the year, but most often during the summer months. The **Discovery Center** (see *Family Activities*) is part visitors center, part museum.

Approximately 10 miles of trails along the slopes and crest of Meadow Mountain provide an opportunity to get away from the crowds of the lake and campground, visit an old mining site, enjoy a couple of vistas, and study a mountaintop wetlands. Be aware that hunting is permitted in the park's backcountry area during regular hunting seasons, and that some of the trails are popular snowmobile routes in the winter and open to mountain bikes year-round.

✳ Lodging

RESORTS 🐾 **Wisp Mountain Resort/Hotel** (301-387-5581; www.wispresort.com), 290 Marsh Hill Road, McHenry, 21541 (Deep Creek Lake). The 168-rooms/suites hotel for the **Wisp Ski and Golf Resort** offers a heated pool, tennis courts, an exercise room, and special golf, skiing, and other package deals. Pets permitted with a substantial deposit. $89–329.

MOTELS AND HOTELS

Grantsville, 21536

🐾 **The Casselman Inn** (301-895-5055; www.thecasselman.com), Main Street (US Alternate 40). The Casselman was built in 1824 as a stop to serve the stagecoaches, covered wagons, and other travelers along the National Road (see "What's Where in Maryland"). The decor and fixtures (Room 5 has an old-fashioned water closet) in the four inn rooms reflect the early days and rent for $48–75. Newer motel rooms have been built next door and have some of the lowest rates in the state, $28–38. The adjacent restaurant (see *Eating Out*) serves Amish/country fare.

McHenry/Deep Creek Lake, 21541

✎ **Point View Inn** (301-387-5555), MD 219 on Deep Creek Lake. The Point View Inn, family run for more than 30 years, looks like a typical motel from the outside. Yet most rooms have a great view of the lake and are furnished with unique and different types of antiques. There are some suites, but even the standard rooms are larger than you will find in many motels. The restaurant (see *Eating Out*) is known for its crabcakes. $90–110.

Panorama Motel (301-387-5230; 1-800-700-9257; www.deepcreektimes.com/panorama), 921 Mosser Road. It is not on the lake, so its rooms and efficiencies have some of the lowest rates in the area. $55–80.

Oakland, 21550
Lake Side Motor Court (301-387-5503, extension 2205; www.deepcreeklakeside.com), 19956 Garrett Highway (US 219 near Thayerville). Low-rate, clean lake-view rooms. $68–75.

INNS

Deer Park, 21550
Deer Park Inn (301-334-2308; www.deerparkinn.com), 65 Hotel

☎ ✎ **Savage River Lodge** (301-689-3200; www.savageriverlodge.com), P.O. Box 655, 1600 Mt. Aetna Road (within Savage River State Forest), Grantsville, 21536. Call for directions.

The lodge, and its 45 acres surrounded by thousands of Savage River State Forest (see text note under *Lodging—Camping*) acreage, is the pet project of Jan Russell and Mike Dreisbach. I like that the facility's construction disturbed the environment as little as possible. The sites for the 18 guest cabins (which can accommodate up to four people) were carved out of the forest but left most of the trees standing. Even at the main lodge, which overlooks the land, Jan and Mike did not cut down trees just to enhance the view. The septic system uses an environmentally friendly method, and even the roadway is designed with water conservation in mind. Although the natural world would be best served by no further development, if we must disturb the land, architects and planners would do well to emulate Savage River Lodge's example.

In addition to self-explorations of the 13 miles of trail (which connect with additional pathways in the state forest), the lodge can arrange all manner of guided outdoor activities: hiking, bicycling, canoeing, kayaking, flyfishing, and more. This is, by far, one of my favorite outdoor-oriented Maryland places. It is also very pet-friendly.

$180; $75 each additional person; $50 for children 2–12 years old. Many packages available.

Road. The inn was constructed as a 17-room family cottage in 1889 by Baltimore architect Josiah Pennington. Many of the family's furnishings are still here, such as a tiger maple dresser and table, a ruby-colored chandelier, and one of the first Sears & Roebuck mail-order sleigh beds. The plumbing is original (the sinks were made in nearby Mount Savage), the tile work in the bathrooms and fireplaces is quite interesting, and I always get a kick out of pulling the chain on the toilet's suspended water box. Mattresses have that distinctive French sag in the middle. French country meals are served by candlelight in the downstairs dining rooms (see *Dining Out*). $115–135.

Oakland, 21550

Carmel Cove (301-387-0067; www.carmelcoveinn.com), Glendale Road (off US 219 near Thayerville). The inn, built in 1945 as a monastery for Carmelite Fathers, provides many complimentary items and amenities: hot tub, billiards, fishing poles for use on the dock, swimming in the lake, canoes and paddleboats, mountain bikes, tennis courts and equipment,

THE LAKE POINTE INN

beverages and snacks (always available), cross-country skis, and snowshoes.

Some rooms have a private deck, fireplace, and whirlpool bath; all have a private bath. Wood furniture and ceilings, along with a stacked stone fireplace, add an overall warmth to the inn. $140–180.

✒ **Red Run Lodge** (301-387-2626; 1-800-898-7786; www.deepcreek-times.com/redrun), 175 Red Run Road (on Deep Creek Lake off Mayhew Inn Road near Thayerville). The 1937 lakefront lodge's eight guest rooms are furnished with antiques and quilts, and each has a private bath. The three rooms on the top floor can interconnect for large groups. The included breakfast is served in a impressive curved-ceiling room overlooking the lake. Other meals are available in the restaurant (see *Eating Out*).

BED & BREAKFASTS

Grantsville, 21536

♿ **Elliott House Victorian Inn** (301-895-4250; 1-800-272-4090; www.elliotthouse.com), 146 Casselman Road. Situated next to the Casselman River and across the street from Penn Alps/Spruce Forest (see Spruce Forest Artisan Village under *To See—Other Sites*). The outdoors members of the family can fly-fish in the stream while other members stroll through the artisans' village.

The 1870 home is furnished in a mix of contemporary and period pieces. All four guest rooms and three cottages have private baths. The living room, the brightest in the house, is where you can spend hours with the crystal chess set.

Mountain bikes available for free guest use. $100–150.

Walnut Ridge (301-895-4248; 1-888-419-2568; www.walnutridge.net), 92 Main Street. Walnut Ridge offers rooms, suites, and a log cabin furnished in a simple country decor, with handmade quilts on the beds. Theme gardens, a hot tub, and breakfast served on the porch provide serene stays. Just a few minutes off I-68, it is also a good choice if you are just traveling through. $80–150.

McHenry/Deep Creek Lake, 21541

Lake Pointe Inn (301-387-0111; 1-800-523-5253; www.deepcreekinns.com), 174 Lake Pointe Drive. The inn is the oldest house on Deep Creek Lake, actually predating the lake by several decades. It now sits just 13 feet from the water's edge, and the wraparound porch, with rocking chairs, is perfect for lazy hours of lake-watching. The 9-foot stone fireplace, rich woodwork, and handcrafted furniture, fixtures, and pottery give the feel of a rustic lodge, but one with modern amenities. All 10 guest rooms have a private bath, air-conditioning, TV with VCR (an extensive collection of videos is available), and telephone. There are also bikes, canoes, kayaks, and a hot tub for guest use. It is one of my favorite Deep Creek Lake places because of the location, laid-back atmosphere, and attentive staff. Orange juice, muffins, and snacks are available throughout the day; hors d'oeuvres are served in the early evening. Breakfast may include scrambled eggs on a puff pastry and/or a fresh strawberry-mango tart. $158–189.

Oakland, 21550

Streams and Dreams (301-387-6881; www.streams-and-dreams.net), 8214 Oakland–Sang Run Road. Host-

HALEY FARM B&B

ed by Don Hershfeld, an aquatic ecologist, and Karen Hershfeld, a fisheries-science graduate and physician assistant, this little retreat sits upon 15 acres bisected by Hoyes Run, a wild trout stream. An extensive deck overlooks the parklike grounds. Guests of the three private rooms have access to refreshments in the parlor, a cedar sunroom, and a gazebo planted upon a small island in the stream. Don offers fly-fishing lessons for individuals and small groups by making use of any one of the four major trout rivers within a few minutes' drive (see *To Do—Fishing*). Be sure to have him tell you the story of the fireflies as the two of you take an evening stroll along the Youghiogheny River. $90–130.

Haley Farm B&B (301-387-9050; 1-888-231-3276; www.haleyfarm.com), 16766 Garrett Highway (between Thayerville and Oakland on US 219). The wraparound porch looks upon the farm's 65 acres and the surrounding mountains. All of the suites and rooms have a private bath, and everybody has access to a Jacuzzi either in the room or on the deck. Wander the property, sit by the fireplace, fish or row the pond, or borrow a bike for an exploratory ride. $130–195.

The Oak and Apple (301-334-9265; www.oakandapple.com), 208 North Second Street. The 1915 Colonial Revival Victorian sits in Oakland's quiet historic preservation district and offers five guest rooms, most with a private bath. Host Jana Brown has tastefully, but lightly, furnished the large rooms, leaving you lots of space to spread out. From my second-floor room, I was entertained by squirrels scampering from one large oak tree branch to another just outside my windows. The rest of my time was spent on the columned front porch watching small-town life roll by. An expanded continental breakfast, with French toast and homemade breads and scones, is served in the formal dining room. $85–115.

SUITES Will O' the Wisp Prestige Condominiums (301-387-5503; www.willothewisp.com), 20160 Garrett Highway (US 219 near Thayerville), Oakland, 21550. The one to three-bedroom condominiums overlook the lake. Indoor pool, sauna, exercise room, and its own sand beach. $92–299.

CABINS Herrington Manor, New Germany, and **Deep Creek Lake State Parks** have cabins that may be rented by the week from Memorial Day through Labor Day, and for 2-night minimum stays at other times of the year. Reservations may be made by calling 1-888-432-2267. (Also see *Green Space—Parks.*)

VACATION RENTALS There are so many rental homes and condos in the area, well over 600, that descriptions of them fill several large advertisement books. Everything from small, rustic cabins to nine-bedroom luxury homes are available. Many are on the Deep Creek Lake shoreline, but others are nestled in quiet, out-of-the-way places. In a sign of the times, some include free computer and Internet access. Most of the individually rented places are listed in the *Vacation Guide,* available from the **Garrett County Chamber of Commerce** (see *Guidance*). However, three companies manage the bulk of the rentals:

McHenry/Deep Creek Lake, 21541

Coldwell Banker Deep Creek Realty Rentals (301-387-6187; 1-800-769-5300; www.DeepCreekRealty.com), 24439 Garrett Highway (US 219).

Railey Mountain Lake Vacations (301-387-2124; 1-800-846-7368; www.deepcreek.com), 22491 Garrett Highway (US 219).

Long and Foster Resort Rentals (301-387-5832; 1-800-336-7303; www.deepcreekresort.com), 23789 Garrett Highway (US 219).

CAMPING

Friendsville, 21531

🐾 **Mill Run Recreation Area** (814-395-3242), Mill Run Road (off MD 53, 4 miles north of Friendsville). Mailing address is RD 1, Box 17, Confluence, PA 15424. Usually open May through September. The only Youghiogheny Lake campground in Maryland, it has a swimming beach, boat ramp, and flush toilets, but no showers. Pets permitted.

Grantsville, 21536

🐾 **Little Meadows** (301-895-5675), Chestnut Ridge Road. Offers improved and unimproved sites, along with rowboat rentals, a playground, and a dump station.

🐾 **New Germany State Park** (301-895-5453), 349 Headquarters Lane. The park is located off New Germany Road. Close to the park's small lake are 39 sites with a playground for the kids. (Also see *Green Space—Parks.*)

🐾 **Big Run State Park** (see New Germany State Park, above, for contact information). Near Savage River Reservoir 16 miles south of I-68 Exit 24 on Savage River Road. Basic sites

with few amenities, but open year-round. Also see Savage River Reservoir under *To See—Lakes.*

McHenry/Deep Creek Lake, 21541

🐾 **Double G RV Park** (301-387-5481), Moser Road. Bathhouse, playground, and dump stations.

Oakland, 21550

🐾 **Swallow Falls State Park** (301-334-9180), 9 miles northwest of Oakland on Herrington Manor–Swallow Falls Road. Showers, modern bathhouse, sanitary facilities. (Also see *Green Space—Parks.*)

Swanton, 21561

🐾 **Deep Creek Lake State Park** (301-387-5563), 898 State Park Road. The more than 100 campsites, with hot showers and modern sanitary facilities, are just a short walk from the lake. Rental cabins also available. (Also see *Green Space—Parks.*)

Note: Thousands of acres of state-forest lands are open to backcountry camping (after payment of a fee). Contact the **Potomac and Garret State Forests** (301-334-2038), 1431 Potomac Camp Road, Oakland, 21550, and **Savage River State Forest** (301-895-5759), 349 Headquarters Lane, Grantsville, 21536, for details.

✳ Where to Eat

DINING OUT **Deer Park Inn** (301-334-2308; www.deerparkinn.com), 65 Hotel Road, Deer Park. Open for dinner. Reservations required. Pascal Fontaine moved his family to Deer Park so that he could concentrate on preparing meals influenced by methods he learned growing up in France. The menu changes often, as he makes use of seasonally available items grown locally. I dined on the succulent confit of duck ($18.50), while my companion praised the beef filet with sun-dried cherry sauce ($22.75). One of Pascal's signature appetizers, corn chowder with applewood-smoked bacon and crabmeat ($6), is an example of how Maryland cuisine is blended into the offerings. $16–24.95. (Also see *Lodging—Inns.*)

🍴 ✎ **Cornish Manor** (301-334-6499), Memorial Drive, Oakland. Open for lunch 11–2, dinner 5 to closing, Tuesday through Saturday. Reservations required. Who would expect two French restaurants in this far western corner of Maryland, and both located in Victorian homes?

From the wall of masks, to the gold-tinted chairs, to the tassels hanging from the ceiling, Christiane Bergheim has put her mark on the decor, while she and her husband, Fred, share the chef's duties. The names of the dishes are as inventive as the meals themselves: Ménage à Trois (scallops, shrimp, and mussels in cream wine sauce—$19.95); Are You Game? (quail in cream and mushroom sauce—$19.50); Flirtation Filet Mignon in Say Yes Sauce ($22.95). The fresh French breads that come with each meal are reason enough to dine here. The almost decadent decor, Christiane's lilting personality, and the great food have turned this into my favorite Deep Creek Lake–area restaurant. $13.50–27.50.

🍴 ✎ **Leone's at Silver Tree** (301-387-4040; www.silvertreecenter.com), 567 Glendale Road, Thayerville/Deep Creek Lake. Open for dinner 5–10 Monday through Thursday, 5–11 Friday and Saturday, and 4–9 Sunday. Leone's is housed in what is believed to be the first place built to cater to tourists after completion of Deep Creek Lake in the early 1900s. The large stone fireplace and log walls may recall a bygone era, but the decidedly fresh menu makes this the most popular Italian restaurant around the lake.

Several items are distinct to Leone's. For an appetizer, try the carpaccio—tenderloin beef over arugula and finished with Parmesan, capers, and white truffle oil ($9.95). My favorite dish is the shrimp Leone, with stuffed crabmeat and a cognac-and-lobster-flavored sauce ($17.95). The "Bambini Menu" is reasonably priced. Arrive very early (or very late) to be seated at one of the lake-view tables. Entrées $13.95–21.95.

Downstairs at Leone's is **Larry's Blues Cellar,** with more of a tavern menu and atmosphere. Live music on the weekends.

EATING OUT

Grantsville

✎ ♿ **Penn Alps Restaurant** (301-895-5985; www.pennalps.com), US 40. Open daily for breakfast, lunch, and dinner. Part of the Penn Alps/Spruce Forest complex (see **Spruce Forest Artisan Village** under *To See—Other Sites*), the restaurant serves what I would call an upscale country/Amish/German fare. Hickory-smoked ham ($9.95), pork with sauerkraut ($9.95), and cabbage rolls ($11.95) are representative dishes on the menu. Seemingly out of place, but I thought delicious, is the chickpea burger ($3.50). Three of the dining rooms were once part of a log stagecoach inn, and the front of the restaurant showcases arts and crafts items. The restaurant is part of a nonprofit organization, so some of the money you spend goes toward good works. Entrées $8.95–15.95.

☙ **The Casselman Inn** (301-895-5055; www.thecasselman.com), Main Street (US Alternate 40). Open for breakfast, lunch, and dinner; closed Sunday. Straightforward, low-cost Amish/country cooking that is popular with locals. Look for fried chicken, breaded fish, grilled ham, and other entrées served with two vegetables for $7–10. The shoofly pie is different from what you will find in Pennsylvania Dutch country. (Also see *Lodging—Motels and Hotels.*)

McHenry/Deep Creek Lake

Point View Inn (301-387-5555), MD 219 on Deep Creek Lake. Open daily. Overlooking the lake, the Point View Inn (also see *Lodging—Motels and Hotels*) is best known for its rainbow trout and crabcakes. (While I and a companion were trying to decide

what to order, the ladies at the next table told us they were thoroughly enjoying their crabcakes.) Lunch can be casual with sandwiches, while dinner choices can include steamed crabs or wild game. The adjacent **Boardwalk Lounge** (see *Entertainment—Nightlife*) is a very popular watering hole. Entrées range from $8.95 to $20.95 to market price.

☙ **Deep Creek Brewing Company** (301-387-2182; www.deepcreekbrewing.com), located behind the visitors center on US 219. Open daily for lunch and dinner. The lake area's first brew pub has a menu that goes on for page after page. The black bean salsa with chips ($4.50) complements any of the eight handcrafted brews. Sandwiches and wraps are available ($5.95–8.50) if you are in a hurry. Entrées range from seafood jambalaya ($14.95) to a 20-ounce porterhouse ($24.95).

RED RUN LODGE

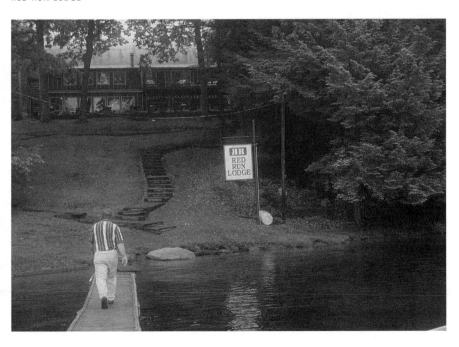

⚓ **Canoe on the Run** (301-387-5933), 2622 Deep Creek Drive. Open for breakfast, lunch, and dinner. A cross between a coffeehouse where you can grab a quick breakfast of baked goodies and a café serving soups, sandwiches, and other finger foods, such as quesadillas and *panini* sandwiches. $4.25–6.25.

Thayerville/Deep Creek Lake

Red Run Lodge (301-387-2626; 1-800-898-7786; www.deepcreektimes.com/redrun), 175 Red Run Road (on Deep Creek Lake off Mayhew Inn Road near Thayerville). The lakefront is the prime reason to dine here. House specialties include Maryland crab soup ($4.25), chicken sandwich topped with crabmeat, bacon, and cheeses ($8.50), and cod fixed a variety of ways ($12.95). Seafood, steak, and vegetarian entrées $7.95–22.95. (Also see *Lodging—Inns.*)

Oakland

Dottie's Fountain and Grill (301-533-0000), 205 East Alder Street. Open for breakfast, lunch, and "afternoon" dinner, Monday through Friday 8:30 AM–3:30 PM, Saturday 8:30 AM–2 PM. Come to Dottie's to experience a time warp. Dottie, the vinyl booths, U-shaped counters, and the menu have been here for more than 30 years. Everything retains the look and feel of when it served as the fountain for a long-gone pharmacy. (The front of the store is now an antiques/gift shop (see **Englander's Antique Mall** *under Selective Shopping—Antiques.*)

Breakfast is served all day, and the most expensive item you can order is less than $5. Hot dogs, cheeseburgers, grilled cheese, and good ol' PB&J are some of the standard lunch items. Try the deep-fried cauliflower instead of french fries. Dinner is a choice of fried chicken, shrimp, or fish. The hand-dipped milk shakes are not to be missed. Sandwiches and entrées $.70–4.65.

Mountain Lake Park

Long Branch Saloon (301-334-4533), 1501 Maryland Highway. Open daily for dinner 5–9:30. One half of this large building is a bar, the other half serves as the restaurant (and dance hall on Friday and Saturday nights—see *Entertainment—Nightlife*). Beef in all shapes—filet mignon, T-bone, Delmonico, and others—is the definite house specialty and is served with salad and potato. Chicken, fish, and sandwiches also available. $8.95–21.95.

COFFEE BARS **Trader's Coffee House** (301-387-9246), US 219 about a half mile south of the Deep Creek Lake bridge, Thayerville/Deep Creek Lake. Open daily at 7:30 AM. Gourmet coffees, breakfast and lunch sandwiches, and fresh-baked goodies. A few sugar-free items, too.

SNACKS AND GOODIES **Old Flour Shoppe Bakery** (301-746-6126), 203 North Main Street, Accident. Open at 6 AM Wednesday through Saturday, 9 AM Sunday. Linda and Lynn Patton and staff begin work at 3 AM so that you can stop by early in the morning for some fresh bread (many varieties) and sinfully rich and sweet baked goodies. The pecan tarts go well with a cup of coffee.

Sugar and Spice Bakery and Cheese (301-334-1559), 2 miles south of Oakland on US 219. Closed Sunday. It looks like someone's private home, but go on in for fresh-baked Amish breads, doughnuts, cookies, pies, and some scrumptious pumpkin rolls.

☞ **Lakeside Creamery** (301-387-2580; www.lakesidecreamery.com), 20282 Garrett Highway, Thayerville/Deep Creek Lake. This is homemade ice cream at its best. There is a rotating menu of about 80 flavors and no way to choose a bad one. Bill Meagher, who oversees the operation, is so particular that he buys different vanilla extracts from around the world. He has found that Tahitian vanilla complements fruit-flavored ice creams, while an extract with a slight alcoholic taste is suited for heavier flavors. Bill is such a recognized authority that people come from other continents for his college courses about the homemade ice cream business. Enjoy your cones or sundaes on the picnic tables overlooking the lake.

✳ Entertainment

FILM **Garrett Eight Cinemas** (301-387-2000), 19736 Garrett Highway (US 219), Thayerville/Deep Creek Lake. First-run films.

NIGHTLIFE

McHenry/Deep Creek Lake
Boardwalk Lounge, (301-387-5555), MD 219 on Deep Creek Lake. In the **Point View Inn** (see *Eating Out* and *Lodging—Motels and Hotels*). Also known as the "Round Bar," this is one of the most happening places around the lake, especially during live-entertainment weekends.
Black Bear Tavern (301-387-6800), US 219, at "The Fort." Live regional bands every Friday and Saturday night. No cover charge 10 PM–2 AM.

Thayerville/Deep Creek Lake
Honi Honi (301-387-9172), US 219, across from Garrett 8 Cinema. This place hops both night and day as they often have live outdoor entertainment from early afternoon on.

Mountain Lake Park
Long Branch Saloon (301-334-4533), 1501 Maryland Highway. The restaurant (see *Eating Out*) tables are rolled away on Friday and Saturday nights to create the largest dance floor in the area. Energetic crowds dance the night away to music supplied by regional musicians.

THEATERS **Our Town Theatre** (301-334-5640; www.ourtowntheatre.com), 121 Center Street, Oakland. The volunteer community theater, housed in a building that has served as a church, armory, and a museum, provides space for teen coffeehouses, recitals, meetings, dances, classes, and theatrical performances.

✳ Selective Shopping

ANTIQUES

Grantsville
Spinning Wheel Antiques and Dream Weavers Antiques (301-895-5938), 161-A Main Street. Mother and daughter Elizabeth Brant and Debbie Klotz have been in the antiques business for well over a decade.

McHenry/Deep Creek Lake
Reminisce Antique Mall (301-387-8275), US 219. Open daily; closed Wednesday from Labor Day through Memorial Day. Furniture, glassware, books, toys, prints, and more from 15 dealers.

Oakland
Mt. Panax Antiques (301-334-9249),

27 Norris Welch Road. About 3 miles south of Oakland. Closed Sunday. Glassware, clocks, and some excellent furniture finds.

Englander's Antique Mall (301-533-0000), Alder and 2nd Streets. Four thousand square feet of antiques and collectibles.

Also see **Book Market and Antique Mezzanine** under *Bookstores.*

Note: A pamphlet available from the **Garrett County Chamber of Commerce** (see *Guidance*) describes a couple of antiques driving tours in the area that will take you by scores of dealers.

ART GALLERIES Garrett County Arts Council (301-334-6580), 206 East Alder Street, Oakland. Closed Sunday. The only fine-arts gallery in the region. Arts and crafts by more than 80 local and regional council members.

BOOKSTORES Expanding Horizons (301-387-5700), 19895 Garrett Highway, Thayerville/Deep Creek Lake. It is a small store, but many volumes and music CDs are displayed in the limited space.

Book Market and Antique Mezzanine (301-387-8778), Oakland. Open Monday through Saturday; sometimes Sunday. A full-service bookstore with best-sellers, classics, and an excellent selection of local-interest books. One of the friendliest bookstores I have visited. Antiques on the second floor.

CRAFTS

Mountain Lake Park
Simon Pearce Glassblowing (301-334-5277; www.simonpearce.com),

265 Glass Drive (off MD 135). Open daily 9–5. A catwalk permits visitors to watch the craftspeople at work on the factory floor. It is amazing to watch as a blob of red-hot, molten silica is turned into a crystal-clear work of glass art.

SPECIAL SHOPS Yoder Country Market (301-895-5148; 1-800-321-5148), MD 669, Grantsville. This market had its beginnings when the patriarch started a butchering business on his farm to supplement his meager income during the Great Depression. Today, Yoder's is known for its sausages, scrapple, bologna, smoked hams, and other meats. The country market is next door to the packing house, so the meats are fresh. Many locals also shop here for the breads and cookies made on premises, or other Amish items such as apple butter, maple syrup, and maple candies produced locally.

Cobblestone Alley (301-387-4644), 2778 Deep Creek Drive, McHenry/Deep Creek Lake. Open 10–6 Sunday through Thursday, 10–7 Friday and Saturday. Besides the usual items found in gift shops, Cobblestone Alley has some locally made items such as Bag Lady Totes, Grandma's Jam House, and Laurel Ridge Pottery (whose deep blue glazes are sumptuous).

FARMER'S MARKETS Oakland Mountain Fresh Farmer's Market (301-334-6960). In the city parking lot off 2nd Street, 10–1 on Saturday and Wednesday, July through October.

WINERY Deep Creek Cellars (301-746-4349), 177 Frazee Road, Friendsville. Tours, tastings, and sales

Wednesday through Saturday from 11–6. Deep Creek Cellars is the farthest west of the state's wineries and, even with its reputation for fine wines, offers its varieties at some of the lowest prices. It's situated on a hillside, so visitors are encouraged to linger, picnic, enjoy the scenic vineyard, and maybe shop in the farm market.

✳ Special Events

January: **Annual Kick and Glide Cross-Country Ski Race and Winter Fest** (301-334-3114), Herrington Manor State Park (see *Green Space— Parks*). Sledding, snowshoeing, snowpeople making, horse-drawn sleigh rides.

June: **McHenry Highland Festival** (301-387-9300), fairgrounds, McHenry. Scottish dancing and solo piping contests. The annual daylong event celebrates the heritage of Scotland, Ireland, Wales, and England and includes sheep dog demonstrations, ethnic food and music, and a military encampment. **Loggers/Forestry Day and Equipment Sale,** fairgrounds. A biennial event that showcases the latest in forestry equipment and techniques. Arts and crafts, and presentations for kids and adults. Smoky Bear always shows up. **Grantsville Days** (301-895-5177), town park, Grantsville. Parade and fireworks, tractor and horse pulls, lots of food, and continuous entertainment.

June through September: **Garrett Lakes Arts Festival** (301-387-3082; www.artsandentertainment.org), various sites. A summerlong celebration of visual and performing arts. Classes, workshops, and concerts with classical and contemporary music. **Music at Penn Alps** (301-895-5985; www.musicatpennalps.com), Grantsville. The annual series features classic to contemporary classical music.

July: **Independence Day Exhibition of Art** (301-746-6115), Accident. Annual juried art competition in a variety of media that has categories open to adults and children of various ages. **Summer Festival and Quilt Show** (301-895-3332), Spruce Forest Artisan Village (see *To See—Other Sites*), Grantsville. The annual event includes visiting and resident artisans, children's activities, and hundreds of hand-stitched quilts made in the region and submitted for the juried exhibition.

August: **Annual Western Maryland Tennis Championships** (301-334-3249), Mountain Lake Park. The clay-court competitions have been held for more than 80 years. **Garrett County Fair** (301-533-2321), fairgrounds, McHenry. **Country Fest and Auction** (301-245-4564), fairgrounds, McHenry. Arts and crafts, all-day gospel music, old-time milking, weaving, and apple cider demonstrations. Hay wagon and pony rides. Petting zoo and pedal-tractor pull for the kids. Auction proceeds from homemade items support the local Mennonite school and church.

October: **Autumn Glory Festival** (301-387-4386), various sites throughout the area. An annual 5-day celebration of fall foliage. Parades, live music, arts and crafts, dances, and lots of food.

INDEX